Lynn Springer

D0819628

Manual For Legal Assistants

Second Edition

Prepared By

The National Association of
Legal Assistants, Inc.

West Publishing Company

St. Paul New York Los Angeles San Francisco

Copyeditor: Marilynn Taylor
Text design: Lucy Lesiak Design
Cover design: Kristin Weber
Composition: Parkwood Composition Service, Inc.

COPYRIGHT © 1979 By WEST PUBLISHING COMPANY
COPYRIGHT © 1992 By WEST PUBLISHING COMPANY
                    610 Opperman Drive
                    P.O. Box 64526
                    St. Paul, MN 55164-0526

Printed in the United States of America
99 98 97 96 95 94 93   8 7 6 5 4 3 2 1

Library of Congress Cataloging-in-Publication Data

NALA manual for legal assistants / the National Association of
   Legal Assistants. — 2nd ed.
       p.   cm.
    Rev. ed. of: Manual for legal assistants. 1979.
    Includes bibliographical references and index.
    ISBN 0-314-80780-2 (hard)
     1. Legal assistants—United States—Handbooks, manuals, etc.
I. National Association of Legal Assistants. II. Title: Manual for legal assistants.
KF320.L4N34   1992
340'.023'73—dc20
                                                     91-18166
                                             ∞   CIP

Dedication

This Second Edition of the National Association of Legal Assistants Manual for Legal Assistants is dedicated to the memory of

Andrew J. Kasic, Esq.
and
Gerald M. Shea, Esq.

As a tribute to their dedication and support of NALA and of the legal assistant profession.

Acknowledgments

The National Association of Legal Assistants, Inc., gratefully acknowledges the contributions of the following persons to the successful completion of this second edition:

Patricia L. Armstrong, CLAS	Wichita	Kansas
Pamela J. Bailey, CLAS	Pittsburgh	Pennsylvania
Lee T. Deuto, CLAS	Jacksonville	North Carolina
Karen M. Dunn, CLAS	Vail	Colorado
Amy J. Hill, CLAS	Raleigh	North Carolina
Karen B. Judd, CLA	Champaign	Illinois
Kay Kasic, CLA	Napa	California
Virginia Koerselman, Attorney at Law	Omaha	Nebraska
Connie Kretchmer, CLA	Omaha	Nebraska
Anthony L. Matens, Private Investigator	Bloomington	Illinois
Sharon M. Pope, Attorney at Law	Hartford	Connecticut
Karen Sanders-West, CLA	Wichita	Kansas

The National Association of Legal Assistants also wishes to renew its recognition and appreciation to the following contributors to the first edition of this manual:

Linda R. Babineaux	Lafayette	Louisiana
Nina Baker	Colorado Springs	Colorado
Ellen H. Batt, CLA	Huntsville	Alabama
Gert Benz	Morristown	New Jersey
Mary Watts Baylor	Sherman Oaks	California
Susan Bierschbach	El Paso	Texas
Julia Brouhard	Galveston	Texas
Jery Bryce, CLA	Lubbock	Texas
Mary Ellen Buehring, CLA	Maitland	Florida
Emma Valborg Carlson, PLS	Humboldt	Iowa
Gabriella Carozzino, CLA	San Francisco	California
Una Clark, CLA	La Mesa	California
Shirley M. Collins	Cupertino	California
Janis C. Davidson, CLA	Birmingham	Alabama
David P. Della Penta	White Plains	New York
Kay Eismann	Mt. Vernon	Oregon
Penny L. Fuestel	West Allis	Wisconsin
Twyla Gab, CLA	Brookings	South Dakota
Pat T. Gibson	Paris	Illinois
B. Jayne Greene	Vinita	Oklahoma
Haru K. Hains, CLA	Manasquan	New Jersey
Kathleen J. Hill, CLA	Tallahassee	Florida
Sally Hingley	Key Largo	Florida
Barbara Hutchisson	New Orleans	Louisiana
Jo D. Johnson	Kalispell	Montana

Dorthea Jorde, CLA	Minot	North Dakota
Glynjo Keefer	Long Beach	California
Bruce A. Kesselman	New Brunswick	New Jersey
Linda J. Kiernan	Buffalo	New York
Geri Land	Tucson	Arizona
Carol McGill	Boulder	Colorado
Violet McNew, CLA	Boulder	Colorado
Eunice Miller	Waco	Texas
Kayla B. Muse	Tacoma	Washington
William R. Park	San Francisco	California
Doris Paxton	Tucson	Arizona
Mary Ann Pickrell	Sunnyvale	California
Margaret Richards, CLA	Topeka	Kansas
Randi Rochow, CLA	Los Altos	California
Madelyn Russell	Davenport	Iowa
Eloise Schneider	Babylon	New York
Mildred Sheffy	Tulia	Texas
James M. Shriver, Jr.	Schertz	Texas
Dorothy Swicord	Irving	Texas
Florence M. Telling, CLA	Bloomfield Hills	Michigan
Jane H. Terhune, CLA	Tulsa	Oklahoma
Ardeth Thomas	Greenfield	Wisconsin
Joanne Toporski	Brookfield	Wisconsin
Rosemary Westbrook	St. Petersburg	Florida
Cathy Zander, CLA	Meridian	Idaho

Lawyers and educators have expressed interest in this book since first it was conceived. A number of these people undertook substantial review and critique of the text for certain chapters and this book is the better for their effort and interest. This group includes the following:

Robert F. Gardner, Esq., Martin, Gibson & Gardner, Sedalia, Missouri
Barry F. Keller, Esq., Keller and Avadenka, Bloomfield Hills, Michigan
Richard L. Meiss, Esq., Law Department, Pacific Gas and Electric Co., San Francisco, California
Lois M. Plowman, Professor, Cerritos College, Norwalk, California
Michael Ropers, Esq., Ropers, Majeski, Kohn, Bentley & Wagner, San Jose, California
Marty Schiff, St. Louis, Missouri

Foreword

The National Association of Legal Assistants, Inc. (NALA) presents this manual as an educational contribution to the legal assistant profession. It was originally developed:

> To serve as a quick reference guide for working legal assistants; and
> For use by schools as a teaching aid in exposing legal assistant students to practical skills and techniques required for entry into the profession; and
> To assist legal assistants in preparing to take the voluntary NALA Certified Legal Assistant Examination.

This revised manual was completed by many dedicated members. These professionals unselfishly gave their time and energy for this very worthwhile project. None of that dedication has gone unnoticed and it is here that NALA gratefully acknowledges these exemplary and concentrated efforts.

This manual is a collection of techniques and procedures which can be used by legal assistants nationwide. It is compatible with the Federal Rules of Civil Procedure; however, the purpose of the manual is not to teach federal law or procedures since there are many excellent treatises available on that subject. This book is not intended to offer specific guidance on any state law or procedure since the fifty jurisdictions differ too widely to capsulize all the laws adequately within one volume.

The techniques described are examples of past successful solutions to actual assignments accomplished by working legal assistants. These should be considered as starting points from which changes, adaptations and modifications can be made by other legal assistants in similar situations.

This manual will serve its purpose if it:

> helps legal assistants achieve a comfortable viewpoint and perspective of themselves;
> inspires them to dedicate themselves to high standards of professional performance and strong ethical and moral commitment to the client and attorney;
> generates enthusiasm and a willing sense of loyalty between legal assistants and their employers.

Table of Contents

2 Introduction to the American Legal System 31

3   Ethics   43

4   Judgment and Analytical Ability   58

5   Legal Research   77

8   Litigation Skills   187

9   The Legal Assistant and Document Discovery Cases   260

Introduction

What is a legal assistant? What does one do? What does a job as a legal assistant entail? How much responsibility can or should one assume? If you are a legal assistant and have not encountered these questions, you are lucky! You may only need this Manual for reference or guidance in a particular area of the law. For those who have questions and for students and those entering the profession, the National Association of Legal Assistants (NALA) offers this practical aid for the legal assistant.

The number of legal assistants continues to increase along with a corresponding need for a workable reference on "what to do" and "how to do it." Realizing that those best qualified to present this information are legal assistants themselves, NALA called upon its members to share their knowledge and expertise. This MANUAL is a culmination of that effort. It is designed to help further your understanding of this profession, as well as its duties, responsibilities, and limits.

What Is the National Association of Legal Assistants?

The National Association of Legal Assistants is a professional association for legal assistants. Incorporated in 1975, NALA had grown by the 1990s to represent over ten thousand legal assistants through its individual members, affiliated state and local associations, and certified legal assistants. The primary activities of the National Association of Legal Assistants include publication of educational materials, such as this MANUAL, presentation of educational seminars and workshops for legal assistants, research and study of the growth, development, and maturation of the legal assistant profession, and administration of the Certified Legal Assistant ("CLA") certifying program, the profession's national credentialing mechanism. The National Association of Legal Assistants is governed by a board of directors consisting of legal assistants from throughout the nation, and its day-to-day activities are carried out by its professional staff in Tulsa, Oklahoma.

In 1986, NALA initiated a biannual survey of legal assistants to begin extensive research of the status of the legal assistant profession. These questionnaires are very detailed in their request for information on the respondents' educational backgrounds and experience, description of the employers, definition of duties and responsibilities, billing rates, and compensation and benefits. Through this biannual survey, NALA has begun to develop a significant study of the profession. In addition to providing a description of this career field every two years, NALA is storing and summarizing a tremendous amount of data showing the growth and development of this field. Much of the information in this introductory chapter is based on these research efforts and the work and contributions of NALA members and committees.

What Is a Legal Assistant?

In 1984, the National Association of Legal Assistants adopted the following definition of a legal assistant:

Legal assistants* are a distinguishable group of persons who assist attorneys in the delivery of legal services. Through formal education, training and experience, legal assistants have knowledge and expertise regarding the legal system and substantive and procedural law which qualifies them to do work of a legal nature under the supervision of an attorney.

---

* Within this occupational category, some individuals are known as paralegals.

This definition has been used to foster a distinction between a legal assistant, as one working under the direct supervision of an attorney, and a broader class of paralegals who perform tasks of a similar nature but not necessarily under the supervision of an attorney.

In 1986, the American Bar Association defined legal assistants as:

Persons who, although not members of the legal profession, are qualified through education, training or work experience, who are employed or retained by a lawyer, law office, governmental agency, or other entity in a capacity or function which involves the performance, under the direction and supervision of an attorney, of specifically delegated substantive legal work, which work, for the most part, requires a sufficient knowledge of legal concepts such that, absent the legal assistant, the attorney would perform the task.

These definitions share many similarities. Both state that 1) legal assistants work under the supervision of a lawyer, 2) legal assistants are qualified through education, training, or work experience, and 3) legal assistants do substantive legal work. The American Bar Association (ABA) further states that the work of legal assistants is of such a nature that "absent the legal assistant, the attorney would perform the task."

These similarities are the ingredients that separate this profession from other occupations and other professions in the legal field. They are the concepts that make the legal assistant profession unique. As mentioned earlier in this section, a distinction is being made between the terms "legal assistant" to refer to individuals who meet these definitions and "paralegal" to refer to other lay personnel working in the legal field whose employment or responsibilities do not meet these definitions. It is important to remember this distinction when discussing the legal assistant profession. There are numerous positions and responsibilities for non-lawyers within the legal profession. However, the membership and services of the National Association of Legal Assistants, including this publication, are designed for those persons whose positions and duties meet the NALA and ABA definition of a legal assistant.

The definition of a legal assistant includes those who free-lance. Rather than being full-time employees of a law firm, these legal assistants work for law firms on a contract basis, primarily through their own businesses or through other contractors. These individuals work on the same professional basis and under the same supervisory provisions as legal assistants who work for only one law firm. During the past ten years, the numbers of free-lance legal assistants and independent contractor businesses have increased. However, the only difference between these legal assistants and those working on a full-time basis for a single employer is the terms of their employment and delivery of services. Free-lance legal assistants are subject to the same, if not more, ethical proscriptions and responsibilities as all legal assistants.

Who Do Legal Assistants Work for?

The vast majority of legal assistants are found in private law firms, although legal assistants are also employed in banks, insurance companies, corporations, government, or are self employed (freelance). They may work under the direction of just one attorney or several, have a private office or no office, have secretarial assistance or no support, travel frequently or never travel. While the majority work full time, some legal assistants work on a part-time or temporary basis or free lance.

One of the questions facing the profession and management studies is that of identifying the relationship between the size of a law firm, as defined by the number of lawyers, and the number of legal assistants. A comparison of our 1988 data with our 1986 data provides little information for making a definitive statement about this relationship beyond the obvious that larger firms tend to have more legal assistants than smaller firms. Interesting in the trends that are developing is that the numbers of legal assistants employed in firms of like size are increasing across the board. For example, in 1986, 12 percent of the firms with twenty-one to thirty attorneys employed over eleven legal assistants; in 1988, this increased to 21 percent of those firms.

We have found that legal assistants generally work in private law firms (80 percent of those surveyed in 1988) on a full-time basis (94 percent) and have a private office (72 percent). Most legal assistants share a secretary with one or more attorneys (41 percent) or with one or more legal assistants (10 percent), and most legal assistants (75 percent) travel to some extent in connection with their work. A majority of legal assistants (69 percent) are supervised by one or more attorneys; however, the number of those supervised by legal assistant administrators is growing. Your working environment will depend in large part on your employer, your geographic region, and how your skills are utilized.

Professional Standards: Education and Experience

With the recent, overwhelming increase in educational programs designed for legal assistant training, a growing number of legal assistants have some sort of formal, post-high school legal educational background. The largest growth area in the 1980s was in two-year associate degree programs. However, more and more colleges and universities are beginning to offer bachelor's degree programs in legal assistant studies. Also, the number of employers requiring a bachelor's degree of entry-level employees is increasing. The growth of educational programs for legal assistants, the impact of which has been demonstrated in many ways and is attributed to many factors, coincides with predictions for a phenomenal growth of the legal assistant profession.

In addition to the training offered through formal education programs, many law firms and other employers provide in-house training for their legal assistants. In-house training refers to attorney education of the employee concerning legal assistant duties. In addition to review and analysis of assignments, the legal assistant should receive a reasonable amount of instruction directly related to his or her duties and obligations. This preparation of legal assistants is important because most codes of ethical and professional responsibility of bar associations require that the attorneys must be assured of the professional competence of their employees.

As a hiring criterion for entry-level employees, many employers require prior legal experience or successful completion of the Certified Legal Assistant certifying examination. In 1984, the National Association of Legal Assistants suggested to the profession the following as the minimum qualifications for a legal assistant:

1. Successful completion of the Certified Legal Assistant certifying examination.
2. Graduation from an American Bar Association-approved program of study for legal assistants.
3. Graduation from a course of study for legal assistants that is institutionally accredited but not ABA approved and requires not less than the equivalent of sixty semester hours of classroom study.
4. Graduation from a course of study for legal assistants other than those set forth in (2) and (3) above, plus not less than six months' in-house training as a legal assistant.
5. A baccalaureate degree in any field, plus not less than six months' in-house training as a legal assistant.
6. A minimum of three years of law-related experience under the supervision of an attorney, including at least six months of in-house training as a legal assistant.
7. Two years of in-house training as a legal assistant.[1]

These minimum qualifications recognize law-related work and formal educational backgrounds, both of which should provide the legal assistant with a broad exposure to and knowledge of the legal profession. This background is necessary to assure the public and the legal profession that the one being identified as a legal assistant is qualified.

What Does a Legal Assistant Do?

A legal assistant is allowed to perform any task that is properly delegated and supervised by an attorney, so long as the attorney is ultimately responsible to the client and assumes the complete professional responsibility for the work product. The chapter on ethics in this manual will explain in greater detail what a legal assistant *cannot* do, as well as the variety of considerations and concepts of law that are involved in working as a legal assistant. Generally, and except as otherwise provided by statute, court rule or decision, administrative rule or regulation, or the attorney's Code of Professional Responsibility, a legal assistant may perform any function delegated by an attorney, including but not limited to the following:

1. Conduct client interviews and maintain general contact with the client;
2. Locate and interview witnesses;
3. Conduct investigations and statistical and documentary research;
4. Conduct legal research;
5. Draft correspondence, pleadings, and other legal documents;
6. Summarize depositions, interrogatories, and testimony;
7. Attend execution of wills, real estate closings, depositions, court or administrative hearings, or trials with the attorney; and
8. Author and sign letters, provided the legal assistant status is clearly indicated and the correspondence does not contain independent legal opinions or direct legal advice.

---

[1] NALA, *Model Standards and Guidelines for Utilization of Legal Assistants,* (1984), revised 1990).

The tasks of legal assistants vary but usually fall within those functions listed above. Empirical studies show a definite trend toward a concentration of legal assistant time in specialized areas of practice due to the tendency of lawyers to move toward specialized practice. However, our 1986 and 1988 surveys offer very strong data suggesting a continuing trend of legal assistants being assigned a variety of tasks and responsibilities in diverse specialty areas. These are not competing ideas or contradictory statements. It is difficult, if not impossible, to segregate the areas of practice of law or to compartmentalize these specialties so neatly that there is no overlap. Legal assistants generally are assigned a wide range of tasks and responsibilities in varied areas of practice. This general statement refers particularly to those who have less experience.

How assignments are given to legal assistants will also vary. Some employers have defined levels of legal assistants; others have no structure. Assignments most commonly come from individual attorneys or through specific departments. Some legal assistants participate in meetings with clients, do legal research, and attend court hearings, while others do not.

Remember, there will be diversity in each and every position filled by a legal assistant. This diversity will depend in large part on the particular requirements for the position, the needs of the attorney, and the background and experience of the legal assistant.

Utilization and Billing

The standards, responsibilities, and utilization of legal assistants received significant endorsement in June 1989, when the United States Supreme Court announced its decision in *Missouri v. Jenkins,* 491 U.S. 274, 109 S.Ct. 2463 (1989). This case, from the Eighth Circuit Court of Appeals, placed several issues before the Supreme Court regarding the general subject of attorney fee awards under 42 U.S.C. Section 1988. The issue related to the utilization of legal assistants was whether or not legal assistant time may be reimbursed at market rates, rather than at actual cost, in attorney fee awards. The question before the Court already assumed that the time was reimbursable under the Code. However, the question of how the time may be reimbursed required the Court to examine the utilization of legal assistants.

Ultimately, the Court agreed with the decision of the Eighth Circuit Court, which had allowed the compensation of legal assistant time at market rates. There are many matters of great significance to the profession in the Court's decision. First is the Court's acknowledgment of the general practice of billing legal assistant time at market rates and that these rates are significantly lower than the hourly market rates for attorney time. Second, the Court allowed the time of legal assistants to be considered in the same manner as all professional fees and separate from costs or expenses associated with a case. Finally, the Court encouraged the use of lower-cost legal assistants wherever possible as a practice that ensures the cost-effective delivery of legal services and reduces the spiraling cost of litigation.

The Court cautioned, however, that "purely clerical or secretarial tasks should not be billed at a paralegal rate, regardless of who performs them." Herein lies the significance of the Court's decision on the utilization of legal assistants. While strongly encouraging the use of legal assistants through its comment and decision, the Court cautioned just as adamantly that when billing for legal assistant time (or time for any other professional), firms should not bill for any tasks that are clerical or secretarial in nature. The assumption is that the costs for these tasks are already included as overhead expenses in the hourly rates of professionals such as attorneys and legal assistants.

The Court's decision in *Missouri v. Jenkins* has been relied on by other courts in reviewing the propriety of attorney fees awards and compensation within that award for legal assistant time.[2]

The following list of factors should be helpful in defining billing practices for legal assistants:

1. The firm customarily bills clients at an hourly rate for legal assistant time.
2. The legal assistant has the necessary qualifications through education, training, professional certification, or work experience to function in that capacity under the direction and supervision of an attorney.
3. The legal assistant time and the services performed are clearly identified and documented in the fee request.
4. The tasks performed by the legal assistant are not clerical or ministerial in nature.
5. The tasks performed by the legal assistant involve substantive legal work specifically delegated by and conducted under the direct supervision of an attorney.
6. The tasks performed by the legal assistant are cost effective in the delivery of legal services in that, absent the use of a legal assistant in the litigation, the attorney would have performed the tasks at a higher hourly rate.
7. There is no duplication of efforts by the use of a legal assistant, as the only necessary time for the attorney is in review and supervision of the legal assistant's work to merge it into the attorney's final work product.
8. The training and expertise of the legal assistant are such that they support the requested hourly rate for the services performed.
9. In specialized or complex litigation where a higher hourly rate may be sought, emphasis should be placed on the legal assistant's experience, expertise, and type and quality of work.
10. Affidavits, other documentation, or evidence are presented on the prevailing hourly rate in the relevant market area for legal assistant services.[3]

Compensation

A legal assistant's compensation will likely depend on the type of employer, such as a private law firm or corporation, and its size; the geographic region; and the number of years of legal assistant experience, education, or other professional achievements, such as the "CLA". Depending on these variables, the legal assistant salary ranges from $20,000 to over $30,000 annually. In its 1988 survey, the National Association of Legal Assistants found an increase of about $3,000 in the average compensation of legal assistants. This average nationwide increase cannot be at-

---

[2] For a discussion of the reliance of the courts on *Missouri v. Jenkins,* see *The Ripple Effect of* Missouri v. Jenkins *Begins: Special Report of NALA President Karen B. Judd,* Facts & Findings, (January 1990).

[3] See Judd, Karen B., *Legal Assistant Time in Attorney Fee Awards: A Separate and Distinct Compensation,* VIII Facts & Findings I, (June 1988).

tributed merely to the two-year time span between the distribution of question-naires; other factors are causing the increase of over 10 percent in average compensation since 1986. Increasingly, lawyers have come to recognize the high cost of replacing a seasoned legal assistant. Because educational institutions are generally better equipped to train legal assistants than law firms are, positions are being filled by legal assistants with more education than ever before. The number of certified legal assistants has increased dramatically within the past few years.

The majority of legal assistants are salaried, frequently work in excess of their employers' normal working hours, and are not paid overtime. Fringe benefits can include vacation, medical or other insurance, parking, professional dues, and retirement plans.

Professional Certification and Activities

Legal assistants work under the supervision of attorneys, and attorneys shoulder the ultimate responsibility for the work product of legal assistants. However, these facts do not relieve a legal assistant of his or her individual obligation to exhibit ethical conduct and responsibility to the legal assistant profession itself. For example, legal assistants must seek to remain current on such subjects as ethical guidelines, opinions, and case law that affect their professional status, to continue their legal education, and to demonstrate their competence as well as their commitment to professional standards. It is through their local, state, and national professional associations that they may address these goals and responsibilities.

The National Association of Legal Assistants offers the nation's only voluntary certification program for legal assistants. This peer-established certification provides a means for legal assistants to demonstrate their knowledge and expertise in this profession and their commitment to professional development. The "Certified Legal Assistant" designation is generally recognized within the legal community as one means of identifying competent legal assistants.

This certification and the use of the "CLA" designation are available to any legal assistant who meets certain eligibility requirements and successfully completes a two-day examination covering the range of skills and knowledge required of legal assistants. All "Certified Legal Assistants" must meet certain continuing education requirements in order to maintain the "CLA" designation. The designation must be renewed every five years.

Legal assistants who pass the certified legal assistants certifying examination may continue their professional accreditation through NALA specialty certification. As of 1990, specialty certification was available in the areas of civil litigation, probate and estate planning, criminal law and procedures, real estate law, and corporations/business law. These advanced specialty certification examinations are available to all Certified Legal Assistants, and continuing education credit is awarded for successful completion of a specialty examination.

Through pursuit of education and competence, legal assistants are able to meet their responsibilities and commitments.

Summary

The word *assist* is the basis for the title "legal assistant." This one word contains the key reason for the emergence of and the ever growing need and demand for qualified legal assistants. Legal assistants *assist* attorneys in the delivery of legal services by performing whatever tasks the attorneys delegate, work that the attorneys would perform "absent the legal assistant." This frees attorneys to do that which only they can do. This "assisting" can be in a direct one-to-one relationship with an attorney, as part of an attorney-legal assistant-legal secretary team, or with a number of attorneys. It is in this spirit of assisting that we must approach the legal assistant profession. This, above all others, is the criterion upon which we will build and expand this new, exciting, promising, and vital career.

1 Communications

1.00   Communication Concept

"Communication," as defined by *Webster's Ninth New Collegiate Dictionary,* is "a process by which information is exchanged between individuals through a common system of symbols, signs, or behavior." Communicating is a skill each of us employs, some more successfully than others. To be a successful communicator, one must study the elements of communication and then develop the ability to use those elements that complement one's personality.

The scientific aspects of communication involve well-identified techniques that can inhibit communication or facilitate it, depending upon the circumstance.

1.01   Ultimate Skill

Communication is one of the most important skills the legal assistant must develop. Legal assistants are charged with the responsibility of assembling and conveying facts and factual situations accurately to attorneys from the data source. This test of communication skill relies not only on the identification of a known or believed "fact" but also the effect on it of any coloration of prejudice, self-interest, credibility, and applicability to the problem. Every "fact" that comes to the legal assistant originates somewhere else, not in his or her own brain. Otherwise, the legal assistant would be the witness rather than the identifier of witnesses. As is discussed in other sections of this book, facts may be testimonial, physical, or material. Relaying needed information to the attorney, both clearly and fully, is the legal assistant's absolute duty; perhaps it is even more important than the duty to find and isolate the important facts from the unimportant or irrelevant ones.

It is true that a legal assistant can accomplish this simply by flooding the attorney with every fact, inference, and circumstance relevant to the case. Doing this without attempting to provide gradations of value to these facts essentially reduces the contribution of the legal assistant to little more than that of a clerk. It is important for the legal assistant to use the fewest words to convey the fullest message to the attorney or, conversely, from the attorney to such other person as the legal assistant is designated to contact. The legal assistant's *function* then is not to serve as an unfiltered conduit of word flow but rather to relay clear meanings and ideas. If there is one formula for communicating that legal assistants should adopt, it is the KISS formula—"Keep It Simple, Stupid." Simple words are easily understood and seldom misunderstood. Short sentences do not confuse readers or listeners, and short thoughts are more easily assimilated than long, involved sentences. Remember that one formula. It will be your salvation in all forms of communication—KISS—the minimum needed for full understanding.

1.02   Methods of Communication

There are increasing numbers of communication techniques, most of which are variations or amplifications of the three most common means of communication available to each of us:

(a) *Nonverbal,* sometimes referred to as body language, or the associative image we project by the posture of our body, the clothes we wear or the way they are worn, as well as the expression on our faces or the manner in which we look (or avoid looking) at others;

(b) *Verbal,* or the process of speaking, either directly to someone or through mechanical devices such as a telephone, dictating machine, tape recorder, television camera, or, in some cases, a computer; and,

(c) *Written,* where we put our thoughts on paper and convey them to someone else.

Communication is also possible by use of any one of the five physical senses of sight, smell, taste, touch, or hearing. However, the message then is frequently shallow and incomplete. A combined use of these senses can afford us a fully textured communication experience with the aggregate impression triggering our "sixth sense" *instinctive reaction.*

Why people instinctively like or dislike others, trust or fear them, are attracted to or repelled by them are questions too complex for us to study definitively. Legal assistants must be aware that the total communication effort is affected by the impressions they give others, whether in the form of body image (good or bad), facial expressions, body language (we'll discuss this later), voice tone, phrasing and vocabulary, or writing style and technique.

Each of these, singly or in combination, affects the legal assistant's professional productivity and effectiveness directly or through stimulation of the "sixth sense."

It is not the decision reached that is critical. What is vital is that the legal assistant consider, test, modify, alter, adapt, or reject concepts in establishing the technique that fits the individual's personality and contributes to strengths while minimizing the effect of weaknesses.

1.03   Basic Communication Skills

It is possible through study to improve the quality of one's communication skills. Numerous courses are available at junior colleges, community colleges, universities, private schools, or through seminars sponsored by professional associations that greatly enhance these abilities. Some of the courses that should be considered by persons entering the legal assistant field are public speaking, debate, appreciation and analysis of English literature, creative writing, and spelling. All will play a distinct part in raising the communication skills of the legal assistant to the highest possible level.

1.031   Public Speaking and Oral Presentations.

Public speaking or acting classes, debate societies, and similar activities will assist legal assistants in learning to think on their feet, to select effective and persuasive words under the press of time, and to *listen* to an adversary or partner.

Public speaking classes teach the skill of organizing a presentation into four steps: (1) the introduction; (2) a bridge from the introduction to the topical matter; (3) the argument; and (4) the closing summation. Following these four simple steps will assist the legal assistant in preparing presentations to attorneys, clients, or adversaries.

The introduction (step 1) in a speech should accomplish three things: introduce the speaker to the audience; bring the attention of the audience to the presentation in comfort or ease (thus the frequent use of a suitable joke to break the tension and build a little rapport); and provide a preliminary statement of the overall topic.

The bridge to the topic matter (step 2) is a departure from the introduction and a transition to the true body of the presentation. Usually this bridge points out to the audience the timeliness, importance, or value of the material the speaker will cover.

The argument (step 3) is the presentation of viewpoint or data. It is organized in logical, progressive steps that allow the audience to follow the reasoning from a basic fact (or assumption) through the analysis, with a definition of all issues, choices, procedures, or proposals), and any major alternatives.

The conclusion (step 4) is a statement of the speaker's decision, recommendation, or request. Frequently, this is presented as a recapitulation where the salient thoughts are briefly restated and a persuasive conclusion is offered.

1.032   Reading and Writing.

Creative writing or literature appreciation classes increase the ability of the legal assistant to write, to read, and to understand what is written. How to select words to convey the precise image desired is learned through the reading of essays, speeches, fiction and nonfiction works, and periodicals and daily newspapers.

Reading and writing legal material is a specialized activity that the legal assistant must study and practice in the course of the day-to-day job. Seek critiques, discussions, and the opportunity to draft material for others to accept or reject, edit, or totally rewrite. Do not take offense: take the suggestions and criticism and modify the technique used to match the style and technique of the office. Legal writing courses may help develop these skills.

1.033   Special Problems.

In communication, special problems must be overcome to accomplish a given purpose. Among those the legal assistant may anticipate are communicating with people with different levels of literacy or different life-styles and backgrounds, with people who are more fluent in a language other than English, and with those who have some form of physical handicap, such as a hearing, vision, speaking, or endurance problem. In each of these situations, it is the duty of the legal assistant to find solutions to the problems. The ability to solve such problems is one measure of his or her value to attorneys.

With the aged and the young, where attention problems may be a difficulty, schedule a series of visits of short duration or handle only one small problem, fact, or issue at a given meeting. For a person of limited literacy, word selection and the pace of conversation must be adapted to the comprehension level of that individual. If foreign languages are a barrier to direct communication, the use of an interpreter is essential for efficiency and desirable for the interviewee's confidence. Similarly, the handicapped who cannot hear, see, or speak have substitute means of communication that should be explored and used whenever possible.

1.04   Nonverbal Communication

This term relates to the image we create around ourselves as a matter of *choice*. It includes body language and sometimes is called the "associative image." It is that aura in which people clothe themselves and by which they project their self-image to others. Body language can be extremely important because the clients who visit law firms frequently differ in age, social status, levels of wealth, and backgrounds.

Law firms operate successfully on the trust of their clients, and each person who is employed by a firm to provide services to clients can reasonably be expected to contribute to that comfortable image of trust. To damage that image with whimsical or bizarre clothing or personal grooming is inexcusable and unnecessary. Each law office generally has some form of standard of dress for both men and women. It should be sufficiently flexible and comfortable so that none of the employees feels unduly constricted, nor should the attorneys feel the firm is being adversely affected or exploited by their employees' manner of dress, grooming, or personal hygiene.

1.041   Facial Expressions.

A legal assistant's demeanor is as important as his or her grooming. A pleasant, cheerful expression will generally elicit a responding smile from even the most unhappy or dissatisfied person.

We seldom fully appreciate the effect of the image we present to the world by the expression we wear on our faces. Actors, of course, make their livings by conveying emotion, attitude, and meaning through their faces. Comedians have built their whole careers on wearing a particular expression. If the legal assistant watches the attorneys' conduct in court, he or she will see that they, too, make use of the same communication techniques with the jury in trying to convey emotion, attitude, or belief to supplement or add impact to the words they are using.

Similarly, each of us, as we pass through our offices, meet each other, clients, or witnesses, and convey something about our attitude simply by looking at them and exposing our faces to their inspection. A legal assistant's attitude signals to the interviewee and to everyone else whether the legal assistant is serious or jocular, cheerful or sullen, interested and attentive, or bored and tolerating. Belief and disbelief often can be conveyed simply by the movement of eyebrows, and acceptance or rejection of a story can be expressed by wrinkles, motions, or lack of motions in the face. Surprise, shock, and revulsion are betrayed by facial expressions. The legal assistant who does much interviewing should perform "mirror practice" so that appropriate expressions can be adopted as needed. Practice allows analysis of the effect the legal assistant may create in the mind of a viewer by a particular grimace, scowl, or smile. It helps to see what the other party sees.

Remember, the most effective tool a legal assistant has in a repertoire of facial expressions is that of interested, cheerful, attentive, professional concentration. It encourages interviewees to talk; it makes the employing attorney believe in the legal assistant's dedication; and it assists the office manager in determining if the legal assistant will properly carry out the functions delegated.

1.042   Hands and Gestures.

Some gestures may be offensive to others. Be careful of such actions as pointing fingers, spearing someone in the chest or shoulder while making a point in a discussion, or touching others. Many people resent the unwanted physical contact and miss the point of the argument because they are preoccupied with the contact.

1.043   Eye Contact and Body Position.

These are vitally important in communication. Books are filled with descriptive terms such as "shifty-eyed liar," the "darting glance of fear," the "stern gaze of righteousness," as well as "a stiff-backed rage," "trembling with terror," or "crouched in shame." These vivid descriptions engender images in our minds based on past experiences or remembered characterizations in plays, movies, and television. It is a fact that various emotional conditions produce physical changes of posture and conduct that others interpret. The legal assistant is concerned with the messages given with the body or received from others. Project supportive, professional competence and avoid reflecting uncertainty, fear, confusion, irritation, or anger, unless there is a tactical need for such display.

1.0431 Nervous System.   The body's autonomic nervous system is a complex mechanism that aids it in preparing for or responding to stress. It is sometimes called the "fight or flight" condition. As stress increases, most people find their heart rate increases, their breathing rate and/or volume of each breath changes, more adrenaline is produced, and the body temperature may rise. Additional perspiration is generated, and muscle tension increases, sometimes causing trembling. The body is preparing itself for combat or escape, depending on the situation and its development.

Legal assistants should observe such symptoms and try to place them in the context appropriate to the situation—normal nervousness in anticipation of a novel experience, fear of the unknown, or fear of being detected in a lie.

Common nervousness can be dispelled by accommodation to the circumstance and the establishment of a comfortable situation. Other physical manifestations should be noted together with the stimuli that generated them. Legal assistants can adjust (or record) the condition, as needed, when it is reflected. The same messages *sent by* legal assistants may be irretrievable, however, and it is necessary to know, understand, and minimize the body language that adversely affects the legal assistants' function. Again, note the conduct appreciated or disliked in others and adopt that preferred conduct.

1.0432 Body Language.   Among the most common types of body language with a high potential for adverse interpretation are:

(a) No eye contact. Avoiding a person's eyes during conversation is very dangerous for a legal assistant. It has been said that the "eyes are the mirrors of the soul." Failure to look in the other person's eyes denies the legal assistant an excellent means of character evaluation and may create a doubt in the other party's mind as to the honesty, candor, or interest of the legal assistant.

Practice looking at people when they talk. Hold their eyes and try to evaluate whether they shift their eyes because they are lying or embarrassed or just because they are nervous. Do they practice the "sincere look" when trying out a tall tale?

Match the stress of the conversation with the appearance of their eyes. Stress causes the pupils to contract in some eyes; others become brighter and wetter, while others jerk back and forth. Joy, pleasure, and friendliness cause some eyes to sparkle.

It is not the whole world of meanings that is most important to a legal assistant professionally but the changes that occur during the talks and the time in the talks when the changes occur.

(b) Standing too close. Most people in Western cultures want some distance between themselves and those with whom they talk. It is an outgrowth of the "territory" theory that anyone who comes too close to you is "invading your territory." Big or tall people who stand very close to smaller or shorter people create both a physical intimidation and a difficult psychological problem of submission and/ or anger. "Arm's length" negotiations imply an equality of bargaining position, physically and psychologically. Legal assistants who like being close to people must gain their trust *first;* then closeness is tolerable.

(c) Slouching, stooping, and leaning. These postures suggest carelessness, lack of interest, and lack of intensity. They are acceptable with friends but should be avoided during first meetings. Erect posture may not prove the person is alert, but its lack makes the *proof* more necessary.

Body language and all its elements are important to a legal assistant in the employer-employee relationship as well as the interviewer-interviewee one.

1.044   The Office and the Image.

Body control, personal grooming, manner of dress, and facial expressions must meet acceptable standards for the office. These standards must also extend to the order and arrangement of the desk or office. This is one place where the old adage "neatness counts" cannot be emphasized more. Neatness assists prompt location of a file when it is needed. It engenders confidence in the minds of visitors to the office, whether they are other legal assistants, lawyers, or witnesses. In many ways, the office and the desk are extensions of the legal assistant's image of him- or herself: organized or disorganized, neat or sloppy. Certainly for interviewees who visit the office on business, the neatness of the office and the fact that all materials relating to their case are immediately available, while the cases of everyone else are discreetly out of sight, engender confidence and the belief in their minds that they are important and that their affairs are important and confidential.

1.05   Verbal Communication—The Listening Portion

Verbal communication denotes dialogue, speaking, *and* listening. It requires the use of the voice and of the ear, the two essential tools in verbal communication. They function twelve to twenty hours of every day in some form or another, and of the two, the ear and its use may be the most important. It is the "inbound" half of a two-way street. Listening is not an easy skill, but it is one that should be practiced at every opportunity by every legal assistant. Most people like to talk, and in talking, they expose themselves to the listener. If the legal assistant will listen and *keep his or her mouth shut,* he or she has greater opportunity to hear what the speaker has to say, to comprehend the words the speaker uses, and to correlate these words with other things the speaker has said before. This allows the legal assistant to accommodate him- or herself to the speaker's particular level of intelligence. The legal assistant is then better prepared to phrase productive questions at the appropriate time.

1.051   Fast Mind—Slow Mouth.

The mind works much faster than the mouth. As a result, many people find their minds telling them to argue, analyze, interject, question, or comment rather than to continue listening for greater and greater detail. There is nothing wrong with the mind going faster than the words of another, provided the narration is not confused by the listener's interjecting comments, thereby making the speaker reflect and fully realize what he or she is saying. The trickiest part about listening is to listen accurately and absorb what is being said, rather than allowing the mind to be distracted with comparisons, analysis, and arguments about what is being said.

1.052   Listen and Note.

The preferred technique is to listen and take notes while visually observing the person doing the talking. The change of facial expression, the onset of blushing, the movement of the eyes, the willingness to meet the listener's eyes or the avoidance of them, all are significant to the person who is listening. Whether it is an attorney giving instructions to a legal assistant for the first time or an interviewee telling a story for the fourth time, it is important to listen closely to what is said.

1.053   Words—The Key to Speaking.

Everyone speaks thousands of words every day. Strangely enough, the number of *different* words used among those thousands of spoken words may be small; the rest are the same words used repeatedly. It is estimated that the average high school graduate uses only seven.hundred different words in the course of normal conversations, and that figure does not increase appreciably with a college education. Twelve hundred is a fairly common number of different words in regular use by U.S. college graduates.

By contrast, a Japanese child entering school for the first time has a working knowledge of approximately six thousand different words. This is due in part to the structure of the Japanese language, in which verbs are combined to create conjugations reflecting tense and other grammatical elements. In English, however, we live through a memory course of strange rules and irregular conjugations of verbs as well as irrational pronunciations of certain combinations of letters. For legal assistants to communicate effectively, it is necessary to learn, appreciate, and correctly use these variations to the highest degree.

1.054   Jargon.

Once a person has attained a position as legal assistant, some alchemy occurs in the personality requiring the adoption of Latin phrases and the jargon of the legal profession in that legal assistant's normal conversations with peers, clients, and others. This is a serious error because people outside of the legal community may not fully understand the meaning of these words; thus, their use tends to confuse rather than clarify the meaning intended by the speaker. A legal assistant needs a broad vocabulary, and toward that end, understanding legal terminology is necessary; however, legal terminology should be reserved for use in technical discussions with peers of the legal assistant where the exact meaning of the legal terms is important.

1.055   Meanings, Words, and Sounds.

One of the unfortunate features of the English language is the number of words that sound the same phonetically and yet carry substantially different meanings. A different complication is words of similar sounds but different spellings. These words can pose very serious problems in the use of electronic dictating or recording equipment.

Despite the limited number of words used by the average American, *Webster's Unabridged Dictionary* modestly describes itself as containing twenty thousand different words. Add to that the amazing complexity of technical languages, such as those of the legal, engineering, and medical professions, as well as the jargons adopted in business and other fields. The volume increases dramatically and so does confusion.

Since legal assistants work in all of these areas, the demand for *learning* vocabulary is strong. However, great discipline should be exercised in the vocabulary that is *used*. Slang and jargon are often regional, having totally different meanings outside a given area. Learn everything but limit use to the right phrase at the right time. Do not simply exercise a specialized vocabulary to impress or awe listeners. Consider words as tools to convey appropriate meaning, not toys with which to satisfy the ego.

1.056   Ethnic Language and Street Talk.

Complicating communication is the proliferation of slang and/or ethnic phraseology and "street talk" in modern language. Many community colleges and some universities are adopting literature classes particularly designed to satisfy the needs of ethnic language students. Whenever possible, legal assistants should be familiar with these vocabularies, particularly when interviewing or contacting these ethnic populations. "Street talk" is ever-changing, as is slang, and staying abreast is difficult at best. A retentive memory, inquiring mind, and patient questioning when encountering street talk can clarify the needed meanings.

1.057   Understanding Is the Object.

Remember, the essence of communication is understanding, by both the speaker and the listener. The legal assistant is at once a highly skilled listener, translator, and speaker. The use of profanity, slang, or ethnic stereotypes by legal assistants is inappropriate. However, the people the legal assistant will encounter may use them, and it may be necessary in the course of those conversations to be able to speak on a comfortable level with such people. The legal assistant must be aware of these language dissimilarities and be able to accept their use without shock, irritation, or condescension.

1.058   Voice Tone and Implication.

Perhaps more important than the words they speak is the manner in which legal assistants use their voices: tone, modulation, inflection, and diction. A word correctly used but incorrectly pronounced loses the meaning ascribed to it. The legal assistant often discusses matters of great importance to people in stressful situations where the listener's critical examination of the legal assistant's verbal response is colored by anxiety. Many clients anticipate failure, and they expect their initial statements will be misunderstood. Support their hopes and dispel their fears as much as possible with a pleasant voice tone that is well modulated, with good diction, and with a relatively cheerful or at least neutral attitude.

1.059   Facial Expressions and Word Meaning.

One delightful feature about person-to-person conversation is the ability to impute shades of meaning to another's words from the emotion displayed on the person's face and from characterizing the individual's voice tone, modulation, and diction as being helpful, supportive, confirming, or argumentative. Once the conversation is filtered through a mechanical phase, such as through the use of a telephone or of dictating or recording equipment, these supplemental clues to the *meaning* of the speaker are lost. Often it is not possible to ask for clarification if the communication is on electronic media. Therefore, careful use of words and language and of voice tone and modulation is critical when conducting a conversation or a verbal communication through mechanical or electronic means.

1.06   Telephone Techniques

The telephone, of course, is the most common electronic or mechanical device in verbal communication. We seldom consider it as an extension of our personality. However, the majority of a legal assistant's first contacts with people will be accomplished over the telephone and it is very important to seriously analyze the manner in which the legal assistant conducts him- or herself on the telephone.

Telephone companies around the nation offer training courses in telephone techniques for people who work in offices and use the telephone as part of their daily business. One of the things they uniformly advocate, and rightly so, is to "put a smile in your voice." There is nothing more aggravating than to call an office seeking information and be switched from one phone to another seeking the one person who can provide the information. This is especially true if each of the people to whom the individual is transferred expresses by voice tone, inflection, or choice of words his or her lack of interest in the particular request or inability to assist the caller.

1.061   Friends or Enemies.

Each time a legal assistant picks up a phone, there is an opportunity to make either a friend or an enemy, and it should be considered precisely in that light; neutrals do not count.

Cooperation usually flows from a confident understanding by one person that the person on the other end of the line is both interested and able to consider his or her problem in a constructive and supportive manner. The legal assistant answers the phone, listens closely to what the person is saying, and considers before responding whether or not the request is reasonable and clear. "Is it a matter that can or cannot easily be answered on the telephone right now?" "Is it better to take a full message now, or switch the caller from extension to extension seeking 'possible sources' of an answer?" Decide, then respond appropriately to the caller. Smile into the mouthpiece; the voice will adapt to that stimulus and help make that person a friend for today.

1.062   Telephone Calls.

When placing or receiving a telephone call, the legal assistant must identify him- or herself by name and title. Notes should be taken of all calls involving clients or other office matters, and a copy of such notes should be placed in the appropriate client file. Any agreements reached or information given or received should be noted. A log of all telephone calls placed and received should be kept, not only by the receptionist but also by the legal assistant, particularly when he or she is accepting or placing calls on behalf of the employing attorney.

1.063   Confirming Letters.

When a telephone call involves matters of legal procedures, docketing, extensions of time to answer, arrangements for production of witnesses or documents, or other material relevant to a particular case, a confirming letter should be initiated immediately following the call. This letter should be a complete recapitulation of the discussed topics and arrangements to be included in the case file for the information and documentation of the attorney, with copies to the office docket control and each affected party in the case. Usual custom calls for the party requesting an accommodation to write the letter; however, legal assistants are best advised to initiate the confirming letter immediately for the protection of their own firms and attorneys. If two letters result, redundancy won't hurt and a difference of opinion in what the agreement was thought to be might be revealed.

1.064   Phonetics.

Telephones and other mechanical or electronic equipment can alter voice tones in the normal speaking mode. As a result, the transmittal of information of any importance, particularly names, addresses, numbers, or initials, should always be double- and sometimes triple-checked to insure accuracy. Letters, particularly, are easily misheard over a telephone or on a tape recording; B, D, P, and V tend to be confusing and indistinct over the telephone. Compensate with phonetic spelling. When there is doubt, use a phonetic alphabet to clarify any ambiguities. The legal assistant who does not know the international alphabet must substitute his or her own, for instance "A as in apple," and "G as in George."

Numbers, too, are difficult to hear clearly over the telephone. "Fifth" and "sixth" can be confused. Therefore, when discussing an address over the phone, first be sure that the other party understands the address and that the listener reads it back to the giver precisely the way it was heard. When there is doubt, use the phonetic alphabet to clarify any ambiguities or count the numbers as in "one, two, three, four, five—fi-yiv street!"

1.065   Aids in Telephone Use.

The telephone should be held so that words are transmitted directly into the mouthpiece and words emanating from the earpiece may be clearly and easily heard. The use of desktop amplifiers that allow for conference calls sometimes is beneficial if more than one person will participate on one instrument; however, the sound from such amplifiers can be eerie and distorted. The use of conference calls that interconnect several telephones so that each person can converse from his or her own office instrument may be used. In each of these cases, the participants must take turns talking.

The legal assistant who intends to use the telephone to take statements from potential witnesses in informal discovery must review and observe the federal laws on the use of tape recording equipment, particularly in connection with telephone company facilities. There is a considerable variety of equipment available that interjects a "beep" into the line periodically during the time the recording equipment is used. To make the statements valuable, they must be prefaced, as any other statement would be, with date, time, name of participant, and whether the work is or is not being done at the request of or for the benefit of an attorney in a given case. *Both* participants must be aware the recording is being made, and *both* must agree to such recording. This acknowledgment should be stated at the outset of such a recorded conversation and repeated before its termination.

Do not forget to memorialize all important nonrecorded telephone conversations with clear, written notes. They should be complete and expository with date, time, and the parties identified even if it is for the file only. Anything involving a case, the attorney, or a client should be summarized with the same elements in a memorandum to the file, or to the attorney, a letter to the client, or both.

Even recorded telephone conversations can more profitably be memorialized by a concise, written *summary* of the call, reserving the tape for future reference, if needed, rather than having the full dialogue transcribed and edited.

1.07   Dictating Equipment

The use of dictating equipment is well established as a time-saving operation in the conduct of work for attorneys and secretaries. This dictation process now extends to a large proportion of legal assistants who must convert their thoughts and notes into some less cryptic and more communicative form of preserved document. Legal assistants must learn the courtesies and practices of good dictation. One of the greatest helps, of course, is to understand fully the dictating equipment to be used, both in its use and its ability to reproduce the human voice. The user's manual supplied with each piece of equipment should be studied by each user *before* attempting to dictate.

Every dictated communication should carry some identifying data at the outset to insure that the material can be identified quickly and easily by the typist at the time of transcription, and, if necessary, later. Among the essential items are the date, the name of the dictator, the dictator's phone number or extension, the case or the topic of the dictation, whether or not there is a specific addressee, whether or not there are copies intended for other parties, and whether this effort is for execution as a draft or final form.

The use of a dictation "log" is helpful to most secretaries, whether they are experienced legal secretaries or novices from typing pools. The log usually has a tape reference number and identifies the dictator, the date, the type of case or topic, how many copies are needed, and the full names and addresses of all parties who are addressees or who will be *mentioned* in the course of the dictated material. This insures that the proper spelling of names and addresses is reflected in the final product. Including on the log any special, technical, or obscure words used in the dictation will save the dictator and the secretary/typist a great deal of time (the latter in research, the former in editing).

1.071   Voice Use.

The next element encountered is *how* the voice is used in dictating material other people will type. The pace of dictation should approximate a normal conversational pace. However, it is necessary to use better diction and pronunciation. Slurring or the use of such noninformational words as "and," "oh," "or," and "er" are not helpful to the typist and, in a long tape, can be both irritating and distracting. Do not use a monotone, but use a modulated voice, as you would in conversation. If possible, place emphasis on the correct words and the usual voice inflections that reflect sentence closings, periods, or question marks.

1.072   The Outline.

An outline of the material to be dictated should be prepared either mentally or on paper before beginning dictation. The entire structure of the ultimate document must be conceived ahead of time, both in content and form. Its format should be thought out and described either on the dictation log or in the introductory portion of the dictated material. Any tabulated material to be included should be referred to, and if it is in a form that can be inserted as a separate sheet or some other variety of material, it should be attached to the dictation log.

The actual dictation should proceed smoothly and quickly, with little dead space on the tape where the dictator is thinking. The speaker must concentrate on enunciating correctly so the typist can correctly understand the words and translate them into written form. Be especially cautious of using words that have unusual or irregular spelling or are technical terms, trade jargon, or of foreign derivation. Note these on the log. See Exhibit 1.

1.073   Verbalizing Punctuation.

The speaking voice has a cadence and pace that must be represented in writing by punctuation marks. Since the conversion of dictation from spoken to written form involves two people, the dictator must see the punctuation that will structure the sentence for the reader, then speak that punctuation for the typist. For example: "paragraph, all in caps, now is the time, colon, your opportunity to buy in quote sunshine acres close quote, is limited, exclamation point, write for details, period, end of dictation" will look like this: "NOW IS THE TIME: Your opportunity to buy in "Sunshine Acres" is limited! Write for details."

Often an experienced secretary, listening to a familiar voice, well modulated and speaking conversationally, can impute commas, semicolons, and capitalization. Very few typists, experienced or not, can hear a *new* voice and correctly punctuate for it. Typing from voice dictation is a reflex process for many typists, and they can perform only as well as the dictator dictates. The combination of modulated voice and spoken punctuation promotes efficiency through clarity and by providing the maximum number of clues to the material possible.

1.074   Review, Edit, and Learn.

It is not enough simply to dictate and pass the completed material over to someone to type. Legal assistants must periodically review the material dictated to detect failures in dictating technique and to improve delivery. No one can learn only from reviewing his or her own tapes. Consult the experts—the typists and secretaries whose work allows them to hear and appreciate the techniques of many dictators. A "partnership" feeling between secretaries and legal assistants can de-

EXHIBIT 1

DICTATION LOG		
Dictator	Date	
Case	Attorney	
	Client Charge	
	Deadline	
Topic		
To	CC	
SPECIAL NOTES: (Names, Addresses, Technical Terms, etc.)		

velop the dictating style of legal assistants into one of great efficiency that is pleasant and fulfilling for the secretaries and the legal assistants.

The legal assistant must be critical of his or her own work and accept the suggestions and criticisms of others with a positive and constructive attitude.

1.08   Written Correspondence

This section will not include legal briefs, pleadings, formal discovery documents, or other materials whose style and form or format can be established from form books or other research material available to the legal assistant and that are generally within the responsibility and editing purview of the attorney. We will discuss those elements of correspondence originated by the legal assistant to the members of the law firm and those documents of correspondence originated by the legal assistant, either individually or for the attorneys, from the firm to other people.

1.081   Internal Correspondence.

The law firm's internal correspondence can take many forms, from slips of paper bearing cryptic notes to full-scale studies and briefing materials. Without exception and regardless of the matter to be communicated, there should be a clear and distinct rule requiring each item of correspondence material to be dated, signed, and, preferably, directed to a specific addressee, even if that addressee is "memorandum to the file." Any correspondence originated in connection with a court action should refer to that case by suitable caption at the outset of the correspondence.

The correspondence may be typed or handwritten, according to the office policy, and may use multi-page carbon materials or a typed master from which photocopies can be made. For correspondence within the office where an answer is requested, the use of multi-page carbon material is helpful. Many firms produce in-house memoranda forms with answering spaces that have carbon sheets between the original and the return answer sheet. The use of this device saves time and allows both parties to have the full text of the original communication and its answer.

1.0811 Buck Slips and Action Tabs.   The use of buck slips or action tabs for transmittal of material directing certain actions from one person to another can save time without losing clarity. Similar slips can be used as a tickler or suspense file for docketed items to provide spaced reminders of anticipated due dates and/or appearances. See Exhibit 2. Where such tags or slips are used, color coding may be helpful: red for urgent, green for advisory, yellow for informational alert, with white for routine only. If such a color system is adopted, discretion in the use of red must be honored because, if everything is *urgent,* then the utility of the color coding is destroyed. The office manual may include a time guide for such codes: for instance, three days or less is red (urgent); three days to seven days is green (advisory); and seven days to fifteen days is yellow (information alert). Some firms use rubber stamps applied to certain colored slips for the same purpose with equally good effect.

1.0812 Memos and Full Documentation.   The preparation of a memorandum to file or to an individual is an important step and should be treated as such. Do not use cryptic notes that rely on mnemonics or association with other words in order to derive the exact meaning of the memorandum. Each document should be sufficiently detailed so that its meaning and purpose are easily discernable by anyone who reads it and it is as understandable next week or next year as it is on the day it is conceived. Each document should be an independent thought. The plan of any memorandum should always follow a logical path of having an introduction, a body, and a conclusion. The extent of these three elements for a given memorandum may vary; however, they should be considered at the outset and honored in the execution whenever possible.

   (a)   The introduction includes the reason for the memo—references to files, conversations or correspondence that might be needed as background.
   (b)   The body is the discussion of matters to be recorded, paragraphed by major thought, or a review of the elements.
   (c)   The conclusion is the recommendation, decision, or statement of status. If any suspense date is involved, it is reflected here, and the means of observing the suspense is shown—the "writer will follow up" or "the docket clerk was notified."

1.0813 Privilege.   In those written memoranda between the legal assistant and the attorney related to a given case, one of the desirable introductory sentences

EXHIBIT 2

ABC LAW OFFICES

TO: _____ DATE _____

    SEE ME _____

    FILE _____

    REFER TO _____

    DRAFT _____

    COPY & CONSULT _____

    SUSPENSE TO _____

    POST DOCKET _____

_____
BY

ABC LAW OFFICES

TO: _____ DATE _____

CASE: _____

COURT _____

PLEADING DUE _____

ANSWER DUE _____

ANSWER TO INTERR # _____

    DUE (ours) _____ (theirs) _____

DEPOSITION OF _____

    SCHEDULED _____

    AT _____

LAW & MOTION _____

    DUE _____

TRIAL SETTING CONF _____

PRE-TRIAL CONF _____

TRIAL DATE _____

to be used is "In connection with the cited case, you directed me to _____, and the following is reported." Since the legal assistant addresses the memoranda to his or her employing attorney, and it is in relation to a particular case, that particular document may carry the attorney-client privilege or the attorney work-product privilege. Whether the attorney at some future date may waive that privilege is not a speculation to be made by the legal assistant at any time, and certainly not when conceiving the document. In each and every case, the legal assistant is working for and under the direction of an attorney, and every step should be taken to insure that the same privileges the attorney exerts on behalf of the client attaches to the work of the attorney's legal assistant.

The policy and procedure of the office may or may not address this problem. If it does not, the question should be discussed with the attorney. An alternative technique may be preferred, such as the use of a rubber stamp saying "Attorney Privilege" or "Confidential" on the top and bottom of every page of such material.

1.0814 Brevity. Correspondence within the office should be brief. It is reasonable to believe we all work toward the same ultimate goal, and the use of excess verbiage or stereotyped language does not contribute to the communication of facts and information between members of the same firm. Simple words, clear and unmistakable, should be used whenever possible within the firm. This does not mean that in-house correspondence should not be phrased logically and persuasively. Candor, truth, and directness have greater value within the firm than in correspondence going outside the firm, which must be phrased more diplomatically and be more generalized. The legal assistant can use technical phrases here or employ the jargon or acronyms so dear to the profession. The only caveat is, use them properly, spell them correctly, and if in doubt, look them up in *Black's Law Dictionary* or a set of legal *Words and Phrases* before trying to include them in an internal memorandum.

1.0815 Project Memos or Reports. Frequently, the legal assistant is directed to study, review, summarize, and make recommendations on a given problem, topic, or volume of data. Such work requires extensive analysis, often supplemented by investigation or research, as well as the submission of a detailed report. Use an outline, such as the one shown below, to organize your thoughts before beginning to write.

TO: _____

FROM: _____   Date of Assignment _____

Assigned by _____

Deadline Date _____

Statement of the Problem:

Assumptions:

Sources of Information:

Analysis:

Alternative Analysis:

Recommendation/Conclusion:

This format requires the legal assistant to assemble the basic data; identify the assumptions (time constraints, personnel costs, task-time allocations) that will affect the conclusions; and clarify the sources of information used (whether books, documents, reports, or interviews) and the resulting dissection and analysis of the material, information, and assumptions. In applicable circumstances, an analysis of each available alternative is made and the full project then reported in terms of a conclusion or recommendation.

In the course of the analysis, footnotes, marginal annotations, or parenthetical citations should be used to refer to factual statements supporting sources or inferences that are significant in the analysis or the conclusion.

Note that this format is an adaptation of the "introduction, body and conclusion" form. Since the study may be lengthy, it may be efficacious to prepare a cover letter to the attorney setting out the problem presented and the recommendation or conclusion and indicating the detailed memo attached. This allows a quick perusal of the essence of the assignment on one page, while making the full report available for more thorough evaluation if needed.

1.082   Correspondence—Out of Office.

All correspondence from the firm to persons outside the firm, whether they are clients, the courts, adversaries, or sources of information, should follow the standard established by the office in the office manual. If no office manual exists, consult with the attorney to determine the form preferred, the conventions of salutation, case citation, signature blocks, and the policies and practices honored by the attorney that are to be followed by the legal assistant. Many attorneys prefer to have all correspondence go out over their signatures, while some attorneys will allow the legal assistant to write and sign correspondence connected with lawsuits as long as such correspondence does not contain legal opinions or give direct legal advice. Some attorneys mix it up. Follow the office procedures. Any questionable correspondence should be reviewed by the attorney for either his or her signature or your own. Letters signed by the legal assistant must clearly set forth his or her title, preferably as part of the signature block.

1.0821 Style and Form.   Frequently, legal secretaries set the style and form of the correspondence. They have developed habitual forms of salutation, citation, paragraphing, signature blocks, attachment or enclosure reference, spacing, and so on and are comfortable with the established procedure. The legal assistant adapts his or her writing to that style if at all possible, because his or her work and the secretary's are complementary. The choice of form, provided the alternatives are equal in clarity, should be made by the secretary or the attorney. If the form is clear, direct, and acceptable to the attorney and comfortable for the secretary, the legal assistant defers to their choice.

The organizational structure of letters leaving the office is extremely important, and each such letter must be composed with care. There is always the addressee identification. There may be a caption, for example, "Re: Smith vs Jones, Your file: XYZ 123, Our file: 77AB132." There may be a salutation (depending on office policy). There is always an introductory sentence or paragraph followed by the body of the correspondence, which should be limited to two or three major points (preferably *one*), and then a concluding paragraph in which the conclusion, decision, or request is stated and a deadline date established for any required action or response.

1.0822 Review for Impact.   Following dictation and typing, read the letter in final form to evaluate its impact. Does it fulfill the intended purpose? Is it clear? Is it concise? Is it sufficiently courteous and expository? Does it sound like you? Does it sound the way it was intended to sound?

The review will expose any cliches or stereotyped phrases that may have slipped in. Composing often is done one sentence at a time, each of which may be great standing alone but poor when combined.

1.0823 Purposes of Correspondence.   The purpose of legal correspondence, particularly that leaving an office, follows the same general principles as business correspondence. It should serve a combination of, or at least *one* of, the following four functions:

(a) To obtain action. The letter should create action by the party to whom the letter is going. This is done by presenting a situation in which the recipient of the letter either must act or, by failure to act, accept the results of inaction. This is insured by establishing a date in the last paragraph of the letter by which an answer or response is expected and required to prevent an alternative action.

(b) To provide information. The letter often is a response to an inquiry or a request by a client, adversary, court, or a source of information for information or futher details. This type of letter tends to be a little longer and may be more discursive or more involved than other correspondence. Any letter whose major purpose is to provide information should contain a concluding sentence or paragraph requesting further contact if the information provided is insufficient or incomplete. It can be as simple as "Please call or write if further information or clarification is needed."

(c) To maintain goodwill. Goodwill should obviously be maintained with the clients, with friendly witnesses, and with sources of information. Not quite so obvious is the necessity of maintaining goodwill with adversaries and with the court system employees. Many legal assistants tend to feel that adversaries are the enemy and, therefore, should be treated with disdain or without substantial courtesy. That attitude is wrong. Even though the adversary may act in a discourteous, abrupt, crude, or offensive manner, there is no excuse for the legal assistant's correspondence to reflect a similar attitude. Remember, the conduct of trials and pretrial discovery activity is often a complex series of maneuvers in which the advocates of the parties take on certain colorations and roles based on the factual situations with which they contend. It is foolish to allow an adversary to force the attorney or legal assistant into playing that kind of game. Correspondence reflecting discourtesy also reflects a lack of professionalism. Many times the present *adversary* in a difficult and contentious piece of litigation will be a *co-defendant* in some future action. The effect on each other of courtesy, tact, and diplomacy—or the lack of them—carries over into the next case. Legal assistants are responsible for the relations between the attorney and any other person of the legal community. The correspondence should *engender,* not destroy, goodwill.

(d) To create a record. The record to be created is one of courteous, disciplined, timely, professional, and appropriate conduct fully recognizing the rules of court. At the same time, the correspondence may create a record advantageous to the legal assistant's employing attorney and his or her client regarding the adversary's unwillingness to comply with those same rules of court. In the case of extensions of time where either side requested or agreed to a request by the other appropriately phrased correspondence will express an attitude either of cooperation or

vexatious behavior. A letter following a telephone call involving delaying tactics can be used in lieu of formal legal motions to create a record forcing the adversary to respond appropriately or face the difficulty of explaining the letter at some future time. The letter can be courteous and effective. The more responsibility the legal assistant carries in any piece of legal service and the more contact he or she has with witnesses, the court, and the adversaries, the more important are his or her efforts to create a record in the files of the court and the parties to the case.

1.0834 Timeliness.   Correspondence should never be postponed. As soon as the need presents itself, draft the letter, have it checked for accuracy, approved or signed, as appropriate, and send it. All letters confirming appointments or arrangements made over the telephone with other law offices, courts, or sources of information should be dictated immediately and mailed within a day or two of the original arrangement. If a suspense date is set in the letter, it is imperative to signal that date in the files of the attorney and the legal assistant. If it affects the docket, be sure to notify or send a copy to the docket or calendar clerk. Uniform understanding by everyone is the acme of communication. ·

1.0825 Grammar.   The composition of legal correspondence follows certain basic rules, among which are the rules of English grammar. The lack of a solid foundation in grammar will inhibit the legal assistant's ability to communicate. Consequently, many legal assistants find writing an onerous burden because their grammar is inadequate for the task. Those legal assistants must undertake to improve their English grammar, their creative writing ability, their vocabulary, and their methods of expression if they expect to advance in the profession.

In the interim, however, work must go on, and the easiest rule to follow in writing letters is to write as you speak. The language used in daily life sometimes may be elliptical in nature, lacking a clearly defined subject, object, or predicate, but it is a form of expression that will usually be comprehensible to the reader. A legal assistant with severe problems in this area must seek and honor the advice of others and write, edit, and rewrite if necessary. In the interim, he or she should write with confidence in the same manner as he or she speaks. The legal assistant is hired, in part, because of his or her ability to communicate, and the only way to improve that ability is to expose the faults to the blue pencil of critics, take note of the weaknesses thus exposed, and attempt to eliminate them in future work. The most comforting thought a legal assistant can have in drafting legal correspondence is that grammar is *important* but generally follows the lead of everyday conversation (by a few years, unfortunately, but it does follow). If the usage in a letter is comfortable to the author, it is probably acceptable as communication and may even be correct grammatically. If it is not, critics may help and seem to enjoy doing so.

1.0826 Stereotypes.   There is a tendency among those who lack confidence in drafting letters to follow guideline books that provide examples of phrases, some of which can be adapted to the legal assistant's needs. This may be a crutch of faulty strength since the legal assistant does not have to create the thought and may substitute triteness for spontaneity. It also allows the legal assistant to rely on the book instead of learning the correct use of the English language. Be certain that such canned letters or phrases are appropriate to the situation and will fulfill the purpose of the letter before adopting their use.

1.0827 Logical Presentation and Limited Topics.   Of more importance than stereotyped methods of referral is a well-organized presentation of the facts in coherent and logical fashion following the three-step structure discussed previously—"the introduction, the body, and the conclusion." Holding each letter to a minimum number of different topics will allow for easy drafting and simplicity of construction. The letter will be comprehensible if not fashionable. Often it is better to write three letters, conveying one or two ideas in each, rather than one long letter containing five or six points. Short letters will be read promptly, while longer ones may be scanned and put aside for later detailed review. If the purpose of the letter was to generate action, its very length may postpone that action.

1.0828 Vocabulary and Spelling.   The writing of letters necessarily involves vocabulary and spelling. No single skill is more important to the legal assistant than the ability to use and spell words correctly. Drafting letters by hand, to be typed later, pinpoints the ability to spell as essential to the finished product. In dictating and proofreading the drafted material, the ability to spell is essential to insure that the material does convey the idea intended by the use of given words. Misspelled words can alter meanings and content dramatically.

1.083   Which Word Is It?

We all are familiar with the simple word "to," or is it "too," or "two"? Each has a distinctly different meaning, is spelled differently, and yet sounds the same. In dictation, each can be confused, and in handwritten notes, the necessity of spelling each of those three words properly is apparent. A great number of other questions may arise over words of similar phonetic sound. A partial listing of some of these are below:

council or counsel	summary or summery
pistol or pistil	chorale or corral
tear or tare	bow or bough
capital or capitol	principle or principal
imminent or eminent	compliment or complement

Recognize these words and their meanings? If not, look them up and consider the difference of meaning implicit in using one for the other. These are but a few. Watch out for the others.

1.084   Typos and Meanings.

There is also the problem with words that are not pronounced the same but have all of the same letters within them or nearly the same letters within them. Minor misspelling or transposed letters change the meaning dramatically. With the word "casual," for example, a transposition of the "u" and "s" turns it into "causal." The word "did," if misspelled, can be "dead" or perhaps "deed." More dramatic would be the word "illusive," which could be misspelled as "elusive" or, even worse, "allusive," each of which has a distinctly different meaning. Will the letter then carry the intended communication?

A legal assistant who cannot spell *must* work intensively and continuously to eliminate or minimize that basic weakness.

1.085   Vocabulary Improvement.

Earlier we mentioned that the average range of words at the instant command of the average American is seven to twelve hundred words. The legal assistant's general vocabulary must be much greater, or it will be insufficient for the normal discharge of his or her duties. There are specialized areas in the legal field that will put demands upon the legal assistant's retentive and recollective abilities, such as the specialized terminology of medicine and all sorts of trade terms in marketing, construction, longshoring, maritime activities, business, engineering, and so on. The ability to learn new words accurately, understand their meanings, and incorporate them into our professional lives is important. Enrolling in English classes that emphasize spelling or creative writing is certainly beneficial and offers a working professional the opportunity to improve his or her command of vocabulary and of spelling under conditions where the effort is professionally judged and critiqued.

Bibliography

Block, Gertrude, *Effective Legal Writing for Law Students, Lawyers, and Paralegals.* 3rd ed. Westbury, N.Y.: Foundation Press, 1989.

Ebbitt, Wilma and Ebbitt, David. *Index to English.* 7th ed. Glenview, Ill.: Scott, Foresman & Co., 1982.

Fowler, H. Ramsey and Aaron, Jane E. *The Little, Brown Handbook.* 4th ed. Glenview, Ill.: Scott, Foresman & Co., 1989.

Gordon, Karen E. *The Well-Tempered Sentence: A Punctuation Handbook for the Innocent, the Eager, and the Doomed.* New York: Ticknor & Fields, 1983.

Hodges, John C., et al. *Harbrace College Handbook.* 10th ed. San Diego: Harcourt Brace Jovanovich, 1986.

Kirkland, James W., et. al. *Writing and Revising: Modern College Workbook.* Lexington, Mass.: D.C. Heath, 1986.

Mager, Nathan and Mager, Sylvia. *Encyclopedic Dictionary of English Usage.* Englewood Cliffs, N.J.: Prentice-Hall, 1975.

Mellinkoff, David. *Legal Writing: Sense and Nonsense.* St. Paul: West, 1981.

Rodale, J. I. and Urdang, Lawrence. *The Synonym Finder.* Emmaus, Pa.: Rodale Press, 1990.

Sisson, A. F. *Sisson's Word and Expression Locater.* Englewood Cliffs, N.J.: Prentice-Hall, 1966.

Strunk, William Jr. and White, E. B. *The Elements of Style.* 3rd ed. New York: Macmillan, 1979.

Venolia, Jan. *Write Right!* rev. ed. Berkeley, Calif.: Ten Speed Press, 1988.

Webster's Ninth New Collegiate Dictionary. Springfield, Mass.: Merriam-Webster, 1988.

Wydick, Richard C. *Plain English for Lawyers.* 2nd ed. Durham, N.C.: Carolina Academic Press, 1985.

2 Introduction to the American Legal System

The American legal system reflects complexity and diversity in its structure and procedure. In the United States, two sovereigns exercise jurisdiction: the United States (the federal government) exercises authority according to the powers granted by the United States Constitution; the state exercises authority through the state and federal constitutions.

In each case, the power exercised is a grant from the people, an expression of the people's choice as to how they will be governed and the limitations upon that governance.

2.00   Law in American Society

An essential element in understanding the law begins with definition. How is law defined? What is law? *The American College Dictionary* defines law as "...the principles and regulations emanating from a government and applicable to a people, whether in the form of legislation or of custom and policies recognized and enforced by judicial decision." *Black's Law Dictionary* also offers a general definition: "...Law, in its generic sense, is a body of rules of action or conduct prescribed by controlling authority, and having binding legal force...." Common to these definitions are 1) rules of conduct, 2) made by a controlling body, usually a government, 3) which are enforceable.

How has this controlling force, that is, the government, earned the right or power to make and enforce rules for a people? The answer can be found in the history and theory of legal principles, a brief overview of which follows.

2.001   History, Theory, Philosophy.

Legal traditions develop from history, theory, and philosophy. Our American legal system is most often thought to be taken only from English systems. However, in the development of Anglo-American law, four basic schools of thought are commonly identified.

2.0011 *Natural Law.*

In ancient times, the great philosophers from Athens—Socrates, Plato, and Aristotle—and the great Roman jurists, including Cicero, believed humankind could discover, by reason, the perfect rules of human conduct that were separate from enacted laws. These "natural laws" are not peculiar to any one people, rather they conform to the inherent nature of all people. These "natural laws" are unchanging rules of conduct discovered only by the rational intelligence of humankind.

Our Founding Fathers, especially Thomas Jefferson and Alexander Hamilton, adopted a revised "natural law" school of thought. They were particularly influenced by John Locke (1632–1704), an English philosopher who wrote on the individual's rights and government's obligations. A good example of Thomas Jefferson's work can be found in the Declaration of Independence:

> When in the course of human events, it becomes necessary for one people to dissolve the political bonds which have connected them with another, and to assume, among the powers of the earth, the separate and equal station to which the laws of nature and of nature's God entitle them, a decent respect to the opinions of mankind requires that they should declare the causes which impel them to separate.
>
> We hold these truths to be self-evident, that all men are created equal; that they are endowed by their Creator with certain unalienable rights; that among these are life, liberty, and the pursuit of happiness.

Our Founding Fathers declared revolution against the king of England based on the thinking that new rules must be established that were consistent with natural rights.

2.0012 *Positive Law/Divine Law.*

Early positivism developed in Europe, reflecting Judeo-Christian traditions and the canon law of the early Holy Roman Empire. Fundamentally, believers held all law is of divine origin and handed down by the sovereign. The positivist focused on four basic principles: 1) law consists of rules, 2) law is different from morals, 3) the sovereign establishes the rules, and 4) legal rules carry sanctions. Although this school of thought was influential, our constitutional principle of separation of church and state was already strongly embedded in American law.

2.0013 Sociological Jurisprudence.   This school of thought is concerned with the effects of law and its justifications. When a law is enacted, the proponents of sociological jurisprudence analyze the effects and reasons for the law by applying methods of the social sciences. The adequacy of a legal system is judged by weighing its effect on society against individual interest, special group interest, and the good of the general public.

2.0014 Legal Realism.   This school, which best describes our American legal philosophy, has its roots in natural law and sociological jurisprudence. The great jurist Oliver Wendell Holmes (1841–1935) was a pioneer of the realist school. Fundamentally, realists examine what the law *is* and not what the law *ought to be.* They use social science to analyze how the law functions and to look for underlying policy.

2.01   Sources of American Law

Federal and state laws come from many different sources. When most of us think of the law, we are generally referring to the statutes or ordinances that are enacted by a legislative body. To understand the American legal system and its sources of law, however, we will have to look further.

The American government is divided into three branches: executive, legislative, and judicial. Each of these branches has several levels: federal, state, and local. Thus, the United States executive branch is headed by the president, the state executive branch by a governor, and the local executive branch by a mayor or similar officer. The same pattern can be found in the legislative branch of government. The United States legislative body is the Congress; the state legislative body is the legislature; and the local legislative body is generally called a city or town council. The judicial branch of government also has three basic levels: the United States (federal) courts, consisting of the U.S. Supreme Court and the lower federal courts of appeals and district courts; state courts reflect this system as well by having a court of last resort, usually referred to as the supreme court, an appellate court, and a trial court. Administrative agencies are sometimes referred to as the "fourth" branch of government because the regulations that they promulgate have

EXHIBIT 3   Sources of American Law

	Four Sources of Law			
	Statutory *(Legislatures)*	*Administrative* *Agencies*	*Common Law* *(Courts)*	*Constitutions*
Federal Level of Government	Congress (Statutes)	Federal Agencies (Regulations)	Federal Courts (Cases or opinions)	U.S. Constitution
State Level of Government	State Legislatures (Statutes)	State Agencies (Regulations)	State Courts (Cases or opinions)	State Constitution
Local Level of Government	City Council (Ordinances)	City Agencies (Regulations)	Local Courts (Cases or opinions)	Charter

the effect of law. Administrative regulations are made at the federal, state, and local levels.

2.011   Common Law.

The individual states of the United States can trace the development of their legal principles, and to some degree their judicial systems, to medieval England. Common law principles have evolved through judicial decision making. The judge applies principles of law through the analysis of prior court decisions. This is known as *stare decisis,* that is, following the reasoning and decisions of earlier courts when presented with a similar fact situation unless a clear, convincing reason exists to depart from the established precedent. Judicial adherence to the principle of *stare decisis* creates consistency in the law. When a similar fact situation arises, the parties and their attorneys can, with some degree of certainty, predict and explain what the law has been and how the courts are likely to decide the dispute. Clearly, there are exceptions because the law does change. This system, however, offers stability and consistency in how legal principles are applied. Because the rules do not change rapidly, attorneys are able to explain to clients what the general law is and how courts have viewed their specific fact situation.

2.012   Statutory Law.

Laws that have been enacted by a legislative body are known as statutes or ordinances. Statutes are enacted by either the United States Congress or a state legislative body. The term *ordinance* is generally used when a city or town council passes a local law. The federal legal system is exclusively statutory in nature. There is no federal common law source. However, federal statutes, when challenged, are interpreted by judges. The state legal system, however, is a combination of statutory law and common law principles.

2.013   Administrative Law.

Administrative law is similar to statutory law (legislation). It is now well established and judicially accepted that Congress and the state legislatures may delegate some of their constitutional law-making authority to administrative agencies. In fact, without these agencies, government could not effectively function. Agencies of the federal government, such as the Social Security Administration, promulgate rules and regulations that have the effect and force of law.

Administrative agencies have the power to exercise quasi-judicial, quasi-legislative, and quasi-executive authority. Their authority is limited by the power granted. Congress can grant to the Social Security Administration, through legislation, the power to hear and decide violations of Social Security regulations. This grant is not unlimited because Congress, under the United States Constitution, is restricted to what it can delegate. In this way, agencies carry out many functions that are simply not possible for Congress to do alone. Because the separation of powers through the three branches of government is fundamental, this "fourth branch" can only function through the authority granted by one of the original branches, specifically, the legislative branch or the executive branch.

2.014   Constitutional Law.

The last major source of law is the constitution. Again, there are basically three levels of constitutions: federal, state, and local. The federal Constitution is the supreme law of the land. All other sources of law—legislative, administrative, and common law—are subject to the principles of the U.S. Constitution. The Constitution embodies general principles regarding the powers granted to the federal government, the powers reserved to the states, and the rights held by citizens, especially in the Bill of Rights, which are the first ten amendments to the Constitution. Because the principles are general, they require frequent interpretation by the judiciary.

In addition to the U.S. Constitution, state and local governments have constitutions. A state's constitution is the supreme law of that particular state; however, it is subordinate to the federal Constitution. Local governments also adopt constitutions, generally referred to as charters.

2.02   Systems

Systems provide structure for processing the various sources of law. There is a judicial system and process, a legislative system and process, and an administrative system and process.

2.021   Federal Court System.

The federal judiciary is established in Article III of the U.S. Constitution. However only the Supreme Court is specifically mentioned: "... The judicial Power of the United States, shall be vested in one supreme Court, and in such inferior Courts as the Congress may from time to time ordain and establish ...." Thus, the federal court system is in large part determined by Congress. In addition, Congress may establish courts under Article I, section 8 of the Constitution, which states that "... Congress shall have the power... To constitute Tribunals inferior to the supreme Court. ..." Congress has established, for example, the U.S. Tax Court under this section of the Constitution. The difference between the two articles is that under Article III, Section 1, judges hold office for life and compensation can not be reduced during their term. However Article I, section 8 makes no statement regarding the length of office or the compensation, thus Congress may establish specialty courts, such as tax or bankruptcy, without appointing judges for life or guaranteeing a level of compensation. Congress cannot establish all courts under Article I, however, because Article III, section 2 describes certain judicial powers granted to the Supreme Court and inferior courts.

The federal court system is composed of four types of courts: district court, a trial court; court of appeals, an intermediate appellate court; Supreme Court, final appellate court; and specialized courts.

2.0211 District Courts.   The district courts are established geographically, with a minimum of one per state (none crosses state lines); currently, there are ninety-four district courts. Larger states, such as Texas, California, and New York, have several district courts within them. District courts are trial-level courts of original jurisdiction. The district court evaluates testimony, hears witnesses, and makes findings of fact and law; most types of trials brought within the federal court system originate here.

District courts are general jurisdiction courts in that they hear most types of cases, unlike specialty courts, such as the U.S. Tax Court or U.S. Court of Claims, which hear only single-subject cases. Judges are appointed for life by the president, subject to confirmation by the U.S. Senate.

EXHIBIT 4   United States Judicial System

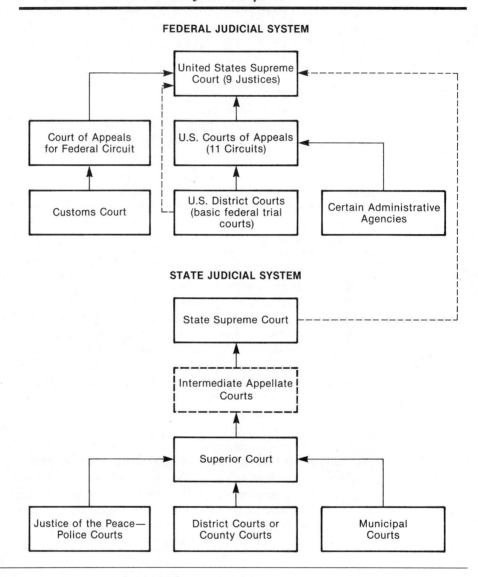

FEDERAL JUDICIAL SYSTEM

STATE JUDICIAL SYSTEM

2.0212 Courts of Appeals.   Courts of appeals (also referred to as circuit courts) were established as intermediate appellate courts to help relieve the workload of the Supreme Court. The United States has thirteen circuits: twelve represent geographic areas plus the District of Columbia, while the thirteenth is known as the federal circuit. The Federal or Thirteenth Circuit Court of Appeals handles appeals from the U.S. Court of Claims, U.S. Court of International Trade, and other specialized federal courts.

Courts of appeals hear cases where the appellant (the party appealing) argues that the evidence did not support the trial court's finding or that the trial court erred in the application of the law. The appellate court reviews the record only; no new evidence is admitted, and no witnesses are heard. This court will hear the arguments of the parties' attorneys, review the record of the trial proceedings, and read written briefs submitted by both parties. The court will make its decision based on this information. Most appeals end here. The next appeal would be to the Supreme Court, which exercises discretion in accepting cases. About 4,500 cases are appealed to the Supreme Court annually; the number actually heard averages less than 300.

2.0213 Supreme Court.   The U.S. Supreme Court is the ultimate interpreter of the United States Constitution. This is the court of last resort, although in most cases, litigants do not have a right to have their appeal heard by the highest court. There are two basic ways appeals reach the Supreme Court: through a writ of certiorari, an order to the lower court to send the Supreme Court the record of the case for review, which may or may not be granted by the high court; or through an appeal of right, which exists in certain cases, such as where a state or federal court of appeals has held a state statute violates the U.S. Constitution.

The Supreme Court has nine justices and exercises both original, or trial court, and appellate jurisdiction. Original jurisdiction is exercised in very few cases.

2.0214 Specialized Courts.   Federal specialized courts have jurisdictions limited to a specialized subject area. Examples of such courts are the U.S. Court of Claims, U.S. Tax Court, and federal bankruptcy courts.

The basic three-tier federal system is generally repeated at the state level.

2.022   State Court Systems.

Although state court systems are not uniform, they share some typical elements. They have trial and appellate level courts and courts with general and limited jurisdiction. Examples of trial courts with limited jurisdiction would be small claims, housing, or municipal courts that enforce local ordinances. Examples of specialized courts would be family or domestic relations and probate courts. The state will also have a trial court with general jurisdiction to hear civil and criminal cases.

Most states have an intermediate appellate court where the losing party has a right of appeal. The appeals court of last resort in most states is the state's supreme court. If the state has an intermediate appellate court, its supreme court may use discretion in accepting cases.

2.023   Legislative Systems.

The power to make law originates with the federal and state legislative bodies. The "supreme law of the land" is the Constitution; all other laws are subordinate. The Constitution states in Article I, section 1, "All legislative Powers herein granted shall be vested in a Congress of the United States, which shall consist of a Senate and House of Representatives." The Constitution grants broad powers to Congress, but those powers not specifically granted to Congress are reserved to the states or to the people through the Tenth Amendment, which says that "the powers not delegated to the United States by the Constitution, nor prohibited by it to the States, are reserved to the States respectively, or to the people." This is referred to as the Reservation Clause.

State constitutions similarly grant the power to legislate to a state body, often referred to as the legislature. This legislative body acts within the power granted by the state constitution or by the power reserved through the Tenth Amendment. Collectively, these powers are the police power of the state because they allow

EXHIBIT 5   How a Bill Becomes Law

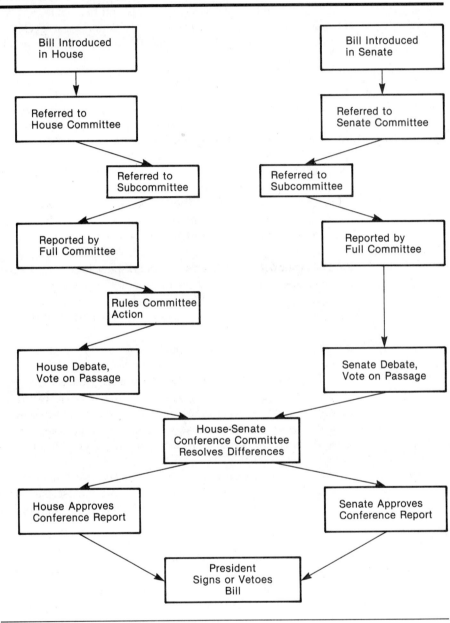

the state to enact laws to promote public health, safety, and welfare. Police power is very broad and permits states, for example, to set standards for licensing professionals, requirements for operating vehicles, and minimum age for marriage and generally to control any areas unique to the state.

State and federal legislative bodies have many potentially conflicting areas of power. However, the Supremacy Clause of the Constitution (Article VI, section 2) makes clear that the Constitution is the ultimate law: "This constitution, and the laws of the United States which shall be made in pursuance thereof; and all treaties made, or which shall be made, under the authority of the United States, shall be supreme law of the land; and the Judges in every State shall be bound thereby, any thing in the constitution or laws of any State to the contrary notwithstanding."

Another article that tries to clarify the relationship between state and federal power is Article IV, Sections 1 and 2. Section 1 states, "Full faith and credit shall be given in each State to the public acts, records, and judicial proceedings of every other state. And the Congress may by general laws prescribe the manner in which such acts, records and proceedings shall be proved, and the effect thereof." This is called the Full Faith and Credit Clause. Section 2 is referred to as the Privileges and Immunities Clause, and it states, "The citizens of each State shall be entitled to all privileges and immunities of citizens in the several States." Both of these sections of Article IV have been interpreted, through case law, by the U.S. Supreme Court.

Laws enacted by Congress are enforced by the judicial and administrative systems.

2.024   Administrative Systems.

Administrative agencies are established by a specific act of either the legislative or executive branch; the U.S. Constitution does not specifically provide for the agencies. Some examples of federal agencies are: Federal Deposit Insurance Corporation, Environmental Protection Agency, Interstate Commerce Commission, Securities and Exchange Commission, Federal Trade Commission, Farm Credit Bureau, Consumer Protection Safety Commission, and National Labor Relations Board. The administrative agencies, which may be under any one of the three branches of government or classified as independent, are often authorized by the act creating them to engage in quasi-legislative, quasi-executive, or quasi-judicial activities. In their quasi-executive status, they manage a particular area of interest of law; in their quasi-legislative role, they promulgate rules and regulations that have the force and effect of law; in their quasi-judicial status, they conduct hearings and render and order the enforcement of decisions.

Under the theory of exhaustion of administrative remedies, a person must seek an administrative agency remedy to a problem, if a remedy is available, before seeking relief through a court system.

2.03   Classifications of Law

Our large mass of laws is difficult to break down into simple classifications to study. Some general divisions can be made, however, that provide a useful introduction.

2.031   Substantive and Procedural Law.

Substantive law includes laws that regulate, define, and establish legal rights and obligations. Examples of substantive law are contracts, torts, criminal law, corporations, real property, administrative, trusts and wills, and constitutional law.

Procedural law establishes the methods of enforcing the substantive laws. Examples of procedural law are federal and state rules of evidence, rules of civil procedure, and rules of criminal procedure.

Basically, the difference between substantive and procedural law is that the former describes what our rights and obligations are and the latter describes how we apply and enforce the substantive rights.

EXHIBIT 6   Administrative Branch, Federal Government

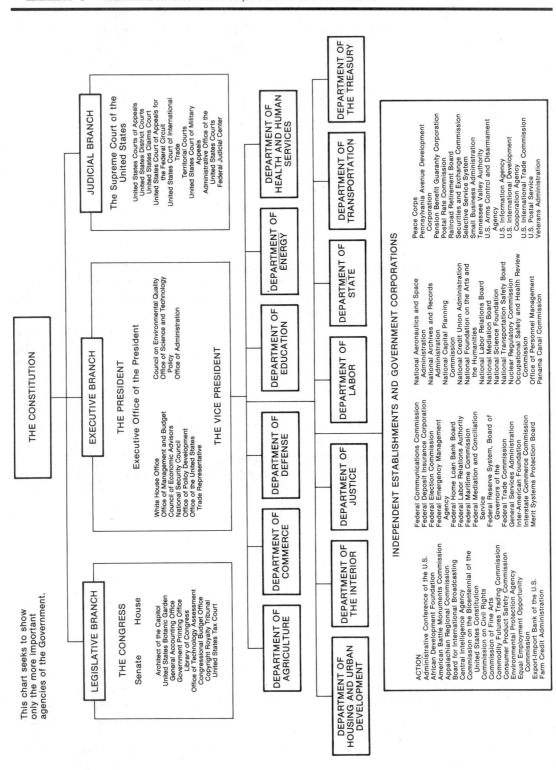

2.032   Public and Private Law.

Public law is best described as the relationship between persons and their government. For example, constitutional law, in part, describes the relationship between the government and the people. Administrative law is another example, as is criminal law. Constitutional law provides the right to vote, a voice in the government; administrative law describes what entitlement might be available through an agency, such as Social Security benefits; and criminal law defines crime against society, even though the crime may be committed against an individual person.

Private law deals with relationships between people. A breach of contract, a tort, wills and trusts, and corporation law are all examples of private law because they affect person-to-person relationships.

2.033   Civil and Criminal.

Civil law embodies the whole area of law that exists between persons or between citizens and their government. Some civil law is public and some is private. A suit by the government against a citizen is public even though it may involve a civil wrong.

In contrast, criminal law involves a wrong against the public as a whole. A person accused of a crime has violated society's standard of conduct. Although the crime may also involve a civil wrong, such as assault and battery, criminal law is public law.

2.04   Remedies

2.041   Law and Equity.

Remedies are the legal means to recover for a wrong. Historically, remedies were divided into legal and equitable. Courts were also divided in this way, so that a court of law could award a legal remedy and an equity court could award an equitable remedy. The courts were limited; if you wanted a legal remedy, that is land, money, or something of value, only a court of law could provide this; if you wanted an equitable remedy, such as an order for a person to perform an obligation under a contract, you had to go to a court of equity.

Today our courts are merged, thus these distinctions are not as important. The judicial system can issue a legal or equitable remedy. However, the adage "no remedy, no right" still pertains. For example, in the area of contract law, if the party feels money damages are inadequate, rescission (an order modifying or canceling the parties' obligations) may be sought.

2.05   Alternate Methods of Dispute Resolution

Two major alternatives to litigation and resort to the judicial system are arbitration and mediation.

2.051   Arbitration.

Arbitration allows a person or persons other than a court to make a binding decision and to make an award regarding the dispute. Most states have arbitration statutes, and the Federal Arbitration Act covers certain areas. Arbitration may be compulsory (mandated by law) or voluntary. Generally, arbitration is quicker and less expensive than litigation. The American Arbitration Association can provide experienced arbitrators for parties in dispute. These experts, who often come from such professional fields as law, medicine, and engineering, can provide inexpensive, speedy solutions to conflicts.

2.052 Mediation.

Mediation is the process of voluntarily submitting the dispute to a third party who will try to reconcile the differences. This process does not involve a binding decision or an award but rather is an opportunity for the parties to compromise. The National Mediation and Conciliation Service provides mediators for labor disputes. Other national and local associations offer mediation services in such areas as family relations and small business problems.

3 Ethics

3.00 Introduction

Ethics are guideposts for measuring conduct and for conforming behavior to meet accepted standards for legal assistants in their role in the judicial system. Ethics, simply put, are proper professional conduct. Ethics are critical for legal assistants and should not be taken lightly. Legal assistants work under the supervision of attorneys in the delivery of legal services. The legal profession traditionally has pursued and maintained a goal of assuring high standards of professional competence and ethical conduct. As part of the attorney team in the rendering of legal services, a legal assistant should pursue and maintain this same level of high standards of professional competence and ethical conduct.

The past two decades have brought many changes and advances in the legal assistant profession and the recognition and increased utilization of legal assistants by attorneys. But this advancement and utilization have also raised questions about what activities a legal assistant may perform and still remain within accepted professional boundaries and ethical limitations. One must ascertain what standards and principles exist for a legal assistant to follow to assure that the conduct and activities performed do not cross the boundary into the realm of potential liability for the unauthorized practice of law. Questions on legal ethics, however, are not always easily answered. Conduct cannot always be simply categorized as right or wrong. A knowledge of ethical considerations will assist in this decision process. The NALA *Code of Ethics and Professional Responsibility,* the NALA *Model Standards and Guidelines for Utilization of Legal Assistants* (annotated), provisions of the American Bar Association *Model Rules of Professional Conduct,* similar state codes of professional conduct for attorneys, and case law are necessary sources for the legal assistant to obtain this knowledge.

The American Bar Association has traditionally provided attorneys with meaningful guidelines for competent and proper representation of their clients and the public interest as a whole. The ABA's most recent formal attorney conduct guidelines are found in the *ABA Model Rules of Professional Conduct,* adopted in 1983. The predecessor to the *Model Rules* was the *ABA Model Code of Professional Responsibility,* which consisted of canons, ethical considerations, and disciplinary rules. Provisions of the former *Model Code* have been incorporated into the present *Model Rules,* and the provisions of each consider substantially similar subject matter or reflect similar concern. To the extent that the ethical considerations and disciplinary rules of the *Model Code* offer further explanation or clarification, they can and should be relied on as a resource for professional standards and as a supplement to the current *Model Rules.* These ethical considerations and disciplinary rules of the ABA only have direct prescription on attorneys and only in those state jurisdictions that specifically adopt them. But all states have at least some equivalent code of professional conduct or responsibility statute governing the conduct of attorneys within their jurisdiction. The legal assistant should be familiar with the provisions of the attorneys' code applicable in his or her jurisdiction because the employing attorney has a responsibility to see that the legal assistant abides by the standards for ethical conduct set out in the code. Rule 5.3 of the *ABA Model Rules* specifically requires that in employing a nonlawyer, the attorney "shall make reasonable efforts to ensure that the person's conduct is compatible with the professional obligations of the lawyer." This requirement is imposed on the attorney because the "assistants, whether employees or independent contractors, act for the lawyer in rendition of the lawyer's professional services" (Comment, Rule 5.3, *ABA Model Rules of Professional Conduct*).

Courts also continually render opinions interpreting the ABA model code and model rules, in addition to disciplinary code provisions for a particular jurisdiction. The American Bar Association maintains a Committee on Professional Ethics, which publishes formal and informal opinions relating to code provisions. State and local bar associations also may offer formal and informal opinions on questions relating to ethical conduct.

Self-regulatory efforts to pursue and maintain professional conduct and provide meaningful guidelines for ethical behavior are also a tradition in the legal assistant profession. In 1975, the National Association of Legal Assistants adopted its own *Code of Ethics and Professional Responsibility,* which is reproduced in its entirety at the end of this chapter. Each of these canons considers similar subject matter and concerns addressed in rules and codes governing attorney conduct generally, as well as attorney conduct in the use of nonlawyers. NALA recognized that the legal assistant's conduct must be compatible with the obligations of the lawyer since the ultimate interests served are the same. Accordingly, Canon 12 of the NALA Code mandates that a legal assistant is governed by the *ABA Model Rules of Professional Conduct* and *Model Code of Professional Responsibility.*

In 1984, NALA determined that with the increased utilization of legal assistants by attorneys, an educational document relating to standards and guidelines for their use was necessary to provide guidance for the legal profession on acceptable conduct for legal assistants. The culmination of NALA's research and efforts in this area is the *Model Standards and Guidelines for Utilization of Legal Assistants* (annotated; 1984, as amended), which is reproduced in its entirety at the end of this chapter. These guidelines were developed from existing case law, professional standards of conduct governing attorneys and their use of legal assistants, and other authorities. In short, the guidelines served to answer three basic questions about legal assistants: who are they, what are their qualifications, and what duties may they perform. Sections IV through IX of the *Model* provide an excellent outline of the ethical standards and principles for legal assistants and guidance for the attorney in utilizing a legal assistant.

3.01 Duties A Legal Assistant May Perform under the Supervision of an Attorney

As noted in the introduction to this book, the NALA definition of a legal assistant includes the caveat that the legal work being performed by the individual is done under the supervision of an attorney. The rationale for inclusion of this aspect will become obvious in the discussion of guidelines, codes, and case law that follows.

What may a legal assistant do? Canon 2 of the *NALA Code of Ethics and Professional Responsibility* addresses this question as follows: "A legal assistant may perform any task delegated and supervised by a lawyer so long as the lawyer is responsible to the client, maintains a direct relationship with the client, and assumes full professional responsibility for the work product." This language is compatible with EC 3-6 of the *ABA Code of Professional Responsibility,* which provides:

> A lawyer often delegates tasks to clerks, secretaries, and other lay persons. Such delegation is proper if the lawyer maintains a direct relationship with his clients, supervises the delegated work, and has complete professional responsibility for the work product.

Various states have included similar provisions in attorney professional responsibility codes. For example, EC 3-6 of the *Florida Code of Responsibility* provides:

> A lawyer or law firm may employ non-lawyers such as secretaries, law clerks, investigators, researchers, legal assistants, accountants, draftsmen, office administrators, and other lay personnel to assist the lawyer in the delivery of legal services. A lawyer often delegates tasks to such persons. Such delegation is proper if a lawyer retains a direct relationship with his client, supervises the delegated work, and has complete professional responsibility for the work product.

The work which is delegated is such that it will assist the employing·attorney in carrying the matter to a completed product either by the lawyer's personal examination and approval thereof or by additional effort on the lawyer's part. The delegated work must be such, however, as loses its separate identity and becomes either the product or else merged in the product of the attorney himself.

Kentucky was the first state to actually adopt a separate paralegal code within its supreme court rules; this code recognizes the use of paralegals and sets forth certain exclusions to the unauthorized practice of law. But the code also expressly mandates that the attorney must supervise the legal assistant and must remain responsible for the work.

For purposes of this rule, the unauthorized practice of law shall not include any service rendered involving legal knowledge or advice, whether representation, counsel or advocacy, in or out of court, rendered in respect to the acts, duties, obligations, liabilities or business relations of the one requiring services where:

a. The client understands that the paralegal is not a lawyer;
b. The lawyer supervises the paralegal in the performance of his duties; and
c. The lawyer remains fully responsible for such representation, including all actions taken or not taken in connection therewith by the paralegal to the same extent as if such representation had been furnished entirely by the lawyer and all such actions had been taken or not taken directly by the attorney.*

---

* Paralegal Code, Ky.S.Ct. R. 3.700, Sub-Rule 2.

In addition to the general professional responsibility codes regulating the use of nonlawyers by attorneys, many states have adopted specific guidelines for the use of legal assistants.[1] These guidelines are generally not part of the attorney's professional responsibility code but have been developed to emphasize the requirement that attorneys must supervise the work that is delegated to the legal assistant and must accept complete responsibility for the final work product. To be fully informed, a legal assistant should be familiar with not only the professional code for attorneys in a state but also with any additional guidelines regarding the use of legal assistants.

3.02 Ethical Considerations in the Work Environment

The ethical considerations for legal assistants do not end with proper delegation and supervision by the attorney. The legal assistant must be conscious of other ethical considerations in carrying out the assigned tasks. The individual must look at more specific principles contained in the various professional responsibility codes for attorneys and legal assistants and the relationship of these concepts to the conduct and activities performed by the legal assistant as part of the attorney team.

3.021 The Legal Assistant in the Client-Lawyer Relationship.

3.0211 Accepting Clients and Setting Fees. Canon 3 of the *NALA Code* specifically prohibits a legal assistant from engaging in the practice of law by

---

[1] See, for example, *Guidelines for the Utilization of Legal Assistants in Kansas* adopted by the Kansas Bar Association; *Guidelines for Legal Assistants,* adopted by the Colorado Bar Association; *Guidelines for Utilization by Lawyers of the Services of Legal Assistants,* adopted by the South Carolina Bar; *Guidelines for Utilization of Legal Assistant Services,* adopted by the State Bar of Michigan.

accepting cases and setting fees. (Also see *NALA Model Standards*, section VI for a discussion of case law regarding such prohibited acts.)

The legal assistant may not establish the attorney/client relationship. While the legal assistant may be involved in obtaining initial information from a prospective client, the attorney must make the final decision to accept the case. The legal assistant must also be extremely cautious in quoting fees for legal services. Making general statements about approximate fees that might be charged for a particular service is a very unwise practice, even when the employer may have an established schedule listing fees for various services. There may always be exceptions to the set fees, and until the attorney has discussed the specific legal problem with the client, neither the services required nor the reasonable fee are certain.

3.0212 Competence and Integrity.

Canons 9 and 10 of the *NALA Code* stress competence and integrity. Rules 1.1 and 8.4 are the counterpart rules in the *ABA Model Rules of Professional Conduct*. As with lawyers, the legal assistant must maintain skills and knowledge and stay abreast of changes in procedures and the law. Knowing how things used to be done and what the law was will not enable the legal assistant to perform competently. The legal assistant is a professional, and to retain that status, a competent legal assistant must maintain a continuous program of self-education and reeducation. Attendance at workshops and seminars in substantive areas of the law and in the legal assistant's specialty is essential. Reading legal publications, case summaries, and professional association publications will keep the legal assistant on the cutting edge. Integrity is a catch-all term prohibiting misconduct generally. The legal assistant must adhere to the precepts of truth, honesty, and loyalty to assist the lawyer in maintaining integrity in not only the lawyer-client relationship but in all activities conducted in the professional capacity.

3.0213 Diligence and Communication.

A legal assistant is often responsible for docket control on matters involving time deadlines. The lawyer will depend on the legal assistant to meet his or her obligation to act with "reasonable diligence and promptness in representing clients," as required by Rules 1.3 and 1.4 of the *ABA Model Rules of Professional Conduct*. The legal assistant will also frequently keep clients updated on the status of cases or matters. And clients often will rely on the legal assistant to get information because they may prefer to talk to the legal assistant rather than the attorney. A legal assistant may explain procedural matters to clients, but making a legal judgment on a client's behalf as to what procedure is best would be improper. If the legal assistant is merely passing on information or a decision made by the attorney, the communication by the legal assistant is not improper. A legal assistant must be on guard in these situations to ensure that he or she does not give legal advice or perform any acts that involve professional legal judgment. Such activities are specifically prohibited by Canons 3, 4, and 5 of the *NALA Code* because the exercise of professional legal judgment is the practice of law.

3.0214 Confidential Information and Privileged Communications.

A legal assistant becomes privy to confidential matters about clients' affairs and information about matters or cases generally in performing job functions. All of this information must be kept confidential and should not be revealed in casual or indiscreet conversations, particularly with individuals outside the workplace.

Canon 7 of the *NALA Code* addresses this ethical responsibility for legal assistants, and the ABA counterpart for attorneys is Rule 1.6.

Privileged communications relate to rules of evidence and involve a third party's attempt to obtain information within the realm of the lawyer-client relationship. A communication made to an attorney in professional confidence is not permitted to be disclosed unless an exception to the general rule allows it. Other similar privileged relationships exist, such as those between physician and patient or husband and wife, which are all established by statute, constitutional mandate, or common law. Any communication made by a client to the legal assistant in confidence will most likely be considered privileged. A legal assistant should not, without the consent of the client, the direction of the employing attorney, or by court order, make any disclosures to third persons of communications made by the client to him or her in the course of professional employment.

This privilege can also extend to work done by the attorney for a client as part of the attorney's work product. The work of the legal assistant, directed, supervised, authorized, and required by the attorney as part of the service provided the client, may also be privileged. The legal assistant must assume that each communication sent or received, each document generated, all notes taken, and so on are privileged and must protect that privilege until the attorney, the client, or the court authorizes or orders disclosure.

3.0215 Conflict of Interest.   Conflict of interest and the avoidance of the appearance of impropriety are important considerations because loyalty is an essential element of the attorney-client relationship. Canon 8 of the *NALA Code* expands the general protection of the confidences of a client to include the avoidance of conflicts of interest or any activities that might present the appearance of impropriety. Rule 1.7 of the *ABA Model Rules* addresses the attorney's responsibility to avoid conflicts of interest.

With the increased utilization of legal assistants, the potential for conflicts of interest heightens. Recognizing that conflicts may arise when a job change occurs for a legal assistant, the ABA Committee on Ethics and Professional Responsibility issued an opinion on this topic:

> A law firm that hires a non-lawyer employee, such as a paralegal, away from an opposing law firm may save itself from disqualification by effectively screening the new employee from any participation in the case the two firms have in common.*

---

* ABA Opinion No. 88-1526 (6/22/88)

This screening seeks to protect the confidences of a client and any information that pertains to the attorney-client relationship. EC4-2 and DR4-101(D) of the *ABA Code of Professional Responsibility* impose requirements on the attorney to exercise care in selecting and training employees to ensure that such confidences are preserved.

Several courts have already been faced with requests for disqualification on the basis of non-lawyers' conflicts of interests, primarily resulting from a job change from one firm to another.[2] Although neither the ABA nor the courts have specified

---

[2] *Kapco Manufacturing Co., Inc. v. C & O Enterprises, Inc.,* 637 F.Supp. 1231 (N.D.Il. 1985); *Williams v. Trans World Airlines,* 588 F.Supp. 1037 (W.D.Mo. 1984); *Glover Bottled Gas Corp. v. Circle M Beverage Barn, Inc.,* 514 N.Y.S.2d 440 (A.D.2 Dept. 1987); *Esquire Care, Inc. v. Maguire,* 532 So.2d 740 (Fla.App.2 Dist. 1988).

how far disqualification may extend, it certainly extends to the new employer in not utilizing the legal assistant in these common cases. The new employer also may not properly attempt to obtain information from the legal assistant that he or she obtained as a result of the prior employment. The legal assistant should be on guard for any situations that might present a conflict of interest as a result of information gained in past employment and should disclose any questionable situation to the employer.[3]

3.0216 Safekeeping of Property.   A final area deserving of mention is the safekeeping of property. Rule 1.6 of the *ABA Rules* prohibits the comingling of funds. Law offices maintain separate trust accounts for holding monies related to client transactions, and strict accounting procedures must be followed in these accounts. The legal assistant is often involved in setting up these accounts or in disbursements and should abide by all procedures required of the law firm in such transactions.

3.022   Transactions with Persons Other than Clients.
The legal assistant's ethical obligations are not confined to activities within the employer's office or involving the clients represented by the employer.

3.0221 Truthfulness in Statements.   Rule 4.1 of the *ABA Model Rules* mandates that false statements cannot be made and facts cannot be misrepresented. Such a responsibility extends to the legal assistant. Of particular importance here is the need for a legal assistant to clearly identify him- or herself, specifically including his or her status as a legal assistant, in any communications, oral or written, to anyone during the performance of his or her job. Such a practice will ensure that there is no misrepresentation regarding the legal assistant's nonlawyer status nor any incorrect inference from the failure to disclose the nonlawyer status.

3.0222 Improper Communications.   Just as attorneys are prohibited from any direct communications with persons and adverse parties known to be represented by counsel (Rule 4.2 of *ABA Model Rules*), legal assistants cannot make such a contact to circumvent that prohibition.

3.023   The Legal Assistant and the Law Firm.

3.0231 Attorney Responsibility regarding Nonlawyer Assistants.   As noted in the introduction to this chapter, Rule 5.3 of the *ABA Model Rules* specifically discusses the responsibilities of an attorney regarding the use of nonlawyer assistants and the need to take measures to ensure the nonlawyer's conduct is compatible with the professional obligations of the lawyer. EC 3-5 of the *ABA Model Code of Professional Responsibility* also relates to the attorney's use of nonlawyers.

3.0232 Sharing of Legal Fees and Partnership.   Rule 5.4 of the *ABA Model Rules* states that legal fees may not be shared with nonlawyer personnel. This rule is not intended to deny legal assistants salary, bonuses, or benefits, even though they may be tied to the profitability of the law firm. Instead, the prohibition applies

---

[3] For a thorough discussion of the considerations for a legal assistant in changing jobs, see Voisin, Vicki, *Changing Jobs: Ethical Considerations for Legal Assistants,* XV Facts & Findings 12 (March 1989).

to any form of compensation that is based on the existence or amount of a particular fee. Thus, a legal assistant's compensation may not include a percentage of the profits of a law firm, nor can the compensation be based on fees received in the general course of business or from a particular client or case. However, subparagraph (a)(3) of Rule 5.4 provides an exception to the extent that the law firm may include nonlawyers in a compensation or retirement plan, even though the plan is based in whole or in part on a profit-sharing arrangement.

3.0233 Listing on Letterhead, Use of Business Cards, and Signing of Letters. Questions arise frequently as to whether a law firm may list legal assistants and other nonlawyers on the firm letterhead, whether such individuals may have business cards also containing the law firm name, and whether legal assistants can sign letters under the lawyer's letterhead.

ABA Model Rules 7.1 and 7.5 govern what information may be provided on lawyers' letterhead. While these rules do not specifically address the listing of nonlawyer personnel, the ABA has issued an informal opinion (89-1527, 2/22/89) stating that the listing of nonlawyer support personnel is not prohibited by the rule or any other rules, provided the listing is not false or misleading. To avoid being misleading, the opinion states, it should be clear that the personnel listed are not attorneys. The same findings are made with regard to business cards for nonlawyers. The primary concern is that measures are taken with respect to any title or other designation of the nonlawyer personnel to avoid confusion about the status of the nonlawyers.

Rules regarding nonlawyer use of business cards and listing on letterheads vary from state to state, and a legal assistant should be familiar with and follow the appropriate rules of the jurisdiction involved. The form and language of any listing on letterhead or business cards should also be approved by the employing attorney.

It is generally accepted that a legal assistant may sign letters on the law firm letterhead. Again, though, the status of the legal assistant must be clear, so the signature should be followed by an appropriate designation of nonlawyer title. The contents of the letter signed must also be considered. No direct legal advice should be contained in correspondence sent under the legal assistant's name. If any doubt exists, the attorney should be consulted on the propriety of sending the letter over the legal assistant's signature.

3.024   The Legal Assistant and Public Service/Pro Bono Activities.

Attorneys have a basic responsibility to provide public-interest legal services without a fee or at a reduced fee (ABA Rule 6.1). To meet public concern about the availability of legal services to the indigent, many bar associations have established programs to provide such low-cost or free services to these individuals. Some legal assistant professional associations are even working with the organized bar associations in these programs. A legal assistant may assist attorneys in the same manner and under the same delegation and supervisory obligations in these public service activities. As with the attorney, the legal assistant is bound by the same standards of professional conduct in offering pro bono services as with any other services.

3.03   The Legal Assistant and the Unauthorized Practice of Law

ABA Model Rule 5.5 specifically prohibits a lawyer from assisting a nonlawyer in the performance of any activity that would constitute the unauthorized practice of law. Canon 6 of the NALA *Code of Ethics and Professional Responsibility* prohibits a legal assistant from engaging in any activity that would constitute the unauthorized practice of law. Canon 1 of the NALA *Code* requires that the legal assistant not perform duties that only lawyers may perform.

The proper starting point for any discussion of the unauthorized practice of law is to have a basic understanding of what constitutes the practice of law. The ABA has been reluctant to formulate a single specific definition of what constitutes the practice of law but stresses (in the Model Code EC 3-5) that it relates to the rendering of services for others that call for the exercise of professional legal judgment. Courts have also attempted to define the practice of law, and in *Davis v. Unauthorized Practice Commission,* 431 S.W.2d 590 (Tex. 1968), the Court stated:

> According to the generally understood definition of the practice of law, it embraces the preparation of pleadings and other papers incident to actions of special proceedings, and the management of such actions in proceedings on behalf of clients before judges in courts. However, the practice of law is not confined to cases conducted in court. In fact, the major portion of the practice of any capable lawyer consists of work done outside of the courts. The practice of law involves not only appearances in court in connection with litigation, but also services rendered out of court, and includes the giving of legal advice or the rendering of any service requiring the use of legal skill or knowledge, such as preparing a will, contract, or other instrument, the legal effect of which under the facts and conclusions involved must be carefully determined.

A cursory reading of this definition might lead one to the inaccurate conclusion that anyone who prepares legal documents could be engaged in the practice of law. The important distinguishing fact, though not present in the *Davies* case, is that a legal assistant performs these functions under the direct supervision of an attorney. In addition, as discussed above, attorney standards of professional conduct recognize the use of nonlawyer personnel in performing many tasks that the lawyer would otherwise do.

Another aspect of the practice of law touched upon in the *Davis* definition is the appearance in proceedings on behalf of clients in courts. The NALA Code of Ethics prohibits the appearance of a legal assistant in court in a representative capacity for a client, unless such appearances are authorized by court or agency rules. The basis for this guideline is the requirement that the legal assistant's work must be under the direct supervision of an attorney. Unless there has been a waiver, either through a court or agency rule, that permits the legal assistant to perform services independently and without the supervision of an attorney, the legal assistant will be crossing the boundary and could be subject to charges of unauthorized practice of law.

The appearance by nonlawyers in a representative capacity in administrative proceedings is allowable by a number of state and federal agencies. The use of legal assistants in administrative proceedings may well be the wave of the future, but before the legal assistant engages in such activities, appropriate steps should be taken to ensure that such appearances are sanctioned by the agency rules, the supervising attorney has authorized and endorsed the appearance, court approval for the legal assistant to appear has been obtained, and, if appropriate, the client has consented to the legal assistant appearing on his or her behalf.[4]

What constitutes a court appearance is somewhat vague, depending on the activities involved in the appearance, and at least one court has held that preparation of a court order and transmission of information to the court was not the unauthorized practice of law because of the ministerial nature of the act.[5] As noted in the NALA Code (Canon 3), exceptions allowing court appearances by legal assistants may exist, and local, state and federal rules applicable for the jurisdiction where the legal assistant works should be consulted. (As noted earlier in this chapter, the Kentucky Paralegal Code specifically allows for some court appearances by legal assistants but only if the client understands the legal assistant is not a lawyer, the lawyer supervises the legal assistant in the performance of his or her duties, and the lawyer remains fully responsible for such representation, including all acts taken and not taken.)

3.04 Adequate Supervision by the Attorney

The requirement that a legal assistant work under the direct supervision of an attorney is embodied in the ethical guidelines, case law involving the unauthorized practice of law, and rulings in disciplinary proceedings against attorneys. As a result of this clear ethical precept for the use of nonlawyers in the delivery of legal services, the National Association of Legal Assistants has incorporated this principle into its definition of a legal assistant, as discussed in the introduction of this book. The importance of adequate supervision by the employing attorney cannot be overemphasized. As is made clear in the guidelines and accepted standards of professional conduct for attorneys, the ultimate responsibility rests with the supervising attorney. The professional codes and case law establish that the attorney must be responsible for the assignment of the tasks to be performed, must supervise the manner in which the legal assistant performs the duties and tasks, and must merge the work products of the legal assistant into the attorney's final work product. The attorney must maintain a direct relationship with the client and a managerial role in the representation of the client.

A failure of the attorney to adequately supervise can result in harsh disciplinary consequences, including disbarment. Sections VI and VIII of the NALA *Model Standards and Guidelines for Utilization of Legal Assistants* provides detailed annotations to case law dealing with the duties of the attorney and instances where sanctions have been imposed for the attorney's failure to perform these duties.

3.05 Summary

The placement of responsibility on the attorney does not relieve the legal assistant from an independent obligation to follow the same professional conduct obliga-

---

[4] The California Bar has issued an advisory opinion regarding the use of a paralegal employed by a law firm for appearances before the Workers' Compensation Appeals Board (WCAB). While under certain labor code sections, nonlawyers are authorized in California to represent applicants before the WCAB, the California Bar's Standing Committee on Professional Responsibility and Conduct was dealing with the effect of the representation by the nonlawyer as an employee of a law firm and on behalf of the firm's client. The committee noted the need for adequate supervision by the employing attorney and the requirement that the client be informed and consent to the use of the nonlawyer.

[5] *People v. Alexander,* 53 Ill.App.2d 299, 202 N.E.2d 841 (1964).

tions required of attorneys and certainly to refrain from illegal conduct. While the provisions of standards and disciplinary rules for attorneys are not binding on nonlawyers, the very nature of a legal assistant's employment imposes an obligation to not engage in conduct that would involve the supervising attorney in a violation of attorneys' codes. This obligation has been codified in Canon 12 of the NALA *Code*.

The legal assistant has further considerations to ensure his or her own protection from potential liability for the unauthorized practice of law. While statutory provisions concerning the unauthorized practice of law will generally not delineate such conduct with exactitude, precautionary steps can be taken by the legal assistant to stay within proper and accepted boundaries.

From the compendium of material discussed in this chapter, the legal assistant can analyze professional conduct by considering the presence or absence of the following factors:

1. Are the tasks the legal assistant performs being delegated by an attorney?
2. Are the tasks and activities of the legal assistant being performed under the supervision of an attorney?
3. Are the tasks being performed ministerial or information gathering for an attorney's use?
4. Are the tasks and activities performed being given final approval and/or personal examination by an attorney, and does the work performed by the legal assistant merge into the attorney's final work product?
5. Has the attorney maintained a direct relationship with the client, or is the legal assistant managing the attorney-client relationship?
6. Has the legal assistant disclosed his or her nonlawyer status at the outset of any professional relationship with a client, other attorneys, a court or administrative agency (and personnel), or members of the general public?
7. Has the legal assistant established attorney-client relationships by accepting cases?
8. Has the legal assistant set the fees for the services to be performed?
9. Has the legal assistant rendered professional legal opinions or advice?
10. Has the legal assistant represented a client before a court when such activity is not authorized by the court or agency rules and when appropriate approval has not been obtained?

National Association of Legal Assistants, Inc. Code of Ethics and Professional Responsibility

It is the responsibility of every legal assistant to adhere strictly to the accepted standards of legal ethics and to live by general principles of proper conduct. The performance of the duties of the legal assistant shall be governed by specific canons as defined herein in order that justice will be served and the goals of the profession attained. The canons of ethics set forth hereafter are adopted by the National Association of Legal Assistants, Inc., as a general guide and the enumeration of these rules does not mean there are not others of equal importance although not specifically mentioned.

Canon 1. A legal assistant shall not perform any of the duties that lawyers only may perform nor do things that lawyers themselves may not do.

Canon 2. A legal assistant may perform any task delegated and supervised by a lawyer so long as the lawyer is responsible to the client, maintains a direct relationship with the client, and assumes full professional responsibility for the work product.

Canon 3. A legal assistant shall not engage in the practice of law by accepting cases, setting fees, giving legal advice or appearing in court (unless otherwise authorized by court or agency rules).

Canon 4. A legal assistant shall not act in matters involving professional legal judgment as the services of a lawyer are essential in the public interest whenever the exercise of such judgment is required.

Canon 5. A legal assistant must act prudently in determining the extent to which a client may be assisted without the presence of a lawyer.

Canon 6. A legal assistant shall not engage in the unauthorized practice of law.

Canon 7. A legal assistant must protect the confidence of a client, and it shall be unethical for a legal assistant to violate any statute now in effect or hereafter to be enacted controlling privileged communications.

Canon 8. It is the obligation of the legal assistant to avoid conduct which would cause the lawyer to be unethical or even appear to be unethical and loyalty to the employer is incumbent upon the legal assistant.

Canon 9. A legal assistant shall work continually to maintain integrity and a high degree of competency throughout the legal profession.

Canon 10. A legal assistant shall strive for perfection through education in order to better assist the legal profession in fulfilling its duty of making legal services available to clients and the public.

Canon 11. A legal assistant shall do all things incidental, necessary or expedient for the attainment of the ethics and responsibilities imposed by statute or rule of court.

Canon 12. A legal assistant is governed by the American Bar Association Model Code of Professional Responsibility, and the American Bar Association Model Rules of Professional Conduct.

National Association of Legal Assistants, Inc. Model Standards and Guidelines for Utilization of Legal Assistants

Preamble

Proper utilization of the services of legal assistants affects the efficient delivery of legal services. Legal assistants and the legal profession should be assured that some measures exist for identifying legal assistants and their role in assisting attorneys in the delivery of legal services. Therefore, the National Association of Legal Assistants, Inc., hereby adopts these Model Standards and Guidelines as an educational document for the benefit of legal assistants and the legal profession.

Definition

Legal assistants* are a distinguishable group of persons who assist attorneys in the delivery of legal services. Through formal education, training, and experience, legal assistants have knowledge and expertise regarding the legal system and

---

* Within this occupational category, some individuals are known as paralegals.

substantive and procedural law which qualify them to do work of a legal nature under the supervision of an attorney.

Standards

A legal assistant should meet certain minimum qualifications. The following standards may be used to determine an individual's qualifications as a legal assistant:

1. Successful completion of the Certified Legal Assistant (CLA) examination of the National Association of Legal Assistants, Inc. (see attached Exhibit A);
2. Graduation from an ABA approved program of study for legal assistants;
3. Graduation from a course of study for legal assistants which is institutionally accredited but not ABA approved, and which requires not less than the equivalent of 60 semester hours of classroom study;
4. Graduation from a course of study for legal assistants, other than those set forth in (2) and (3) above, plus not less than six months of in-house training as a legal assistant;
5. A baccalaureate degree in any field, plus not less than six months in-house training as a legal assistant;
6. A minimum of three years of law-related experience under the supervision of an attorney, including at least six months of in-house training as a legal assistant; or
7. Two years of in-house training as a legal assistant.

For purposes of these standards, "in-house training as a legal assistant" means attorney education of the employee concerning legal assistant duties and these guidelines. In addition to review and analysis of assignments, the legal assistant should receive a reasonable amount of instruction directly related to the duties and obligations of the legal assistant.

Guidelines

These guidelines relating to standards of performance and professional responsibility are intended to aid legal assistants and attorneys. The responsibility rests with an attorney who employs legal assistants to educate them with respect to the duties they are assigned and to supervise the manner in which such duties are accomplished.

Legal assistants should:

1. Disclose their status as legal assistants at the outset of any professional relationships with a client, other attorneys, a court or administrative agency or personnel thereof, or members of the general public;
2. Preserve the confidences and secrets of all clients; and
3. Understand the attorney's Code of Professional Responsibility and these guidelines in order to avoid any action which would involve the attorney in a violation of that Code, or give the appearance of professional impropriety.

Legal assistants should not:

1. Establish attorney-client relationships; set legal fees; give legal opinions or advice; or represent a client before a court; nor
2. Engage in, encourage, or contribute to any act which could constitute the unauthorized practice of law.

Legal assistants may perform services for an attorney in the representation of a client, provided:

1. The services performed by the legal assistant do not require the exercise of independent professional legal judgment;
2. The attorney maintains a direct relationship with the client and maintains control of all client matters;
3. The attorney supervises the legal assistant;
4. The attorney remains professionally responsible for all work on behalf of the client, including any actions taken or not taken by the legal assistant in connection therewith; and
5. The services performed supplement, merge with and become the attorney's work product.

In the supervision of a legal assistant, consideration should be given to:

1. Designating work assignments that correspond to the legal assistant's abilities, knowledge, training and experience;
2. Educating and training the legal assistant with respect to professional responsibility, local rules and practices, and firm policies;
3. Monitoring the work and professional conduct of the legal assistant to ensure that the work is substantively correct and timely performed;
4. Providing continuing education for the legal assistant in substantive matters through courses, institutes, workshops, seminars and in-house training; and
5. Encouraging and supporting membership and active participation in professional organizations.

Except as otherwise provided by statute, court rule or decision, administrative rule or regulation, or the attorney's Code of Professional Responsibility, and within the preceding parameters and proscriptions, a legal assistant may perform any function delegated by an attorney, including, but not limited to the following:

1. Conduct client interviews and maintain general contact with the client after the establishment of the attorney-client relationship, so long as the client is aware of the status and function of the legal assistant, and the client contact is under the supervision of the attorney.
2. Locate and interview witnesses, so long as the witnesses are aware of the status and function of the legal assistant.
3. Conduct investigations and statistical and documentary research for review by the attorney.
4. Conduct legal research for review by the attorney.
5. Draft legal documents for review by the attorney.
6. Draft correspondence and pleadings for review by and signature of the attorney.
7. Summarize depositions, interrogatories, and testimony for review by the attorney.
8. Attend executions of wills, real estate closings, depositions, court or administrative hearings and trials with the attorney.
9. Author and sign letters provided the legal assistant's status is clearly indicated and the correspondence does not contain independent legal opinions or legal advice.

Exhibit A

To become eligible to sit for the Certified Legal Assistant (CLA) examination, candidates must meet one of the following requirements:

1. Graduation from an ABA approved legal assistant training course or graduation from a legal assistant training course at a school which is institutionally accredited;

2. Graduation from a legal assistant course neither approved by the ABA nor at an institutionally accredited school plus two (2) years experience as a legal assistant;
3. A bachelor's degree in any field plus one (1) year experience as a legal assistant;
4. Seven (7) years law related experience under the supervision of a member of the bar. (Note: This optional requirement is open through December 31, 1991.)

Once admitted to the program, the applicant must successfully complete an eleven hour examination covering general skills required of all legal assistants plus knowledge of four substantive areas of the law.

The CLA designation is for a period of five years and if the CLA submits proof of continuing education in accordance with the stated requirements, the certificate is renewed for another five years. Lifetime certification is not permitted.

CLA is a service mark duly registered with the U.S. Patent and Trademark Office (No. 1131999). Any unauthorized use is strictly forbidden.

Bibliography

American Bar Association, *Model Code of Professional Responsibility* (1969, as amended).

American Bar Association, *Model Rules of Professional Conduct* (1983, as amended).

Judd, Karen B., *Beyond the Bar: Legal Assistants and the Unauthorized Practice of Law,* VIII Facts & Findings 1 (NALA), (May-June 1982).

National Association of Legal Assistants, *Code of Ethics and Professional Responsibility* (1975, as amended).

National Association of Legal Assistants, *Model Standards and Guidelines for Utilization of Legal Assistants* (Annotated; 1984, as amended).

Voisin, Vicki, *Changing Jobs: Ethical Consideration for Legal Assistants,* XV Facts & Findings 12, (March 1989).

4   Judgment and Analytical Ability

4.00 Introduction

The scope and diversity of job duties delegated to legal assistants depend upon the trust and confidence the lawyer accords the legal assistant as an individual, not as one of a class generically titled "legal assistant" or "certified legal assistant." This trust and confidence are earned recognitions of the personal attributes of the individual, including intelligence, a cheerful attitude, a willingness to assume responsibility, communication skills, ethical and moral standards, imagination, reliability, analytical ability, and good judgment.

The utility and value of a legal assistant to the lawyer depend more on the last two personal skills than all the others. Weakness in analytical abilities or judgment capabilities seriously limits the duties a lawyer delegates to the legal assistant, for the entire legal process requires these two qualities.

Analyze is defined as "to study or determine the nature and relationship of the parts by analysis." *Judgment* is defined as "the process of forming an opinion or evaluation by discerning and comparing." Try that concept on an employer. "Yes, sir, I've formed an opinion by 'determining the nature and relationship of the parts by analyzing, discerning, and comparing'." The attorney's response may be: "Now tell me what you've done."

Legal assistants and attorneys work in an atmosphere of *good* and *bad* judgments. These two modifiers expand that formerly passionless and risk-free definition of judgment into a qualitative evaluation of the action that flowed from the "formation of the opinion." That is the nature of legal work—participation and action, rather than mere observation or comment.

Judgment is necessarily followed by a decision from which some act flows. The result is then measured to determine whether a particular judgment in a particular situation was good or bad.

For instance, one does not need to go to law school nor enroll in an extensive course for legal assistants to understand that if an automobile driver deliberately runs a red light, a police officer may issue a citation calling for a fine or trial; if a person deliberately shoots and kills another person, an arrest for murder may result; breaking and entering a residence and the removal of a television set or jewelry may result in a jail sentence for theft. Everyone is generally acquainted with good and bad judgments and the consequent acts and results that can flow from them.

This chapter stresses more definitive aspects of judgment and analytical ability as they relate to legal assistants in large and small law offices and in simple and complex cases.

4.01   How to Develop Good Judgment

If good judgment in any given situation involved facts, statistics, or objects, each considered without self-will, opinions, biases, prejudices and preferences, tempers, egos, and feelings, then a computer could be used to sort all the factors and select the optimum decision. Computers, of course, have little insight, no compassion or consideration of the benefits of timely and ingenious "white lies," and little flexibility or adaptability to changing situations.

Reliable good judgment and productive analytical ability are developed by exercise and practice and, even more important, through mistakes. Good judgment requires the leavening of experience with analytical ability and other personal characteristics, such as compassion and flexibility, applied within a framework of the following basic guidelines:

(a)   Understand the chain of command;
(b)   Understand the scope, instructions, and authority delegated;
(c)   Appreciate priorities;
(d)   Honor time commitments;
(e)   Recognize exceptional situations;
(f)   Accept guidance, directions, and comments constructively; and
(g)   Enthusiastically observe moral and ethical standards.

Let us now consider these guidelines individually.

4.011   Understand the Chain of Command.

Every law firm has a hierarchy of personnel and specific reservations and/or delegations of responsibilities. Clearly, the librarian is responsible for the selection, purchase, and maintenance of the materials in the library. Sometimes, the office manager is the coordinator for "extra help," overtime, or other personnel adjustments and is responsible for equipment purchase, service contracting, petty cash expenditures, travel arrangements, and so on. The senior attorneys and their secretaries have certain stated, or unstated but well understood, prerogatives, and other attorneys, secretaries, and legal assistants have another set of prerogatives or guidelines. It is essential that areas of authority and responsibility of the office as a whole be generally understood by the legal assistant, including the avenues for inquiry, suggestions, and requests. For example, in a firm with a well-established and rigidly controlled file system that requires every file to be returned to the file room daily, except with specific permission, the legal assistant should learn the background of the current procedure from the files supervisor before attempting to introduce changes in the procedure through the attorney. The legal assistant, lacking the historical perspective, cannot know the crying need for the system before it was instituted nor appreciate the difficulties surmounted putting it in. It is bad judgment to attempt to resurrect an old system without knowing its history and without having substantial justification and a well-founded plan for changing it. Personal opinions and convenience simply do not qualify as justifications, even though the legal assistant's suggested system worked beautifully and masterfully in other and even larger firms.

As the legal assistant becomes more and more familiar with office organization and distribution of operational authority, his or her good judgment is demonstrated by posing appropriate questions to the properly responsible parties. Conversely, the legal assistant becomes aware of gossip mongers or troublemakers among the personnel, particularly in large law firms, and develops tactics to use in dealing with these people.

Learning the hierarchy or chain of command ensures that few, if any, inadvertent cases of "going over the head" of a responsible person occurs. Completion of such a study gives the legal assistant the proper perspective of the office and prepares him or her to handle the other guidelines effectively.

4.012   Understand the Scope, Instructions, and Authority Delegated.

Legal assistants are an ambitious group who generally will accept all the responsibility delegated to them and additionally create, or even usurp, other areas of responsibility. They also devise new methods and procedures not previously tried and proven, which can be effective in certain situations.

Many legal assistants begin thinking of themselves as the lawyer's good right arm, sometimes in the shadows but always there. That frequently becomes true but never suddenly nor without a period of apprenticeship and the gradual demonstration of reliable judgment and analytical ability. Never will an overly aggressive or presumptuous legal assistant achieve a high level of responsibility as the "good right arm" as quickly as one who proceeds with caution, preparation, study, and deliberation.

Legal assistants entering a law office must become aware of and understand the office concept of the legal assistant, as well as the kinds of duties performed; who directs their work and whose work (if any) they direct; if they can spend funds, and, if so, to what dollar limit; and if they can contract for the firm, and, if so, what kinds of contracts (travel, document copying, photography, model making, and so on.) They must obtain information concerning how billable and nonbillable hours are recorded; who makes decisions about billable expenses; how the secretarial support system functions for the legal assistant; the mail system; the docket system; and any other system that may directly or indirectly affect them.

No matter how restrictive, inefficient, or ridiculous the system first seems, the legal assistant makes every effort to follow the stipulated procedures while establishing his or her own level of respect in the office. Most of the poor or inefficient practices encountered in an office are the compromises of past internal struggles or "hand-me-downs" of long ago that remain through inertia. The legal assistant will find sufficient challenge in adapting to the delegated work without expending energy and generating animosity over internal affairs until those affairs are within his or her scope of responsibility. In other words, legal assistants must be flexible enough to adapt to the internal situation until they have an opportunity to make proper, thoughtful, and constructive suggestions for change to the appropriate person at the proper time.

Once the office concept and general administration procedures are understood, the legal assistant seeks to understand both the kinds of cases the lawyer handles and the preferred techniques for every procedure in which the lawyer intends to involve the legal assistant. The next most important area of concern is the comfortable and effective accommodation of the lawyer, the legal assistant, and the secretary in all phases of the working relationship; this is a changing and vitally important team that requires consideration and participation from all three parties.

The legal assistant becomes familiar with the attorney's schedule in order to adapt his or her own efforts with the lawyer's work habits. Some lawyers prefer the first hour to be undisturbed for handling mail and dictation, others the last hour. Some prefer to have the legal assistant meet with them once a week for a general review of all active files, and others prefer more frequent meetings for case-by-case discussions; others are "hit it while I'm hot" advocates who are likely to say, "We'll do it right now, regardless of your previous assignments." Here again, flexibility and patience are important characteristics of a legal assistant.

Legal assistants specializing in real estate must be familiar with the real estate laws in their state, mortgage rates, property descriptions, title information, closing statements, zoning board regulations, local, state, and federal regulations or statutes concerning purchasing, leasing, landlord-tenant situations, and all other pertinent areas of real estate law.

Corporate legal assistants must be familiar with state and federal laws concerning corporations and procedures for incorporation, including: tax and other laws pertaining to different types of corporations, such as domestic, foreign, Chapter S, closed, nonprofit, charitable or eleemosynary corporations; stock splits and stock options, dividends; pension plans; minutes of meetings of shareholders, directors, and incorporators; mergers; acquisitions; blue sky laws; and certain requirements of the Securities and Exchange Commission.

Legal assistants involved in estate planning must necessarily keep abreast of the ever-changing tax laws affecting estate planning for particular clients and be familiar with proper auditing procedures; valuation of assets; preparation of federal and state tax returns; proper acquisition of bank accounts; insurance proceeds; Social Security regulations; and many other areas.

The same is true in all other specialty areas—the legal assistants first are thoroughly familiar with the area or areas in which they work. Then they apply judgment and analytical ability in a particular area or areas.

While there are many specialty areas in which legal assistants operate, there is one area of specialization that could encompass any one or all of the other specialty areas, and that is litigation. A litigation legal assistant, of necessity, becomes involved in real estate, probate, estate planning, and family law; or possibly in real estate and corporate, criminal and corporate, criminal and tax, or other combinations, or in only one area, depending on the cases. For that reason, we shall use the area of the litigation specialist to illustrate the concept of judgment and analytical ability. The same principles can be applied in any other specialty area but can be explored in more depth in the area of litigation. Therefore, as we explore the remaining five guidelines, the illustrations we use will deal primarily in litigation.

Litigation legal assistants must be familiar with the rules of federal and state courts, either criminal or civil, depending on the bulk of office practice. If the court rules state (for civil matters) that "all law and motion matters must be filed forty-eight hours prior to the hearing," a legal assistant must determine whether this means forty-eight actual hours or "no less than two full working court days before the hearing." Similarly, court rules or local interpretation give rise to such questions as: "Does the court accept pleadings on 8½″ × 14″ paper, 8½″ × 13″ paper, or only 8½″ × 11″ paper?" "Will the court allow legal assistants at the counsel table during trial?" Other similar questions may arise to an inquisitive legal assistant. The failure to resolve such questions may confound the best efforts of the legal assistant, result in embarrassment to the lawyer, and frustrate a tactical objective.

4.013   Appreciate Priorities.

Priorities in legal assisting lie first in the court docket, including deadlines, orders, and applicable city, state, and federal rules and regulations, and then in personal preferences. Also of importance are less well-defined priorities, the most vexatious of these being the priority of work production accorded the various personalities within the firm. It is obvious that the managing partner with a job to be expedited will receive all the necessary resources to complete the assignment in a timely and diligent fashion. Less clear and compelling is the need of a junior attorney's legal assistant for extra help in completing a long-term project on schedule. Yet the objective merit of the situations appears to be the same. This lack of individual importance and power makes it more important for the legal assistant properly to evaluate and predict the need for assistance before the situation becomes a panic than for the managing partner to utilize his or her valuable time making such predictions. Too, the occasional panic situation usually is a failure at the legal assistant or operating levels of the office. Such foresight is helpful not only to the lawyer but also to the office manager, who is responsible for coping with unanticipated peaks in workloads created by "Please expedite" or "panic" operations.

Choosing between two necessary activities for first attention and effort is the most difficult priority judgment a legal assistant makes. Which should be done first—develop the document control plan or assemble all the documents? Draft additional interrogatories or summarize the depositions? Thoughtful analysis can lead the way to making the decision, provided the legal assistant conquers the "but-I-like-to-do-this-more-than-that" attitude. The work obviously cannot be predicated on the likes and dislikes of lawyers, legal assistants, or secretaries, since all aspects must be done sooner or later. Ignoring logical priorities results in creating additional problems, such as doing necessary but boring and disliked work under inordinate and unnecessary time pressures. The usual result of panic work often is poor quality and lost time due to material being improperly prepared, proofed, and/or corrected. Unreliable and incomplete material is of little or no use to the employing attorney and seriously affects his or her trust and confidence in the legal assistant.

4.014   Honor Time Commitments.

Time is the most important commodity of a lawyer. It determines his or her work schedule, which may be planned many weeks in advance. In private practice, it is a primary basis for certain charges to the client. Court rulings, codes, and statutes all provide for certain periods of time to elapse in the normal course of pleadings, motions, discovery, trial, and appeal. A legal assistant who is consistently and conscientiously aware of the importance of time is highly valued. It is true that many time periods may be waived or extensions granted; however, the lawyer should not be forced into seeking such favors from the adversary or seeking the indulgence of the court because of the failure or inability of the legal assistant to perform. A legal assistant usually knows well before a deadline whether a project can meet a specified schedule with the resources currently in use. If the schedule cannot be met, the legal assistant should not hesitate to request or recommend additional help, overtime, or a combination of both.

4.015   Recognize Exceptional Situations.

Every legal assistant, after some time with a firm, may become a secondary target (in the absence of the case attorney) for requests, questions, and demands that involve routine matters clearly within his or her knowledge and functional ability to resolve. Other requests, questions, or demands may constitute serious questions of the propriety of the legal assistant responding either affirmatively or negatively. These instances usually involve such questions as, "If I do this, will it be all right," or "What do you think I should do?" or "If I don't know how to act on this immediately, will the chance be gone?" These all pose ethical problems regarding the unauthorized practice of law by the legal assistant. Let us consider three basic problems in this area:

PROBLEM No. 1

The client is involved in litigation with a lessee in possession of a cattle ranch over the issue of who pays for the maintenance of cattle guards and drainage lines on the ranch. Recent flooding has endangered the foundation of an equipment building used by a sublessee who has offered to share the corrective costs with the client to prevent the building's collapse during anticipated additional rains. The client wants to know if such participation will adversely affect the lawsuit. The attorney is completely out of touch for the next three days.

Query: How can the legal assistant handle the situation? Offer advice? Stonewall the client with "The lawyer won't be back until Monday. I'll have him call you." How does the legal assistant decide what course to follow?

Commentary: The client may weaken his legal case by making any contribution to solving the drainage problem, since it may act as a waiver of his claim against the lessee; conversely, failure to participate may contribute to substantial additional damage. Clearly, the legal assistant cannot make a direct recommendation. An alternative may exist if another attorney is available who can be briefed by the legal assistant and then review the case file to offer the client appropriate legal advice. Otherwise, either the client must act on his own or the legal assistant must try to contact the case attorney. Even if the lawyer and legal assistant had previously discussed this particular problem, and participation was approved, only the attorney knows the self-protective language to inject into any agreement between the owner and the sublessee on this matter.

PROBLEM NO. 2

Preparations are nearly complete for allowing an adversary to inspect documents under a "Request to Produce" that required "each and every copy" of a specified variety of records and files. Some 3,700 pages of material, already screened, are ready. Two hundred and fifty pages of privileged material have been removed, and the appropriate list prepared, when the client reveals that a wholly owned subsidiary has nearly an exact duplicate file, plus several individual personal files reasonably responsive to the request. Seventy-five work hours have already been expended, and the inspection is scheduled for the day after tomorrow.

Query: What does the legal assistant need to do to allow the lawyer to select a course of action? Can the legal assistant suppress this information until it is too late to act on it? Should the legal assistant simply throw up his or her hands and leave for the day?

Commentary: This is not an unusual occurrence in document production cases. The obvious alternatives include: 1) instituting a priority rush program to process the additional material (and later explaining how it first was missed); 2) seeking a postponement; 3) promising future production; or 4) ignoring the documents in hope that the adversary will not discover them. Each alternative should be presented with factual data (such as hours of work involved and cost) and the legal assistant's candid recommendation to the attorney.

PROBLEM NO. 3

A client is involved in difficult contested divorce involving substantial assets in real estate, stocks, bonds, annuities, and other property. In the course of interviewing and assembling the property and asset descriptions, it becomes apparent that the client has been siphoning community property assets into a separate fund over the past two or three years. It has been skillfully done, and only the legal assistant's intimate involvement and careful analysis allowed the discovery.

Query: Does the legal assistant punish the client by advising the attorney? Become a part of the client's fraud by remaining silent? Or send an anonymous note to the adversary attorney ensure that the client gets his just desserts?

Commentary: There are no decisions to be made here, no matter how many alternatives can be created intellectually. The legal assistant has a moral and ethical obligation to apprise the attorney of these unpleasant facts and to rely on the attorney's moral and ethical standards to guide his or her subsequent actions. This is not a totally unusual situation for legal assistants to encounter. It may not be diversion of assets (as in this example) but some other aspect of human weakness, avarice, greed, lack of virtues, or unscrupulous business practices. It should not affect the legal assistant's execution of duties for the employing lawyer.

Each of these situations presents urgent motivation for the legal assistant to do something; however, none of the alternatives in any of the cases has a completely satisfactory complexion. The legal assistant chooses the course of least danger to the attorney, even though it results in a less-than-optimum solution to the problem as he or she perceives it. Remember, the client's adversary is also skillful, intelligent, and hardworking.

These are but a few of many exceptional situations that will arise in a law office from time to time. After many such experiences, a legal assistant's *good* judgment will become second nature, provided there is no compromise with loyalty to the lawyer and observance of good ethics.

4.016   Accept Guidance, Directions, and Comments Constructively.

Few people enjoy criticism, yet the most common on-the-job training program for legal assistants is similar to the frontier method of teaching children to swim by throwing them bodily into the lake and shouting, "All right, sink or swim!" The "sink or swim" method exposes the legal assistant to a variety of situations he or she can neither understand nor control. Its proponents claim it engenders intense interest, self-control, and determination to overcome common errors of procedure and/or judgment. Its detractors point to the unnecessary friction, anxiety, wasted work, and self-doubt that the "sink or swim" method creates. Criticism *after training* is helpful, corrective, and constructive. Criticism without training is damaging and counter-productive.

The beginning period for a new legal assistant in a firm can be a positive or negative experience, depending on the training and the pattern of correction and criticism he or she receives.

Everyone profits from mistakes and errors, provided the "whys and wherefores" are understood and result in growth. Some attorneys, legal secretaries, office administrators, and legal assistants are gracious and helpful when they realize they incorrectly presumed the new legal assistant knew what to do and how to do it in all procedures. Others who are less kind may make caustic comments to hurt and belittle, rather than to educate.

The intelligent legal assistant will absorb both kinds of comments with patience and resolve to learn from the experience. An even more intelligent legal assistant will delve more into how he or she could avoid this type of incident in the future and will be willing to learn more about the surrounding issues, taking any extra steps necessary to convince the attorneys and other law office personnel that legal assistants are an integral and important part of the effective delivery of legal services.

Legal assistants need help, suggestions, guidance, and—most important—constructive criticism to improve their skills and to serve as a reminder of the legal activity they have yet to learn and master. The same can be said of attorneys and other law office personnel.

Judgment often is learned through painful post-mortems—the examination, after the fact, of alternatives that had not been considered. In other words, the legal assistant did not appreciate all the legal issues involved, did not assemble, analyze, and evaluate all the facts or factual circumstances, or simply did not delve deeply enough into background or peripheral matters. The unsatisfactory result is due to failure of the legal assistant's comprehensive analytical ability.

PROBLEM NO. 4

A simple lawsuit involving the blowout of an oil well during drilling, under circumstances where an error by the drilling crew appears to be the cause, has been filed against the drilling contractor by the client oil company. The issues are simple negligence and contractual indemnity. One of the officers of the drilling contractor has left that firm and lives and works out of state. He was not present at the blowout, but his deposition is scheduled in Houston. An appropriate commission has been obtained, and one of the firm's junior attorneys is drafted into replacing the case lawyer at the deposition, for it seems to be a routine deposition. At the deposition, little was learned that was not learned from the crew. The witness clearly was not experienced, did not volunteer anything, had no personal records, did not refresh his memory prior to deposition, and relied on what he was told by others. The deposition therefore proved to be simple, straightforward, and unproductive.

Query: What if the witness were known before deposition to be an author of *Blowouts and Blowout Prevention;* taught seminars in safe drilling practices; served on the board of the American Petroleum Institute; and was sought as a technical consultant on special construction problems of blowout equipment? Would his opinion on blowout training equipment and procedures on the drilling rig have more or less weight? Would the deposition outline have sought more "expert opinion" than "hearsay"? Could he, as a company officer with special expertise, be charged with only ordinary knowledge of the industry standards in blowout prevention training of crews and equipping rigs? Would that knowledge *ahead of time* have helped the attorney? Helped the *case?* Helped the *client?* Prior to taking of the deposition, an efficient legal assistant should inquire into all these things and draft questions the young attorney may wish to ask at the deposition.

4.017   Enthusiastically Observe Moral and Ethical Standards.

Every profession that exists to serve people has recognized its obligation to provide this service within certain standards of proper conduct. Doctors follow the Hippocratic oath, lawyers the *Model Rules of Professional Conduct*; pharmacists, real estate salesmen, bankers, and other professionals all create (or have created by legislation or regulatory agency) guidelines for proper and proscribed conduct. The direct beneficiary is the patient, the client, the customer, the "civilian" who uses the offered service.

This is as it should be, and these constraints on conduct are ones that legal assistants cheerfully and enthusiastically endorse, accept, and observe, for the legal assistant profession serves *two* levels of users, lawyers and clients. The only endorsed, published, and adopted code of ethics in the profession was written by the ethics committee of the National Association of Legal Assistants in 1975 and is discussed in detail in Chapter 3 on Ethics.

4.02   Analytical Ability

Analyzing is the process of orderly sorting and categorizing information, from which relevant facts are discerned as applicable to a given situation. The ability to analyze is essential to the legal assistant. Creative thinking, imagination, and inspiration are excellent attributes; however, the prosaic, methodical assembly of every relevant fact or evidentiary fact is also essential. Analytical ability that cannot be demonstrated to the satisfaction of the employing attorney in direct relation to a particular case or set of circumstances surrounding a particular case obviously has no merit or usefulness. However, if a legal assistant can supply the attorney with reliable control and retrievability of analyses of facts, testimony, or source information, then the legal assistant's system and analytical ability are invaluable to the attorney.

In commencing the analysis of facts and/or testimony in a case, the legal assistant must be aware of the essential elements of the case before beginning the evaluation of relevant facts. For instance, a case of misrepresentation is founded on proving at least the following seven points:

1. The representation was to a material fact.
2. The representation was false.
3. The falsity was known to the party making it.
4. The representation was made with the intent to induce the other party to act.
5. The representation was relied upon by the party to whom it was made.
6. The acting party was ignorant of the falsity of the representation and reasonably believed it to be true.
7. The acting party suffered damages as a result of the act.

There may be side issues of intentional or negligent misrepresentation and oral or written contract to be considered as well. The legal assistant therefore has factual categories established, each of which relates to the issues that must be proved or refuted (depending on the client's position). Otherwise, the pattern of facts assembled by the legal assistant is worthless to the lawyer.

Suppose this case involved the purchase of machinery designed for a specific agricultural harvesting function and the representation involved the cost of purchase and maintenance, the speed of operation, reliability, and the capability of operation by only two people. Is it relevant that the operation damaged 50 percent of the crop? Yes! Items of proof will be necessary for the issue. Is it relevant that the machine works so slowly that the prime picking period cannot be exploited without two of the machines? Yes! Again, proof may be documentary or testimonial. Is it relevant that its dimensions prevent it from being stored in existing equipment buildings? Probably not, unless some additional representation on ease of storage can be developed. Building an additional shed may not be a supportable item of damage.

This categorization of relevant topics to which evidentiary materials and testimony are related serves as the basis for preparing deposition plans and for abstracting or summarizing transcripts of depositions, particularly the topical summaries (see Chapter 9 on litigation skills). Even the list of deponents should be organized and logged in clear and expository form. An example of one such partial index is Exhibit 7.

Note that the form allows the accumulation of data on each deponent and the status of the deposition in the office pretrial and trial proceedings. Some of these

EXHIBIT 7

Index of Depositions
Case No. 70-828
Last Posted 6/18/72
Legal Assistant, J & D

Deponent	Date Taken	Deponent Employed by	Deposition Transcript	Deposition Summarized	Topical Index	Corrections	Exhibits
Allen, James N.	1/27/69	City of New York	x				
Anderton, James L.	7/28/69	Pacific Co.	x	x	x		
Arnoulde, Arnie Lou	9/7/68	City of Detroit	x				x
Aunndell, Joseph P.	6/8/68	The Gee Co.	x	x	x	x	x
Barker, Edward L.	1/9/67	City of Dallas	x	x	x		
Barton, Lester	5/7/68	The Lean Co.	x	x	x		x
Bean, Kendrick Lewis	9/4/69	City of Atlanta	x	x	x		
Black, Frank O.	6/5/69	Pipe Corp.(1) (formerly the Gee Co.)	x	x		x	

depositions had little case value and were not processed (see Allen, James N.), while others involved the full gamut of processing—deposition, transcript, summary, topical index, corrections posted, and exhibits attached (see Aunndell, Joseph P.). The attorney or legal assistant can, by a quick glance, tell the exact status of the deposition of each witness.

Analysis of factual situations in simple cases often is more challenging than in complex cases, for the simplicity of the case issues places a premium on identifying each relevant evidentiary fact and assigning it a value that reflects its help or hindrance to the client's case.

Consider the following hypothetical case and proceed through an interview or fact-gathering session:

Mr. Jones called an attorney and made arrangements to be represented in a personal injury suit arising from an automobile accident. He is uninsured and has been served with a complaint as the defendant in the suit. After the initial interview with the attorney, the legal assistant is the first person in the office with whom he will fully discuss the accident. He arrived by appointment and, after a few minutes of casual conversation, discussion of the case and the gathering of information begin. The initial questions seek background information, such as name, address, telephone number, place of employment, and marital status. Since this is a case involving an automobile accident, it is essential to ask questions about his driving record, how long he has been driving, and what is the model, make, and condition of his car, where it was repaired, and whether it was in prior accidents. These background questions will give insight into the client's nature. For instance, if Mr. Jones has never had a traffic citation in his thirty years of driving, presumably he is a careful driver. If his driving record discloses a number of citations, then clearly there are times when Mr. Jones has disregarded the law. Also, what kind of a car does he drive and what color is it? Psychologists have determined that there is a link between the type and color of a car a person drives and the individual's personality; for example, a souped-up red car indicates an aggressive person, while a conservative model and color suggests a conservative individual. Is the client a steady worker, or does he flit from job to job? Is he happily married, miserably married, or in the process of a divorce? The answers to these questions should be used to assist in evaluating the answers the client gives in response to questions related to the facts of the case. Mr. Jones admits to two speeding citations in the last eighteen months. He drives a bright yellow car with a large, modified engine with two four-barrel carburetors and is, according to him, "the fastest thing on the road." He is between jobs, and he does not approve of his wife's job. The interview proceeds into the discussion of the case.

L.A.:   Now Mr. Jones, where did this accident occur?

JONES: In the driveway of Sam's Go-Go Bar.

L.A.:   What was the date, the day of the week, and the time of the accident?

JONES: It was April 24, 1976, a Saturday, and it was just before closing time, around 1:45 A.M.

(His testimony established that the accident occurred on private property, on a weekend and late at night. A few questions on weather, lighting, visibility, vehicle conditions, and so on should be asked.)

L.A.:   Mr. Jones, had you been in Sam's prior to the time of the accident?

JONES: "Yes, I had been there. My wife works as a go-go girl for Sam, and I pick her up after work.

(Now the legal assistant knows why Mr. Jones was at Sam's, but the question arises, "If he picks his wife up after work, why was he leaving before closing time?")

> **L.A.:** According to the complaint, Mr. Smith says that you deliberately drove your car into the side of his as he was leaving the parking lot and that, after you hit his car, you left your car and attempted to pull him from his vehicle. Please tell me what really occurred, in the sequence it happened.

> **JONES:** Well, I didn't see his car in the driveway, and I only left my car to go over to him to see if he was injured.

There are now two entirely different and conflicting accounts of the same accident. The accident could have occurred as the client alleges. (It could also be that he did not admit the plaintiff had been overfriendly with Mrs. Jones in Sam's, that he became enraged, left Sam's to follow the plaintiff, and in a fit of temper did hit the plaintiff's car and assault him.) With the background information regarding Mr. Jones and his account of the accident, it is now time to proceed with more detailed inquiry for corroboration, identification of other witnesses, and so forth. This is pursued circumspectly, without expressing doubt or accusation.

Keep in mind that clients usually will present their cases in a manner that places them in the best light. They do not do this intentionally; it is a subconscious rationalization to avoid embarrassment or criticism for their actions. In the case of Mr. Jones, continue to question him to gather more facts and information to substantiate his presentation of the accident. If there is any doubt about the actual facts of the case, independently question the witnesses to the accident and/or to events that occurred prior to the accident. This information, along with the information given by Mr. Jones, will allow the legal assistant to analyze the facts and reach an accurate conclusion that will be helpful to the lawyer in representing Mr. Jones properly or by providing a basis on which the attorney can further investigate other avenues of defense or settlement. The prime rule of legal assisting is "Never let the attorney be surprised by harmful information!" Find it and defuse it so the attorney can adapt to its impact.

In more complex cases, "Requests for Production of Documents" sometimes seek invoices, purchase orders, employee lists, time cards, expense accounts over a period of time, books, records, histories, and other comparative data surrounding the particular action. Responses to these requests may result in boxes and boxes of materials or may state that certain records will be available for counsel to inspect or reproduce at a particular time and place. Here, again, the ability of the legal assistant to index and analyze comparative data will be of invaluable assistance to an attorney.

In minimal time, the attorney can instruct the legal assistant on the issues involved and the comparative data needed. The legal assistant may then spend days or weeks going through statistical data, documents, manuscripts, depositions, records, invoices, or purchase orders, making comparative analyses and chronologic sortings and gathering other information. It may be that the adverse party's attorney has produced computer printouts in answer to a request for certain documents or information from these documents. A legal assistant must then become familiar with computer printouts, how to read them, and how to trace the source documents from which the printouts came, comparing the printouts with the source documents in order to verify the exactness of the information furnished on the printouts. In this verification, a legal assistant may be able to point out inaccuracies from source documents to the computer printout, thereby tremendously aiding the attorney through use of his or her good judgment and analytical ability. Document cases are discussed in more detail in Chapter 8 on litigation skills and Chapter 9 on document discovery cases.

Complex litigation, particularly multiple-party actions, can create problems with simply keeping track of the pleadings, the discovery motions and orders, trial testimony, and transcripts, let alone the evidentiary material. The legal assistant can assist both the lawyer and the legal secretary by formulating and supervising the organization and cross-indexing of material for simple reference and retrieval. This is no small or insignificant task.

It may be desirable to have indexed copies of all pleadings filed in court, including the date on which filed. This index supports a file containing nothing but copies of these pleadings, marked by a numbered tab on each pleading, corresponding with the number listed in the index of pleadings. (See Exhibit 8.) The index includes a description of the pleading filed, the date it was filed, the pleading number assigned and tabbed on the pleading, and any other desirable information. A cross-index of pleadings could be prepared as to topics. In the case of a multi-party suit, prepare a file that would contain all complaints, properly tabbed and indexed; another file for all answers to complaints, properly tabbed

EXHIBIT 8

Index to Pleadings
Filed in Case 70-823

Document Number	Document	Date Filed	Volume
8	Plaintiff's Rule 34 Request for Document Prod.	7/11/70	II
9	Order on Preliminary Pretrial Conference	7/16/70	II
10	Withdrawal of appearance of Danny J. Jones	7/15/70	II
11	Order Consolidating Cases 823 and adding counsel	7/16/70	II
12	Answers of the Lean Co. to Plaintiff's Interrogatories No. 1	8/09/70	II
13	Answers of Pipe Corp. to Plaintiff's Interrogatories No. 1	8/09/70	III
14	Answers of Clamor Co. to Plaintiff's Interrogatories No. 1	8/09/70	III
15	Answers and Objections to U.S. Co. to P's Int. No. 1	8/09/70	III
16	Def's Response to P's Rule 34 Req. for Doc. Prod.	8/09/70	III
17	Answers of ASGO to Plaintiff's Int. No. 1	8/09/70	III
18	Defendant's Objections to Plaintiff's Interrogatories No. 2	8/09/70	III
19	Answers and Objections of Clamor to P's Int. No. 2	8/09/70	III
20	Answers of OUTGO to Plaintiff's Interrogatories No. 1	8/09/70	III
21	Arno's Ans. & Objections to P's R. 34 Req. for Doc. Prod.	8/12/70	III
22	Arno's Answers & Objections to Plaintiff's Int. No. 1	8/12/70	III
23	Answers of Met Gov't of Anywhere to Def's. Joint Int. of June 25, 1970	8/12/70	III
24	Joint Response of Plaintiff's to Def's Joint Int.	8/12/70	IV
25	Answers of CA to Def's Joint Int. of June 25, 1970	8/12/70	IV
27	Def's Memo R. 37 to Compel Ans. by P's to Def's Joint Int. and Other		
28	Relief	9/17/70	IV
	Plaintiff's Motion & Support of Class Actions	9/18/70	IV
29	Memo of all Def's in Opposition to Cl. Action	9/20/70	IV
30	Arno's Reply to Plaintiff's Rule 37 Motion	9/20/70	IV
31	Def's Memo in Opposition to P's Motion for Order pursuant to Rule 37	9/23/70	IV
32	P's Response to Def's R. 37 Motion & Memorandum	9/23/70	IV
33	Agreement Lt. between Met. Gov't of Anywhere and Messrs. Brown and Moulder dated 1/21/70	9/24/70	IV

and indexed; another file for all interrogatories; another for all answers to inter-rogatories; and still another for plaintiff or defendant objections. Other files, each properly tabbed and indexed, are created as needed. A legal assistant would then be able to retrieve any pleading or document on a moment's notice. The same would be true of any other supporting documents in the files, including documents on microfilm, if any. For the most effective instant retrieval, index both chrono-logically and topically.

If the trial is expected to be of some duration, thought should be given to the economics of requesting daily transcripts. If this is done and it usually is advisable and economical in multi-party cases, a legal assistant could see that an alphabetical index to witnesses is prepared on a daily basis. The index would include names of the witnesses, the date they appeared on the stand, names of interrogating attorneys, volume and page numbers of testimony of all witnesses, whether on direct examination and by whom, whether on redirect examination and by whom, whether on cross or recross-examination and by whom. (See Exhibit 9).

In some instances, testimony at trial may be presented via depositions. This, too, should be noted in the index. Also, if the file contains a deposition, abstract, or topical index of the deposition of certain witnesses, that should be noted. Here again is another avenue of comparison and analysis.

In addition to the index of trial witnesses, an index of the entire trial transcript would be beneficial. (See Exhibit 10.) In instances where there are multitudinous exhibits filed during trial, if arrangements can be made prior to trial with the trial judge to procure on a daily basis copies of the exhibits entered, a legal assistant could then supervise the reproduction, tabbing, and indexing of all exhibits, fur-nishing copies to the attorney, properly indexed and tabbed, and returning the original exhibits to the court prior to trial the next day. (See Exhibit 11). An index of these trial exhibits should reveal to the attorney the dates, volumes and page numbers in the transcript on which the particular exhibit was identified, marked, received into evidence, and mentioned; the interrogating attorney and witness on the stand at the time; a brief description of the exhibit; the plaintiff or defendant exhibit number as actually filed in court; and the legal assistant's tabbed document number. Not all exhibits are entered in sequence of plaintiff and defendant num-bers in court; therefore, a legal assistant would prefer an independent chrono-logical numbering system (from the attorney's trial book, see Chapter 8 on litigation skills), at the same time noting the court's exhibit number.

Obviously, this requires round-the-clock assistance. In this instance, the legal assistant would be supervising a good working crew that might have to work in shifts to render the ultimate assistance during the trial.

Not all trials require this kind of massive assistance, indexing, and cross-referencing; however, the signs pointing to the need for such can be discerned early in the case from the number of parties, the complexity of issues, the volume of witnesses, and the factual material to be presented to the judge or jury for decision. Then, too, there are cases where the matter obviously will be appealed by one party or the other, whatever the outcome. Detailed transcripts and indices are invaluable to the attorney in relocating the points of contention to be appealed and the testimony, factual data, and exhibits supporting his or her view.

4.021   Basic Rules.

Analytical ability relies on a few basic rules with which all legal assistants should be familiar:

EXHIBIT 9	**Alphabetical Index to Trial Witnesses From Daily Transcript—Beginning June 3**				

		Volume and Page Numbers			
Defense Witnesses	*Date*	*Direct*	*Cross*	*Redirect*	*Recross*
Anderton, James N.	7/26	XXXI-8102-JONES			
	7/27	XXXII-8155-JONES	XXXII-8188-BROWN 8302-KING	XXXII-8311-LEWIS	
Bozels, Lewis A.(A)	7/20	XXVII-7006-RICHARDS -7090-LEWIS -7095-RUGGLE	XXVII-7090-KING		
	7/21		XXVIII-7164-KING -7214-BROWN	XXVIII-7216-JONES	XXVIII-7227-KING
Bush, Carson T.	7/26	XXXI-8068-JONES	XXXI-8090-BROWN	XXXI-8101	XXXI-8102
Carl, Craig (d)	7/26	XXXI-8045			
Chaney, G.P. (d)(I)	7/20	XXVII-6840	XXVII-6980		
Davids, Fred R. (I)	7/20	XXVII-6827	XXVII-6835		
Eaton, Sol. R. (I)	7/18	XXV-6384	XXV-6399-KING	XXV-6406-LEWIS	XXV-6406-KING
Feld, John Robert (I)(A)	7/28	XXXIII-8545			
Friend, Harry (I)(A)(d)	7/27	XXXII-8371			
Garnett, Ralph R. (I)(A)	7/28	XXXIII-8460-JONES	XXXIII-8486-KING	XXXIII-8503-JONES	
Grey, John P. (I)	7/18	XXV-6409			
	7/19	XXVI-6581	XXVI-6625-RICHARDS XXVI-6732-THOMAS	XXVI-6735-BROWN -6742-RICHARDS -6744-THOMAS	XXVI-6744-JONES
Gunnar, Alfred (d)(A)	7/28	XXXIII-8447			
Henney, David C.	7/24	XXX-7626-JONES -7640-JONES	XXX-7639		

(I) Topical index in file.
(A) Abstract in file.
(d) Testimony by deposition.

4.0211 *Understand the Final Objective of the Analysis.* It is important to understand the final purpose of the analytical effort. One situation might require a broad study of a complex manufacturing process in order to comprehend the relationships of people, plans, and documents—obviously a major learning effort—before undertaking any analysis of the evidentiary material.

A different situation exists when the final objective is to provide demonstrative exhibits for use in helping a jury to understand the lawyer's case. Little learning is involved, though a testing of different mediums might be needed, such as photography, sketches, graphs, charts, maps, videotape, and models.

If the need is simply to identify and retrieve exhibits easily and quickly that were introduced in single depositions, solve that problem alone in lieu of expanding it into a case-wide indexing system. Do not develop complex procedures

EXHIBIT 10 Index to Trial Transcripts

Volume I—June 1, 1970—Pages 1–650

Opening Statements By	Page No.
Thomas Jones	250
David Smith	325
John King	405
Edward Brown	485
Joseph Richards	520
Donald Lewis	559
Robert Ruggle	580
Tommy Thomas	500

Volume II—June 2, 3, 4—Pages 651–1280

Continuation of Opening Statements By

David Davids	651
Mack McLean	702
Rettus Reading	750
Testimony of SAM SHAM, by DEPOSITION, with questions read by D. Smith and answers by T. Jones	775
Proceedings outside presence of jury	790
June 3—Continued reading of DIRECT EXAMINATION by Smith	800
Testimony of BARRY BROWN—DIRECT EXAMINATION by T. Jones	905
June 4—Continued DIRECT of BROWN by T. Jones	1025
VOIR DIRE by Ruggle	1190
—by Thomas	1195
Continued DIRECT by T. Jones	1200
VOIR DIRE by Lewis	1273
Continued DIRECT by John King	1275

when there is no need for them. If the utility of the deposition exhibits requires only identifying duplicates (many times several witnesses will identify the same object or document, and it thus bears individual exhibit numbers), a detailed history or summary of each exhibit may be unnecessary. A workable, understandable cross-reference system of duplicate exhibits would suffice. Effective analysis fits the need of the case.

4.0212 Comprehend the Resources Available. Analysis sometimes can be accomplished only within the mind of one person; other times, it requires the assembly of information, data, documents, records, photos, and so on to allow sorting, copying, indexing, and physical comparison. Large and complex tasks sometimes may be handled in increments. For instance, one person is responsible for creating a chronologic history, while another person assembles and collates all witness statements for points of agreement or conflict and yet another person copes with analysis and cross-referencing data from interrogatories, requests for admission, and so on.

Obviously, if the legal assistant is assigned to the task alone, with no extra help or funds available, then extra document reproduction, microfilming, scale model construction, and so on may be unrealistic. Each necessary act or function must be scheduled to fit available equipment and personnel hours, and realism in time estimates and dollar values is essential. The legal assistant who without protest acquires more projects than can be honored hurts the employing attorney

EXHIBIT 11

Plaintiffs' Exhibit No. 13
(Our Document No. 18)
Schedule showing prices per net ton for centrifugal
pipe for water—Specs. S32.7—USC 003948

Date	Description	Action	Transcript Page Nos.
6/11	Jones on Brown	identified	1028
		marked	1030
		mention of having been received	1052
		mentioned	1069, 1070, 1072
6/15	King on Grey	mentioned	1575
7/8	King on Mark	mentioned	5859, 5861, 5862–63
7/13	Lewis on Mark	mentioned	5886
7/14	Lewis on Mark	mentioned	5889, 5890, 5891

Plaintiffs' Exhibit No. 14
(Our Document No. 19)
Schedule showing prices per ton East Coast prices f.o.b. Our Town
for 3″–13″ from Union City USC 938475

Date	Description	Action	Transcript Page Nos.
6/11	Jones on Brown	identified	1029
		marked	1030
		mention of having been received	1052
		mentioned	1069, 1070, 1072
6/15	King on Grey	mentioned	1565, 1567, 1569, 1570, 1572, 1573
7/8	King on Mark	mentioned	5519
7/13	Lewis on Mark	mentioned	5886, 5889, 5830, 5899

Plaintiffs' Exhibit No. 15
(Our Document No. 20)
Schedule showing prices per net ton for centrifugal
pipe—West Coast prices f.o.b. Anywhere, USA 4″–11″
from Union City—USC 039485

Date	Description	Action	Transcript Page Nos.
6/11	King on Brown	identified	1028
		marked	1030
		received	1052
7/8	Jones on Mark	mentioned	1069, 1070, 1072
7/13	Lewis on Mark	mentioned	5857, 5859, 5861, 5863

Plaintiffs' Exhibit No. 16
(Our Document No. 21)
Page of Appendix showing up-to-date listing
for price book pages: CO 4112

Date	Description	Action	Transcript Page Nos.
6/11	King on Brown	identified	1079
		received	1080
		mentioned	1081

and commits cumulative professional suicide. Effectiveness is measured by successfully completed projects.

4.0213 Determine the Function of the Materials or Documents to Be Handled.   Legal assistants do not analyze abstract philosophies but testimony, recorded events, groups of documents, production systems, material objects, and/

or locations. If the material involved is evidentiary in nature, it must be preserved, protected, and prepared for production at trial. If the analytic process requires use of that object, a surrogate must be developed, a duplicate obtained, or a model created. For instance, an original evidentiary document is stored in the safe, but a photocopy is adequate for the legal assistant's analytical purpose. It can be written upon, recopied (with a legend as described in the litigation skills chapter), or annotated. The analysis may be to summarize and simplify the utility of a document, a few documents, or all the documents, and it is important to create the proper framework to meet the need established by the attorney.

If the need is to summarize depositions, then primary concentration should be placed on these summaries. Plans should not extend to cross-referencing Requests for Admission to the deposition testimony (even though it may become necessary at a later date). If the legal assistant feels such a cross-reference would be a possibility, then a note to this effect could be placed on a list of possible things to do.

4.0214 Establish the Parameters of the Project. These parameters may be the rules of law in the case by which topical breakdowns can be established; the number of hours to be dedicated to specific projects; the date of origin of the action that is the earliest date documents can carry and still be relevant to the case; the related professions that have an impact on the standards of the industry involved in the case (a general contractor may be charged with safety orders on excavation, steel work, reinforced cement, electrical wiring, heating, cooling and environmental controls, worker's compensation, Occupational Safety and Health Act regulations, and so on); or possible expert witnesses who could be utilized, for example economists, statisticians, actuaries, psychiatrists, research analysts, and computer programmers.

4.0215 Consider Time as a Major Element in Choosing Techniques, Systems, and Detail. An extraordinary system that can be operated perfectly is worthless if it does not produce results on time. One of the frustrating elements of legal assisting is working within short time frames that require austere and even incomplete solutions because of a lack of early planning, funding, or appreciation by the attorney. The attorney, in fairness, is constantly beset with Hobson's choice in dedicating time and money to projects that may prove unnecessary. In some instances, the attorney does make such dedication simply because he or she understands that his method is "recommended by experts" in the field without attempting to adapt the recommendation to the particular problem at hand. Discretion, then, becomes, the watchword for legal assistants in determining time and monies expended for projects in particular phases of discovery. A prudent and efficient legal assistant will also be aware of time- and money-saving devices for the attorney, as well as the client, and seek to identify necessary projects from unnecessary ones.

4.03 Summary

Following the basic principles only aids the legal assistant in analyzing factual situations. Analysis requires a good memory and the ability to link facts, testimony, or objects together in relationship to the issues of the case. Some legal assistants do not perceive the similarities or conflicts that arise in testimony and reports and should not accept or be assigned to such cases where this ability is vital. Effective legal assistants persevere in reading and measuring each statement, reported act, or event against others, constantly thinking, "If this is so, how can that be true?" and then proceed to examine, study, and review to establish the answer. A good legal assistant who, after examining, studying, reviewing, and attempting to establish an answer, finds nothing conclusive will not hesitate to say so. Being able to say "I found nothing" is sometimes as important as saying "This is what I found."

Good judgment and analytical ability are developed attributes of successful legal assistants and frequently are best appreciated and criticized retrospectively. It is the result of those attributes that is noticed. Judgment improves with experience, and both good and bad judgments contribute to the improvement. Interested legal assistants grasp every opportunity to make unimportant or inconsequential judgments in the course of their careers to test the attitudes of the lawyer, their co-workers, and the firm and to develop a feeling for the responsibility and authority they are permitted to exercise. Such minor tests expose the legal assistant to others in the office and provide the feedback that allows him or her to identify sources of assistance or opposition in various activities.

Judgment and analytical ability go hand in hand with prudence—thought in acting and planning. What is excellent for one law office may be a disaster for another. Personnel valued by one law firm may be the bane for another. A particular method of filing and storage of files may work fine in one office but would not meet the needs of another office.

The legal assistant works for people and with the problems of people. Prudence, discretion, respect, and consideration for others—coupled with a driving interest, professional pride, and the desire to perform satisfactorily—will compel the legal assistant to consider each assignment, analyze it, and use the best judgment possible. No more—and no less—is expected.

5

Legal Research

5.00   Introduction

Learning to research a legal problem can be compared to learning a sport. For example, there are literally thousands of people who can explain the mechanics of the golf swing—how to address the ball, how to grasp the club, what muscles to use, and so forth. In theory, it seems that once the student has a clear picture of the mechanics and a chance to communicate to his or her brain what is desired, all that is necessary is to put the ball on the tee and hit a drive that results in praise from the instructor. Everyone, however, recognizes the fallacy of this theory. Expertise is the result of diligent practice. As with all learning processes, teachers and materials are available to explain legal research, but in the final analysis, it is a matter of finding the most effective method for the particular need. The ability to perform effectively is not an instantaneous result of understanding the techniques and mechanics of research. There are, however, universal principles and basic techniques that are essential to researching a legal problem effectively.

The legal assistant should not be discouraged if, after reading this chapter, his or her efforts do not bring such immediate success that the attorney praises his or her brilliance. In all likelihood, the initial assignment will take much more time than anticipated and the odds are against achieving perfect results at first. Those efforts will not be wasted, however, as they contribute to a practical foundation in research and provide opportunities to try different methods and identify the most effective. As familiarity with the research material and resources increases, the time required to find the law and analyze the case decisions will diminish. The individual's research techniques will become more refined, and even less time will be needed to research a given fact situation. Experience, practice, and constructive criticism by others will help the legal assistant develop expertise in stating facts and opinions in professional, concise legal writing, which the attorney will appreciate.

The law library is overwhelming and complex at first glance, but as the legal assistant becomes acquainted with it, it will become a friend. While most lawyers maintain a library sufficiently complete to meet the needs of their practice specialty, other libraries are highly specialized and sophisticated with multiple copies of source material and several varieties of sources on the same topics. Just looking at the different topic titles and sets of books to determine exactly what sources of information are available in the library, understanding how the library is arranged, and finding the specialized sections is time well spent. It simplifies research planning and improves confidence. If there are other law libraries available to the public in the area (such as law school, county, district, state, or federal libraries), write or visit them; meet the librarians; and take note of the procedures that allow access to use, or borrowing of material. Competence in library use is the key to success in legal research.

This chapter is merely an introduction and is not intended to be a complete course in legal research. It will provide the inexperienced legal assistant with a working background of the mechanics of research but will not satisfy the highly sophisticated needs of an attorney or a fully trained and experienced legal assistant. Most beginning legal assistants will receive very limited and specific research assignments in the beginning. The parameters of the research will be clearly defined, some research sources suggested, cases cited, and, perhaps, past research efforts of others made available for guidance in form, style, and preferred format. These will help in determining beginning points or checkpoints during the research and reporting tasks. The tasks will increase in difficulty and complexity as the legal assistant demonstrates skill and craftsmanship and gains the attorney's trust and confidence.

If the legal assistant is diligent in his or her efforts, he or she will acquire confidence in his or her ability to research and will function with the professionalism that is expected. It is a very rewarding experience, and the challenge is exciting; however, it requires full understanding of the research objective by the legal assistant and can be accomplished only if the lawyer identifies each of the legal principles and legal issues that are inherent in each assignment.

5.01 Principles of Legal Research

Legal research is an integral part of the practice of law, and its impact on a case can be critical. It is essential that all research be accurate and include the most current data available. The authority controlling the status of the law can change very quickly as decisions come down from higher courts; therefore, the importance of fully updated research cannot be overemphasized.

A working rapport must be established between the lawyer and the legal assistant. Mutual respect and trust are essential. The lawyer must necessarily discuss the problem or subject of the research with the legal assistant thoroughly, including his or her views on the problem, the legal principles, the legal issues involved, the scope of the research, the fact situation, and the time deadline. These must be completely understood by the legal assistant, who then can proceed. Bear in mind at all times that the research, in essence, may become the lawyer's research, and it must be thorough and exact, or it will have to be redone completely by the attorney. Leave no stone unturned, no case or statute (and the updated pocket parts) unread, and no conflict unresolved without being clearly pointed out. If confusion sets in, seek help.

5.011   Case Law and Statutory Law.

The legal assistant must become comfortable with the dual origins of law and legal principles that may influence the client's case. There is "case law" and "statutory law" to consider in most situations. Be aware that the courts, at both the federal and state levels, must apply statutory law where applicable, even in the face of contradictory case law. The only exception to this hierarchy is when a court determines that the statute is inconsistent with the state or federal constitution. Further, when applying case law, the courts are obligated to follow appropriate precedents unless the present circumstances can be distinguished in some way. This method of adhering to the same legal principles in similar cases is the doctrine of *stare decisis* ("let the decision stand"). The product of this doctrine is the ability of the public to examine existing legal standards and predict with some degree of accuracy the likely outcome in a current situation. As mentioned previously, when following an existing legal standard, the court must give preference to statutory law over case law. With respect to goals in legal research, this translates to the following equation: 1) search for applicable statutory law, then 2) search for case law (especially if there is some basis upon which the statutory law is likely to be declared unconstitutional).

5.0111 Case Law.   Case law is based in part on the legal principles developed in the judgments of past cases dating as far back as medieval England. The exception to this is case law developed in the state of Louisiana. This state has its legal origins in France, and the case law has been developed over the years based upon French legal principles. However, while the legal terminology may be different, there are many striking similarities in English and French legal principles.

In essence, the opinions of judges in past cases set down legal principles to be followed in future cases. These principles are known as *precedent*. Precedents are generally accepted standards of action or nonaction expected of everyone in the conduct of social and business intercourse. They establish parameters for measuring infringement of one person's rights by another's actions. The trial courts provide a forum for a party complaining of such an infringement to present facts and arguments against the one who has allegedly wronged the complainant. Similarly, the alleged wrongdoer can present explanation or defenses as to why his or her conduct was not improper. The jury is charged by the judge to follow the law that he or she explains to them and to return a verdict based on the facts presented and consistent with the requirements of the explained law.

Most judicial opinions that are reported (published) are those of appellate courts, which establish standards for entire jurisdictions, such as the federal court system or the courts of a particular state. As a result, these are the precedents that can be cited as authority in subsequent cases. When cases are appealed, one of the parties to the original lawsuit seeks review of what took place in the trial court on the basis that the law was misapplied or that the judge or jury abused the limits of their authority. The appellate court, usually a panel of three or more judges, reviews the record of the trial court, including the evidence presented at the trial level and any objections that were made to the actions of the trial court judge or jury. If the appellate court finds that the trial court judge or jury acted in such a way that a party was prejudicially affected, it will reverse the decision. If it is found that the trial court did not exceed the parameters of its authority, the decision is affirmed. In either event, the appellate court generally issues an opinion that is published and recounts the pivotal facts, the decision of the appellate court, and its legal authority for the decision. This legal authority is usually in the form of statutory law or case law precedent and, in most cases, has been submitted by the parties to the suit in support of their cause.

As a general rule, state court cases can only be appealed to the highest court of the state. The exception to this are cases that have federal constitutional issues. In some circumstances, these cases may go to the United States Supreme Court for final disposition. Similarly, federal trial court cases are appealed to the circuit courts of appeals. In some situations, the Supreme Court may review the decision.

When researching case law, it should be kept in mind that the law of one's jurisdiction is usually controlling; the law of other jurisdictions may be used to influence and persuade the court, but the court has no obligation to follow it. For example, if one is performing research for a case that is pending in a particular state, the statutory law and appellate decisions of that state are controlling. However, the law of other states or the federal courts may be cited as persuasive authority.

It is important to understand that appeals may be made on nearly any area of the law involved with the trial, such as the basic legal questions involved; the procedural rules, including but not limited to jurisdiction and discovery procedures; introduction of witnesses or evidence; instructions to the jury on the law to apply; and standards. Only the issues tried, appealed, and ruled upon at the appellate level may be properly cited as authority from the appellate decision. All the rest is dictum: interesting in showing how the appellate court reached its decision but not binding. It may be helpful in determining how the court might rule on a given matter in the future, even persuasive in arguing that another court should so rule, but it is not law.

5.0112 *Statutory Law.* Statutory law is different from case law in that statutes are the stated intention of a legislative body to create a standard of permitted or proscribed conduct. The U.S. Constitution, the Bill of Rights, and the subsequent amendments to the Constitution are controlling as the primary written expression of the rights of individuals, and state and federal laws must be consistent with them and encourage the observance of similar desirable objectives. Each state also has its own constitution upon which its statutes are based, and these must be consistent with the federal Constitution as well. Counties, as subordinate governmental units of the state, are granted certain powers by the state to legislate rules of conduct within the county with ordinances and codes. Cities and towns are organized under the permission of the state and are granted certain powers to create rules necessary to the execution of their public responsibilities. Each of these entities follow the same basic process of creating a law, whether titled as such or called a "rule," "regulation," "ordinance," or "code." The first draft of a proposed statute (usually called a *bill*) is introduced by a legislator. The bill may subsequently be amended, amplified, or clarified by a legislative committee. In bicameral legislatures, such as the U.S. Congress or most state legislatures, the draft bill will be examined in both houses. In county or city governments (usually unicameral), a committee, a commission, or the legal counsel of the entity will examine and report on the draft to the appropriate entity, such as the county board of supervisors or the city council. Public hearings or notices with periods of time for comment are usually required, then a vote on the final draft of the measure is taken. In the U.S. Congress and most state legislatures, passage by both houses then forwards the measure to the chief executive for signature. If signed, the measure becomes a law. If the bill is vetoed, the legislature has a limited period of time in which to override the veto. The vote to override in both houses must be a greater majority than required for normal passage, usually two-thirds rather than a simple majority.

This same procedure is followed to a limited extent by federal and state regulatory agencies. These bodies create a form of law through regulations or rules that interpret, define, or clarify statutes passed by the legislature. The rule or regulation is drafted and published for public comment in the Federal Register or the state's official publication. There may also be public hearings. When finally effective, the rule is published in the appropriate official rules and regulations of the administrative agency. In adopting a particular rule or regulation, the administrative agency tacitly implies that they are authorized by the statute or statutes they interpret, define, or clarify, that no conflicts with other laws exist, and that the law is enforceable.

Laws may be public or private. If the topical matter pertains to citizens in general, it is public law. If the topical matter is of interest or benefit to a very limited number of people or a class of people and if it does not impinge on the rights or responsibilities of the general public, it is considered a private law. An example of a private law is one that provides for the naturalization of an individual in other than the usual circumstances. Temporary laws may also be enacted; these include appropriation and disaster relief bills.

All laws of Congress are bound into volumes at the end of the legislative session as part of the Statutes at Large (also known as session laws). These are chronologically organized and include all the laws passed in a given session.

5.0113 Codes. Codes are collections of statutory or regulatory law by jurisdiction and sometimes by subjects of law within a jurisdiction. A similar term used by some states is *revised statutes*. These collections are updated frequently to include new statutory law and to reflect amendment or repeal of existing statutory law. These codes are organized to facilitate the research process. Typically, all of the laws on a particular area of legislation, such as motor vehicles, are placed under a single heading. This is sometimes known as a title or chapter. The titles are arranged in alphabetical order and then assigned consecutive numbers as well. For example, *"agriculture"* would be one of the first numbered titles since it begins with A. The main headings are also arranged in alphabetical order. Within each heading, all of the laws on the particular subject are individually numbered. Thus, new laws can be added to the subject simply by adding new numbers. In addition, each code is accompanied by an extensive subject index that assists the reader in locating the needed information. For example, if one wanted to locate the law that indicated a driver's duty when road conditions are dangerous, one would look in the subject index for such topics as motor vehicles, automobiles, and traffic. Below each main topic are more specific references to the individual laws on the subject. When the correct heading and subheading are located in the index, a two-part number will be found. This generally corresponds to the number assigned to the main heading and the number assigned to the particular law.

Included with the actual text of the statute in the code may be a reference to the initial publication of the statute in the session laws. This enables the reader to locate historical information about the passage of the statute. Many codes are also annotated, which simply means that a brief description and reference to any judicial opinions that have interpreted the statute follow the text of the statute. These can be helpful in determining how the statute has been applied in specific past situations and consequently how it is likely to be applied in a present situation.

5.0114 Legislative Intent.   Each statute exists for the purpose intended by the entity that passed it. Where the language of a particular statute cannot be clearly understood, or, as is more often the case, opponents claim different meanings for the same words, the researcher may have to look back into the recorded minutes of hearings, committee discussions, and legislative rhetoric to define the original purpose. Many times this is an onerous task, which involves tracking the statute back to its origins as a bill, through committee and public hearings, even to the personal files of the original author of the proposed legislation. In some cases, a federal statute is so important that the U.S. Government Printing Office will publish all the written materials pertaining to it in one or more volumes. The historical data, debates, and comments can be a great aid to the researcher. Administrative agencies also have archives of historical information concerning rules they establish from the date of their proposal until publication. It may be necessary when contending with administrative agency rules and regulations to research first the rule, then the agency's own enabling legislation to ensure the agency is not exceeding its own authority as shown by the legislative intent in the statutory law that created the agency.

5.02   Five Steps of Research

While efficiency and productivity in legal research can only be the product of extended practice, some basic steps can help the researcher locate valid authority more quickly and easily. After years of performing legal research, many practitioners still follow these basic steps as a normal course of action. The five basic steps are:

(1) analyzing the facts and identifying the problem and subject of research;
(2) recognizing the issues or points of law involved;
(3) finding the law and expanding the research to access all necessary information, including adverse authority:
(4) updating the search; and
(5) reporting the research.

5.021   Step One: Analyzing the Facts.

Know the factual situation completely and know the client's objective. There may be occasions when the legal assistant will be able to discover an alternative way of obtaining the client's purpose when direct methods, as the client may have proposed, cannot be used. For example, if a man wants an advertising sign erected on his building and city ordinances prohibit certain kinds of signs, there may be an alternative way to accomplish the desired advertising to his satisfaction. Legal research will be easier if the facts and desired end result are clearly understood.

Analyzing the facts and identifying the problem and/or subject are musts. Every legal problem arises from a factual situation; the facts determine whether there is a legitimate cause of action or a valid defense. The facts are the basis of the document to be prepared, such as a will, a bill of sale, a lease agreement, or a complaint.

(a)   The first essential element in the factual analysis is to identify the parties involved. Determine whether they have any special standing under the law, such as a tenant, a landowner, or a particular class of people (such as all the purchasers of Product X) or whether they are immune from suit.

(b)   Next, determine the subject matter, such as real or personal property, bodily injury and damages, issues of governmental regulation, or contract execution.

(c)   Then determine the basis of the action or issue, such as negligence, breach of contract, or strict liability.

(d)   Now determine what types of relief are available, such as temporary restraining order, specific performance of the contract, or compensatory money damages.

(e)   Determine the defenses to the claim. Consider the facts and evaluate whether the claim has merit and whether any extenuating circumstances, facts, or law might legally exonerate the opponent, such as self-defense, comparative or contributory negligence of the plaintiff, or impossibility of performance of the contract.

5.022   Step Two: Identifying the Law.

When defining the law problems and areas, try to determine (a) what court or agency has primary jurisdiction; (b) if there are statutes, codes or administrative agency rules or regulations involved; and (c) whether it is a substantive or procedural law problem.

5.023   Step Three: Finding the Law.

Finding the law and expanding the search to include all necessary information is the next step and the point at which the true research begins. Again, there are many approaches open to the legal assistant. One of the most useful actions at this point is identifying all related terms, synonyms (same or similar meaning), and antonyms (opposite meaning) for the subject of research. Legal research is aided tremendously by the existence of subject indexes for most authorities. However, one must know what terminology the author used when preparing the index. By first identifying a number of possibilities, the speed of research can be increased while at the same time decreasing the level of frustration at not being able to locate the proper authority.

If the research problem is in an area of law unfamiliar to the legal assistant, the first step would usually be to read some secondary authority that contains a general commentary and explanation of the subject. (See Section 5.04 Sources of the Law in Research.) This allows the legal assistant to become familiar with the general nature and past history of and approaches to the problem and to decide which path the research must follow. The secondary authority generally cites cases and sometimes statutes. These can often provide a starting point for the research. Identifying the leading case on an issue provides a key to many other cases that follow, distinguish, or depart from the leading case holding. At the very least, these sources contain basic principles and relevant terminology and can provide a general familiarity with the subject matter. Because the majority of legal research resources can be accessed through various types of subject indexes, this basic knowledge can greatly assist the researcher when searching for commentary, case law, or statutory law.

Following examination of secondary sources, it is often necessary to go to the codes and reported judicial opinions of the jurisdiction whose law is being applied in the case under research. While more attention is given to this in the subsequent discussion, it is briefly noted here that codes are accompanied by extensive subject indexes that allow easy access to the particular statute sought. Similarly, all published judicial decisions are briefly described and arranged by subject in what is known as a *Digest*. A digest also has a subject index (called a "descriptive word index") that allows the researcher to locate the specific subject area of research. A key element in both statutory and case law research is knowledge of the relevant terminology. What one might consider the appropriate subject heading for a topic might vary significantly from the actual heading used in the legal resources. Familiarity with the subject, as well as such aids as a legal thesaurus, can take much of the frustration out of this aspect of legal research.

5.024   Step Four: Updating the Search.

Updating the search accomplishes two very important objectives. First, it confirms that the legal authority is still accepted as valid by the legislature and the judiciary. Second, it allows the researcher to learn of any subsequent statutes or judicial opinions on the subject that may not yet have been incorporated into the code or published. The most commonly accepted method of updating is through a process referred to as "Shepardizing." This describes the use of *Shepard's Citations* to locate all references to or approval, amendment, or repeal of published statutory or case law. (See Section 5.06 Use of *Shepard's Citations* or Shepardizing.) In addition to examining the subsequent treatment of the case or statute in *Shepard's Citations,* one should also read the actual text of the case or statute to determine if there are any distinguishing characteristics that may affect its applicability to the case at hand. With respect to statutes, it is important to note the date upon which the statute became effective to ensure that it was in effect on the relevant dates in the case being researched.

The completeness of the updating is of paramount importance, since the research must reflect the law as it is currently interpreted. The review of advance sheets, pocket parts, and supplements of codes or statutes is essential. The legal assistant who cites a case as authority for a positive position and later is proved to be in error because a more recent decision reversed the cited authority may find overnight that the attorney's confidence has been lost, along with any further assignments in this interesting and highly important work area.

Caveat: Most cases involve the law as it was on the date of the occurrence; for example, changes in the vehicle code or other law are seldom retroactive. Therefore, be certain to research the applicable law individually from the current date back to the origin of the cause of action. There can be some shocking exceptions. For example, in *Li v. Yellow Cab Co.,* 13 Cal.3d 804, 119 Cal.Rptr. 858, 532 P.2d 1226 (1975), a case establishing in California the system of comparative negligence to assign responsibility and liability for damage in direct proportion to the degree of negligence of each of the parties, the California Supreme Court concluded that the rule of contributory negligence (which had prevailed for years in California law) was overturned and that a rule of limited retroactivity should prevail. The court held that in view of the many pending cases involving matters similar in issue to that in *Li* at the trial and appellate levels, *Li* would apply to all cases in which the trial had not begun before the date the decision became final but would not apply to any case in which trial had begun before that date. It also provided that if any judgment were reversed on appeal for other reasons, the opinion would be applicable to any retrial. Another example is California Code of Civil Procedure Section 1048, Severance and Consolidation of Causes, which was completely reworded in 1971 to be operative July 1, 1972. The new act applied to actions commenced on or after July 1, 1972, but not to actions pending on July 1, 1972, and provided that any action to which the act did not apply would be governed by the law as it would exist had the act not been enacted.

Admittedly, these are exceptions, but this type of limited retroactivity or limited applicability of operative dates must be considered in any research.

5.025   Step Five: Reporting the Research and Commenting on the Adversary's Position.

Everything done must be reported concisely to the attorney, including the positive research and, if the work effort goal is to rebut the position of another, the research and review of every case cited in support of the adversary's position. Do not accept at face value the adversary's cited positions or authorities as either factually or legally correct statements of the positions taken by the courts in the cited cases. Citing cases out of context, from headnotes, or only from synopsis is a common, though dangerous, activity. Similarly, citing dictum from a case as though it were a tried and considered issue is a technique the legal assistant can avoid only by reading the case in its entirety.

Reviewing the adversary's cited cases provides several benefits, one being an appreciation of the adversary's legal reasoning and/or legal foundation. Many times the legal assistant may find the adversary cited a case that does not help the adversary's position nearly so persuasively as it does the client's; also, other cases favorable to the client's position may be found in Shepardizing the cases developed in the adversary's citations. These finds occur when the legal assistant reads the full case text, not just the headnotes, to be certain the context of the citation is applicable, the interpretation is correctly reported, and it is current law and not a case that has been overturned by subsequent decisions. If the cases cited in the initial document are not valid authority or have been incorrectly interpreted, the report of research must point out these facts as well as the reasoning and cases supporting the legal assistant's own conclusions.

While a report on all the research is essential, carefully think about and consider each bit of information accumulated and decide whether to include or exclude it. This is critical to the clarity of the end result and conclusion. Research requires an intelligent and active mind and the ability to analyze information and to concentrate all efforts singlemindedly and fixedly on the goal.

Practice in legal writing requires familiarity with legal writing styles. Go to the library and read some decisions at random. Learn to analyze the case content. The first few cases may not make any sense, but familiarity with the legal writing style and careful rereadings will create skill in analysis, perception, and measuring the written cases against a given issue. It also will increase the legal assistant's ability to detect relevance or analogy between the reported cases and the factual situation in the instant problem.

The office file of past legal research reports can offer pointers on style and form for the legal assistant to follow. Briefs filed in appellate proceedings can clearly show the organized manner of expression that may be helpful or desired by the office. Adapting to the style preferred in the office simplifies the lawyer's review of the finished effort since the form of the report is familiar and he or she can concentrate on the substance of the report or memorandum.

Finally, while most research will entail only a review of authority and will not be incorporated in any formal pleading, the purpose is to provide the lawyer with case law, statutory law, and statements sufficient to enable him or her to measure the law against the facts, thereby reaching a final determination and stating a positive position. Even drafting pleadings requires research, as do law and motion matters, particularly the points and authorities for such documents. In any event, the written product should be clear and to the point, and the writing quality should be above reproach. An evaluation of the factors should be presented in an appropriate, logical and effective manner, and the legal assistant must be confident of the position recommended. Strong decisions in opposition to the proposed point of view must be brought to the attention of the attorney, as well as any distinctions between those cases and the instant problem. If at any time during the research procedure, the legal assistant becomes unsure of a point, it must be discussed fully and freely with the attorney to resolve the doubt, redirect the effort, or get back on the right track. If the attorney won't help, the legal assistant is working in the wrong office.

5.03   Basic Research Procedures and Practices

Certain basic beneficial procedures should be instituted at the start of a career in research to avoid duplication of effort; they also will be invaluable later as starting points.

5.031   Retention of Legal Research.

This sounds self-explanatory, but it is not necessarily a simple matter. Some offices maintain complete legal memoranda files, and all research in the office is categorized, indexed, and filed in a control file. If the office has such a file, the legal assistant must become familiar both with the file and the indexing system. Clearly, it is important to take advantage of the past research contained within the file. In large firms, this is often one of the functions of the law librarian. Some firms with such files also have procedures to continuously update the material, or selected categories of material, depending on the specialties of the office. If the employer does not maintain such a file, take the initiative and start one. In any event, the legal assistant must adapt to or devise a suitable system and maintain his or her own research for use in the future, taking care to update the cites in any past memorandum or report before again citing that material as authority. Each update is posted to the research file as well. If the legal assistant is working in a specialized field, such as malpractice, it is helpful to read the West advance sheets on that topic as they come into the office.

5.032   Compilation of a Personal Case Book.

As the legal assistant researches problems and as new decisions are handed down, he or she should file or record the citations in a case book by topic. Also, when researching a problem which is common from both "for and against" sides, that is, filing a claim with a public entity, as opposed to relief from the requirement of filing a claim, or filing a late claim, note the case as applicable to both sides. This book normally is not a detailed description of the case but, rather, a loose leaf notebook with general categories, such as malpractice, fraud, or strict liability, and contains the cite or code sections and the particular point of law to which it applies together with a few lines setting forth the theory.

Examples:

PRODUCTS LIABILITY—Lessor of Personal Property . . .
Doctrine of strict liability in tort applicable.
Fakhoury v. Magner, 25 Cal.App.3d 58, 101 Cal.Rptr. 473 (1972) lessor of
    furnished apartment liable for injuries when couch partially collapsed.
Price v. Shell Oil Co., 2 Cal.3d 245, 85 Cal.Rptr. 178, 466 P.2d 722 (1970)
    lessor of truck and ladder to plaintiff's employer liable when ladder
    collapsed.

5.033   Devise a Workable System to Avoid Duplication in Research.

When legal assistants begin their initial efforts to research, many find themselves returning to the same case several times. This is wasted effort and should be avoided. This seems to happen most frequently in the updating process, where the legal assistant is reading many cases and Shepardizing. (See Section 5.06 Use of *Shepard's Citations* or Shepardizing.) Many methods can be utilized, such as keeping lists of citations or titles as cases are read. Find a method and use it faithfully. Consistent use will make even a poorly conceived system helpful and a well-conceived system invaluable.

5.034   Save Time and Steps.

One essential tool for beginning research is a legal dictionary or combination dictionary/thesaurus. Dictionaries provide meanings, origins, spellings, and pronunciations. A legal thesaurus can provide synonyms to aid the legal assistant in locating information during research and in writing in a more concise and professional manner. One such source is *West's Legal Thesaurus-Dictionary.* This concise paperback is complete in its reference to legal terms and manageable in size, making it a useful library or desk reference tool. The legal assistant must become familiar with the law dictionary, and a review thereof will show that there are many different laws to consider, such as law of arms, law of nations, law of the case, and law of the land. Browse through it and enjoy it. In order to understand the law and to conduct the search of the law, it is important to understand the legal system of the country and to be comfortable with its vocabulary. The glossary of this manual is a collection of some of the basic legal terms that will be encountered. An excellent and comprehensive source is *Words and Phrases,* a multivolume dictionary published by West Publishing Company, which can provide subtle meanings not apparent in an ordinary legal dictionary. Its greatest value is in its citations of the cases where courts have defined and construed the particular meaning of certain words and phrases. Consider how helpful such meanings are when trying to defend an *intoxicated* person: *Words and Phrases* both defines the word and provides citations from certain courts of the meaning of the word *intoxicated* and the cited cases, when read, clarify the elements of proof the prosecutor must present.

5.035   Be Familiar with the Hierarchy of the Courts and the Reporting Systems.

All states have an order of court systems as well as rules of court and guidelines for appellate procedure. For example, California has five courts; small claims court, municipal court, superior court (all of which comprise the trial level courts), the courts of appeal, and the supreme court (the appellate-level courts). Each court has established rules of court that must be followed. The appellate procedures provide for appeal to the next higher court, for example, from superior court to court of appeal. The decisions of the trial-level courts are seldom published; the decisions of the appellate-level courts usually are. For example, *California Appellate Reports* (in several series) contains the decisions of the California Courts of Appeal, and *California Reports* contains the official supreme court decisions. The legal assistant must be familiar with the state's court system and which decisions are published, the reporting systems of the courts' official reports, and the corresponding commercial (unofficial) reporters and the decisions they cover. For instance, the official reports of the California Courts of Appeal and of the California Supreme Court are discussed above. The West Publishing Company's national reporter system contains two series of unofficial reports of great value to the legal assistant. The *Pacific Reporter* contains the unofficial reports of the California Supreme Court, as well as reports of other western states, but does not contain reports for the California Courts of Appeal. The separate *California Reporter* (still of the national reporter system) contains cases both of the courts of appeal and of the supreme court. Therefore, most California legal assistants, in researching California law, rely on the *California Reporter* rather than the *Pacific Reporter.*

Similarly, the federal court system has a hierarchy of trial and appellate courts and separate and distinct reporter systems, official and unofficial.

5.04   Sources of the Law in Research

Generally, the law is contained in two types of authority—primary and secondary. Law books and finding aids are categorized in the same manner—primary and secondary.

5.041   Primary Authority.

Primary authority is that which is valid authority as to the exact status of the law on any given point, in any state or area and at any given time. The most persuasive primary authority that can be cited is that of the official report of the highest court, state or federal, (above the trial-court level) that has rendered a decision on the point of law being researched. This may be cited as the controlling law. Examples of this type of authority are the U.S. Supreme Court decisions or the supreme court decisions of the state in which the issue is located; then the Constitution (state or federal); codified laws; Statutes at Large or session laws; administrative rules, regulations, orders and decisions; and court rules and court decisions in the state where the issue is located. Similar authority from other jurisdictions may be persuasive authority on matters not previously decided in the state but is not mandatory authority.

5.042   Secondary Authority.

Secondary authority is any compilation of opinions and/or comments by various authors setting forth their interpretation of the law. This kind of authority is most helpful as an aid in research but does not have the force and effect of law. Examples of this type of authority are annotated case reports, annotated codes and statutes, "restatements" of various laws, encyclopedias, looseleaf services, index books, dictionaries, digests, form books, treatises, and periodical literature.

Secondary authority is a basic tool. It provides insight into the disputed issue and, many times, quickly directs the researcher to the primary authority being sought. There are occasions when secondary authority can be cited and effectively used to sway or persuade the court to accept a given position as the correct one, but it should be clearly referenced to the attorney as a secondary authority—distinctly different from case law or statutory law or any administrative agency rule. In so-called test cases (a case where the particular legal issue has not been tried and appealed in the state before), where there is no substantive or case law, it may be the only authority available.

5.05   Search Methods—Finding the Law

It is impossible to include in this chapter a detailed discussion of each and every search aid available to the serious researcher. This will review the types of materials available and give a brief discussion of the general categories. Entire books are devoted to this topic (see the bibliography of this chapter). In addition, the National Association of Legal Assistants has a comprehensive cassette course entitled "Legal Research for the Legal Assistants, Guide to the Use of the Law Library." It covers the subject, case, statutory, and administrative approaches to the law and contains four professionally recorded cassette tapes to supplement approximately a hundred pages of written material.

5.051   The Subject or Text Approach.

The subject or text approach to the law requires the use of general information sources (secondary authority). In the absence of a specific case or a definite starting place, this is probably the logical starting point. Some of the sources are:

5.0511 Dictionaries.   There are various kinds of dictionaries, including single-volume and multivolume glossaries. The single-volume type is represented by *Black's Law Dictionary, Ballentine's Law Dictionary,* and, of course, *Webster's Dictionary.* The definitions in the law dictionaries are usually derived from court opinions and are quoted verbatim with citations to the cases, and sometimes the discovery of one case on a subject leads to all other cases on the topic. The best known of the multivolume dictionaries is probably *Words and Phrases* by West Publishing Company. This set covers, as nearly as possible, every word and phrase defined by the federal and state courts in opinions rendered since 1658, and the words and phrases are listed in alphabetical order. A smaller version of *Words and Phrases* is produced for some states, for example, *Florida Words and Phrases.* These sets are kept up to date by annual pocket parts and revisions. Other standard law dictionaries may be in the firm's library. Dictionaries are secondary authority but can be used to find reference to primary authority.

5.0512 Textbooks, Treatises, and Law Reviews.   As the primary authorities became more voluminous, lawyers, students, and others began to follow the development of the law in certain fields. As attorneys became more knowledgable, they began to write treatises and textbooks relating to certain areas of the law. The bibliography at the end of this chapter provides an idea of some of the texts and references available on legal research. Textbooks are available on nearly every area of the law, including discovery procedures, evidence and punitive damages.

Periodically, judges, attorneys, and law school professors jointly agree that the law in a particular area needs clarification, modernization, or adjustment to the demands of our changing, complex society. Study groups are formed, such as the American Law Institute, and produce definitive restatements of a law for the area under study, such as the Restatement of the Law of Torts or the Restatement of the Law of Contracts. This type of authority is secondary and is not the law itself, but it is a strong and persuasive presentation of the way the law should be. Such studies have, in the past, become the law by a court agreeing and overturning the existing law or by being codified and the code being enacted by the various jurisdictions. The Uniform Commercial Code is the result of such a restatement and codification procedure. The restatements are widely respected as quotable authority, though secondary, because of the distinguished and highly respected authors who participate in their preparation and because of the sound logic and legal reasoning they represent. Such authority has value to the attorney particularly if directly on point in the instant case, whether in direct conflict with past case law or not.

Law schools publish law reviews, such as the *Cornell Law Review,* the *Harvard Law Review,* and the *Hastings Law Review.* Law reviews contain articles written by professors, lawyers, and students usually including detailed analysis of a particular problem, area of law, or particular case, with copious commentary and voluminous footnote references to primary and secondary authorities on the topic. These materials are secondary authority in that they contain one person's discussion, opinion, viewpoint, and conclusions after examination of the footnoted sources; the theories expressed, therefore, are not universally accepted, so the cases cited in support of their opinions should be read.

5.0513 Newspapers. Local newspapers may contain references to state and federal opinions (for example, publicized decisions on the disconnecting of life-sustaining apparatus for the terminally ill). There also are newspapers that deal only with legal matters, such as *The Recorder,* the *Los Angeles Daily Journal,* the *New York Law Journal.* These are also secondary, though valuable, sources of current information.

5.0514 Legal Encyclopedias. Many researchers find legal encyclopedias are the best secondary source of information and an excellent place to start research. Encyclopedias give an overall view of the given legal topic and, when properly used, provide an enormous amount of background information, sometimes set out the necessary elements or meaning for any given term, and get the legal assistant off on the right foot in finding the law. Because they contain numerous case citations, the legal assistant who studies them will have a general feeling for the point being researched as well as a place to start the case research to determine the present state of the law. Normally, encyclopedias are multivolume publications, arranged alphabetically and indexed. They are updated continually with cumulative pocket parts or replacement volumes. Here again, do not cite cases from encyclopedias without reading the cases.

Two general legal encyclopedias are available: *Corpus Juris Secundum* and *American Jurisprudence*. *Corpus Juris Secundum* (*C.J.S.*) is published by West Publishing Company. It generally is known as *C.J.S.* and purports to cite all American cases. Footnotes in these volumes are extensive. Since this is a West publication, it carries references to the West topic and key numbers, which allows easy transition from one to another of the West publications. As a bound volume created from past cases, extensively edited and proofed, the information is very informative but may be out of date. Every item of interest in the basic volumes must be checked by reference to the cumulative annual pocket parts and by seeking out updated case citators to find any cases on the same matter that may have been decided since the publication of the pocket part. An example of pages in a *C.J.S.* volume and its updating pocket part are shown in Exhibits 12 and 13. These exhibits clearly show the number of cases in the product liability field that occurred between the publication of the 1972 bound volume and the 1990 Annual Cumulative Supplement on the one topic of "———— Knowledge of Defect or Danger as Affecting Duty to Warn."

Three search methods can be applied to *C.J.S.* through the (1) descriptive word index, the fact method of search; (2) the topic analysis method, through its topical outlines; and (3) the words and phrases method or words sprinkled throughout. A separate "Words and Phrases Defined" listing in alphabetical order is located at the back of each volume.

American Jurisprudence 2d (Am.Jur.2d), published by the Lawyers Cooperative Publishing Company reports selected cases. It also contains a general index system. If the researcher is familiar with the area of law, he or she may proceed directly to the volume that contains that topic. If the researcher has difficulty using this method, the volume itself has a volume index (to be used in the same manner as the general index volumes). In the front of every volume of *Am.Jur.2d* are tables of statutes and parallel references. These tables indicate where the statutes cited in the volume are located and the references covered by articles formerly in the first edition of this work. Cross references are cited to: *American Law Reports (ALR); U.S. Supreme Court Reports, Lawyer's Edition; U.S. Code Service; Am.Jur.Legal Forms; Pleading and Practice Forms;* and *Proof of Facts and Trials.*

Out of the national legal encyclopedias have evolved state legal encyclopedias, examples of which are *California Jurisprudence, Texas Jurisprudence, Florida Jurisprudence,* and practice sets, such as *Indiana Law and Practice* and *Florida Law and Practice.*

The value of encyclopedias becomes obvious through examination and use of the books since they give extensive coverage of the law in broad treatment covered by known cases within specific jurisdictions and footnoted to those cases.

5.0515 Indexes, Words, and Phrases.

Almost every publication contains an index. Some indexes also contain a section entitled "Words and Phrases" containing significant words and phrases used within that publication, in alphabetical order. These are useful in leading the reader quickly to the proper section of the publication.

There also are special indexes for legal periodical literature and periodicals, as well as law review citations. Among these are Jones-Chipman's *Index to Legal Periodical Literature* (covering the period from 1803 until it ceased publication in 1937); *Index to Legal Periodicals* (covering the period from 1926 to date), and *Shepard's Law Review Citations.* These sources can be found in larger libraries, such as law school, county, state, or federal law libraries.

EXHIBIT 12

At least constructive knowledge is required,[41] and such knowledge is usually sufficient.[42] One may not escape liability because of lack of knowledge where he has omitted to inform himself as to what his duty was.[43]

§ 5(1). Knowledge or Notice of Defect or Danger

In order for an act or omission to be negligent, the person charged therewith must generally have, or be reasonably chargeable with, knowledge that it involved danger to another.

Library References

Negligence ⊂⊃10, 24, 48.

Since negligence necessarily involves a violation or disregard of some duty, as discussed supra § 4(1), which is known to the person charged therewith, as considered supra § 4(13), it follows that knowledge of the facts out of which the duty arises is an essential element for consideration in determining whether one has exercised reasonable care or has been guilty of negligence,[44] at least in the case

quoted in Norris v. Macon Terminal Co., 198 S.E. 272, 275, 58 Ga. App. 313.
Idaho.—**Corpus Juris cited in** Nash v. Meyer, 31 P.2d 273, 281, 54 Idaho 283.
Md.—**Corpus Juris quoted in** Adams v. Carey, 190 A. 815, 821, 172 Md. 173.
Tex.—St. Louis, S. F. & T. Ry. Co. v. Gore, Civ.App., 69 S.W.2d 186, error dismissed—**Corpus Juris cited in** Texas & P. Ry. Co. v. Wylie, Civ. App., 36 S.W.2d 238, 242.
Wis.—Shaw v. Wisconsin Power & Light Co., 40 N.W.2d 498, 256 Wis. 176, 13 A.L.R.2d 1390—**Corpus Juris cited in** Moen v. Madison Rys. Co., 225 N.W. 821, 822, 199 Wis. 168, followed in 225 N.W. 822, 199 Wis. 171.
45 C.J. p 651 note 69.

"Negligence presupposes a duty of taking care, and this in turn presupposes knowledge or its equivalent. . . . There can be no neglect to perform a duty unless the person sought to be charged with negligence has knowledge of the condition of things which requires performance at his hands."
Me.—American Lumber Sales Co. v. Fidelity Trust Co., 141 A. 102, 105, 127 Me. 65.

41. N.Y.—Silver's Lunch Stores v. United Electric Light & Power Co., 255 N.Y.S. 515, 142 Misc. 744, modified on other grounds 261 N.Y.S. 714, 146 Misc. 554.
Constructive knowledge of defect or danger see infra § 5(3).

42. N.Y.—Sherman v. Western Transp. Co., 62 Barb. 150.
45 C.J. p 651 note 70.

43. N.Y.—Sherman v. Western Transp. Co., 62 Barb. 150.

44. U.S.—**Corpus Juris Secundum cited in** U. S. v. Marshall, C.A.Idaho, 230 F.2d 183, 189—Mattson v. Central Electric & Gas Co., C.A. Neb., 174 F.2d 215, certiorari denied 70 S.Ct. 142, 338 U.S. 868, 94 L.Ed. 532, rehearing denied 70 S.Ct. 238, 338 U.S. 896, 94 L.Ed. 551.
Ariz.—Alires v. Southern Pac. Co., 378 P.2d 913, 93 Ariz. 97.
Cal.—Lejeune v. General Petroleum Corporation of California, 18 P.2d 429, 128 C.A. 404.
Duval v. Rowell, 269 P.2d 249, 124 C.A.2d Supp. 897.
Colo.—**Corpus Juris cited in** Girardot v. Williams, 80 P.2d 433, 434, 102 Colo. 456.
Conn.—Gipstein v. Kirshenbaum, 174 A. 261, 118 Conn. 681.
Del.—Rhein v. Wark & Co., 174 A.2d 132.
Ga.—Georgia Elec. Co. v. Smith, 134 S.E.2d 840, 108 Ga.App. 851—Whitaker v. Jones, McDougald, Smith, Pew Co., 26 S.E.2d 545, 69 Ga.App. 711—**Corpus Juris quoted in** Norris v. Macon Terminal Co., 198 S.E. 272, 275, 58 Ga.App. 313.
Idaho.—**Corpus Juris cited in** Nash v. Meyer, 31 P.2d 273, 281, 54 Idaho 283.
Ill.—Fier v. Chicago Orpheum Co., 14 N.E.2d 860, 295 Ill.App. 247.
Ind.—Kennedy v. Southern Fire Brick & Clay Co., 159 N.E. 1, 86 Ind.App. 629.
Iowa.—Woodworth v. Iowa Cent. Ry. Co., 149 N.W. 522, 170 Iowa 697.
Ky.—Howard v. Fowler, 207 S.W.2d 559, 561, 306 Ky. 567.
Md.—Texas Co. v. Pecora, 118 A.2d 377, 208 Md. 281—**Corpus Juris quoted in** Adams v. Carey, 190 A. 815, 821, 172 Md. 173—**Corpus Juris cited in** Moore v. American Stores Co., 182 A. 436, 440, 169 Md. 541.
Minn.—Wire v. Williams, 133 N.W.2d 840—Manteuffel v. Theo. Hamm Brewing Co., 56 N.W.2d 310, 238 Minn. 140—Rue v. Wendland, 33 N.W.2d 593, 226 Minn. 449.
Miss.—Columbus & G. R. Co. v. Coleman, 160 So. 277, 172 Miss. 514—Jabron v. State, 159 So. 406, 172 Miss. 135—Williams v. Lumpkin, 152 So. 842, 169 Miss. 146.
Mo.—Clayton v. May Department Stores Co., App., 184 S.W.2d 735—**Corpus Juris cited in** Monsour v. Excelsior Tobacco Co., App., 115 S.W.2d 219, 222.
N.C.—Craver v. Franklin Cotton Mills, 145 S.E. 570, 196 N.C. 330.
Ohio.—Lowe v. Hippodrome Inn Co., 165 N.E. 749, 30 Ohio App. 520.
Pa.—Wermeling v. Shattuck, 76 A.2d 406, 366 Pa. 23.
Tex.—**Corpus Juris cited in** Texas & P. Ry. Co. v. Wylie, Civ.App., 36 S.W.2d 238, 242.
Vt.—**Corpus Juris Secundum cited in** Thompson v. Green Mountain Power Corp., 144 A.2d 786, 789, 120 Vt. 478.
Wis.—Shaw v. Wisconsin Power & Light Co., 40 N.W.2d 498, 256 Wis. 176, 13 A.L.R.2d 1390—**Corpus Juris cited in** Moen v. Madison Rys. Co., 225 N.W. 821, 822, 199 Wis. 168, followed in 225 N.W. 822, 199 Wis. 171.
45 C.J. p 651 note 75.
Anticipation of presence of:
Licensee see infra § 63(37).
Trespassers see infra § 63(13).
Knowledge of:
Condition of property see infra § 63(77).
Defect or danger to:
Infant trespassers see infra § 63(66).
Invitees generally see infra §§ 63(53)–63(54).
Persons in stores see infra § 63(124).
Presence of:
Children generally see infra § 63(77).
Infant trespassers see infra § 63(66).
Licensee see infra § 63(37).
Property owners as to acts or omissions of third persons see infra § 92.
Known presence of trespasser in position of danger or peril see infra § 63(16).
Liability of manufacturers see infra §§ 100(1)–100(5).

Actual or constructive knowledge
Negligence may be predicated only upon knowledge, actual or constructive.
U.S.—Texas Consol. Theatres v. Pittman, C.C.A.Tex., 93 F.2d 21, rehearing denied 94 F.2d 203, certiorari dismissed 59 S.Ct. 40, 305 U.S. 3, 83 L.Ed. 5.
Tex.—Ebersole v. Sapp, Com.App., 208 S.W. 156.
Houston Lighting & Power Co. v. Brooks, Civ.App., 319 S.W.2d 427,

of common-law negligence involving a violation or disregard of some duty which is known by the person to be charged therewith.[45]

Accordingly, the general rule is that, in order that an act or omission may be regarded as negligent, the person charged therewith must have knowledge or notice that such act or omission involved danger to another[46] or that there was some

reversed on other grounds 336 S.W.2d 603, 161 Tex. 32—Compton Transport Co. v. Jones County, Civ. App., 292 S.W.2d 895, err. dismissed—Luck v. Buffalo Lakes, Civ. App., 144 S.W.2d 672, error dismissed, judgment correct—Texas Consolidated Theatres v. Slaughter, Civ.App., 143 S.W.2d 659, error dismissed—Burke v. State Fair of Texas, Civ.App., 93 S.W.2d 765.

Relevancy to determination
Knowledge of danger is relevant to a determination of negligence.
U.S.—Fitzgerald v. U. S. Lines Co., C.A.N.Y., 306 F.2d 461, reversed on other grounds 83 S.Ct. 1646, 374 U.S. 16, 10 L.Ed.2d 720, rehearing denied 84 S.Ct. 26, 375 U.S. 870, 11 L.Ed.2d 99, motion denied 84 S.Ct. 655, 376 U.S. 901, 11 L.Ed.2d 604.

Exoneration by ignorance; culpable ignorance
Ignorance of facts exonerates from liability, unless such ignorance is culpable; culpable ignorance is that which results from a failure to exercise ordinary care to acquire knowledge.
Tex.—Ebersole v. Sapp, Com.App., 208 S.W. 156.
Luck v. Buffalo Lakes, Civ.App., 144 S.W.2d 672, 676, error dismissed, judgment correct.

Test of negligence is whether defendant either knew or, as reasonably prudent person, should have known of plaintiff's peril.
Or.—Lindsey v. Southern Pac. Co., 399 P.2d 152.

Duty to avert danger
The duty to take steps seasonably to avert danger is predicated on knowledge of the danger or its equivalent.
Conn.—Lambert v. City of New Haven, 30 A.2d 923, 129 Conn. 647.

Act of omission
A defendant cannot be charged with an act of omission when he is not aware of any condition which requires him to do such an act.
Md.—Toy v. Atlantic Gulf & Pacific Co., 4 A.2d 757, 176 Md. 197.

Dangerous character of thing dealt with
(1) In absence of contractual relation between party complaining and defendant charged with injury, there must be knowledge of the dangerous character of the thing dealt with, in order to make defendant liable for injuries.
N.M.—Reif v. Morrison, 100 P.2d 229, 44 N.M. 201.
(2) Manufacturers and vendors see infra §§ 100(1)–100(5).

45. Mo.—Monsour v. Excelsior Tobacco Co., App., 115 S.W.2d 219.

46. U.S.—**Corpus Juris Secundum cited in** Missouri-Kansas-Texas R. Co. v. Ingram, C.A.Okl., 322 F.2d 286, 291—**Corpus Juris Secundum cited in** U. S. v. Marshall, C.A.Idaho, 230 F.2d 183, 189—Alaska Freight Lines v. Harry, C.A., 220 F.2d 272, 15 Alaska 457.
Ark.—Guille v. Snyder, 263 S.W. 403, 165 Ark. 221.
Cal.—Barber v. Gordon, 295 P. 377, 111 C.A. 279.
Colo.—Girardot v. Williams, 80 P.2d 433, 102 Colo. 456.
Fla.—Carter v. Hector Supply Co., 128 So.2d 390—Carls Markets, Inc. v. Meyer, 69 So.2d 789.
La.—Spiers v. Consolidated Companies, 132 So.2d 879, 241 La. 1012, certiorari denied 82 S.Ct. 602, 368 U.S. 986, 7 L.Ed.2d 524.
Md.—Aleshire v. State to Use of Dearstone, 170 A.2d 758, 225 Md. 355—Texas Co. v. Pecora, 118 A.2d 377, 208 Md. 281—**Corpus Juris quoted in** Adams v. Carey, 190 A. 815, 821, 172 Md. 173.
Mass.—Gould v. Slater Woolen Co., 17 N.E. 531, 147 Mass. 315.
Mich.—American Airlines, Inc. v. Shell Oil Co., 94 N.W.2d 214, 355 Mich. 151.
Minn.—Wire v. Williams, 133 N.W.2d 840—Peterson v. Truelson, 83 N.W.2d 236, 249 Minn. 530—Manteuffel v. Theo. Hamm Brewing Co., 56 N.W.2d 310, 238 Minn. 140—McDonald v. Fryberger, 46 N.W.2d 260, 233 Minn. 156—Despatch Oven Co. v. Rauenhorst, 40 N.W.2d 73, 229 Minn. 436—Rue v. Wendland, 33 N.W.2d 593, 226 Minn. 449.
Mo.—Davidson v. St. Louis-San Francisco R. Co., 229 S.W. 786.
Corpus Juris Secundum cited in Rauch v. McDonnell Aircraft Corp., App., 303 S.W.2d 226, 231—Greenwood v. Bridgeways, Inc., App., 243 S.W.2d 111—Whealen v. St. Louis Soft Ball Ass'n, App., 198 S.W.2d 371, affirmed 202 S.W.2d 891, 356 Mo. 622.
N.Y.—Hubbell v. South Nassau Communities Hospital, 260 N.Y.S.2d 539, 46 Misc.2d 847.
Or.—**Corpus Juris Secundum quoted in** Stuhr v. Berkheimer Co., 349 P.2d 665, 667, 220 Or. 406—Belknap v. Klaumann, 178 P.2d 154, 181 Or. 2.
Pa.—**Corpus Juris cited in** Schlichtkrull v. Mellon-Pollock Oil Co., 152 A. 832, 834, 301 Pa. 560.
Monske v. Mazaleski, Com.Pl., 54 Lack.Jur. 189.
Tex.—Byrd v. Trevino-Bermea, Civ. App., 366 S.W.2d 632—Phillips v. Texas & P. Ry. Co., Civ.App., 223 S.W.2d 258, error refused no reversible error.
Vt.—**Corpus Juris Secundum cited in** Winter v. Unaitis, 204 A.2d 115, 119, 124 Vt. 249.
Wash.—**Corpus Juris Secundum cited in** Leek v. Tacoma Baseball Club, 229 P.2d 329, 331, 38 Wash.2d 362—Heber v. Puget Sound Power & Light Co., 208 P.2d 886, 34 Wash.2d 231—**Corpus Juris cited in** Burr v. Clark, 190 P.2d 769, 773, 30 Wash.2d 149.
Wis.—Wadzinski v. Cities Service Oil Co., 80 N.W.2d 816, 275 Wis. 84—Weber v. Interstate Light & Power Co., 68 N.W.2d 39, 268 Wis. 479—Shaw v. Wisconsin Power & Light Co., 40 N.W.2d 498, 256 Wis. 176, 13 A.L.R.2d 1390—**Corpus Juris cited in** Moen v. Madison Rys. Co., 225 N.W. 821, 199 Wis. 168, followed in 225 N.W. 822, 199 Wis. 171.
45 C.J. p 652 note 76.

Actual knowledge required
N.Y.—Sealey v. Finkelstein, 206 N.Y.S.2d 512.

Foundation of liability
(1) The foundation of liability for negligence is knowledge.
Neb.—Whittington v. Nebraska Natural Gas Co., 128 N.W.2d 795, 177 Neb. 264.
(2) The foundation of liability in negligence cases is knowledge of the peril which subsequently results in injury.
U.S.—Petition of Reading, D.C.N.Y., 169 F.Supp. 165, affirmed, C.A., Reading v. Beauden, 271 F.2d 959.
Cal.—Schwerin v. H. C. Capwell Co., 34 P.2d 1050, 140 C.A. 1.
Fla.—Springer v. Morris, 74 So.2d 781—Lindsay v. Thomas, 174 So. 418, 128 Fla. 293.
Ky.—Meeks Motor Freight v. Ham's Adm'r, 193 S.W.2d 745, 302 Ky. 71.
N.D.—**Corpus Juris Secundum cited in** Schmitt v. Northern Imp. Co., 115 N.W.2d 713, 722.
S.D.—Ford v. Robinson, 80 N.W.2d 471, 76 S.D. 457.

Knowledge contemporaneous with infliction of injury
Fla.—Lindsay v. Thomas, 174 So. 418, 128 Fla. 293.

Actual or constructive notice
(1) No duty to act arises until one has notice, actual or constructive, that failure so to act will probably result in injury to another.

EXHIBIT 13

§ 4(11) NEGLIGENCE
Page 504

65 CJS 56

Skill ordinarily required of architects
Ill.—Miller v. DeWitt, 208 N.E.2d 249, 59 Ill.App.2d 38, affd. in part and revd. in part on oth. grds., Sup., 226 N.E.2d 630, 37 Ill.2d 273.

Duty to keep abreast of times
Ill.—Miller v. DeWitt, 208 N.E.2d 249, 59 Ill.App.2d 38, affd. in part and revd. in part on oth. grds., Sup., 226 N.E.2d 630, 37 Ill.2d 273.

Perfect plans not required
Ill.—Miller v. DeWitt, 208 N.E.2d 249, 59 Ill.App.2d 38, affd. in part and revd. in part on oth. grds., Sup., 226 N.E.2d 630, 37 Ill.2d 273.

page 505

31,30. Ill.—Miller v. DeWitt, 208 N.E.2d 249, 59 Ill.App.2d 38, affd. in part and revd. in part on oth. grds., Sup., 226 N.E.2d 630, 37 Ill.2d 273.
Iowa—Evans v. Howard R. Green Co., 231 N.W.2d 907.

Duty as to contractor
Ill.—Miller v. DeWitt, 208 N.E.2d 249, 59 Ill.App.2d 38, affd. in part and revd. in part on oth. grds., Sup., 226 N.E.2d 630, 37 Ill.2d 273.
31,35. Ill.—Miller v. DeWitt, 208 N.E.2d 249, 59 Ill.App.2d 38, affd. in part and revd. in part on oth. grds., Sup., 226 N.E.2d 630, 37 Ill.2d 273.

§ 4(13). —— Knowledge of Duty

40. U.S.—Johnson v. Aetna Cas. & Sur. Co., D.C. Fla., 339 F.Supp. 1178.
Ariz.—Wright v. Demeter, 442 P.2d 888, 8 Ariz.App. 65.
Ill.—Penrod v. Merrill Lynch, Pierce, Fenner & Smith, Inc., 385 N.E.2d 376, 24 Ill.Dec. 464, 68 Ill.App.3d 75.
Ohio—Thompson v. Ohio Fuel Gas Co., 224 N.E.2d 131, 9 Ohio St.2d 116.

§ 5(1). Knowledge or Notice of Defect or Danger

page 506

44. U.S.—Sabine Towing & Transp. Co. v. St. Joe Paper Co., D.C.Fla., 297 F.Supp. 748.
Cal.—Oakes v. Geigy Agr. Chemicals, 77 Cal.Rptr. 709, 272 C.A.2d 645.
Fla.—Gibson v. Avis Rent-A-Car System, Inc., 386 So.2d 520, on remand App., 388 So.2d 55.
Ga.—Crosby v. Savannah Elec. & Power Co., 150 S.E.2d 563, 114 Ga.App. 193—Seaboard Coast Line R. Co. v. Clark, 176 S.E.2d 596, 122 Ga.App. 237.
Mich.—Samson v. Saginaw Professional Bldg., Inc., 224 N.W.2d 843, 393 Mich. 393.
Ohio—Reinke v. Lenchitz, 537 N.E.2d 709, 42 Ohio App.3d 163.
Wash.—Perry v. Seattle School Dist. No. 1, 405 P.2d 589, 66 Wash.2d 800.

Actual or constructive knowledge
Ind.—Hunsberger v. Wyman, 216 N.E.2d 345, 247 Ind. 369.

Moral duty
U.S.—Ford Motor Co. v. Dallas Power & Light Co., C.A.Tex., 499 F.2d 400.

page 507

46. U.S.—State v. McFetridge, C.A.Ill., 484 F.2d 1169.
Cal.—Fries v. Broadway Federal Sav. & Loan Ass'n of Los Angeles, App., 65 Cal.Rptr. 460.
D.C.—S. Kann's Sons Corp. v. Hayes, App., 320 A.2d 593.
Fla.—Peeler v. Independent Life & Acc. Ins. Co., App., 206 So.2d 34—Luckey v. City of Orlando, App., 264 So.2d 99.
Ga.—Chapman v. Phillips, 145 S.E.2d 663, 112 Ga. App. 434—Raborn v. Richmond County Hospital Authority, 213 S.E.2d 534, 134 Ga.App. 153.

Ind.—Hunsberger v. Wyman, 216 N.E.2d 345, 247 Ind. 369.
La.—Hicks v. Nelson, App., 182 So.2d 151—Foreman v. Vermilion Parish Police Jury, App., 258 So.2d 652.
Md.—Bauman v. Woodfield, 223 A.2d 364, 244 Md. 207.
Mo.—Wells v. Goforth, 443 S.W.2d 155.
Neb.—Maxwell v. Lewis, 186 N.W.2d 119, 186 Neb. 722.
N.Y.—Toner v. Constable, 306 N.Y.S.2d 323, 61 Misc.2d 586, mod. on oth. grds. 307 N.Y.S.2d 231, 61 Misc.2d 591.
Ohio—Moore v. Denune & Pipic, Inc., 269 N.E.2d 599, 26 Ohio St.2d 125.
Pa.—Jones v. Treegoob, 249 A.2d 352, 433 Pa. 225.
R.I.—Hennessey v. Suhl, 333 A.2d 151, 114 R.I. 311.
S.D.—Waggoner v. Midwestern Development, Inc., 154 N.W.2d 803, 83 S.D. 57.
Tex.—Board of Trustees, Tarrant County Jr. College v. National Indem. Co., Civ.App., 484 S.W.2d 399, err. ref. no rev. err.
Vt.—Largess v. Tatem, 291 A.2d 398, 130 Vt. 271.

Actual or constructive notice
(1) N.Y.—Stevens v. Loblaws Market, 278 N.Y.S.2d 703, 27 A.D.2d 975.

Knowledge describes orbit of duty
Md.—Owens v. Simon, 226 A.2d 548, 245 Md. 404.

Actual knowledge not shown
Cal.—Wingard v. Safeway Stores, Inc., 176 Cal.Rptr. 320, 123 C.A.3d 37.
La.—Ducote v. Voorhies, App., 350 So.2d 1289.
N.Y.—Yates v. Chrysler Corp., 433 N.Y.S.2d 837, 79 A.D.2d 656.

page 508

47. U.S.—Hall v. E. I. Du Pont De Nemours & Co., Inc., D.C.N.Y., 345 F.Supp. 353—Cincotta v. U.S., D.C.Md., 362 F.Supp. 386.
Ga.—Hyde v. Bryant, 151 S.E.2d 925, 114 Ga.App. 535—Herring v. Hauck, 165 S.E.2d 198, 118 Ga. App. 623.
La.—Champagne v. Harahan Lions Club, Inc., App., 243 So.2d 292.
Okl.—Barnhart v. Freeman Equipment Co., 441 P.2d 993.
48. Conn.—Baker v. Ives, 294 A.2d 290, 162 Conn. 295.
Ga.—Somers v. Tribble, 154 S.E.2d 620, 115 Ga.App. 282.
Pa.—Heck v. Beryllium Corp., 226 A.2d 87, 424 Pa. 140.
49. N.Y.—Fiocco v. Doerflinger, 431 N.Y.S.2d 795, 106 Misc.2d 381.
Pa.—Com. v. McFarland, 308 A.2d 126, 226 Pa.Super. 138.
50. U.S.—Lopez v. A/S D/S Svendborg, C.A.N.Y., 581 F.2d 319.
Ga.—Chappman v. Phillips, 145 S.E.2d 663, 112 Ga. App. 434.
Mo.—Edwards v. Springfield Coca-Cola Bottling Co., Inc., App., 495 S.W.2d 489.
Vt.—Forcier v. Grand Union Stores, Inc., 264 A.2d 796, 128 Vt. 389.
51. Conn.—Nolan v. Morelli, 226 A.2d 383, 154 Conn. 432.
Fla.—Dolan Title & Guaranty Corp. v. Hartford Acc. & Indem. Co., App., 305 So.2d 296.
Ga.—Chastain v. Fuqua Industries, Inc., 275 S.E.2d 679, 156 Ga.App. 719.
54. N.C.—Jenkins v. Helgren, 217 S.E.2d 120, 26 N.C.App. 653.

page 509

55. Tex.—Oldaker v. Lock Const. Co., Civ.App., 528 S.W.2d 71, err. ref. no rev. err.

§ 5(3). —— Implied, Constructive, or Imputed Knowledge or Notice in General

59. La.—Penn v. Inferno Mfg. Corp., App., 199 So.2d 210, writ ref. 202 So.2d 649, 251 La. 27—Travelers Indem. Co. v. Sears, Roebuck & Co., App., 256 So.2d 321.
Mo.—Catalano v. Kansas City, App., 475 S.W.2d 426.
60. Tex.—Jackson v. Associated Developers of Lubbock, Civ.App., 581 S.W.2d 208, err. ref. no rev. err.
61. U.S.—Daigle v. Point Landing, Inc., C.A.La., 616 F.2d 825.
62. Ga.—Colonial Stores, Inc. v. Donovan, 154 S.E.2d 659, 115 Ga.App. 330.
Md.—Hensley v. Montgomery County, 334 A.2d 542, 25 Mo.App. 361, 94 A.L.R.3d 1148.
N.M.—First Nat. Bank in Albuquerque v. Nor-Am Agr. Products, Inc., App., 537 P.2d 682, 88 N.M. 74.
63. U.S.—Rhode Island Hospital Trust Nat. Bank v. Swartz, Breasenoff, Yavner and Jacobs, C.A.Va., 455 F.2d 847, app. after remand 482 F.2d 1000.
Cal.—Contini v. Western Title Ins. Co., 115 Cal.Rptr. 257, 40 C.A.3d 536.
Conn.—Warren v. Stancliff, 251 A.2d 74, 157 Conn. 216.
Iowa—Boge v. Jack Link Truck Line, Inc., 200 N.W.2d 544.
Vt.—Largess v. Tatem, 291 A.2d 398, 130 Vt. 271.

page 510

65. Vt.—Lane Const. Corp. v. State, 265 A.2d 441, 128 Vt. 421.
66. Md.—Palms v. Shell Oil Co., 332 A.2d 300, 24 Md.App. 540.
68. U.S.—Mamiye Bros. v. Barber S.S. Lines, Inc., C.A.N.Y., 360 F.2d 774, cert. den. 87 S.Ct. 80, 385 U.S. 835, 17 L.Ed.2d 70.
Ga.—Rockmart Bank v. Hall, 151 S.E.2d 232, 114 Ga.App. 284—Elebash v. Whitley, 151 S.E.2d 196, 114 Ga.App. 294.
Ill.—Lewis v. Stran Steel Corp., 311 N.E.2d 128, 57 Ill.2d 94.
La.—Deris v. Finest Foods, Inc., App., 198 So.2d 412.
69. U.S.—Ohio Cas. Ins. Co. (Venango Federal Sav. and Loan) v. Bank Bldg. & Equipment Corp. of America, D.C.Pa., 300 F.Supp. 632—Campbell Soup Co. v. Springdale Farms, Inc., D.C.Ark., 338 F.Supp. 279.
Ill.—Pantaleo v. Gamm, 245 N.E.2d 618, 106 Ill. App.2d 116—Ryan v. Robeson's, Inc., 251 N.E.2d 545, 113 Ill.App.2d 416.
Minn.—Berry v. Haertel, 170 N.W.2d 558, 284 Minn. 400.
N.M.—Williams v. Herrera, App., 496 P.2d 740, 83 N.M. 680.
N.Y.—White v. Long Island Lighting Co., 302 N.Y. S.2d 463, 32 A.D.2d 792.
Wash.—Wood v. Postelthwaite, 496 P.2d 988, 6 Wash. App. 885, affd. 510 P.2d 1109, 82 Wash.2d 387.

Opportunity as equivalent to knowledge
Vt.—Lane Const. Corp. v. State, 265 A.2d 441, 128 Vt. 421.

page 511

73. Ky.—Bowlin v. General Tire & Rubber Co., 445 S.W.2d 602.
Tex.—Murray v. O & A Exp., Inc., 630 S.W.2d 633.
73.5. U.S.—Di Gregorio v. N. V. Stoomvaart Maatschappij "Nederland" D.C.N.Y., 411 F.Supp. 331, affd. 531 F.2d 1143.
74. U.S.—C.J.S. cited in Wagner v. Grannis, D.C.Pa., 287 F.Supp. 18, 25.
Ga.—U.S. v. Aretz, 280 S.E.2d 345, 248 Ga. 19.

Some states, in addition to the indexes in the volumes of the state codes and statutes, have other indexes that may prove more adaptable to the individual researcher's thinking. For example, the state library (usually in the capitol city) may publish a special directory listing the types of legislative documents within the library and providing procedural guidance on searching the library for the volumes and on the types of information within them, their availability for loan, the methods of arranging to check out the books, and the names and phone numbers of persons in the library who can assist the researcher. Additionally, there are commercial sources for more detailed indexes that can be helpful. For instance, the Recorder Printing and Publishing Company of San Francisco, California, published *Larmac, Consolidated Index to the Constitution of Laws of California,* a very comprehensive index with an effective subject cross-index. Other states have similar publications. Indexes sometimes are difficult to use for finding the specific area of interest. An alternative then is to use the table of contents, which will lead to the general area of interest, and persistence and review of the general material will suggest or lead to the specific subject of interest, if it is contained in the legal publication.

5.0516 Digests. Legal digests are arranged much like legal encyclopedias, except that they do not contain a summary of the law or a particular point. Legal digests are really indexes to the law. The *American Digest System,* published by the West Publishing Company, constitutes the most comprehensive index to American decisions that is available. The system is based on a topic and key number classification scheme that divides the entire body of law into seven major headings, thirty-two subheadings, and over four hundred digest topics. There are over 75,000 sub-topics, each representing decisions accumulated under the topic-key number system.

The topic name and the key number, together, serve as a research reference for points of law abstracted from reported judicial decisions. The digest paragraphs are short summaries of the decisions arranged to help locate the decision and its holding(s). Digests also have indexes and tables of cases, as well as "Words and Phrases" compendia, which refer the reader to judicial definitions of words and phrases in court opinions.

An example of the indexes found in digests is Exhibit 14. This exhibit clearly reflects the helpful organization and explicit outline of the matters covered or excluded, suggests sources for near-synonymous topics and outlines, and provides topic and key number references to the material covered. Anyone interested in "proximate cause of injury" quickly finds the same topic and key number within the text as shown in Exhibit 14.

5.0517 Other Sources. Unorthodox methods that some researchers find expeditious will be mentioned only because they can be effective for persons with particular research needs. Every method is only a tool to accomplish a task, and each should be designed to fit the individual and the special task when possible.

One unorthodox method takes advantage of a resource that some states have and some do not: the approved state books for forms or pleading and practice and/or points and authorities. There are many form books commercially published for pleadings and for preparation of legal documents for the client. When one is asked to draft a motion for summary judgment, for example, the state forms of pleading and practice book details the specific items that must be included for a meritorious motion to be acceptable. It often cites the code section, rule of court, and so on that makes such a requirement. A state-approved points and authorities book can provide the form and language of any issue and cite the actual case giving rise to the acceptable authority. Naturally, the cases must be read to ensure that they are on point and do support the proposed motion.

Another method that can be effective is best demonstrated by an example:

Suppose the legal assistant has the assignment to review a complaint to determine whether an action for strict liability against the client has been properly stated and to draft interrogatories sufficient to reveal the existence of facts known by

EXHIBIT 14   Texas Digest 2d, Volume 38

NEGLIGENCE

SUBJECTS INCLUDED

Failure to use due care, either in respect of acts or of omissions, in performance or observance of a duty not founded on contract, which failure is the proximate cause of unintended injury to the person to whom such duty is owing

Nature and extent of liability for such injuries in general

Nature and effect of negligence or other fault on the part of the person injured contributing to his injury

Comparison of negligence of the parties

Imputation to the person injured of others' negligence

Civil remedies for such injuries

Criminal responsibility for such negligence in general, and prosecution and punishment thereof as a public offense

SUBJECTS EXCLUDED AND COVERED BY OTHER TOPICS

Death, actions for damages for, see DEATH

Manslaughter by negligence, see AUTOMOBILES, HOMICIDE

Particular kinds of property, negligence in care and use of, see MINES AND MINERALS, WATERS AND WATER COURSES, ANIMALS, SHIPPING, COLLISION, and other specific topics

Particular kinds of works, public improvements, etc., negligence in construction and use of, see RAILROADS, BRIDGES, HIGHWAYS, MUNICIPAL CORPO-RATIONS, and other specific topics

Particular personal relations, occupations, employments, contracts, etc., negligence in respect of duties incident to, see ATTORNEY AND CLIENT, EMPLOYERS' LIABILITY, PHYSICIANS AND SURGEONS, CARRIERS, LANDLORD AND TENANT, BAILMENT and other specific topics

For detailed references to other topics, see Descriptive-Word Index

---

Analysis

I. ACTS OR OMISSIONS CONSTITUTING NEGLIGENCE, ☞1–55.
    A. PERSONAL CONDUCT IN GENERAL, 1–15.
    B. DANGEROUS SUBSTANCES, MACHINERY, AND OTHER INSTRUMENTALITIES, ☞16–27.
    C. CONDITION AND USE OF LAND, BUILDINGS, AND OTHER STRUCTURES, ☞28–55.

II. PROXIMATE CAUSE OF INJURY, ☞56–64.

III. CONTRIBUTORY NEGLIGENCE, ☞65–101.
    (A) PERSONS INJURED IN GENERAL, ☞65–83.11.
    (B) CHILDREN AND OTHERS UNDER DISABILITY, ☞84–88.
    (C) IMPUTED NEGLIGENCE, ☞89–96.
    (D) COMPARATIVE NEGLIGENCE, ☞97–101.

the adversary that support the cause of action. Some researchers are very successful in immediately finding the essential elements to prove strict liability by consulting their state *Book of Approved Jury Instructions (BAJI)*. (*BAJI* books are accumulations of standardized jury instructions approved by the court as to form and language for presentation to the jury by the judge before the jury is sequestered to consider and decide a case. The theory of framing jury instructions has led inevitably to creating succinct expressions of each essential element that must be proved for a cause of action to be supported by a jury verdict. Since the pleadings are generally phrased in very broad terms, the *BAJI* is a guide to framing interrogatories to develop the exact facts that support or attack the allegations as well as the facts on which the adversary counsel relied to hold the client in as a proper party-defendant or (as often is the case in strict liability) as a cross-defendant.

5.052 The West Topic and Key Number System.

The topic and key number system of classification is a comprehensive law classification system used by researchers to locate points of law or legal principles in any of the West Publishing Company encyclopedias, digests, unofficial reporters (such as the national reporter system volumes), and annotated codes. The major topic headings are shown in Exhibit 15. A quick perusal of the topic and key number chart reveals there are many topics within each division and each topic is further subdivided according to the legal principles or the points of law that fall within its scope. Finer breakdowns within the individual subtopics naturally result, and each subdivision topic is given a key number. Every case reported in the West system is provided with headnotes that summarize the salient points decided in the case. Basically, the headnotes of every published decision are reviewed and the elements within the cases are given topic and key number references. Thus, all cases with the same elements will be assigned the same topic and key number and will involve fact situations or points of law that have some similarity. West then takes the topic and key numbers from all the cases and consolidates them into digests. West publishes digests, and a researcher must first check the appropriate digest; for example, for an action in Montana, the appropriate one would be *West's Montana Digest.* These digests are kept up to date with cumulative annual pocket parts and supplemental pamphlets, as are cases through current volumes and advance sheets with indexes for the various reporters. The most complete digest published by West is the *American Digest,* which indexes and classifies all American case law, state and federal. This digest is published every ten years in units called decennials.

West also publishes digests that individually cover the decisions of different courts, such as *The Supreme Court Digest* and the *Modern Federal Practice Digest.* The ultimate value of the topic and key number system is that once a lawyer or researcher locates a particular topic and key number, he or she has the key to every reported American case that has litigated that given point or principle of law. If a state digest is checked and there are no cases under the topic and key number assigned a particular point, the researcher knows that question has not been decided or litigated in the state and then can extend the search to cases of other states and courts. *Caveat:* Careful consideration must be made of the selection of the topic word under which a search for the key number is made since our vocabulary is filled with near synonymous words and the absence of a topic and key number should not be accepted without exhausting the reasonable synonyms.

Certain invaluable methods for finding the correct topic and key number are outlined below.

5.0521 *Descriptive Word Method.* The descriptive word method is the most effective unless the researcher has the name of a case on point or already knows the topic that deals with the issue of interest. Every case decided is based on a fact situation, and the aim is to find other cases based on the same, or similar, fact

EXHIBIT 15   Digest Topics

Abandoned and Lost Property	Bills and Notes	Credit Reporting Agencies
Abatement and Revival	Blasphemy	Criminal Law
Abduction	Bonds	Crops
Abortion and Birth Control	Boundaries	Customs and Usages
Absentees	Bounties	Customs Duties
Abstracts of Title	Breach of Marriage Promise	Damages
Accession	Breach of the Peace	Dead Bodies
Accord and Satisfaction	Bribery	Death
Account	Bridges	Debt, Action of
Account, Action on	Brokers	Debtor and Creditor
Account Stated	Building and Loan Associations	Declaratory Judgment
Accountants	Burglary	Dedication
Acknowledgment	Canals	Deeds
Action	Cancellation of Instruments	Deposits and Escrows
Action on the Case	Carriers	Deposits in Court
Adjoining Landowners	Cemeteries	Descent and Distribution
Administrative Law and	Census	Detectives
Procedure	Certiorari	Detinue
Admiralty	Champerty and Maintenance	Disorderly Conduct
Adoption	Charities	Disorderly House
Adulteration	Chattel Mortgages	District and Prosecuting
Adultery	Chemical Dependents	Attorneys
Adverse Possession	Children Out-of-Wedlock	District of Columbia
Affidavits	Citizens	Disturbance of Public
Affray	Civil Rights	Assemblage
Agriculture	Clerks of Courts	Divorce
Aliens	Clubs	Domicile
Alteration of Instruments	Colleges and Universities	Dower and Curtesy
Ambassadors and Consuls	Collision	Drains
Amicus Curiae	Commerce	Drugs and Narcotics
Animals	Common Lands	Dueling
Annuities	Common Law	Easements
Appeal and Error	Common Scold	Ejectment
Appearance	Compounding Offenses	Election of Remedies
Arbitration	Compromise and Settlement	Elections
Armed Services	Condominium	Electricity
Arrest	Confusion of Goods	Embezzlement
Arson	Conspiracy	Embracery
Assault and Battery	Constitutional Law	Eminent Domain
Assignments	Comsumer Credit	Employers' Liability
Assistance, Writ of	Consumer Protection	Entry, Writ of
Associations	Contempt	Equity
Assumpsit, Action of	Contracts	Escape
Asylums	Contribution	Escheat
Attachment	Conversion	Estates in Property
Attorney and Client	Convicts	Estoppel
Attorney General	Copyrights and Intellectual	Evidence
Auctions and Auctioneers	Property	Exceptions, Bill of
Audita Querela	Coroners	Exchange of Property
Automobiles	Corporations	Exchanges
Aviation	Costs	Execution
Bail	Counterfeiting	Executors and Administrators
Bailment	Counties	Exemptions
Bankruptcy	Court Commissioners	Explosives
Banks and Banking	Courts	Extortion and Threats
Beneficial Associations	Covenant, Action of	Extradition and Detainers
Bigamy	Covenants	Factors

EXHIBIT 15   Digest Topics (*Continued*)

False Imprisonment	Joint Adventures	Pardon and Parole
False Personation	Joint-Stock Companies and	Parent and Child
False Pretenses	Business Trusts	Parliamentary Law
Federal Civil Procedure	Joint Tenancy	Parties
Federal Courts	Judges	Partition
Fences	Judgment	Partnership
Ferries	Judicial Sales	Party Walls
Fines	Jury	Patents
Fires	Justices of the Peace	Paupers
Fish	Kidnapping	Payment
Fixtures	Labor Relations	Penalties
Food	Landlord and Tenant	Pensions
Forcible Entry and Detainer	Larceny	Perjury
Forfeitures	Levees and Flood Control	Perpetuities
Forgery	Lewdness	Physicians and Surgeons
Fornication	Libel and Slander	Pilots
Franchises	Licenses	Piracy
Fraud	Liens	Pleading
Frauds, Statute of	Life Estates	Pledges
Fraudulent Conveyances	Limitation of Actions	Poisons
Game	Lis Pendens	Possessory Warrant
Gaming	Logs and Logging	Post Office
Garnishment	Lost Instruments	Powers
Gas	Lotteries	Pretrial Procedure
Gifts	Malicious Mischief	Principal and Agent
Good Will	Malicious Prosecution	Principal and Surety
Grand Jury	Mandamus	Prisons
Guaranty	Manufactures	Private Roads
Guardian and Ward	Maritime Liens	Prize Fighting
Habeas Corpus	Marriage	Process
Hawkers and Peddlers	Master and Servant	Products Liability
Health and Environment	Mayhem	Prohibition
Highways	Mechanics' Liens	Property
Holidays	Mental Health	Prostitution
Homestead	Military Justice	Public Contracts
Homicide	Militia	Public Lands
Hospitals	Mines and Minerals	Public Utilities
Husband and Wife	Miscegenation	Quieting Title
Illegitimate Children	Monopolies	Quo Warranto
Implied and Constructive	Mortgages	Railroads
Contracts	Motions	Rape
Improvements	Municipal Corporations	Real Actions
Incest	Names	Receivers
Indemnity	Navigable Waters	Receiving Stolen Goods
Indians	Ne Exeat	Recognizances
Indictment and Information	Negligence	Records
Infants	Neutrality Laws	Reference
Injunction	Newspapers	Reformation of Instruments
Innkeepers	New Trial	Reformatories
Inspection	Notaries	Registers of Deeds
Insurance	Notice	Release
Insurrection and Sedition	Novation	Religious Societies
Interest	Nuisance	Remainders
Internal Revenue	Oath	Removal of Cases
International Law	Obscenity	Replevin
Interpleader	Obstructing Justice	Reports
Intoxicating Liquors	Officers and Public Employees	Rescue

EXHIBIT 15   Digest Topics (Continued)

Reversions	States	Trover and Coversion
Review	Statutes	Trusts
Rewards	Steam	Turnpikes and Toll Roads
Riot	Stipulations	Undertakings
Robbery	Submission of Controversy	United States
Sales	Subrogation	United States Magistrates
Salvage	Subscriptions	United States Marshals
Schools	Suicide	Unlawful Assembly
Scire Facias	Sunday	Urban Railroads
Seals	Supersedeas	Usury
Seamen	Taxation	Vagrancy
Searches and Seizures	Telecommunications	Vendor and Purchaser
Secured Transactions	Tenancy in Common	Venue
Securities Regulation	Tender	War and National Emergency
Seduction	Territories	Warehousemen
Sequestration	Theaters and Shows	Waste
Set-Off and Counterclaim	Time	Waters and Water Courses
Sheriffs and Constables	Torts	Weapons
Shipping	Towage	Weights and Measures
Signatures	Towns	Wharves
Slaves	Trade Regulaiton	Wills
Social Security and Public	Treason	Witnesses
Welfare	Treaties	Woods and Forests
Sodomy	Trespass	Workers' Compensation
Specific Performance	Trespass to Try Title	Zoning and Planning
Spendthrifts	Trial	

situation that will provide authority with which to argue the client's case. In classifying and indexing cases, the West editors use words describing the facts of a case, and these words are arranged alphabetically in volumes called "Descriptive Word Indexes" which will, in turn, direct the researcher to the topic and key number involving cases with similar facts or legal issues. To use this search method, the researcher must analyze the fact situation and list key words and phrases describing the essential elements. The researcher may have difficulty analyzing problems and choosing descriptive words at first, but the skill will develop with practice. West suggests that most descriptive words naturally group themselves around the five elements common to every case, namely:

(a)   Parties
(b)   Places and things
(c)   Acts or omissions that give a basis for the action or issue
(d)   Defenses that might apply to an action or issue
(e)   The ultimate relief sought

The problem for most researchers at the start is to select words that are the same as a significant descriptive word to which West has assigned a key number. The pamphlet *West's Law Finder, a Legal Research Manual* contains an excellent example of the process (see Exhibits 16 and 17). *West Digest* uses a similar method of topic analysis, as seen in Exhibit 18. Additionally, at the beginning of each digest topic is a note specifying the scope of the topic and a complete breakdown of all subtopics, which are arranged numerically. Each subtopic bears what is called a key number. These numbers are often preceded by a drawing of a small key. This

Copy of page 19, *West's Law Finder,*
EXHIBIT 16 *a Legal Research Manual.*

mind that most descriptive words naturally group themselves around the five elements common to every case, namely:

1. PARTIES
   Aliens, Children Out-of-Wedlock, Landlords, Physicians, Sheriffs
2. PLACES AND THINGS
   Playground, Theater, Office Building, Roller Coaster, Puck, Automobile, Engagement Ring
3. BASIS OF ACTION OR ISSUE
   Negligence, Breach of Contract, Slander, Restraint of Trade, Title to Property, Admission of Evidence
4. DEFENSE
   Act of God, Assumption of Risk, Contributory Negligence, Usury
5. RELIEF SOUGHT
   Damages, Injunction, Eviction, Rescission, Divorce

———————

At a professional wrestling match the referee was thrown from the ring in such a way that he struck and injured plaintiff who was a front row spectator. Does plaintiff have a cause of action? The following analysis shows how the descriptive words for this problem should be selected.

1. PARTIES—Spectator, Patron, Arena Owner, Wrestler, Referee, Promoter
2. PLACES AND THINGS—Wrestling Match, Amusement Place, Theater. Show
3. BASIS OF ACTION OR ISSUE—Negligence, Personal Injury to Spectator, Liability
4. DEFENSE—Assumption of Risk
5. RELIEF SOUGHT—Damages

The following are actual excerpts from the Descriptive-Word Index of the 6th Decennial Digest showing how several of the above words refer to Theaters 6 which is the Topic and Key Number that carries the wrestling injury cases in all Key Number Digests.

Descriptive-Word Index

ASSUMPTION OF RISKS—Cont'd
Automobiles—
  Burden of proof in action for injuries from operation or use of highways. **Autos 242(8)**
  Evidence of assumption of risk by occupant. **Autos 244(56)**
  Guest passenger, host's failure to look. **Autos 224(1)**
Hockey spectator. **Theaters 6**
Hunting party members. **Weap 18(1)**
Motorboat race, voluntary entry. **Collision 15**
Operation of doctrine. **Neglig 105**
Passengers. **Carr 323**
Patron of amusement device. **Theaters 6**

Swimming pool patron. **Theaters 6**
Tenant. **Land & Ten 168(1)**
Tenant's injuries, evidence. **Land & Ten 169(6)**
Tractor operator voluntarily assisting truck driver. **Autos 202**
Willful and wanton conduct of defendant. **Neglig 100**
Workmen's compensation—
  Abrogation or modification of defense. **Work Comp 772, 2110**
  Failure of employee to elect to come under act. **Work Comp 2114**
Wrestling match spectator injured by referee thrown from ring. **Theaters 6**
ASSUMPTION OF SKILL
Master as chargeable with knowledge

is simply a reminder that the number and title that follow are part of the organized group of topics and subtopics, as seen in Exhibit 19.

Beginning at page 21 of *West's Law Finder* (Exhibit 16), the researcher is shown how the descriptive word method works:

(a) "Parties" equals spectator and a synonym patron, or arena owner, or wrestler, or referee, or promoter, all words that might have been the issue parties in past litigation. Other synonyms could be gen-

EXHIBIT 17

Copy of page 21, *West's Law Finder,*
a Legal Research Manual.

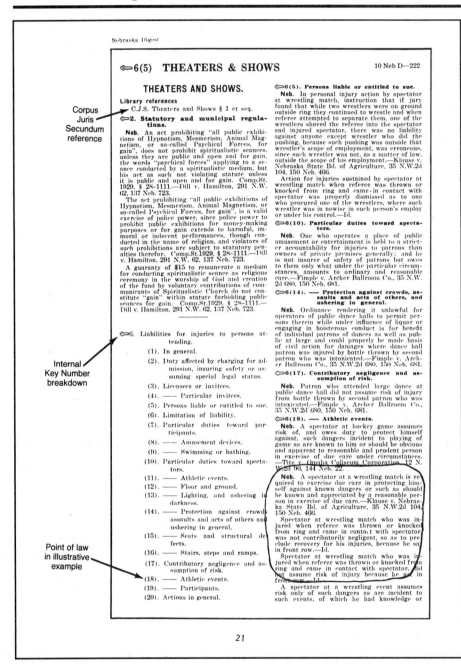

Nebraska Digest

6(5)   THEATERS & SHOWS   10 Neb D—222

THEATERS AND SHOWS.

Corpus Juris Secundum reference

Library references

C.J.S. Theaters and Shows § 1 et seq.

2. Statutory and municipal regulations.

Neb. An act prohibiting "all public exhibitions of Hypnotism, Mesmerism, Animal Magnetism, or so-called Psychical Forces, for gain", does not prohibit spiritualistic seances, unless they are public and open and for gain, the words "psychical forces" applying to a seance conducted by a spiritualistic medium, but his act as such not violating statute unless it is public and open and for gain. Comp.St. 1929, § 28–1111.—Dill v. Hamilton, 291 N.W. 62, 137 Neb. 723.

The act prohibiting "all public exhibitions of Hypnotism, Mesmerism, Animal Magnetism, or so-called Psychical Forces, for gain", is a valid exercise of police power, since police power to prohibit public exhibitions for money-making purposes or for gain extends to harmful, immoral or indecent performances, though conducted in the name of religion, and violators of such prohibitions are subject to statutory penalties therefor. Comp.St.1929, § 28–1111.—Dill v. Hamilton, 291 N.W. 62, 137 Neb. 723.

A guaranty of $15 to remunerate a medium for conducting spiritualistic seance as religious ceremony in the worship of God and creation of the fund by voluntary contributions of communicants of Spiritualistic Church do not constitute "gain" within statute forbidding public seances for gain. Comp.St.1929, § 28–1111.—Dill v. Hamilton, 291 N.W. 62, 137 Neb. 723.

Internal Key Number breakdown

6. Liabilities for injuries to persons attending.

(1). In general.

(2). Duty affected by charging for admission, insuring safety or assuming special legal status.

(3). Licensees or invitees.

(4). —— Particular invitees.

(5). Persons liable or entitled to sue.

(6). Limitation of liability.

(7). Particular duties toward participants.

(8). —— Amusement devices.

(9). —— Swimming or bathing.

(10). Particular duties toward spectators.

(11). —— Athletic events.

(12). —— Floor and ground.

(13). —— Lighting, and ushering in darkness.

(14). —— Protection against crowds, assaults and acts of others and ushering in general.

Point of law in illustrative example

(15). —— Seats and structural defects.

(16). —— Stairs, steps and ramps.

(17). Contributory negligence and assumption of risk.

(18). —— Athletic events.

(19). —— Participants.

(20). Actions in general.

6(5). Persons liable or entitled to sue.

Neb. In personal injury action by spectator at wrestling match, instruction that if jury found that while two wrestlers were on ground outside ring they continued to wrestle and when referee attempted to separate them, one of the wrestlers shoved the referee into the spectator and injured spectator, there was no liability against anyone except wrestler who did the pushing, because such pushing was outside that wrestler's scope of employment, was erroneous, since such wrestler was not, as a matter of law, outside the scope of his employment.—Klause v. Nebraska State Bd. of Agriculture, 35 N.W.2d 104, 150 Neb. 466.

Action for injuries sustained by spectator at wrestling match when referee was thrown or knocked from ring and came in contact with spectator was properly dismissed as to one who procured one of the wrestlers, where such wrestler was in nowise in such person's employ or under his control.—Id.

6(10). Particular duties toward spectators.

Neb. One who operates a place of public amusement or entertainment is held to a stricter accountability for injuries to patrons than owners of private premises generally; and he is not insurer of safety of patrons but owes to them only what under the particular circumstances, amounts to ordinary and reasonable care.—Fimple v. Archer Ballroom Co., 35 N.W. 2d 680, 150 Neb. 681.

6(14). —— Protection against crowds, assaults and acts of others, and ushering in general.

Neb. Ordinance rendering it unlawful for operators of public dance halls to permit persons therein while under influence of liquor or engaging in boisterous conduct is for benefit of individual patrons of dances as well as public at large and could properly be made basis of civil action for damages where dance hall patron was injured by bottle thrown by second patron who was intoxicated.—Fimple v. Archer Ballroom Co., 35 N.W.2d 680, 150 Neb. 681.

6(17). Contributory negligence and assumption of risk.

Neb. Patron who attended large dance at public dance hall did not assume risk of injury from bottle thrown by second patron who was intoxicated.—Fimple v. Archer Ballroom Co., 35 N.W.2d 680, 150 Neb. 681.

6(18). —— Athletic events.

Neb. A spectator at hockey game assumes risk of, and owes duty to protect himself against, such dangers incident to playing of game as are known to him or should be obvious and apparent to reasonable and prudent person in exercise of due care under circumstances. —Tite v. Omaha Coliseum Corporation, 12 N. W.2d 90, 144 Neb. 22.

Neb. A spectator at a wrestling match is required to exercise due care in protecting himself against known dangers or such as should be known and appreciated by a reasonable person in exercise of due care.—Klause v. Nebraska State Bd. of Agriculture, 35 N.W.2d 104, 150 Neb. 466.

Spectator at wrestling match who was injured when referee was thrown or knocked from ring and came in contact with spectator, was not contributorily negligent, so as to preclude recovery for his injuries, because he sat in front row.—Id.

Spectator at wrestling match who was injured when referee was thrown or knocked from ring and came in contact with spectator, did not assume risk of injury because he sat in front row.—Id.

A spectator at a wrestling event assumes risk only of such dangers as are incident to such events, of which he had knowledge or

21

erated if a search for each proved negative. As it is, patron immediately leads to the topic "Theatre" and the key number 6.

(b)   "Places" equals wrestling match, amusement place, theatre, and show, and could include auditorium, arena, or others. "Theatre," however is the title of a topic on point.

EXHIBIT 18   Texas Digest 2d, Volume 38

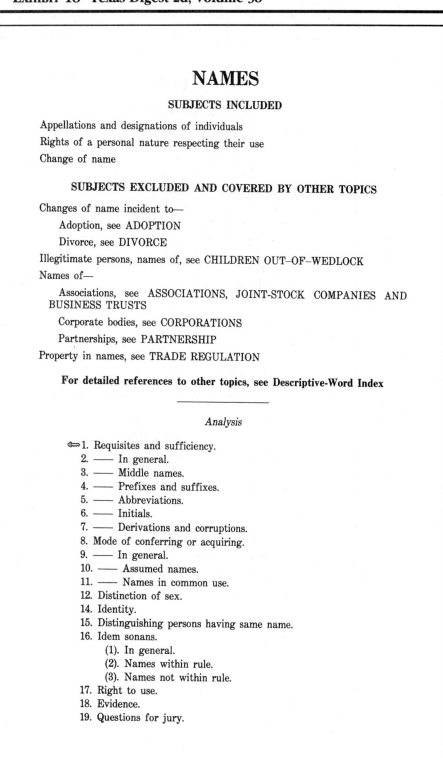

NAMES

SUBJECTS INCLUDED

Appellations and designations of individuals

Rights of a personal nature respecting their use

Change of name

SUBJECTS EXCLUDED AND COVERED BY OTHER TOPICS

Changes of name incident to—

    Adoption, see ADOPTION

    Divorce, see DIVORCE

Illegitimate persons, names of, see CHILDREN OUT–OF–WEDLOCK

Names of—

    Associations, see ASSOCIATIONS, JOINT-STOCK COMPANIES AND BUSINESS TRUSTS

    Corporate bodies, see CORPORATIONS

    Partnerships, see PARTNERSHIP

Property in names, see TRADE REGULATION

For detailed references to other topics, see Descriptive-Word Index

---

Analysis

☞1. Requisites and sufficiency.

    2. —— In general.

    3. —— Middle names.

    4. —— Prefixes and suffixes.

    5. —— Abbreviations.

    6. —— Initials.

    7. —— Derivations and corruptions.

    8. Mode of conferring or acquiring.

    9. —— In general.

    10. —— Assumed names.

    11. —— Names in common use.

    12. Distinction of sex.

    14. Identity.

    15. Distinguishing persons having same name.

    16. Idem sonans.

        (1). In general.

        (2). Names within rule.

        (3). Names not within rule.

    17. Right to use.

    18. Evidence.

    19. Questions for jury.

EXHIBIT 19
Copy of page 24, *West's Law Finder*, a Legal Research Manual.

New York Digest

LOTTERIES

SUBJECTS INCLUDED

Schemes for distribution of prizes by lot or chance among purchasers of shares therein or chances to obtain a prize

Grants and operation of lottery franchises and privileges

Management and regulation of lotteries, whether conducted under such franchises or directly by the government

<u>Rights and liabilities of owners or managers, and of purchasers or holders of shares, tickets, or chances</u>

Constitutional and statutory prohibitions of lotteries

Validity and effect of agreements relating to lotteries, and rights, liabilities, and remedies of parties to such agreements

Unlawfully conducting, advertising, etc., lotteries, as public offenses, and liability therefor, civil and criminal

SUBJECTS EXCLUDED AND COVERED BY OTHER TOPICS

Mailing matter concerning lotteries, see POST OFFICE

Wagers and gaming in general, see GAMING

For detailed references to other topics, see Descriptive-Word Index

---

RESEARCH NOTE
Practice Commentaries, Penal Law, McKinney's Consolidated Laws.

Analysis

I. REGULATION AND PROHIBITION, ☞1 8.

II. LOTTERY FRANCHISES, CONTRACTS, AND TRANSACTIONS, ☞9–15.

III. PENALTIES AND FORFEITURES, ☞16–19.

IV. CRIMINAL RESPONSIBILITY, ☞20–30.

    (A) OFFENSES, ☞20–27.

    (B) PROSECUTION AND PUNISHMENT, ☞28–30.

II. LOTTERY FRANCHISES, CONTRACTS, AND TRANSACTIONS.

    ☞9. Franchises and privileges.

    10. Scheme and mode of distribution.

    11. Holding and management.

    12. Contracts and transactions connected with lotteries in general.

    13. Advertisements.

    14. Sales of tickets or chances.

    15. Rights and remedies of holders of tickets or shares.

(c) "Basis of Action" produces "Personal Injury" (to a spectator).
(d) "Defense" finds an easy entry under "Assumption of Risk."
(e) "Relief Sought" produces references to several sources of information.

5.0522. Topic Method.   The topic method involves locating the topic under which the point of law has been previously classified. Before relying on this method, be very familiar with the key number classification system. Researchers, particularly those just beginning, very often arrive at the wrong topic. Study and analyze the key number system law chart (Exhibit 15); almost invariably it will lead the researcher to the correct topic. If problems still exist, refer to the alphabetic list of digest topics that appears in the front of each digest volume and the *C.J.S.* indexes. In using the descriptive word indexes, the researcher may have difficulty locating the precise key number needed, but they will always lead the researcher to the proper topic, and sometimes, to additional topics for consideration. Every digest has a topic analysis that begins with a "scope-note." Perusal of the scope-note will often quickly reveal whether the selected topic matches the case factual situation. For instance, presume a client has complained of being fired from her job. This will require a search to determine her rights as an employee. Perusal of the key number system law chart (Exhibit 15) suggests the transaction fits best in the category of "Master & Servant."

5.0523 Table of Cases Method.   The table of cases search method is useless unless or until the researcher has the name of at least one case that deals with the particular point of law of concern. The name of a case allows the researcher to go immediately to the table of cases in the appropriate state key number digest, reporter key number digest, or the *American Digest* and find from that case what topics and key numbers were used. Once the proper topic and key number are located, all other American cases dealing with the same general point become available for review, analysis, and report.

5.053   The Statutory Approach to Law.

Once an initial review of the secondary source material has been completed on a particular issue, the legal assistant has a general understanding of the problem and in all probability has discovered some cases on point and found references to one or more statutes or codes. When researching a problem involving a statute, a good rule of thumb is to first read the statute (including all updates) and relevant annotations that may be listed after the statute. As mentioned previously, an annotation is a brief description of a judicial opinion.

Locating a statute is a relatively simple procedure. Statutory laws can be divided into three subdivisions:

(a) Federal—United States Constitution, congressional legislation, treaties, executive orders, administrative rules and orders, and court rules;
(b) State—state constitutions, session laws, uniform laws, administrative rules and orders, and court rules; and
(c) Local—municipal charters, county and municipal ordinances and court rules.

When statutes are initially published, they are arranged in chronological order according to the date of passage. However, the statutes passed in a particular legislative session are ultimately incorporated into statutes that were in existence prior to that legislative session, thus creating an ever-growing and changing collection of laws. Because these change so frequently, they are arranged topically. Consequently, if one is familiar with the appropriate terminology relating to a particular subject of law, one can locate all current laws on a specific topic through the use of a subject index to the statutes. Various names for these collections of statutes are used by the different states and jurisdictions. Very often the terms *code, annotated statutes, compiled laws,* or *revised statutes* appear in the title of the publication. There are a large number of codes in this country, and each may be composed of one, five, or even several hundred volumes, as in the case of the United States Code Annotated. Additionally, some states subdivide their state codes into smaller codes, such as a code of civil procedure, a code of criminal procedure, an insurance code, and so on. A researcher who is encountering a code for the first time should try to become familiar with the organization of the state code, including any smaller codes, and become comfortable with the form and style of the text. At the beginning of the code will be noted the order in which the topics are arranged as titles, parts, or chapters, as well as the system of numbering of the sections and subsections.

The difference between chronologic (such as statutes at large and session laws) and the topical arrangements of codes is of primary importance to the researcher for speed of location, clarity of reading, and ease of updating.

5.0531 Federal Reports.   Research involving federal opinions is highly technical and advanced, seldom requested of the beginning researcher and legal assistant, and will not be discussed in detail. It is important, however, to be aware of common sources of federal statutory and case law.

The United States Constitution was signed in 1787 and became operative in 1789. It was the origin of federal law and, as amended, still stands as the supreme law of the land. Most Americans are affected continuously by its provisions, and the discussion of cases and terminology arising directly from the rights guaranteed to individuals by the Constitution (for example, freedom of speech, freedom of the press, and due process) regularly appear in the media. The Constitution is the highest authority available, and the Supreme Court is the final arbiter in disputes over its provisions. All other federal and state statutes must conform to the guarantees of this document or they will fall. West's *U.S. Code Annotated (U.S.C.A.)* has several volumes devoted only to the Constitution and the cases that have arisen from disputes over its provisions.

As bills are enacted by Congress, they enter the Statutes at Large, and may, if permanent, general, and public in nature, be included in the U.S. Code. Official copies of the U.S. Code can be obtained through the U.S. Government Printing Office. Each such provision as it becomes law can be found in the *Congressional Record* and may be located through the *Congressional Information Service/Index.* Unofficial reports include the *U.S.C.A.* and the *U.S. Code Congressional and Administrative News,* both by West Publishing Company, and the *U.S. Code Service,* published by the Lawyers Cooperative Publishing Company. Additionally, there are numerous publishers of loose-leaf services that monitor and publish new laws and updated material for subscribers in particular fields of law, such as trade regulation, taxation, antitrust, environmental law, labor, and occupational safety and health law. Any firm that has a substantial specialty will have access to such a service, both at the federal and the state levels.

Each publisher supplies the legal community with a particular style and format they believe is helpful, easy to use, and clear to its readers. The *U.S.C.A.* supplies the researcher with a variety of routes to the significant material of the statutes and cases referring to them. It is a multivolume set, and each volume contains all or a portion of the U.S. Constitution or the U.S. Code. Each volume contains a title page describing the extent of material covered in the volume and is supplemented by detailed tables of contents and indexes. An example of one of *U.S.C.A.*'s title pages and the facing page, which lists the fifty titles within the U.S. Code, is shown in Exhibit 20.

The *U.S.C.A.* also contains a special index of the popular name of each law enacted by Congress, references to the date of its passage, any amendments, the chapter and statute reference to the statutes at large, its public law designation (if any), the titles and sections under the U.S. Code, and any alternative names under which it is listed. (See Exhibit 21).

Since only nineteen of the fifty U.S. Code titles have been reenacted into law in their codified form, it is essential to be able to move between the U.S. Code and the Statutes at Large. The *U.S.C.A.* provides such indexes that advise the researcher of the year and the session of Congress in which the law was passed, the statute volume in which it is recorded, the date of passage of the statute, and its public law number, along with the sections and pages all cross-referenced to the *U.S.C.A.,* as shown on Exhibit 22.

Administrative agencies must publish their rules and regulations in the *Federal Register*. It accumulates this material chronologically, and therefore, the codification of those various rules of the multitudinous agencies is accomplished by the *Code of Federal Regulations (C.F.R.),* the official record for such law. The *C.F.R.* is well indexed and revised annually. Such frequent revisions require spaced publication of the issues of revisions of the titles. The updated volumes list the *C.F.R.* sections affected by cumulating the changes from 1964 forward. Anything older is found in a special volume, *C.F.R. Sections Affected 1949–1963,* published by the U.S. Government Printing Office in 1966. The *C.F.R.* has indexes allowing the researcher to move to the U.S. Code, the Statutes at Large, the proclamation, the executive order, or the reorganization plans on which the particular rule or regulation relies for authority. The *C.F.R.* also is organized by topic with title numbers corresponding to the U.S. Code, thus making it easier to locate administrative pronouncements on specific statute.

To assist a researcher in delving into the governmental regulatory and administrative agency maze, the U.S. Government Printing Office annually publishes the *United States Government Manual.* This manual describes all executive branch and regulatory agencies and cites the statutes under which they function, their subordinate units, and other organizational data, as well as the types of information each agency can provide.

Many of the loose-leaf services, mentioned in passing above, follow the publications of these agencies and supply their subscribers with the most recent changes in timely fashion.

5.0532 Federal Court Rules. Federal courts establish rules of procedure to guarantee a uniform system of presentation of cases. These rules are subject to controversy and interpretation, and the courts are sometimes requested to decide the meaning of a rule. In 1940, the West Publishing Company began publishing court decisions interpreting and construing the rules in a series of volumes called

EXHIBIT 20

UNITED STATES CODE
ANNOTATED

Title 28

Judiciary and Judicial Procedure
§§ 1446 to 1650

Official Revision and Codification of the
Laws relating to the Judiciary and Judicial Procedure
Under Arrangement of Official Code of
the Laws of the United States

with

Annotations from Federal and State Courts

ST. PAUL, MINN.
WEST PUBLISHING CO.

Federal Rules Decisions. Court resolutions of questions about the proper interpretation of rules will be found in the *Federal Rules Decisions.* Another publication, *Federal Rules Service,* published by Callaghan and Company, has a similar arrangement of decisions on federal rules. Either is excellent for use in researching the federal rules of civil procedure. Of course, the U.S. Government Printing Office publishes *Rules of Civil Procedure for U.S. District Courts* and all other federal rules. This official publication, like all other official publications, provides only the text of the material without reference to cases. The unofficial publications of

EXHIBIT 21

TITLES OF
UNITED STATES CODE
AND
UNITED STATES CODE ANNOTATED

---

1. General Provisions.
2. The Congress.
3. The President.
4. Flag and Seal, Seat of Government, and the States.
5. Government Organization and Employees.
6. Surety Bonds.
7. Agriculture.
8. Aliens and Nationality.
9. Arbitration.
10. Armed Forces.
11. Bankruptcy.
12. Banks and Banking.
13. Census.
14. Coast Guard.
15. Commerce and Trade.
16. Conservation.
17. Copyrights.
18. Crimes and Criminal Procedure.
19. Customs Duties.
20. Education.
21. Food and Drugs.
22. Foreign Relations and Intercourse.
23. Highways.
24. Hospitals, Asylums, and Cemeteries.
25. Indians.
26. Internal Revenue Code.
27. Intoxicating Liquors.
28. Judiciary and Judicial Procedure.
29. Labor.
30. Mineral Lands and Mining.
31. Money and Finance.
32. National Guard.
33. Navigation and Navigable Waters.
34. Navy *(See Title 10, Armed Forces)*.
35. Patents.
36. Patriotic Societies and Observances.
37. Pay and Allowances of the Uniformed Services.
38. Veterans' Benefits.
39. Postal Service.
40. Public Buildings, Property, and Works.
41. Public Contracts.
42. The Public Health and Welfare.
43. Public Lands.
44. Public Printing and Documents.
45. Railroads.
46. Shipping.
47. Telegraphs, Telephones, and Radiotelegraphs.
48. Territories and Insular Possessions.
49. Transportation.
50. War and National Defense.

II

EXHIBIT 22

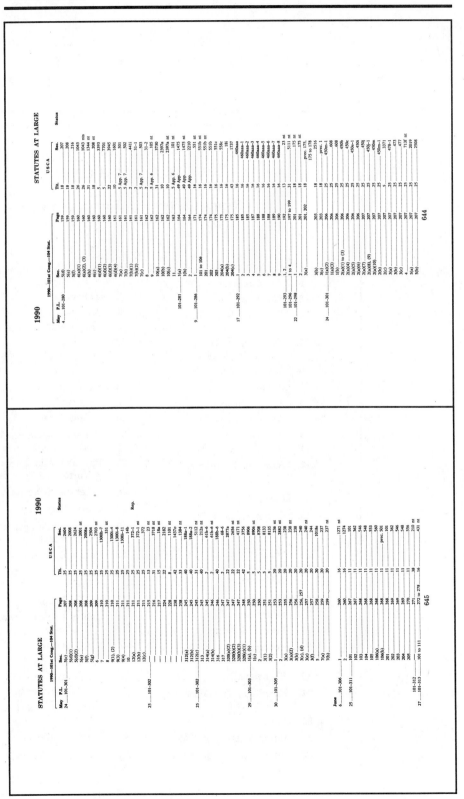

the commercial firms, such as West Publishing Company, provide the rules with expository and explanatory material in the form of the footnoted cases.

5.0533 State Reports. Each state has a similar range of statutory authority controlling or directing the lives of its citizens. The same basic procedures for proposing legislation, introducing bills, and enacting them into law is followed whether the state legislature meets annually or every other year. The executive branch of the state government (the governor and the regulatory and administrative agencies) generates executive orders and rules and regulations in a manner similar to the federal system. In many cases, however, there are areas of overlapping responsibilities between the state and federal jurisdictions that must be considered by the researcher. Some of these areas are education, health and welfare, housing, occupational health and safety, and utility regulation. Great care must be exercised to determine the exact problem and whether it is responsive to state statute, federal statute, or both. The basic sources of state statutory law are:

(a) State constitution. The constitution of each state is the ultimate source of the laws for that state. Here, again, check to be certain some article or section has not been amended or repealed. The state's highest court, the supreme court in most states, is the final authority on the interpretation of the state's constitutional provisions, though some of those rulings may be appealed for decision by the U.S. Supreme Court where a conflict between rights under the state and the U.S. Constitution are alleged.

(b) State codes and statutes. These are the laws of the state, passed by the legislature and signed by the governor (or passed over his or her veto). Once the governor signs the legislation, the statute is published as a session law and consolidated chronologically with the current legislative session's accumulation. If the particular bill provided for the acceptance of a code in its codified form, it will be found both in the chronologic and the code version of the law. The researcher will find parallels between the research aids for the federal system and the research aids for the state statutory law. Each state has a printing office that supplies official copies of the statutes and codes. Similarly, there are commercial publishers that produce the unofficial publications. In California, for example, there are two publications that cover the state's codes: *West's Annotated California Codes,* by West Publishing Company, and *Deering's California Codes,* published by Bancroft Whitney Company. California's codes are divided topically much like the U.S. Code and the *U.S.C.A.,* as shown in Exhibit 23. The arrangement of the content is similar to the *U.S.C.A.* in that it provides quick reference in the code to the statutes for each section, the historical notes, library references, and the derivation of any section, as well as the West topic and key number references for research in other West sources. (See Exhibit 23.) Clearly, care must be taken to ensure the latest amendments are included. Each volume is updated annually with pocket parts containing amendments to the sections in the volume, as well as additional annotations. (Annotations are compilations of cases and historical matter dealing with various aspects of a code or statute, with short summaries of decisions and case citations. They contain cases ruling both for and against.) Always check the volume to determine its date of publication and for a pocket part. If there is a pocket part, check to see if there have been any changes. If there is no pocket part, it may be the most recent replacement volume. However, if there are several years between the publication date in the front of the volume and the time of the research, take the extra step of checking for a missing pocket part. The librarian in the office or

EXHIBIT 23

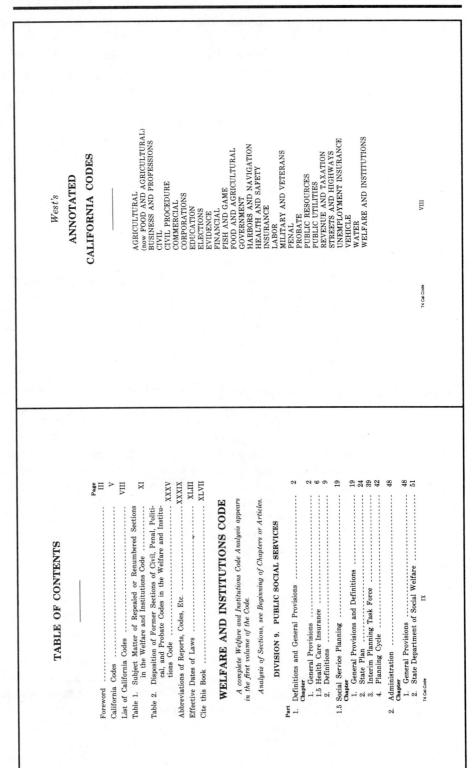

West's

ANNOTATED
CALIFORNIA CODES

AGRICULTURAL
(now FOOD AND AGRICULTURAL)
BUSINESS AND PROFESSIONS
CIVIL
CIVIL PROCEDURE
COMMERCIAL
CORPORATIONS
EDUCATION
ELECTIONS
EVIDENCE
FINANCIAL
FISH AND GAME
FOOD AND AGRICULTURAL
GOVERNMENT
HARBORS AND NAVIGATION
HEALTH AND SAFETY
INSURANCE
LABOR
MILITARY AND VETERANS
PENAL
PROBATE
PUBLIC RESOURCES
PUBLIC UTILITIES
REVENUE AND TAXATION
STREETS AND HIGHWAYS
UNEMPLOYMENT INSURANCE
VEHICLE
WATER
WELFARE AND INSTITUTIONS

74 Cal Code   VIII

TABLE OF CONTENTS

WELFARE AND INSTITUTIONS CODE

A complete Welfare and Institutions Code Analysis appears in the first volume of the Code.

Analysis of Sections, see Beginning of Chapters or Articles.

DIVISION 9.   PUBLIC SOCIAL SERVICES

74 Cal Code   IX

in the nearest major law library can be of assistance. The volumes also contain legislative history, cross-references, and collateral references. Each book of codes and statutes reflects the effective dates of the statutes and the date the statutes were passed in a given year. Exhibit 24 displays the type of annotations, statutory language, and historical and cross-referencing information that is typically included in annotated statutes.

State regulatory and administrative agencies are empowered by the legislature that created them to propose and publish (after public comment or hearing) rules and regulations necessary for the discharge of their responsibilities. Often they also are empowered to enforce their own regulations, subject to appeal, of course. Many times these state agencies parallel federal ones and must work in concert with them on matters of mutual concern but within their specified areas of juris-diction. *Caveat:* Research in statutes alone is ineffectual unless the cases (cited in the annotated code volumes) are studied to determine how the courts construed and interpreted the rules. It is obvious that finding cases analogous to the re-searcher's problem is helpful, whether the decisions support or refute the client's desired position. The attorney, armed with the past decisions, can adapt the theory, choice of jurisdictions, and strategy or at least advise the client of the most effective and economic course of action.

5.054   Case Approach to the Law.

Case research is clearly the backbone of all legal endeavors in the United States. Even in cases of "first impression," where the court never before has heard or decided the disputed issue, the decision is influenced by the principles and rea-soning of the courts in past similar cases and decisions. Sometimes, a dissent (the individual opinion of a judge disagreeing with the majority decision) becomes the choice of later judges who recognize that changes in social structure or mores call for a change in the law. These landmark cases do not come about without persuasion based on logic and the views presented in past decisions, by study groups (such as the American Law Institute), and in law review articles, among other sources. Reading and distinguishing the cases is essential. Reporting the results of the research in easily recognizable form contributes to the value of the research by aiding the reader's understanding and appreciation of the views and conclusions of the researcher/writer.

5.0541 Case Citation.   The uniform procedure for citing cases is: (a) by the parties surnames (full names of business entities should be included); (b) the volume number of the reporter containing the case: (c) the abbreviated name of the reporter; (d) the page number where the case begins: (e) the parallel citation (if the case is published in two separate law reports); (f) the date: and, if necessary, (g) the court that rendered the decision. The latter is required if the reporters (official and parallel) in which the case is published contain decisions of more than one court. It is essential to know which of the courts rendered the decision because the authority of one court may be more persuasive than another or even mandatory. The Harvard Law Review Association publishes *A Uniform System of Citation,* which illustrates the proper way to cite cases, statutes, and other legal authorities. The researcher is cautioned to follow these rules rather than to follow the form used in an authority. It is not uncommon for incomplete citations to appear within a published authority.

EXHIBIT 24

---

28 § 1449   REMOVAL OF CASES   Part 4

6. Denial of request

Plaintiff was not entitled to order directing production of arrest report dealing with his arrest in criminal prosecution on basis of which he presently claimed deprivation of civil rights where report was not part of state court record and state recording officers had advised plaintiff that record could be subpoenaed at appropriate time from police evidence custodian. Smith v. Philadelphia Police 39th District Spec. Invest. Squad, D.C.Pa.1969, 48 F.R.D. 341.

Plaintiff's motion for production of search and seizure warrant introduced at his trial in state criminal prosecution which was basis of his instant action for deprivation of civil rights was denied where in response to an earlier motion in state court seeking same document plaintiff had been sent by clerk of state court a copy of the only warrant in the state court file. Id.

§ 1450.   Attachment or sequestration; securities

Whenever any action is removed from a State court to a district court of the United States, any attachment or sequestration of the goods or estate of the defendant in such action in the State court shall hold the goods or estate to answer the final judgment or decree in the same manner as they would have been held to answer final judgment or decree had it been rendered by the State court.

All bonds, undertakings, or security given by either party in such action prior to its removal shall remain valid and effectual notwithstanding such removal.

All injunctions, orders, and other proceedings had in such action prior to its removal shall remain in full force and effect until dissolved or modified by the district court.

June 25, 1948, c. 646, 62 Stat. 940.

Historical and Revision Notes

Reviser's Note. Based on Title 28 U.S. C., 1940 ed., § 79 (Mar. 3, 1911, c. 231, § 36, 36 Stat. 1098 [derived from R.S. § 646; Mar. 3, 1875, c. 137, § 4, 18 Stat. 471]).

Changes were made in phraseology.

Federal Rules of Civil Procedure

Attachment or sequestration in federal court after removal, see rule 64, this title.
Continuation of section, see note by Advisory Committee under rule 81.
Jury trial in removal actions, see rule 81(c).

Library References

Removal of Cases ⏝95, 119.

C.J.S. Removal of Causes §§ 235–241, 268–271.

West's Federal Forms

Motion to dismiss, see § 1215.
State court proceedings, preservation, see § 1192 Comment.

Notes of Decisions

I. **GENERALLY** 1–30
II. **ATTACHMENT, BONDS, UNDERTAKINGS OR SECURITY** 31–70
III. **INJUNCTIONS** 71–100
IV. **ORDERS AND OTHER PROCEEDINGS** 101–117

312

"Parallel authority," mentioned above, refers to the fact that some cases are printed in more than one publication. When this occurs, one will be designated as the official reporter and the other as the unofficial reporter. As a general rule, the state-authorized publication is the official or parallel cite and the commercially published copy of the decision is the unofficial cite. When the same decision is published in more than one location, the citations are referred to as parallel cites. *A Uniform System of Citation* includes a table of the federal and state governments and indicates the appropriate method of citing to the official (and unofficial, if any) publication. It should be noted that many states no longer publish their own cases and instead adopt the commercial publication as the official citation. In these states, the case is published in one location, so there is only one citation reference to a report. Parallel cites are not generally used in the statutory citation of laws that have been incorporated into a code.

Citations should omit the first names or initials of natural persons who are plaintiffs or defendants (except in administrative cases), but the entire name of fictitious entities, such as companies or corporations, should be used. For example, cite *Smythe v. Jones,* NOT *John Smythe v. Earl Jones;* BUT *J. M. Smythe Co. v. Smith and Sons Inc.,* NOT *Smythe v. Smith et al.*

5.0542 *Federal Reports.* Certain federal cases are reported both officially and unofficially. U.S. Supreme Court cases are reported officially in *U.S. Reports. Caveat:* Volumes one through ninety must be cited with the name of the official court reporter who compiled the volume and the volume number, for example, *Marbury v. Madison,* 5 U.S. (1 Cranch) 137. There were a number of different reporters over the years who imposed their own numbers on the volumes they compiled. Citing their name and volume obviates any confusion. The unofficial reporters include the *Supreme Court Reporter* by West Publishing Company (a portion of the national reporter system), which began at Volume 106 of the *U.S. Reports,* and the *Lawyer's Edition of the U.S. Supreme Court Reports,* published by the Lawyers Cooperative Publishing Company. Some researchers like West's reporter since it incorporates the topic and key number system in the annotation, while others prefer Lawyers Cooperative's series because they include a summary of the arguments of counsel on both sides of the question.

The U.S. Supreme Court publishes its decisions immediately on ruling on an issue as a "slip" decision; slip opinions are available electronically or by mail subscriptions. Subscribers to the mail service receive their copy about two weeks after the decision is announced. There are unofficial loose-leaf services that fill the same function but even more quickly than the official report. Both West and Lawyers Cooperative supply advance sheets to their subscribers containing the decisions as they will appear in the forthcoming bound volumes.

U.S. Courts of Appeals decisions are originally published in nominative reports (reports carrying the name and volume number of the reporter who compiled them) for each federal court, both district courts and circuit courts of appeals, creating a confusing and voluminous problem. West Publishing Company accumulated the most important federal decisions, both of district and courts of appeal cases, and published them in a thirty-volume set called *Federal Cases,* dated up to 1880. U.S. district courts and courts of appeals stopped publishing volumes of decisions, and now publish some (but not all) their decisions as slip opinions. West accumulated the slip opinions and published them in bound volumes as the *Federal Reports* until 1932. In that year, West began the *Federal Supplement,* which accumulated the selected district court and customs court decisions, leaving the *Federal Reporter* to cover only the decisions of the courts of appeals, court of patent appeals, and the court of claims.

In 1940, West began publishing the *Federal Rules Decisions* series, which covers decisions of all the federal courts on procedural law matters as well as articles or speeches on the topic.

The Lawyers Cooperative Publishing Company entered the federal case reporting business by instituting its *American Law Reports—Federal,* which includes specially selected and annotated federal court decisions. Citation to these "unofficial" reporters, whether West's or Lawyers Cooperative, is usually acceptable under local district or appellate court rules, a matter easily checked by examination of the court rules in the jurisdiction of the researcher's interest.

All the West publications, the *Supreme Court Reporter,* the *Federal Reporter,* and the *Federal Supplement,* are part of the national reporter system and use the topic and key number system.

5.0543 *The State Court Reports.*   Most states have official reports. In California, for example, there are two official reports: *California Reports,* containing reports of cases decided by the California Supreme Court since March 1850, and *California Appellate Reports,* containing reports of cases determined in the state's district courts of appeal since May 1905. Not all state decisions are published in the official reports, because the supreme court can mark some decisions "Not to be Published in Official Reports."

California decisions too recent to be bound are reported in paperback volumes called "advance sheets," that contain both supreme court and appeal decisions, appropriately paginated as they will be in their respective future bound volumes.

Many states do not have a satisfactory method of reporting recent decisions, and the delay in publication of the decisions is a distinct disadvantage to the lawyer and the researcher. As a result, about one-fifth of the states have discontinued production of an official state reports system in favor of a commercial series, which is more efficient to use, current, and indexed. In such states, the series is designated as the official reporter of the state; for example, the *Southern Reporter, Florida Cases* is the official reporter for Florida in lieu of the *Florida Reporter,* which ceased publication in 1948.

The *Southern Reporter, Florida Cases* is a unit of West Publishing Company's national reporter system, which includes the federal units described above and the following state and regional reporters:

Atlantic Reporter: contains cases for Connecticut, Delaware. Maine, Maryland, New Hampshire, New Jersey, Pennsylvania, Rhode Island, and Vermont.

North Eastern Reporter: contains cases for Illinois, Indiana, Massachusetts, New York (court of appeals only), and Ohio.

North Western Reporter: contains cases for Iowa, Michigan, Minnesota, Nebraska, North Dakota, South Dakota, and Wisconsin.

Pacific Reporter: contains cases for Arizona, California (supreme court only), Colorado, Idaho, Kansas, Montana, Nevada, New Mexico, Oklahoma, Oregon, Utah, Washington, Wyoming, Alaska, and Hawaii.

South Eastern Reporter: contains cases for Georgia, North Carolina, South Carolina, Virginia, and West Virginia.

South Western Reporter: contains cases for Arkansas, Kentucky, Missouri, Tennessee, and Texas.

Southern Reporter: contains cases for Alabama, Florida, Louisiana, and
Mississippi.

New York Supplement: contains cases for New York only from 1887 to the
present.

California Reporter: contains all California cases from the supreme court, the
district courts of appeal, and the appellate division of the California Superior
Courts since 1960.

Since the inception of the national reporter system in the late 1800s, the states
(which had or have official reporters) had parallel reporters—one official and the
other unofficial, the commercially published edition. Many decisions reported in
the unofficial reporters were not reported in the official reporters; this, together
with the headnoting system, makes research in the unofficial publications a bit
more thorough and informative than that allowed in the official reporters. Unofficial reporters published by West will contain the same topic name and key
numbers that are used in all West digest series, making it possible to research the
same issue in several jurisdictions very quickly.

All reporters, whether official or unofficial, include similar elements in their
publication format, such as:

(1)   The docket number assigned by the court and the date of the decision;

(2)   The full caption of the case;

(3)   A summary of the case;

(4)   Headnotes;

(5)   Identity of counsel for the parties, including any counsel submitting briefs
as *amicus curiae* (friend of the court); and

(6)   the actual opinion.

The actual opinion of the court on the subjects at issue is the only "authority"
in the reports. Unless otherwise indicated,the summary is prepared by the editor
of the reporter to assist the researcher in deciding whether to read the entire
opinion or not. While this is helpful, it is not authority and, conceivably, may be
in error. The headnotes (short paragraphs with numbers) list the legal issues and
points of law covered in the opinion but are not authority. The headnotes are
prepared by the editor and are a great aid in quickly determining (1) whether the
opinion deals with or relates in any way to the researcher's current specific problem
and (2) where in the opinion the particular point of law covered by the headnote
is discussed. They are also very important when updating research by Shepardizing
(See Section 5.06). The actual language in the opinion must be checked to verify
that what the summary and the headnotes indicate is truly supported by the opinion
text.

The opinion usually starts with the name of the judge writing it (though
opinions may be written as *per curiam* decisions—those written expressing the
court's view, (even if all the judges were not there, or as *en blanc* views—those
written with all members of the court present and agreeing on the decision). The
opinion is followed by a statement of the fact situation of the case, analysis of the
points of law argued by the various parties, and the court's opinion and decision
on each point raised. The court then states its decision(s) on the case as a whole.
Because judges sometimes disagree, a decision may also carry one or more dissenting or minority opinions. The footnotes can also be helpful in finding supporting cases. Many lawyers start by reading the decision at the end of the report
as an aid in understanding the language of the opinion that resulted in that decision.

5.06 Use of *Shepard's Citations* or Sheparding

Query: "Can the cases and laws be brought up to date? Have any of the cases been reversed on appeal or overruled by subsequent cases? Have the laws been amended or repealed? In essence, is our authority really valid authority?"

Shepard's Citations are published for the cases in the United States Supreme Court reports, federal reports, National Labor Relations Board (NLRB) reports, some other federal departments reports, the national reporter system, and state reports. This material is accumulated through searches of the various court decisions, agencies' decisions, opinions of attorneys general, articles in legal periodicals, and annotated reports.

Shepard's publishes for statutory citations as well, including the United States Constitution, United States Code, United States Statutes at Large, treaties and other international agreements, United States court rules, state constitutions, codes, session laws, municipal charters, ordinances, and state court rules.

Every reported case is collected and examined at Shepard's, and the cases and statutes mentioned in each reported case are recorded and printed under their own citations in the Shepard's publications. By this process, the history of the cited cases and laws is developed. Editors read the cases and, where required, note the history and treatment of the case. A table of abbreviations for consultation is provided at the front of each volume. If the same case is affirmed on appeal, a lowercase *a* appears in front of the citation; *cc* represents a connected case that is a different case but arising out of the same subject matter; capital *D* stands for dismissed, *m* for modified, *r* for reversed, *s* for same case. Capital *S* for superseded case, and parentheses indicate parallel citations. In the treatment of the case, *c* indicates criticized, *d* distinguished, *e* explained, *f* followed, *h* harmonized, *j* dissenting opinion, capital *L* limited, *o* overruled, *p* parallel, and *q* questioned. If any of these symbols appears at the front of a citation, for example, "s 167 FS 405," (see Exhibit 25 under Vol. 364, page 339), check the table of abbreviations at the front of the volume to confirm what the abbreviation means.

Frequently a case will cite another case for only *one* point of law in the cited case that may have had as many as twenty points of law analyzed in headnotes. In order to indicate to the researcher that the citing case discussed only one point of law, a smaller number, called a superior figure, appears before the page number a little elevated from the line of type to show which headnote relates to the discussion in the citing case: for example, "377 US[1] 555" (see Exhibit 25 under Vol. 364, page 339).

As stated before, the resources of the law library will control the scope of the research to a large extent. This chapter covers a variety of the Shepard's publications in the hope that the legal assistant has access to some of the titles or at least similar titles so that he or she may apply the techniques to the resources at hand.

5.061 Case Research.

The scope of case research in *Shepard's* can be limited to the state jurisdiction, expanded to neighboring states, to federal cases, or to all reported cases in accordance with the titles selected.

5.062 State Shepard's Citations.

Shepard's Citations cover every state with volumes listing every case in that state that has been subsequently discussed in any later case in that state or federal

EXHIBIT 25

UNITED STATES SUPREME COURT REPORTS						Vol. 364
Cir. 4	237FS1566	456FS3673	j306F2d1476	255So2d69	379US1143	j568FS1461
537FS393	CtCl	506FS32	313F2d138	Md	380US1540	Cir. 1
—297—	198CCL624	541FS1872	314F2d1228	226Md600	383US1311	376F2d1541
s278F2d446	461F2d1379	76FRD3600	355F2d1362	174A2d783	j383US1672	570F2d11075
Cir. D.C.	Mo	82FRD4609	362F2d1120	NY	385US1130	295FS1206
292F2d756	352SW681	94FRD3241	410F2d81	33Msc2d521	387US1108	385FS1882
293F2d153	NY	Cir. 7	445F2d832	227S2d87	d391US1384	405FS11394
294F2d221	13Ap2d209	346F2d3251	191FS1683	Ore	393US1391	j451FS1154
j294F2d228	215S2d191	f525F2d1764	d222FS1986	229Or246	j393US589	70FRD1655
547F2d699	Pa	408FS41161	238FS1757	230Or6	j396US453	Cir. 2
Cir. 2	497Pa63	68FRD4385	242FS1298	235Or66	j398US1193	j294F2d144
380F2d777	498Pa535	85FRD20	326FS530	366P2d886	400US1126	j379F2d497
205FS836	439A2d103	98FRD721	Cir. 3	367P2d400	j400US1283	482F2d1265
—298—	448A2d1048	13BRW860	486F2d11105	383P2d1004	400US1389	c482F2d266
s371US807	Wis	18BRW4798	330FS1496	Pa	402US141	510F2d514
s371US907	53Wis2d400	Cir. 8	361FS21	222PaS372	403US15	e510F2d1522
s371US944	192NW897	476F2d260	28FRD440	295A2d100	d403US1149	j510F2d530
s374US203	47ABA458	Cir. 9	28FRD495	Wash	j403US1177	512F2d49
s177FS398	**—310—**	316F2d4789	39FRD1340	63W2d323	j403US1225	e191FS1184
s184FS381	(5LE8)	337F2d1750	Cir. 4	387P2d80	j403US1264	196FS1762
s195FS518	(81SC13)	f399F2d895	344F2d1742	**—336—**	405US170	202FS1744
s201FS815	s361US958	481F2d41190	351F2d41422	**Case 1**	j406US1576	202FS1754
Cir. 3	s364US938	487F2d1675	202FS1664	s76Nev157	407US1194	202FS755
j465F2d863	s270F2d290	708F2d41492	218FS1597	Nev	j407US1483	d211FS1466
Cir. 9	s301F2d133	38FRD2197	237FS165	s350P2d724	j408US1390	j211FS1468
77FRD36	379US1158	Cir. 10	Cir. 5		409US1521	j211FS1473
Cir. 10	401US4335	446FS4908	286F2d1752	**Case 2**	412US1751	d214FS1901
689F2d914	406US417	76FRD346	290F2d1398	s18Il2d506	413US1368	j229FS1779
Md	j449US926	Alk	290F2d1431	Ill	j418US1778	d238FS1926
228Md247	52FC@1271	499P2d602	291F2d1420	s165NE322	j418US1808	260FS1208
228Md259	Cir. D.C.	632P2d543	297F2d1417	**—337—**	422US378	d266FS1325
179A2d702	424F2d4907	DC	319F2d1366	**Case 1**	425US1142	j271FS116
179A2d709	Cir. 2	305A2d530	322F2d1159	s364US925	j425US1148	271FS1499
—299—	392F2d384	468A2d1342	335F2d1197	s170OS393	426US1254	290FS1883
s279F2d289	522F2d158	Ind	346F2d1874	Ohio	429US1266	j311FS155
s290F2d858	f541F2d1952	263Ind195	405F2d1949	s165NE642	430US1165	341FS1148
Cir. 6	568F2d4906	325NE843	585F2d1741		430US1170	d377FS11166
311F2d47	668F2d108	Mich	249FS1379	**Case 2**	430US1179	386FS7
—300—	226FS2372	99McA858	331FS1289	s359Mch430	j430US1181	429FS1212
s271Ala22	349FS705	390Mch656	426FS1375	Mich	j430US1511	473FS1495
Ala	359FS914	213NW136	514FS11204	s102NW552	433US1414	476FS323
s122So2d280	440FS1092	298NW870	Cir. 6	**—338—**	442US1272	f535FS11017
—301—	445FS4722	Mo	340F2d1730	**Case 1**	j442US283	Cir. 3
(5LE1)	506FS4308	572SW867	662F2d1434	Mo	446US162	j535F2d1812
s185Kan274	63FRD50	Ohio	305FS11185	s335SW118	e446US185	563F2d1582
Kan	66FRD4228	33@A228	Cir. 7	**Case 2**	j446US102	564F2d1141
s341P2d1002	82FRD4	293NE329	322FS519	s171OS192	j446US127	d648F2d1182
Cir. D.C.	23BRW283	Ore	Cir. 8	Ohio	j446US214	233FS1620
419F2d1312	Cir. 3	271Or311	401FS17	s168NE409	j458US652	262FS1828
Cir. 1	312F2d3372	532P2d4	Cir. 9	**—339—**	51USLW	j262FS1857
f254FS1255	407F2d673	Tenn	d343F2d1221	(5LE110)	[4858	419FS1273
369FS1114	420F2d41276	637SW884	369F2d1300	(81SC125)	51USLW	468FS1951
Cir. 2	534F2d569	Wash	371F2d1783	s362US916	[4861	536FS1584
190FS1625	663F2d4425	100W2d349	495F2d916	s270F2d594	j51USLW	567FS11515
Cir. 3	346FS4994	670P2d243	d203FS1725	s167FS405	[5116	Cir. 4
356F2d1654	382FS474	MFP§6.16	213FS1356	j366US573	Cir. D.C.	397F2d141
347FS1254	484FS409	**—325—**	Cir. 11	369US1229	395F2d587	442F2d1572
Cir. 5	519FS1562	(5LE20)	224FS1249	369US1244	452F2d11306	459F2d11097
333F2d1640	561FS4137	(81SC6)	Calif	j369US1284	459F2d1247	j459F2d11100
523F2d1286	58FRD447	s362US909	228CA2d697	j369US1335	465F2d1638	j459F2d11109
319FS522	81FRD3662	s271F2d194	44CA3d355	d372US1376	j481F2d530	462F2d1068
Cir. 6	89FRD64	j375US212	39CaR763	j372US1386	j489F2d11174	j462F2d1078
421F2d1765	96FRD4235	379US1672	118CaR518	376US156	520F2d170	463F2d56
489FS143	Cir. 4	51USLW	Conn	376US158	j559F2d694	j473F2d11021
Cir. 9	484FS312	[4103	153Ct78	j376US159	593F2d1111	573F2d1190
377FS152	37FRD4435	63MC935	171Ct276	376US168	661F2d1303	588F2d1424
Cir. 10	Cir. 5	66MC1561	214A2d366	377US1296	255FS1299	664F2d919
513F2d137	413F2d1281	67MC2155	368A2d230	377US1555	j333FS1590	710F2d1135
620F2d779	616F2d1747	Cir. 1	Fla	j377US1613	349FS1729	198FS1503
	639F2d41284	434F2d1122	139So2d403	j377US1744	d354FS11030	245FS1245
	661F2d152	608F2d18	Ill	378US1287	374FS1377	d267FS267
	Cir. 6	608F2d120	79IlA594		376FS1352	269FS848
	429FS183	Cir. 2	399NE175		411FS1654	d276FS1668
		297F2d111	La		568FS1460	313FS386
			260La46			*Continued*

297

system. The state *Shepard's* edition also incorporates any state case that is not reported in the National Reporter System (primarily those decided prior to 1887). *A.L.R.* and legal periodical citations are included in the Citator. The first time a case is mentioned in *Shepard's Citations,* the parallel citation to the National Reporter System is given but not repeated in subsequent volumes.

Every unit of West's National Reporter System has a companion Shepard's Citator. To use the contents, convert the state citation to the regional reporter citation. Under the reporter citation will be listed every case discussed in any later case in that regional reporter and all other reporters in the National Reporter System as well as federal reporters. *A.L.R.* and *American Bar Association Journal* citations are also included. The first time a case is mentioned in *Shepard's Citations,* the parallel citation to the state reports is given but not repeated in subsequent volumes.

5.063   Federal Shepard's Citations.

Shepard's United States Citations and Shepard's Federal Citations list every case citing the federal cases in alphabetical order by state, given the state or National Reporter citation.

To research a federal case in Florida, for instance, consult the proper federal *Shepard's* and find a Florida case or a *Southern Reporter* citation. Then take that citation to the *Florida Shepard's Citations* or the *Southern Reporter Citations* and research that case through the state or regional system.

5.064   Statutory Research.

Knowing the wording of a law may be insufficient to resolve a controversy between litigants, and resorting to court interpretation of the law is required. *Shepard's Citations* exist for state and federal statutory research, giving the citations to cases interpreting the laws as well as editorial notations as to changes in the law by legislative bodies.

Armed with the proper citation to state or federal constitutions, codified law, or session laws, it is possible to determine what courts have mentioned the laws in their opinions as well as subsequent changes in the law. Cases holding a law unconstitutional will have *U* prior to the citation alerting the researcher to this important fact. Tables of abbreviations at the front of the volume explain the meaning of the symbols used in the text. Again, law review articles, attorney general opinions, and *ALR* annotations specifically identifying the law will be cited in *Shepard's.*

Laws frequently are known by popular names but cannot be identified in indexes that way. *Shepard's* incorporates a "Table of Acts by Popular Names or Short Titles" in its statutory division as well as in a separate publication, *Shepard's Acts and Cases by Popular Names.* This is frequently the best source to consult for the proper statutory citation.

Municipal or county ordinances are included in the state *Shepard's Citations* when they have been interpreted and construed by the courts. These are usually arranged in alphabetical order by geographical unit and then alphabetically within the unit by catchword identification of the ordinance. Usually an index accompanies these for easy identification.

5.065 Court Rules.

State and federal court rules can be Shepardized either in the state *Shepard's Citations* or the *Shepard's Federal Citations*. The latest cases are cited under the number of the rule along with changes in the rules and periodical citations.

5.066 Administrative Decisions.

Shepard's United States Administrative Citations include other decisions by administrative agencies, such as the tax court, Interior Department, Federal Communications Commission, Federal Trade Commission, Treasury decisions, opinions of the Attorney General of the United States, and many others. Again, these decisions will be included if they have been mentioned specifically by name in later decisions. Notes will accompany the citations of subsequent changes in the points of law considered.

5.067 Shepard's Federal Labor Law Citations.

This very specialized system includes decisions and laws relating to labor. NLRB decisions and orders form the basis for the content. Extensive coverage of periodical literature is included. One of the distinct advantages of this title is the reporting of the parallel citations for the different commercial services publishing editions of labor materials.

Patents and trademarks are also the subjects of specialized treatment in *Shepard's United States Citations*.

5.068 Law Review Articles.

Shepard's Law Review Citations lists law review articles by citation and subsequent articles and court decisions that cite the original article. This permits one to locate a good article on a given subject and then trace it through later literature for other good articles on the same subject.

New in 1974 was *Shepard's Federal Law Citations in Selected Law Reviews*. This compiles references from nineteen law reviews to federal court cases, federal rules decisions, and the U.S. Constitution, U.S. Code, and federal court rules. From these federal sources of primary authority, it is now possible to pinpoint law review articles that mention them specifically by name.

5.069 Supplements.

Supplements to *Shepard's Citations* take the form of bound volumes and cumulative paper pamphlets in red or ivory color, with individual advance sheets in white. As information accumulates, the red pamphlet is revised and reissued with instructions to discard previous pamphlets. Be sure to check the notice on the front cover of the pamphlet as to the parts of the series that make up the whole unit of *Shepard's Citations*.

Total reliance on *Shepard's Citations* without substantiation from other sources could be fatal. *Shepard's* gives the history and treatment of a case by judges in later decisions. It does not cite all cases on a point of law. It should not be used as a substitute for a researcher bringing the search up to date through the reporter or statute being searched. *Shepard's* is designed as a complementary aid to research. Cases can cite other cases, not for the point of law involved, but for the amount of damages or some other phase of the case; therefore, cases cited in *Shepard's* must be checked for their pertinence to the question at hand. On the other hand, a case can completely change the areas of the law by a grand, sweeping statement that "all former decisions not in accord with this opinion are overruled." If such statements include no reference to cases affected (either by name or citation), they never will appear in *Shepard's Citations*.

The use of *Shepard's Citations* may yield more cases on the subject of inquiry and shed some light on the direction the law is taking in the area. In addition, it should turn up related sources that were not uncovered in prior research. Finding a case in *Shepard's Citations* may at first glance seem to be confusing, but it is easily resolved by consulting the back side of the title page to each volume. This page indicates the volumes of citing materials included in the *Shepard's* volume. Start with the first volume of *Shepard's Citations* (of any series) and examine the contents indicated on the spine. If the case or statute is of early vintage, in all likelihood it will be in this volume. Examine every subsequent volume for newer cases, law review articles, and other sources that cite the given case or statute. However, if the case is a relatively recent one, it may not be in the first volume. Advance forward through the volumes until you find the first mention of the case citation of interest. This procedure should become apparent when the volume itself is used, not just read about.

5.07 Review of the Basic Research Process

1. If unfamiliar with the particular area of law, locate a reference that discusses it, such as a legal encyclopedia or other commentary.
2. Identify a number of different terms that pertain to the topic of research. A legal thesaurus or dictionary may be helpful in doing this.
3. If the research question involves or is likely to involve a statute, go to the subject index of the appropriate code and use the terms previously identified to locate the appropriate reference to a statutory chapter (title) and section number.
4. After locating the statute, read the text and examine any relevant annotations that might follow.
5. If the issue is not statutory, or if there are no annotations, go to the digest. Again, use the identified terms with the descriptive word index (subject index) of the digest. These will help locate the topic and key number (section) for finding annotations or case summaries (also called headnotes) on the specific subject.
6. After reading the annotations, select those most applicable to the case at hand and locate the complete decision in the reporter system by using the citation given in the annotation. This citation will contain the case name, the reporter volume and page, and the year of the decision.
7. After reading the complete judicial opinions, note those that most closely resemble the research issue and general facts of the case at hand. Generally, those decisions that come from the same jurisdiction and most closely parallel the case being researched will be the most persuasive.
8. Prepare the correct citation for those authorities that are going to be used to respond to the research issue. Then go to the *Shepard's Citations* volume for the reporter where the case or statute is published, and using the volume and page number, locate the *Shepard's Citations* volume for that particular case or

statute. The volume and page will appear in boldface and any subsequent references will appear immediately below.

9. In all stages of research, be aware that most publications, whether commentary, statutes, digests, or *Shepard's,* contain supplements or pocket parts with the most up-to-date information. These must be consulted to determine the most current law on a particular subject.

5.071   Let's Research.

As you prepare to do your research, get ready to be alert, dig out facts needed to prove the client's side of the case, alert the lawyer to strong cases adverse to the client's position, and find or distinguish cases in rebuttal. Above all, be prepared to accept constructive criticism. Such criticism is an invaluable learning aid, and a lawyer who takes time to give thoughtful advice and constructive criticism is one who is interested in helping the legal assistant advance and improve. One common criticism of a new legal assistant's work is that it does not express the lawyer's own personal style. In both legal research and legal writing, a legal assistant should try to style his or her work in a way that complements the attorney's. Don't be offended if the lawyer doesn't accept the offered writings in every instance or totally rewrites a proffered offering; try to think as the lawyer does and gear the style of the work product to his or her liking.

The research examples given here will be simple; they are illustrations of the sequence of researching and will pertain to one point of law only.

5.072   Facts Example No. 1.

In 1984, Sam Smith sued General Hospital and some physicians for malpractice. In 1985 the suit was settled and a dismissal was filed.

In 1987, the legal assistant's employer filed suit on behalf of General Hospital for money owed by Sam Smith as a result of the prior hospitalization in the amount of $1,800.00. Sam filed an answer and cross-complaint alleging malicious prosecution, among other things. The prayer of the cross-complaint exceeded the Municipal Court dollar limit and the action was transferred to the Superior Court. The legal assistant is asked to determine whether the cross-complaint states a valid cause of action for malicious prosecution and if this issue can be properly raised by way of cross-complaint.

The review of Sam's cross-complaint reveals that Sam alleges the amount of the bill ($1,800.00) was included in the settlement of the malpractice action and General Hospital waived that amount as part of the settlement. The employing attorney's position is that the settlement included only the cause of action for malpractice, that the release signed by Sam released only General Hospital and contained no provisions for waiving the amount of the bill, and that the hospital had not authorized the inclusion of the outstanding $1,800.00 bill in the settlement.

Beginning with a secondary source, such as *Corpus Juris Secundum* (also see 5.052, Secondary Authority and 5.061d Legal Encyclopedias, supra) or in California perhaps, *Witkin, Summary of California Law,* Eighth edition, the legal assistant determines that to establish a cause of action for "malicious prosecution of a civil proceeding" a plaintiff must plead and prove three points:

(a) that the prior action was commenced by or at the direction of the defendant and was pursued to a legal termination in his (the Plaintiff's) favor;

(b) that the prior action was brought without probable cause, and

(c)   was initiated with malice.

In reading the secondary sources the legal assistant noted the cases cited or referred to and now begins reading them. The legal assistant quickly learns that malicious prosecution is a cause of action not favored by law. Shepardizing (see Shepardizing, supra) develops cases the legal assistant reads and finds that malicious prosecution cannot be raised by way of cross-complaint. The legal assistant's memorandum to the lawyer might be:

5.073   Research Memorandum.

Memo to Ace, Attorney at Law, from Deuce, Legal Assistant
Re: Smith v. General Hospital
1/26/87
Report of research on the question—Can Malicious Prosecution be raised by cross-complaint?

NECESSARY ELEMENTS TO PROVE: (1) That the prior action was commenced by or at direction of defendant and pursued to legal termination in plaintiff's favor; (2) that the prior action was brought without probable cause; and (3) was initiated with malice. The cross-complaint fails to state facts sufficient to constitute proof of any of the necessary elements and their inability to plead favorable termination of a prior action appears to be fatal. *Bertero v. National General Corp.,* 13 Cal.3d 43, 50, 118 Cal.Rptr. 184, 529 P.2d 608 (1974); *Tool Research & Engineering Corp. v. Henigson,* 46 Cal.App.3d 675, 120 Cal.Rptr.29 (1975).

MALICIOUS PROSECUTION SHOULD NOT BE ALLOWED BY WAY OF CROSS-COMPLAINT IN THE MAIN ACTION: The case of *Babb v. Superior Court,* 3 Cal.3d 841, 92 Cal.Rptr. 179, 479 P.2d 379 (1971), involved the question of whether a defendant in a civil action might file a cross-complaint seeking declaratory judgment; that in the event the action terminated favorably to him the action be adjudged to have been instituted and prosecuted maliciously and without probable cause. The trial court overruled a demurrer contending that favorable termination of the prior proceeding is a necessary precondition to the maintenance of a malicious prosecution action, on the ground the cross-complaint was not premature since it sought only declaratory relief. The Supreme Court reversed the ruling and ordered the lower court to vacate its order and sustain the demurrer without leave to amend. This decision was based on the "conclusion that precedent, principle, practicality and policy forbid such a cross-complaint, which entails the risk of discouraging legitimate claimants . . .". The Court stated, at page 846:

> First, there is a certain metaphysical difficulty in permitting a counterclaim for malicious prosecution since theoretically that cause of action does not yet exist.

The Court further stated, at pages 847 and 848:

> Third, the *rule of favorable termination is supported by strong policy considerations.* (5) Since malicious prosecution is a cause of action not favored by the law, it would be anomalous to sanction a procedural change which not only *would encourage more frequent resort to malicious prosecution actions, but would facilitate their use as dilatory and harassing devices.* Abolition of the requirement that malicious prosecution suits be filed as separate actions after termination of the main litigation would surely increase the incidence of such suits, since filing a cross-action requires less time, expense, and preparation than does initiation of a separate action. Furthermore, the introduction of evidence on the issues of malice and probable cause may prejudice the trier of fact against the plaintiff's

underlying complaint, or enhance the possibility of a compromise verdict. Even if, as here requested, consideration of those issues is deferred until the principal action has been completed, an outcome of that trial adverse to the plaintiff may unduly enhance the defendant's chances in his malicious prosecution action. Finally, as was the case here, the plaintiff and his attorney may be joined as cross-defendants in the malicious prosecution suit. This not only places the attorney in a potentially adverse relation to his client, but may well necessitate the hiring of separate counsel to pursue the original claim. (See Note, supra, 58 Yale Law Journal 490, 493, and fn. 13.) *The additional risk and expense thus potentially entailed may deter poor plaintiffs from asserting bona fide claims.*
(Emphasis added.)

It is hornbook law that the plaintiff in a malicious prosecution action must plead and prove that the prior judicial proceeding of which he complains terminated in his favor.

"... Because of this requirement it is obvious that a defendant cannot cross-complain or counter claim for malicious prosecution in the first or main action, since a claim cannot state a cause of action at that stage of the proceedings. This appears to be the rule, not only in California, but generally." *Babb v. Superior Court,* 3 Cal.3d 841, 845–846, 92 Cal.Rptr. 179, 180–181, 479 P.2d 379, 380–381 (1971).

Failure to plead prior favorable termination is fatal; cross-complainants cannot allege a favorable determination of the underlying action.

5.074   Facts—Example No. 2.

John Law, a California highway patrolman, was injured while making an arrest and attempting to prevent Willy Henry from falling down. Law subsequently filed a civil suit against Henry and John Smith for personal injury. Law's employment records were subpoenaed, and the state of California claimed they were privileged. Determine whether the claimed privilege applies, and draft a letter in support of the contention that they are not privileged, if so indicated. The state claims privilege under California Government Code section 6254 and California Evidence Code section 1040. Begin the research by reading the code sections cited.

It appears clear they to not apply to a private citizen who files a civil suit for injury. Then read the California Code of Civil Procedure's applicable sections relating to discovery and confirm that the records are not privileged under those provisions.

5.075   Memorandum and Draft Letter.

Memo to Ace, Attorney at Law, from Deuce, Legal Assistant
6/6/86
Re: Privileged records—draft of letter to state
Gentlemen:

We are in receipt of your records, forwarded to Naida Love, C.S.R., with your letter of May 11, 1986. We are also in receipt of the declaration attached thereto for the records withheld and deemed privileged, signed by Jack W. Lewis, state services analyst. You cite as authority for claiming privilege Government Code section 6254(b) (c) (f) and Evidence Code section 1040. We submit that under the fact situation in this lawsuit, the privilege does not apply to "(3) Correspondence and reports pertaining to the December 10, 1984, injury which occurred on duty and from which Officer Law sustained a lower back injury. Injury Record card excluded." We are not concerned with the records listed in the balance of the declaration.

In support of our position, we call your attention to the following facts:

1. Enclosed is a copy of the amended complaint for personal injury filed by John Law. You will note that the charging allegations are that John Smith provided defendant Willy Henry with alcoholic beverage during the course and scope of his employment, that defendant Henry negligently and wrongfully assaulted, battered, and struck plaintiff about the face, head, back, body, and legs, causing severe bodily injuries, frightened plaintiff, and placed plaintiff in great fear for his life and physical well-being. In addition, the complaint alleges that these acts were done with malice and ill will and with the intent and design of injuring and oppressing plaintiff. The claim for punitive damages in the complaint has been dropped by stipulation of counsel. These injuries allegedly were the result of acts required of plaintiff in the course and scope of his employment. Further, in verified answers to interrogatories, plaintiff contends that defendant violated "ordinances, codes and statutes relating to reckless driving, speeding, improper lane change, failure to yield to a red light, resisting arrest, failure to obey lawful order of police officer, drunk driving and public drunkenness, and assault and battery."

2. Mr. Law is claiming back pain at the conclusion of putting the defendant in the car and that he later developed left leg problems. Further, he had surgery that he relates to this accident and may need further surgery. Asked why the facts surrounding the arrest as described by him in deposition were not included in his arrest report, he pointed out it is the Garden City's California Highway Patrol office policy not to charge intoxicated persons with resisting arrest or assault and battery on a peace officer unless the officer has actual signs of injury, such as lacerations, broken bones, etc., and, therefore, he felt the facts stated by him in deposition were not relevant to the charge of driving under the influence. He further testified that he reported the incident at the jail to his superior, Sgt. Lager, and later that evening the sergeant completed an injury report.

3. Your cited subdivisions to Government Code section 6254 (b) (c) and (f) are not applicable in this instance. Subsection (b) relates to "pending litigation to which the public agency is a party or to claims made pursuant to Division 3.6 (commencing with section 810) of Title 1 of the Government Code. . . ." In this instance, the "public agency," or the California Highway Patrol, is not a party, nor is this suit filed against public entities or public employees (section 810). Rather, it is a private lawsuit by a California Highway Patrol officer for injuries resulting of an arrest made by him while on duty as an officer. Subsection (c) relates to personnel, medical or similar files, the disclosure of which would constitute an unwarranted invasion of personal privacy. Here, again, we submit that by filing a civil action for personal injuries as a private citizen, plaintiff Law has subjected himself to the normal discovery available to defendant to prepare a defense to the suit and, thus, correspondence and reports pertaining to the injury are a proper subject of discovery to substantiate the injuries and the circumstances surrounding same and that he has, in essence, waived the privilege regarding his reports and work records relating to the injury. This material is relevant and should be produced. Subsection (f) does not appear to state a privilege insofar as this lawsuit is concerned.

4. Your cited Evidence Code section 1040 refers to "official information," which is defined as "information acquired in confidence by a public employee in the course of his duty. . . ." We submit that the correspondence and reports pertain to the December 10, 1984, injury of plaintiff Law. We suggest that they are, in view of his personal civil lawsuit, business records and should be produced as such under the provisions of California Evidence Code section 1560. Further, provision (b)(2) provides for privilege if disclosure of the information is against public interest because there is a necessity for preserving the confidentiality of the information that outweighs the necessity for disclosure in the interest of justice. Our position is that the withholding of this information would be against public interest and prejudicial to the defendants in preparation of their defense.

Defendants cannot obtain this information through their own efforts, and under the facts, the necessity for disclosure in the interest of justice outweighs the necessity for preserving the confidentiality of the information.

We will appreciate your forwarding the material described under number (3) of your declaration relating to privileged and withheld records.

These are but two examples the legal assistant anticipates; the possibilities are endless.

5.076   Research Memorandum—Example 3.

Memo to Ace, Attorney at Law, from Deuce, Legal Assistant
Re: *Smith v. Johnson*
8/9/90

Report of research on the question, can a civil action for malicious prosecution be brought against a complaining witness in a criminal case?

SHORT ANSWER: When a criminal action is dismissed in favor of a defendant and if the court is of the opinion that the prosecution was commenced for malicious reasons, the court has the authority to enter judgment against the complainant for the costs of the prosecution. Il.Rev.Stat. Sec. 38-200-5 (1984).

NECESSARY ELEMENTS TO PROVE: (1) That an original criminal or civil judicial prosecution by defendant has been initiated; (2) that the prosecution was terminated in favor of the plaintiff; (3) that there was an absence of probable cause for such proceedings; (4) that there was the presence of malice by the defendant; and (5) that in malicious prosecution actions based on civil proceedings, the complainant must allege and prove special injury. *Gonzalez v. Chicago Steel Rule Die and Fabricating Company,* 62 Ill.Dec. 577, 106 Ill.App.3d 848, 436 N.E.2d 603 (1982).

In the present case, the relevant facts are that Mr. Smith was accused of stealing money from the church where he served as a deacon. The minister of the church, Rev. Johnson, pressed criminal charges, and Mr. Smith was arrested. Mr. Smith's ordinary occupation is bank teller. Immediately after his arrest, Mr. Smith was discharged from his employment due to the nature of the charges. Prior to trial, it became apparent that a case could not be proven against Mr. Smith, and the case against him was dismissed. Mr. Smith has asked that we initiate a lawsuit on his behalf against Rev. Johnson for malicious prosecution. Mr. Smith is of the belief that Rev. Johnson initiated the criminal charges in retaliation and as an attempt to discredit Smith, who was advocating the dismissal of the reverend from the church.

Based on the statute and the requirements indicated in the *Gonzalez* case, it is my opinion that an action against the reverend is viable. A criminal action was commenced on the basis of the complaint of Rev. Johnson. The action was dismissed in favor of Mr. Smith. There is evidence of malicious motivation by Rev. Johnson, and Mr. Smith's loss of employment and wages should suffice as the required special injury. It is my recommendation that we proceed in Mr. Smith's behalf.

5.08   Modern Technology and Legal Research

The reliance by courts and lawyers on precedent, the recorded accounts of the decisions in past litigation, as well as the gradual proliferation of statutes (whether amplifying old law or creating new), have made big business out of libraries and publishing houses. The increasing volume of decided cases and learned dissertations on facets of the law, the growth in regulatory agencies with their obligatory rules and regulations, increasing numbers of law schools and students, and the continuing legal education courses across the country all assure that the production of law source, reference, and citator books will greatly expand in the years ahead. It also ensures that an adequate law library is no mean investment to create or to maintain. Large firms, of course, find it necessary to equip their libraries with more than one volume of some law books, even of some sets of books. It is one of the observed, but untitled, laws that whenever a particular law book is desperately needed to check an authority, form, or reference for a last minute filing at court, that book will be checked out or misfiled within the library or another attorney is also engaged in a last-minute research project in the same volume.

Other types of library problems are the need for a dedication of labor time in posting and updating the reference books with pocket parts, rearranging shelves to make space for new acquisitions and replacement volumes, restoring books to the proper shelf, and performing emergency searches for wanted but checked-out volumes. The space needed to create a law library is another consideration. At current commercial property rates in metropolitan areas, the financial impact of space alone is substantial.

The modern technologies of photography and computers can be applied to solve some of these nagging problems.

5.081   Photography, Microfilm, Microfiche, and Microform.

Photography can reduce printed pages to the size of a typewriter's letter *m* with resolution quality that allows a lighted viewing screen to restore the image to clear, readable size, even allowing the production of hard-copy prints of the image. Whole volumes can be reduced onto one or several cards or rolls.

Microfilm usually refers to the reduction of material into photographs on film rolls. Several thousand page-size images can be stored on one roll. The roll of film can be equipped with keyed film image counters that allow the indexing of its contents.

Microfiche began as transparent cards with sleeves into which microfilm strips were slipped, allowing the assembly to be handled as a four-inch-by-six-inch card, easily filed and easily adapted to the assembly of one increment of information or topic. The reader equipment is less expensive than for microfilm, since no transport mechanism is needed and focusing problems are minimized. Copying requires slightly different equipment, however.

Microforms are microfiche further reduced to exceptionally small size, allowing hundreds or thousands of images on one card. West Publishing Company uses one such form, "ultrafiche," to provide units of the national reporter system to subscribers. Each volume (approximately 1,450 pages) is on one ultrafiche card. The readers for the process have a nine-inch-by-twelve-inch screen and can be mounted on a library table or office desk. Separate equipment is needed to make paper copies.

Such devices as these eliminate the need for space to store the several thousand volumes involved, a major space and economic benefit. They also reduce the problem of the "borrowed but not returned volume." If more than one volume is needed or if two or more sets are required for the office, the economies and conveniences of these technologies are obvious.

5.082   Computer-Assisted Research.

Perhaps the greatest strides in legal research have been made in the area of computer access to resource materials. The developments in the last few years alone are phenomenal and can only be expected to continue. It is entirely conceivable, if not probable, that in the not too distant future, most bound-volume libraries will be replaced by computer terminals with access to the resources located in databases (collections of information that can be retrieved through a computer) on-site or across the country. Already these terminals are an integral part of most comprehensive libraries.

One of the major computer research systems is Westlaw, created by West Publishing, which provides access to such sources as statutes, the West digest series, the national reporter system, *Shepard's Citations,* and *Black's Law Dictionary.* Another similar system is Lexis, offered by Mead Data Central. There is also a system similar to *Shepard's Citations* known as Auto-Cite, offered by the Lawyers Cooperative Publishing Company. One of the more recent developments is West Publishing's CD ROM Libraries, which allow research for a specific jurisdiction rather than a nation-wide scope, a much less expensive system. CD ROM will be discussed in greater detail below. Additionally, certain governmental entities have similar computer research systems. In all of these systems, the user inputs a query into the system, and receives an information response relevant to the query. This is seemingly a simple process. However, as with all legal research, a particular skill must be developed in formulating the appropriate question in order to gain the most valuable information and the least amount of irrelevant information.

The first step is to understand how the system works. The user will have a computer terminal with a monitor and a keyboard and a telephone. The terminal is connected to a special telephone that sends the information projected on the screen—the user's queries, for example—and receives information back from the computer-based library. If the user wishes to receive a hard (paper) copy of the information obtained, a printer is also needed.

Though the query process will be discussed briefly here, the reader who anticipates using a computer research system is encouraged to obtain and study a tutorial or reference manual, such as the *Westlaw Reference Manual.* An example of a computer tutorial is *Westrain.* There are similar tools for the other systems. *Westrain,* which can be used on any personal computer, is a step-by-step approach to effective computer research that can be employed at the user's own pace and convenience.

The process of legal research is quite similar for most systems. For the purposes of demonstration here, reference will be made to the Westlaw system. As with any type of legal research, the first step is to identify the jurisdiction whose authority is being sought. For example, if research is being done for a case pending in Pennsylvania, the researcher would be primarily concerned with the legal standards issued by the courts and legislature of that state. In computer research, this step is known as identifying the "field." Once the correct field has been entered into the computer, all queries will be directed to the law of that field.

The next step is to formulate the query. Because the cost of computer research is based on the time the system is in use and because research should be performed efficiently, it is important to adequately prepare before accessing the system. In all legal research, including that which is computer-assisted, it is necessary to determine the issue with as much specificity as possible. Once the issue has been defined, the researcher must select those terms relevant to the issue and identify any variations or synonyms of them.

To arrive at variations that might be used in place of the original term, the researcher needs only to identify the root of the term and follow it immediately with an exclamation point (!). This instructs the database to produce all authorities in the field that contain the root of the word and any variation. If the only relevant variations differ by only a few letters, an asterisk (*) can be used within the original term at any place where a different letter might appear in a variation. The system automatically searches for plurals, so these need not be identified as variations.

After the terms and their variations are selected, it is important to connect the terms properly. This will aid in limiting the information retrieved to relevant authorities. The system interprets a space between letters as the word *or;* for example, the system would interpret a query of "malicious prosecution" to mean locate any authority containing the word *malicious* or the word *prosecution,* but not both. Thus, one should be especially aware of spaces in the query before inputting it into the system.

Connectors are symbols that tell the computer how closely terms in the query must appear to one another in order to be retrieved. For example, the symbol "/s" between two terms means that the terms must appear within the same sentence of an authority before the system will retrieve it. Similarly, the symbol "/p" means that the terms must appear within the same paragraph of an authority before the system will retrieve it. The "/s" symbol is so limiting that relevant cases or statutes may be missed, while the "/p" symbol may cause numerous irrelevant authorities to appear. Basically, a knowledge of the subject and the likelihood of authority will guide the researcher in determining which connectors or combination of connectors to use between terms.

When an authority is retrieved, the terms of the query will be highlighted where they appear in the authorities. It is possible to retrieve only the citations of the authorities or to examine the specific text of each authority.

The researcher who has a specific citation of a relevant authority may call up that citation without going through the query process by using the "find" command or by doing a field search. To do this, the name of the statute or case, the volume, page, and report citation, or both, if available, are input. The computer will then retrieve all cases in the field by that name; if the volume and page are available, the specific case will be called up. *Insta-cite* can be used to provide the researcher with direct and indirect history in the particular case.

Step 4.   Identify variations of the terms that might be used in authorities on this issue:

Elements—element

Malicious—maliciously, maliciousness, malice
Prosecution—prosecute

Step 5. Construct the query.
         Element requirement factor component and or /p malic! malevolent
         wanton and /p prosecut***

Step 6. Input the query, review the headnotes, and select the decisions that appear to address the issue most directly.

Step 7. If the results are not satisfactory, modify the query and input it.

Step 8. Call up the complete decisions of the selected headnotes and review.

Step 9. Shepardize those decisions that will be used as authority.

At virtually any point, the research process can be converted to standard book research. For example, if the printed materials are also available, it may be more cost effective to perform the research by computer through Step 7 and then read and Shepardize the decisions in the actual books. This compatibility with book research is an additional benefit of computer-assisted research.

Another component of computer-assisted research is CD ROM Libraries by West Publishing Company. The development of this system has made computer research affordable for virtually any size firm or organization. The concept is quite simple. Compact discs containing research materials for a particular subject of law or jurisdiction are loaded into a compact disc player attached to a personal computer and the information on them retrieved by the computer. As with Westlaw, one can retrieve headnotes, cases, statutes, and so on. However, because the user purchases only those discs his or her library needs, there is no cost for access through telephone lines to the Westlaw database or for access to all published statutes and cases nationally. Because approximately three hundred thousand pages of information can be contained on a single disc, space requirements are extremely low, compared with a standard library. Additionally, updated discs allow the researcher to retrieve the most current information. CD ROM also has word processing capabilities that enable the researcher to lift information from the disc and incorporate it into a brief or other document.

As the efficiency and cost of computer research continues to improve, its use is becoming more and more widespread. Computer research may soon be more cost-effective than the expense of book space and updates of hardbound volumes in the ever-expanding subject of law.

5.09   Research Delegation Considerations

At first the legal assistant's research projects will be basic and carefully detailed in scope, purpose, form, and time allowed for completion. Typically the problem may be one requiring little interpretation, such as "identifying each state code section or reference relating to riparian water rights . . . ." The project has easily defined parameters and can be checked easily by the attorney in order to verify the accuracy and thoroughness of the legal assistant's work. A second assignment might be "locate each riparian water rights case decided since 1850 and distinguish each to our present case issue of beneficial water use, briefing chronologically those cases which *mention* this issue."

Legal research requires skill, perception, hard work, and a candid and forthright recognition by the legal assistant of his or her own limitations. The lawyer has a fund of knowledge obtained both at law school and in practice which allows him or her relatively quick recognition and appreciation of the sometimes complex and/or convoluted views expressed in some case opinions. The legal assistant cannot, without equivalent training and experience, expect to, or *be expected to,* perform with the same insight, legal writing skills, and appreciation of legal expressions as the employing attorney.

Both the attorney and the legal assistant must adopt a mutually confident and comfortable posture which recognizes these differences in training and performance.

Some lawyers do not use legal assistants to do research; however, all who do are very careful in their choice of what research they allow legal assistants to do.

5.10   Research Tasks

The assumption must be made in allowing a legal assistant to do legal research that the legal assistant is trained, well-informed, and capable of doing such research. A working rapport and understanding must be established between the attorney and the legal assistant. The following checklist is actually one of capabilities. Most of the tasks can be performed either by the attorney or the legal assistant; however, some require more knowledge and insight than a legal assistant might have or more than his or her training will allow. Other tasks can and should be performed by a legal assistant as a great time saver to the attorney, some of which are:

Tasks	Attorney	Legal Assistant
Given a fact situation and a point of law, go to appropriate sources to find relevant cases; update those cases to see if there have been any decision changes regarding that point of law.	X	X
Given a fact situation and a point of law, find statutes or ordinances bearing on the issue and update statutes through supplements and session laws.	X	X
Given a fact situation and a point of law, determine whether there are constitutional considerations.	X	
Given a particular question or point of consideration, find relevant sections of constitution (federal and state).	X	X
Given a West key number, a fact situation, and a point of law, read summaries of cases listed under this number to find relevant cases.	X	X
Read cases and prepare a brief synopsis of each.	X	X
Organize research results into memo form.	X	X
Write a brief.	Primarily an attorney's job; however, a legal assistant can assist in drafting and supplying technical information, such as legal descriptions, cites, and organizing exhibits.	
Check cites and Shepardize a brief.	X	X
Prepare a table of authorities for a brief.	X	X

5.11   Summary

The more experience and expertise the legal assistant demonstrates, the more complex the research possibilities will become. BE ABSOLUTELY CERTAIN to understand what is expected and avoid assignments totally beyond current skills and knowledge, as this will result in disaster both for the legal assistant and the employing lawyer.

One of the basic concepts of the role of the legal assistant is to enable the lawyer to provide legal services at less cost to the client. The competent research of legal assistants will enhance this aim, and the legal assistant will become a valuable member of the staff in the law office.

Bibliography

Cohen, Morris L. *Legal Research in a Nutshell.* 4th ed. St. Paul: West, 1985.

How to Find the Law. Ed. Morris L. Cohen and Robert C. Berring. St. Paul: West, 1983.

How to Use Shepard's Citations. Colorado Springs, Colo.: Shepard's Citations, n.d.

Jacobstein, J. Myron and Mersky, Roy M. *Fundamentals of Legal Research.* 3rd ed. Westbury, N.Y.: Foundation Press, 1985.

Jacobstein, J. Myron and Mersky, Roy M. *Legal Research Illustrated: An Abridgement of Fundamentals of Legal Research.* Westbury, N.Y.: Foundation Press, 1987.

Price, Miles O., et al. *Effective Legal Research.* 4th ed. Boston: Little, Brown & Co., 1979.

Rombauer, Marjorie Dick. *Legal Problem Solving: Analysis, Research, and Writing.* 4th ed. St. Paul: West, 1983.

Sprowl, James A. *Computer-Assisted Legal Research: West Law and Lexis.* 62 ABA Journal 320–323, 1976.

Statsky, William P. *Legal Research and Writing: Some Starting Points.* 3rd ed. St. Paul: West, 1985.

Statsky, William P. *Legislative Analysis and Drafting.* 2nd ed. St. Paul: West, 1983.

Statsky, William P. *West's Legal Thesaurus-Dictionary.* St. Paul: West, 1985.

A Uniform System of Citation. 14th ed. Cambridge: Harvard Law Review Association, 1986.

West's Law Finder: A Legal Research Manual. St. Paul: West, 1990.

6 Interviewing Techniques

6.00   Introduction

No one call tell another person how to interview. At best, one can relate procedures and techniques that have been successful in the past and point out certain inherent hazards and problems and their potential solutions.

The ideal interviewer has a photographic memory, total recall, and knowledge of English and other languages, the law, politics, science, business, and the trades; is meticulous, highly trustworthy, empathetic, and a superb actor; could sell doormats to Robinson Crusoe, and is attractive with a commanding but comfortable personality and an appreciative sense of humor and radiates great dignity.

Few of us meet that ideal, but all of us can be effective. We adapt ourselves to the people we meet and concentrate on using our strongest assets to the fullest while improving our weakest skills. We learn from everyone and study the techniques of others to try to develop a style of interviewing for ourselves that produces good results and allows us to function confidently.

To conduct an interview presupposes that the interviewer controls the direction, purpose, and pace of the dialogue. This is not easy with bombastic extroverts or self-important executives, but it can be accomplished with good humor, provided the legal assistant has a definite goal and procedure in mind and adheres to the plan. As skill and experience increase, the legal assistant can allow such dominating personalities to feel in control while following the course the legal assistant has laid out.

The legal assistant's technique will develop by trial and error, requiring adjusting approaches used in the past with good results and the ability to prepare for interviews. Maintaining flexibility and adapting and adjusting during the interview are essential.

Practice, review, critique, study, and observation of others are required to become a good interviewer. Patience and perseverance are essential.

6.01   The Interview: What It Is and What It Is Not

The interview is a special form of verbal exchange between two persons transferring information from one to the other, usually toward a common objective. It is not a conversation but a polite, unofficial form of interrogation. Interrogation is a system of questions and answers where one person obtains the maximum amount of facts about an event, transaction, plan, or concept within the personal knowledge of the person being interviewed.

The process sorts out evidentiary facts of personal knowledge from beliefs founded on conjecture, inference, deduction, mistake, error, or assumption. It is used to develop leads to other witnesses; to establish the presence or absence of corroborating physical evidence; to identify the merits of a given situation; and to explore possible remedies.

Interviewing requires the exertion of control and direction by one party to accomplish a particular objective. The legal assistant is the one charged with gathering the data; therefore, the legal assistant must control, direct, and set the pace of the interview.

We all conduct interviews of various kinds on a daily basis. Employment interviews, tax counseling, applications for credit, shopping, filing complaints with governmental agencies all require the exchange of information toward an objective between two people. The very volume of interviews conducted leads to the belief that many can be "canned" in format and stereotyped in procedure. Simple forms of interviewing may be handled in such a manner; however, the legal assistant who conducts an interview in connection with the delivery of legal services cannot approach the task in that fashion.

The problems of each client are unique to that client, and not surprisingly, each situation has unique qualities that canned formats fail to accommodate. Flexibility and imagination, combined with skilled questioning by a legal assistant with a good memory, will produce more reliable results than any canned set of questions and forms.

The professional interviewer uses forms and canned procedures to expedite the gathering and recording of the data but does not allow the forms and procedures to control the interview. This is a person-to-person process requiring the legal assistant to use sensitivity, understanding, consideration, patience, and a cooperative sense of purpose for the benefit of the attorney, the client, and the witness.

Legal assistants always meet people seeking information or services they traditionally expect to be supplied by an attorney. It is an adjustment for witnesses and most clients to understand that assembling data is a skill that does not require the delivery of legal advice or the practice of law and therefore does not require a practicing attorney. A proper introduction and explanation eases that adjustment.

Many governmental agencies use legal assistants as the initial contacts for persons seeking advice on their legal rights under particular legislation or directions on how best to expedite matters on such topics as welfare, tribal rights, applications for use of federally controlled land, employment disputes, military veterans' rights, and verification of prior military service.

Public service law offices usually have legal assistants meet persons who are seeking legal guidance. Their problems may be as diverse as seeking assistance for someone in jail; advice on violations of their civil rights, immigration problems, or tenant-landlord disputes; or directions for how best to set up an ad hoc committee to negotiate with a governmental agency. Each of these encounters creates an instant interview. Such unexpected situations can be very difficult for the legal assistant, because there is no time to prepare for the interview and the situation for the interview is not ideal.

Legal assistants employed by private law firms or in law departments of corporations seldom encounter potential interviewees under surprise circumstances. The legal assistant usually meets the potential interviewee after a preparatory period during which the legal assistant has done some research on the matters to be discussed.

An interview, for the person being interviewed, is usually a unique, sometimes worrisome, even terrifying event. It nearly always relates to a matter of great importance to the individual. A legal assistant must approach every interview by understanding that the party being interviewed is in a stressful situation.

To minimize the stress, avoid conduct that can be interpreted by the witness as creating pressure. Give an impression of relaxed efficiency, not nervous haste. Smile and demonstrate real interest, rather than gloom, worry, or distraction. Be thoughtful, courteous, and responsive, not inconsiderate, rude, or remote.

This is not a burden or a requirement to "play act." A sincerely interested attitude will generate trust and confidence in the mind of the interviewee and his or her reserve will disappear. Suddenly the interviewee actually will be an interesting person, important to the legal assistant as well as to the case.

A thorough, well-prepared and well-conducted interview often will produce sufficient information for an attorney to offer the needed advice or the client/ applicant to obtain the benefits requested. In other cases, one interview leads to others to develop the full factual history of an event or transaction, complete with the colors of lawful or unlawful conduct, error, prejudice, mistake, and/or confusion. The attorney is aided by the legal assistant who treats every interview as a full-scale project worthy of preparation, skillful execution, review, corroboration, clarification, and report. The interview is not a vehicle to demonstrate the legal assistant's high level of education, wide vocabulary, heavy workload, or command of legal jargon. Interviewing is a learned skill requiring carefully considered and intense preparation and continuous and responsive adaptation by the legal assistant to the interviewee while pursuing the testimony needed. It extends past the interview to a concise report and critique of the interview and a thorough evaluation of the interviewee by the legal assistant. This information may be all the attorney will have in substantive form in the early stages of the legal process, and obviously, the quality must be good.

Interviews generally are one-on-one conversations but occasionally may be group meetings. It is axiomatic, however, that the more participants in an interview, the less thorough the interview of each person will be and the less likely the interviewer will obtain the truly individual thoughts, impressions, and personal recollections of each of the interviewees. The stronger personality, the most authoritarian official, or the most capable debater in the group will create the impression that the rest will adopt in group interviews. Such settings often deny the attorney and the legal assistant the identity of the dissident voice or the value and merit of any single viewpoint, particularly if that viewpoint is a threat to any group member's ego, authority, or reputation. A spoken consensus can inhibit the later revelation of a convergent view. Group meetings should be relegated to a conversational introduction of the legal assistant by the attorney to those persons attending the meeting and a broad statement of the problem. This introduction establishes the legal assistant's function, identifies the persons responsible for cooperating with the attorney and the legal assistant, and outlines the types of information needed. Interviews, however, should be conducted one-on-one or as close to that ideal as circumstances allow.

6.02 The Participants

6.021   The Legal Assistant.

The legal assistant is the person for whom this book is written; therefore, we shall refer to the interviewer as the legal assistant. You may be a student, a legal assistant, or a legal secretary, but we will call you a "legal assistant." It is your responsibility to extract information from one person and convey it to another. It will require your greatest communication, judgment, and analytical abilities.

6.022   The Client.

Clients may be people seeking the advice of an attorney, applying to government agencies for information or aid, seeking assistance from public service law firms, or any other person needing legal service and encountering a legal assistant in the delivery of that service. The client usually is the best source of information on a matter. The depth or accuracy of a client's known facts will vary from complete and accurate to virtually worthless. Seldom will one interview complete the legal assistant's contact with the client; however, each interview is considered as a separate important step. Clients take themselves and their problems very seriously, as they should, and often feel that their opinions and allegations are the truth, that the damages due them in compensation should be measured by the affront to them rather than through penciled calculations on paper. Often this results from a deeply felt but unstated faith that Murphy's Law—whatever can go wrong will go wrong—will operate against them unless they battle for their due. Most clients are fine people who revert to reasonable standards of behavior on learning that the attorney and legal assistant will help them succeed in their efforts so far as the facts, the law, and professional ethics and abilities will allow.

6.023   Friendly Witnesses.

Witnesses categorized as friendly are usually related to the client by blood, viewpoint, common business interests, occupation, or social acquaintance. They usually require little pressure to speak freely and fully but present rather polarized opinions that must be considered in the evaluation of their information. They are helpful in corroborating the client's viewpoint and offer a means of evaluating the information of adversary or hostile witnesses.

6.024   Official Witnesses.

Official witnesses are necessary to many cases because of the positions these individuals occupy. They may be municipal employees, state employees, federal employees, officers of corporations; they may belong to associations, business groups, ad hoc citizen committees, or other forms of organized, identifiable bodies. Depending upon their position on the issues, they may be friendly, impartial, or hostile. For instance, if the dispute is over a zoning matter and the witness is an official on the planning commission, he or she may have taken a formal public stand on the issue that may be supportive or antagonistic to the client's position. If the client's position coincides with the witness's, the legal assistant may receive more voluntary cooperation than otherwise. Ideally, official witnesses are impartial and objective. They neither enhance nor inhibit the development of information for either side of the dispute but offer only those facts of which they have personal knowledge or which can be ascertained from their files, where those files are open to the public.

6.025   Expert Witnesses.

Experts are encountered in many ways by legal assistants and frequently are interviewed in depth prior to being identified as expert witnesses. Often there is a need for an expert consultant rather than a witness. The expert witness can usually be identified as either friendly or hostile, depending on which side is paying his or her fee, though few experts are hostile on a personal basis. Occasionally, the legal assistant may be able to interview experts who have no interest in the case at hand and who simply offer information as requested. In these cases, the information is generalized and nonspecific and frequently serves only to identify the expert's field.

Expert witnesses tend to have a narrow band of information relative to any given case and generally should not be used to generate information outside their areas of expertise. Interviews of experts usually are conducted to obtain a feel for their method of oral presentation, to ascertain their impact on the listener, and to allow the legal assistant to play devil's advocate to test the expert's thoroughness of preparation and response to a cross-examiner's critical questions. Expert witnesses are identified by their ability to cope effectively and dispassionately with attacks on their credibility and the soundness of their conclusions.

6.026   Hostile Witnesses.

Who knows why hostile witnesses are hostile? Some witnesses, of course, the legal assistant can anticipate will be antagonistic to the purposes of the interview since they are aligned with the client's adversary. They are not necessarily hostile, however, in their conduct toward the legal assistant or toward the attorney. The objectively hostile witness poses a difficulty only in the extent of the information he or she is willing to divulge, the circumstances under which he or she divulges it, and the total lack of volunteered information. The truly hostile witness is one whose emotional character intrudes into the dialogue with the legal assistant. Truly hostile witnesses may be on either side of the case, and they may be witnesses the legal assistant expected to be objective or neutral.

No one knows why one person likes or dislikes another on sight and without apparent justification. It is a challenge to the legal assistant to identify the source of the discomfort causing the witness to display hostility with the resultant lack of information. If the witness allegedly is on the client's side, it is possible that a basic, visceral personality conflict has arisen between the legal assistant and the witness. Clearly, if the legal assistant cannot solve this problem or doubts the validity of the information obtained, he or she must seek help from the attorney. Perhaps another interviewer will be more successful.

Do not equate offensive language with hostility. Some witnesses speak profanely, even obscenely, as a matter of habit. If such remarks are so offensive that the legal assistant cannot function, he or she may be too sensitive for this type of work. However, if the remarks appear to be directed at the legal assistant personally, some action is required. Legal assistants do not have to endure personal abuse or vilification, and where it occurs, a polite termination of the interview is appropriate and desirable.

It is always important to identify the cause of a witness's hostility. It may relate to the case, the attorney, or the client and therefore be significant. It may relate only to the legal assistant, and that is important also but less so than the other reasons. If the legal assistant projects arrogance, superiority, or condescension, the witness may naturally respond hostilely. It is vitally important to the legal assistant to identify any such handicaps and alter the mannerisms giving others such impressions or causing hostile reactions.

6.03 Interview Preliminaries

The legal assistant who encounters the walk-in person seeking aid or advice has little or no opportunity to prepare for the interview. It is presumed that such a legal assistant has a full grasp of the limits of his or her authority and responsibility and a complete repertoire to handle the various types of inquiries he or she is charged to receive. Checklists, forms, and resource material must be at hand to allow immediate reference for those problems the legal assistant will encounter routinely.

All other legal assistants should thoroughly prepare before an interview if at all possible.

6.031 Introductions.

The introduction of the legal assistant to the witness is extremely important in setting the relationships of the legal assistant, the attorneys, the client, and the witness in proper perspective. Where the introduction is to the client, it naturally should be performed by the attorney employing the legal assistant. The introduction should not be effusive but professional and reflect that the attorney has full confidence in the capacity and capabilities of the legal assistant. Ideally, this introductory phase will be preceded by the attorney's discussion with the client of the reason for introducing a nonlawyer into the legal service program being provided the client.

In all introductions where the lawyer is not present, it is incumbent upon the legal assistant to delineate clearly the differences between lawyers and legal assistants and the function served by the legal assistant in the contemplated interview. It goes without saying that the legal assistant should always listen closely to the manner in which he or she is addressed by the witness; often, after indicating to the witness that he or she is a legal assistant, he or she will hear the interviewee refer to him or her as an attorney. When this occurs, it must immediately be brought to the attention of the party that the interviewer is not an attorney but a legal assistant conducting the work at the request of an attorney for the benefit of the client.

If the witness is unfamiliar with legal assistants or the case, the legal assistant must ensure that the witness is fully aware of the object and purpose of the interview, the parties, and the legal assistant's connection to the matter.

6.032 Establishing the Purpose of the Interview.

Establish the purpose of the interview early on. One major area of client interviewing is preparing for or responding to litigation. Such preparation may frequently develop sufficient information to clarify the issues and lead to the settlement of the dispute that brought the client to the office. It is equally important in providing service to the client to resolve the problem in a timely and equitable manner without litigation, if possible, as it is to file suit and prevail at some uncertain date in the future.

Supplying nonlitigation-type legal services is another category frequently requiring interviews. These include such things as organizing corporations; creating estates or trusts; handling probate, difficult and complex sales, business mergers, and applications to governmental agencies; drafting contracts; and assisting in employer-employee matters. In these services, legal assistants equipped with training, research, and preparation can aid fast, definitive determinations.

6.033   Review of Law and Facts.

Research and review the general area of the law anticipated to arise in the case, if time allows. Obviously, if the client intends to file for a variance for zoning in the county, it does little good for the legal assistant to become an expert in city zoning law. Similarly, if an environmental impact report is required for a project, the legal assistant's expertise in political expenditure disclosure matters is irrelevant.

The attorney will alert the legal assistant in sufficient time to allow some review of the probable area of interest. The legal assistant must recognize his or her own limitations and seek the advice of the attorney when approaching a new or unfamiliar area of activity. The need for knowledge cannot be overstated, and the legal assistant must have the confidence to face the attorney and say, "What do you recommend I read or study to prepare?" or "I'm not familiar with this type of case; can you brief me or point me toward reference material I can study?"

A review of public or private documents, including the attorney's notes, if possible, regarding the matter to be discussed with the client is essential to provide for the effective, economic, and efficient conduct of the interview. Otherwise, the client will have to begin at point zero and tell yet again the basic information already in the office file.

The review may involve a multitude of facts in the form of documents, statements, and/or citations of code, statute, or case law. The legal assistant's review system may employ some form of tabulation of existing facts with the supporting references. Each fact can be listed chronologically on paper with corroboration on the left side of a dividing line down the center and the conceived attack or developmental questions on the right. For instance, if the dispute is a construction contract and the client seeks specific performance, the contract may be the physical fact with the client statement corroborating it. The attack questions on the right side might include "Novation?" "Rescission?" "Down payment made?" "Is the contract capable of performance?" "Labor strikes affect the contract?" "Ingress and egress possible?" "Zoning okay?" "Building permits okay?" or "Does client have title?"

6.034   Checklists and Forms.

If the law office has checklists and forms covering the area of legal service desired by the client, the use of appropriate ones by the legal assistant during the interview may be of great assistance in expediting the matter. It is better to have more forms and checklists on hand than will actually be needed since they can easily be returned to stock, rather than interrupting the interview to obtain a form. For instance, many jurisdictions have standard preprinted forms approved by the courts for filing pleadings, motions, notices and agreements, such as in divorce proceedings. The availability of such forms virtually mandates their use to ensure smooth, efficient management of the case. Use them. If the case is bodily injury, the names and addresses of doctors, hospitals, insurance companies, employers, and witnesses, among others will be needed, and the use of a form for assembling the data is efficient both in time and completeness. Naturally the legal assistant will need forms (easily standardized) authorizing the release of otherwise privileged information from the client's doctors, hospitals, therapists, accountants, and employers. Think ahead, save time, and be professional.

6.035   The Interview Site.

Selection and arrangement of the interview site may be problems unless adequate notice is obtained. When possible, the interview should be in an uncluttered conference room of the appropriate size for the interview. It should be comfortably furnished and arranged to avoid distraction or unease. During the interview, the legal assistant seeks to hold the interviewee's attention to the issues at hand. Eliminate unnecessary files or material not related to that interview. The room should be equipped with all necessary miscellaneous supplies, such as scratch pads, pencils, a carafe of water, and glasses.

If the interview cannot be conducted in such a conference room but must be at the legal assistant's desk, clear the desk of all other materials. Put away correspondence, files, and reference materials. Create the impression that the interviewee's case is the most important thing at that time. Arrange for the phone to be answered elsewhere.

Not every interview can be conducted under controlled conditions, but where conditions can be controlled, they should be. Interviewing is difficult enough without allowing distracting influences to inhibit or interrupt the dialogue between the interviewer and the witness.

Arrange the chairs and tables so that the legal assistant sits either side by side with the witness or at the corner of the table. Placing the table directly between the interviewer and the witness creates a physical barrier and the classic posture of confrontation—eye to eye. Barriers and confrontation, whether actual or implied, physical or psychological, are not productive of the feeling of rapport the legal assistant will need to achieve total cooperation in uncovering the true facts.

6.036   Recording.

Ideally, every interview should be tape-recorded; however, the decision to use recording equipment depends on the opinion of the attorney, the attitude of the client or witness toward the device, and the circumstances or purposes of the interview. It is a consideration, however, that should be made individually for every case and cleared with the attorney. The tapes serve as a marvelous teaching aid for the legal assistant who will find on review that he or she sooner or later commits all of the interviewing offenses subsequently described herein. There are good arguments both for recording and not recording the interview.

6.0361 Drawbacks.   One problem with recording is that some witnesses will speak freely only if "not on the record" and will refuse to execute written statements or allow their story to be recorded. Another drawback is that a long statement will require changing tapes, which tends to interrupt the witness, sometimes reminding him or her that his or her words may be ill-conceived but perpetually recorded or, at the least, breaking the witness's train of thought. Finally, the statement containing information adverse to the client's case may now be available to the adversary through formal discovery.

6.0362 Benefits.   Some benefits of recording include the ability: to review and refresh memories of the legal assistant, the attorney, and the witness at every stage of the case; to impeach later inconsistent statements; and to inhibit tendencies of the witness to speculate, extrapolate, and/or interpret at a later time in a departure from the story that served as foundation for the client's case. Occasionally, a strong favorable statement will aid in early settlement of a case that otherwise might have to be tried. For all practical purposes, the interview should be recorded in some manner, be it by tape recorder, longhand, shorthand, or some other method. Unless the interview is extremely short, relying on one's memory is not efficient.

6.04   General Considerations for Every Interview

6.041   Jargon and Slang
The language used should be comfortable for the interviewee. Legal assistants should be careful in using legal jargon, as this can be uncomfortable for a witness with no legal background.

Special jargon used by the interviewee must be identified and explained. As these terms are encountered, precise and exact meanings must be elicited from the witness, not only to inform the legal assistant but also to ensure that the witness is using them correctly and in the proper context.

6.042   Listening.
The legal assistant must listen to the interviewee. The most common danger that the legal assistant encounters is that of not listening. This is a disservice to the interviewee directly, for in his or her world, this event is unique and represents some form of tragedy, unfair situation, or onerous burden. The legal assistant with an attitude of disinterest offers no hope and little cooperation by failing to pay attention to the substance of the interviewee's story. Every legal assistant working on behalf of an attorney has the responsibility to listen fully, attentively, and patiently to those people seeking the attorney's advice.

Truly attentive listening will reveal the known facts, the erroneous beliefs, and the mistaken interpretations. These should be heard in context, without argument or correction, until the full account is told. Correction of a minor but glaring error of understanding during the narration of the witness will have a negative effect. It may unnecessarily create an argument on the fact; it may unnerve the witness so badly that the interview may have to be terminated; the legal assistant loses the opportunity to learn the background of the matter; and, worst of all, the legal assistant begins talking while the interviewee listens—an inversion of roles.

6.043   Empathy and Interest.
The legal assistant must generate a feeling of empathy and understanding as well as sincere interest in the interviewee. Lack of interest by the legal assistant probably results in a lack of perception of the issues and the basis of the remedy being sought.

6.044   Supportive Questioning.
During the course of the interview, supportive questioning helps the interviewee to provide all the information he or she has. The questions should be posed in ways that elicit cooperative narrative explanation. Phrases or words that are argumentative or tend to show a lack of belief in the witness's story will generate anger, self-consciousness, and lack of cooperation. It is easy to alienate people by asking blunt questions or confronting them with previously stated views that con-

flict or disagree. Utilize question phrasing that will elicit a voluntary explanation in narrative form from the witness.

Supportive questioning can proceed during the initial story-telling phase of the interview with such phrases as "And then what happened?" "Who said that?" and "What did he say then?" Subsequent questioning may follow. "I'm a little confused now, did you write the agency or call them on June first?" "Did this follow his letter or did his letter follow this?" "Now that we know this, how can we prove it to the other people?" Many times the subsequent explantion will clarify otherwise conflicting points. Seek the interviewee's help in resolving conflicts, rather than accusing him or her of erring or lying.

6.05   Inhibiting Factors in Interviewing

6.051   Leading Questions.

Legal assistants continually suffer the problem of having to interview witnesses with poor memories. Many people confuse the sequence of events or their occurrence in relation to a specific time or date. The longer the span of time between the event being recalled and the interview, the less accurate the recollection is liable to be. It is important to carefully interview in order to establish whether the witness truly recalls that to which he or she is testifying or is simply providing the answers he or she thinks the client or the legal assistant is seeking. The use of leading questions by the legal assistant can be responsible for otherwise truthful and reliable people turning into unreliable and uncomfortable witnesses. The use of such questions as "You did see the accident, didn't you?" when posed to a friend of the client may well generate agreement as an obligation not a belief. Asking a question that allows the witness to provide a narrative answer might change that one question into several others. "Where were you when the accident happened?" "How far were you from the point of impact?" "Which way were you looking when you heard the sound of the squealing tires?" Doing this is more work, but it will produce more reliable answers than leading questions. Use of questions based on the six basic interrogatives—who, what, when, where, why, and how—will help avoid leading the witness.

6.052   Confabulation.

Confabulation is a special word employed in psychiatry and lie detector use to denote the capacity of individuals to manufacture the necessary joining of events in a narrative between known elements of fact in order to make a coherent, believable story. All witnesses who submit to interviews of any variety, whether by voluntary appearance or by subpoena, seek to be believed. The problem of having knowledge of fractured events usually leads a witness to impute the connective incidents that lead from one known fact to another and that make the story logical and less subject to challenge. The legal assistant who understands this phenomena will carefully establish the known facts and allow the interpolated events to be proven by corroboration from other sources.

6.053   Handling the Deceptive Witness.

Sooner or later, the legal assistant will find that he or she cannot reconcile the facts known with the story told by the witness. A tactful questioning technique may fail to develop explanations to account for the discrepancies. Repetition and review may convince the legal assistant that the witness is deliberately and knowingly telling lies, concealing the truth, or misrepresenting the sequence of events. In this event, the interview should be closed, and the legal assistant should consult with the attorney as to what steps should be taken. Referring the matter to the attorney may seem to be an expression of defeat, but it is not. The legal assistant's job is to assist the attorney. When the legal assistant seeks help, he or she is using good judgment if the situation is beyond his or her expertise.

6.06   The Interviewees' Motivation to Speak

6.061   Ego Satisfaction.

Many witnesses derive a high level of ego satisfaction in the public recognition of their knowledge and willingness to testify in any given action. Sometimes it may be limited solely to recognition by the client, an employer, or a small group of people in an ad hoc committee, but sometimes it is even more ephemeral. It is the attention given by people in a different profession who weigh the witness's words as if they were carved in stone and who apparently will rely upon the representation in resolution of a dispute.

The willingness to testify for this reason is never verbally admitted but may be deduced by the legal assistant from the conduct of the witness.

6.062   The Desire to Be Liked.

Some witnesses are speaking solely because they are called and they are going to do what they think the interviewing party wants them to do, whether that person is the client, the attorney, or the legal assistant. Usually, these people are very honest and are most easily recognized by their effusiveness and how they fill conversational blanks if the legal assistant lets the silence build. The legal assistant will notice that the witness will watch the interviewer very closely and attempt to read the legal assistant's mood from facial expressions or the phrasing of questions. Responses are generally directed to improving this transient relationship. The desire is to do what is expected and to be liked for it.

If leading questions are used, the witness will give the answers the questions suggest. The legal assistant should use the six basic interrogatives "who, what, when, where, why and how" to make sure the witness at least generates his own line of suggestion.

6.063   Altruism.

Altruism as a motive in witnesses is undoubtedly present and occasionally identified. More and more, people are rejecting the theory of "not wanting to get involved." They feel that justice must be done, and they are willing to give up facts in their possession, provided it will not be too inconvenient. Usually, these witnesses are relatively objective, they seldom have any interest in the outcome or proceeding, and many times they are strangers to the principals of the case. They are, perhaps, the most credible witnesses the legal assistant will encounter since there is no personal gain at stake. Official witnesses come close to this identification.

6.064   Novelty and Excitement.

Some witnesses, of course, participate only because of the novelty of the event and the excitement of being a part of a form of litigation. It is almost as though they were gathering material to write a book or for the next cocktail party.

6.065   Catharsis.

Some witnesses and many clients find that the interview is an opportunity to purge their souls. It is a form of catharsis and satisfaction of conscience that has been long delayed. They relate everything they know, believe, or suspect about the circumstance. Sometimes they are so effusive that it is difficult to record all of the information they are attempting to provide. Subsequent questioning may reveal the story is a fabrication pieced together by deduction and rumor. The legal assistant should accept this as a reasonable, understandable, and basic human failing, if a time-consuming and frustrating one. There should be no anger or criticism of the witness who suddenly recants the earlier story and makes a clean breast of the situation. This effectively begins the interview all over again with a new set of parameters by which the credibility of the witness is measured.

6.066   Loyalty and Friendships.

The motivation for some witnesses is based on personal friendship with one principal of the case. Some people feel obliged to choose sides, while others, by virtue of some dim process of mental reasoning feel there is a winning side or a losing side and attempt to join the winners. Their testimony, while voluntary, is colored by these motivating factors, and frequently the substance of their testimony is suspect.

Where loyalty is suspected to be leading a friendly witness away from strict bounds of truth and personal knowledge, a discussion of the hazards implicit in the attorney's relying on questionable facts and testimony usually results in reconsideration.

6.067   Extrinsic Reward.

The most difficult motivation the legal assistant will confront is the one that drives the witness to testify for some extrinsic reward. The expert witness, of course, receives a fee; however, there is little personal stake in the outcome of the case, and the expert receives payment for the research, analysis, and testimony needed by the parties, the court, and jury in understanding the case issue.

Other witnesses, however, may find there is a *special* (perhaps secret) reward in being on the winning side. It may be a coveted job with the firm involved in the litigation; it may be a dollar interest in the proceeds of the litigation; it may be a favorable recommendation by one of the principals to some other organization. A typical example would be a criminal case where one criminal testifies against, or on behalf of, another in exchange for immunity from prosecution, recommendations to the parole board, or the promise of employment following release. Family disputes may suffer similar problems, especially if there are estates involved. The legal assistant must avoid suggesting that a witness will receive any extrinsic reward for his or her testimony through the attorney or through the client.

If a witness offers information in exchange for money or other reward, the legal assistant should advise the witness that the decision must be made by the attorney in charge. It is unethical to buy testimony or information. As a practical matter, the source's credibility is poor, the benefit to the case is questionable at best, and the effect on the judge and jury can be disastrous if the purchase becomes known. A witness selling information is an amoral opportunist and probably contacts every party in the case and is prepared to edit his or her information appropriate to the party's interests.

6.07 Questioning Techniques

6.071   Question Construction.

The interviewer should use simple, easily understood words. Use straightforward questions that do not have multiple issues. Each question should generate one answer and should not combine more than one unknown quantity. Use questions that require narrative answers rather than a yes or no.

For instance, consider the question: "Were you at the corner of 15th and A Streets, Seattle, Washington, on February 12, 1991, when an auto accident occurred in which John Doe was injured?" Such a question lends itself to a single-word answer of yes or no. A no answer leads to at least five or six other questions to determine which *part* of the question is being answered. Perhaps the witness was not at that corner; he or she may have been in a building overlooking the intersection. Perhaps he or she was confused as to what the date was and honestly believes that it was not February 12, 1991. Perhaps he or she saw an incident at that location but did not know that John Doe was involved.

The phrasing of questions in a manner that allows yes or no answers can be a mistake. It presupposes an ability to correctly formulate pertinent, relevant, clear questions totally understood by the witness and capable of single-word answers. It is far better to use the six interrogatories—who, what, where, when, why, and how. For instance, ask the question "Where were you on February 12, 1991?" and allow the witness to answer in narrative form. It may be necessary to lead him or her through a sequence of acts over a span of time, but at least concerning the witness's presence in the intersection on the given night, both the interviewer and interviewee understand what night it was and whether or not the witness really was there. Similarly, the question "while you were there, what did you see?" requires a narrative answer that later can be evaluated and clarified with further questions. Questions are designed to elicit information. That requires the witness to talk at his or her own speed and in his or her own language and to create his or her own frames of reference in time, place, and event. Phrase the questions so the witness expresses his or her recollections in an understandable and comfortable manner that provides a solid foundation for successive questions.

6.072   Judgment Statements.

Special care must be used when the witness offers judgment-type statements. These may involve estimates of distance, time, color, or capability of doing or not doing something. For instance, the witness says "He was a hundred feet away." Explore the accuracy of that estimate of "a hundred feet" by having the witness estimate distances. Use easily estimated or checked distance. Many residential city streets are thirty feet wide, curb to curb. Multilane business district streets can be sixty to one hundred feet. Have the witness estimate the distance, *at the scene* if possible, or mark the locations of the important reference points on a witness sketch and then measure the distance. Do *not* let an important witness lock into a footage figure without checking the reasonableness of the distance.

Time estimates can also be dangerous. "It just took a minute" must be explored to determine if "a minute" was sixty full seconds or a split-second, or simply a figure of speech. Ask the witness to recreate the time feeling by saying, "I'll time the full minute; you tell me if it is too long." Use a sweep second hand or a stop watch and sit quietly through the full period the witness estimated. Seldom will it feel correct. Have the witness reenact (role play) the time period he or she felt while it is timed (out of his or her sight). Record the period and discuss this with the witness.

Descriptions can be treacherous if the witness's first offerings are accepted at face value. Have the witness offer a description, then check its salient points. Remember, people are identified by race, sex, age, height, weight, general physical build (slim, stocky, stout, fat, etc), hair color, eye color, and outstanding physical characteristics or distinguishing marks. These latter two characteristics may involve scars, disfigurements, hairstyles, glasses, limping, use of crutches or braces, tattoos, and/or use of cosmetics, wigs, jewelry, and watches.

Physical objects, too, sometimes must be described. Autos and colors are troublesome elements. Red does not mean quite the same thing to everyone. Therefore, it must be well defined. Car makes and models and year of production are very difficult but should be determined, perhaps by visiting a used car lot or new car salesroom with the witness to locate similar or identical cars.

Conduct may require some definition. If the witness says the plaintiff or defendant was "acting strangely," how was the strangeness manifested? Glassy, unfocused eyes? Staggering? Unresponsive to direct questions? Grimacing from pain? Sorrow? Shock? It is difficult to put into words, but easier in the interview than on the witness stand during cross-examination by the adversary counsel.

Occasionally, the witness will be found to have hard evidentiary facts on which to base a statement. For instance, an elderly lady who lived on a street commonly used by teenagers for drag races had developed the habit of timing passing cars between two known points with a stopwatch and mathematically calculating their speeds so she could file a complaint with the police. In an accident case, her testimony was crucial to show proximate cause of the collision. Compare that situation with a group of nondriving teenagers at a hamburger franchise who alleged their schoolmate, though admittedly jaywalking, was struck by a "speeding" truck driver. None of the witnesses was over fourteen years of age, none had any driving experience, none could offer a basis for the "speeding" evaluation, and the physical evidence was in conflict with the testimony.

6.073   Recapitulation.

Following the witness's narration and the legal assistant's subsequent narrative-generating questions, the witness's previous statements should be recapitulated. Restate the major elements of his or her testimony and make certain the witness agrees with the conclusions. This should be repeated until the *witness* is satisfied that the *interviewer* understands what the witness said.

6.08   Special Problems

6.081   Language.

The language the legal assistant uses, the selection of vocabulary, and the ability to phrase questions may not match the language, vocabulary, and level of articulation of the witness. It is incumbent on the legal assistant to seek a comfortable range of vocabulary that will allow an effective, thorough transfer of thoughts and information.

6.082   The Young and the Old.

Very young and very old witnesses pose some special problems.

Children should never be interviewed without the consent of their parents, and they frequently speak more easily if their parents are with them. The presence of a parent complicates the process because a child frequently will watch the parent for guidance or approval of what he or she is saying. It presents an interesting problem for the legal assistant to prepare the parent properly for the interview so the parent will avoid coaching by word, gesture, or attitude how he or she wants the child to testify. One technique is to arrange the chairs so the legal assistant and the child are sitting side by side at the table or desk and the parent is to the rear of the child and out of sight. This does not work if the parent repeatedly interjects comments, however.

It may be necessary to conduct interviews of older persons under circumstances that are a little unusual for the legal assistant. Many times it will be in the home of the witness. Interviewing an aged witness in his or her own environment may be more advantageous than putting the witness to the difficulty of traveling to an office for the interview. This possibility should be considered if a very aged or infirm person must be interviewed.

6.083   Personality Clash or Lack of Rapport.

Incompatibility between the interviewer and interviewee should be promptly identified by the legal assistant. If such a personality conflict arises, a courteous inquiry should determine if the witness would feel more comfortable with a different legal assistant.

The incompatibility may blossom during the interview as a result of the legal assistant's style or manner of interviewing. If possible, identify and modify the cause of the problem.

6.084   Profanity and Abuse.

Occasionally the legal assistant will encounter a witness who cannot speak without being profane or abusive. It is incumbent on the legal assistant to restrain his or her emotions and not reply in kind. The legal assistant's whole purpose is to elicit information, so while the witness's speech may be laced with expletives and offensive phrasing, once the witness is talking, keep him or her talking. The more the witness says, the more information he reveals. The attorney may never use the witness; however, he or she may be able to use the data. The information obtained from the witness may lead to a more presentable witness or source of evidence.

6.085   Correction of Erroneous Information.

It is not unusual to find that the initial interview given by a witness is incorrect or incomplete. A second interview may be needed during which the legal assistant may be able to clarify the erroneous allegations or account of events given by that witness.

Of greater importance is determining the foundation for the error and the witness's motivation for representing the erroneous facts. Generally, when this type of situation becomes known, the witness is very cooperative in resolving the difficulties. But it does result in essentially a dissection of the entire first interview to learn what was in error and what was correct.

6.086   Telephone Interviews.

A special problem is the witness who cannot be seen in person and must be interviewed over the telephone. Recording equipment is recommended. The legal assistant must discuss the use of the recording equipment *before* using it with the potential witness. Permission must be obtained to record the call, and then, periodically during the interview, the legal assistant should refer to the fact that the dialogue is being recorded. At the conclusion of the interview, confirm that the witness agreed to the recording of the interview.

The disadvantage of the telephone interview, of course, is that the interviewer cannot observe the person's appearance of demeanor when answering the questions. As every interviewer will find, the saccadic movements of the eyes and the tendency to blush or look away, among other actions, are symptoms of a *change* in the witness's normal style of conversation and often are indications of embarrassment, confusion, or lying. These manifestations are helpful in evaluating witnesses but are lost over the telephone.

The telephone interview can be very helpful in identifying important witnesses at little expense. If they know little or nothing, the recorded telephone statement eliminates them as potential adversary witnesses or expensive deponents.

For some neighborhood canvassing, official agency file checks, or witness identification and location, the telephone cannot be surpassed in utility, timeliness, or economy.

6.09   The Interview Proper

6.091   The Meeting and the Beginning of Rapport.

From the moment the legal assistant first meets the interviewee, a rapport should be created. The short period of time between first meeting the person in the attorney's office or at the door and taking him or her to the interview site should be a purposeful period in which the legal assistant puts the interviewee at some ease regarding the process to be undertaken and engages in casual dialogue during which the legal assistant gains insight into the personality of the interviewee. The exchange of pleasantries, comments on the weather, inquiries into the traffic situation or how the ball team did are not time wasters but rather exchanges allowing the legal assistant to ascertain the presence or absence of hostility, language difficulties, or the capacities of the interviewee. It permits the interviewee to evaluate the legal assistant to some extent and overcome the initial apprehension inherent in an average citizen meeting one of the mysterious workers in the arcane field of law.

Coffee, tea, or a glass of water may be offered at this time to good effect. It allows the interviewee to do something with his or her hands and to build that little bridge between his or her private world and the legal assistant's private world. Rapport is the relationship of harmony between people working toward a common goal. The legal assistant's appearance, sincerity, cheerful attitude, and demonstrated courtesy and interest in the witness will aid in dispelling the witness's fears and in generating rapport.

If an interpreter is needed, the legal assistant should anticipate this and have one available.

As the legal assistant reaches the point where the interview is to begin, an inquiry into the witness's feelings or objections to recording equipment is appropriate. If recording equipment is to be used, there are some conventions that should be observed when beginning the recording:

(a) The legal assistant (or investigator) introduces him- or herself, gives the date, location and purpose of the interview, and provides the case reference or title; for example, "This is Robert Smith, a legal assistant employed by John E. Jones, attorney for Mrs. Alice Brown, who is the Plaintiff in *Brown vs. ABZ Corporation.* The following will be a tape-recorded interview with Mrs. Brown in a conference room of Mr. Smith's office. Today is April 3, 1989; it is now 10:05 a.m."

(b) The witness to be interviewed should be introduced; for instance, "Mrs. Brown, please state your full name and spell your last name." Allow her to answer. Then ask, "Mrs. Brown, will you allow us to record the discussion we have planned to have today?" The next question may be "Our discussion will deal with the events that gave rise to this legal action. Will you freely and voluntarily relate your best knowledge and recollections of this matter?"

(c) Each person present in the room must also be introduced and asked to respond verbally as to identity, relationship to the case, reason for presence, and willingness to have any and all of their words recorded.

(d) If a tape log is used, the tape identification should be spoken onto the tape, both early (during the initial introduction preferably) and at the conclusion of the tape.

(e) All interruptions of the recording should have the time (hour and minutes) read onto the tape at the point when stopped and the reason for stopping. The date and time of resumption and a brief restatement of the people present should be made when resuming the recording.

(f) Some jurisdictions require that witnesses be supplied with copies of their statements when preserved in writing or by recording. Some witnesses will agree to make a statement only if they can have a copy of it.

(g) At the conclusion of an interview, the legal assistant should reinforce the voluntary nature of the statement and that it was knowingly recorded and ask whether the witness wishes to add, delete, or clarify anything discussed during the interview.

Where the interview may have more than two people participating, it is important that the microphone be positioned to pick up each voice equally. When various people speak intermittently on tape, each person should state his or her name before injecting comments. This allows comprehensible transcription of the tape. This sequence should be followed in a case where *favorable* testimony is anticipated. If the expected testimony may be harmful, it may be better to conduct an oral interview while taking notes. Then if the data is not harmful, it can be capsulized or abbreviated on tape or by a written, signed statement. The attorney directs the technique preferred.

6.092 Beginning the Interview.

Following the introductory period and the attempt to build rapport with the interviewee, the legal assistant begins taking down preliminary data. This process serves to normalize emotion in most interviewees because these things are routine, well-known, not in dispute, yet essential to the identification of the person, the location, the dates, indispensible parties to the matter at issue, and the purpose of the interview.

Now is the time to take custody of copies of photographs, sketches, drawings, or documents that this particular witness may have brought to the interview. Each of these items should be described on the tape and physically identified. If necessary, the legal assistant should have copies made of the documents provided so that either the witness or the legal assistant can read the identification data for each item into the recording equipment and, when necessary, identify the significance of each item while the other reviews a copy of the same material.

6.093 The Body of the Interview.

Usually an interviewee has a preconceived idea or sequence of thought to present. The most effective way of gauging the value of a witness is to encourage a free narration in the form he or she wants to tell it.

The legal assistant takes notes of points that attract his or her attention as needing corroboration or further detail, that are in conflict with other facts already known, or items of information the particular interviewee would have difficulty in obtaining firsthand. The legal assistant's contribution to the story should be supportive in nature, through nods of the head, "and then what" type questions, or saying "Yes?" Many people, once they begin talking, like to talk, and the difficulty the legal assistant may have is keeping the witness from straying too far afield on peripheral issues or irrelevant matters.

Once the interviewee has told the story the way he or she wishes, clarification and explanation can and must be initiated by the legal assistant to separate facts of personal knowledge of the interviewee from those of supposition, inference, or rumor.

Every witness, whether a volunteer or a reluctant one, wants to be believed. This desire to be believed often creates problems for legal assistants, attorneys, and their clients. Witnesses seldom know a full, detailed, coherent story of *all* the facts pertaining to any given transaction or event. Even a client (usually the best source of information on a given matter at issue) seldom knows *all* of the things that occurred and created the disputed matter. Similarly, everyone lives life moment by moment, coping as well as possible with the exigencies of the business, situations, or events. Few take notes, and each tends to relate his or her sad stories to audiences of chance or choice, friends and relatives for instance. It is only human nature to take the known facts and fit them to a scenario that makes sense. This permits coherent stories and the usual feeling of "if it is logical and reasonable, it probably did happen and people who hear me will believe me." This tendency for witnesses to make up facts in order to fill a logical scenario of how a given event happened may cause the legal assistant to evaluate the testimony improperly.

Therefore, once the legal assistant has heard the story offered by the witness, the true interrogation begins. Gentle it is and gentle it should be; however, the points raised by the witnesses must be identified as personal knowledge, inference, or supposition. Search for corroboration of every point of the story through skillful questioning of the witness. One witness may know of other witnesses, remember photographs, recall the use of maps, or identify documents, some of which may be present in the interview room.

An essential element to be covered at this time is whether the witness has previously provided any written or recorded statement to anyone about the case at issue. The firm's policy will determine how the witness should handle any approach by the adversary for an interview. It may be to cooperate or to decline to give another statement, referring the requesting party to the client's attorney. Remember, two inconsistent statements can make an honest witness appear to be lying, stupid, or both to a jury.

6.094   Conclusion.

The interview should be concluded on friendly terms with the understanding that additional information may be needed in the future. Obtain agreement on a completion date of any checklist that the witness has agreed to execute and mail to the office. The legal assistant should put that date in his or her own diary.

The legal assistant should accompany each participant back to the door of the office or to the next person (within the firm) the witness is to see. Never abandon a witness on completing this first interview. *Rapport* is a condition to be nurtured throughout the case, not just the first interview.

6.10   Summary of the Interview

Now the difficult part of the interview begins. The legal assistant prepares a summary for the attorney with a succinct description of the interview and its basic facts. It may be necessary at some future time, if the interview was recorded, to have the interview transcribed fully. Beyond the recapitulation of the important facts both supporting and refuting the client's position, the following additional important elements should be included in every summary of the interview.

6.101   Evaluation of the Witness.

The witness should be characterized in appearance, deportment, language skills, articulation, and the probable impression the witness would make on a judge, jury, or a regulatory board, as the case may be. Of crucial importance to the attorney will be the legal assistant's opinion of whether the witness is credible and truthful; credible but untruthful; *not* credible but truthful; or not credible and not truthful.

These opinions may be based on such indications as inconsistencies in the story, knowledge the witness has no way of having but insists is *direct* knowledge, physical mannerisms the legal assistant interpreted as evasive or signs of lying, or only a visceral disquiet toward the witness. The attorney needs the evaluation and its foundation to supplement his or her own opinion or to alert him or her to areas needing special consideration.

6.102   Elements of Proof.

Every element of proof offered by the witness must be evaluated. The evaluation should be separated into testimonial proof and documentary or demonstrative proof. For each statement that could have a bearing on the issues considered, points of corroboration or points of refutation should be outlined.

Testimonial proof always needs valuation as "inferred," "deduced," "hearsay," or "firsthand, personal" knowledge.

6.103   Possible Remedies, Responses, and Additional Potential Defendants.

The matters discussed between an attorney and his or her legal assistant may include many the legal assistant cannot discuss with the witness or the client, such as potential remedies. The legal assistant, in interviewing the client, always seeks to have the client articulate as many acceptable remedies or recourses as possible. The legal assistant does not *suggest* or *comment* on the probability of success or propriety of pursuing those potential resolutions. To do so verges on practicing law. This hazard does not exist between the attorney and the legal assistant, and the attorney needs the thoughts and comments of the legal assistant, if only as a spur to his or her own considerations.

Identification of potential additional defendants is always important, of course, whether the client is the plaintiff or the defendant.

Investigation, discussion, and mediation of disputes can often resolve the issues without suit. In some cases, the client's position can be advocated for him or her in a forum that has not been considered. And, of course, litigation is always evaluated in terms of the probability of success, provided the original story is supported by additional facts; the possibility of receiving the desired recovery by judgment; and the potential for timely settlement on favorable terms prior to judgment.

6.104   Leads to Witnesses and Evidence.

The last item on the summary should be a list of potential witnesses and/or the documents or objects needed but not on hand. If arrangements can be made to obtain them easily, little comment is needed. However, if time, geography, the technical nature of the matter, or other considerations exist, these should be pointed out.

6.11   Confirming Client Interviews by Letter

Every client interview should be confirmed by a letter to the client, particularly where there is supplementary material being requested and a due date has been established. These items shown in a letter are a great assistance to the attorney and should be written for his or her signature. Due dates should be noted first on the legal assistant's own schedule and then on the attorney's calendar to assure that the follow-up is made.

6.12   Collation of Testimonial Data against the Essential Elements of Proof

The purpose of every interview is to identify the testimonial evidence expected to be used in the course of legal services being provided. Perhaps this evidence, at some future time, will be prepared in the form of a written declaration appended to a pleading or application submitted to a regulatory body. Perhaps it is testimony that will be preserved by deposition or by written interrogatory at some future time. It represents what the witness is expected to say under oath from the witness stand if called upon in the course of trial or hearing.

Every case has certain essential elements, and the testimony of each potential witness must be measured against the elements of proof of the client's case. One of the most effective things a legal assistant can create is a collation or index of facts relating the essential elements of proof for each issue in the client's case to the people who are willing to testify to it. The presence of two, three, four, or five witnesses who have substantially similar views on given points raises the probability that the alleged facts are truthful or untruthful and that the jury will be persuaded by the testimony. This is a basic form of information the attorney needs in making his or her judgment on how to present the case for the client, how many and which witnesses to call, and the points he or she expects each to make in developing the case for the judge or the jury.

Interviewing is a constantly changing challenge and perhaps not a perfectable art form. Just as each case has different facts, any two or three witnesses have individual and different ways of perceiving and testifying to any given fact, event, or proposal. The challenge is obtaining the *truth* from all the talk. Altogether, interviewing can be one of the most satisfying parts of legal assistant work for those who enjoy people and like to listen, think, and talk toward a purpose. The legal assistant's ability, style, and effectiveness should grow with each interview.

7 Investigation

7.00 The Gatherer of Facts

The gatherer of facts in a situation where a client is seeking services or advice from an attorney may be any one of a broad range of people. The attorney clearly has the first responsibility of gathering sufficient facts on which to base his or her opinion as to the proper course of action to pursue. Additionally, since the attorney is not an expert in many other fields, he or she may employ the services of such gatherers of facts as accountants, engineers, doctors, real estate appraisers, or any of the whole gamut of professional people peculiarly suited to provide the special type of information required. In cases where litigation or some form of legal representation or advocacy may be required, the employment of an investigator may be indicated. Investigators may be called "private investigators," "insurance adjustors," "police officers," or "legal assistants." Clearly there may be other titles in other jurisdictions that denote the same function. However, these people are all alike in the purpose they serve. They do not dispense legal advice but take directions from an attorney to follow the legal theory that he or she has created and support or refute that theory through the careful and thorough assembling of all pertinent and relevant evidentiary facts within their ability to locate, identify, corroborate, and report.

Investigation basically is going where specific information is suspected to be, determining whether or not it exists, and collecting it if it does. This may involve searching official records, unofficial records, or quasi-official records of any form, type, or nature. It may involve obtaining the testimony of those people who have direct, peripheral, or hearsay information bearing on the matter at issue. It may involve creating evidence in the form of photographs, drawings, reproduction of documents, models of places, things, and conditions, or preserving physical objects for later use. This is done in an efficient manner, without intending to harass anyone, and solely to accomplish the basic purpose of supplying the attorney with reliable information of a factual nature on which to base his or her legal conclusions and advice to or advocacy for the client. The investigator should be thorough in this fact-finding process. If that is done, the attorney can then select and rely on the information he or she deems important. Investigations should also be conducted in such a way that witnesses are willing to submit to follow-up interviews by either the investigator or the attorney.

7.001 Informal Discovery—Basic Elements.
Investigation is "informal discovery" in the sense that it is a unilateral collection of facts ordered by one attorney, not the court, and without specific notice to the adversary. Whether the investigation consists of one or two letters and phone calls or a full team of field investigators, the basic principles are the same:

(a) Define the issues in dispute.
(b) Identify the essential elements of proof involved in the case.
(c) Identify the facts needed to prove each of the elements.
(d) Analyze the potential sources and locations of evidentiary factual data and/or witnesses that may contribute or impede the establishment of the facts.
(e) Elect the method of investigation most likely to produce timely, reliable results commensurate with time, distance, economy, and the importance of the data to the case.
(f) Find, preserve, and present both the evidentiary facts (with foundation) to the attorney and an explanation of nonavailability of those that could not be obtained or established.
(g) Reevaluate, reinvestigate, and develop data needed and/or revealed right up to conclusion of the case.

7.002   Judgment and Ethics.

In the course of this work, a substantial amount of judgment is required of the investigator. It is not enough simply to produce evidence; it must be done in an ethical and acceptable manner. The investigator should never stoop to burglary, robbery, embezzlement, extortion, corruption of any variety, or blatant misrepresentation in order to obtain facts, physical evidence, or cooperation from witnesses. There is a fine line between dissembling and misrepresentation, but the legal assistant must distinguish it. Particularly in litigation, it is important to be able to go to court with clean hands and an honest case. The legal assistant, even when acting as an investigator, must follow the attorney's policies and guidelines in contacting parties to obtain information, documents and other items connected to the case. If any of the parties is represented by an attorney, the legal assistant must discontinue all communication except through that party's attorney. The investigator, and particularly a legal assistant who is acting as an investigator, works at the direction of and under the control of the attorney. Illegal or improper conduct reflects on the attorney and, in serious cases, may jeopardize his or her right to practice law. Private investigators and independent adjustors usually are regulated by state law, licensed by a state agency, insured, and bonded. Unethical or illegal conduct by them will jeopardize their own businesses, as well as their licenses.

7.01   The Investigation Plan

The investigation plan is a preliminary examination of the problem presented to the attorney and the considerations that are to be made in developing the form of work to be done by the investigator or the legal assistant in generating the information needed to provide the service to the client.

Among the major considerations to be discussed at the outset is whether or not the firm is acting in behalf of the plaintiff, the defendant, or an applicant. The needs are different in most cases, and the time element involved varies widely according to the circumstances under which the investigation is to be made. If the client is the plaintiff, the investigation can be made before the complaint is served and often before a claim is presented to the potential defendant. Most litigious matters begin with the plaintiff's attorney having a tremendous advantage since the only time compulsion is to insure that the claim or case is filed prior to the expiration of the applicable statute of limitations. This usually provides plenty of time in which to perform the investigative tasks necessary to establish firmly the factual foundation of the right of the client to the remedy selected. Another advantage is that the client usually has a substantial number of facts ready at hand. As the injured party, he or she has personal knowledge of the circumstances that caused the action to arise, the names of witnesses, the types of documents involved, and the potential issues that the attorney will define. This is a major headstart for an investigator in assembling the evidentiary facts necessary to proving the case.

The defendant, on the other hand, has a different set of problems. Time frequently is a handicap if the action is one that began sometime in the past and a response is statutorily required within a short period of time. While the plaintiff's investigator could speak freely to each person in seeking witness statements, the defendant now is precluded from talking to the adverse party (or the party's employees) without the agreement of the plaintiff's counsel. Thus a substantial source of testimonial fact is denied the defendant through informal discovery.

Applicants generally are not in a litigious mood but are assembling data required by statute or code in order to comply with the minimum requirements of a governmental entity. Time may be a problem, but it seldom is a crushing load on the investigator. Accuracy and thoroughness are just as important as in any other form of legal action. Intervention in administrative hearings by interests opposed to the applicant's objective is more and more common, particularly where the environmental regulations are involved; these interventions can require "crash" programs to develop information countering the unanticipated allegations of the intervenors.

The plan always considers the possible theories of action the attorney contemplates at the outset. From these, the essential elements of proof can be identified and serve as guidelines to the investigator in seeking out the testimony and factual support for the attorney's positions. The elements of proof are easily obtained in most jurisdictions by consulting the approved jury instructions, the appropriate code or statute to be litigated (or the standards to be met in applications), or the texts and commentary that define the common law actions. Identities, locations, and physical evidence are always critical for the investigator to consider, examine, obtain, and preserve.

7.011   The Plan Outline.

The plan outline always covers the following:

1. What facts are believed known? How can they be proved? Supported?
2. What facts must be corroborated?
3. What evidentiary facts are needed to prove?
4. How do we locate and establish them?
5. Where may the needed evidentiary facts or information be found?
   Federal, state, local governments, agencies, commissions
   Business, trade, and professional associations
   Private firms' or businesses' records
   Public domain sources (libraries, newspapers, TV stations)
   Individuals' files, memories, and knowledge
6. How best can the inquiries be made?
   By telephone
   By letter
   By physical contact, examination, or interview
   Through employment of associated investigators who will perform informal discovery tasks
   By formal discovery methods
7. When must it be available for the attorney?

7.012   Inhibitors of Investigation.

The investigation may be inhibited by a variety of factors, such as cost, the geographic location where the investigation must take place, document volume, or the time available for the work.

7.013   The Cost versus the Value.

The method of investigation has a tremendous impact upon its economics. Obviously, if a legal assistant can conduct the investigation by letter or telephone from the office, the cost will be minimized. If it requires the employment of a special outside investigator on a retainer for a substantial period of time, the cost of proving the elements of the case may outweigh the value of the information. Formal discovery may be more economical and effective.

7.0131 Geography.   Geography can be a barrier to investigation if time or cost is a major element in the choice of technique. Witnesses can be located in remote areas by physically going there and talking to people, examining records, directories, and so forth, but only occasionally can they be located by telephone or letter. Locating relevant documents from large volumes in diverse locations requires time and knowledgeable eyes and is best accomplished by an investigator fully versed in the case background and issues. Telephones and letters are weak substitutes for physical examination.

7.0132 Volume of Material.   If the matter is one involving large volumes of documents for review and analysis, alternative means of accomplishing that task should be explored. Alternatives to it being done internally by the attorney's existing staff include the temporary employment of a special staff for this particular project or the use of the client's own personnel under the supervision of a legal assistant. (See Chapter 9, Litigation Skills, and Chapter 10, Document Discovery.)

If only a few documents are involved, the investigator must be careful to insure that each step of locating and acquiring them is carefully documented to create a foundation for the attorney's later use. The "best evidence rule" requires the original of a given document to be offered in evidence. Only when the original cannot be located may copies be substituted. Some copy may be admissible under the business records exceptions to the "hearsay rules" (Federal Rule of Evidence 803). The legal assistant or investigator cannot make such assumptions or expect the attorney to rely on documents collected without some foundation established by the answers to such questions as: Where was the document located? Who was custodian? Why was the document in the file? If a copy, is it a notarized or certified copy? Where is the original? Where is a duplicate original? Who might have one? The lawyer will also need the legal assistant's opinion of what evidentiary fact the document established. Perhaps in a contract case, it represents a contemporaneous memorial of the requisite "meeting of the minds" or acknowledges the tender of the consideration, or perhaps it is persuasive that the defendant's defense of "mistake of material fact" was not a mistake at all but a well-understood gamble. In a matter in probate, the document might represent support for a contention that the decedent had made a true gift *inter vivos* that should allow an asset to be exempted from the estate.

Each document in a case can be more than informational if the legal assistant continually seeks to locate and preserve the documents that, with proper foundation, constitute evidentiary facts proving or disproving the essential elements of the case, corroborate or refute testimonial evidence, or support or refute the credibility of the witnesses.

The foundation may be established easily at the time the document is found by any of several methods:

1.   In public records, the easiest is to obtain a certified copy from the custodian.
2.   Records of private firms may be obtained with a short statement of the custodian identifying the document, the file, the firm, and the custodian with a notarization of the statement and document by a notary public.

3. Records of the client should be fully identified by file, location and the identity of the person who will testify as to how, why, and where the document was kept.
4. Where certification or notarization is impossible, obtain full details of the document—identity, custodian, file identity, and purpose—for formal discovery proceeding.

The legal assistant never submits a document to the attorney without some foundation for it or without a statement why the legal assistant thinks it is significant, helpful, or dangerous.

7.014   Formal and Informal Discovery and Privilege.

Investigation, as a term, reflects that work done by an investigator or a legal assistant in the informal discovery process for the benefit of the client. This is distinguished from the formal discovery process made available through the code sections of the jurisdiction and the rules of the court in which the case is being handled. Formal discovery procedures are interrogatories, depositions, requests for admission, requests for production of documents, and all of the related law and motion matters associated with those functions. Informal means are those conducted solely for the attorney by his or her employees and without consulting, or needing to consult, the adversary counsel in the process. Much of the information obtained is privileged or "work product," since it is obtained for and by direction of an attorney in contemplation of litigation. The legal assistant and the investigator must insure that they handle all of the material obtained and their reports in a manner that will not breach that privilege. The waiver of privilege is exclusively the right of the attorney. Ruling on privilege is the duty of the court.

The physical evidence, photography, documents, and statements of witnesses (if written or recorded) will not usually be privileged and thus will be available to the adversary through formal discovery. It is a constant fact of life for the investigator to consider when locating information adverse to the attorney's client. The investigator's memorialized recollection or report of examination for the attorney may be the best method of alerting the attorney to the adverse data without creating a discoverable windfall for the adversary.

7.0141   Investigator Notes and Reports.

In the investigation process, the legal assistant or investigator must take copious notes to ensure accurate rendition of the learned information to the attorney. Opinions differ on the preservation of these notes.

One viewpoint is that all the detail is obtained for inclusion in a confidential memorandum to the attorney, and once they have served that purpose, the investigator's notes should be destroyed. The rationale is that notes usually are abbreviated, sometimes cryptic, seldom narrative, and often undated and unsigned. Whether the notes are privileged or not is questionable—especially if used for memory refreshment in any manner. If the privilege protection is lost months or years after the notes were made, the investigator may find that explaining the cryptic, abbreviated entries can be personally embarrassing and/or damaging for the attorney's case. Therefore, the conversion of the notes into a privileged memorandum in full narrative detail shortly after the notes are made is safer and more beneficial to the attorney and without the risk, provided the notes are destroyed. Because even an informal memorandum to the attorney may be subject to disclosure by discovery requests, the legal assistant or investigator should request direction from the attorney before preparing a memorandum.

Seldom must an investigator or legal assistant testify at trial or deposition, but occasionally, he or she may be called upon to explain photos that were taken, sketches that were made, or a physical examination made of the scene or of document files. When this happens, the legal assistant's natural reflex is to review all the documents available to prepare for the proceeding. That reflex may be wrong. Talk to the lawyer first. Remember, anything personally reviewed to refresh a memory may have to be made available to the "noticing" or cross-examining attorney in the formal proceeding. A better procedure is for the attorney to review the memoranda, then interview the legal assistant or investigator in a dry run of the pending examination. He or she can refresh the legal assistant's or investigator's memory with questions while preserving the privilege of the report or memoranda.

7.02   Public Relations in Investigation

Investigation activities create contacts with a wide variety of people in private and public roles. The manner in which the legal assistant impresses them reflects favorably or unfavorably upon the employing office and attorney. The legal assistant's manner of speech and dress, the arrangement and honoring of appointments, the efficiency displayed in the conduct of the business, particularly in public offices, all are dynamic indications to those contacted of the images of legal assistant and the attorney's office. The rule then, of course, is: "Be pleasant, be cooperative, be firm, but be reasonable." Doggedness does not necessarily require rudeness. Thoroughness does not require argumentative behavior. The importance of the matter is no excuse for arrogance by the legal assistant.

If the legal assistant understands and can present an understandable request to others, half the problem is solved. Before asking people for assistance, the legal assistant must have a reasonable grasp of the kind of help expected. If the legal assistant enters a city planning office and asks for assessment information, two people's time (the legal assistant's and the city employee's) has been wasted. Prepare ahead, plan, and try to work efficiently, *in concert* with others, and make reasonable requests. Avoid the "panic" searches, certifications, and/or filings that irritate everyone and reflect poorly on the office.

The people the legal assistant contacts, particularly in public offices, are people the legal assistant can expect to see again and again. "Official witnesses" are people who are custodians of documents and files repeatedly needed. It is essential, for success as an investigator, to meet these people with a deep appreciation of the information they have, their expertise in locating and producing that data, and their willingness to assist the legal assistant's work. Appreciate it, even when their efforts seem feeble, inefficient, or untimely. As with us all, they have personal and professional problems to which the legal assistant is neither privy nor in a position to judge.

The successful investigator is one who hides irritation and accepts help cheerfully, graciously, and with obvious friendly gratitude. The next trip to that office will result in smiles, friendly words, and the best assistance to which anyone is entitled. An arrogant, irritable, or abrasive personality will find that the information sought must leap out of the books, walk down the counter, and sit itself in front of him or her virtually without assistance. Cooperation is the watchword and the essential element any investigator requires from those contacted. The way to obtain it is to give cooperation and consideration.

This does not mean one should be fawning or obsequious. The legal assistant's pleasant assurance that the fair and necessary request will be fairly and fully honored by the responsible party gives dignity and pleasure to both parties in performing their respective jobs.

7.03   In-Office Investigations

7.031   Telephone.

The legal assistant who must gather information within the office is not precluded from conducting investigations. The telephone has a tremendous range and potential for information gathering. It also has handicaps in that the person with whom the legal assistant is speaking is invisible, making it difficult to evaluate credibility solely by the voice tones and words.

Visit the county clerk's office and learn what kinds of records are kept there. Make at least one trip to the courthouse in the company of a more experienced person who will explain the offices in the building and detail the files there. Knowledge of their manner of recording and retrieval could be of great assistance, particularly if the names of responsible persons in the offices are obtained and recorded on a phone list.

Similarly, assessors' offices, public defenders' offices, law libraries, secretary of state offices, the corporation filings offices and others all have tremendous amounts of information and various files that can be tapped telephonically in many cases if the legal assistant knows the questions to ask, the phone numbers to call, and the manner to display in seeking assistance.

The state and federal agencies publish directors of phone numbers (at nominal cost) and usually have a general information number as well to assist everyone in locating the correct source for particular kinds of data.

In some large cities, the local telephone system may have a central directory center where telephone books from its own system and those of participating interconnected systems are available.

Often it is not necessary to call a particular governmental office, commission, or department. Many firms perform research functions for clients within the governmental files of state and federal agencies. Identifying these firms will allow the legal assistant to verify or obtain a wide range of data from such things as drivers' licenses, car ownerships, legislative intents, official filing forms of federal agencies (or other types of governmental entities) to proposed legislative bills. This usually can be accomplished for nominal cost at tremendous geographic distances from the legal assistant's office. The inquiries must be clearly framed as to topic, scope, and acceptable costs *before* they are initiated, or the document expected to cost five dollars worth of paper may grow into several expensive boxes of material.

Sometimes a governmental agency produces periodic reports and sends them automatically to subscribers. For instance, the National Oceanic and Atmospheric Administration, Environmental Data Service, National Climatic Center, Asheville, North Carolina, publishes monthly climatological data, by state, in *certified* form.

If the legal assistant personally achieves a high level of reliability and trust in repeated direct contacts with personnel in such offices and agencies, it will be possible to call a person by phone and ask for a timely search, photocopying, mailing, and billing of specific information. The first time this occurs favorably, the value of past contacts and the personal manner of making them suddenly comes home.

Asking others to search records is efficient and reliable when the volume of material to be screened is small and the facts or issues are clearly defined and easily recognizable.

If the issue or fact is affected by the context of the documents, personal examination is required, and the telephone inquiry should be avoided.

7.032 Correspondence.

Correspondence is another vehicle of investigation from within the office with the added advantage that there is a record created that is easy to follow up in the file. Most offices have created files of form letters of inquiry for basic types of information relating to the kinds of cases they handle. These letters may include requests for such things as medical records from doctors, employment records from employers, accident reports and other reports of investigation from police or regulatory bodies, or studies from governmental agencies.

Witnesses can be contacted with "form" questions that serve to identify those with helpful information. Sending stamped, self-addressed envelopes together with the prepared forms makes it as easy as possible for prospective witnesses to provide the basic information needed to determine whether or not they should be contacted personally for further details.

This technique is relatively inexpensive but can result in varied responses from the addresses. It is not a good technique for important or complex cases where solid evidentiary representations by each potential witness are required.

7.033 Physical Examination.

Physical examination by the legal assistant is the *best* form of inquiry, whether it is reading documents or inspecting the damaged home or vehicle, grazing land, or the scene of an accident. Personal observation allows automatic and reliable comprehension of related testimony, perception of related exhibits, and quick recognition of error, confusion, and mistake.

7.04 Interviewing Witnesses

Chapter 6, Interviewing Techniques, of this manual discusses many of the problems associated with interviewing people who may be witnesses in a given case. We did not at that time discuss the difficulty of locating the witnesses nor the problems presented by conducting interviews at some location other than one under the full control of the legal assistant.

Potential witnesses are identified in many ways. Some are revealed by their names on official records, reports, or within private documents that comprise part of the evidence in the case. Often the client, friendly witnesses, or hostile witnesses will refer to other people who they believe have knowledge of the circumstances. Frequently they do not know the location of the person's residence, and in many cases, the information they do have regarding the individual is stale.

It is advantageous to identify witnesses, locate them, and interview them in the informal discovery process of investigation, since this offers the lawyer an opportunity to determine the extent of the person's knowledge and whether it is helpful or damaging to the client's own position. The formal discovery process of deposing a witness unfortunately requires notice to the adversary counsel of the existence of the person and the possibility that his or her testimony is important to the case. It is also expensive. Therefore, developing systems of locating and interviewing potential witnesses outside the office is an essential ingredient of investigation.

The two main identifying items most effective in locating witnesses are residence and occupation. Once the legal assistant has some idea of the area in which the potential witness resides, the sources that come easily to mind are the telephone book, the voters' register, and the city directory (if the community in which the person lives is served by a city directory service). If none of these sources works out, then inquiry must be made of persons who can reasonably be expected to be acquainted with the person. This may include all of the other witnesses previously interviewed on matters relating to the case and during which discussion they did not mention the person's name. Questions as to the identity and location of the new potential witness may bring forth the fact that the name is misspelled or mispronounced, that it is a nickname, or that it is only a diminutive of the real name. In that case, the legal assistant reinstates the program of checking the phone book, voters' register, and city directory.

Once the general area of the person's residence is located, a house-by-house canvass of the neighborhood may be the only way to develop a specific address, whether current or past. If the investigator obtains an address that is not a current one, the possibility always exists of seeking the assistance of the post office for an address correction. The U.S. Postal Service provides forwarding address data when requested in writing (See Exhibit 26). However, the Postal Service is required only to forward mail to new addresses for one year.

If the potential witness is very important and the usual sources of identification have failed, locating the witness then depends on contacts. The legal assistant usually will have established a wide range of contacts within the business community and may be able to enlist the assistance of utility companies, city services, merchants, or newspapers for the past address. Some of these sources will not release information without a subpoena. The subpoena can be a useful tool, although it may alert adversaries to the purpose of the information being sought. Once a firm name and at least one address for that person is obtained, the credit bureau of the community may provide a reliable source of identifying past and present addresses. Under current laws regarding fair credit reporting, the credit bureau may have to reveal the legal assistant's interest to the individual, but that is not a particular concern in most cases. Motor vehicle and vehicle operator license bureaus often can furnish reliable data directly or through private services at nominal cost.

If the residence cannot be determined, the legal assistant must work through the potential witness's occupation, and the problem becomes much more complex. If the occupation can be tied to a particular company, it sometimes is possible to obtain the address from the personnel department of that company. However, this possibility is diminishing with the right to privacy laws inhibiting the release of information. One possibility, depending on the approach and the reaction of the person to whom the legal assistant makes the inquiry, is to obtain names and phone numbers of persons who were co-workers of the potential witness. These people may be able to provide some idea of residence, current location, and

EXHIBIT 26

UNITED STATES POSTAL SERVICE
Field Division
St. Paul, MN 55101-9998

COA INQUIRY

TO: Postmaster   Date: _____

In Accordance with the provisions of the Freedom of
Information Act, I request the new address of:

        Name:_____

        Old Street Add._____

        City_____State_____Zip_____

Fee: $1.00
Receipt # _____
The $1 fee is not refundable if the address is not found.

Signature:_____

Street Address: _____

City & State:_____

Zip Code:_____

_____
                    FOR POSTAL USE ONLY

_____
Sta/Br or Office

Zip Code_____Rt.#_____

        New Address:_____

                    _____

                              Zip_____

---

whether or not the person whose name the legal assistant has is indeed the potential witness being sought.

Many professions are regulated and/or licensed by the state and regulatory agencies may provide the basic identifying data on inquiry or through submission of an equivalent of the Freedom of Information Act inquiry used with federal agencies. Examples of licenses or regulated professionals and activities are: physicians, pharmacists, private investigators, taxi drivers, land surveyors, certified shorthand reporters, private guard services, lobbyists, real estate brokers, and mortgage brokers.

Unions and union hiring halls sometimes may be helpful through their records or through canvassing people who appear at the halls for job assignments. Professional associations, such as engineering societies, bar associations, legal assistant associations, or academic honor groups, can provide leads to addresses or associates as well.

Occasionally, an avocation can point the legal assistant toward record centers. Bowlers often belong to the American Bowling Congress or the Women's International Bowling Congress. Pilots are licensed by the Federal Aviation Administration. Golfers frequently join state or national golfing associations. College graduates often join alumni groups or booster clubs of their alma maters.

A last resort is to contact others with the same last name listed in local telephone books. It is possible they are related to the witness being sought.

If the witness seemingly has disappeared, there are private detective firms that specialize in "skip-tracing." When the witness is critical to the case, the cost is reasonable.

Once the witness and his or her location have been identified, the problems just begin. Contacting the witness and inducing him or her to discuss the matter and provide a statement are "sometime" things. Unlike the circumstance where the witness may be interviewed in the legal assistant's office, there is little control over the environment of the interview. Frequently, time pressures are upon the legal assistant because the interview is being fitted into the witness's schedule and the legal assistant is seeking cooperation under circumstances where it is not enthusiastically volunteered.

Courtesy, sincerity, and a dogged willingness to adapt the interview to the convenience of the witness will stand the legal assistant in good stead. The interview may be conducted in one room of a home while a noisy fight is going on in another room among the children or their pets. It may be necessary to interview the individual in the kitchen because the television set is operating in the living room. Occasionally, the legal assistant can arrange to interview the individual at lunch time or during a work break and sometimes immediately after work, sitting in the car of the witness or the legal assistant for the few minutes made available.

These conditions, obviously, are not conducive to the contemplative, thorough, and deep-ranging discussions the legal assistant would like to conduct. Furthermore, it may be advantageous to conduct a preliminary oral interview of the individual to determine the extent of his or her knowledge and whether the information is favorable or unfavorable to the client's position before memorializing it on magnetic tape or in written form. If the legal assistant is experienced and trusted by the attorney, the decision to memorialize the interview will be in the legal assistant's hands. This decision often must be made summarily, depending upon the time constraints imposed by the potential witness.

Evaluating the witness in terms of impact on the jury, impact of the testimony on the client's case, and whether or not the witness will change the story under pressure of cross-examination is one of the major benefits of personal contact and interview of the potential witness. The attorney will also be interested in the legal assistant's general impressions of the witness, such as the witness's appearance and how the witness projects him- or herself.

That evaluation should be quickly summarized following the interview, based on those fresh impressions and the legal assistant's best judgment. It should include all the elements discussed in Chapter 6, Interviewing Techniques, and may be amplified by a value accorded to the information the witness possessed. What evidentiary value is the story standing alone? What other evidentiary fact does it corroborate or refute? What conflicts in fact, opinion, or allegation does it create? If you were a juror, would you believe the testimony? The witness? Neither? Or both?

7.041   Special Problems.

As we discussed in Chapter 6, some witnesses create special problems that the legal assistant must consider at the outset. In addition to the problems of taking statements or interviewing children or with particular handicaps, other categories of witnesses will be difficult for the legal assistant in the context of the interview site or because of a witness's temporary physical and/or mental condition.

These include witnesses who are in hospitals or under medication at the time of the interview, who are prisoners in custody, and who are willing to provide information but are unwilling to be identified as the source.

Those latter persons may be government officials who volunteer information that may be in the public purview but by virtue of its obscurity would not be requested in the course of a normal investigation or contacts who, knowing of the legal assistant's particular interest, exceed the limits of their responsibility to assist the legal assistant by generating more information than would be obtainable by a routine request. These contacts are referred to as "confidential sources," and their identity must be protected if the legal assistant agrees to accept their information. The major danger in using confidential sources is the inadvertent exposure of them to others related to the case.

The experienced investigator or legal assistant who has developed confidential sources, whether they happen to be neighbors who are volunteering information of a private and personal nature regarding the adversary's client or government officials who have generated some information from their own and other departmental files, must keep these sources strictly confidential, even from the attorney. This information may be extremely helpful to the legal assistant in determining leads for other investigative steps, but its nonattribution precludes it from being a potent weapon of evidentiary fact in the case. Its value in assisting the legal assistant and lawyer in other phases of formal discovery cannot be measured since it places the attorney in a superior position of knowledge in framing questions for interrogatories or during depositions and in framing subpoenas for production of documents.

7.042   Experts.

Investigations of areas beyond the expertise or personal experience of the investigator will require basic consultation with an expert. This occurs only after the following steps have been taken:

(a)   Identification of the need for expert help. Some cases require help to identify the theory of liability to be pursued, to identify the evidentiary facts to be established, or to analyze or examine some of the evidence involved in the case. Medical malpractice, product liability, construction fraud, and other types of cases require insight into the standards of the industry, common practices, and the type of conduct or procedures suspected of causing the situation at hand. Chemists, engineers, physicists, economists, demographers, and others may be the experts the legal assistant must consult to establish a framework from which the attorney may deduce the existence of a desirable and productive course of legal action.

Later on, damages, compensation, or recourse, for example, may compel the use of other experts to provide insight into the fairness of proposed settlements or to prove those elements to a judge or jury.

(b)   Location of an expert. Law firms often have a list of experts, some for consultation and some for both consultation and use as witnesses. Not all experts are suitable for both purposes, and not all expert witnesses are the most knowledgeable people in their field. When seeking an expert's information, the best expert available should be obtained since the expert will contribute to the attorney's and the legal assistant's understanding of the technical material around which the factual issues revolve.

If the legal assistant must locate an expert without the benefit of an office expert file or recommendations from a knowledgeable source, consider the following:

1.   *The Lawyers Desk Reference* lists expert firms and individuals by their specialty and basic services offered (analysis, examination, exhibit preparation, testimony, and so on), together with addresses and phone numbers.
2.   Public libraries have reference sections, sometimes available by appointment only, where trade or specialty publications can be perused. Experts frequently are authors, and occasionally the legal assistant may be able, through perusal of trade publications and related teaching texts, to learn much of the background of the technical matter while accumulating data on potential experts.
3.   Trade libraries are fertile sources for locating knowledgeable authors. Utility companies, oil companies, merchandisers, contractors, and others often have professional associations or societies that maintain libraries for their members and will allow nonmembers to use the facilities on request.
4.   Universities, colleges, foundations, and think tanks all maintain faculty lists by academic discipline. This information is easily obtainable, often with a biographic sketch for each member, including literary credits and lists of the articles and/or books authored.
5.   Municipal, state, and federal regulatory agencies whose activities impinge on the area or material in which the legal assistant has an interest can be sources for identifying those people with whom they have had experience in administrative hearings.
6.   Professional, academic, trade, and industry associations and societies maintain membership lists that may serve as a starting point in seeking comments on the reputation of their individual members, a beginning in establishing the qualifications of an expert. The legal assistant can start the inquiry of the membership secretary by seeking the "best known" member in that organization.
7.   A review of similar cases, especially where successful results have been obtained, usually will reveal the names of qualified experts who testified in them.
8.   The telephone book can serve as a starting point for locating an expert, provided the community supports the kind of activities requiring the expertise

needed in the case. This essentially is a form of canvassing to find those people who will listen to the problem and volunteer their own services or refer the legal assistant to someone else. It is the least satisfactory of the methods, since many volunteers are not as expert as they believe themselves to be, though they may be very knowledgeable.

Once located, the expert must be made fully aware of his or her function for the attorney, the sources of information he or she can or cannot use, whether he or she is to prepare formal reports or transmit his or her information to the attorney orally from his or her own notes, and the fee and expense arrangements, particularly if there are limitations.

7.043   Obtaining a Statement.

In those instances where an interview is to be conducted of a person known to have favorable information regarding the case and that the legal assistant wishes to memorialize through written or recorded means, a decision must be made. Should the legal assistant make an appointment ahead of time or simply confront the individual under circumstances where the interview will probably be allowed? This decision is a major one, because the appointment process allows the potential witness to do either one of two things, one good and the other bad. The first is to assemble documents, notes, memorabilia, and other materials that will serve as memory aids in the forthcoming interview; the second is to prepare mentally to provide only that minimal information he or she wishes to discuss.

Encountering a witness as a surprise often has the benefit of spontaneity and precludes anticipatory thoughts and considerations of self-interest that sometimes inhibit frank and forthright discussion of the information at his or her disposal. Sometimes the witness suffers the knee-jerk reflex of "I don't want to be involved!" and the surprise is a disadvantage.

The skillful investigator or legal assistant can cope with the adverse circumstances of either of these situations through the application of the techniques we have discussed in Chapter 6, Interviewing Techniques. The first rule of interviewing and statement taking is "get the witness talking." Once talking begins and a favorable rapport has been established, the legal assistant's skill and knowledge should assist him or her in controlling the direction and productivity of the interview.

The decision whether the statement should be written or recorded, or in unusual circumstances, recorded under oath by a certified shorthand reporter, is dependent upon the legal assistant's particular technique and the importance of the matter at hand. In many ways, written statements are desirable, particularly if they are holographic and not simply the legal assistant's paraphrasing of the witness's story. If the legal assistant writes it out, a sufficient number of minor errors must be included in the text to require the witness to correct and initial the errors on each of the pages of the written statement, in addition to his or her signature on the last one. A good technique is to require an initial or signature at the bottom of the last line of each individual sheet to prevent additions and to reflect that the witness did see each page. Frequently, the witness will request a copy of the statement, which, if promised, must be provided. Many jurisdictions require that a copy of the statement be provided the interviewee. The purpose is to prove the witness saw and approved each page of the statement and agreed with it.

The essential information in the statement is the full identity of the witness, including name, age, home, address, occupation, employer, employer's address, work and home phone numbers, and the relationship of the witness to the case or the event at hand. This relationship should be described in narrative form; for instance, as a "witness to the event," as an "accountant in the accumulation of records regarding the costing of the project," or as a "participant in the discussions which resulted in the agreement," the breach of which caused this particular action. A statement must be included that the interviewee is providing the statement freely and without coercion or promise of reward.

If the statement is being recorded, there must be an acknowledgement at the beginning (and at the end) that the tape recorder, disc recorder, belt recorder, or whatever other device used is being operated with the knowledge and agreement of the witness. The full identity of the participating personalities is dictated at the beginning as well. This includes the legal assistant and anyone else whose voice is interjected on the record. The location at which the statement is being taken should also be identified. Mention should be made of observers, their identity, and their reasons for being present. For instance, if the interview is with a child and the parent is present, this should be indicated on the statement form, whether written or recorded. Any individual, who is identified at all is identified as fully as the basic witness, excepting the legal assistant who usually is identified as "Albert Investigator employed by attorney (name) inquiring into the matter of (case title) or (incident description)."

A helpful technique, time permitting, is to play back the entire taped statement to the witness and then record a supplementary dialogue that may resemble this: "This is Albert Investigator again. We have reviewed the entire tape and Mr. Witness, do you recall anything you would like to add, clarify, or amplify? Does anything come to mind that has been omitted? Did you have any trouble understanding what was said on the recording? Is that a fair and clear account of what you recall at this time concerning the case?"

Naturally, the legal assistant seeks a verbal response to each of such questions and then audibly states the interview is being terminated "at (time) o'clock on (date) in the (home of witness)."

One of the major objectives in statement taking is the identification of other persons who have or may have knowledge of the issue or access to data important to the case. No interview is complete without asking the individual to search his or her mind for the names of others who know anything about the circumstances discussed in the interview. Whether or not the legal assistant will be able to locate each of those people should not be a consideration in making the request of the witness being interviewed. Ask for sufficient data to provide leads as to where people are and/or how to contact them. It is truly surprising the number of people who have phone numbers, addresses, old envelopes, and such memorabilia that will assist you in this task.

Even nicknames, diminutives, or first names, without any other data, may be of help later on. Take notes, preserve the information, or record the interview. The pieces all fit together sooner or later.

After the statement is taken, it is also important to learn from the witness of any other statements he or she may have given (written, recorded, or otherwise), who took the statements, and what questions were asked of the witness.

Statements in memorialized form may be used before or during trial. Before trial, the recorded statement allows the accumulation of and reference back to all facts without the distortions caused by loss of memory or remoteness in time. At trial, statements (whether sworn or not) may be used to impeach the testimony of witnesses who testify differently on the stand than they did during the interview. Impeachment is an attack on the truthfulness of the witness. This potential value cannot be minimized since juries frequently determine cases on the credibility of witnesses as it is displayed to them from the stand.

7.044   Negative Statements.

Negative statements are those that are passively helpful in the case and not adverse to the client's interest. In many incidents, there are a great number of potential witnesses who *might* have seen the event in its early state, during its actual occurrence, or only its aftermath. Such incidents as disputes in a neighborhood, fisticuffs in a bar, or automobile accidents usually have a number of potential witnesses around the scene. Few of them actually see or have knowledge of evidentiary value for either side in the case, but all should be asked what, if anything, they saw. The majority will give negative statements. This requires the legal assistant conscientiously to attempt to locate each potential witness by canvass interview. The simplest method is to carry a tape recorder and contact everyone in the area who conceivably might have seen the accident, identifying each one and obtaining a statement from him or her that he or she either "did (or did not) know anything about the case," "did (or did not) see it," and "did (or did not) know anyone who did see it or know anything about it."

This type of canvass is sometimes known as the "neighborhood check," but since it may involve such activity as consulting the patrons of a bar, the workers in a plant, or the patrons of a public park, that term may be misleading.

The canvass must be done at the same time of the day as the incident occurred and on the same day of the week, at a minimum, though several passes are preferable. Many potential witnesses in any given incident "cycle" through a neighborhood or a particular location in the course of their normal duties. Newspaper and mail carriers, delivery truck drivers, children going to or coming from school, and commuters all follow roughly the same paths at particular times of the day or on particular days of the week. If the legal assistant conducts a neighborhood check at two o'clock in the afternoon for an incident that occurred at two o'clock in the morning, the legal assistant clearly will miss those cyclical people whose schedules do not meet the one the legal assistant is imposing on the scene.

When attempting to identify potential witnesses, the legal assistant lets his or her imagination run rampant. In an accident case with very few witnesses, explore the possibility that door-to-door salespeople, real estate solicitors, or customers at a gasoline service station may have knowledge of the incident. In the course of this work, the legal assistant becomes certain that investigation follows the truism of "90 percent perspiration and 10 percent inspiration." Leg work, leg work, and checking, checking and double-checking is the formula for effective investigation.

7.045   Questionable Statements.

There are other circumstances where valid, evidentiary statements cannot be taken, and among them, although this is a judgment decision in each case, are those involving individuals suffering such extreme emotional shock that they are not coherent; people deeply under the influence of alcohol or other drugs; patients suffering the effect of medication that tends to isolate them from reality; and people of obviously questionable mental stability or development. If the legal assistant elects to take statements from such people, they must be qualified with a full description of the circumstances under which they were taken. Usually the decision will be to proceed with the statement if the process does not adversely affect the witness; the attorneys can argue value later.

7.046   When Not to Take a Statement.

The memorializing of adverse information from a witness, whether friendly, neutral, or hostile, usually is not desirable. Formal discovery procedures usually require the production of all nonprivileged statements when requested by the adversary. Witness statements usually are not privileged. Client statements may or may not be privileged, depending on the form and manner in which they were taken.

Even if the legal assistant knows an individual is lying, memorializing the adverse information in that statement is not usually in the best interests of the case. If the legal assistant knows the witness is lying and can prove it, he or she should save that ammunition for a later time, when the adversary introduces the witness, for instance.

The legal assistant cannot take a statement from nor interview in depth any person who is *known* to be represented by counsel in *the matter at issue*. If the legal assistant begins an interview without knowledge that the individual is represented, he or she should continue that interview until such time as a statement or notice of representation is made by the individual. At that time, especially if the interview is being recorded, the legal assistant must clarify the record to the extent that legal representation was unknown until that moment and then ask the individual to identify his or her counsel fully, the circumstances of the representation, and whether or not it is related to the matter at issue. If it is, the legal assistant must immediately terminate the statement and advise the employing attorney of the situation.

7.047   Formal Statements.

These occur in many cases of advocacy or litigation where an affidavit, a declaration, or a sworn statement are of value. Each of these documents has certain utility in different procedures and should be part of the legal assistant's consideration in an investigation plan. A declaration is simply a written statement prepared and signed by an individual that includes a statement that it is voluntarily made under penalty of perjury. Frequently, these declarations are drafted by the investigator or the legal assistant, read, edited, approved, and executed by the declarant. They may be attached as exhibits to filings in law and motion matters or in applications to regulatory agencies, petitions for rights, and so forth.

Affidavits are statements taken under oath by a certified shorthand reporter or signed under oath in the presence of a notary public.

It may be necessary to interview someone geographically removed from the site of the office or the trial location under circumstances where the legal assistant wishes to preserve that testimony for later use at trial. If so, it is necessary to move out of the informal discovery phase and into the formal discovery device of depositions to allow the adversary to participate in that interview. The ability to cause a witness to leave the normal place of residence or business and report to another place for such sworn statement by subpoena is limited by the statutes of the jurisdiction. Sometimes a witness will volunteer, provided expenses are paid, to make a trip beyond subpoena range. However, such expenses may be substantial and include travel, meals, and lost wages as well as the statutory witness fee, if any.

The affidavit differs from the deposition primarily in that the adversary has no opportunity for cross-examination. Thus, the affidavit may at some time be useful but does not have nearly the impact or admissability of the deposition. When considering the use of sworn testimony, the legal assistant consults the attorney to determine the utility of the desired document.

7.05   Obtaining and Preserving Evidence

Evidence is that testimony or material that proves or tends to prove a specific fact. It may be testimonial in the form of the personal recollections of a person with firsthand knowledge of the matter; it may be documentary in the form of letters, notes, memoranda, tape recordings, photographs, movie strips, videotape, microfilm, or other recorded and retrievable information.

Evidence may be physical, such as a broken mechanical part, skid marks on the ground, an appliance that did not work correctly or failed to work at all, or, the tools or devices used to commit the offense that is the subject of the action.

Evidence also may be demonstrative. Demonstrative evidence includes sketches, diagrams, maps, models, reconstruction, tests, or pieces of equipment identical to the time involved in the case.

7.051   Identification.

Identifying potential evidence is perhaps the most difficult duty of the investigator. An investigator at an accident scene works under certain time constraints before the cleanup activity begins, and there is always a substantial amount of confusion regarding the circumstances of the event as well as the number and variety of people interested in the matter. Police, fire department, and public safety personnel all have responsibilities in any accident involving major property damage or injury to life.

The first step most investigators follow at an accident scene is to preserve that scene as best they can through immediate photography and/or sketches. This frequently requires a quick orientation sketch on which a diagram of the camera angles and distances is plotted. (See Exhibit 27.) One technique for creating good proportionate sketches is to carry a quad-ruled tracing paper pad. After a basic sketch with the major geographic features (whether of an intersection or a room) is made, it is torn off the pad and slipped beneath the next sheet. Retrace the major features and add the specific data desired for that sketch. One sketch may be the photo reference sketch; another might be the positions of the vehicles (if it is a traffic collision); and a third may be a clear basic sketch with the data supplied by each percipient witness. That data might include the location of the witness, the first point at which the witness saw each vehicle, and the locations of other vehicles or witnesses. These witness sketches can be amplified by adding trees, shrubs, buildings, parked vehicles and supplemented by the investigator standing where the witness was to determine whether the story of the witness is physically possible. A composite sketch can be used to locate each witness graphically. (See Exhibit 28.)

The diagram may be used to record such things as skid marks, significant buildings, vegetation, safety control devices, and the relationships of the objects involved in the incident. At an explosion scene, for instance, where a gas heater is considered to be the origin of the explosion, a photograph including both the

EXHIBIT 27   Photograph Index Sketch

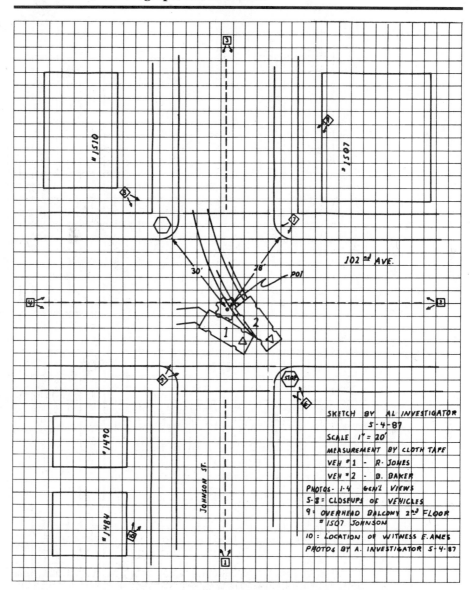

thermostat and heater in one picture is desirable, if possible. If not, a sketch must be used to carefully reconstruct that relationship, keying the multiple photographs together with the sketch.

At accident scenes involving automobiles, the locations of the road ways, traffic control devices, visual obstructions (trees, fences, bridges, parked cars), skid marks, point of impact, and positions at rest of the involved vehicles are essential. While photographs can do this to a certain extent, detailed sketches are also necessary. (See Exhibit 29.) In extremely important cases, these details should be surveyed

EXHIBIT 28   Witness Location Sketch

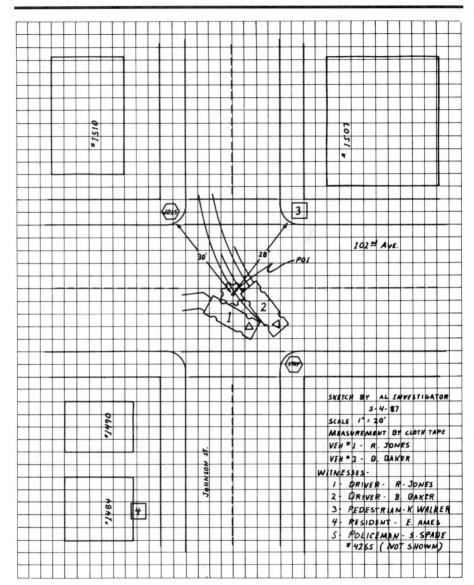

by a qualified surveyor to ensure the accuracy and later admissability of the sketch at trial.

Unfortunately, the investigator is rarely able to get to the accident scene before the vehicles are removed. The investigating police department usually makes a diagram of the accident scene, which is attached to the police accident report. Such a report and diagram can be obtained from the police department and will assist the investigator in creating additional sketches. Police departments also sometimes prepare accident reconstruction reports and diagrams that can be excellent resources for scale drawings.

EXHIBIT 29   Basic Scene Sketch

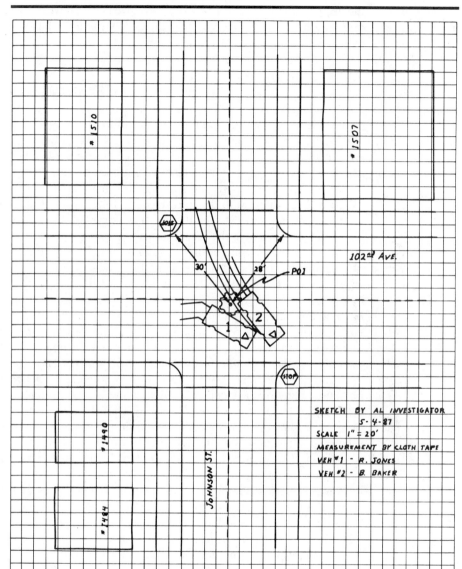

7.052   Physical Evidence.

Every time an object is identified as potential evidence, the investigator faces the problems of how to acquire, preserve, and identify it for future reference and retrieval for introduction at trial, and create the foundation for its admissibility. In many cases, the investigator does not have legal title to the evidence he or she wishes to take into custody. Frequently, the ownership of the item is in question, and the propriety of taking custody calls the investigator's judgment to the test. In most cases of doubt, take custody of the documents, objects, or things and leave a receipt indicating the investigator's name and identity and the means by which people can contact the investigator if they wish to exert their ownership rights in the matter. Often police, fire, or safety investigators will be on the scene, and notification can be left with them if they allow the investigator to take possession of the item.

7.053   Control and Retrieval.

Possession of the item of evidence carries the responsibility of control and assuring the future identification of the object as being *that very item*. The investigator imposes upon the object some minor but unique marking to allow absolute and unequivocal identification of that particular object as being the one taken into custody on the date and at the time involved. The investigator thus must create a document that details the manner of taking custody and of marking this item for future reference as well as establishing the first step in the chain of evidence, which will terminate with the introduction of the item at trial. Many investigators carry copper wire and lead seals with a sealing tool. The wire is passed around the object, then through the seal. The sealing tool squeezes the seal tightly around the wire and can impress designs, a logo, or numbers on the soft lead. For larger objects, nylon cable-ties can be obtained in a range of sizes. Some objects are too large or unsuitable for such seals, and a unique marking can be engraved on the object; initials and the date are best. Small objects can be placed inside plastic bags or envelopes and sealed with tape on which the date and initials can be written. Any system may be used, so long as it provides a means of distinguishing that one object from all others similar to it and a credible basis for testifying that the object is the one collected as evidence on a given date.

From the time that object is identified as potential evidence, its custody must be substantiated by a document trail showing every transfer of custody from the point of the incident or event to the trial. That chain is based on the investigator or legal assistant creating that first step in proper, ethical, and careful manner and recording each subsequent transfer in detail.

Caveat: Documents pose a special identification and storage problem for the investigator. They are most valuable to the attorney in their unaltered state. Yet the investigator usually must attach them to a report, describe them, provide a foundation for their use, and refer to them as "attached." When the document is a letter, written memorandum, or pamphlet, many investigators mark the document "EXHIBIT _____" or "ATTACHMENT _____" and staple it to the report. Convenient? Yes! But very poor technique, since the attorney now has an *altered* document, and the convenient title "EXHIBIT _____" or "ATTACHMENT _____" must be explained in the future.

A better technique is to place the document in a transparent envelope (or even an opaque paper one) and apply the "EXHIBIT _____" or "ATTACHMENT _____" label to the envelope together with a thorough description of the document (date, document type, author, addressee, topic or title, number of pages, and any attachments), as well as a short statement of the source of the document, the custodian, and the relevance of the document to the case. Alternatively, a "face sheet" can carry this information. A photocopy of the document can be used as a "work copy" during preparation of the case.

Underlining, marginal annotation, or writing on the document cannot be allowed to happen to the *original* document (whether the true original, a duplicate true copy, or a photo copy). *Evidence* must be preserved in the *discovered state*. If a copy is made, it *must be marked as a copy,* preferably with a marginal label

"Copy of a document in the file ＿＿＿ vs. ＿＿＿." This avoids the problem of creating yet another piece of *evidence* that could confuse the future admissability of the original document at the trial.

Other forms of documents, such as movie films, tape recordings, even photographs are not quite so susceptible to contamination as paper documents; however, safeguards should be considered for any item that may become evidence at trial.

7.054   Storage.

Once the document or object is in custody, it cannot simply be placed in a file cabinet in an uncontrolled environment where anyone can obtain access to it, remove it, alter it, or damage it. Therefore, the investigator or the attorney must provide a safe and controlled environment within which the object is stored. Each event between the time of taking custody and its introduction to trial where people wish to examine the object should be recorded in detail to include the date and time, the person authorizing the particular examination or movement, the person benefiting from such activity or movement, the duration, and the return of the object to the place of storage. Anyone taking possession of the object must sign for it with a statement that it will be safeguarded and returned or preserved in the exact same condition. Polaroid photos may be appropriate for memorializing the transfer. A suitable form for controlling evidence is shown on Exhibit 30.

EXHIBIT 30   Evidence Log

Evidence Log			
Case:		Event:	
Evidence:			
How Acquired:		Date:	
		By:	
Identifying Marks:			
	By ＿＿＿＿＿＿＿＿ Date ＿＿＿＿＿＿		
Storage Location:			
Custodian	Date	Released To	Date/Purpose

7.055   Testing and Examination.

Often evidence connected with an event over which litigation is to transpire must be tested, examined, or disassembled to validate it as evidence. Sometimes the examination, disassembly, or test will damage or destroy the object. If this situation arises, the attorney will ensure that the adversary and all other parties to the action have an opportunity to have representatives present. The investigator generally is charged with taking custody of the item, removing it to the place of examination, and documenting the steps of the examination. The purpose of the examination and the anticipated method should be planned and the scenario described and noticed in timely fashion to all parties of the action to allow them or their experts to participate or observe the necessary examination. The whole process may be recorded through the use of still photographs, movies, or videotape. The investigator records the presence of all witnesses, including their full identification and their association with their respective parties in the matter. All experts should be fully identified as to name, address, specialty, and employer. Remember, any examination, testing, or disassembly of the item that destroys or changes the physical characteristics of the item and is not accomplished with the knowledge, consent, and participation of all of the parties may prevent the use of any developed information at trial.

7.06   Surveillance and Activity Checks

Occasionally, there will be a need to verify the activities of certain parties to a lawsuit. This type of investigation is usually done when plaintiffs or claimants are alleging disabilities that either preclude them from certain activities or limit abilities to perform particular tasks.

Surveillance should be conducted by trained investigators who have the experience and equipment to properly perform this type of investigation.

Sometimes the alleged disabled party can be caught working around the yard or involved in sporting activities with little or no sign of physical limitations. A serious limp that was quite obvious in the doctor's office sometimes can miraculously disappear outside. Videotaped proof of these activities can be later used in the courtroom to raise questions of truthfulness in regard to the alleged disabilities. However, this kind of investigation may be expensive and may yield no useful information.

Divorce and child custody disputes may require "domestic" surveillance. In states where grounds for divorce are required, surveillance may be used to establish the needed evidence to determine certain grounds, such as adultery. Surveillance in child custody cases may yield helpful evidence regarding the fitness of the adverse parent.

Activity checks are usually conducted by talking with neighbors or other persons who make frequent observations of the plaintiff or claimant. Though these checks may provide helpful information, they will often alert the plaintiff or claimant that an investigation is being conducted. For this reason, activity checks should be done as the last or later part of the investigation.

7.07   Demonstrative Evidence

Demonstrative evidence in the form of sketches, drawings, or surveys created as a means of preserving transitory physical evidence in retrievable form will require a certain amount of documentation for use at future times. The presence of a scale and the date and the name of the person who rendered the drawing is essential. The means and method of making the measurement represented in the drawing will be subject to question and must be supported by the proper foundation. The date of the examination and measurements is essential, particularly if it is different from the date of the event in question. It is helpful to support these drawings with photographs of the same area.

Demonstrative evidence that is a model, a replica, a reconstruction, or an exact duplicate of the object involved in the case requires the same establishment of the dates, times, scale, methods of calculation, sizes, and measurements. The accuracy of the representation probably still will be subject to questioning. Many of these demonstrative evidence procedures are very expensive and obviously should be discussed with and authorized by the attorney before they are undertaken.

7.071   Sketches and Drawings.

Certain injury litigation cases and regulatory agency actions can benefit from the use of renderings by artists. Medical illustrators are talented at clarifying what otherwise might be very difficult explanations of X rays (even if produced as positives) by converting them into easily understood colored drawings at relatively little cost. Illustrators can show a proposed development or project in simplified (even idealized) form to assist the presentation for permits, zoning actions, and so forth.

7.072   Photography.

Photography is both a blessing and a curse in litigation. It is a truism that almost any photograph related to an event is potentially admissable at trial. The opposite side of the coin is that almost any photograph may be subject to argument over its admissability. The judgment of the person taking the photograph and his or her expertise are always subject to question. The average investigator or legal assistant who chooses to take his or her own photographs rather than to employ professional photographers must be prepared to defend the representations in the photographs. For this reason, many investigators have resorted to snapshots taken with simple, nonadjustable or instant cameras. If the investigator is an expert, he or she understands that the use of an adjustable lens camera that allows shooting wide-angle, normal-angle, and telephoto views of the same scene alters perspective as focal length changes. In order to ensure that the investigator defend the photographic representation, he or she should employ some form of photo log.

For every photograph taken, the focal length, f-stop, film speed, film type, filters, and whether or not artificial lighting equipment was used should be recorded. If possible, each photograph should be related to a sketch indicating the location of the camera and the direction it was pointed to get the view in the photograph. (See Exhibit 27).

The use of filters is arguable at best and difficult to explain to a jury. At worst, the photograph will be excluded. If filters are used, an unfiltered shot of the same view should be made. A great deal of judgment must be exercised by the investigator or legal assistant in deciding whether or not to shoot photographs.

Obviously, if the client is a plaintiff and the accident investigation involves an automobile collision with injury, photographs of the amount of blood spilled in the vehicles may be desirable. If the client is a defendant, gory photographs can be no help at all. It is not enough to take them and destroy them because then the photographs and the destruction must be explained. The skilled legal assistant considers the evidentiary value of each photograph he or she intends to take—both its benefits and its detriments—and then decides whether the benefits outweigh the detriments.

Counsel for plaintiffs often find photographs of bodily injuries very early in the incident are shockingly persuasive to the jury to demonstrate the obvious pain and suffering caused by the injury. It is important to consider the type of camera and film used in making these photographs. For instance, a black-and-white photograph of a person showing massive bruises of an extremely dark nature may be the result of the use of film specially sensitive to the color red and generating a higher contrast than otherwise may be present. Similarly, color photographic film can have show red, blue, or green very strongly, depending on the representation desired by the person taking the photograph.

The use of lighting will often have an effect on the photograph. Daylight provides one form of reflected light accepted, while incandescent light tends to throw a warmer red-toned color on the same object. Fluorescent light tends to provide more yellow-green, and flash bulbs, depending on their size and nature, affect the color quality of the image produced. Infrared film can be highly informational in cases involving vegetation growth, decline, and death or in heat gain and loss disputes.

When the investigation begins some time after the incident, a wide variety of sources of photographs should be explored. The police often take photographs, as do fire departments, coroner's officers, and newspapers, wire services, and freelance photographers. The more important, dramatic, and longterm incident produces a veritable flood of photographs to which the legal assistant can gain access. Occasionally, a neighborhood canvass can locate snapshots of the immediate area.

It is always possible, and often desirable, to employ a professional photographer to take selected photographs for specific purposes. They are relatively expensive, but professionals can usually qualify their photos for introduction as evidence. Be specific in the request for the number, sizes, type of film, and views desired. Every photograph should benefit the case or the understanding of the jury.

Do not ignore the possibilities of overhead views obtained through aerial photos from a wide variety of sources. The U.S. Coast and Geologic Survey has a tremendous collection of recent and historical aerial photos in different scales. The U.S. Department of Agriculture, too, uses aerials in its studies. Forestry departments, state and federal highway projects or departments, city and county public works and planning departments turn more and more to aerial photographs for planning, zoning, and traffic study work. Many have aerial photographs of diverse locations. Any area subject to land management or reclamation probably has been photo-mapped by the U.S. Department of the Interior. These governmental sources generally provide fine, full-frame prints at nominal cost but with a bureaucratic time delay problem. Using private aerial photograph sources often permits enlargements of all of a negative or only a portion, at the lawyer's election. The cost is a little greater for the custom work but is well worth it.

Individually, photographs from an upper-story window or rooftop can be helpful. A photograph from a chartered airplane may be desirable. It is difficult for these photographs to be used to scale, however, and that is one of the major benefits of professional aerial photographs—the exact determination of scale.

7.08   Preserving Recorded Statements

Earlier in this chapter, and in Chapter 6 on interviewing techniques, the use of recording equipment for statement taking was discussed, together with its benefits and hazards. The preservation of the recorded statement is a special problem since it is a form of evidence. A special storage facility for such recordings should be maintained, together with a numbering system, a log, a cross-reference to the case file, and a suspense device to dispose of the recording following resolution of the case. An easy system combines the last two digits of the year, the initials of the investigator, and the number of the tape (an increasing sequential series) to be affixed to the tape. (See Exhibit 31).

7.073   Video.

The video camera is quickly becoming a very valuable investigative tool. It is useful in illustrating accident scenes, roadway views taken from a vehicle traveling on the roadway, statements of witnesses, depositions of expert witnesses not available to testify at trial, and "day in the life" videos of disabled plaintiffs.

Accident-scene videos should adhere to the same standards required of regular photographs. When illustrating roadway views, the camera operator should be prepared to testify about the position of the camera and the general speed of the vehicle while the recording was being done.

Witness statements will be taken under the same general rules as the audio-recorded statement.

Videotaping of the expert witness, such as doctors, should be done according to state or federal rules of procedure. Most rules will demand that the operator of the video equipment make an opening statement, on camera, prior to the beginning of the deposition. The operator is usually required to state his or her name and address, the date, time and place of deposition, the caption of the case, the name of the witness, the party on whose behalf the deposition is being taken, and the party at whose instance the deposition is being recorded on an audiovisual recording device. After completion of the video, the operator should complete an affidavit stating the length of the deposition and that the videotape has not been altered nor edited in any manner.

"Day in the life" videos should be recorded in the natural environment where the disabled plaintiff can illustrate daily routines. The video should, in a discrete manner, show the plaintiff in general daily routines, such as getting out of bed in the morning, taking care of personal hygiene, preparing and eating meals, and doing other chores. These videotaping sessions should not be rehearsed. Opposing counsel should generally be given notice that such videotaping will be done. These "day in the life" videos can be very instrumental in representing to a jury the plaintiff's life in terms of pain and suffering and his or her general loss of enjoyment of life. While the scenes may be unpleasant, so are the plaintiff's injuries.

7.09   Discovery through Investigation

The informal discovery (investigation) by the legal assistant or the investigator is primarily to assist the attorney in developing the lines of inquiry that should be followed in formal discovery and in evaluating the responses of the adversary to the questions and motions posed in the formal discovery actions.

EXHIBIT 31 Tape Log Slip

Case Number and/or Name				Recorded By
Day, Hr. & Date		Tape No.		Reel Size:
Recorder No. & Type:			Tape Speed 7½ 3¾ 1⅞ ¹⁵⁄₁₆ S	
Typing Requested		By	Reason	
Typed By:		Trans. No.:	Date Typed:	
Counter Rdg.		Description of Recording		
Side 1	Side 2			
		Date of Accident RECORDER LOG SLIP FIELD OPERATION		

EXHIBIT 31 Completed Slip Sent to Typist for Transcription of Tape

Case Number and/or Name *Jones v. Baker* *Sup. Ct 91-4880*				Recorded By *A. Smith*
Day, Hr. *Monday 4:30 pm* & Date *July 29, 1991*		Tape No. *91- AS -37*		Reel Size: *Cassette*
Recorder No. & Type: *Sony SK-9*			Tape Speed 7½ **3¾** 1⅞ ¹⁵⁄₁₆ S	
Typing Requested *9-14-90*		By *B. Lawyer*	Reason *Comply w/discovery*	
Typed By:		Trans. No.:	Date Typed:	
Counter Rdg.		Description of Recording		
Side 1	Side 2			
00-246 *246-250* *250-end*		*Statement of Ed Ames, eyewitness to accident* *Blank* *accident scene description* Date of Accident *5-21-91* RECORDER LOG SLIP FIELD OPERATION		

Remember, no item of evidentiary fact will stand alone at trial. Each fact needs corroboration, and one of the best ways of corroborating a fact is to ask questions of the adversary under oath. Whether this is done through interrogatories, requests for admission, or in depositions is the choice of the attorney. Each is effective.

Investigation provides the basis for specific and explicit questions to be posed to the adversary. It changes interrogatories from broad-based, shotgun, or generalized questions to specific, detailed, pointed inquiries of specific interest.

Further, the investigation serves as a fountain of knowledge to assist the attorney in creating the deposition plan for any potential deponent. Statements taken of adversary witnesses often can be used in preparing the attorney to generate sworn testimony and depositions that might otherwise be overlooked. They will reveal motivation, relationships, background, and post-incident activities of intense interest to the attorney. The rule is to know as much about the witness and what he or she is going to say, before the questions, as it is possible to know. The use of testimonial statements, physical evidence, and photographs are essential to proper preparation of the attorney for the confrontation in the deposition procedure.

7.10   Service of Subpoenas

Investigators and legal assistants may also be requested to serve subpoenas on witnesses needed to testify at hearings or trials. Although a favorable witness may offer to testify without a subpoena, one should still be prepared and served on the witness. Once witnesses are subpoenaed, they are no longer appearing in court voluntarily, which might have made their testimony suspect as biased witnesses. Applicable state or federal rules should also be reviewed so that the proper witness and mileage fees are tendered to the witness when he or she is served. The legal assistant or investigator should also check the rules regarding the manner in which subpoenas can be served and by whom.

Subpoenas should also be served on witnesses even if they have already been subpoenaed by the adverse side. This is done to ensure the witnesses will appear on your behalf since the adversary may later tell the witnesses they are not required to appear under the subpoena issued by the adversary.

Subpoenas should be served far enough in advance to allow witnesses sufficient notice to arrange their schedules for the appearance date. The subpoena should be thoroughly explained to the witness. Frequently, the subpoena date and time merely reflects the starting date of the trial. Arrangements should be made with the witness on how and when to contact the witness (by obtaining work and home telephone numbers) to advise him or her of the actual date and time his or her testimony will be required.

The attorney may also request the investigator or legal assistant review with the witness before testifying any prior statements given by him or her. This may be accomplished by allowing the witness to review any prepared transcript of his or her statement or by reinterviewing the witness.

7.11   Investigation of the Jury Panel

Every jury panel may be obtained from the jury commissioner prior to the scheduling of a specific courtroom and date of trial of any particular case. Usually, the list is two hundred or more prospective jury members. The investigator may be called upon to vet the jury panel. Many firms now obtain jury commissioner lists and create limited background information on each jury member. These reports can be purchased, and if a firm handles a high volume of trials in one city, it may

be a wise investment. To vet or investigate the members of the jury panel individually is not particularly difficult, but it is expensive and time-consuming.

Obvious sources are voters' registers, tax records, credit bureaus, and, depending on access, the credit records of the client. If the client is a corporation
supplying services to the public, ensure that none of the persons on this jury panel
is known to the client company in any *adverse* way. Depending on the time
available, a check can be run on the plaintiff and defendant registers of the state
trial courts, both civil and criminal, to determine if any of the jury members shows
up in those registers in recent months or years. Knowing that a particular juror
owns or does not own his or her own home, is or is not a good paying customer,
is litigious minded, or has been a defendant in criminal matters is of assistance to
the trial attorney in attempting to determine prejudice or bias on the juror's part.
The voters' register generally provides information on age, residence, occupation,
and political persuasion. All such facts, depending on the case, may be important
to the attorney.

Bibliography

Buchanan, John C. and Bos, Carole D. *How to Use Video in Litigation: A Guide
    to Technology, Strategies, and Techniques.* Englewood Cliffs, N.J.: Prentice-
    Hall, 1986.

Casualty Investigation Checklists. 3rd ed. Ed. Pat Magarick. New York: Clark
    Boardman Co. Ltd., 1985.

Dudnik, Robert M. *Anatomy of a Personal Injury Law Suit.* 2nd ed. Ed. Francis
    H. Hare, Jr., and Edward M. Ricci. Washington, D.C.: Association of Trial Law-
    yers of America, Education Fund, 1981.

Federal Civil Judicial Procedure and Rules. St. Paul: West, 1991.

Kirk, Paul L. And Thornton, John I. *Crime Investigation.* New York: Wiley, 1985.

Philo, Harry M. *Lawyers Desk Reference.* 7th ed. Rochester, N.Y.: Lawyers Coop-
    erative Publishing Co., 1987.

Statsky, William P. *Introduction to Paralegalism.* St. Paul: West, 1986.

8 Litigation Skills

8.00   Introduction

Litigation is the focal point of the U.S. legal system. In one way or another, everything that lawyers do revolves around litigation. They are either working to prepare a legal dispute for trial or working to avoid a legal dispute that could lead to trial. Regardless of the area of practice where a legal assistant finds himself or herself, he or she must have a basic working knowledge of the litigation process in order to function effectively.

The types of duties that a legal assistant may be expected to perform in the field of litigation vary widely. A legal assistant may interview clients and witnesses or may perform investigative functions that involve searching public records or locating potential documentary evidence from other sources.

Litigation involves substantial research. While the ability to research is a skill that requires extensive training and practice, legal assistants can acquire a level of expertise that is invaluable to a busy trial attorney. Attention to detail, critical analysis of statutes and court opinions, and superior written communication skills are essential for the legal assistant who performs legal research.

The legal assistant with solid written communication skills may also be heavily involved in preparation of court pleadings and related documents. While many pleadings, such as notices, are fairly simple and routine, others require some creativity on the part of the drafter, along with substantial familiarity with substantive and procedural law.

Another major contribution of legal assistants in an active trial practice is in the area of discovery. All discovery requires someone to oversee its organization, to systematize it, and to monitor its implementation. Legal assistants are especially well qualified to undertake these important tasks. Under the supervision of a lawyer, a legal assistant can draft interrogatories and other discovery requests, assist clients in preparing responses to the discovery requests of the opponent, and prepare summaries and digests of discovery documents as the case progresses. Although legal assistants are generally prohibited from asking questions during a deposition, they play a valuable role in developing the outline of questions to be used at the deposition and in taking notes and keeping track of exhibits during the deposition itself.

Attending to details connected with the trial, such as keeping track of witnesses, having subpoenas issued, and organizing the trial notebook, is often the legal assistant's duty. A legal assistant also provides an invaluable resource for the attorney at the time of trial by keeping track of exhibits, taking notes, and performing other tasks that do not involve the practice of law.

Generally speaking, legal assistants cannot represent clients in courts of law. They may represent clients before an administrative agency, however, if the rules governing that particular agency permit nonlawyer representation. Assuming that nonlawyer representation is permitted and that both the attorney-employer and the client consent, it is critical that the legal assistant in this situation master the necessary advocacy skills and have a strong working knowledge of the substantive and procedural law involved. Nevertheless, many lawyers are reluctant to allow anyone other than themselves to represent their clients in any setting. This is not a reflection on legal assistants so much as it is a reflection of the attorney's commitment to provide personal representation to clients at hearings and trials, regardless of the arena.

8.01   The United States Legal System

The United States legal system (except Louisiana) is founded in common law principles that the colonists brought with them from England. Louisiana follows a civil law system based upon the Napoleonic Code that its settlers brought from France. Under common law, cases are decided by comparing the facts and issues with similar cases that were decided previously. The process of analyzing or synthesizing cases in this manner is referred to as *stare decisis,* or following the rule of precedent. Common law may also be called case law or opinion law, referring to the opinions of judges. While common law principles remain fairly constant, their application to particular cases may change over a period of time to reflect the changing needs of the society it serves.

The difference between the common law system and Louisiana's civil law system is not so much a difference between what is right and what is wrong as it is a difference in procedure, though each system does have some substantive laws that are unique to it.

Common law does not operate in isolation within our legal system. Each governmental unit (federal, state, and local) has adopted a document that defines and limits its powers in relation to its citizens. At the federal and state levels, this document is called a constitution. A local government, such as a city, may adopt a charter for this purpose.

The U.S. Constitution dictates the method of government adopted by the founders, the governmental branches (legislative, executive, and judicial) created by it, and the specific powers that each branch is authorized to exercise. The legislative branch is authorized to make laws; the executive branch, to enforce laws; and the judicial branch, to interpret laws. This is known as the separation of powers among the three governmental branches. The federal Constitution and most state constitutions include a Bill of Rights that specifically defines those individual rights that no governmental branch can take away.

The federal Constitution gives Congress the authority to legislate in specific areas, such as interstate commerce and federal taxation. The U.S. Supreme Court is the only court specifically authorized by the Constitution, although Congress is given authority to create such other, inferior courts as it determines are necessary.

Since most state constitutions follow a format similar to that used in the U.S. Constitution, many parallels can be drawn between the two systems of government. Yet, federal and state governments exist independently of each other. Their authority or jurisdiction is distinct. For further discussion, see Chapter 5, Legal Research.

8.011   Court Systems.

At both the federal and state levels, court systems have been established for judicial resolution of legal disputes. Each court system is generally organized in three levels: trial courts, intermediate appellate courts, and supreme courts. Some decisions and appeals, heard and adjudged in state courts, may be appealed further to the U.S. Supreme Court if a federally protected right is involved and if the Court consents (grants certiorari) to hear the case.

8.012   Federal Court System.

The federal court system covers the United States, Puerto Rico, the Virgin Islands, and Guam. The federal trial courts serving these areas are the U.S. District Courts, which are geographically located to serve each of the fifty states and Puerto Rico with one or more courtrooms in each state. These courts have federal jurisdiction over civil and criminal matters. U.S. District Courts that have both federal and local jurisdiction serve the District of Columbia, the Virgin Islands, and Guam.

Courts are organized with judges and courtrooms assigned to departments within the court. The more population and litigation, the more courtrooms and judges. Trials may be held, depending on the issues, before a judge, a jury, or specially selected and qualified masters whose powers and limitations are defined by the district court making the appointment.

EXHIBIT 32   Federal Court Structure

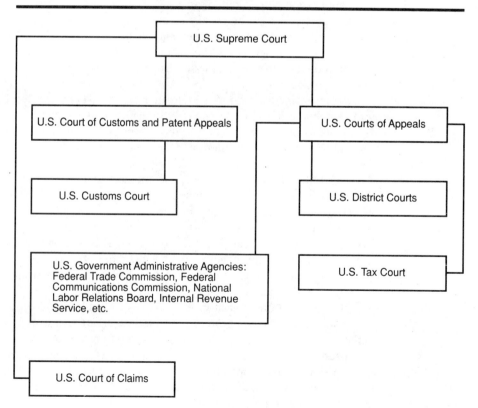

The U.S. Court of Claims is a separate and distinct entity and renders judgments on the validity of certain types of claims against the United States. Also separate from the U.S. District Court, the U.S. Tax Court renders judgments in federal taxation matters.

A separate U.S. Customs Court deals exclusively with matters of imported merchandise and the activities of customs collectors. The U.S. Court of Customs and Patent Appeals hears appeals and reviews decisions of the Customs Court, the Patent Office, and the Tariff Commission.

The U.S. Courts of Appeals are organized into eleven judicial circuits, with one court of appeals for each circuit. There may be more than one division within a single circuit. Three judges are designated from all the judges in the division to sit in each case in each division. Appeals are not heard before juries but before the judges of the division. At least two judges are always present, but the judges may sit *en banc* (all three judges present). When two of the three judges assigned to a particular case agree on an outcome, the decision is binding.

The Supreme Court of the United States consists of the chief justice and eight associate justices. It has original jurisdiction in cases affecting ambassadors, other public ministers, and consuls and in those cases where one of the fifty states is a party. It has appellate jurisdiction in all other cases. The Supreme Court itself is subject to some regulation by Congress. Article III, Chapter 21 of the U.S. Constitution establishes the powers and limitations of the federal judiciary. Sections 1251–1257, Title 2A, Chapter 81 of the U.S. Code confer appellate jurisdiction on the Supreme Court. It is characteristic of all federal law that every matter in civil or criminal litigation is covered by written laws passed by the Congress. There is no federal common law.

Certain circumstances allow the removal of some cases or issues from state courts into federal courts, such as diversity of citizenship among parties. Where diversity of citizenship exists and the federal court accepts the right of removal as one properly exercised and procedurally correct but where no federal question is involved, the U.S. District Court will apply the law of the appropriate state, whether it is common law, civil code, or the statutes of the state.

The administrative agencies of the federal government carry out the directions of the president as a part of the executive branch. Each was established and authorized by a specific legislative act (enabling act) passed by Congress. Within the boundaries of its particular enabling act, each administrative agency adopts rules and regulations to carry out its purpose. In addition, it is empowered to hold hearings and to render binding decisions in quasi-judicial proceedings that resemble trials. Hearing officers in contested matters may be administrative law judges, referees, hearing examiners, commissioners, or other persons authorized by the agency. Hearing officers are not generally required to be attorneys. Although their work is not controlled or directed by the courts, all appeals from their decisions proceed directly to the U.S. Courts of Appeals. Examples of administrative agencies are the Federal Communications Commission, the Federal Trade Commission, the National Labor Relations Board, the Federal Aviation Administration, the Occupational Safety and Health Administration, and the Equal Employment Opportunity Commission.

8.013   State Court Systems.

State courts handle an immense volume of litigation, both civil and criminal. Largely because of the defendant's constitutional right to a speedy trial, most courts give priority to criminal cases. This causes some problems in scheduling and rescheduling civil cases, both for procedural matters leading to trial as well as for the trials themselves. It is not unusual to have civil trial dates canceled or postponed on the court's calendar because of a sudden influx of criminal cases. Attorneys and legal assistants recognize that the litigation process has inherent elements of uncertainty that require an attorney to be ready for trial on schedule, in full knowledge that the trial may not begin on schedule. This uncertainty is the basis for at least a portion of the pressures experienced by the litigation team as trial dates draw near.

From state to state, trial court systems may differ (particularly in titles) but probably fit the following general outline:

State Supreme Courts have minimal, if any, original jurisdiction. The bulk of their workload derives from their appellate jurisdiction over civil and criminal cases that are appealed from state superior courts and state administrative agencies. From five to nine judges, depending on the state, provide appellate review based upon the record made at the trial court level and intermediate appellate court level, if any. No jury exists at this level, and no new evidence is received. In some states, citizens have an absolute right of review by the state supreme court. In others, supreme court review is discretionary with the court itself.

Superior courts (sometimes called district, circuit, or sessions courts) are usually established in each county, parish, or similar region and have sufficient judges and courtrooms to handle the population or litigation within that particular county. Occasionally, judges are "borrowed" from other counties to handle heavy

EXHIBIT 33 State Court Structure

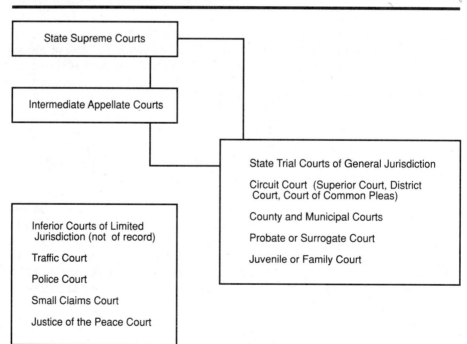

litigation loads. Superior courts generally handle the trial of all felonies, as well as civil litigation over a minimum dollar amount, such as five thousand dollars. In many states, this court is one of general jurisdiction, which means that there is no minimum or maximum dollar amount for the civil suits that it handles. These courts may also handle appeals from inferior courts as a separate and distinct responsibility.

County court or municipal court is a lower-level court that hears criminal misdemeanor cases and civil cases having a maximum dollar value. Sometimes this court has a separate small claims court, which is limited to very small dollar amounts (five hundred dollars or less, for instance), does not provide for trial by jury, and does not allow parties to be represented by attorneys.

8.014   Jurisdiction.

The complexity of law and its administration, together with the multilevel regulation of modern life, often make it hard to identify the best forum in which to present the client's case. Even after all the forums have been identified that have authority to hear a particular matter, difficult decisions often remain.

A state may have laws that parallel those of the federal government in certain areas, such as antitrust statutes, securities regulation, equal employment opportunity, and utility regulation. If so, the lawyer must decide whether to lodge the client's claim at the state or federal court or the administrative level.

A decision on whether to file a civil action in state superior court or in county court may depend on the dollar value of damages and the length of time necessary to bring the case to trial. While trials usually can be completed more quickly in county court, a successful plaintiff may still need to register the judgment with the superior court before it will be given full faith and credit by other courts in other jurisdictions. This is a critical factor when it appears likely that judicial enforcement will be required to collect the judgment.

Further decisions must be made if the potential defendant (or defendants) is domiciled outside the geographical jurisdiction of the forum court. In that case, facts must be established that will give the forum court personal jurisdiction over the defendant. Most states have long-arm statutes that authorize jurisdiction over persons who commit torts within the forum state (such as causing an automobile accident) or who do other things to establish minimum contacts with the forum state.

Even if all of the parties live in the same state, it may still be necessary to decide which court has proper venue to hear the case. Venue relates to the place where the case should be tried, assuming that there is more than one division or department of a court that has jurisdiction. When venue becomes an issue, it is usually resolved by balancing convenience to the plaintiff, convenience to the defendant, where the events occurred, and where the witnesses and other evidence are most readily available.

8.02   The Advocacy System and the Legal Assistant

Lawyers and law firms often find that they simply cannot economically perform each and every service required by clients in processing the many phases of litigation. Discovery has become more encompassing and attorneys are more skillful in identifying possible sources of evidence and information. The skills and abilities of the legal assistant who has been trained to accumulate, analyze, collate, and cross-index factual information and to draft discovery requests ranging from the simple to the complex result in high productivity for the attorneys who take advantage of this resource.

Lawyers who do not use legal assistants are at a serious disadvantage when engaged in discovery activities with adversaries who do. The tempo of discovery pressures is accelerated. It forces the attorney to devote a higher percentage of his or her time to factual matters in the case, while the adversary reinforced by legal assistants can spend more time on the law, tactics, and strategy of trial or even other cases.

Legal assistants should seek instruction from the lawyer on the substantive law and sometimes on court procedures and practices for each case on which they will work together. Naturally, the legal assistant will review the law, procedural rules and court rules periodically anyway, preferably at the outset of every new case. This ensures that the legal assistant is an effective litigation team member and allows the legal assistant to anticipate the needs of the case and to comply with all of the time elements, forms requirements, and policies that will affect its outcome.

The beneficiaries of the legal assistant's work are simultaneously the client, the attorney, and the legal system as a whole. The legal assistant, by performing functions normally performed by the lawyer, accelerates the pace of discovery and the ultimate resolution of the case. The legal assistant improves the attorney's perception of the factual information developed in discovery by organizing it and digesting it into compact summaries that are cross-referenced to exhibits. This helps the attorney make cogent, concise, and persuasive presentations of those cases that must be tried, and it allows thoughtful consideration and evaluation of the entire case: facts, law, timing, suitability of settlement, along with evaluation and selection of the settlement options.

8.03   Specific Litigation Skills

Clearly, the benefits an attorney gains from using a legal assistant increase as the legal assistant achieves more skill, knowledge of legal procedures, exposure to different situations, and awareness of the techniques and tactics preferred by the supervising attorney. Those skills that a legal assistant may develop in the course of employment by a particular attorney or law firm can include drafting complaints and subsequent pleadings; drafting motions and related documents; performing legal research and investigation; conducting interviews; and managing the information accumulated in the case file. Each of these activities enhances the utility of the legal assistant to the attorney and the attorney's clients.

As a case progresses, facts may develop that clearly indicate that the case should not be tried, either from a plaintiff's or a defendant's point of view. The legal assistant, by carefully monitoring the factual development through discovery efforts, is in a unique position to identify such a situation as soon as it occurs, to refer it to the attorney, and to assist the attorney in quick resolution of the settlement options that may be available.

8.04 Preliminary Considerations in Litigation

Long before the pleadings are prepared and filed, the attorney and those assisting him or her on the litigation team must make some basic decisions about the case that will have long-reaching effects. During or very shortly after the client's first interview, the facts of the case must be analyzed to determine whether the client has a cause of action; the legal theories and remedies that may be available to resolve the client's claim, as well as potential defenses that may be raised by the opposing party; and a preliminary calculation of the damages or other relief to which the client may be entitled.

The attorney must develop the legal theory or theories that will provide the framework for all that follows, from drafting the complaint through the trial itself. Virtually everything that is done must be done within the context of the applicable legal theories. Experienced trial attorneys use checklists of the requirements for each legal theory of recovery and for each defense that may be used, in order to avoid overlooking important details. As each requirement is drafted into the complaint or presented at trial, it is checked off to be certain that nothing is missed. For each element on the checklist, supporting facts must be outlined, along with all sources that prove the fact (make it more likely than not in civil cases; cause a reasonable doubt in defense of criminal cases). This may be one or more witnesses and/or one or more exhibits.

The checklist will be expanded, contracted, summarized, and cross-referenced many different times and in many different ways throughout the course of the litigation. However, at the preliminary stage, the checklist is important more because it exists than because of what it contains. It will provide the foundation for constructing appropriate legal theories, which, in turn, will result in a purposeful and thorough litigation plan.

The following list contains possible legal theories that might be used in preparation of a checklist. It is not intended to be exhaustive but rather only as a starting point from which a more complete legal theory checklist can be tailored to a particular lawyer's practice.

- A. Law Action Theories
    1. Contract
    2. Personal Injury Torts
        a. General Negligence
        b. Products Liability
        c. Premises Liability
        d. Professional Liability
        e. Governmental Liability
        f. Worker Compensation claim
    3. Other Torts
        a. Intentional Torts
        b. Defamation (Libel/Slander)
        c. Fraud/Misrepresentation
- B. Equity Action Theories
    1. Mandamus
    2. Injunction
    3. Rescission
    4. Reformation
    5. Specific Performance

      6.   Equitable Trust

C.   Damages Recoverable

    1.   Compensatory Damages
    2.   Restitution Damages
    3.   Punitive Damages
    4.   Liquidated Damages
    5.   Lost Profits
    6.   Diminished Earning Capacity (reduced to present value)
    7.   Future Medical Expenses (reduced to present value)
    8.   Interest
    9.   Attorney Fees

D.   Defenses/Limitations to Recovery

    1.   Performance
    2.   Satisfaction/Accord and Satisfaction
    3.   Statute of Limitations
    4.   Statute of Frauds
    5.   Privity of Contract
    6.   Prior Breach (of contract)
    7.   Duress
    8.   Impossibility of Performance
    9.   Illegality of Purpose
    10.   Laches
    11.   Agency/Independent Contractor Status
    12.   Contributory Negligence
    13.   Comparative Negligence
    14.   Assumption of Risk
    15.   Indemnity/Contribution
    16.   Economic Waste
    17.   Statutory Limitation of Damages
    18.   Governmental Immunity
    19.   Third-Party Liability
    20.   Exhaustion of Remedies (administrative)

A portion of the legal theory checklist is reproduced below to demonstrate how it might be expanded.

3.   Other Torts

a.   Intentional torts
    (1)   Act by Defendant
    (2)   Intent
    (3)   Causation
    (4)   Damage

b.   Defamation (Libel/Slander)
    (1)   Defamatory Statement (Written/Oral)
    (2)   Plaintiff Identified or Identifiable
    (3)   Publication to Third Party
    (4)   Plaintiff's Reputation Damaged
    (5)   Calculation of Loss to Plaintiff

c.   Fraud/Misrepresentation
    (1)   False Statement/Misrepresentation of Fact
    (2)   Knowledge of Falsity by Defendant (for fraud only)

    (3)   Intent that Plaintiff Rely
    (4)   Plaintiff's Reliance Justified
    (5)   Damage to Plaintiff

8.05   Pleadings and Pretrial Motions

In addition to the substantive legal theories and rules, the litigation team must be familiar with the procedural rules that govern a particular case. At the federal level, all courts are governed by the Federal Rules of Criminal Procedure for criminal cases and by the Federal Rules of Civil Procedure for civil cases. Federal trial courts (U.S. District Courts) are permitted to adopt local court rules to supplement the federal rules; however, they may not replace the federal rules or materially change the character of the federal rules.

As an example of this interaction, Rule 12(b) of the Federal Rules of Civil Procedure permits motions to be filed to test the sufficiency of the complaint. The rule goes on to list specific bases that can be included in such a motion. A particular federal district court would be permitted to adopt a local court rule requiring all Rule 12 motions to be filed in triplicate. This type of local rule does not change the character of the federal rule, but it does add another requirement.

State court systems also have procedural rules, many of which closely resemble the Federal Rules of Civil Procedure. State rules of civil procedure, for instance, are adopted either by the highest court of the state or by the state legislature. Similar to the federal system, many local courts are permitted to adopt local court rules so long as the local rules do not supplant state rules of procedure.

Since state rules of procedure may deviate from the federal rules and since local court rules may supplement either the federal or state rules of procedure, the litigation team must become familiar with the particular rules of procedure that apply in its jurisdiction. The discussion that follows uses the Federal Rules of Civil Procedure as its general basis.

The pleadings in a case consist of the complaint, the answer, and the reply. The pleadings inform the court of the allegations or contentions of each party and assist the court in formulating the issues. The pleadings (1) establish the court's jurisdiction or authority to adjudicate the controversy, (2) briefly state the facts that provide the basis of the plaintiff's claim against the defendant, (3) briefly state any affirmative defenses that the defendant claims against the plaintiff, and (4) demand relief.

A complaint (sometimes called a petition in state courts) is drafted on behalf of the plaintiff to formally notify the court and the defendant of the basis for the plaintiff's claim. It is filed with the clerk of the court and is served upon the defendant, along with the summons notifying him that he must answer the complaint within a specified period or a default judgment will be entered against him. The plaintiff's prayer for relief may request damages of a stated amount, an equitable remedy, or any other relief the plaintiff may be entitled to receive.

When the complaint is received, the defendant's lawyer analyzes it for legal sufficiency. The defendant may challenge the legal sufficiency of the complaint by filing a motion to dismiss (called a demurrer in some state courts) with the clerk of the court and by serving a copy of the motion on the plaintiff, usually by mailing it to the plaintiff's attorney. In a motion to dismiss, the defendant asserts that the case should not be tried at all because of a specific defect. The defect may be lack of subject matter jurisdiction of the court, lack of personal jurisdiction of the defendant, improper issuance of summons, improper service of summons upon the defendant, or a failure to state a claim upon which the relief can be granted. The motion to dismiss and all other pretrial motions are set for hearing by the judge assigned to the case.

If the complaint survives the preliminary motions designed to test its sufficiency, the defendant must file a written answer with the court. The answer may contain admissions, denials, affirmative defenses, and counterclaims. If the defendant admits a particular allegation in the complaint, there is no need to prove that fact at the time of trial. If the defendant denies a particular allegation in the complaint, a factual issue is created, and the plaintiff must prove the fact at the time of trial unless he or she is able to do so before then. Allegations contained in the answer that may bar (prevent) the plaintiff's recovery are called affirmative defenses.

When the defendant states a cause of action in the same suit that seeks relief against the plaintiff, this is called a counterclaim. If the defendant's cause of action arises from the same facts as plaintiff's cause of action, the defendant's counterclaim is compulsory. In other words, if the defendant's claim is based on the same facts as the plaintiff's claim, the defendant must file the claim against the plaintiff in the existing action, or the defendant can never file it. If the defendant's cause of action against the plaintiff is based upon a different occurrence or a different set of facts, the defendant has a permissive counterclaim. This means that he or she may file it in the same case if he or she chooses to do so, but the defendant is not required to do so. With a permissive counterclaim, the defendant may file an entirely separate suit now or at some future time.

The legal assistant will often be faced with the task of organizing and becoming familiar with a complex litigation file that involves multiple parties and voluminous pleadings. In sorting out the various parties and their claims, it is helpful to keep in mind that a counterclaim always means that a defendant is alleging a claim against a plaintiff. A cross-claim always means that one defendant is alleging a claim against another defendant. A third-party complaint always means that a defendant is alleging a claim against a new party to the lawsuit. Third-party complaints cannot be filed without the court's permission.

After the defendant's answer has been filed, the plaintiff may file a reply if the answer contains factual allegations that were not contained in the complaint. In the reply, the plaintiff responds to the new factual allegations by admitting them, denying them, or stating any affirmative defenses that may exist in relation to them.

The key to drafting an effective pleading is to include only those matters that are absolutely necessary and to state facts in a simple, concise way. Never admit unnecessary facts that may later become embarrassing obstacles in the proper presentation of the client's case. Save righteous indignation and legal arguments for the trial brief. These have no place in pleadings filed with the court.

Depending on the jurisdiction, other pretrial motions may be used to refine the allegations contained in the pleadings and to weed out those claims and defenses that are without merit. Among these are a motion for a more definite statement; a motion to strike (referring to statements in a pleading that are redundant, immaterial, or scandalous); and a motion for judgment on the pleadings (called a motion for summary judgment in some state courts).

8.06 Discovery and Pretrial Preparation

While the issues are being joined through the process of written pleadings and pretrial motions, formal discovery may also be undertaken by the parties. Formal discovery includes interrogatories, depositions, requests for production of documents and other things, and requests for admission.

Other than those facts withheld for impeachment purposes and those facts that are privileged, the underlying philosophy of the Federal Rules of Civil Procedure and their state court counterparts is that all relevant facts should be available to all parties prior to trial, provided that the party has properly requested this information. If each party has access to all evidence prior to trial, the presumption is that many cases will be settled. The presumption may be correct, since only a very small percentage of cases result in a full trial on the merits. The formal discovery process lends itself especially well to the skills of the legal assistant member of the litigation team.

8.061 Interrogatories.

This procedure allows each party to require other parties in a case to answer written questions, under oath, within a specified time period. The procedures are self-executing. In other words, if properly prepared and served on the other party, the interrogatories are as effective as a court order without the judge of the court seeing them. With delivery of the interrogatories on the responding party begins a specific time period within which a response must be returned. Extensions of time may be agreed upon between the propounder and the responding party. If the responding party fails to answer some questions or answers incompletely, the propounding party must decide (within a specific time period) whether to file a motion in the court to compel further answers, to ignore the problem and submit another set of interrogatories, or to exercise another discovery option.

Drafting, answering, analyzing answers, drafting objections, and responding to objections in interrogatory work are all appropriate legal assistant efforts, both in ensuring full compliance with the discovery demands of other parties and obtaining the maximum economic benefits of discovery initiated on the behalf of the client.

8.062 Depositions.

A deposition is the oral (occasionally, written) examination of a witness by an attorney for a party in the case, under oath, and in the presence of a certified shorthand reporter (sometimes called a court reporter or depositions reporter) who records each question and its answer by shorthand or more commonly, a stenotype machine. Some jurisdictions allow the reporter to use a tape recorder.

Lawyers for all other parties are present and may also examine or cross-examine the witness. The reporter than transcribes the deposition, assembles it into a booklet, and mails copies to each legal counsel who requested a copy and one copy to the witness (deponent). The witness has a short period of time to review the transcript, make appropriate corrections, and return it to the reporter. The reporter prepares the corrections, notifies each counsel of the corrections, and files the corrected deposition booklet with the court. This allows the witness to correct errors made by the reporter in transcription. It does not allow the witness to change the testimony that he or she gave. The booklet is composed of numbered pages of paper on which each line also is numbered to allow easy reference to the testimony.

Depositions are another self-executing device, within certain limits. A witness may be served a subpoena individually (if not a party to the action, the witness *must* be served) or made available by agreement between counsel. Witnesses usually cannot be compelled by subpoena to travel more than a specified distance to give their depositions or to travel from state to state; therefore, the attorneys often must travel to the witness.

Witnesses may be compelled to bring documents within their control to the deposition, and those documents (or copies) may be entered as exhibits to the deposition transcripts. Photographs, sketches, and so on may also be introduced by counsel for the various parties through the witness at the deposition and attached as exhibits to the transcripts.

A witness who reviews documents or records to prepare for the deposition may find that the attorney who sought the deposition is entitled to see the material used and even to have every such document or record attached to the deposition as an exhibit.

Most attorneys prefer the deposition to other discovery methods because it provides an opportunity to explore fully the personal knowledge and impact of the witness on the case. The opportunity to observe demeanor of the witness, the manner of oral expression, and his or her nervousness or belligerence, and ability to think and respond under stress, and the opportunity to ask the "hard" questions and receive a spontaneous and responsive answer under oath all are important to the attorney in gauging the credibility of the witness and the value and probable effect of the witness' testimony on a jury.

The legal assistant's contribution to the effort may include identifying witnesses; drafting deposition outlines; preparing friendly witnesses for deposition; identifying areas of inquiry regarding documents, evidence, and other witnesses; organizing potential exhibits and exhibit logs; attending depositions to take notes; assisting in reproduction of exhibits; preparing post-deposition summaries; and collating conflicts in the sworn testimony of witnesses from their depositions.

8.063   Requests for Admission.

A request for admission is usually a late-in-the-game procedure designed to elicit the agreement of the adversary of the truth of a fact, the falsity of an allegation, the identity of documents or other physical evidence, and so on.

The purpose is to simplify the trial by eliminating the need of proving each of the items. If, during the course of discovery, sufficient information has been disclosed to support the admission requested, yet the answering party refuses to make the admission, then the propounding party may be able to recover the costs of proving in court each of the requested but denied admissions.

The legal assistant aids the attorney in this discovery technique by collating facts, contentions, answers to interrogatories, exhibits in depositions, documents from requests for production, and so on and by drafting appropriate requests for admission.

Similarly, the legal assistant can review the same kinds of material and provide the attorney with a reliable foundation on which to decide how to answer the adversary's requests for admission.

8.064   Requests for Production of Documents.

Requesting a party, usually the adversary, to produce documents can be done early or late in the discovery process in virtually any kind of case. It is essential in every case to examine each document individually for its intrinsic value proving or tending to establish any fact, act, or procedure; confirming or refuting the testimony of witnesses; fixing dates and/or sequences of events; and so forth. Additionally, each document may refer to other documents, other personalities, or other sources of information not previously detected.

Requests for production of documents are self-executing but may be complicated in business litigation by the need to protect disclosure of trade secrets or other proprietary methods or procedures. There are procedures by which protective orders can be obtained that limit the publication of the confidential material solely to the purposes necessary to the case.

Many cases involve limited categories of documents, such as medical records, employment records, or military service records—all easily definable and specific in nature and character. These are susceptible to a subpoena *duces tecum* requiring the custodian of the records to appear and produce the records for examination and copying. Since the custodian seldom originates the records, his or her only testimony is the manner of routine filing and storage of the records to create the foundation for the introduction of the documents as evidence under the business records exception to the hearsay rule (Federal Evidence Rule 803). The courts recognize the routine nature of such procedures, and most court rules allow the subpoena to be exercised by a notary public who takes the subpoena from the attorney and serves it on the custodian, who then surrenders the records to the notary public. The notary copies the records, validates the copies as being true copies of the records covered by the subpoena and sends copies to the requesting attorney (and sometimes other parties by prior agreement), and returns the original records to the custodian.

Whichever system is used, the legal assistant can aid the lawyer by carefully reviewing and summarizing the documents, particularly medical records, and by establishing a control system for produced documents (both the client's and the adversary's) that identifies, controls, attributes origin, and permits timely retrieval of the relevant documents.

The advent of sophisticated business litigation caused the document case to become a major field of legal assistant endeavor. Whether it is a class action, a labor matter, a corporate contract dispute, an antitrust action, or a products liability case, the volume of paper involved (and the necessary evidentiary facts contained therein) may explode into volumes far beyond simple manageability by an attorney and a trial book. The legal assistant, by providing organized document categorization, indexing, collation, and retrieval abilities, may be the salvation of the case.

8.065   Damage Calculation, Verification, and Settlement Offers.

The major element in every form of litigation is the remedy being sought. In many cases, this takes the form of some calculation of money damages. Procedures to identify valid amounts and categories of damage are indispensable to the attorney in attempting to evaluate the case, whether for settlement or for trial. This essential activity is important, whether the work is for plaintiff or defendant, and often the determinations, depending on timing, will result in a quick, timely, just settlement of a particular case early in the proceeding before substantial expenses have been incurred by either side.

It is a function particularly within the capabilities of legal assistants to assemble, organize, and cross-check claimed damages or to coordinate the efforts of accountants, financial or economic analysts, actuaries, and others in that effort.

8.066   Trial Books.

The attorney's trial book is a succinct accumulation of the data and references the attorney believes necessary or helpful in the actual trial process. It necessarily is a compressed but comprehensive organization of the identities of parties, witnesses, counsel, and others; legal briefs, opening statements, legal motions, points and authorities, jury instructions, evidence rules; admitted facts; witness statements, depositions and examination plan for each witness; technical references, exhibits, foundation or objections to exhibits as evidence, evidence log; and so forth.

Each attorney operates in a slightly different manner, but the legal assistant by effective collating, indexing, summarization and cross-checking contributes to the reliability, inclusiveness, and utility of the trial book.

There are many texts and sources (particularly continuing education of the bar) that explain each of these activities; however, the majority are written specifically for the attorneys and the court from the attorney's viewpoint. The legal assistant must consider participating with the lawyer in forming the trial book long before trial to accumulate effectively in easily retrievable form the data the lawyer will need.

8.07   Interrogatories

8.071   Concept—Code and Statute.

Interrogatories are a discovery device specifically authorized in the Federal Rules of Civil Procedure under Rules 33 and 37. Rule 33 sets out the availability of the discovery method and procedures connected with interrogatories. It essentially provides that any party may serve any other party in a law suit with written interrogatories that must be answered within a specific time limit. These are self-executing discovery devices; each question must either be answered separately and fully in writing, under oath, or an objection to the question must be filed. Such an objection must be detailed and must be made within the time limit permitted for responding. The rule provides that interrogatories may be used at trial "to the extent permitted by the rules of evidence." This points up the fact that interrogatories may extend to matters that will not be admissible in evidence at trial.

Rule 37 provides the recourse to force a party who has failed to answer interrogatories to answer them responsively. A proceeding under Rule 37 may be accompanied by a request for the costs of making such motion (sanctions), and it allows the court to make an award against the party who has failed to respond properly to the discovery request.

Every state has a similar rule, whether or not it is a rule of civil procedure. Many of the states have adopted rules carrying precisely the same language and section numbers as the Federal Rules of Civil Procedure, including Alaska, Arizona, Colorado, Hawaii, Idaho, Kentucky, Montana, Nevada, West Virginia, and Wyoming. Other states, however, rely upon rules, codes, or statutes containing substantially similar provisions as the federal rules. Even Louisiana has a Code of Civil Procedures, statutes 1491 and 1551, which are substantially the same as the federal rules.

8.072   Rules of Court.

Whatever the federal or state rule is, there also may be conditions or limitations imposed by the rules of the court in which the action is filed. These generally pertain to the form of the interrogatory and its answers. More and more common is a state court rule similar to the federal court rule of requiring the engrossment of the question and the answer to interrogatories in the interest of clarity and simplifying both the court's and the lawyers' files. In this procedure, the propounded interrogatory format allows sufficient space between questions to permit the insertion of appropriate answers.

Other courts simply require the responding party to type the question ahead of the answer being supplied. This allows the court, or any of the parties, to look at one document and find, in successive order, question and answer, question and answer, and so on. Few courts, however, have solved the problem of supplemental answers, and few require engrossment of supplemental answers with the original questions and answers.

In this day of photocopy and computer copy equipment, the "cut and paste" system has simplified the process. It is highly desirable in responding to interrogatories to perform engrossment for the attorney's own file, even if the court does not require engrossment as a condition of filing the answer.

Under the federal rules, a party may serve more than one set of interrogatories but may be required to number the interrogatories sequentially in order. In other words, "Set one" may include questions from one to sixty-five, and "Set two," filed at a later date, begins with question sixty-six and extends to the completion of that set. In many ways, this is a desirable practice, whether in federal or state courts. It allows quick and easy reference to questions from the onset of the case to its conclusion. The legal assistant finds it is a highly desirable system since it allows easy collation of one answer to another on a related point. Far better to be able to refer to "Questions 1, 12, 38, 125, and 265" on the same point, rather than "Set one, Questions 1 and 12; Set two, Question 3; Set three, Questions 10 and 25." This procedure, if the attorney will allow it, assists the legal assistant and, ultimately, benefits the attorney.

8.073   Canned Interrogatories.

Law offices generally have an "interrogatory file" of sets of questions generally suitable for certain types of cases, such as "Bodily Injury—Automobile Collision," "Wrongful Death—Airplane Crash," "Breach of Contract—Mechanics Lien Filed," which includes questions seeking essential data that do not depend on the unique facts of the case. Many collections have been published of questions by categories (for example, identity of people, identity of corporations, automobile condition and maintenance records, and aircraft ownership, registration, and maintenance) from which suitable questions may be selected and used.

Often whole sets of such canned or patterned questions have been printed up ahead of time or stored in computerized files in offices with a practice specialty. Inexperienced or lazy legal assistants or lawyers then select "nearly suitable" sets, type in the proper captions, and mail them out to the adversary. The danger of this practice is the possibility that a large portion of the questions may be inappropriate, and the adversary may object to the entire set as inappropriate, unintelligible, irrelevant, and unjustly burdensome. An example might be a car-pedestrian accident where the questions sent to the plaintiff (pedestrian) seek data about "the other car" or "plaintiff's automobile's speed at the time of the collision," its "mechanical condition," or "its maintenance record."

Use of canned or patterned interrogatories can be helpful, expeditious, and appropriate, provided the set is edited for the individual case and circumstance. Usually some specific additional questions are necessary to fit the case facts to the canned set anyway.

The legal assistant, by careful editing and alteration, increases the attorney's effectiveness in the case by foreclosing the adversary from justified, if minor, complaints and/or objections.

8.074   Interrogatories as Part of the Discovery Plan.

Interrogatories are only one function in the discovery effort against an adverse party. Effective discovery is the result of thoughtful planning in determining whether development of factual data is appropriate to this form of discovery. Almost anything can be asked, relevance to the issues or the possibility of leading to relevant facts being the only tests, and these tests are liberally construed.

The *timing* of written interrogatories in the discovery process must be co-ordinated with depositions to ensure the maximum impact from the effort. Similarly, many items may be better developed by independent investigation (informal discovery) with the resultant benefit of not exposing the attorney's specific interest to the adversary. While anything *may* be asked, interrogatories generally are expected to serve specific functions and to match or supplement the attorney's discovery plan.

Filing interrogatories without a plan smacks of an attempt to create "busy work" for the adversary while appearing to advance the client's case. This conduct is unprofessional and usually unproductive because the effort is not pointed or planned; the questions are general and lack specific application to the issues of the case. When such a set is received, the legal assistant can easily recognize that the adversary is far behind in case planning and analysis.

8.075   Major Objectives.

The major objectives of interrogatories easily fulfilled are:

8.0751 Identify People or Entities.   These may be parties, witnesses, custodians of records, experts, or principal officers and directors of corporate bodies. Similarly, identifying "people" also involves identifying fictitious people, such as partnerships, corporations, company names, or entities recognized at law that are business, government or eleemosynary organizations.

"Identity" of natural people includes (or may include) family name, given name, middle names; hereditary suffixes (Sr., Jr., the III); professional titles (M.D. or Ph.D., for instance); maiden names of married women; adoptive names; nicknames or diminutives in common use; pen names or professional names; aliases used for any reason (a stepfather's name used by a child who was never legally adopted or a fictitious name used by a criminal to evade capture, for instance); and the inclusive dates of use of any name other than that legally recorded one.

Other identifying factors include: age; Social Security number; current home address; home address at the time of the incident at issue; employer; education; relationship to the case and to the parties in the case or the legal counsel in the case (for instance, next-door neighbor of plaintiff, cousin of defendant, cross-defendant, expert witness employed by plaintiff, or independent third-party witness).

The identity of a fictitious entity requires characterization of the entity as a corporation, partnership, association (incorporated or not), family-owned company, or solely-owned company (either of the last two might operate under their own names or fictitious names) and whether the entity is an independent operation, has subsidiaries, or is a subsidiary of another entity. The degree of ownership and control is important as well as the identities of the controlling interests (whether individuals or other companies), contractual ties, management chain, commonality of management, directorship, or financial control. The location of legal organization (incorporated in the state of Delaware; partnership filed in Louisiana; or solely-owned company with fictitious name registered in Santa Clara County, California, for example), and its principal office location, branch office locations, address for legal service; financial status (stock sold on New York Stock Exchange; closely held corporation; partnership of one general partner and two limited partners; and so on).

8.0752 Identify Documents and Objects.

The relevant documents may be very limited in nature and easily characterized by the responding party through date, author, addressee, type of document, subject matter of the document, and/or file number. In other cases, it may be necessary to identify the size and character of the file, the filing system identification, and storage location for subsequent examination and/or production.

When document identification is requested, the identity of the current custodian of each category of documents also is requested to include name, business position or title, business address, and preferred mailing address. The document custodian at the time of the event at issue should similarly be requested to furnish the name of his or her current location within and/or outside the company.

8.0753 Establish Facts or Lead to the Discovery of Facts.

Many incident cases are tried on facts solely in the personal knowledge of witnesses. Some witnesses are *parties*. Since interrogatories can be served *only* on parties, it is possible to elicit through written interrogatories those facts within their knowledge. Often the questions are designed to elicit identification of sources of facts beyond the personal knowledge of the parties. Those sources (witnesses, usually) are interviewed regarding their knowledge either by informal discovery or by deposition.

A major benefit in this type of interrogatory is the fact that the answer of the responding party must be verified under oath and may used at the trial if the testimony is later changed. Such an interrogatory may call for all the facts developed by the party, the party's counsel, or anyone acting on the party's behalf.

8.0754 Identify Contentions.

Properly timed and phrased interrogatories require the adverse party to state the contentions on which he or she relies in advancing his or her claim of liability or nonliability, damages, or refutation of damage. From these responses, the merits of the adverse party's position may be deduced or weaknesses identified. Contention interrogatories usually have follow-up questions requesting identification of the facts on which those contentions are based.

The contentions may deal with whether the issue is one of law or fact and, if fact, the evidentiary facts on which the party relies, the source of the evidentiary facts, whether corroborated by documentary or physical evidence, and so forth. If the contention is not based on evidentiary facts, the attorney then may prepare to contest the issue based on the legal rules, the statutes, past precedents, and arguments to sway the court into landmark decisions distinguishing or overturning existing law.

The legal assistant drafting responses to such interrogatories must be aware of answers filed to the complaint and to prior interrogatories or requests for admission. There are few more embarrassing moments for a legal assistant than to prepare draft answers to a contention interrogatory or an interrogatory bearing on an important issue only to have the lawyer point out that the issue was substantially admitted in the filed answer to the complaint. One of those few moments, however, might be when the legal assistant's employing attorney relies on the draft answer and then is reminded by adversary counsel that the contention in issue was effectively disposed of in the pleadings.

8.0755 Narrow the Issues for Trial.   Cogent, timely interrogatories will force the exposure of information from the adversary under oath and thereby identify issues that either may be disposed of before trial or will be disputed matters in court.

The purpose of discovery is to eliminate the need for jury or court adjudication of undisputed facts. Also, if the matter is solely one of law, the court can determine the matter without a jury since the jury considers and renders verdicts only on the facts of a case; the court (judge) decides issues of law and instructs the jury.

8.076   Benefits of Interrogatories.

8.0761 Piercing the Corporate Veil.   Pursuit of the major objectives listed above have many distinct benefits to the party who intelligently uses this device. The plaintiff suing a corporation can, through interrogatories, "pierce the corporate veil" and identify that particular person, file, or policy most important to the establishment of the facts of the case. The corporation must provide all the information and facts available to it (and to its counsel) on a given question; thus, the interrogatory is a highly effective tool for the individual plaintiff against an economically superior adversary.

The careful, methodical creation of appropriate interrogatories, whether one set or many, and analysis of the responses can provide a factual foundation for productive depositions and requests for production of documents by establishing organization, chain of command, policies, practices, standards of the industry, applicable regulations, file systems, and so on.

If a diligent discovery effort has been conducted to identify the cause of an accident, but neither interrogatories nor depositions have elicited explanations of the event from the parties or percipient witnesses, and if independent investigation and expert witnesses have developed theories rather than facts, yet the accident could not occur if everything and everyone operated reasonably and properly, the attorney may have the data to support a *res ipsa loquitur* pleading. The *res ipsa* pleading, if accepted in a civil tort case for negligence, shifts the burden of proof from the plaintiff to the defendant; however, the plaintiff must show (1) that the accident should not occur in the absence of negligence by someone; (2) it did not occur as the result of negligence by the plaintiff; (3) that the instrumentalities as well as the means for determining what went wrong were totally within the defendant's control; and (4) that good faith and diligent efforts to learn what went wrong and caused the accident were unproductive. The legal assistant must therefore look for productivity of facts from interrogatories as well as for a pattern of factual suppression or nondisclosure in this discovery medium coupled with sparse returns in the informal and other formal discovery activities to support the *res ipsa* plea.

8.0762 *Overcoming Language Problems.* Written interrogatories are an excellent means of surmounting communication obstacles of the adverse party. It matters little whether the obstacle is illiteracy or lack of English facility (sometimes a deadly problem in depositions), blindness, deafness, senility, incapacity due to illness, injury, or the side effects of medication. The written interrogatory must be answered by the party through such assistance as is necessary. The opposing counsel has the burdens of obtaining responsive answers from his or her client, the client's agents, or from the file and of submitting the answers in timely fashion. The questions and answers are in English, verified and under oath or, if in a foreign language, accompanied by an English translation.

8.0763 *Foundation for Summary Judgment.* Cogent, pointed, and extensive interrogatories are a legitimate and effective means of exposing one who files an exaggerated or specious lawsuit. Similarly, it is an ideal and economic way to force the arrogant, but unresponsive, tortfeasor into a posture of truthful disclosure on the issues. The objective here, of course, is to force quick and timely resolution of the matter without extensive legal proceedings and their attendant cost. The correct and timely use of interrogatories often will elicit sufficient information that, being given under oath, can be used by the lawyer in support of a motion for summary judgment when that action is appropriate.

8.077   Pitfalls.

For every benefit, there may be a pitfall. The use of interrogatories can create at least the following problems:

8.0771 *Forcing the Adversary to Prepare the Case.* The untimely submission of extensive interrogatories of a highly pointed nature, especially where the adversary's case has substantial merit, may force the adversary attorney to prepare that case much earlier than otherwise. The attorney, of course, makes the tactical decisions; however, drafting the interrogatory frequently is delegated to the legal assistant. In the early development of the discovery plan, the merits of the case as they are appreciated by counsel must take into account the effect that extensive and detailed interrogatories may cause. It is a fact of life that many lawsuits are filed on "bare bones" allegation and seldom with a full set of supporting facts. Often both sides have good points in their favor and weaknesses in their positions. Discretion in answering and drafting interrogatories is appropriate.

8.0772 *The Paper War.* The filing of extensive and unnecessary interrogatories may spur the adversary into a similar response and create a "paper war." This is harassing and nonproductive in that it requires both legal assistant and attorney time with little benefit to the clients. This effect can be minimized by asking only cogent and relevant questions with obvious and limited purposes and by avoiding the trap of using reams of patterned or canned interrogatories of a general nature (sometimes called "boilerplate filings").

8.0773 Casual Handling.   Inexperienced legal assistants and occasionally attorneys under heavy calendar pressure will accept interrogatories from the adversary and forward them to the client for answer. Upon return, the answers are typed and filed without careful review or analysis of the questions or answers supplied. Since the answers are required to be under oath, the client is bound by the answers in future court proceedings, and it is difficult and embarrassing to attempt to correct even inadvertent errors.

Similarly, the execution of an answer solely from the attorney's work file without consultation with the client or knowledgeable sources is extremely dangerous. It is imperative that the attorney and/or legal assistant carefully peruse the questions that are posed and decide the best source of an answer, if any answer is to be given. Further, the answers must be checked for consistency with answers to pleadings, prior statements, depositions, and so forth before they are finalized.

8.0774 Unverified Answers.   Unverified answers, though not proper, often occur through failure (inadvertent or deliberate) of the responding party to execute the verification to which the propounding party is entitled. They cannot occur, however, unless the propounding party fails to check the answers to determine that they were submitted in verified form. Unverified answers are *not under oath* and do not have the same force and effect as an admission against interest, as the civil procedure rule intended. Due to the self-executing nature of interrogatories, the failure to detect the unverified answers and to move appropriately to compel verification in timely fashion may require resubmission of the interrogatories to the adversary in order to obtain the value desired. Occasionally, a stipulation will correct the defect.

The attorney who uses legal assistants will usually designate either the legal assistant or the legal secretary to check incoming answers for verification; however, the professional legal assistant recognizes that errors can occur and double-checks each set independently of office procedure or custom.

8.0775 Incomplete or "To Be Supplied" Answers.   Incomplete or "to be supplied" answers are very dangerous for the responding party. The propounding party has a right to complete answers. Any indication by the responding party that the answer is incomplete or will be supplied at a later date creates a burden that must be honored in the future.

The propounding party should follow up such an answer to ensure the answer is supplied. The legal assistant for either party has a significant burden to calendar the matter properly and be prepared, as discovery comes to a close, to resolve such incomplete answers.

Consider the effect of a plaintiff trying to get into court who, during discovery, files a "to be supplied" answer to an interrogatory of the defendant. Discovery reaches the closing stage (usually about thirty days prior to the trial) when the defendant moves to postpone the trial because the plaintiff has not completed response to the defendant's discovery. In many jurisdictions, the case might be removed from the calendar until discovery was completed and a new court trial date requested. Court backlogs are often months long, sometimes years. Dragging a case out may not be an exemplary means of representing a client, yet it may be an effective means of delaying the financial burden of a judgment and is seldom subject to sanctions of the court or bar association, provided the attorney has legitimate grounds for the postponement.

The lawyer and legal assistant are a team that effectively moves the case forward and denies the adversary these types of "sitting duck" grounds for postponements and delays.

8.0776 Unresponsive Answers.   Unresponsive answers are fairly common. Though they may contain a lot of words, they may not answer the question asked. The propounding party's responsibility is to review the answers and determine whether or not they are acceptable. If not, there is a limited period of time in which to compel responsive answers. Due to the self-executing nature of the interrogatories, an attorney who allows that period to pass without action waives the right to have the unresponsive answers corrected.

The legal assistant who reviews the answers as they arrive can be of great assistance to the lawyer on this point alone. Analysis of the question and its answer may reveal the question to be unclear, ambiguous, or capable of various meanings. The answer may be patently an evasion, a misunderstanding, a typographical error, or an inadvertent misstatement. Such an analysis will suggest the corrective action needed: a motion in court, a phone call to the adversary counsel, or a new set of more specific and clarifying interrogatories.

8.078   Motion to Compel Further Answers.

A motion to compel either complete answers or further answers is permitted by Federal Rule of Civil Procedure 37. The corresponding state rule or code section allows substantially the same motion. In every case, the rules of court outline the minimum requirements necessary for filing such a motion. In almost every case, the moving party must submit several documents. There is a notice of the motion, the motion itself, points and authorities supporting the motion, and a declaration by the attorney as to the legitimacy of the motion. One of the most common errors is the manner in which the court is made aware of the question asked, the answer provided, and the reason that particular response is unacceptable to the propounding party. Most courts have adopted rules that require the following content in the motion:

(a)   State the full text of each interrogatory that is not fully answered, then

(b)   Immediately following each question, quote the answer given by the answering party and/or the objection thereto in full; and then

(c)   Provide a short statement of the moving counsel's contention that the interrogatory is not fully answered and/or the reasons why the responding party's objection should be overruled. The attorney may cite any points and authorities applicable to his or her position; and

(d)   The moving party must serve the documents, along with the notice of the motion and any other papers required by law, upon the party or parties against whom the motion is directed within the time period prescribed.

The burden is upon the party receiving the answers to interpret them correctly as being responsive or unresponsive, to determine whether the objections have merit or not, and to initiate such appropriate action as he or she feels legitimate. Allowing the statutory time period to pass without action will waive the right to file a motion to compel further answers on that set of interrogatories. The attorney's declaration usually must show that the information is reasonably believed to be available to the responding party and that the information sought is relevant to the proceedings and/or calculated to lead to the discovery of admissible evidence. Further, there must be a statement denying that answering the interrogatory will be *burdensome,* a *harassment,* or *oppressive,* if the adversary used those terms in objecting to the interrogatory. The courts are generally very lenient with interrogatories and usually will instruct responding parties to respond to the questions correctly and fully on an individual basis so long as there is not an extraordinary burden and so long as the questions do not constitute *oppression.* Oppression can mean inordinate expense for the value of the information provided or extraordinary work effort in ferreting out the information or determining the existence of information over long spans of time or through huge masses of paper with little or no probative value in the action at hand.

If the responding party has created an unnecessary burden (the motion to compel) on the propounding party in order to obtain the requested information, sanctions (the costs of the motion and appearances in court of the attorney) may be sought and obtained against the responding party. As a general and practical rule, courts are hesitant to grant sanctions early in a case or for failure properly to respond only to one set of interrogatories. A pattern of obstructive behavior or unwillingness to participate fairly and cooperatively in the process, however, may result in the court assessing financial sanctions against the noncooperating party.

8.079   Drafting Interrogatories.

Drafting interrogatories is one duty frequently assigned to legal assistants by the attorney and, mechanically, is one simply performed, provided the legal assistant is fully conversant with the facts in the case, the pleadings (complaint, answer, and reply), and has done some research into the elements of the cause of action involved. The kind of case will often direct the legal assistant to sources of pattern interrogatories or to the law firm's interrogatory file for questions that have worked very well in the past for the same type of case. Incident- or accident-type events lend themselves to certain styles of questioning. Contract disputes generate another set of typical questions. Product liability and antitrust cases often require extensive questions with different thrusts in several sets of interrogatories.

The "form books" written for preparing interrogatories are very helpful to the legal assistant, particularly to the inexperienced one, and should not be ignored. Neither should they serve as the *sole* source of information for the creation of questions. Previous sets of interrogatories used within the law firm on similar cases may be of great assistance in selecting questions phrasings from past cases (so long as both the legal assistant and the attorney have weeded out the nonproductive, argumentative, and ambiguous ones). Each set has some common elements.

8.0791 Introductory Paragraph.   Every set of interrogatories has an introductory paragraph in which the propounding party states that the responding party is directed to answer the following questions. In multiple-party cases, this introductory paragraph may be directed at each adversary party separately or to the parties jointly with instructions that each must answer separately.

8.0792 Definition of Terms.   Following the introduction may be a definition of terms used in the interrogatories. The definitions will include the identities of individuals or corporations, fictitious names, and so forth, which may be abbreviated or reduced to a one-word representation or acronym. For instance, if the suit happened to be against the United States Bureau of Reclamation of the Department of the Interior, "a definition might state the phrase 'USBR' when used within these interrogatories refers to the United States Bureau of Reclamation, Department of the Interior." This ensures that the propounding and answering parties both are using the same definition, eliminates ambiguity, and reduces length and unnecessary words. Similarly, if the defendant in the case is the fictitious firm, The National Textile Corporation of the North American Continent, a single-word identification such as "National" or an acronym "NTCNAC" may be used after the definition is supplied.

Similarly, words that will be used repetitiously throughout the questions may be defined at this time to good effect, both for clarity and for understanding. The word *documents* may be defined as "letters, memoranda, notes (whether handwritten or typed), studies, reports, bound books or volumes, photographs, tape recordings, belt recordings, disc recordings, or other forms of memorialized material in stored form are, without limitation, included within the term *documents*.

Another opportunity to shorten questions is the word *identity* by defining it as the following: " 'Identity' when requested in relation to a *natural* person in these interrogatories, requires the full name, age, home address, home telephone number, business or occupational title, place of employment, address of employer, business telephone number, and Social Security number, as minimum elements when available. 'Identity' when referring to documents requires the following minimum information to be provided: date, type of document, author, addressee, major topic or title of the document, the number of pages comprising the document plus any attachments or exhibits incorporated by reference therein."

To avoid unnecessary verbiage in referring to an *accident,* the identity of the accident may be provided in the definition of terms by something similar to the following: " 'Accident' when used herein refers to that incident which occurred on _____ day of _____ month in 19__ in which two vehicles collided at the intersection of _____ Street and _____ Avenue in the town of _____, Arkansas, and is the focus of this lawsuit, unless otherwise specified." Definitions of this general type allow the subsequent questions to be phrased with a minimum of words and a maximum of meaning, specificity, and to command productive answers. In very complex litigation, there is a tendency to expand the definition of terms to such length that they become unwieldy and difficult to remember, either by the plaintiff or the defendant. Where this occurs, the definition of terms has lost its purpose and may create a situation where the answering party may respond with an objection on grounds of burdensomeness and oppression.

8.0793 Numbering System.   At the outset of drafting the interrogatories, it is important to establish the numbering system to be used and then to follow it. Whether each question will receive a separate arabic number or whether a decimalized system (a parent question followed by a decimal subsection) or an arabic number with alphabetic subparagraphs is to be employed is immaterial so long as the decision is made early in the process and strictly followed. In federal court, it is necessary to number all questions sequentially in order, even when moving from one set of interrogatories to another, for the convenience of the parties and the court. This is a technique that may be required in some state courts and is a great convenience to the legal assistant. If it is not required but permitted, use of the sequential numbers through several sets of interrogatories is a great help later on in collation of answers against issues of fact and allegations.

8.0794 *Considerations in Drafting Interrogatories.*

(a) Timing. Probably the most important single aspect to be considered in drafting interrogatories is the timing of the set being propounded. A number of considerations of the types of questions to be asked bear both tactically and strategically upon the conduct of the case.

Early in the case, it is important to identify people, locations, sources, and documents. It is not so important to seek the contentions of the adversary. If it is not an accident case (an isolated incident) in which facts are peculiarly within the knowledge of the party, questions seeking facts may make the adversary counsel perform research for his or her own information, if not to answer interrogatories, far sooner than otherwise. Similarly, contention questions asked early require the adversary attorney to sit down and weigh the legal positions very carefully.

Conversely, interrogatories submitted to the adversary late in the case concentrate on contentions and on the facts on which they rely. Questions regarding identities (late in the case) may be used primarily to check on such informal discovery the adversary may have conducted since the case began regarding which little information was provided in the earlier interrogatory sets or may identify expert witnesses, or only the discovery of documents or evidence that bears on the matters at issue.

(b) Question format. Another consideration is the format of the questions to be used. While interrogatories presuppose questions, they commonly are phrased in "demand-like" terms, such as "Please state . . . ." As a professional exercise for the legal assistant, it is much better to practice writing interrogatories in question format to avoid the possibility of creating a statement that does not require a response. For instance,

> "If you will do so without a motion to produce, attach copies of the above documents to the set of interrogatories."

This statement is seen quite frequently in hurriedly and thoughtlessly prepared interrogatories. It requires no answer, it requires no attachment of interrogatories—it's a useless, wasted statement. Far better if it were a subquestion to a series of questions regarding documents, such as:

> "3.d. Will you attach copies of the documents described above without the necessity of a legal motion to produce?
>   3.e. If so, please attach such copies to your answers."

In this manner, the answering party has either to provide all of the identifying data requested or attach copies of the documents to the interrogatories; in either case, the party must respond.

Alternatives are to spell out in the definition of terms the option to attach the documents or to identify the document, the storage location, and the custodian with sufficient specificity to allow filing an appropriate motion to produce. These alternatives, though attractive, are poor choices that provide the adversary with room for "inadvertent omission" or an objection to "complex, confusing, and oppressive instructions."

(c) Relevant time span. In propounding questions to the adverse party, it is important to consider the time span to be covered in the questions. Whether an

accident, business litigation case, or antitrust case, many of the records, conduct and actions of the party precedent to the event causing the litigation are important. However, seeking information preceding the event that gave rise to the action must be, in some way, relevant.

It is important that the inquiry into past events, documents, and conduct be sufficiently comprehensive to discover anything that is relevant or is capable of producing leads to admissible evidence in the case; however, it is also important to balance that need with the practical reality that a shorter period of time will involve a smaller volume of material for reasonable search. A short, relevant period may encourage the adversary party to respond to the request rather than to stonewall it, object to it, or provide partial or incomplete answers. This type of decision can be made only by the attorney; however, a careful analysis of the *probability* of usable data for the long and short period should be made. The legal assistant should be prepared to make a well-founded recommendation on the period of time to cover for the various kinds of material sought. Some records have a reasonable life of only one year, some three years; some financial data must be preserved for seven years, and some corporate data may be permanent and/or perpetual (life of the corporation plus a statutory period). The purpose is discovery of factual data, not exercises in law and motion filings, and only reasonable requests will produce effective discovery.

(d) Tense in questions. Lawsuits concern matters in the past, and the phrasing of interrogatories in the proper tense is extremely important. If the current practice of a party is sought, the question must ask, "What *is* the practice. . . ." If the past practice is important, then it must ask, "What *was* the practice of the company. . . ." Consider only the time involved. The use of wrong verb tense results in a truthful but useless answer and wastes time. The service of the interrogatory requires a few days, whether by hand or through the mail; then the responding party has thirty days in which to answer. Naturally, an extension may be requested and may be provided for any long or complex series of questions or because of illness, conflicting assignments of the adversary party's counsel or so on. A poorly prepared question conceivably could waste anywhere from forty-five days to several months of time in the preparation of the case. Sloppy questions are expensive in terms of time. Remember, also, that discovery closes before the trial, and all answers must be in by then. If a sloppy question is asked and the answer is due shortly before the close of discovery, it may be impossible to serve the rephrased question to obtain the needed information.

(e) Simple questions. Keeping the question simple, partly through using the definition of terms described above and restricting the use of adjectives and adverbs, will result in answers to the questions, rather than evasions or objections.

For instance, if the case involved an excavation by the defendant in which a pipeline was struck and damaged, the tendency to ask a question like the following might arise:

> "Did an employee of the defendant during excavation on June 12, 1979, strike, damage, and sever a five-inch cast-iron water pipeline three and one-half feet below the surface of Jackson Street, Oklahoma City, Oklahoma?"

The question is capable of easily being answered "no" in a truthful manner by the defendant. It is possible the defendant did not know it was a "cast-iron pipe"; it is possible he did not know he had "struck, broken, and damaged" it; it is possible he did not know how deep it was.

It is far better to have the information in several questions:

"Did an employee of the defendant strike a buried pipeline on _____ day? How deep was the pipe buried at the point of contact? Where did he report the contact to have occurred? (Please provide street, location, distance laterally from the south side of the road, distance from the nearest intersecting street, or alternatively, provide photographs and sketches that may have been made regarding this event.)"

Trying to write one clear, but complex, question, rather than a related pattern of simple questions—each with a specific, clearly focused object—is dangerous, may be unproductive and time wasting, and may still require additional questions in clarification.

(f) Belief questions. Such questions as "Why did he do . . ." or "Why did he say . . ." are particularly unproductive, especially in the early stages of the case. Almost every such question will produce answers like "He believed he had a right to . . ." and "He said it because he believed it to be true." Depositions are usually far more productive than interrogatories because of the spontaneity of the answers and because the deponent must respond to the question without an opportunity to consider the "best" answer and the adversary counsel cannot edit, phrase, or clarify the answers.

After drafting a question, or a series of questions, test them by answering them as unresponsively as possible. If the propounding party can answer the question unresponsively, a responding party should have no difficulty in providing the same type of answers, perhaps in full truth and perhaps by rationalization.

(g) Spelling. Good spelling is essential in writing interrogatories. Misspelling the name of the party or of any witness, the street, town, or any other identifiable feature, document, or matter of inquiry will result in an answer that negates the value of the question. It is true that a stipulation may be entered into correcting the spelling; however, it is equally true that a professional should be able to draft and double-check written matters in a timely fashion to preclude the need for seeking favors of the adversary. Effective lawyers prefer to grant courtesies to the adversary rather than seek them.

8.0710   Types of Information Sought by Interrogatories.

Among the things that will be essential to establish in the course of the trial and can be developed through interrogatories are the following:

8.07101 Identities of Parties.   Identity and family description to include full name, date of birth, Social Security number, height and weight, and color of hair and eyes. In some situations, the attorney may ask questions about nicknames, maiden or adoptive names, aliases, professional names, pen names, and identifying characteristics such as scars, tattoos, and/or deformities or disabilities, citizenship status, naturalization dates, immediate family, immigration sponsor, and so forth.

8.07102 Addresses.   Addresses, both residential and business. Normally, questions on current residence and business addresses present few problems; however, the same may not be true regarding prior residences and prior employment. Interrogatories provide the responding party an opportunity to consult records and give complete and thorough answers; at deposition, the witness may not recall and decline to speculate or guess.

8.07103 Educational Background.   It may be relevant to inquire into the educational background of the witness. The time period involved must be considered. The attorney will always consider the purpose and value of such request before determining the total extent of inquiry to be made.

8.07104 Marital and Parental Status.   Marital status and parenthood can be significant as well as the status of the marriage (common domicile, legal separation, pending interlocutory decree, reconciliation, and so on) and the domicile and dependence of children or other close relatives.

8.07105 Employment History.   Evaluation of damages or the ability to respond to damages may make inquiry appropriate regarding past employment, including names and addresses of the employers, dates of employment or self-employment, hours worked in a typical week, the job titles and description of the work performed, rate of pay, and monthly income received. Along these same lines, the reasons for termination of employment may be significant. In the case of a plaintiff, such inquiry might be necessary to establish the financial basis for calculating the effect the incident had on future prospects of employment in the same lines of work, effect on advancement, and effect on future income. Such data might be helpful in evaluating different settlement options and so on.

8.07106 Military Records.   Occasionally, military and draft records can be helpful, such as medical history, discharge status, and disciplinary records.

8.07107 History of Crimes or Citations.   Conviction of crimes or infractions of statutory rules that have any kind of bearing on the case can be explored. The crime of perjury, for instance, is highly significant in any case. Violations involving alcohol or drugs also could be significant.

8.07108 Compliance with Regulatory Rules.   Compliance with or citations for violations of administrative rules, building codes, standards of health and hygiene may be a proper area of inquiry, depending on the case.

8.07109 Ownership Interest in Real Property.   Ownership interest in real or chattel property may be highly relevant and pertinent to the case. In a slip-fall case, the owner of the real property is clearly involved—perhaps not liable but involved. So, too, might be a lessee, a sublessee, or even a tenant, depending on the circumstance, the contracts involved, any indemnities, and so on. Therefore, the questions can be drafted, and the attorney will decide whether to discard or serve them.

8.071010 History in Civil Litigation.   Past history as a plaintiff or defendant in a civil action or accidents may be sought through interrogatories, particularly if they are relevant to the case at hand. A plaintiff with a history of eight lawsuits for the same type of back injury may be discovered.

8.071011 Official Identity of Fictitious Persons.   Obviously, if the defendant, or sometimes the plaintiff, is a business, a fictitious person, or a person doing business under a title not linked with his or her own name, inquiry into the identity of the organization, structure, officers, or managerial personnel is appropriate.

Similarly, the authority under which the organization does business (such as articles of incorporation), partnership agreements, or the filing of the fictitious name with the appropriate regulatory agency are all suitable for inquiry and proper questioning. Distribution of stock, identity of any required public reports, agencies that regulate or license the business, standards of the industry, and the agency or association that sets the standards can be elicited by proper questions.

8.071012 *Insurance Coverage.* Types of insurance coverage; the carrier and the limits that are involved in such coverage; whether the insurer has raised any defenses to the assertion of coverage by a party to the action; whether the accident occurred in the course and scope of the defendant's employment; and whether any subrogation rights are claimed are proper areas of inquiry. Knowing the extent of insurance coverage may be significant in settlement discussion and the decision of whether to settle. In some states, the plaintiff can file an offer to settle the case near insurance policy coverage limits, which forces the insurer to consider the merits of the case carefully and the probability of the judgment size in a timely fashion in order to keep good faith with the insured defendant. Cases have occurred where an opportunity to settle was refused; the case was tried, and a judgment rendered in excess of the settlement offer and of the policy limits. The insured defendant then sued the insurer on a "bad faith" theory and prevailed.

Thus, accurate and timely insurance data, damage calculation and verification, and early consideration of a reasonable settlement offer are necessary.

8.071013 *Consumption of Alcohol or Drugs.* In accident cases, certain questions regarding the events prior to the accident are appropriate. Among these are ones probing the consumption of drinks or drugs of any kind that have or could have any effect on the physical capacity of the individual. Where such questions are asked, the time preceding the event, the frequency and quantity of consumption, the place and location where the products were ingested, and the witnesses who were present during the consumption are all important to ascertain. The quantity and quality and name or type of drug, medicine, or beverage taken, whether or not any of these were obtained by doctor's prescription are needed, as well as the identity of the doctor and of the pharmacy providing the medication. This information gives rise to questions regarding the mental or physical condition for which the medication was prescribed, the duration of the treatment, and the effect the medication is supposed to have on the person's physical capabilities and mental capacity. The defendant's activities during the period immediately preceding the accident should be established, as well as the presence or absence of witnesses who can attest to such events and activities.

8.071014 *The Accident Scene and Conditions.* The description of the accident scene itself is important. It will encompass all the basic elements to fix the event in time and place, including: the date, time, and exact location of the accident; the weather conditions at the time; visibility; if the location is in a public area; and all of the surrounding traffic conditions that may have contributed to it, such as the sidewalks, street surfaces, the presence or absence of curbs, the presence or absence of shrubbery, fences, street lights, holes, posts, traffic signals, warning signs, crosswalks, guards, custodians, and so forth.

8.071015 *How the Accident Occurred.* (Sometimes this is better handled at deposition.) Ask *how* the accident occurred. The plaintiff or defendant certainly is one of the witnesses who must have a good grasp on how the accident mechanically occurred and should be asked to describe it and name each element that contributed to the accident, such as a physical object, meteorological conditions, or physical incapacity. At this time, ask a series of questions in an attempt to identify any documents, reports, photographs, or other devices used to memorialize the accident, the conditions, or circumstances around them.

8.071016 *Knowledge of the Adversary's Statements.*

Each party always poses questions to the adversary as to whether they talked with or heard any statement by the (or any) other party (the propounding attorney's client) concerning the accident at any time. Partly this determines whether they have an opinion as to what the adverse party (client) may have said, whether those statements were admissions against interest, and, if so, whether there were any witnesses to what was said.

8.071017 *Party's Conversations with Others.*

It is important to ask the other party (or parties, plaintiff, defendant, or co-defendants) if they have given any statement or had any conversations with other persons (investigators, police officers—anyone other than their attorney) about the accident, and, if so, to identify that person and the date, time, and place the conversation took place, the substance of the conversation both in what the party said to the individual and what the individual responded. If a written statement or some other memorialized transcript of the dialogue has been created, seek the location of that record, who the custodian is, and how it can be obtained.

8.071018 *Identities of Witnesses.*

It is essential always to seek the identity of any witnesses known to the other party.

8.071019 *Identities of Experts.*

Identification of any expert is appropriate. Questions will identify them, any reports they may have submitted, and whether or not any have been retained to provide testimony at trial or assistance in the investigation.

8.071020 *Existence of Photographs, Maps, Sketches, and Models.*

Occasionally, maps, diagrams, and models will be made specifically for the trial by one party or the other. Appropriate questions will develop whether such items exist, the current location, the types of such representation, and the name, address, and location of the person who prepared them. Similarly, physical evidence may play a part in the case, and appropriate questions can and should develop whether such physical evidence is held by the party or his or her counsel. The propounding party is entitled to inquire into the nature of each item, the time and place the evidence was obtained or acquired and the name, address, telephone number, and place of employment of the person who is custodian of the evidence at the current time. A follow-up question of whether inspection of the evidence will be permitted is essential.

8.071021 *Plaintiff's Damages and Life-style.*

The questions posed by the defendant will go very deeply into the damages allegedly sustained by the plaintiff. If the case is one of contract, business dispute, or property damage, interrogatories may well serve to document the loss and identify the supporting bills, estimates, expert appraisals, and so on.

When the case involves minor bodily injury, the medical treatments, records of hospitalization, doctors' reports, out-of-pocket-costs, and indirect but consequential costs can also be identified by written questions.

In every case where "pain and suffering" is a significant element of damages, interrogatories are a poor medium for developing sworn data. "Pain and suffering" includes more than the minimum definition of the two words. It extends to the current and future effect on the plaintiff's life-style, including hobbies, sports, volunteer work for groups and organizations, travel, perhaps the ability to sit comfortably through a symphony, to walk several miles a day along the seashore, or to concentrate long enough for competition chess or bridge. The attorney will undoubtedly seek that information through deposition.

8.0711   Exhibits to Interrogatories.

The attachment of exhibits to interrogatories can be a very helpful technique. It can also complicate the interrogatory procedure if there is poor planning of control and retrieval of the exhibits and the relevant questions and answers related to them.

At the outset of the discovery plan, some general estimate of the numbers of exhibits pertinent to the case should be made and numbering and control techniques chosen.

8.07111 *Case Exhibit Control Log.*   One effective system for controlling exhibits is the use of a case exhibit control log, which identifies each exhibit introduced by each party. It should run chronologically and permit the attorney to advance his or her own exhibits in numeric or alphabetic sequential order, whether in the complaint, the answer to the complaint, or in the interrogatories, depositions, requests for production of documents, or requests for admission (see Exhibit 34).

8.07112 *Interrogatory Exhibit Log.*   An alternative is to maintain an exhibit log for each discovery operation: interrogatories, depositions, requests for admission, and so on (see Exhibit 35).

The objective is to instill order into what can become a chaotic situation. Compare how simple reference to twenty exhibits introduced in the various proceedings can be if numerically in order (Plaintiff's Exhibits 1–20) with a situation where three were introduced in the complaint (Plaintiff's Exhibits A, B, and C), eight introduced in Plaintiff's Interrogatories to Defendant Set No. 1, (Exhibits 1, 2, 3, 4, 5, 6, 7, and 8), two in Plaintiff's Interrogatories to Defendant Set No. 2, (Exhibits 1 and 2), four in Deposition of Mr. L. Jones (Exhibits D1, D2, D3, and D4), and three in Plaintiff's Requests for Admission (Exhibits 1, 2, and 3).

Calling for Exhibit No. 2 (in the latter case) and the relevant foundation requires extensive description of the exhibit to ensure obtaining the correct Exhibit No. 2, then some research to find the foundation material.

Using a sequential numbering system requires close cooperation and discipline among the attorney, the legal assistant, and the legal secretary. If the case has more than one attorney assigned to it, the need for clear understanding of the procedure is increased. Everyone must be committed to making the system work.

8.0712   Answering Interrogatories.

Responding to interrogatories is peculiarly the responsibility of the client's attorney (whether the client is an individual or officer of the corporation). The legal assistant

EXHIBIT 34

CASE EXHIBIT CONTROL LOG

CASE:

ATTORNEY: DATE LAST POSTED:

CLIENT: LEGAL ASST.:

Plaintiff	Defendant	Description of Exhibit	How Introduced (Deposition, Interrogatory, etc.)

primarily assembles the factual data and may provide draft answers from which the responses are created. "Responding" and "answering" interrogatories are not necessarily the same. "Answering" includes *expository answers, fully complete as to all relevant known data;* however, that definition may include "volunteered" information that is beyond the exact call of the question or that is public information equally available to both sides. Such an answer may include the attachment of exhibits, documents, photographs, and declarations or the legal reasoning of the attorney and/or conclusions of law or fact, even self-serving argument.

"Responding" may include a refusal to answer interrogatories on a legal basis or may include only that portion of an answer that is within the personal knowledge and understanding of the client or of the attorney as independent facts without the color of subjective interpretation or protection of privilege.

EXHIBIT 35

		MASTER EXHIBIT LOG—INTERROGATORIES	
CASE:		DATE LAST POSTED:	
ATTORNEY:		LEGAL ASST.:	
Plaintiff	Defendant	Interrogatory Set and Question	Description of Exhibit

For instance, a question may seek "any and all evidence in your possession." The word *evidence* is one with a specific legal meaning and is not within the ability or authority of *one* attorney to determine. It usually is the title given by a trial judge to qualified exhibits introduced during the trial. Unless the propounding attorney stipulates blindly that each item identified in the answer will be accepted as an evidentiary exhibit at trial without protest, the responding attorney can avoid identifying anything in the response on the grounds that "the court identifies items or exhibits as evidence."

This poses a special responsibility on the legal assistant to ensure that all sources of information readily available to the client or the attorney are carefully searched and that properly inclusive responsive answers are drafted for the consideration and editing of the attorney and the client. This requires a careful analysis and full understanding of the interrogatories received.

Generally speaking, it is necessary to read every set of interrogatories at least three times before answers are drafted. The purpose of these reviews are as follows:

8.07121 *Reading—Two Times.*   The interrogatories are first read immediately on receipt, and they are not read analytically or argumentatively but from beginning to end, as a novel would be. This allows an appreciation of the flow and scope of the interrogatories and suggests the approach of the adversary party and the overall thrust of the set of questions: for example, does it seek facts, does it seek identities, does it seek contentions, are the questions pointedly specific or generalized and broadly inclusive, does it aim at clarifying proximate cause or at the defense of assumption of risk?

Following the initial reading, a careful question-by-question reading of the set is initiated by the legal assistant *independent* of the attorney. Some questions are of straight factual nature, while other questions appear to be mixed questions of fact and law, particularly susceptible to interpretation by the attorney; the third type of questions is those of pure law interpretation. The legal assistant makes notes during the analysis to include the probable responding responsibility as "legal assistant," "attorney," or "client."

8.07122 *Attorney and Legal Assistant Conference.*   The legal assistant schedules a planning meeting with the attorney to formalize the answering procedure. The attorney probably will have read the interrogatories (or may read them during the course of the meeting), and decisions then can be made about how to proceed in the case. The responding responsibilities noted by the legal assistant are affirmed or modified, and decisions on how to handle the "client" answers can be made—call the client to the office, mail a set of the questions with instructions to return by mail, or mail a set of questions and schedule a meeting at a later time for coordinating answers.

8.07123 *Source of the Answer.*   Following the attorney and legal assistant review of each question, the legal assistant must try to decide the *source* of the information for answers to the questions the attorney delegated to him or her. If it is the case file, the information can be extracted, and the answers drafted and presented for approval, editing, or rejection by the attorney.

Where the potential answer depends partially on a legal interpretation by the attorney, the factual data called for by the question should be assembled in draft form and a meeting scheduled with the attorney to discuss the interrogatory.

If the client is a corporation, it may be necessary to distribute certain specific interrogatories (questions) to various departments within the corporation and establish deadlines for the return of appropriate information in order to meet the time schedule imposed by the courts. A follow-up procedure is essential to have the answers fully drafted well in advance of the answer date. Many times the department will conclude that the information does not have to be provided and will want the attorney to object. The answer, of course, is "Get the data first!"

8.07124 *Burdensome and Oppressive Questions.*   Where questions pose severe burdens of time, money, staff work, travel, or so forth, in order to assemble the data required for answers, the attorney will consider objecting. Usually, the legal assistant is well versed in the facts of the case and the sources of information that interrogatories of this nature will require. Where it is anticipated that the search for the information required by interrogatories will be—or may be—"burdensome and oppressive," the legal assistant must assemble factual data on the nature of the burden to assist the attorney in deciding whether to object or to assemble all or a portion of the information for the answers. The foundation for such a decision is an estimate of the time and expense that assembling the data will require.

8.07125 *Time Schedule and Draft Response.*   The legal assistant is responsible for the time schedule of the response, the assembly of facts from the various sources, and the drafting of proposed inclusive answers together with data on question semantics that the attorney may wish to consider in editing, a collation of facts and sources for each answer, and any cross-referencing of questions or proposed answers to other questions, other answers, other sets of interrogatories, and so forth. Once the data is assembled and the answers drafted, a meeting with the attorney is held, and each question-and-answer group is analyzed. The draft is then edited and retyped in final form.

8.01726 *Final Draft.*   The final typed answers must be proofread with great care to ensure that the exact answers desired are properly produced, that all questions have a sufficient response, and that a last check for consistency and absence of conflict among the answers is made.

8.0713   Answering Responsibility and Control.

Where questions will be answered by a variety of sources, it sometimes is helpful to photocopy the entire set of interrogatories and supply each source with those questions he or she will answer factually. A long or complex series of pattern interrogatories (one basic question followed by related subsections based on alternative anticipated answers) can be controlled most effectively by photocopying the full set, then cutting and pasting each question onto a sheet (or two or three) of paper punched for three-ring binders. As the source's material is received, it is filed behind the question until it is time to draft answers. This system is helpful to the secretaries in engrossing answers, if thoughtfully done.

Alternatives are to punch two holes in the top margin of the set and mount the questions on the left hand side of a file folder and the data and draft answers on the right; or punch the set (without cutting and pasting) for three-ring binders, then assemble the data behind numbered dividers corresponding to the questions.

Any system is useful if it permits good control of due dates, orderly accumulation of factual data, and timely identification of problems, delays, and burdensome procedures. The whole function is to assist the attorney to respond on time.

8.0714   Engrossing Questions and Answers.

Federal Rules of Civil Procedure require the question and the answer to be engrossed in the filed answers. This practice is very helpful to all parties and to the courts and jury in the conduct of a case. Many state courts have adopted the same rules.

Many courts suggest and many attorneys routinely propound interrogatories with a substantial space between questions and/or subquestions. The space is intended to allow insertion of the answer after the question. Some firms have each question on a separate sheet of numbered paper. This allows their interrogatory files to be maintained simply and interrogatories assembled by selecting the proper sheets and numbering the questions appropriately.

Alternatively, the legal assistant can cut and paste and then photocopy interrogatories to create a work file and the secretary's master draft ready for the addition of answers.

8.0715   General Considerations.

8.07151 Duty to Respond.   The responding party to interrogatories, properly served, has a duty to answer each question separately, fully, responsively, and under oath, the only limitation being that the information requested be relevant to the subject matter of the action and/or reasonably calculated to lead to the discovery of admissible evidence. The exceptions, of course, are where the information is privileged, such as through attorney/client relationship or the work product of the attorney, or where the answer would be a burdensome and oppressive load on the respondent. Failure to answer a properly phrased, relevant interrogatory within the time allowed may result in an order to compel answers. Worse than that, the failure to *respond* on time may waive the attorney's right to *object* to answering any interrogatory for which a proper objection might have been made in a timely fashion.

8.07152 Form of the Answer.   Interrogatories sometimes appear repetitious, since the form of the question is changed slightly to ensure that the entire area of interest is covered and that the responding party, in avoiding an answer to one question, will be forced to respond to another. Unfortunately, this sometimes allows answering one interrogatory by reference to the answer of another interrogatory.

Occasionally, some counsel will refer in answers to interrogatories to pleadings, other documents, depositions, or other answers in previous interrogatories. This is sometimes called "the chain letter" answer, and it comes from finding the "Answer to Interrogatory 65," which refers to the "Answer of Interrogatory 37," which refers to the "Answer of Interrogatory 12," which refers to the "Answer of Paragraph III of the Complaint" and to the "deposition" of a witness. In order to learn exactly the answer to Interrogatory 65, it is necessary to work back through the entire chain of questions to the answer to the complaint and then attempt to determine whether the answer is truly responsive back down that chain to the ultimate question. This type of chain letter answer has been the topic of motions to compel in federal and state courts. In some cases, they have been held nonresponsive. Few courts believe that such chain letter answers are good practice. The weakness in this course is that the reference to the earlier answer must be truly responsive, and the earlier answer must be full and precise for the later question—a difficult task at best.

8.07153 Content of an Answer.   Once a party decides to answer an interrogatory, the answer should be clear, concise, and directly responsive to the question. Answers that are verbose yet evasive of the question encourage the opponent to seek a motion to compel together with sanctions for the need to so move. This wastes both parties' time and money and creates a poor climate in which to conduct the case.

The answer, of course, is limited only by the information that the responding party has at hand. It is not necessary to provide information that is unavailable to the client or over which neither the client nor the attorney has control. The question becomes one of degree of knowledge.

A corporation is peculiarly susceptible to a harsh interpretation of the duty to answer. While it may take substantial inquiry within the corporation to find, all information available to any employee of the corporation is equally available to the corporate entity and to its counsel.

8.07154 *Time to Answer.*   Every jurisdiction, whether federal or state, provides a specific period of time in which a response to the interrogatories must be filed. The response can be an objection to the entire set of interrogatories; it can be an answer to every question within the interrogatories; it can be a combination of answers to some interrogatories and objections to other interrogatories; and it can be a combination of answers and objections to some specific questions with partial information provided anyway, despite the objection.

A common practice, especially when there are complex questions requiring substantial amounts of time and effort, is to object to the question and yet provide a partial answer within the proper time limit. This places the propounding party in a difficult position of attempting to determine just how beneficial a motion to compel further answers would be. Obviously, the objection must be taken on reasonable grounds, and any information provided must be accurate, detailed, and responsive to some portion of the question asked.

Where additional time is needed to answer questions, a request to the propounding party for an extension may be made by telephone or by letter, and in most cases, one will be granted. There is no particular rule on the period of time to be granted as an extension. It is negotiated between the lawyers or their representatives. A technique that has been successfully used in many areas is to grant time to *answer* the interrogatories but not to *respond* to them.

The distinction is that the statutory time period allows any of the responses discussed above to be filed with the court. An extension of time *to answer only* in effect requires the responding party to waive the right to object or, alternatively, to timely file an objection to specific questions or the entire set. Where a limited extension of time to answer is given, that agreement should be confirmed the same day with a letter to the responding party from the propounding party signed by the counsel.

8.07155 *Grounds for Objection.*   Where the legal assistant finds the interrogatory extremely complicated, difficult to understand, or requiring excessive amounts of effort, research, audit, assembly, collation, and reporting of information to answer the interrogatories properly, objection to the interrogatories may be considered. It is necessary, therefore, that the legal assistant understand that the grounds for objection are essentially those of injustice. For instance, it is immaterial that the information requested may require hearsay, since interrogatories have a much broader range than admissible evidence at trial. The purpose is to discover or lead to the discovery of admissible evidence, not necessarily to provide it, though any answer given may be used against the respondent. If an objection is to be raised, it must be couched in phrases the court will honor, and those always must include a showing of some form of injustice to the responding party.

The attorney is the authority on objections and whether to file them. The legal assistant may find at the conclusion of the meeting in which the decision has been made to object that the attorney will say, "Give me the draft answers and objections tomorrow by ten, please, so they can be typed and filed by four."

Familiarity with some of the language can save substantial rewriting if the office does not have a set of standard "objection" phrases available.

(a) Continuing Answers. For interrogatories that require "continuing answers," the objection may be in something like this form: ". . . objects to this entire set of interrogatories on the grounds that the request to treat these interrogatories as a continuing obligation would create an unjust burden and oppression upon him." Under Federal Rules of Civil Procedure, the propounding counsel who wishes to obtain "continuing interrogatories" must petition the court specifically in a separate and distinct motion.

(b) Confusing Instructions. If the propounding party has a preface that includes confusing sub-instructions, it may constitute a basis for objection by the responding party that may be phrased something on this order: ". . . object to the form of the instructions controlling these interrogatories on the grounds that the instructions are so complex and contain so many sub-instructions of such detail that they require the respondent to spend unnecessary, extra, and unjustified time and effort to ascertain that the impact of reference on succeeding interrogatories is correctly appreciated and the instructions are therefore unjustly burdensome and oppressive."

This serves as a warning that, where instructions are going to be included within complex sets of interrogatories, they must be relatively few and clearly and reasonably phrased; otherwise, the propounding party is going to have a difficult time either obtaining an answer or having a motion to compel further answers sustained by a court.

(c) Public Records. Public records and documents are often sought by the propounding party and resisted by the responding party. The mere fact that the documents are a public record, equally available to both sides, is not a legitimate objection unless the objection is phrased in this sort of manner: ". . . the requested information is a matter of public record and in public documents that are not in defendant's possession or control and is equally available to plaintiff so that requiring defendant to locate, copy, and furnish such information would be an unjust burden and be oppressive to him."

(d) Irrelevancy. Some interrogatories go far afield and may intrude on areas not relevant to the issue at hand. In such case, an objection may stand on the basis of relevance, but it must be combined with a statement that the question ". . . is not reasonably calculated to lead to the discovery of admissible evidence." The burden then goes on the propounder to "move to compel" and to show the relevance and the reason behind the question as well as a connection to the discovery of admissible evidence. Such a motion will very likely be overruled by the court. Abusing this particular objection in subsequent sets of interrogatories, however, will probably result in sanctions being imposed against the respondent.

(e) Uncertainty and Ambiguity. Where an interrogatory is drawn in an uncertain and ambiguous manner to the extent that the attorney and legal assistant must impute meaning to the words, there is a basis for an objection that may be phrased in this fashion: "Interrogatory No. _____ and particularly the phrase '_____' is so ambiguous, uncertain, and unintelligible that defendant cannot frame a meaningful reply and objects therefore to the form of the question."

Probably the propounding party will not pursue this in a motion to compel. The easiest solution is to rephrase the question in a more intelligible fashion and serve it again. Alternatively, the responding party could answer this question by imputing to it the meaning most favorable to the client's case, objecting to the form of the question in the manner mentioned above, and then providing an answer consistent with the attorney's views of the client's best interest. This places the propounding party on a double hook of attempting to compel further answers to a poor question when a free and willing offer of some information has been obtained.

8.07156 *Contention Interrogatories.* Among the types of questions that may be asked in interrogatories, usually late in the case and shortly before trial, are contention interrogatories in which the attorney asks the adversary party for an explanation of his or her legal and factual contentions. These may be phrased in very simple terms, such as in Exhibit 36.

The basic question can be numbered to fit the numeric sequence of the set or case as desired.

Other alternatives are to pose a pattern of interrogatories based on a specific factual allegation and requiring the adversary to agree with the truth of the statement, to specifically deny the truth and expansively detail the grounds for the denial, or to admit the denial is not based on factual or evidentiary grounds. The format might appear as is shown in Exhibit 37.

With the pattern established, statements can be inserted to force the adversary into admitting their truth or, alternatively, pinpointing areas of disagreement and the factual foundation on which he or she relies. For example, insert the statement "Defendant was driving his own automobile in the proper traffic lane at a lawful rate of speed immediately preceding the collision with plaintiff's car" or "There are no independent witnesses who have expressed the belief that plaintiff violated defendant's right of way."

Such statements, if not contested, can dispose of many issues that otherwise would be tried in court. If the statements are contested, the patterned subparts and subsequent questions elicit an identification of the areas of disagreement, factual basis for the opinion, witnesses, whether an investigation was conducted, and so forth.

EXHIBIT 36

Do you contend that Plaintiff did not violate the right of way of the Defendant in the accident that is the focus of this lawsuit?

A. If so, please state:

(1) Each fact on which you base your contention.

(2) The identity of each person who has supplied you with information or testimony on which you base your contention. Identification requires names, address, telephone number, and relationship to plaintiff as a minimum.

(3) The location and description of any documents, objects, or other evidentiary facts or materials that you believe to support your contention.

(4) The custodian of any documents, objects, or other evidentiary facts or materials identified in (3) above.

EXHIBIT 37

Do you contend that the following statement, or any portion thereof, is not true?

If your answer to No. _____ is in the affirmative, state which portion thereof you contend is not true.

Is your contention (described in No. _____) based upon or supported by any facts known to you that are contrary to or inconsistent with the claimed truth thereof?

If your answer to No. _____ is affirmative, state:

a.   The evidentiary facts that support or tend to support your contention;

b.   The names of each person; and

c.   Identify each document on which you rely.

If your answer to No. _____ is negative, state whether you have conducted any investigation or inquiry as to the truth or falsity of said statement.

If your answer to No. _____ is negative, state with particularity all bases, reasons, and grounds for your nonfactual contention contrary to or inconsistent with the claimed truth thereof.

The execution of a few critical statements in contention interrogatories of this variety, which must be answered under oath, may eliminate a substantial number of issues from the trial, particularly if the submission of the interrogatories and the answers are very close to the trial. They are far more beneficial than requests for admission, since they allow the follow-up questions in explanation of a denial of the base question.

If contention interrogatories are used early in the trial, the attorney attempts to determine a better foundation for a vague or uncertain pleading and tries to require the adversary counsel to state the issues with specificity to simplify the progress of the case. It is difficult to elicit much supporting data of the contentions until the discovery process has matured, however.

8.07157 Collation and Analysis of Interrogatories.   The legal assistant is charged with recording all questions posed to the client. It is necessary to accumulate both the questions and the answers and to relate them in some collated form to the issues or the elements of proof in the case. Both elements of proof of the issues and the elements of proof of the defenses expected should be accumulated.

Every case begins with an allegation. Discovery leads both parties into admissions under oath and statements against interest that reveal the conduct of the parties and, to a certain extent, where the responsibility for any given event lies. The collation of this information—together with informal discovery testimony, the physical evidence, and demonstrative evidence that has been developed—will serve to pinpoint the issues to be determined at trial. It will expose defenses for the defendant and points of fact for the plaintiff when it is carefully and diligently pursued.

8.07158 *Adversary Answers to Interrogatories.* It is important for the legal assistant to analyze carefully and immediately on receipt the answers provided by the adversary to the client's interrogatories. Evasiveness in answering and non-responsive answers must be pinpointed immediately since there is a very short period between when the answers are filed and any motions to compel further answers can legitimately be made. Occasionally, the answers to interrogatories are incomplete or unresponsive but without a pattern of obvious deception or intent to deny the information called by the interrogatories. As a custom in analyzing answers that appear in this fashion, it is appropriate to note and measure what was sought in the question and what was provided in the answer.

Where the relationship is reasonable, sometimes the matter can be resolved by phoning the adversary counsel's office and asking if the incomplete answers were inadvertently provided without detailed checking and by volunteering an extension of time in which to answer. This conduct usually is well received. (This tactic is employed only with the approval and authority of the attorney, of course.)

In cases where the answers are patently nonresponsive and deliberately incomplete, the same procedure may be followed, if the legal assistant's attorney agrees, and the offer of additional time is made in writing and uses a phrase similar to: "This will confirm the telephone conversation between my legal assistant, Mr. Jones, and Ms. Smith of your office regarding your incomplete Answers to our Interrogatories Set No. 2 in which we offered to extend the time for your answers for fifteen days. It is assumed that the time for us to file a motion to compel further answers will be tolled until we are notified that your answers will stand as submitted or we receive the correct answers."

A device of this nature places the burden on the responding party to decide whether to stand on the answers or provide additional information. Similarly, it protects the right of the legal assistant's counsel to go to court and move to compel the respondent to provide further answers yet shows cooperation and courtesy and may elicit the requested information in the fifteen-day period without having to spend time preparing a motion, filing it, obtaining a date for hearing, the attorney appearing and arguing the matter (provided it is not continued), having the matter submitted and ruled upon at a later date, and the respondent being ordered to answer further within a specified period. Conceivably, those answers may not be responsive either, and the process may have to be repeated.

8.07159 *Utility of Interrogatories.* Any expression made by the attorney or the client in answer to interrogatories is usable by any other parties in the action as an admission against interest of the client. The phrasing of answers in a self-serving manner is not particularly beneficial to the client for his or her own use as an evidentiary offering unless, at some future date closer to trial, contention interrogatories or a request for admission are submitted asking that those answers are accepted by the adversary as true. In other words, a party cannot use his or her own answers to another party's interrogatories as *proof* of the fact in issue, although an adversary may be able to use those answers (because they are under oath) as proof of a fact against the respondent.

This situation emphasizes the importance of knowing the foundation of each answer supplied and that the answers are as factually correct and consistent as possible.

Analysis of the other party's answers is extremely helpful to the attorney, particularly where the interrogatories incorporated documents attached as exhibits and answers were obtained that specifically or impliedly affirmed the documents as true or correct copies of originals. If the originals cannot be found, some foundation has been laid to introduce the exhibits as "secondary evidence" at trial.

8.071510   Additional, Supplemental, or Correcting Answers.   Frequently, in the submission of answers to interrogatories, not all of the information is available within the time limit specified. In such cases, it is appropriate to indicate "supplemental information will be provided" or "is to be supplied," "documents will be supplied at a time mutually convenient to counsel on request," or similar phrasing where the information is not being provided, no objection to the production is raised, and it is promised for delivery in the future. Where such commitments are made, it is important to record the promise and to follow up on fulfilling it.

After a reasonable time, the responding party should either voluntarily provide the information, or the propounding party should inquire, in writing, when it will be provided.

A sequence of letters seeking completion of the promised discovery over a period of time may serve as a sufficient foundation for a motion to compel at a later time, together with an award of sanctions for dilatory or unresponsive performance by the adversary.

The legal assistant always suspects that "to be supplied" answers conceal important data in a case and should keep close track of and repeatedly follow up on such matters with the attorney and the adversary's office.

Where it is learned that information previously supplied in answer to interrogatories is incorrect, a supplemental answer correcting that information should be supplied (requested of the adversary, if appropriate) in order to clarify the record. It is extremely difficult to make such corrections of inadvertent error at trial. The attorney, the court, and juries dislike it. The legal assistant constantly keeps track of the factual matters developed in a case and, as factual conflicts are identified, brings them to the attention of the attorney. The legal assistant can prepare drafts of supplemental answers or stipulations to correct and clarify the situation.

Interrogatories are effective and productive forms of discovery whose force and effect can be amplified or diminished by the legal assistant's skill, organization, control, and ability to retrieve data for the attorney. They are an outstanding means of demonstrating imagination, judgment, analytical ability, and tenaciousness.

8.08   Depositions

Depositions are a primary tool of discovery in civil proceedings. They are the mechanism by which a party or a witness is examined orally under oath by counsel for each party to the action. The Federal Rules of Civil Procedure provide a mechanism for such depositions in federal cases (Rule 30). State courts generally have parallel provisions within their codes or statutes. Federal Rule of Civil Procedure

31 provides for depositions on *written* questions, which can be used for witnesses located some distance from the court or the offices of counsel. However, face-to-face depositions are preferred.

8.081   Lawyer's View of Depositions.

Lawyers generally favor depositions over most other forms of discovery for information *within* the personal knowledge of a witness or party to the action. Questioning the witness, under oath and in the presence of the attorney, affords the lawyer an opportunity to evaluate the witness in terms of credibility, spontaneous response, and depth of knowledge. Unlike with interrogatories, the witness must respond spontaneously, in his or her own words, to the questions and generally cannot consult other counsel for a favored phrasing of particular answers.

In incident (accident) cases, the witness' testimony of how the accident happened may be the only basis the jury has of judging the case. The appearance, articulation, and credibility of the witness is of supreme importance to the case. Depositions on oral examination afford the counsel for each of the parties an opportunity to examine and cross-examine the witness and to measure the impact of the witness on the case before entering the courtroom. Questions at depositions are not limited by the same rules of admissibility of evidence as testimony at trial and therefore nearly all relevant questions or those that may lead to the discovery of admissible evidence are permitted.

8.082   Depositions and Legal Assistants.

Depositions provide an extraordinary opportunity for the legal assistant to display knowledge of the case, insight, thoroughness, organization, judgment, and analytical ability.

Depositions should involve both the attorney and the legal assistant and should be a part of a discovery plan, carefully scheduled, timed, and executed. The plan should include the *types of information* anticipated from each potential witness and the order of deposing them. Sometimes it is best to depose the adversary party first, to create a sworn record before the opinions and recollections of independent witnesses are heard. This prevents or limits rationalizations, correction of any misinterpretations, or refreshing recollections by the adversary.

A deposition outline of important or salient points is created prior to the commencement of the deposition. This outline is generated by evaluating all of the facts known in the case and anticipating the areas in which the witness should be knowledgeable. It is important in creating the outline to annotate it in a manner that allows the lawyer, during questioning, to measure the deponent's answers against wholly known and established facts. The outline may be a sheet of paper with an appropriate heading at the top showing the case name, the deponent's name, the date, location, and the page number. A vertical line is drawn to divide the sheet of paper in half. This allows space on the left for annotation of important points and/or known data the attorney wishes to review during the deposition and space on the right to record the answers provided by the deponent and/or placement of corroborative type information sufficient to assist the attorney in measuring the honesty and credibility of the witness or to record introduction of exhibits (see Exhibit 38).

The attorney independently creates an outline, compares both, and adds such data as he or she desires to his or her own outline, if one is used. The legal assistant may make suggestions on the introduction of exhibits at the time of

EXHIBIT 38

DEPOSITION OUTLINE

CASE: Smith v Jones   DEPO DATE: 6 January 1990

DEPONENT: Albert Smith, plaintiff   LOCATION: 1421 - 6th Avenue
                                                   Sacramento
ATTYS: E. Gibson for Jones
        N. Mason for Smith

Items to cover	Known facts?
ID: Albert Smith Age Res SSN	√ 43 2130 "I" St., Sacramento 238 - 45 - 9726
Educ:	Wilson HS, Sacramento
Employ:	State of Calif. Dept. of Highways 51 - 79

---

planning the deposition and (once the attorney determines the exhibits to be used) assembles a set of three copies, one for the lawyer, one to give the court reporter, and one for the deponent to review and to refer to, if any discussion of the item is planned. The copies and the original, if available, for each exhibit are packaged in an envelope or file folder. The packages are arranged in order of their planned introduction.

The attorney and the legal assistant may discuss the upcoming deposition in substantial detail to foster familiarity with the factual data developed, specialized language, critical areas to be covered, and any credibility tests to be used.

8.083   Depositions, Subpoenas, and Service.

Deponents generally must be subpoenaed unless they are adverse parties. Parties usually attend the deposition without service of a subpoena, by notice to or arrangement with counsel. In either event, it is necessary to understand the limitations imposed by the court for the service of the subpoena. Federal and state courts do not allow parties in a lawsuit indiscriminately to impose burdensome travel requirements on potential witnesses. Federal Rule of Civil Procedure 45 imposes specific mileage limitations for categories of witnesses in certain types of proceedings. The state courts, similarly, impose limitations on the distances over which a subpoena is effective. Proper service requires the location of the witness to be fixed and the place of taking the deposition to be adjusted when necessary to the convenience of the witness. Occasionally, it is possible to arrange for a witness to travel farther than the court order subpoena can normally enforce. The witness always is entitled to a statutory witness fee and mileage from home to the place of deposition at a court-fixed rate. Where a witness cooperates by traveling greater distances than required, loses wages, or incurs special expenses for the convenience of the lawyers and parties, arrangements to reimburse out-of-pocket costs can be made without tainting the witness's credibility and testimony.

The service of a subpoena carries with it the responsibility of insuring that it is properly executed. Proper execution requires that the subpoena set forth the purpose of the subpoena. For instance, to take a deposition on oral examination, the subpoena will indicate that the person is required to "appear to testify." Alternatively, if the person is a witness to testify and is in custody of certain documents that are of interest to the case, the subpoena must specify that he is "to appear to testify and to produce documents." The subpoena must provide a description of the general categories of documents that are requested and a declaration by the attorney that they are necessary to the deposition, relevant to the case, and either constitute potential evidence or may lead to the discovery of admissible evidence in the case. Where such a subpoena is issued, the witness must appear with all of the documents specified in the subpoena and be prepared to discuss them.

A check payable to the witness for one day's witness fees (depending upon the current statutory reimbursement specified in the court rules) and mileage (one way to the place of the examination) must be proferred when the subpoena is served.

Some state courts require that the fees be presented only if requested. It is proper and prudent in most cases to ensure that the person serving the subpoena has the check made out in advance or carries sufficient cash to provide the witness with those funds immediately on request. Otherwise, the subpoena may be unenforceable. Further, it is not enough simply to hand the document to the prospective witness and walk away. It is important that witnesses know what they are to do, where they are to do it, and what is expected of them when they arrive. The legal assistant who performs the service can explain these facts to the deponent. Otherwise, the legal assistant must ensure that the process server is professional and familiar with the service desired. U.S. Marshals, of course, may be used in federal court cases. Occasionally, sheriff's departments will deliver subpoenas for state court actions.

The firm seeking the deposition usually arranges for the place of the deposition and the appearance of a court reporter or, if permitted, the use of video- or audio tape equipment.

The room should be large enough for all persons attending and equipped with necessary tables, chairs, ashtrays, carafes of water and glasses, electric power plugs (if recorders, slide projectors, or so on are to be used), and identified access to rest rooms.

The availability of photocopying equipment, waiting areas for other witnesses scheduled the same day, and the presence of telephones in the deposition room should also be considered. Phones should be muffled if they are expected to ring, and arrangements for remote answering are preferred.

8.084   Attending Depositions.

Wherever possible, the legal assistant should attend the deposition with the lawyer. Legal assistants can serve many purposes in the process, whether it is making copies of documents brought to the deposition by the prospective witnesses or simply taking another set of notes on the flow of the questions and answers during the course of the deposition. Further, if the depositions later are to be summarized, it is very helpful for the legal assistant to have been present during the questioning, for many passages seem ambiguous or obscure in transcript form.

Many jurisdictions permit legal assistants to attend depositions, and some corporate legal assistants may be allowed at deposition as "specially designated representatives of the client" under provisions of the civil procedure or evidence codes.

The conduct of an extensive deposition, particularly in business or antitrust litigation, may require hours, days, or even weeks. The presence of two people taking notes, both of whom are intimately knowledgeable with the facts of the case and the deposition outline, is of great assistance to the lawyer. When breaks are taken during the deposition, the lawyer and the legal assistant can compare notes, revise the deposition plan, and check on which points have been covered, have not been covered, or have arisen as surprises.

In complex cases, the introduction of exhibits can present major problems in clarity, utility, organization, and identification. A legal assistant can contribute to the process in each of these areas for the direct benefit of the lawyers, the witness, and the deposition reporter.

8.0841 Deposition Exhibits.   Exhibits in depositions can include photos or documents obtained prior to the deposition, photos and/or documents produced at deposition in response to the subpoena, or documents created during the deposition (most commonly, these are sketches, diagrams, or drawings).

Exhibits are introduced to have their nature, origin, content, and identity established under oath or to provide clarification of matters difficult to describe verbally, such as photographs of an accident scene, blueprints of a mechanical device, or a diagram of an organizational structure. Often the introduction of copies of such things as letters, contracts, bills of sale, and warranty statements can establish a foundation for later introduction of the exhibit as secondary evidence if the original or a duplicate original cannot be located.

Certified shorthand reporters, in the absence of other directions, mark exhibits as "P" for plaintiff or "D" for defendant in numeric sequential order as they are introduced in each separate deposition. Others use numbers for plaintiff exhibits and letters for defendant exhibits.

(a) Deposition Exhibit Register. A system of exhibit identification requires sequential numbering (or lettering) of all exhibits introduced on a case basis, beginning with the complaint and ending with requests for admission. It poses a substantial burden on the lawyer and/or the legal assistant to log each exhibit in and maintain the sequential integrity throughout the various discovery procedures. Whether the decision is made to log the exhibits by single deposition, sequentially through all depositions, or sequentially by case, a log of this type can be used at deposition to record those introduced through the *one deponent*. A copy can be given the reporter to ensure the transcript matches the lawyer's notes and exhibit log (see Exhibit 39).

EXHIBIT 39

DEPOSITION EXHIBIT REGISTER

CASE: DATE:

LOCATION: ATTORNEYS:

DEPONENT:

PLNTF. EXH.	DEFT. EXH.	DESCRIPTION OF EXHIBIT	NOTES

If the exhibits are numbered sequentially by *deposition,* the entries made by the legal assistant might look like those shown in Exhibit 40.

If the numbering sequence was by case, the numbers in the "Plntf. Exh." column might be "P 12, P 13, or P 14" or higher.

If a sequential system is used, a master log must be employed to ensure control of the numbers, the exhibit description, and the witness or deponent by which it was introduced (See Exhibit 41).

If a *case* master log is used, the column "Witness/Deponent" can reflect "Defendant Interrogatory Set No. 1, Question 12," "Answer to Plaintiff Interrogatory Set No. 8, Question 36," or "Plaintiff Request for Admission, Set No. 2, Request No. 18," and so on in abbreviation or code.

EXHIBIT 40

DEPOSITION EXHIBIT REGISTER

CASE: Smith v. Jones   DATE: 6 - 14 - 92

LOCATION: Hilton Hotel   ATTORNEYS: J. Brooks - Smith

San Francisco   V. Gallo - Jones

DEPONENT: A.E. Robinson

PLNTF. EXH.	DEFT. EXH.	DESCRIPTION OF EXHIBIT	NOTES
P1		Contract of sale dtd	(Robinson relied on K
		5 - 10 - 91 signed by Smith	in performing duty as
		and Jones, 13 pages with 3	Jones' agent.)
		addenda; Addendas A, B,	
		and C	
P2		Change Order # 10532, dtd	
		6 - 23 - 91 signed by Jones	
		and initiated by Robinson	
P3		Daily log book of Robinson	Copied at deposition,
		from 5 - 18 - 91 to	original retained by
		10 - 12 - 91	deponent.

While each side can control only the numbering sequence of its own exhibits, logs of this type record chronologically and descriptively all exhibits in the case and simplify retrieval of such exhibits. Reliable identification, control, and retrieval are the prime functions of legal assistants, whether facts, interviews, or exhibits are involved.

8.085 Preparing Friendly Witnesses for Depositions.

One of the major benefits that a legal assistant can provide a lawyer is preliminary preparation of friendly witnesses who are to be deposed by the adversaries. It is important that such witnesses be advised of the nature and process of depositions. Usually the lawyer will discuss these matters with the prospective witnesses and may direct the legal assistant to review any and all documents the witnesses are to produce and to establish the foundation of their knowledge for each of the documents. This should occur not less than a day and preferably two or three days preceding the scheduled deposition.

EXHIBIT 41

Plntf	Def	Witness/Deponent	Description of Exhibit
		MASTER EXHIBIT LOG - DEPOSITIONS	
		Case: Smith v Jones Date Last Posted: 6/15/92	
		Attorney: V. Gallo Legal Asst.: Bob Brown	
P 1		Deposition Robinson	Contract of sale, 4/10/91, sgd by Smith and by Jones w/ 3 attach A, B, & C.
P 2		"	Change Order 10532 . . . . .

A careful screening of the documents should be made to identify any privilege that might apply. Objections may be raised to certain types of records of a personal or professional nature, such as medical records not directly connected to the case at issue, some tax records, or certain types of professional or "trade secret" records. Whenever documents in these categories are detected, consultation with the lawyer is necessary to determine the proper course of action.

In some cases, the documents may be withdrawn and not exposed to the adversary parties; however, their existence must be identified in minimal form and the reason for their withdrawal set forth during the preliminary phases of the deposition. In some special cases, a protective order may be required of the adverse parties before the documents are surrendered for examination in connection with the deposition.

The legal assistant, at the request of the lawyer, may be able to review the factual matters of the prospective deposition with the witness and take the position of devil's advocate to walk the witness through the type of questioning he or she likely will encounter. This provides an active and role-playing practice in how to answer deposition questions. It is important to help the witness to avoid generalities, speculation, guessing, acting as an expert in an area where he or she has no substantial grounds for expertise, and volunteering information not specifically required by the question.

Similarly, the use of judgmental words is discouraged, and the witness is reminded to give only honest, responsive answers in the fewest possible words to the adversary attorney's questions. It is important for the witness to understand that the "friendly" attorney has a limited role in the deposition. There is little defense against the other attorney's questions, unless they are totally irrelevant or constitute abuse, harassment, or humiliation of the witness. Almost all other questions must be answered responsively, unless a protective order limiting the topics is first obtained. Such orders are granted only in special circumstances.

The witness always should allow the questioning attorney to complete the question and provide a short space for the friendly attorney to interpose objections, if any, before answering.

8.086   Tips for Deponents.

Most offices supply witnesses with some guidance in how to handle themselves at deposition. Exhibit 42 is an example of such a guideline. Most witnesses are reassured that they need only tell the truth as best they can recall it. Some want to review documents, reports, drawings, photos, and so forth. Such review is seldom helpful, and few lawyers want the witnesses to do that for it makes such "refresher" materials subject to examination by the adversary attorney. Review even of documents that must be provided by subpoena should be preceded by attorney or legal assistant examination.

The legal assistant's prime function is to dispel anxiety and the fear of the unknown or of going on the record and to assist the witness in avoiding words that can be an embarrassment, such as "judgment words."

"Judgment words" include such phrases as "I waited a minute, then . . . ." A minute is a full sixty seconds, and the witness had better be aware of just how long sixty seconds really are if that phrase is to be used. Help the witness appreciate it by saying, "Was this really how long it was?" and then timing a full minute. If the word is meant only to reflect a short, unmeasured time period, that must be understood and an alternative word chosen. Similarly, speeds, colors, distances, heights, weights, and so forth are all areas of potential inaccuracy or unsupported opinion that a deposing attorney can use to rattle or discomfort a witness. The legal assistant identifies each such judgment word and seeks to establish the witness's foundation for such statement. Personal characterizations may be troublesome, too—for instance, "That boy's always been a smart aleck!" or "Everybody knows he's a drunk!" No one can change a witness's basic manner of expression, but a few helpful hints can sometimes be the difference between a credible or discredited witness.

8.087   Mechanics of a Deposition.

Mechanically, the taking of depositions is a relatively simple process once the subpoena has been properly issued and served and arrangements have been made for a place for the taking of the deposition and the appearance of a qualified reporter. Reporters are usually notary publics, empowered to give oaths, qualified to provide a written transcript of all of the words said during the course of the examination, and to prepare a booklet of that transcript, attaching any documentary exhibits introduced during the deposition.

EXHIBIT 42

"DURING YOUR DEPOSITION"

A. Tell the *truth,* tell only the truth. Do not manufacture elements of a story just to make the story logical and credible. Telling deliberate falsehoods can lose the case. Telling the truth requires more than refraining from lying. It means telling the most accurate recollection possible in response to a question. You can always honestly testify what you recall. The memory of events may fade, but they do not *change* with time; therefore, testimony has little reason to change.

B. Do not guess! If you do not *know* the answer, say so. That is the truth.

C. If you are *asked* to guess or estimate, phrase the answer so it is clearly understood it is not *volunteered* and is only a guess or estimate.

D. Be certain you understand the question before you try to answer. A confused answer to a misunderstood question is embarrassing and disconcerting. If you have a doubt of what the question really seeks, ask the attorney to restate or rephrase it.

E. *Take your time.* Do not hurry your answer. Pick your words to form the answer you want to give in the way you want to give it.

F. Answer the question—just the question. Use as few words as possible. Do not let silence from the attorney or facial expressions stimulate you into further explanation. Do not volunteer more information than the question asks.

G. Answer audibly. The court reporter only writes down words, not nods or wags of the head. Speak loudly enough for everyone in the room to hear.

H. Review all your personal data. Know your name, where you live, your phone number, how old you are, where you work and for how long, when you were married, and so on.

I. Do not fence, argue, or lose your temper. The lawyer has a right to ask you questions, some of which you might not like. You may not like him or her personally, but you cannot hurt the lawyer or his or her feelings. He or she is doing a job getting information about the case from you, and he or she hopes you will lose your composure and make his or her job easier.

J. Be courteous. It makes a good impression on everyone, lawyers, judges, and juries. Say "yes, sir" and "no, sir." Avoid joking, smart remarks, and sarcasm. A lawsuit is a very serious matter and needs courteous cooperation to be resolved.

K. Do not look at your lawyer for help. He or she cannot help you answer the questions. Looking for help also causes the questioning lawyer to believe you want to hide something.

L. Give a positive answer when you can. Do not let the other lawyer catch or intimidate you by asking *if you will swear* by your answer; you are already sworn to tell the truth by the reporter.

M. If you are a plaintiff in an accident case, do not exaggerate, overemphasize, or dwell on how careful or cautious you were. Ordinary, everyday, common-sense care is all the law requires.

Counsel for each of the parties is present (or has an opportunity to be present through proper service or notice of the deposition) and may ask questions of the deponent. Generally, the attorney who requested the deposition conducts the examination, and the other parties have the opportunity, in turn, to examine or cross-examine the witness on points of interest to them.

The witness will be sworn by the reporter at the outset of the deposition, and the attorney who subpoenaed the witness then explains the ground rules of depositions to the witness. This generally includes a caution that anything said by the witness is being recorded under oath and may be used at a later time in a court of law to challenge anything he or she may say at that time that is different from what is said during the course of the deposition. Similarly, the attorney will advise the witness that there is no intent to trap or to take unfair advantage of the witness but simply to obtain honest and forthright answers to the questions propounded. (Not all attorneys, however, observe the spirit or the letter of this procedure.)

Further, the witness is asked to respond verbally to all questions and advised that responses made solely by head movements are unacceptable. The reporter must record the answers, and that requires an audible response.

Usually the attorney will ask the witness not to answer any questions he or she does not understand and inform the witness that if he or she does answer a question, it is presumed that he or she did understand the full import of the question and its nuances. The witness is cautioned that if he or she does not understand the question, the witness should ask to have it rephrased so that it can be understandable and unambiguous.

At this point, the attorneys generally enter into a stipulation that the witness will have thirty days (or some period of time) after submission of the transcript to submit corrections, additions, or clarifications of the transcript and to sign it; however, if the transcript is not signed or corrected within that time, it may be used at trial as though it had been signed. The witness may waive the right to review the deposition transcript.

Each attorney and person present in the room is identified, together with his or her relationship to the case. When all the parties and counsel are satisfied that the preliminaries have been observed, the true examination begins. In each case, the attorney propounding the questions will be identified by the reporter either on a line identifying him or her as "Question by attorney _____," followed by the marginal abbreviation "Q," or in the subsequently submitted transcript, the attorney's name will be shown on the left margin indicating the questions he or she asked.

Exhibits will be introduced in the transcript and should be described verbally by the attorney to ensure the same object or document can be recreated with accuracy from reading the text of the transcript. Document identification is greatly aided by numbering, described in other portions of this manual. (See Section 8.10, Requests for Production of Documents.)

The transcript of the questions and answers will be prepared in booklet form with each line numbered from one to twenty-five or so. Each page is sequentially numbered. An index will be included that lists each exhibit introduced. The exhibits usually will be attached at the back of the book. One or two pages of lined but unnumbered paper is included at the back of each booklet for attorney comments or for the witness to enter corrections. The reporter is charged with custody of the exhibits, following up on the submission of the transcript to the witness, and filing at a subsequent date the deposition transcript with the court. Copies of the transcript may be ordered by each party or counsel.

8.088   Summarizing Depositions.

Depositions, by the very nature of their question-and-answer format, involve many, many pages in order to record properly one evidentiary fact of testimony. They are bulky, difficult to use in the courtroom and, therefore, frequently summarized either by the attorney or by the legal assistant. The form of the summary varies according to the scope of the deposition, the importance of the case, and the number of issues in the case. The legal assistant can save substantial time for the lawyer in this activity. The old saying "Make haste slowly" certainly applies to deposition summaries. Among the rules to establish as a personal discipline are:

1. Learn about the issues in the case. Ideally, the attorney will outline the areas of critical concern and provide a copy of the outline used in the deposition. The major headings frequently reveal the salient areas of interest.
2. Read the entire deposition like a novel before beginning to summarize. No attempt should be made to analyze in detail; just obtain a general feeling of the flow of information, the kind of data revealed, and whether the attorney followed the deposition outline.
3. Attempt to schedule an unbroken period of time to complete the summary. Continuity and quality suffer from doing a little here and there.

8.0881 Sequential Summary. The most common form of summaries is sequential (chronological, logical), which is simply a page-by-page paraphrasing of the information contained in the deposition, eliminating extraneous material and referencing the evidentiary facts of testimony to the page and line on which they appear, as well as annotating the appearance of any exhibits or references to any documents.

In essence, this is simply a reduction of volume, both of pages of material, rhetorical verbiage, and the "fencing" or "game playing" dialogue employed by some witnesses and attorneys.

Its weakness is a lack of order in the entries by triable issues. Unless an attorney is very disciplined and a little lucky, even following an outline will not result in all the data on any one issue being developed in one set of questions and answers. A deposition is an interrogation with all the problems of memory refreshment and afterthought that occur from the witness's detailed retelling of a story and/or the accidental revelation of a fact the attorney had not considered at the outset. Thus, the facts are mixed in the transcript.

Summarizing the account without changing the meaning can be accomplished in several ways, but the two most common are:

1. Reading, digesting, and then paraphrasing a complete segment of text into a concise restatement of the pertinent facts. This works exceptionally well for such topical segments as "Identity," "Educational background," "Employment background," and sometimes "How the accident happened." It is much less satisfactory for cases involving complex issues of contract, product design, antitrust elements, and so forth.
2. In such complex situations, using the ellipses or "three-dot" system, where an extracted incomplete quote or paraphrased comment is recorded, such as " . . . he had read the instructions in detail . . .," " . . . had four hours of on the job training . . .," "he saw the apparatus disassembled during June 1989 . . .," and so forth. A comparison of the two styles is shown on the following Exhibit 43.

The second system allows more specific referencing of page and line to the comments and risks less meaning change than the editorial paraphrasing, but it is choppier to read and has less story quality.

Recording the summaries is done in two basic ways: "sheet" accumulation and "slip" accumulation. Sheet accumulation is titled from the form of the summary, on a full letter-size sheet of paper (either handwritten or typed) organized as in Exhibit 43.

Each page is suitably identified to key it to the case, the deponent, the legal assistant, the date, and the other pages of the summary. It allows an organized,

EXHIBIT 43

DEPOSITION SUMMARY FORM			Page 2
CASE: Smith v. Jones Dixon Sup Crt #234 567 Deponent: Albert Hackston Date: 7/25/91			Atty: G. Baker L/A: N. Luono
Pg 3	Line 10	Summary	Exhibits & Notes
		(Paraphrase system)	
3	10	Hackston had read the instructions in detail and received 4 hours of OJT before operating the machine. In June 1989 he watched the disassembly and reassembly of the machine. It was frequently serviced, and he specifically recalled preventive maintenance was performed on Sept. 8, 89.	
		(ellipses method)	
3	10 13 18	. . .he had read the instructions in detail. . . .he had 4 hours of OJT before using it. . . .saw the apparatus disassembled and reassembled in June 1989. . .	
4	6	. . .he was present when preventive maintenance was performed Sept. 8, 89.	

NOTE: The form is always identified by case, attorney, legal assistant, date, and deponent, as well as by the page numbers of the summary itself.

repetitious recording of the deposition's essential elements needed for easy use and reference and the page and line where an item of information or exhibits are found.

Whether the summary is handwritten or typed, the use of such a format allows quick, reliable retrieval and checking of data.

"Slip" accumulation is favored by many attorneys who do their own summarization and can be as quick and a little more flexible than the sheet system. The summary is not made one item after another on a single sheet of paper; instead, each comment is entered on a slip of paper or index card. One such slip might look like Exhibit 44. On completing the summary, the slips may be sorted in page order and typed sequentially or sorted first topically, then by page order within topical elements, and typed so that the summary is separate sheets devoted to each topical element, such as "Identity," "Damages—General," "Damages—Special," "Doctor's Reports," "Therapy," and so on.

Note that the slip method provides far sketchier identification of data. It is incredibly easy to make a complete waste of a summary by losing one or two slips, particularly if the legal assistant did not attend the deposition and even more so if the legal assistant did not read the deposition in full before summarizing.

8.0882 Topical Index. The second form of deposition summary is not a true summary but an *index* of topical elements. This usually is composed from the sequential summary by identifying categories of information of which the witnesses had personal knowledge and creating a page-line index. The topical index then fits on one or two sheets of paper and might look like:

	Topic	Page	Lines
1.	Identity	1	6–12
2.	Education background	2	2–12
	a. Training O.J.T.	4	17–20
3.	Employment history	5	13–20
		6	1–14
		7	3–18
	a. Employment with plaintiff	7	19–20

This sort of index can easily be created from the sequential summaries, whether sheets or slip type, provided the legal assistant clearly understands the issues of the case or has specific instructions on categorizations from the attorney.

8.0883 Topical Summary.   The topical summary is simply an expansion of the topical index, in that each of the references made by the witness to one of the issues is expanded into an edited and paraphrased narrative form limited to each issue. Anyone reviewing the summary can tell the scope and extent of the deponent's knowledge of each issue. The slip system allows this summary to be created easily simply by sorting the slips by issue and typing in order.

8.0884 Post-Deposition Summary.   One form of summary that does not rely upon the transcript booklet is the "post-deposition summary." When both the attorney and the legal assistant attend a deposition, it is good practice for each to render his or her deposition notes into summaries immediately following the deposition. They do this independently from their own individual notes and memories and then compare them at a later time. The deposition booklet from the reporter may be days, weeks, even months, in appearing, and by that time, a

EXHIBIT 44 Deposition Summary Slip

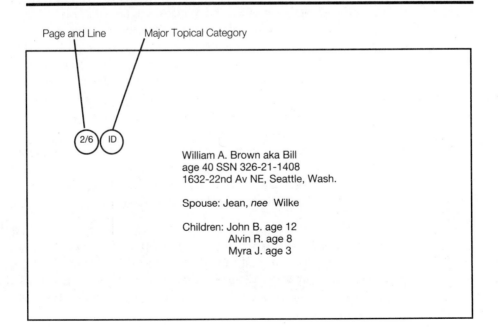

Page and Line   Major Topical Category

(2/6)(ID)

William A. Brown aka Bill
age 40 SSN 326-21-1408
1632-22nd Av NE, Seattle, Wash.

Spouse: Jean, *nee* Wilke

Children: John B. age 12
          Alvin R. age 8
          Myra J. age 3

substantial amount of discovery may have occurred, whether by interrogatory or by other depositions, that could obscure the value of the witness's information if a prompt and timely summary is not prepared. Frequently, these summaries will be nearly identical, but occasionally, substantive differences will arise from interpretations of questions and answers. These summaries always are helpful to the attorney.

8.09 Requests for Admission

Federal Rule of Civil Procedure No. 36 permits each party to serve a request for admission of the truth of facts and/or the genuineness of documents on the other party. The purpose is to limit the number of issues and facts to be proven at trial or the necessity to create a further foundation for the introduction of evidentiary materials and documents. Such requests are founded on matters developed during previous discovery procedures, interrogatories, depositions, or requests for production of documents. Usually, when a foundation has been developed, the answering parties will admit the truth of the facts or the genuineness of the documents, but there is no compulsion to do so. They may put the propounding attorney "on strict proof." When such proof is forthcoming at trial, the propounding party may ask the court to award the costs of the proof (such as the transportation of a witness or the expert witness's fee).

The answers to requests for admission must be verified, and the legal assistant always checks incoming answers for that verification.

8.091. Timing.

Requests for admission are usually employed following extensive discovery. The legal assistant contributes to the effectiveness of this process by assembling from previous discovery efforts those facts and documents important to the case, that have not been specifically acknowledged by the other parties. This may include documents introduced at the depositions of witnesses or the client. It may also include requests for admission propounded by the other parties to obtain reciprocal admissions to the fact, document, or thing since answers to requests for admission are binding only on the *answering* party.

8.092 Form.

Requests for admissions are usually posed in positive statements to which the answering party answers with "admitted" or "denied." It is possible to encounter other answers, such as "Defendant can neither admit nor deny the truth of the matter because. . . ." Requests for admission may be filed as one set or several sets. Multiple sets pose a numbering problem similar to that of interrogatories. Federal court rules usually require sequential numbering for clarity and control, a good idea for use in all courts and a great idea for legal assistants charged with control and retrieval of the admissions.

8.093 Combined with Interrogatories.

Some jurisdictions permit combining requests for admission and interrogatories. The document caption should reflect this, as in the following manner: "Request for admission Set No. _____ and Interrogatories Set No. _____." The technique is to pose each request for admission and a follow-up interrogatory as a form of pattern inquiry to obtain the admission or the denial and its foundation in evidentiary fact or legal contentions.

8.094   Collation of Denials and Cost of Proof.

The legal assistant collates all denials of requests for admission and coordinates with the lawyer on the method of proof. Once the plan of proof is selected, the legal assistant establishes a record of the costs associated with the proof of each disputed fact or document to serve the lawyer as the foundation for seeking recovery of the costs of proof, if appropriate.

8.10   Requests for Production of Documents

Documents are both loved and feared by attorneys. Cases begin with a person telling an attorney of the "injustice of it all" and seeking help in gaining redress, often presenting letters, contracts, and bills in support of the story.

As the case progresses, other documents surface, some by design, some by accident, many in connection with various forms of informal discovery and others through formal proceedings. Occasionally, a case is truly a "document" case where something more than casual revelation of memorialized material is handled, ideally in an organized, thoughtful, and effective manner.

Besides exhibits to the complaint, interrogatories, and depositions, two other circumstances call for special consideration and handling of documents: the subpoena *duces tecum* and the request for production of documents.

8.101   Subpoena *Duces Tecum*.

Federal Rule of Civil Procedure 34 provides that a subpoena may be issued to the custodian of certain documents to appear together with the records and be prepared to discuss the manner of origin and filing of the documents.

As a practical matter, many of these necessary documents are routine business records generated by neutral parties, and no dispute over the admissibility of the records exists: for instance, medical records of a plaintiff in a bodily injury lawsuit or employment, education, or military service records. It is common practice (on mutual agreement) for such subpoenas to be issued to a firm specializing in attorney's legal services to serve the subpoena on the custodian, take custody of the records, copy and notarize the relevant documents, deliver the copies to the attorneys, and return the originals to the custodian.

Documents obtained in such a manner have no value until *processed*. Processing involves the detailed, page-by-page examination of the material and abstraction of pertinent points. The legal assistant often performs that task, whether the material is technical in nature or simply business chronologies. A preliminary review includes:

(a)   Is the pertinent time period covered?

(b)   Do the records deal with the person, company, or entity directly or only by reference?

(c)   Do the records deal with the issues in the case?

(d)   Do the records refer to other records neither attached nor already obtained?

(e)   Do the records require expert help in interpretation or understanding?

Many legal assistants can review technical records and establish summaries based on chronologies that pinpoint the exact areas of technical help required. For instance, the medical records of a thirty-five-year-old plaintiff widow in a bodily injury case may have a medical history of several volumes from doctors, hospitals, therapists, and so on. Only a minor portion of that volume may pertain to the instant case, but all must be reviewed to identify previous medical episodes that involve the same area of injury and that might affect the doctor's prognosis for recovery in the case at hand. One technique that works well is to review all of the file, annotating and flagging the portions requiring more qualified medical training, then contacting through medical or nursing associations either interns or registered nurses to review the flagged areas and suggest possible interpretations. Such data allows specific inquiry of the expert physician employed by the attorney or a determination of whether a physician specialist is needed.

All such medical records include billing records as well, and the legal assistant can easily accumulate, total, and compare the actual billings with those submitted by the plaintiff.

Other specialty records afford the same opportunities to examine the documents and determine the need for expert consultants, technical training, and so forth.

8.102   Requests for Production of Documents.

It is easy to understand how the gradual accumulation of documents through interrogatories, depositions, and requests for admission and the subpoena *duces tecum* can lull an attorney or his or her legal assistant into the belief that the "document" case, from one thousand pages on up, can be handled by the same manual procedures, only scaled up just a bit. It may be possible to do that, but is that the most effective way? What if it involves ten thousand pages? What if it develops twenty-five thousand pages from each of two co-defendants and fifteen thousand from plaintiff? Document cases are or can be lost in the planning stages and require far more than a "let's wing it" attitude from the attorney and the legal assistant.

Federal Rule of Civil Procedure 34 permits the service of a request for production of documents on other parties to the case. States have similar rules, and both provide defenses against unnecessarily broad, burdensome, or irrelevant requests; however, if the case requires access to documents, the court will allow the access, review, and copying.

8.103   Basic Considerations.

In most litigation, the volume of documents is relatively small and manageable; however, there are certain basic considerations to be made in each case:

1. The adversary is entitled to those documents that he or she can describe with sufficient specificity to allow the client, the client's counsel, and the legal assistant to identify, provided the scope of the request is not burdensome and oppressive and the material is not privileged.
2. The attorney and the legal assistant must review each document page before allowing the adversary to see it in order to ensure that no privileged documents, trade secret material, or documents not specifically requested are included.
3. The documents to be produced must be reviewed chronologically in context as well as in their "as found" condition to appreciate whether or not the production has been well and truly made by the client. Files have a way of

being lost, misfiled, retired, and destroyed that only is detected by chronologic review. These events must be explained, of course.

4. The identification of the sources of each document produced must be established and maintained throughout the production process. Whether the document origin was the client's own reading file or the record copy of the secretary of the corporation, such characterizations are very important as foundation in case the document must be offered in evidence in support of the client's case.

8.104. Control Systems.

Small document volumes allow the use of careful but relatively unsophisticated control systems. Perhaps the documents (say, one thousand pages in six or eight separate files) can be carried to the document production room in the folders in which they originally were filed, bearing only a penciled identification of the custodian, room number, and so forth on the file cover. The documents can be shown to the adversary, and only the documents selected by the adversary need be specially handled subsequently. An alternative system is to number all the documents considered responsive to the order and allow the adversary to request copies by document number. Either may work well.

In either case, an index of the numbered pages must be made. One such index is shown in Exhibit 45. Note that the example indicates *all* the documents were numbered. It clearly shows the nature of the documents; inclusive number groups reflect documents from different sources or origins. It reflects when the screening took place and by whom. A column is provided to allow entries noting whether the adversary saw or requested any of the documents. Note that no entry under "Code" is shown. Perhaps there was no privileged material in these files or other special characteristics.

Original documents must be treated with substantial care to avoid changing the character of the document from its "as found" condition; however, the application of an identification number with a progressive hand-numbering stamp usually is not objectionable and simplifies the subsequent handling of documents in the case.

Every request for production of documents should produce an index of the documents involved, whether the client's or the adversary's, and it is very helpful when reviewing the adversary documents to carry a numbering device to the scene of the examination and number each document of interest to the attorney, thereby creating a list against which the production can later be measured. Some adversaries will not allow their documents to be numbered. When this occurs, the legal assistant will have anticipated that lack of cooperation and brought along a battery-powered tape recorder into which the essential identification of a desired document can be read. Remember, basic document identification includes: type of document, date, author, addressee, number of pages, and attachments. If there are characteristic file numbers or subject titles, they may be included. If the identity is to be dictated, set up a pattern of the information and follow the pattern in dictation to allow later transcription in tabulated form.

This is also the time to determine whether the adversary is withholding any documents under a claim of privilege. If so, he or she should provide a list that identifies each such document, as discussed in Chapter 9, Document Discovery Cases.

EXHIBIT 45 Litigation Skills

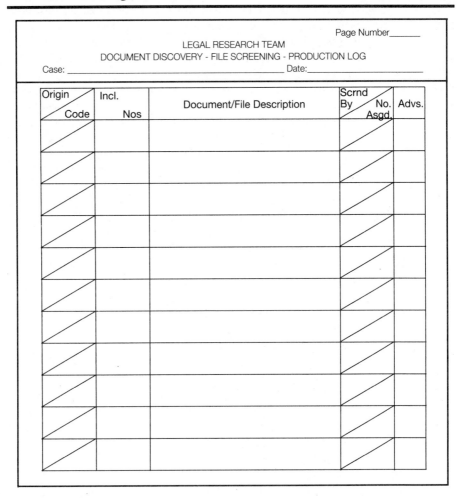

| | | Page Number_____ |
| LEGAL RESEARCH TEAM |
| DOCUMENT DISCOVERY - FILE SCREENING - PRODUCTION LOG |
| Case: _____ Date:_____ |

8.11 Damage Calculation, Verification, and Settlement Offers

Every lawsuit has an object, and the most common civil tort objective is compensatory damages in dollars. The plaintiff is obligated during trial to prove the actual damages sustained. Usually these damages can be documented by actual bills, canceled checks, employment or payroll records, city assessment billings, or, alternatively, estimates of experts on the method and/or the cost of restoring the plaintiff to the position he or she would have enjoyed but for the circumstance at issue.

In bodily injury cases, the damage remedy has two elements. The first is the actual and prospective costs of the medical treatment and therapy associated with the plaintiff's recovery from the injury, and the second is an element called "pain and suffering." This latter element includes a recovery for the physical agony of the trauma itself; the anticipated and predictable future pain, disability, and deterioration of physical condition directly attributable to the instant case; the denial of hobbies or pleasurable interests and the disruption and denial of choice of life-style (for instance, a broken hip may forever bar an amateur marathon runner from competition, or an injured back may deny an interior decorator the ability to rearrange furniture on impulse and without assistance). Clearly, every case contains elements of damage both of an objective nature and those of a subjective, speculative, or cerebral or emotional nature. Even business cases can contain both. For instance, in a dispute over a commercial building construction contract, there may be elements of actual, necessary building alteration and/or reconstruction and another element related to "return on investment," or, perhaps, a higher than usual vacancy rate or greater than anticipated difficulty in attracting long-term lessees.

Each case has it own elements of damage that must be considered objectively both by plaintiff and defendant attorneys and any involved legal assistants. In every case, there are considerations of settlement. Both sides must weigh the probability of success or failure in proving liability and/or damages at trial, and both must value the case in dollars and cents to their clients. For instance, a plaintiff who has an excellent liability case with only nominal damages must consider the amount of the recovery against the costs of trial, the time involved, and the possibility of an adverse judgment. On the other hand, a defendant (perhaps a large corporation) with an excellent case on liability confronted by a highly sympathetic plaintiff with obvious, grievous, and expensive injuries must make similar evaluations from a different, but equally pragmatic, viewpoint.

8.111   Offers.

Settlement offers usually are tendered by the plaintiff to the defendant as an extension of the plaintiff's burden to "prove the damages," though it is true that defendants do invite such offers and sometimes even suggest possible settlement dollar ranges. If the parties do not volunteer such negotiations, some courts schedule a pretrial meeting of the parties and their respective counsel solely for discussion of possible settlement.

Codes of civil procedure (or the equivalent) of some states provide for offers of settlement to induce the parties to propose reasoned, good faith settlement offers to the adversary. The inducement to act in good faith lies in allowing the proponent to recover the costs of trial from the adversary (who refused the settlement offer) *if* the ultimate jury award equals or exceeds the offer. For instance, if the plaintiff offers under the code section to settle the case for fourteen thousand dollars and the defendant declines and if the jury award is fifteen thousand dollars, the plaintiff may seek recovery of the trial costs.

Such a code section has a statutory time limit on acceptance and is particularly effective where a defendant is represented by an insurance carrier with undisputed coverage and the offer is within policy limits while a prospective jury award may exceed the policy limits. The insurance company must weigh the merits of the case itself with its responsibility to the insured defendant to maintain "good faith" in indemnifying him or her while representing the defendant's interest. The decisions are not made whimsically or carelessly. The legal assistant can make a significant contribution in this area.

8.112   Arithmetic.

Since every damage claim involves some calculation of loss, the legal assistant can assist the validation of the arithmetic used in the process, not just the totals of dollars, but the foundations of each subtotal. It is surprising how often decimals become misplaced, a bill is double-entered on the adding machine, or handwritten figures are erroneously totaled.

8.113   Analysis of Bills.

The plaintiff (sooner or later) supplies the defendant with copies of all bills, checks, receipts, estimates, and so on supporting the claim or offer. The legal assistant should ensure (whether working for the plaintiff or defendant) that only legitimate and relevant bills are used. The bills should be assembled first into categories and then in chronologic order.

A detailed examination of the bills should be made to separate bills related to diagnosis from those of treatment—whether the case is medical or not.

Sixteen thousand dollars sounds like a lot of trouble, pain, and serious injury. However, if one hundred dollars is for emergency medical treatment, seven hundred dollars is for periodic office visits to the doctor with little substance reflected in the medical history jacket, and eight hundred dollars is for periodic X rays with little or no substantive diagnostic value, the attorney obtains a different scale of value on the case from the total dollar figure suggested.

In cases that are not medical, the costs of estimates by professionals may be included. For instance, the damage to a home was supported by estimates and bills totaling twenty-eight hundred dollars, but included in that figure were bills for estimating from nine contractors, each charging one hundred dollars for the estimate. The building damage is only nineteen hundred dollars, and nine estimates might be considered a little excessive, even if the costs of the estimates were a legitimate element of recovery.

8.1131   Duplication.   Few plaintiff's bills are all of the same type. In a bodily injury case, there will be bills (some paid and some owing), some vouchers showing insurance payments, some receipts for cash payments, canceled checks, charge account or credit card purchase slips, cash register tapes with handwritten notes identifying the purchase, and so on. The earlier sorting of these various bills into chronologic sets allows comparisons of dollar amounts and dates to eliminate duplications that increase the dollar value of the case. Consider the inclusion of the hospital bill for emergency treatment, the plaintiff's check in payment, and the voucher of the insurance carrier for reimbursement in the damage total. Such inclusions may be innocent and thoughtless, or they may be preconceived and deliberate. The legal assistant sorts these out to avoid placing the employing attorney (if representing plaintiff) in an embarrassing situation. Similarly, the defendant's legal assistant prevents the plaintiff's attempt to puff up the damage figure without challenge.

Careful comparison of the medical history notes against the doctor's office billing may reveal the bills include charges totally unrelated to the incident at issue that should be deleted from the damage total. For instance, a man suffering a minor knee injury who is treated by his family doctor may also be treated for allergy problems on a repetitive basis before and during the knee injury episode. All office visits, treatment, lab work, and other procedures related to the allergy condition must be excluded.

8.114   Special Considerations.

The legal assistant working in the damage area must be aware of certain situations where routine measures of value and damage make little contribution to the lawyer's efforts. Flexibility and imagination are needed.

8.1141 Death Cases.   How can a death be valued? How can money restore the survivors to the position they were in prior to the death? Actuaries can tell us the expected life span of an individual, economists and other experts can postulate that certain statistical methods provide an accurate estimate on the earning capacity of people of "X" ethnic groups, sex, age, education, and fields of endeavor. The U.S. Census Bureau has compiled figures considered reliable in anticipating such development and expectations. With such basic data in hand, the application of a norm to the case at hand can be undertaken. For example, a twenty-five-year-old, white father of two with a high school education and a job in a progressive company can be expected to earn not less than $750,000 in his working life. This is adjusted by creating a facsimile of the specific individual's career in the company, with normal advancement, to retirement and then a separate calculation for income from retirement and Social Security.

The housewife's damage includes her marital interest in the earnings (including retirement benefits), the loss of consortium, companionship, and familial support in rearing the children, as well as out-of-pocket costs connected with the injury and death.

Each child is entitled to support, parental companionship, and so on. The legal assistant must consult with the attorney to determine the basis of each element and the method of validation.

The legal assistant for the plaintiff's attorney may wish to generate a settlement portfolio including all the financial facts, letters of confidence and appreciation from the employer, including statements on probable advancement, salary scales, career paths, retirement, and so forth. One section may include photos of the family as individuals, as a group in various activities at home and on vacation and at school, civic and religious functions. Included might be photos of the accident, newspaper clippings, or other material that dramatize the impact of the loss on the family emotionally as well as financially. Legal assistants representing the defendant must review all such materials, particularly the financial calculations, and consider any adjustments of such projections, particularly where based on the *special* qualities of the deceased.

8.1142 Court Approval.   Many damage claims where settlement is possible require the concurrence of the court and sometimes the appointment of a guardian or trust administrator. Such a procedure is most common in cases involving minors or those who are incompetent in their own affairs. The procedures and requirements differ from case to case and state to state but where encountered, the legal assistant reviews the current requirements of the courts to ensure the settlement can proceed smoothly and correctly.

8.1143 Continuing Damages.   Some cases involve a situation that cannot be remedied, and the damages are continuing or cumulative in nature, such as the contamination of an underground water source or the accidental industrial poisoning of a person where the poison's damage is a function of time of exposure and the material is slow to be expelled from the body. Such matters mean the lawyer and legal assistant must explore every available recourse for means of proof, or refuting such proof, estimating duration and effect, and identifying measures to correct, mitigate, or minimize the situation.

8.1144 Alternative Recoveries. Damages usually are seen as a one-time cash payment placing the injured party where he or she would have been, but for the injury.

In many cases, the aggregate dollar amount is so great that the defendant is incapable of responding to such a judgment even if fair and reasonable. Bankruptcy is the result, and the plaintiff still lacks compensation. In other cases, a large cash settlement may be insufficient to cover the rapidly expanding cost of future necessary medical care. An alternative settlement is needed. In the death case cited previously, endowments to guarantee the children's education as a part of the settlement might be considered. The mother might consider an investment portfolio with a projected (even guaranteed) annual income as a portion of the settlement. Discharge of a mortgage, prepaid medical care plans, or real estate investments—all are possible alternatives to be explored to avoid destroying the defendant while compensating the plaintiff in a just fashion.

8.1145 Diminishment for Early Recovery. Cases settled for cash or at trial judgment always begin with calculation of *all* the dollars lost, including the *future* dollars lost. Future dollars are always adjusted, first upwards to reflect the impact of inflation and then downward to reflect the benefit obtained in receiving a large piece of capital now, rather than piecemeal over a number of years. Clearly, the death case previously mentioned points out that the $750,000 the decedent would earn over forty years would not have the same value as that amount invested now and returning 10 percent per year to the survivors. In effect, they would have benefited unjustly from the death to the extent that 10 percent of $750,000 times forty years equals $2,000,000. There are economists and investment experts who can provide reliable foundations for calculating such adjustments.

Every case has a unique set of facts and damage elements. The legal assistant validates legitimate cost, analyzes the propriety of claimed damage elements, seeks expert help in valuing the loss, and explores alternative methods of settlement where appropriate.

8.12 Trial Books

Trial books are a particularly personal and individual creation of each attorney. Some use three-ring loose-leaf notebooks with dividers, others use multipart file folders, and still others use special ledger-type hardboard covers within which legal- or accounting-size sheets can be added. Whatever the form, the trial book is the lawyer's plan of trial and reference manual for all matters of law and fact related to the trial. It may involve one or more volumes, depending on the size and complexity of the case. It will include at least the following:

8.121 Identities.
This will be one to three sheets on which the name of every personality in the case is recorded together with addresses, phone numbers, and the individual's exact relationship to the case. Always included in detail are the names of the parties, their counsel, and their investigators and/or legal assistants; every identified or probable witness, indicating whether a plaintiff, defendant, neutral, or expert witness (along with their local addresses and phone numbers if brought into town for the trial). There may be references to persons, firms, agencies, and so on that

may become involved in the case (a drayage company that will move a scale model into the courtroom at a particular time, for instance).

8.122   Law Section.

This may include an index and appropriate tabbed dividers for such legal documents as opening statements, briefs, memoranda of points and authorities, jury instructions, law and motion matters, case citations, and authorities on anticipated points of dispute.

8.123   Case Presentation.

Each attorney expects to prove certain facts or introduce certain evidence at specific times or through specific witnesses.

A plan must be devised to organize the questioning of each witness and the introduction of evidence in a coherent, persuasive manner, easy for the judge or jury to understand and relate to the case issues.

Many attorneys first brief the case by cause of action to identify the essential elements of alleged conduct and the legal foundation for each cause of action. Then the answers and affirmative defenses are briefed; the admissions on both sides are posted (from the answer to the complaint and from requests for admission or interrogatories of all parties), and the remaining disputed elements isolated.

A trial brief is created that outlines not only the attorney's own perception of the posture of the case but countermeasures for the discerned positions of the adversary. Once established, the trial plan falls easily into order by collating the available sources of testimony against the factual and legal demands of the trial brief. The plan then reflects the order of presentation and the points to be covered, cross-indexed to witnesses or other sources of information in the order of desired presentation.

8.124   Witness Section.

Every potential witness has a separate section with a fact sheet carrying all the identifying personal data, the dates of each statement and/or deposition, answers to interrogatories attributed to him or her, a "conflicts" index if any conflicting points or story have been detected, and identification of each exhibit that witness may be used to introduce. A summary of each statement and/or deposition is included in chronologic order, perhaps highlighted with tabs or color markings of significant passages and cross-indexed to the separate file of statement and deposition transcripts.

Some attorneys like to separate the witness section into plaintiff and defendant sections and prepare special cross-examination outlines and/or impeachment points for the adversary witnesses and rehabilitation outlines for weak, but necessary, friendly witnesses. These outlines serve to memorialize important details for quick review and provide sufficient space for additional entries.

8.125   Evidence and Exhibit Section.

This lists every exhibit, for both sides, and may be in the form of a log—sometimes one for the plaintiff and one for the defendant. Usually, a court requires the attorneys to provide a list of exhibits to be introduced ahead of time, particularly those where the foundation is established by stipulation, so that the court clerk can assign identification numbers to them and all parties and the court can proceed in the case with minimal confusion.

The log bears each exhibit's number for identification (sequentially in order of introduction); a description of the exhibit; the witness by which it is to be introduced; the needed foundation for admissibility as evidence (possibly the evidence citation); whether the attorney expects to object (cross-indexed to the foundation for the objection, the evidence rule and so on); and a column to record the exhibit's introduction for identification and another for its acceptance or rejection as evidence.

8.126   Jury Panel.

The jury commissioner usually publishes a roster of potential jury members with sufficient identification to allow some background inquiry (as described in Chapter 7, Investigation). The attorney assembles that data and a twelve-block chart for use during *voir dire* to identify correctly each empaneled juror as one with no apparent identifiable bias against the client.

The twelve-block chart is organized just as the chairs in the jury box and, upon completion of the jury selection process, reflects the name, age, address, occupation of each juror, and the attorney's notes regarding each. Alternate jurors, if used, are identified in separate blocks and annotated in the same fashion.

The trial book varies from lawyer to lawyer, partly as a function of the manner in which they learned their trial practice and partly through their own ideas of emphasizing their trial effectiveness. For instance, one attorney splits his witness direct examination and cross-examination section into two volumes, one blue and one red. The red one contains all the conflicts and impeachment materials and references. While the testimony proceeds along the desired lines, the blue book is prominently displayed and used. When an attack on the witness's testimony is needed, the red book is ostentatiously obtained and used. The cumulative impact of the procedure on jurors, even the adversary counsel, is apparent, for each time the red book appears, the jurors sit up, pay attention, and await the exchanges with heightened interest.

Some attorneys ensure that every legal reference, objection, or instructional request is consistent with the reference book used by the judge hearing the case. Judges have confidence in authorities with which they are most familiar. Two very good judges in the same court, though in different departments, may use different reference books. Both judges and reference books honor the same substantive law; however, the lawyer who cites an authority from the judge's preferred reference book is most persuasive, if only because the judge can quickly check the form and foundation of the citation. The advantage is small, but it is one smart lawyers do not waive.

It sometimes requires dual citation in the trial book, however—the authority the lawyer originally chose and a cross-cite to the judge's preferred reference book.

8.127   The Legal Assistant and the Trial Book.

The legal assistant's contribution to the trial book may be the organization of the indices, the entry of factual material, the cross-referencing of facts, and the organization for retrieval *on demand* of the back-up material for the trial book sections, such as;

(a)   Testimony transcripts, tape recordings, signed statements, declarations, and affidavits listed in the witness section.

(b)   The case books, statutes, law review articles, the benchbook, regulations, or textbooks on which the attorney relies, available either as the entire volume or copied portions.

(c) The exhibits, organized, maintained, and easily available, including summaries of depositions, requests for admission, and one-line summaries of interrogatories.

Some matters in the law section may be delegated to the legal assistant for drafting, such as jury instructions—particularly in jurisdictions where a detailed book of approved jury instructions is available and citation of the exact language from approved instructions is quite persuasive. Similarly, the cross-citing of the attorney's anticipated authorities to the judge's preferred reference book may be drafted for the attorney's consideration. Where such matters are delegated, they must be completed in timely fashion to allow the attorney to review, edit, and verify those entries on which the case relies.

8.13   The Legal Assistant at the Trial

Trials are as varied as people and have just as diverse a selection of personalities. One trial may simply contest the damages involved with the liability issue already admitted.

Other cases may be solely a trial of the legal issues or only of the factual issues, the damages or remedy having been established beyond dispute or by stipulation.

Criminal trials may involve only one defendant and one violation of code or statute or may be complicated by multiple issues and defendants.

Business litigation, product liability, and antitrust cases may involve complex and interdependent issues of law and fact, extensive discovery that generates hundreds or thousands of pages of potential exhibits, scores of witnesses, multiple defendants and, perhaps, hundreds of plaintiffs, cross-defendants, and cross-plaintiffs. There may even be interested parties who seek standing as a friend of the court (*amicus curiae*) and file legal briefs for the court's consideration.

The duties delegated to a legal assistant depend on the case. The prime determining factors are always (1) how much help the lawyer feels is necessary and (2) whether the legal assistant is the proper person to supply the needed assistance.

Among the duties easily satisfied by a legal assistant are:

8.131   Witnesses, Control, and Liaison.

It is natural for witnesses to be nervous and apprehensive before a trial. They have had to disrupt their daily lives to attend. Such disruption is particularly difficult in trials that will take only one, two, or a few days but are delayed awaiting a courtroom assignment. The legal assistant makes periodic contacts with the witnesses and keeps them apprised of the stage of the case, not its substantive matters. This allows the witness the utmost personal freedom possible without discussing the case itself. Some witnesses might have come to town for the trial, and the legal assistant may coordinate transportation, lodging, and/or meals for them. Having the witness available at the right time is important.

8.132   Fees, Costs, and Expenses.

The legal assistant frequently monitors all the fees, costs, and expenses associated with the trial. These may include jurors' fees, jurors' meals, meals for witnesses, attorneys, and the client, parking fees, subpoena and witness fees and mileage, photocopying charges, public stenographer fees, and hotel/motel charges. The attorney, the legal assistant, and the firm's office manager or bookkeeper should determine the manner of handling such matters on each case.

8.133   Evidence Log.

The legal assistant should maintain an independent log of every exhibit introduced by the plaintiff or the defendant and record its marking for identification, the foundation and offering as evidence, any objections, and the court's ruling. At the daily (usually evening) recapitulation meeting, the attorney and the legal assistant reconcile their logs to ensure they are consistent. (If the legal assistant is allowed at the counsel table, the attorney will check his or her and the legal assistant's witness log and exhibit logs before dismissing a witness.)

Naturally, the legal assistant is in charge of the exhibits and must be ready to produce a desired exhibit as the attorney is ready to introduce it, particularly where special arrangements are needed, such as the provision of videotape machines, movie projectors and screens, scale models, and large sketches, drawings or photographs.

When possible, the legal assistant follows the testimony of each witness against the topical summaries previously prepared from statements or depositions to check off anticipated testimony or to highlight story changes or conflicts.

8.134   Daily Recapitulation Meeting.

Every day following adjournment of the court and after the witnesses have been released, the legal assistant participates in the review of the day's proceedings. Logs and the lawyer's and legal assistant's notes are compared, and final arrangements and plans for the next day's activity are outlined. Necessary witnesses are notified or subpoenaed when appropriate, and arrangements for transportation and so forth are consummated.

8.135   Trial Notes.

When the legal assistant attends trial, the legal assistant usually will be asked to take notes of the testimony and particularly of the employing attorney's cross-examination of the adversary's witnesses. This is one period where the lawyer cannot fully anticipate the form or content of the response, and careful recordation of the substance of the testimony by the legal assistant will aid the lawyer at the recapitulation meeting. One effective method is to use a lined, spiral-bound 8½-by-11-inch pad, fifty to eighty pages thick (or more than one, if for a complex case). Each page should be numbered with a progressive numbering stamp. If time permits, the top margin of each page should be marked with a rubber stamp imprinting:

Case:

Date: Time:

This information will be entered as the case goes along, thereby creating a chronology of the case presentation. A vertical line one quarter or one third of the way from the right edge of every page will create a margin for noting exhibit introduction, important admissions, important conflicts, and such that the legal assistant perceives.

When trial begins, the legal assistant fills in the case name, date, and time, along with the court and the judge, and then records the names of the court clerk, the court reporter, the bailiff, the adversary attorneys, and experts, and the presence or absence of parties. For example:

Case: Smith vs. Jones   Sharto Sup. Crt #123 645 Dept. 3
Date: 6/14/90   Time: 0930 AM   Judge C. E. Jones

When the opening statements are made, the note taking begins, tying the statements to the attorneys who offer them. When the first witness is called, the entry may look like "Darrow calls Thompson to the stand." Unless someone interposes a comment or objection, the substance of the witness's testimony is recorded as it is given.

Objections are noted in the right margin, together with the judge's ruling.

As exhibits are offered, that is entered both in the right margin and on the evidence/exhibit log for identification. As objections are raised and ruled on, they are logged in the notebook but not on the log. If the item is admitted, a notation of that is made in both places. Since the pages of the notebook fill quickly, the initiation of each page offers an opportunity to enter the time, and that chronology and the recorded recesses (logged in the notes both at the time granted and the time trial resumed) can be of aid in estimating the need for alerting witnesses to come to the courthouse and for use in looking back through notes during the recapitulation meetings. When the trial is over, the notebook, together with the evidence (copies) and the lawyer's trial book, is stored for use in appellate procedures and so forth for the time specified in the office manual.

8.136 Polling the Jury.

When a verdict is rendered that surprises the lawyer, interviewing the jurors to identify the reasoning behind the verdict is important. What fact, exhibit, or testimony caused the result? Whom did they believe? Why did they not believe the client or the client's witness? Usually, there is a reasonable and understandable basis for the decision. Sometimes it is simply common sense. For instance, in a condemnation case, the landowner wanted two million dollars, and the public agency offered only two thousand dollars, while both sides had experts pound away on their respective but opposing valuation theories. It is not surprising a jury would award the landowner two hundred thousand dollars in a decision, recognizing the difference in the two valuations, one so unreasonably high and the other so unreasonably low, and honoring the spirit of honesty in settlement, if not the facts submitted by the adversaries.

In other cases, the severity and continuing nature of an injury to an individual may lead a jury to decide for the injured party on a compassionate basis and point only to the flimsiest thread of causal connection to the defendant's conduct.

Infrequently, the decisions are rendered against the client because of tactics that outrage the sensibilities of the jury. They may be committed by the attorney in a correct procedure, even a necessary one (such as a driving impeachment cross-examination), an obvious lie by a critical witness, or even a pattern of behavior by the client in the case that the jury acknowledged as legal but unworthy of being rewarded by it in the verdict.

The polling is best done immediately after the jury is discharged but can be pursued later. Each juror is interviewed and the notes are all collated for what value such a postmortem may provide.

8.14   Comments

While this chapter does not explore all the varied ways a legal assistant can assist an attorney in litigation, the scope of opportunities should be challenging to the legal assistant because the variety is great, the personal rewards are gratifying, and the compensation for the competent can be comfortable.

The lawyer-legal assistant team thrives on the mutual respect and loyalty of the principals to each other. With it, the lawyer can, and often will, delegate jealously protected functions to the legal assistant, secure in the knowledge that if it can be done, it will be done and done on time, fully, ethically, and done the way the lawyer wanted it.

Few litigation legal assistants will perform every function described in this chapter during the course of every case. Some will never perform some of these functions, because the lawyer will reserve them to himself or herself as his or her responsibility to the client.

The new legal assistant must expect assignments to be simple at first, followed by more complex and challenging ones. Intermixed will be a full gamut of relatively mundane, routine, and unglamorous assignments that are not much fun to execute but are essential to the proper handling of a given case. A document case is typical. With hundreds or thousands of pages of dull, uninteresting material to screen, review or categorize, the temptation is to do less than an outstandingly thorough and comprehensive job. Those duties are the character tests that separate the great legal assistants from the wage takers. Anyone can be happy, eager, cheerful, and productive with fascinating assignments, but the pleasant, thorough, productive, and reliable legal assistant who does the drudgery as well as the fun jobs is the one who will, in time, escape most of the boring jobs simply because he or she is too valuable to use on those jobs that do not require his or her demonstrated drive, efficiency, innovation, and reliability.

Bibliography

Baer, Harold, and Aaron J. Broder. *How to Prepare and Negotiate Cases for Settlement,* rev. ed. Law-Arts Publishers, New York, N.Y. 1973.

Black's Law Dictionary. 6th ed., West Publishing Company, St. Paul. 1990.

*Corpus Juris Secundum. West Publishing Company.

*Federal Practice and Procedure. West Publishing Company.

Federal Rules of Evidence for U.S. District Courts and Magistrates, as Amended to November 1, 1988. West Publishing Company, St. Paul. 1988.

Hare, Francis H. Jr., and Edward M. Ricci (eds.). *Anatomy of a Personal Injury Lawsuit.* Association of Trial Lawyers of America, Education Fund. New York, N.Y. 1981.

Magarich, Pat. *Casualty Investigation Checklists.* Clark Boardman Co., Ltd., New York, New York. 1985.

Rules of Civil Procedure for the U.S. District Courts, with Forms, August 1, 1987.

Trial magazine. American Trial Lawyers of America.

U.S. Government Printing Office. 1987.

*Uniform Laws Annotated. West Publishing Company.

*U.S. Code Annotated. West Publishing Company.

*Words and Phrases. West Publishing Company.

9 The Legal Assistant and Document Discovery Cases

9.00   Introduction

"Discovery" is a process in litigation allowing both sides to ask questions or to require the production of documents of their adversary so that both sides can make their decisions of the liability and damages in a case based on the best information available to them. The theory is that both sides will reach similar conclusions without trial where each has all the facts the other has.

In a major document case, the request for production of documents, whether initiated by the client's lawyer or by the adversary's lawyer, is fraught with difficulty, expense, and a great deal of labor. It is designed to make available all the relevant facts in the case that have been memorialized in documents. Certain basic steps should be followed to obtain the maximum benefit from the least amount of effort.

The attorney and the legal assistant must be harshly realistic about the value, the need for and the utility of the discovery plan they select. They must weigh the time and cost against the anticipated benefits. It does little good to expend large amounts of time and money creating a system that does not substantially contribute to reaching the goal in the case.

Document discovery cases and the systems developed to serve them are non-delegable responsibilities of the attorneys, requiring intensive thought and consideration very early in the cases to produce effective and reliable results. Once committed to a given course, it is very difficult and expensive, both in time and money, to change that path.

Time is the most critical element; once gone, it cannot be replaced, not even by adding more people. The best work is conducted with intensity but not panic. The consistency and reliability of the selected system are all important.

9.01   The Discovery Plan

The initiation of discovery requires the attorneys and the legal assistants to consider jointly the problems anticipated in implementing any discovery plan for documents. There are two sides to this consideration: the client's documents and how to handle them and the adversary's documents and how to handle those. Decisions on the system to employ and the staff required will vary according to a number of factors discussed below.

9.011   Plaintiff or Defendant.

Whether the client is the plaintiff or the defendant in the case will play a part in staffing choices. If the client is the plaintiff, usually there is adequate time before filing the complaint to locate all of the client's documents and to arrange them in a reasonably ordered fashion. In this case, it is possible to work with a much smaller staff than when the client is the defendant responding to an aggressive plaintiff and suffering from the constraints of time created by court orders. Similarly, the selected discovery staff should keep the pressure on the adversary to *respond* to discovery—a true advantage.

9.012   Time Problems.

Time constraints may arise from many sources. The statute of limitations effective in the case may have a bearing on the organization of personnel and equipment. The service of a request for production of documents with a statutory period in which to respond may present timing problems. It is axiomatic that the shorter the period of time in which to accomplish the production, the larger the staff needed and, generally, the more limited the choices of the manner in which the production will be performed.

9.013   Volume.

Documents in business litigation, product liability, and antitrust cases may vary from only one thousand pages of material to two hundred thousand or more pages of material. Document volume has a major effect on the difficulty of production and will make demands both on the attorneys and the legal assistants in terms of the system employed and the manner of handling the documents (which are discussed later). Generally, one to two thousand pages can be handled easily using either lists of documents or cards created for each document as a control device. A small team of one or two people can be used and becomes very familiar with the individual documents. Control and retrieval of the documents are thereby simplified.

As the volume of documents increases, the ability of the team to recall the important documents with certainty diminishes, regardless of the size of the team. If time is a problem, the team may be larger, and consequently, the number of "duplicate documents" that exist in all files may not have the same impact on the discovery team as they would if only one or two people worked on them. Generally, with a file of from two thousand to twenty thousand pages, "document discovery cards" (which are discussed later) are helpful to handle the files properly. The team, again depending on the time frame in which it has to operate, may vary from one or two to as many as fifty people.

The rule in document discovery is the *smaller* the crew, the *better*. A small team gives each person a high degree of familiarity with the file, but it also means the prolongation of relatively boring work and a greater potential impact on the effort if the team loses a member.

9.014   "Technical Skills" Cases.

The technical nature of the case and the content of the documents comprising the document discovery effort have great impact on the nature of the discovery team put together to handle the suit. Routine business correspondence, contracts, drafts of contracts, letters and memoranda, and so on, can be handled by the average legal assistant with reasonable training time and familiarity with the subject of the suit. If the matter contains extensive and technical engineering reports or highly complex studies and mathematical calculations related to those studies, the use of an engineering-qualified legal assistant or an engineer on loan from the company department in which the suit originated may be absolutely essential.

Other special document problems can arise involving economic data, tax matters, or accounting documents peculiar to a large firm in which computer printouts and/or prenumbered forms might be adapted directly into the system without "special" or additional identifying data.

9.015   Locating Responsive Documents.

Among potential discovery production problems is the location and production of *all* responsive documents, when that is the order given by the court. In other cases, only *one representative copy* of a particular type of document is required. The attorney must assist in determining the need for *all,* rather than single, *copies* of exemplary material. Similarly, when the client is the plaintiff, document search parameters must be set with consideration given to the opposing attorney's concept of the case and the *probable* defenses of the adversary and documents to be requested. *Once* through the files is difficult, but twice through is very expensive and time-consuming. The search must be thorough to identify *all* the documents within the guidelines established. Production of *complete* files is essential. Files of a fragmentary nature are extremely difficult to explain in discovery proceedings and will create many difficulties for the discovery team later in tracking the normal handling of such documents.

9.016   Geographic Dispersion.

One of the most difficult problems to overcome in document production is that of geography. Files generally are dispersed among offices of a large corporation or the departments of small companies in a manner relating to their functional and liaison duties. Sometimes the relationship is so tenuous that it is difficult to anticipate where the documents are; this poses a substantial problem in the identification and location of those documents. The legal assistant's imagination should range as widely as the ability of the photocopy machine to produce documents in considering the possible resting places of the potentially responsive material. It may be in a central file room, in one or more offices of individuals, or in storage. Consider each possibility, and then during the physical search ask each person, "Who else might have copies of this?" "Who do you send material to?" and so on.

9.017   Physical Space, Equipment, and Budget.

The space in which the work is performed, the equipment with which to conduct the effort, and the budget with which the team attempts to operate all impose certain aids or restraints on the team's ability to produce results. It does little good to rage against problems beyond one's control, and the legal assistant's equanimity in adjusting to any limitations will assist the discovery effort and present a positive and effective attitude.

9.018   Documents—Evidence or Company Operation.

The need to produce documents in a suit will require the attorney to take custody of this potential documentary evidence. However, the client's daily work must go on as well with as little handicap as possible. Photocopying is simple and fast; however, simply copying the original material creates new documents potentially responsive to the case. Consider placing a legend on the copies of responsive documents and giving these "legend copies" to the operating office for convenience. The legend may be "Copy of an original in the lawsuit file _____ vs. _____."

9.019   To Number or Not to Number.

Once the potentially responsive and relevant documents are identified, the problems of future reference to each one must be addressed. The documents may be marked with a unique identifying number, alphabetic character, or an alphanumeric combination before any photocopying, sorting, or other handling is undertaken. Tactical or strategic considerations or the personal preference of the attorney may dictate otherwise.

Early numbering disposes of one laborious job in the beginning of the case and simplifies the recognition of individual documents and their subsequent copies, the comparison of apparent duplicates, and the use of many file indices, or other techniques. It allows quick relation of the document to its point of origin through the minimum number of reference elements, such as type, date, author, addressee, and topic. Many attorneys prefer *not* to number the documents until the adversary has had an opportunity to see the documents in the case. This creates difficult—but not insurmountable—control and identification problems for the legal assistants. Its worst feature is that it postpones the labor of numbering until after the inspection by the adversary, and often this means that a huge volume of documents must be numbered under a time constraint, as opposed to the more comfortable system allowed by the technique of numbering them as they are found.

9.0110   Privileged Documents.

Documents are identified and segregated early in the production effort if they carry any "privilege," whether of attorney-client, attorney work product, or any proprietary information or trade secrets. The legal assistant may aid this operation if given proper instructions in what to look for, the criteria to be used in evaluating the existence or absence of privilege. It is the attorney's responsibility to provide this guidance at the outset of the case in terms the legal assistant can follow and to provide adequate supervision throughout the process.

9.0111   Issue Recognition.

When the client is the plaintiff, it may be necessary early in the discovery operation to code the documents according to the issues of the case. This requires the attorneys to identify the case by issues and in terms that are understandable to the legal assistants and applicable to the documents. A substantial amount of early analysis or "prethinking" by the attorneys and some familiarity with the documents involved in the case are needed for this.

When the client is the defendant in a case, issue recognition is often accomplished later on since all the issues are rarely well defined at the outset of the litigation. Instead, sortings are performed by each paragraph of the document production request, and the issues may be imputed to some degree from an analysis of the nature of the documents requested.

9.0112   Personnel Choices.

Deciding which types of personnel to use in gathering and indexing the required documents must be done early in the process. The use either of legal assistants or of personnel indigenous to the office where the records are stored may be effective; however, for the attorney's convenience and greatest confidence, legal assistants have proven to be the most reliable and thorough. Where indigenous employees are used, even closer supervision is necessary to ensure that *all* the records are produced and properly sorted.

9.0113   Control Devices.

Since the documents may range in volume from one thousand to two hundred thousand pages or more, the choice of control devices must be explored and decided early. Failure to do this will result in duplication of work and the expenditure of unnecessary labor to correct poorly based early judgments. Among the varieties of control devices that can be used are:

(a)   typed indexes of documents using reference items, such as date, author, and addressee;

(b)   the use of surrogate documents, such as the "Attorney's Document Discovery Control Card";

(c)   personality cards;

(d)   numbering the documents at the outset or at some later point in discovery;

(e)   typed indexes using the numbers for each document;

(f)   the number of copies to be duplicated (if any) and the *sortings* of those documents.

9.0114   Legal Assistant Conceptual Contributions.

The attorney in each case cannot set down each thought and consideration that goes into determining the discovery plan and must rely on assistance in generating enough data to allow intelligent decisions to be made. The legal assistant is often required to perform a reconnaissance of the files and to participate in speculating on paths the litigation will take. When a tentative choice of system is made, the legal assistant often may be required to generate a step-by-step procedure of the document discovery plan selected and attempt to generate estimates of time, personnel, space, equipment, and cost for consideration by the attorney in making his or her decision. The legal assistant should be knowledgeable concerning the mechanical processes and fight if necessary for using those in which he or she has faith; but in the end, it is the attorney's decision.

9.0115   Attorney Reviews and Audits.

The attorney must satisfy himself or herself that the directions he or she has given the legal assistant for performing the document search are effective and that the legal assistant is doing it as the attorney wishes. This is accomplished by conducting spot checks or audits of the work being done. The legal assistant should welcome such checks; it minimizes wasted work and reveals any weaknesses in communications.

9.0116   Documenting the Plan.

Once selected, the plan should be outlined in detail (in writing) with the control devices and procedures well explained. These terms to be used, acronyms, logos, codes, abbreviations, and so on all must be analyzed and the initial selections memorialized. The plan document will serve as a guide for use and modification as the case progresses.

9.02   The Common Principles of Document Discovery Programs

Document discovery programs always involve a minimum of five basic activities to be considered in the planning stages, whether the ultimate effort is small and simple or huge and complex. These essential elements, or common principles, are as follows.

9.021   Locate.

Potentially responsive files or documents must be located geographically, in general terms, within the organization required to produce them. Perhaps they are distributed throughout a corporation in several departments and, in many cases, retired record centers as well. The location search should be wide-ranging to ensure that it includes all the documents conceivably responsive either to the attorney's plan of litigation, the adversary's document request, or the anticipated scope of requests yet to be received. The search plan must be logical and capable of being described on demand.

9.022   Identify.

Once the files containing the responsive documents are located, the process of initial screening and examining them page by page is conducted to identify the specific documents that fit the requirements of the production request, whether in hand or anticipated. No matter the volume of the documents involved, there is no shortcut for examining each document page by page. The identification process is not complete until all potentially responsive documents are distinguished and separated from responsive documents that may be privileged and from irrelevant documents.

9.023   Control.

Once the documents have been identified as relevant to the case at hand/or potentially responsive to the document request, some control of the custody and/or travel of each individual document, or any copies of it, must be initiated. The surest method is to number the selected documents as soon as the "responsive" identity is confirmed. Once each document is numbered with a unique number, alphabetic character, or alphanumeric combination, the team's ability to perform the subsequent steps of the discovery plan is greatly enhanced. Numbering also allows easy notation of the routing of the documents or copies.

   If numbering is not used, a more complex system of "out-carding" or "cover sheet" attachment may be instituted for documents or copies that must be separated from the basic files. The relationship of a document to the file from which it was taken *cannot* be lost.

Similarly, preserving the documents in the same condition in which they were discovered is extremely important. If the document is 105 pages long and stapled, its production should be made in the same fashion. If the document is a bound volume of assembled and stapled individual documents, this condition must be represented to the attorneys for their determination of subsequent processing. It is possible that the custodian of that particular bound document may have to be consulted to determine whether the documents are related in some fashion or are simply bound for convenience. The legal assistant *does not make* this determination.

From this point forward, it is essential that whichever system of control is adopted, the legal assistant ensures its integrity so that at some future time any questions about the procedure will assist in establishing that the system of production is fully in accord with discovery requirements and is not arbitrary, whimsical, or unreliable. The legal assistant cannot change the character of the documents by assembling or disassembling stapled or bound material without the concurrence and direction of the attorney.

9.024   Retrieve.

Documents are discovered during the course of a case to determine those that contribute to establishing facts or the reasoning that led to events, practices, procedures, or representations at issue in the case. The assembly of documents without the ability to use them effectively later in supporting the client's case or refuting the adversary's case is virtually worthless.

The ability to retrieve any given document or set of documents reliably and timely from the assembled mass of produced material or reference material included within a document discovery file is vital. Additionally, where documents become exhibits in a case, the authors, addressees, and persons who have seen or acted upon the content of the document are potential witnesses and may need to see and examine those documents to refresh their memories. The ability to retrieve documents can be the difference between supporting or destroying a witness or winning or losing a case.

Documents often are assembled in a fashion that is solely a convenience for the department file clerk or an individual who has created his or her own personal reference file. The assembly of a large number of these accumulations can result in a hodgepodge of nonchronologic material in no particular order. Since the document discovery file generally must serve the purpose of relating one document to another and documents seldom are generated simultaneously, a *chronologic sorting* of copies of all of the responsive documents is *always* necessary. The peripheral benefits of chronologic sorting will be the identification of duplicate or near-duplicate documents resulting from the juxtaposition of all duplicate or near-duplicate documents. It allows comparison of drafts, marginal annotations, or distribution comments that individually may mean little but together reflect policy, decision, responsibility, and so on.

A last form of retrieval is the extraction of *all* privileged material, including *all* duplicates, from the gross discovery file prior to the examination of the files by the adversary. Remember, once the privilege is waived, it is gone forever. Such extraction of privileged material is not whimsical or casual and must follow certain identifiable guidelines. The attorney generally will provide those guidelines at the outset of the case, and each selection of privileged material by the legal assistant should be supported by a brief "privileged documents summary sheet" executed at the time of the selection. These sheets assist the attorneys in their review of the material. Ultimately, a list of all privileged documents withheld may be required, and the summary sheets generate the proper information in the proper order for editing and submission.

9.025 Return.

Following conclusion of the lawsuit, or in some cases before the suit is concluded, documents considered unnecessary to the permanent file are returned to the custodians from whom they were taken. Since lawsuits require extended periods of time and, in the course of such lawsuits, any given document may become the "best evidence," it is prudent to retain custody of the original documents until the last moment of the case. This, unfortunately, denies access to the original documents for the working departments of the corporation that produced them. To mitigate the effect of removal of the documents, a piece of paper bearing the legend "Copy of original document in the file _____" is taped face down to the glass of the copying machine, and then, as the original documents are photocopied, the legend is transferred to each page of the copies. One set of this legend-marked document is returned to the department custodians for their daily use until the conclusion of the lawsuit. Good practice suggests that on return of the original, this legend copy be destroyed.

9.03 Options within the Common Principles

9.031 Locate.

9.0311 Attorney and Legal Assistant "Prethinking." The attorney and the legal assistant responsible for the production should carefully discuss the case to ensure they both understand the issues (actual or probable) of the case and the parameters for the reconnaissance of files and the subsequent screening and selection of files that will follow. The attorney has the burden at this time of ensuring that the analysis is couched in phrases easily translatable into action by the legal assistants. It may be necessary for the attorney to assist in the early review of documents to obtain a perspective on the types of documents involved in the case in order to make the subsequent decisions. The types of documents, as well as the volume, often determine the control system used in the case.

9.0312 Deducing the Sources. Once a firm concept of the types of documents to be produced has been developed, the sources of the information to be screened must be deduced. In a large corporation with many departments, there are over-lapping areas of responsibility, and these interrelationships must be fully under-stood both by the attorneys and by the legal assistant team. In a case with a minor number of issues, only one, two, or three departments may be involved and the assembly of documents thereby simplified. A full list of all departments and sources of records to be screened and/or produced must be tabulated and agreed upon by the attorneys and legal assistants since this initial step may determine the completeness of the response to the adversary's document request (whether in hand or anticipated).

9.0313 *Reconnaissance.* The reconnaissance of files begins initially with notice to the custodians of those files that such a search is under way as a requirement of the legal case. In large corporations, contact with the highest officer having responsibility for the affected departments is desirable, sometimes by letter and other times by personal meeting. If the departments and the responsible parties are limited, a group meeting may be arranged at which the case, its ramifications, and the scope of the document search may be discussed to ensure maximum cooperation of the functional departments with the legal assistant team.

It is important to identify in each department or subsection the custodian of the majority of the records in a central file room or other depository. The appointment of one person by the department manager to be the liaison for the legal assistant team is very beneficial. Similarly, an initial list of those personnel within each department who may be involved in the case by reason of their title, position, or past activities for responsible parties is a great assistance in ensuring that the *individual* files of the personalities or potential witnesses in the case will be examined for responsive material.

In the reconnaissance of files by the legal assistants, either of two courses may be adopted for time-scheduling purposes. The department can make a preliminary survey based on file titles, area of activity, or other relevant reference to the case at hand and provide a "linear-inch" file estimate, annotated by room number and reference characteristic of the file; or the legal assistant team may, with the assistance of the assigned department liaison, individually go through the files under the guidance of the custodian, examine those file folders and titles of apparent interest, and select those potentially responsive. The selection is inclusive when in doubt. ("Linear-inch" is the actual measurement of the files in place. Page volume is estimated from that measurement.)

9.0314 *Screening Files.* As each file folder is recognized as one to be screened, it is entered on a log that characterizes the location from which it was taken, the custodian who provided it, and the nature of the file itself. If the file has a number and a title, that identification should be used for clarity. An estimate of the space involved should be made as well, such as a "one-half-inch linear measure" or one full transfer box. This is important because at some later date if a decision to a number is made, it may help to cross-reference the inclusive numbers to these individual files. (See Appendix A, Exhibit 53.)

9.0315 *Taking Custody.* Once the file folders, binders, boxes of retired records, or whatever form the documents are in are located within the department, "out cards" are prepared by the legal assistant team and left with the custodian of documents. The legal assistant team then takes the gross files into custody for transport to a work area.

9.0316 *The "Evidence Room" Work Area.* The work area for the legal assistant team should be removed from normal activity of the departments and of the functional personalities in a case. The room should be considered an "evidence room" with restricted entry and a firm control over the entry and removal of documents within it.

9.0317 *Processing "On Site."* In some cases, documents are so vital to the department operation that it may be necessary to process them on site in the department. If so, portable copying equipment, microfilming, and both numbering and legend-marking procedures must be considered in detail. Remember to co-ordinate the effort with the custodian to minimize friction and interference with or by department personnel. Again, the purpose is to take custody of the evidence and leave a working copy.

9.032   Identify.

9.0321 *Identifying the Gross File.*
Once the potentially responsive but un-screened file enters the working area of the legal assistant team, it should be accorded a unique identifying number. Among the variety of unique numbers or characteristics that can be used, the following are suggested:

1. The file folder may be placed within another file folder that is marked either with an alphabetic or numeric character. That should be recorded on the log cross-referenced to the source from which the document was taken. If the forms are correctly prepared, this can be a new entry on the same log on which the screening was conducted. (See examples in Appendix A, Exhibits 51, 54, and 55.)

2. If the volume of documents is substantially large, use pocket folders on which an alphabetic or numeric code, room number, department number, and/or name of the custodian can be entered. This folder is not part of the discovery project documents but simply a container in which the potentially responsive material is stored until the screening process begins.

3. If the documents are of sufficient volume that they may be easily stored in a transfer box, the box itself may be marked either with an alphabetic or numeric code or by the room, department, and/or custodian name. The identification is cross-referenced to the source from which the documents were received. Some "retired" file systems involve a unique number that may be used as the identifier for the screening log.

9.0322 *Reading the Material.*
With the potentially relevant documents in hand and sufficiently characterized to ensure that their origin will not be forgotten or lost, the legal assistant team is now prepared to read all of the enclosed doc-uments within each folder for relevance to the case or responsiveness to the discovery requirements. Every page must be examined and measured against the criteria established by the attorneys for responsiveness to the case or the discovery request. The legal assistants read to include documents within the parameters and do not exert highly critical judgment to exclude documents from the discovery request. Phrased another way, "potential relevance" or "potential responsiveness" is the criteria legal assistants should use in the initial sorting process.

9.0323 *Legal Assistant Training for Selection.*
The judgments made by the legal assistant are not casual and should not be made on an uninformed basis. The attorneys should arrange for careful consideration of the scope of the search they wish conducted, based on the issues of the legal pleadings. The legal assistant in charge, with the assistance of the attorneys and the professional people recruited as consultants in the case, conducts training programs to ensure that the legal assistants performing the screening operation have a working knowledge of the language and functions expressed in the documents to be read. The training process may be a day, two days, three days, or more depending on the extent of the

documents, the complexity of technical terms, the number of legal issues, and the experience of the legal assistants. The legal assistant includes a document by its perceived responsiveness to an issue. Its inclusion can be indicated by a stamp or a pencil mark on one corner of the face sheet reflecting the issue or paragraph to which it is responsive.

9.0324 Selection and Sorting.   Initial sortings of potentially responsive material can often be made in the screening process. All documents are organized in boxes, preferably lying on the long edge, for the legal assistants to read. If the volume of documents is very large, marker cards can be used to ensure the legal assistants are reading the documents progressively in order and covering all of the documents in any file. This card should be identified with the name of the reader, sufficiently tall so it can project vertically above a file, and distinctive in color to allow instant recognition as a "reading place card." The selection of responsive documents is initially indicated in the raw files by standing them vertically on their edges in the boxes.

The documents should not be disassembled during this initial screening process. No stapled document should be taken apart to characterize some portion of it as responsive and another portion as irrelevant. Where files must be transported from the screening location to another place for advice or the consideration of another party, an "out card" fully identifying the document, dated, signed by the screener, and reflecting the person to whom the document was directed must be inserted in place of the document. The integrity of the individual files must be maintained, even though it is somewhat cumbersome and time-consuming.

9.0325 Identifying and Segregating "Privilege."   This is the best time to identify potentially privileged material, if those criteria have been established by the attorneys and understood by the legal assistants. The production form "Privileged Document" (see Appendix D, Exhibit 72), which reflects the number of privileged pages, is substituted for each privileged document. Again, legal assistants read to include, or exclude, privilege. What initially appears to be a privileged document may not be, and when this occurs, its "privileged" designation is removed, and it is returned to the responsive file. The legal assistant must check to ensure that all copies are properly redistributed and the "Privileged Document" production forms pulled and destroyed. Any indices on which these were listed also must be corrected.

9.0326 The Decision to Number.   Once the screening is under way and before the responsive documents are extracted from those that are irrelevant and/or not responsive, the decision whether to number those documents must be made. Numbering of documents prior to production to the adversary has great advantages for the legal assistant team (and by extension, the attorneys for whom they work) in that it simplifies the control problem of the documents. If the document may now be numbered, a legend copy with a number can be inserted in the file at the time the original is extracted. The legend copies and the irrelevant documents soon will be returned to the department from which they came, and the numbered legend copy allows easy reference between that department, the lawyer, witnesses, and other users from then on.

The numbering system does present difficulties. Some irrelevant documents may be numbered that later would not be produced to the adversary but might have to be explained. Further, if numbering is elected, the decision must be made on whether to use various production forms in the document discovery process. Some attorneys dislike this because the production documents may become numbered documents (when a powered mechanical numbering device is used) that may have to be explained at some future time. Production documents will be discussed in more detail in another section.

Numbering presents one major tactical difficulty for the attorneys. A major document production effort suggests that the adversary will be equally diligent in sorting the documents. In this process, the adversary will find—in fact, must find—that not all documents with numbers have been produced. Gaps will occur where there are numbering errors, where production documents are involved, where irrelevant documents were initially included and later extracted and so on. It is a legal question whether a numbering system is an attorney work product and whether the adversary can simply make request for those documents within specified number gaps as constituting a foundation of relevance in the case. This is not within the scope of the legal assistant's decision-making process but within that of the attorney.

Numbering at the outset of a production case is especially helpful. It improves control and simplifies referral, retrieval, and sorting. If numbering is to be postponed to some future time, photocopies of the responsive documents should be limited to reduce to a minimum the duplicates or near duplicates that later will have to be located, purged, or substituted by more easily identifiable numbered copies.

In the event the attorney selects a "no numbering" system, the responsive documents selected by the legal assistants and reviewed by the attorneys are now ready for photocopying. Each document photocopied should have a legend on the side, at the top or bottom of the page in a distinctive location that reads essentially "Copy of an original in the file _____ vs. _____." This will minimize many problems in future discovery searches on subsequent document discovery requests or in furnishing copies to associate counsel, expert consultants, potential percipient witnesses, and others.

Perhaps the "no numbering" system can better be appreciated with the following example:

Assume a moderate-sized case with few issues and approximately 25,000 pages of assorted kinds of responsive documents and their copies:

2,000 pages of drawings, sketches, photos;

5,000 pages of recording charts covering a five-year period for 20 different installations;

4,000 pages of regulatory agency material, public filings, applications, and so on;

6,000 pages of industry practices, studies, standards, public documents, trade publication reference material, and so on;

3,000 pages of internal company standards, specifications, practices, guides, training material, and the like;

800 pages of internal company memoranda;

500 pages of letters between the company and the adversary;

2,000 pages of accounting data, invoices, computer printouts, and so on;

1,500 pages of historical summaries, studies, and analyses;

300 pages of independent contractor opinions;

<u> 150</u> pages of privileged material.

25,250 pages total

The majority of this material is innocuous, responsive to the discovery request but insignificant to the issues of the case. The issues are clear, few, and related to one incident.

Since the documents are manageable due to the large numbers of easily identifiable documents in each category, it is tactically acceptable and economically sound to allow the adversary to examine it all and *number in the adversary's presence only the documents he or she selects.*

Contrast that with a case spanning years of time, the same number of documents but all related to a series of contracts, the meetings between parties, drafts and redrafts of contract provisions, letters, and understandings and the meanings of the contract provisions—and much of it potentially privileged. The choice of system would likely differ.

9.033. Control.

Control in document cases involves more than ensuring the original documents are not lost or misplaced during the course of the case but also ensuring that the photocopies of documents are properly organized in working files that are useful to the attorneys in the progress of the case.

9.0331 Indexes.   Indexing is probably the key to control in all document cases. Whether or not the indexing is done by date, document type, author, and addressee, by a numeric or an alphanumeric system, or by some other coding method, organizing the documents into workable forms is essential. The forms must be recorded and sufficiently clear in the mind of each person working on them that the entire file system has utility and convenience both for the attorneys and the legal assistants who operate it.

9.0332 Types of Files to Create.   Among the types of files usually necessary are the following:

(a) The Original Document File (less privileged). It is best to maintain this in the same sortings as the documents first were found, less the privileged documents but including cross-reference sheets substituted for them. Ideally, the documents will be numbered and the file thus can be maintained in *numeric* order. If production documents were used, the production documents should be left in place, especially if they also were numbered. (If production documents were both used and numbered, a log of the production documents and their numbers should be created. It is simple at that time to title that index "Numeric Sequence Justification Roster and Commentary." [See Appendix A, Exhibit 58.] Within that log, show misnumbers, the addition of alphabetic suffixes when pages have been passed over or left unnumbered inadvertently; the numbers assigned to production forms; and the numbers assigned to irrelevant documents that have been extracted from the responsive document file.)

(b) Chronologic File (legend copy, less privileged). A *chronologic file* is always necessary on document cases. This is a file of photocopies (each bearing the legend discussed earlier) and sorted, irrespective of topic, strictly in a chronologic order. Preferably, this file will contain no privileged documents, no production documents (except "Privileged Document" substitute sheets), and no irrelevant documents.

Ultimately, when complete processing of the file has occurred, there will be no *duplicate* documents in the chronologic file. It will be copies of "prime" documents only. "Prime" documents are the best evidence available, originals or duplicate originals.

(c) Privileged Document File (original documents plus all copies). A *privileged document file* will be necessary. This will be separated physically both from the original file and the chronologic file, preferably in a locked file cabinet. Each duplicate of the privileged documents will be located, and those duplicates should be bound together with the one original selected as the prime document. Cross-reference sheets "Privileged Document(s)" (see Appendix D, Exhibit 72) are placed in the original and chronologic files in place of the documents. Each privileged document (or group of duplicates) is filed appended to a "Privileged Document Summary Sheet." (See Appendix D, Exhibit 73, Exhibit 74, or Exhibit 76.)

(d) Irrelevant Document File (original and copies). This is composed of documents selected by inadvertence, that relate to issues that have been eliminated from the case, or that contain factual but irrelevant material agreed upon by stipulation between the attorneys. This material is extracted from the working files (and from the original file with an appropriate cross-indexing card replacing it) and separated physically from any of the other files.

(e) Duplicate File (legend copy only). Whether a *duplicate file* is maintained in the true sense of the word or the duplicates are filed in with the irrelevants is a matter of choice. In most large organizations, especially since the advent of the photocopying machine, most significant documents have three or four identical or near-identical duplicates located within the organization. The document discovery team is obligated to locate and, if required, produce those documents for the adversary's inspection. Early on in this process, a determination of what constitutes a duplicate is necessary. A *true* duplicate is one with no marginal annotations, distribution stamps, underlining, question marks, or any other differences from the prime document. The existence of many duplicates creates a burden on the team during the retrieval process, and if the percentage of duplicates is high, a separate numerically ordered file is often a very effective depository. If "document discovery cards" (see Appendix B) are used, cross-reference sheets will be unnecessary.

9.0333 Control Devices.   Once the copying of documents begins, the efficacy of the control system elected will determine the amount of staffing necessary to manage the file.

(a) Numbering. The numbering system is the most efficient control device of all because it can be accomplished very early in the discovery process, usually when the most time is available for the mechanical operations by the legal assistants of the team. A number stamped on the document by a progressive hand stamper or any of the variety of powered numbering machines offers the advantage of always being unique and affording a quick and easy means of reference to that document. The incorporation of an alphabetic character, either as a prefix or suffix to the document number, is possible. Numbering allows for the orderly cross-referencing of duplicates, privileged documents, or other material for review by the attorneys.

(b) Surrogate Documents (ADDC). Numbering, too, allows the creation of surrogate document cards that can be used to do retrieval searches and cross-indexing of groups of stapled documents. The "Attorney's Document Discovery Card" (ADDC) can be composed to assemble certain types of information relative to a given

document and placed in a handy form for ready reference. Further details on the use of such a card will be discussed below. (See Appendix B.)

9.0334 *Document Room Control.* Control of documents in the document room or work area is essential to the program. The purpose of the document files created by the team is to serve the needs of the attorney.

It is essential that if a document (original or copy) leaves the document room for any purpose, whether it is to be sent to an attorney for review, a technical expert for review or consideration, supplied for studies, or supplied for review by adversaries under a court order, its passage from and to the document room be logged and supported by some "out card" that reflects the date, who asked for the document, who transported the document, where it was sent, and who had custody of it at that point. (See Appendix D, Exhibit 79 for an example of a sheet for attorney review.) This sounds burdensome and difficult, but it is essential to check and recheck that the document is not lost or mislaid.

9.0335 *Purposes of the Control Program.* The purpose of the document control program is to ensure the following points:

1. That no document is made available to the adversaries without having been reviewed by the legal assistants and by the attorneys.
2. That no privileged document is ever accidentally exposed to the adversary in the course of the proceeding.
3. That every document responsive to the case is produced as required but that every appropriate defense to production of any document is exercised by the attorneys before its surrender.
4. That every highly significant document, whether helpful or harmful to the client, is referred to the employing attorneys for evaluation before the adversary sees it.
5. That every document obtained from the adversary is correctly handled and cross-referenced in relation to the issues and to the "friendly" documents in the case.
6. That documents are maintained in an order allowing retrieval of any document as needed by the attorneys in timely fashion.

9.034 Retrieve.

9.0341 *Withdrawal of Documents from the Files.* Retrieval involves a withdrawal of documents from the document file by specific document or by sortings as requested by the attorneys or required in compliance with proper requests by the adversary. In order to accomplish this, the minimum files and sortings discussed under "control" above are essential.

9.0342 *"Nice to Have" File Sortings.* The following "nice to have" sortings will simplify the conduct of the case:

(a) Issue File. This is a file by *each issue of the case* as defined by the attorneys. This sorting is accomplished subsequent to the initial sorts mentioned above. The attorneys assist the legal assistants in determining what the issues will be; any previous "pencil marking" of the issues can be converted into a production effort simply by perusing the chronologic file of documents or the attorney document discovery cards and recording the number of the document by the issue that made

it responsive. Frequently, this rereading will show that a document pertains to more than one issue and additional copies must be made, one for each desired issue file. These documents are bound in three-ring, looseleaf binders, if possible, chronologically in order, and reviewed by the attorneys and technical personnel as needed.

(b) Document File by Personality. In preparing for depositions to be taken of the prospective witnesses, sortings are made of *each document connected with any witness.* Every document mentioning the witness as author, addressee, or carbon-copied recipient or in the text can be located and compiled in a book. This can be accomplished either by perusal of the chronologic sorting of the documents, the "Attorney Document Discovery Cards," or the "Personality Cards." (See Appendix C.) Generally, these documents are set up in three-ring binders chronologically in order and occasionally chronologically in order by issue. These files are used to allow percipient witnesses, before deposition, to refresh their memories of the documents they have seen and to allow them an opportunity to research the document especially when any document has been obtained by the adversary through discovery. The same preparation may be accomplished for adversary witnesses in order to provide the employing attorneys with a line of questioning based on solid representations from the documents.

(c) Chronologic File of Documents Released to the Adversary. If the volume of documents requested by the adversary is small, it may be advantageous to create three-ring binders chronologically in order of those documents requested and obtained by the adversary. These may be broken down further by issue, by pro- spective witness, and so on. Otherwise, an index of documents fulfills the need.

(d) Exhibit Files. Every *document introduced* for the client or by the adversary *as an exhibit,* either to pleadings, at deposition, or at trial, must be identified and indexed with a historical background on the document, cross-referenced to other related documents, or to witnesses.

(e) Summary File. This is an *assembly of documents* used either by legal assistants or other personnel, such as expert witnesses or technical personnel, to provide *summaries.* There should be a report of those summaries footnoting the documents and attaching the referenced documents.

(f) Not Produced but Cited Documents. In cases where the adversary has produced some documents that refer to other documents not produced or show attachments not attached, a special sorting of these documents may be appropriate at some time, together with the cross-indexing information needed. In some cases, very significant documents within the client files will refer to documents requested of but not provided by the adversary. These are identified and included in that type of file. The indexes should be very specific as to the dates of the request, dates of the response, and the supporting but conflicting references. This may go so far as to use colored highlighting on the documents for quick and easy reference by the attorneys. In screening, a production form "Production Discrepancy" (see Appendix A, Exhibit 57) may be helpful in accumulating the data.

(g) Personality File. This may be a list, a set of cards, or 8½-by-11-inch sheets used to record each name that appears in the case, whether elicited from documents or testimony. (See Appendix C.) It provides an organized means of assembling the bits and pieces of identity to help establish whether an individual is going to be a witness. Properly created, the index can reflect each document the individual has seen, received, or authored.

9.035 Return.

Every case comes to conclusion through settlement, judgment, and/or rulings or appeal. At various times in the process, the attorneys have opportunities to conclude that certain categories of documents may be returned to the appropriate document custodian. Certainly at the conclusion of the case, the documents must be returned to the client's document custodians.

9.0351 Use of the Screening Log. The correct execution of the screening log (see Appendix A) during the initial stages of the case establishes the relationship of each document with the appropriate custodian and simplifies the return of the document. Documents should be returned in the same fashion (stapled, bound, in binders, and so on) as they were surrendered. At the time of return, any documents entered as evidence in the court file can be so annotated on the legend copy of the document in the custodian's file. Each return should be logged and receipted.

9.0352 Retention of Indexes. Every document index and receipt created in the case should be bound and stored in the case file to serve as a guide for future cases or to answer questions regarding documents the client might have at a later time.

9.0353 Destruction of Photocopies. Once the case is concluded and all originals have been returned to the custodians, the photocopied files should be destroyed. Destruction is exactly that: torn up, shredded, or burned, not simply placed in the trash for casual disposal. Any documents or their copies covered by protective orders also should be obtained from the adversary and from the court file, the originals returned to the client's custodian and the photocopies destroyed.

9.04 Production Documents

9.041 General Concept.

Production documents are those sheets that serve primarily as dividers of groups of documents to ensure that the integrity of the original files is maintained. When documents are obtained from functioning departments of companies, they are usually found in folders, three-ring binders, stapled, bound, or in various forms of semipermanent binding. Legal assistants doing document screening should not whimsically or arbitrarily change these binding characteristics. One way to maintain these characteristics during the process of numbering, copying, and filing is to use cover sheets reflecting the nature of the overall document. Among the titles of production forms to be used might be the following:

9.0411 "Begin Bound Document." This is a sheet placed ahead of photocopies made of a bound document, such as a hardbound book, a government pamphlet, or any other document that normally is an assembly of permanently bound pages. This sheet is followed by a sheet "End of Bound Document." (See Appendix D, Exhibit 64.)

9.0412 "Begin Stapled Document." This is placed ahead of a series of pages stapled together before the copying process. As the staple is pulled, the integrity of the stapled document might be lost without this particular sheet. The one that follows the last page of this document would be the "End Stapled Document." (See Appendix D, Exhibit 65.)

9.0413 "Begin Three-Ring Binder."   This is placed ahead of a document found assembled in a three-ring binder and may be supplemented, if there are divider tabs within the binder, by production sheets saying "divider Tab" and carrying the title of the divider tab. The whole assembly at the end of the binder would be followed by "End Three-Ring Binder." (See Appendix D, Exhibit 66.)

9.0414 "Reduced-Scale Document."   This sheet might be inserted just ahead of a large document that has been photocopied in reduced size and scale to a more manageable document. It is only used where the document can be reduced to one page (either legal or book size). This will alert everyone that a document in the *original* file is larger than the one at hand. For handling computer printouts, economic tabulation sheets, engineering drawings, and so on, this type of sheet is convenient and important. (Appendix D, Exhibit 67.)

9.0415 "Document Too Large to Copy."   In some cases, a drawing or other document is too large to be copied, even with reduction, on a single sheet of paper. When this happens, the legal assistant must paste several copies of portions of the document together to achieve one larger one. It is important for persons using the file to know that what they are seeing is not an accurate representation of the original document. (See Appendix D, Exhibit 68.)

9.0416 "Begin Stapled Series of Stapled Documents."   Many times, stapled documents are assembled by purpose or by chance either in central files or in personal information files of individuals under circumstances incomprehensible to the legal assistant reviewing the document. It is inappropriate for the legal assistant to disassemble these documents. Thus, the condition of this assembly of documents is shown by the introduction of this sheet. It would immediately be followed by "Begin Stapled Document" and then "End Stapled Document," "Begin Stapled Document," and so on through the total assembly of the stapled series. The last production document would be "End Stapled Series of Stapled Documents." (See Appendix D, Exhibit 69.)

9.0417 Microfilming.   If the file is of such magnitude that it is being microfilmed to create an archive, there may be a need for a production document entitled "Document Not Copied or Microfilmed." This would be used for bound documents if the microfilmer is incapable of copying bound ones, those too large to be copied by the microfilmer, and roll charts or other odd-sized or -shaped documents actually not incorporated in the microfilm archive but sequentially numbered for file integrity and reference. (Appendix D, Exhibit 70.)

9.0418 Privilege.   A privileged document is one characterized by the legal assistants following the criteria established by the attorneys. This is interpreted inclusively, rather than exclusively. All privileged documents later must be reviewed by the attorney, and the privilege is either supported or waived, or the document is reclassified as unprivileged. This production document is inserted in place of the document it represents in the original file and in *each* of the photocopied files subsequently assembled. (See Appendix D, Exhibit 70.) All of the copies made are packaged with the original and covered with a "Privileged Document Summary Sheet," which will show the following information:

> Date; number, if one exists; author; addressee; carbon-copy recipients (including blind carbons and routed copies); number of pages in the document; title or subject of the document; and the privilege being exerted (attorney-client, attorney work product, trade secret, and so on); and the numbers of all duplicates listed on the prime document's summary sheet. (See Appendix D, Exhibits 68, 69, 70, and 71.)

The summary sheet, together with the privileged document, is referred to the attorneys on a schedule determined early in the discovery process for their review, concurrence, waiver, or reclassification.

9.0419 Other.   Other production document forms may be generated as needed.

9.05 Surrogate Documents

9.051 Attorney Document Discovery Card.

Surrogate documents are sheets of paper or cards generated to take the place of documents in the file for search purposes. An example would be 5-by-8-inch card on which is recorded sufficient data to allow sorting of cards in chronological order, determining all documents authored by a given party, or identifying all of the letters that went from the client company to someone else on a particular topic. (See Appendix B, Exhibit 59.)

The organization of the card is not particularly prescribed so long as it honors the necessity of identifying a document by certain essential elements, which are:

(a) The document number. If a numbering system is used, then the numbers must be recorded in a prominent spot, (upper left-hand or upper right-hand corner of the card); thus, the card may be sorted numerically so that it will match the original document file.

(b) The date. All documents must be identified by date, and this becomes a problem when deciding how to represent that date in some cases. Particularly on handwritten notes, some telephone slips, and roughed-out, handwritten drafts, for instance, only a month and a day may be shown. In many cases, the probable date of the document can be deduced by its position within the files and its juxtaposition with other dated documents. In some cases, a draft may be appended to the finished product, and a very close approximation of the date logically can be imputed. The ideal way to represent the date is with six digits and a seventh space that is marked when the date has been deduced from some extrinsic relationship of that document to others in the file. In some cases, the representation of the date can be made only from context, since there is no other indication available. Such deduction should be supported by notation on the back of the card. If the date is not obvious from the content or placement of the document, it is better to leave it undated and create a separate file of documents to be researched, identified, and incorporated chronologically when a foundation has been established. For quick date search, writing the date by year, month, and day is most effective.

(c) Total pages. A space should be provided on the surrogate document to show the total number of pages in the document. This is important since apparent duplicate documents can be confirmed only if the number of pages is precisely the same. This is especially true of such things as computer printouts or other statistical data where minute examination of each entry would be needed to ensure that each entry is the same in each of two documents. Usually, document page counts are three figures or less.

(d) Document type. One of the more difficult classifications or identification of documents is the document type. Document types are determined in rather arbitrary fashion by analyzing the kinds of documents likely to be encountered in the course of the case and assigning certain arbitrary identification to them. A common stereotyping is to call all letters *between* the client firm and outside interests, firms, or personalities "letters," while all correspondence *within* the client firm or between personalities employed by the client firm are "memoranda." Each of these categories may have extant drafts; some of them may be handwritten or may be simply notes. For purposes of quick recording, it is customary to create a numeric or alphabetic code for document types, which may be expanded as other significant ones are discovered. Among those to be considered are: letters, memoranda, studies, reports, graphic materials (such as drawings, sketches, plans, and surveys), newspaper clippings and photographs, minutes of meetings, and summaries. A separate glossary of such characterizations will be necessary to ensure consistent characterizations of document types by attorneys and legal assistants.

(e) Document quality. Frequently during the screening process the team will find that a responsive document is of such poor legibility that if it were produced, some question might be raised as to whether or not it was a copy. Therefore, an entry "document quality" may be an element to include. This will assist in pointing out torn documents, partially illegible documents, or ancient carbon copies where the carbon has gradually rubbed off, making them nearly impossible to read, let alone copy.

(f) Document sensitivity. In some cases, commentary in a letter or marginally annotated on it is so emotion provoking in the context of the case that it is "damaging," "very informational," "significant," and/or "privileged." These are simple gradations to make, and subtle shading should not be attempted in this area. Frequently, the legal assistants are limited to "privileged" entries under "document sensitivity."

(g) Personalities. Every document is created by someone. Therefore, "personalities" is a category of information to be recorded on the surrogate document. Not only is it necessary to identify the individual but also the context (author, addressee, copy recipient, one who received it by distribution block routing, or perhaps a person mentioned in the body of the document). These may be shown by initial, such as:

T for To (addressee)
F for From (author)
C for Copy (carbon copy or distribution block recipient)
M for Mention (if the person's name appears in the document text)
A for Attendee (at a meeting, the minutes of which are the document)

The system should make allowance for the need to deduce the personalities' identity from initials, nicknames, or handwriting. People's names, although individual to them, are not particulary unique, so it is important that they be linked by the peoples' affiliation with some organization. This is particularly difficult in the context of legal representation. Many documents between attorneys read like

Greek unless the affiliation with the parent or client companies is known. Therefore, the logging of personalities usually requires a *context* entry; the first and middle initial, and the last name (spelled out in full if possible); and the *affiliation,* whether a company, governmental agency, or ad hoc citizens' group, for example. Because of the length of company titles, some mnemonic code or acronyms can be used. For instance:

United States Department of Justice	USDOJ
United States Senate	USSEN
General Motors	GENMTR or GM
United Airlines	UAL
National Broadcasting Company	NBC
Radio Corporation of America	RCA

(The use of easily identified, commonly known acronyms aids consistency and accuracy when more than one legal assistant is used.)

The acronym list is constantly updated to each team member and attorney with each addition to ensure uniform reference to a given entity.

(h) Related Documents. Every document conceivably relates in some way to another document. Therefore, a logging on the surrogate document of the relationship between documents may be important. This is particularly true in discovery operations where many documents may be found stapled together yet have their own individual character, context, and importance, and each requires individual treatment because the document may stand on its own. It is important for the legal assistants, however, to be able to indicate the manner in which they found the document originally: whether documents were appended to it or it was appended to another. Many documents have attachments created solely for them. Other appended ones are not necessarily in good chronologic or topical association.

Distinction can be accomplished by having a coding technique reflect whether one document is attached to another, is related in some way by reference directly or implicit in the context, and/or is a duplicate of another. If the case is large and time allows, it is possible to reflect by *relationship* whether one document is in *response* to another. If there is a numbering system, the manner of entering this information is greatly simplified since only two elements are needed—the relationship entry and the document identification number. It may be that this quick reference ability is the strongest argument for numbering documents. When working with a "related document" concept for a simple document to which one other is attached, it will be necessary to make out a card for each document, one shown as having an attachment and the second one (for the attached document) showing the parent document. This properly sets the context of the two documents to each other yet allows each to be evaluated, sorted, and analyzed individually. It allows the perusal of the coded surrogate document to reflect the relationship of the evidentiary documents when originally found by the legal assistant.

(i) The major subject or title. All documents tend to have a major topic, subject, or title, and where this can be ascertained objectively and briefly written on the card, it may be of great assistance in sorting the document at some future time, particularly where the document has a readily recognizable title such as "Contract for construction . . ." or "Study of. . . ."

(j) Issues. If coding for issues or sorting the documents by issue, include a provision on the card to indicate issues by number or by topic. Similarly, if sorting the documents by document discovery order, a provision to indicate that appropriate paragraph on the surrogate document is very helpful.

(k) Use of the document. One major function of a surrogate document is to track the use of that document in the course of the case: whether it was made available to the adversaries; whether or not they copied it; whether it became an exhibit in a pleading, deposition, or at trial; whether it was produced *to* you or *by* you. All of these can, with proper planning, be reflected on the card.

Surrogate documents are created as the legal assistant reads a document to determine its responsiveness to the issues of the case or to the document discovery requirement (whether in hand or anticipated). In completing this particular form, a preferred system is to read the document fully and complete the objective elements of the document discovery card at the same time. At the end of a day or reasonable period of time, all of the document discovery cards should then be taken to a copying machine and photocopied. The copied sheets are three-hole punched and filed in numerical order because the document discovery cards will be variously sorted or filed chronologically. This results in a numeric set of card copies and a chronologic set, which provides an interesting and sometimes helpful way of moving from one mode to another in searching for specific documents requested by the attorneys. Copying on a daily basis prevents it from becoming an onerous duty, keeps the file up to date, and allows the storing of the documents to continue apace.

9.052   Personality Index Card.

Since documents are the products of people, the creation of personality cards for each of the names mentioned in the course of each case is essential. At the time the surrogate document is being created, a card for every *different* name appearing on the document should also be initiated. (See Appendix C.)

Provision on the card should include last name, first initial, first/middle name, and middle initial. All are included because a party may be referred to by initials on one document and by name on another, and it may take three or four documents before anyone is certain of the exact or preferred name of a given person.

The business position of the individuals and their company affiliations, addresses, and phone numbers all should be accumulated as encountered and posted to show the month and year of the information.

The card always should indicate the *first* document where the name of the individual appears. Ideally, the personality index will be an 8½-by-11-inch page and, with numbered documents, there would be sufficient space ultimately to record every document in which the person was author, addressee, or copy recipient or is mentioned. All of these are categories of documents that individuals may encounter provided they are percipient witnesses in the case.

9.06   The Document Discovery File and the Computer

9.061   Introduction.

"Let's put the documents in the computer!" is a phrase heard increasingly in law firms, partly because of increased knowledge about the amazing ability of computers to sort, collate, and report on stored facts in split seconds and because antitrust, business litigation, product liability, employment discrimination, and class action cases are more prevalent than years ago and involve countless documents.

Just the thought of reading each and every one of these documents can be depressing. Even worse is recalling and retrieving the important ones from the pile. Computerizing begins to look like the ideal situation. However, those contemplating the use of the computer must fully understand that computerization involves acceptance of certain basic precepts and limitations:

(a) Computerization does not reduce total work effort but increases it.

(b) Computerization increases costs of handling the files.

(c) Computerization requires early intensive concentration by the attorney on the scope and issues of the case, the nature of the discovery documents, and the computer program parameters to be employed both by the computer personnel and the legal assistant team.

(d) Computerization of the file requires greater staff time early in the case than a normal manual file index system, both in training and operating.

(e) Computerization's benefit to the attorney is providing nearly instantaneous identification for retrieval of significant documents based on characteristics loaded into the data base. For example, consider a file volume of three hundred thousand pieces of paper of mixed types (letters, memos, reports, studies, minutes of meetings, and so on). The attorney wants to locate "John Doe's memoranda to the file re: meetings held in the spring, or possibly the summer of 1986." The computer can supply such a list (overlapping the time parameters) within seconds. Depending on the equipment and program, it might appear as a line (or several lines) of identifying data in a special format on a monitor screen, the full text of each memorandum called to the screen in chronological order, a line of identifying data for each document printed out in chronologic order, or only the numbers of the memoranda pages printed out, all depending on the early choices of machines, loading programs, and report formats.

Then, why put documents on the computer if it is costly, too much trouble, time-consuming, and seemingly complicated? Since it is the result that counts, instant retrieval may mean the difference between winning or losing the case.

9.062   Computerization Does Not Reduce the Total Work Effort but Increases It.

This proposition is logical and requires little explanation. In a document production effort (as described earlier in this chapter), every document must be found, identified, controlled, evaluated, and preserved for retrieval. Computerization does not change that but adds other layers of special effort to it—loading the essential data into the computer, validating the data loaded, and requesting coded (or clear language) reports from it. The original document is still the potential evidence in the case and the computer cannot substitute for it, only simplify finding it repetitiously during discovery and trial.

9.063   Computerization Increases the Costs of Handling the Files.

The increase in handling will mean greater costs than with a noncomputerized system. The operation of the computer is also expensive. Program design, program testing, creating loading forms, loading data, retrieval reports, and the salaries of the people who maintain the program and/or the computer are all added costs. The type of computer program, the type of computer equipment, and whether the computerization can be done in-house by the law firm, by the client, or through a contract with a vendor all bear on the costs to be considered. Computerization can add 10 to 25 percent to the discovery effort expenditures, depending on equipment and program sophistication.

9.064   Computerization Requires Early Intensive Concentration by the Attorney.

The responsible attorney must block out substantial time in the period where the computerization proposals are being formed and the scope, objectives, and generic document types and topical substance involved are being identified or determined. He or she must contribute to, evaluate, clarify, reject, and accept the proposals, conceptual approaches, and parameters of computer input and output generated by the computer systems analyst and the legal assistant. The skeleton of the system must be designed at the outset of the case with sufficient latitude provided to flesh out (with appropriate additions and/or deletions) the form of the discovery file as the case develops. Too complex and sophisticated a system may never be completed in time to serve the case needs, while too austere and inflexible a program may inhibit the lawyer's exploitation of the computer's ability to retrieve and collate stored data.

9.065   Computerization of the File Requires Greater Staff Time Early in the Case Than the Usual Manual File Index System, Both in Training and Operating.

A manual file index system can be established in broad topical outlines and decimalized additions and subdivisions can be added as the need appears. Nomenclature and filing terms are conventional and few, with little need for strict consistency in the method of recordation of the data. Usually, a mix of hand-printing, cursive writing, and typed material can be found in most manual document discovery file index systems. That changes dramatically with computerization. Everyone involved must learn and observe conventions peculiar to computers—acronyms, codes, even the form of hand-printing or typing that must be used with computer-related forms. *Everyone* must use the *same* symbols in the *same meaningful way,* or the computer system either will reject the offering as errors (if the system is properly designed) or the retrieval ability of the program will be seriously compromised. In addition to finding, identifying, and coding the documents that are normal to any case, loading the data into the computer system must be done through specially designed procedures, and those procedures must be validated to ensure that the data is in the computer data base and retrievable—all before the computer can be used or useful in the case.

The extraordinary need for consistency among all persons involved in converting documents into machine-readable form creates a continuing need for training and for quality control audits of the input to detect errors and create corrective measures.

9.066   The Benefits of Computerization.

The benefits of computerization for complex litigation involving huge volumes of documents and multiplicity of parties, issues, or witnesses are difficult to appreciate in the abstract, even during the early stages of the case. The value of the system is not apparent until the vast majority of significant data has been loaded into the computer and verified as accurately done. Then the flow of succinct collations, in loose sheet or bound form, is awe-inspiring. The production of several pages that identify a major adversary witness and all the documents he or she prepared, received, considered, testified about, identified as genuine, acknowledged as relevant, argued about, or took issue with can be of great assistance to an attorney in supplying the foundation for an evidentiary offering or resisting one. If another level of sophistication allows posting a summary of deposition, cross-referencing conflicts between testimony and documents or conflicts between the testimony of two witnesses, the potential benefit becomes obvious.

Consider also a trial of months, where the daily trial transcripts are coded into the computer by salient facts, exhibits, and issues, and a recollated update is obtained daily or weekly to allow all associated attorneys to keep abreast of testimony, evidence, and issue development without having to sit in court each and every day.

Basic to computerized files at trial are the creation of numeric and chronologic lists of all significant documents in the case. The computer allows additions during trial and update reports on call. These lists can be precoded to reflect importance, past use of documents as exhibits in depositions, and probable use as evidentiary exhibits at trial. The report format can be designed to allow posting the offering of a document for identification, any objections and appropriate rulings, the foundation of the offer, and the acceptance or rejection of the document as evidence.

In lengthy, complex trials, the need for newly created collations of documents supporting, resisting, or providing background on unanticipated issues or witnesses is extreme. Computers with appropriate loading and retrieval plans accomplish these necessary sortings over and over with speed and ease.

These sortings and collations all contribute to the goal of assisting the attorney. They allow the attorney to concentrate on the law, the issues, the facts, the witnesses, the trial tactics, and the strategy instead of wrestling with the tasks of evidentiary foundation, preparation of historical or topical summaries, and other more mundane duties.

Now that we understand the background and technicalities of computerization, we can begin again to say, "Let's put the documents in the computer."

The legal assistant's thorough knowledge of the attorney's needs and his or her participation in creating the guidelines for the computerization of the file are the legal assistant's qualifications to become the translator for the lawyer to the computer's data base and to exploit the near-instantaneous retrieval capacity of the computer. The legal assistant thus can and will provide the proper and timely stimulus required for the system to function effectively as a "person and computer" team.

9.067   Outline of Evaluation Factors in the Computerization Decision.

(a)   Computerization system to use.
  (1) Full text (the entry of the entire document in machine-readable form into a computer access system).
  (2) Coded entry of document data into a computer access system.
  (3) Machine-readable coded card sorting procedures.
(b)   Selection of computer system source.

       (1) Client's in-house computer or equipment.

       (2) Law firm's in-house computer or equipment.

       (3) Vendor-contractor computer or equipment.

  (c) Document types and volume to computerize; "lawyer-like" sortings of the documents.

  (d) Estimate, proposal, and contract.

  (e) Discovery/Computerization team recruitment, training, and auditing.

  (f) Security.

       (1) Natural disaster.

       (2) Negligent damage.

       (3) Negligent compromise.

       (4) Theft, espionage, and intentional damage.

9.068   Discussion of Evaluation Factors in the Computerization Decision.

9.0681 Proper Selection of Computer System.   The selection of the computerization system involves basically a choice of two information retrieval methods. *(a) Full Text.* The first is a method in which the full text of the separate documents is loaded into the computer and retrieved by calling for a search of the full text library by significant words used in the document. The significant words may have been loaded into the computer library for search comparison as a glossary with special-meaning instructions on synonyms or as part of special or trade phrases.

The benefit of this system is the ease of loading the data, since the need for training of personnel is limited to selection of responsive or significant documents. No coding, subjective evaluations, or colorations are required. The creation of the library of significant words can be done by a very small group of lawyers, legal assistants, and technical consultants.

The problems of the system are numerous, but the most important are:

(1) The system can accommodate *only* machine-readable data. This usually means information in word form, typed with optical character reading (OCR) type fonts, computer-generated typed material (which usually is in OCR form), or such data stored on magnetic tapes, discs, or other storage medium. Thus, an original document typed in the elite type font of a standard typewriter must be retyped with OCR fonts or into a machine-readable mode for loading into the computer.

(2) Since only machine-readable data can be entered into this system, photographs, charts, forms, graphs, and drawings cannot be loaded. However, a summary of these documents in OCR form can be loaded, but great care and caution should be taken in summarizing.

(3) Also of major importance is the inability of the full text system to load document oddities of great importance, such as marginal annotations, distribution block characterization or routings, doodles and underlining, interlineation of corrections or suggested phrasings on drafts, all of which may, in some instances, be highly significant to the interpretation of the meaning of the document or a response to a document.

(4) The most dangerous weakness of the full text system is the word-comparison search technique. Even in legal research of statutes or court decisions (such as offered by Mead Data Systems' Lexis and West Publishing Company's Westlaw) where the language is relatively predictable and limited to acceptable terms of legal writing, the phrasing of a search request must incorporate a word loaded

into the computer ahead of time whose use is significant in meaning. Many words are so common that they are eliminated as useless in a search because the computer must compare the words of the search request to every word in the document. If there are three elements in the search request linked together, the search of all documents is done at least three times. If the selection of elements is poor, the reported file may be so large that it is a waste of computer time. Because commercial documents may refer to one significant item by various synonyms, trade jargon nicknames, or program numbers, it is essential that these equivalents be identified ahead of performing the retrieval search and either the computer instructed that a search for one is a search for all the equivalents or the search request must specify each and every equivalent. For instance, consider a product liability case on an allegedly dangerous toy. The toy was originally titled "Project 1780-64" during development and placed in production under "Charge No. NY 10-472." Its name was originally the "Wonderful Widget" but was changed after the first year to the "Wacky Widget." Ordering from retailers was by "Item 6320, Wacky Widget, Model 2." Internally, the "Widget" was fondly referred to as "WW", "WW2," and "The Wack." This results in at least nine methods of referring to the principal object in the litigation, a search request would not develop any document that referred to the product as "that thing," "John's brainstorm" or "blasted catastrophe" unless one or more of the specified nine equivalents occurred within the same document.

(b) Coded Entry System. The coded entry computer system substitutes a surrogate document for the original and uses a combination of conventions, codes, acronyms, and words to assemble data in organized form for loading into the computer. These often are called "loading forms." They may be paper or card stock on which a lawyer, legal assistant, or other person enters the data for someone else to type through a keyboard directly onto magnetic tape, disc, or other machine readable medium. In the latter case, a monitor display usually affords a specified format for entry of a data to assure consistency of the input.

The benefits of this system include the ability to control the search parameters closely and to code a synthesis of the significant documents according to their substantive content, regardless of their form, whether letters, memos, photos, studies, sketches, or pre-printed forms. Further, it is simple to enter additional sorting data, such as their use as exhibits in depositions, to the complaint, to the answer, to interrogatories, and so on. I allows combining all documents into one data base for subsequent sortings and printouts and precludes anyone (lawyer or legal assistant) from relying solely on a computer image (whether on the monitor or a printout) rather than the evidentiary documents.

Several problems are inherent in this system:

1. The attorney may have trouble accepting the need to give early planning and analysis of the case to set the coding and search parameters a higher priority over a workload of more mature cases. It is understandably difficult for an attorney to devote concentrated time at such an early point in a case, given the uncertainties of issues, facts, and legal theories characteristic of suits with relatively vague and inconclusive pleadings.
2. The long lead time between selecting computerization and the loading of sufficient data into a verified program before useful output is obtained can be frustrating.

3. The demands imposed in selection and training of personnel to perform the coding of data into the data base and the stringent quality control, consistency audits, error correction and inevitable program modifications such systems require are time-consuming and costly.

4. The dedication of time, thought, imagination, and practicality essential to creation of parameters for loading data into the base is hard to anticipate. Usually, the fewest possible elements produce the maximum effectiveness in speed and consistency of loading. The "loading form" may look like the surrogate document "Attorney's Document Discovery Card" (see Appendix B, Exhibit 59) slightly modified for machine-readable input (See Exhibit 51).

The major differences between surrogate documents for manual systems and those for machine systems are the additions of certain necessary conventions for instructing the computer where to enter, where to delete, where to change, or where to add data. For instance, see Exhibit 46 and note the card has one block (Block Number 9) with a preprinted number entry. This is the "Record Types" under which the data is entered or searched. Record Type Number 1 is for "Identity" entries; Record Type Number 5 is for "Personality" entries; and Record Type Number 7 is for "Related Documents." Each of these provide for inclusion of data of an objective nature extracted from perusal of the documents. Very few subjective evaluations or decisions are needed and those are limited to identity entries under Blocks 24–25, 26, 27 and 28 and under Record Type Number 2 "Major Subject/ Title," where brevity requires an ability to summarize cogently. This card was developed to supplement another that contained a Record Type 4 and a Record type 6 on which subjective codes related to legal issues, defenses, and percipient witnesses could be entered. Retrieval reports can request compilation of data from any or all record types entered in whatever collation form desired.

9.0682 Selection of a Computer System Source.

(a) Client's Computer. Many clients employ computer systems of varying complexity and sophistication. Some systems may be purchased or leased and located on the client's premises. In other cases, the client will have contracted services through a vendor who provides time-sharing on a remotely located computer. The client may have the staff to operate the system or may add temporary employees to do the work. Such a system has obvious problems of priority of work effort, training, and control of the people operating the system but usually is more economical for the client. Unless control, management, and security of the program rests with the lawyer and the legal assistant in charge, the loss of intensity can affect both the dollar cost and the ultimate utility of the computerization effort.

(b) Law Firm's In-house Computer. Nearly all law firms have an in-house computer system. This probably is ideal if the equipment capacity and availability match the needs of the case. In-house capacity postulates in-house understanding of systems analysis, programming, report generation, computer input and output and the employment of computer-knowledgeable litigation support personnel, whether legal assistants, programmers, or word processors.

(c) Vendor-Contractor Computer. The third source is the vendor-contractor arrangement. A number of independent firms supply litigation support programs, from document discovery plans through hardware, software, personnel selection and training, and the supervision of the whole coding and/or loading process. Generally, they will provide all or any portion of the services and willingly contract

EXHIBIT 46

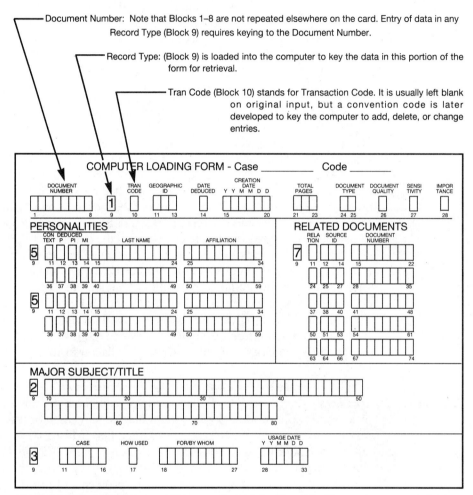

This is the "Attorney's Document Discovery Control Card" modified for use in a computerized system as a loading form.

to do everything and anything the lawyer wants. Some aspects of any contracting of these services, however, must be approached with caution and/or skepticism.

Every price, every time standard, every volume standard considered by a vendor in its proposal is a qualified estimate generated by a very short-term study of the proposed project. The client, the lawyer, and the contractor all are guessing at the outset of a case. Thus, the estimates of dollars, time, and volumes are potentially misleading in terms of the ultimate cost and the ability of the system to perform on time with the correct document volume.

The vendor's sales force and systems analysts may not be the people who actually perform the work. It is essential to meet the people who will analyze, design the system, train the staff, and conduct the quality control and security programs for the life of the case or a good portion of it. Selecting a vendor's people on perception, attitude, interest, and flexibility (assuming their technical skills are adequate) is vital to a successful program with timely problem solutions.

Competitive bids seldom provide any benefit in terms of dollars, time, volumes, or efficiency but do offer another set of vendor's employees for evaluation if the lawyers have any reservation about the first vendor's personnel.

9.0683 Document Types and Volumes to Computerize.

Not all cases consist either of document types or volumes of material suitable for computerization. For instance, in an antitrust price-fixing case where there are hundreds of thousands of numbered invoices, bills of lading, receipts, purchase orders, and other material and only a limited volume of material requiring "subjective" analysis, it might be better to set up the major volumes of different document types in numeric or chronologic order and microfilm or microfiche the material to create an archive and a work file and then store the originals as evidence. A supplementary manual system for the subjective documents may be perfectly adequate for the attorney's needs.

This kind of analysis and decision making must be generated in the reconnaissance of files (discussed earlier) that is conducted while preparing the document discovery plan.

Another issue is the desire to make "lawyer-like" sortings of the documents. Developing a coding plan for a computerized system nearly always results in the lawyer expressing a desire to code the documents by legal theories. This may be expressed as an intellectual daydream, "Wouldn't it be great to have all the documents sorted by 'horizontal integration' or 'denial of market access' or 'ultra hazardous endeavor'?" It always comes from someone who has not physically reviewed the generic documents that do or will comprise the discovery file. Many times the "legal theories" advanced are the ultimate facts to be proved in the suit, and almost never will a document, on its face, reflect sufficient information, standing alone, to support such a subjective identification by lawyers, let alone by legal assistants.

If the attitude persists, the legal assistant is entitled to receive from the lawyer articulated guidelines for applying those legal theory criteria to the documents. This has proven to be nearly impossible at the outset of a case.

A good objective coding system will allow orderly production of documents with provision for entering additional characterizations as the case progresses and documents take on their colorations as significant or insignificant, damaging or innocuous, and so on.

9.0684 Estimate, proposal, and contract.

The computerization proposal, whether an offer or formal proposal by a vendor or an estimate by the client's or lawyer's in-house personnel, must be analyzed for the dollar and time bases giving rise to the ultimate commitment. Basic to every proposal are the salaries paid the document discovery computer loading team and the "minutes per page of documents" necessary to process the documents and create the computer loading form. The salary structure must be examined to ensure it is competitive for the area and adequate to attract quality people.

Scaling the "task-time" of the document processing should be the result of separate and simultaneous tests by the attorney and the legal assistant who will have to make the system work. Each should take a substantial sample (say, 2,000 pages) and actually process them according to the intended program. The purpose is to develop a realistic figure for the processing of documents. If the material results in a figure of 5 pages per document and an "objective element only" coding rate of one document in six minutes, then the universe of documents (120,000, for instance) will require 720,000 minutes, or 12,000 hours. Assuming the sustained work rate of competent coders to be 6 hours per day, it will require 2,000 person-days to code all the documents. Ten coders can then process the file in 200 team-days, or less than one team-work year (a work year is about 220 working days). Realistic adjustments must be planned for personnel attrition, illnesses, errors, and error corrections. Provision must be made for production quality control, quality consistency audits, and program adjustments and changes. Interference with document processing by the ongoing discovery operations of the case should also be taken into consideration.

No estimate or proposal is capable of considering all the potential unknowns in a case. For instance, what happens to a half-processed file if the plaintiffs seek and obtain permission to amend the complaint by adding two more causes of action based on revelations during discovery? The processed documents will have to be reevaluated if subjective coding by issues was elected at the outset.

Such unforeseen developments can result in unanticipated costs, which emphasizes the necessity for a realistic, skeptical examination and testing of each estimate and/or proposal at the outset so that decisions can be made as best as possible on a dollar-versus-value basis.

9.0685 Discovery Computerization Team Recruitment, Training, and Auditing.

Recruitment can be handled in-house or through temporary help agencies. In either event, a "work sample" test is helpful in selecting people. The work sample may be a selected group of twenty to one hundred documents of varying types bundled into a file either bound or in an envelope. Copies of the same documents should be used for each applicant. A set of instructions should be provided that might direct that

(a) all names be circled.
(b) all dates be underlined.
(c) all references to money, dollar costs, expenditures, budgets, and so on be indicated on the left margin with an asterisk.
(d) that the number of different names shown in the document be written in the top right corner of the top page of the document.
(e) other elements be identified as desired.

The work sample must be carefully checked before being presented to the applicant and a master file carrying all the correct entries for each page created. This is compared against the applicant's test file to measure error rates and the time used by the applicant. The test will weed out inaccurate or inordinately slow applicants. Standards must be high and must be maintained. It is better at the outset to quickly identify those who can follow instructions, whether fully understood or not, reliably and productively, from those who cannot. Inconsistency, error, and exceeding slowness are deadly to the document discovery effort. A separate test for reading comprehension, vocabulary, handwriting, and printing is desirable.

Among groups of people who do very well in document work are biologists, anthropologists, museum or library workers, historical society members, and persons with backgrounds in research. A fertile recruitment source for part-time workers is the retired personnel of the client or spouses of company employees. Part-time jobs mean more people are needed to perform the equivalent of full-time work. However, part-time workers are less prone to fatigue and boredom.

Training of selected applicants must involve more than "do this and then do that." The team members must feel like a team. An orientation on the factual history of the case, the legal issues, and the anticipated defenses, as well as an opportunity to meet each of the attorneys, is indispensable to the project. Training usually is staged by succeeding degree of complexity. It includes training on all the machinery to be used, photocopiers, numbering devices, microfilmers, microfilm or microfiche readers; the filing systems to be screened; company organization; and the team's filing and handling systems, as well as basic instructions of how to select, code, and process the various documents.

Refresher sessions will be needed to update procedures, correct detected errors, and give the attorneys a chance to talk directly to the discovery team and ensure they are in it together.

Every team must have an auditor assigned to monitor, spot-check and even "work behind" each team member to ensure consistency in use of the selected coding parameters and other procedures. The audit is a check to assist each team member, not simply to criticize. It helps detect weaknesses in the training presentation and in the coding manual supplied each team member. It identifies ambiguities that creep into the program through documents that may fit more than one category. The audit will reveal the quality and quantity of work produced by each person and can serve as a foundation for dismissal of the lazy or careless worker, an unpleasant but essential task.

9.0686 Security.   Every computerization project adds to the control problems of a document discovery effort and increases the need for security against natural disaster, negligent damage, and negligent compromise of the computer file. It represents a substantial dollar investment and work and time expenditure.

Natural disasters include fire, flood, and power supply aberrations that can damage or destroy the computer, the computer tapes, and/or loading forms. When computer data is loaded on tapes, "mirror" duplicates can be made at little cost and stored in a separate location as a security archive against accidental disasters. Similarly, microfilm and microfiche duplicates can be separately maintained.

Negligent compromise of a computerized system can be minimized by controlling the numbers of coding manuals created and distributed and by limiting the report generation responsibility to certain members of the team. Every computer system can be programmed to grant access only through the use of key words, number codes, Social Security numbers, and names. The production of reports must also be closely monitored to create as few as possible and to ensure that each report generated is shredded when superseded by another—not thrown away but physically destroyed.

Little can be done to prevent intentional theft, espionage, or sabotage of the computerized file outside of the normal security steps. A determined crook can and will penetrate the usual business office protections of client's business, vendors' facilities, or law firm's offices. The only extra security step possible is to detect that such an entry has occurred. Lock all the doors, filing cabinets, vaults, and desks that contain essential data and/or evidentiary documents. Being burglarized is bad, but being burglarized unknowingly can be fatal to the case.

9.069 Comment.

It is a fact of life that mechanical sorting of record or reference data in litigation greatly enhances the presentation of a given case. The most difficult portion is at the outset when the commitment is made to a "pure" system (either full text, coded, or machine-readable) or combination of machine-readable with manual systems. The essential file reconnaissance, analysis, system consideration, dollar-versus-value judgment, and staffing proposals must be made at a time of first impressions of the case, and such decisions can best be described as informed "guesstimates." Such decision-making is very difficult to justify to a client and emphasizes the need for careful, realistic, and thorough consideration of the problem and all alternatives by the attorney and the legal assistant.

9.07 Microfilming

Document discovery often involves mountains of documents that may be necessary in a case being tried miles or thousands of miles from the file repository. Microfilming can solve the transportation problem by reducing document volume from several boxes to one attaché case. Some film rolls (4-by-4-by-1-inch) will hold seven thousand sheet impressions (about three file boxes).

Some companies use microfilm for permanent retention of records, destroying the originals after the microfilming has been checked to ensure all the images were readable.

Microfilming involves several considerations, whether the system uses 16 mm, 35 mm, 70 mm or 140 mm film, portable systems using simple cameras, or sophisticated equipment.

Should roll or microfiche systems be used? Rolls hold many hundreds or thousands of images per roll and can be used with an indexing device to locate any given image quickly. Microfiche provides easy portability of small numbers of documents. One 4-by-6-inch fiche may contain one large document (i.e., drawings) or a series of up to one hundred images arranged in strips that can be examined one by one through inexpensive and portable microfiche readers.

Certain measures must be taken in memorializing data on microfilm, especially if there is any potential for original documents to be lost or destroyed. Every roll of film must be marked at its beginning and end with certain production forms, or "targets," that identify the film but still protect any confidentiality or privilege. Microfilming also requires disassembling of stapled documents or files, and the use of the Production Forms described previously (see Appendix D) is appropriate.

The use of some special microfilming targets is shown graphically in Exhibit 47.

The "Start Roll No. ___" target is self-explanatory, as is the "End Roll No. __."

The "Declaration" target is a protective measure to reinforce that the documents have not become public property solely by being involved in this lawsuit or by being microfilmed (see Exhibit 48).

The "certificate" target (see Exhibit 49) is inserted as a safeguard in the event the originals become lost or scrambled. If microfilming is the first processing step after screening, this target may provide sufficient foundation for introduction of the microfilm copy as secondary evidence or to refute a claim by the adversary of tampering with the produced documents.

EXHIBIT 47   Essential Elements In Every Microfilm Roll

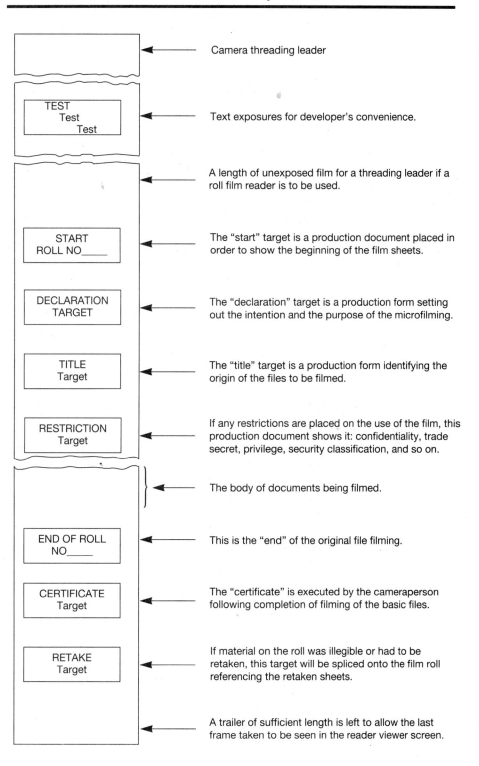

Camera threading leader

Text exposures for developer's convenience.

A length of unexposed film for a threading leader if a roll film reader is to be used.

The "start" target is a production document placed in order to show the beginning of the film sheets.

The "declaration" target is a production form setting out the intention and the purpose of the microfilming.

The "title" target is a production form identifying the origin of the files to be filmed.

If any restrictions are placed on the use of the film, this production document shows it: confidentiality, trade secret, privilege, security classification, and so on.

The body of documents being filmed.

This is the "end" of the original file filming.

The "certificate" is executed by the cameraperson following completion of filming of the basic files.

If material on the roll was illegible or had to be retaken, this target will be spliced onto the film roll referencing the retaken sheets.

A trailer of sufficient length is left to allow the last frame taken to be seen in the reader viewer screen.

EXHIBIT 48

DECLARATION OF INTENT AND PURPOSE

I, _____ employed by _____ , do hereby declare that the records microfilmed herein are the actual records of _____ created during the normal course of business and they were surrendered to their attorneys for use in the lawsuit _____ vs. _____ as the needs of the case and the orders of the court require. This is not a waiver of any confidentiality or privilege, and the custody of the documents by the attorneys does not constitute publication of them.

It is the specific intent of the Company and its attorneys to limit the use of these documents to the minimum publication possible and to return the documents to the Company on completion of the case.

Date _____ 19_____   _____
    (Month)   (Day)   (Year)   (Signature)

Place _____   _____
    (City)   (State)   (Title)

                                       _____
                                         (Organization)

"Title" targets (see Exhibit 50) may be needed for each file to memorialize the folder identification; there may be several "Title" targets on one microfilm roll. Space is left to right in comments, such as "Continued from Roll No. ___."

Some moderate-sized cases can benefit from numbering the documents and microfilming them in order, thereby using the microfilm for the numeric archive and sorting the original documents into chronologic order for the work file, a dangerous but convenient practice.

Microfilming the adversary's documents often is the best and most reliable production method since the team photographs relevant documents as discovered and carries away the image rather than listing all the desired documents and asking the adversary to produce them later. It is much more efficient, and the adversary often does not know which documents were copied and which were not.

Microfilming always should be considered as a security measure against natural or negligent disasters that could destroy the original file.

EXHIBIT 49

CERTIFICATE OF AUTHENTICITY

THIS IS TO CERTIFY that the microphotographs appearing on this film file, starting with

_____ and

ending with _____ ,

are accurate and complete reproductions of the relevant records of the

_____ of the _____
          (Department)   (Company)
as delivered. Production documents have been inserted to reflect the form in which they were received.

Date Produced _____   _____
            (Month)   (Day)   (Year)   (Camera Operator)

Place _____
     (City)   (State)

EXHIBIT 50

TITLE TARGET

Documents from the file/folder _____

of the _____

(Department, Office, etc.)

of the _____

(Company)

in chronologic file from _____ to _____

(Mo., Day, Yr.)   (Mo., Day, Yr.)

or in numeric order beginning at No. _____

Bibliography

Black's Law Dictionary, 6th edition. West Publishing Company, 1990.

Federal Rules of Evidence for U.S. District Courts and Magistrates with Amendments Effective Dec. 1, 1990. West Publishing Company, 1990.

Manual for Complex Litigation, 2nd ed. Federal Judicial Center Staff, 1986.

Rules of Civil Procedure for the U.S. District Courts, with forms, Aug. 1, 1987. U.S. Government Printing Office, 1987.

Appendix A: Document Discovery—File Screening—Production Log

EXHIBIT 51

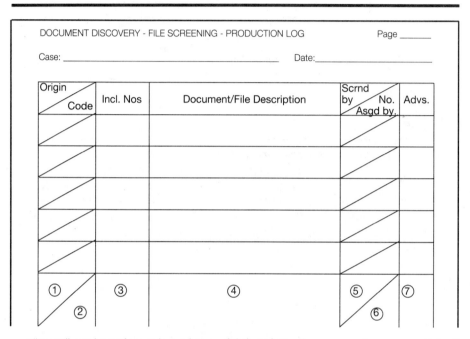

¹ "Origin" may be a title, a code number, an alphabetic letter, the room number, or so on that will uniquely characterize the source of the material to allow its proper return in the future. Codes or alphabetic identifiers require an index.

² "Code" may be used to record production by issue, by paragraph of discovery order, or by percipient witness, provided a separate index is maintained.

³ "Incl. Nos" means inclusive numbers and reflects the beginning and ending numbers of the document or file as assigned following the legal assistant's review and selection of responsive material.

⁴ "Document/File Description" is just that, succinct but complete.

⁵ "Scrnd by" is the name of the person who made the gross file review at the point of origin.

⁶ "No. Asgd by" is the initials of the person who numbered the selected responsive materials and entered the inclusive numbers in 3 above.

⁷ "Advs" reflects the date the numbered, nonprivileged but responsive material was examined by the adversary. If some material was copied for the adversary, a separate index may be required or a special mark may be made in this square to reflect the difference between examination and/or copying.

EXHIBIT 52

Page Number_____

DOCUMENT DISCOVERY - FILE SCREENING - PRODUCTION LOG

Case: _____ Date:_____

Origin / Code	Incl. Nos	Document/File Description	Scrnd by / Asgd by	No.	Advs.

EXHIBIT 53

EXAMPLE   Page Number____1____

LEGAL RESEARCH TEAM
DOCUMENT DISCOVERY - FILE SCREENING - PRODUCTION LOG

Case: _____JONES v. SMITH_____ Date: _2-2-88____

Origin Code	Incl. Nos	Document/File Description	Scrnd by / No. Asgd by.	Advs.
ENGRG Rm 8	0001 – 0572	Contract 4671-71 w/drawings change orders, invoices claims and correspondence	JED 2/4/88 / BP 2-6-88	
Rm 9 A	0573 – 0688	Info file - Contract 4671-71 A: G L Sanders project file custodid	JED 2/4/88 / BP 2-6-88	
Rm 9 B	0689 – 0923	CHANGE ORDER DWGS B = E. J. NEWMAN - Design Draftsmen	JED 2/4/88 / BP 2-6-88	
Rm 10 A	0923A – 01123	Purchase ORDERS & REQUISITIONS A- B.L. HAMMER, BUYER	JED 2/4/88 / BP 2-6-88	
Rm 10 B	01124 – 02721	SPECIFICATIONS-SUB CONTR PROPOSALS, CORRESPONDENCE, CLAIMS B= N.K. Young - Contract Administration	JED 2/4/88 / BP 2-6-88	
Rm 10 C	02722 – 03668	Personal File- Contract 4671-71 C= J.L. SMITH, PRESIDENT	NML 2/3/88 / CK 2-9-88	
Rm 12 A	03669 – 05928	"AS BUILT" DWGS, INSPECTOR LOGS, TIME CARDS, COMPUTER OUTPUT ON JOB SCHED, PROGRESS. (BOUND VOLS BY MONTH), LOG	NML 2/6/88 / GD 2-9-88	
	—	BOOKS, WEATHER RPTS, DELAY CLAIMS, LABOR FORCE RECORDS A= COMPTROLLER FILES		

EXHIBIT 54

CASE _____				
LEGAL RESEARCH TEAM FILES — LOG OF FILES REMOVED				
Department _____		Page No. _____		
Room No. _____				

FILE LOCATION	FILE DESCRIPTION	DATE TAKEN	DATE RETURNED	INITIALS

This form is used for inventorying documents as they are removed from a particular repository (central file room, individual office, or so on). Note it does not make provision for numbering or coding, as does the log in Exhibit 51, Appendix A.

EXHIBIT 55

			CASE _____
		LEGAL RESEARCH TEAM FILES FILE REVIEW — NUMBERING — PRODUCTION LOG	
Alpha. Code	Numeric	File Description	Initial, Date, and Box No.

When documents are initially obtained, whether from client or adversary, the numbering can be controlled by a form like this or that in Exhibit 51, Appendix A.

EXHIBIT 56

LEGAL RESEARCH TEAM—LOG OF FILES REMOVED/RETURNED				Case _____	
Code	Box No.	LOCATION / DEPARTMENT / NAME	Date Removed/Name	Date Returned/Name	Remarks

One form of control sheet for moving files to and from the document discovery "Evidence Room."

EXHIBIT 57 Production Discrepancies

		CASE _____	
	LEGAL RESEARCH TEAM FILES		
Documents Requested	Documents Supplied	Documents Not Supplied	Reason for Failure to Supply Documents

EXHIBIT 58

			CASE _____
		LEGAL RESEARCH TEAM FILES	
		NUMERIC SEQUENCE JUSTIFICATION ROSTER **AND EXPLANATORY COMMENTARY**	
Alpha.	Numeric	COMMENTARY: Describe the sequence aberration and the reason the number was *not* assigned to a responsive document (production form, etc.).	Date and Initials of Person

This form is used to accumulate all aberrations of numbering that occur and to offer explanations for them while they are easy to identify. It may never be used unless an aberration must be explained in court. It includes such things as skipped numbers, skipped pages that have alphabetic suffixes, and production forms that become numbered.

Appendix B: Attorney's Document Discovery Card

EXHIBIT 59

[1] Document Number is eight spaces long, sufficient for most numeric or alphanumeric systems. The last space is bold-lined as a reminder that it is to be used for suffix entries only.

[2] Geographic ID is used only when the scope of discovery is so broad that a special code for diverse locations is needed.

[3] Creation Date is derived extrinsically from the document. It is written with the year first to allow easy future compatibility with computer systems. Note that a block is provided for entry of a mark to show the date was deduced and not taken directly from the document.

[4] Document Alias is an alternative title when a document has become an exhibit in a pleading, deposition, trial, or so on. The entry is short and probably will be an acronym.

[5] The Major Topic entry has blocks provided up to seventy characters long anticipating a future computer need. The line allows further entry, but the capacity of computer record types may not accommodate the excess.

[6] A provision for Deduced Personality identification is made.

[7] Last Name spaces total only ten, though some names may exceed that count. This card is used in conjunction with a "Personality Index Card," which is used to fully record the name of case personalities. This entry is geared to a possible computerization of the file and necessarily is long enough to identify the name but short enough to allow numerous entries for a computer. The technique here is to print the name as fully as the space will allow.

[8] Affiliation has limited space and relies on the same technique described in 7 above, except that acronyms may be employed, provided that a separate index of the acronym and its full identity is maintained. Wherever possible, existing recognizable acronyms should be used. For instance, USS usually is United States Steel; USBR is the United States Bureau of Reclamation, a subdivision of the Department of the Interior; and RCA is Radio Corporation of America. The principle of adopting identifiable trade logos or acronyms should be followed.

[9] USAGE allows the entries showing the use to which a particular document was put and when. An acronym for the usage may be required (an index of the acronyms, too) and the date. Note the date uses the "year first" composition.

EXHIBIT 60

EXAMPLE   ATTORNEY'S DOCUMENT DISCOVERY CARD -   CASE *Jones v Smith*

Document Number	Geographic ID	Date Deduced	Creation Date Y Y M M D D	Total Pages	Document Type	Document Quality	Sensitivity	Document Alias
0 0 0 0 3 4 2	A B C	1	9 1 0 6 3 0	0 0 4	H M		P	

MAJOR TOPIC/SUBJECT/TITLE/DESCRIPTION

A T T Y A D V O N C O N T R A C T # 4 6 7 1 - 7 1

PERSONALITIES

Context	Deduced P	PI	MI	Last Name	Affiliation	Relation	Related Documents Document Number	Usage New Used
F	A	/		L I N C O L N	L I N C O L N	A	0 0 0 0 3 4 5 A	
T		J	L	S M I T H	S M I T H É C o	A	0 0 0 0 3 4 8	
C		G	R	T H O M P S O M	R C I A - I D E N V			
C	I	G	L	S A N D E R S	S M I T H É C o			

Date Used

New Used

Date Used

EXAMPLE

NOTES: Document is 4 pages long, beginning with page 342, and was written by attorney A. (No middle initial) Lincoln, on June 30, 1991. It is a handwritten memorandum, privileged,and discusses his advice on a contract. There were two attachments, one beginning with page 345A (obviously a numbering irregularity) and another beginning with page 348.

The document apparently went to a principal officer of a defendant company (check Personality Index Card for detail).

Query: What effect will the "copies" to Thompson and Sanders have? Who are they and has the copy waived the privilege? Sanders name was not apparent but deduced.

Additions to the Attorney's Document Discover Form

EXHIBIT 61   **for use in Computerized Discovery Files**

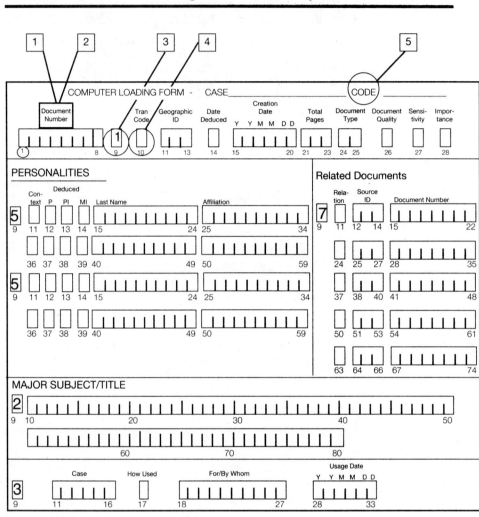

[1] Each space is accorded a number to allow later "gang" loading of corrections, group changes, and so on.

[2] The Document Number is the base indicia for all data in each of Record Types involved. Note that the spaces numbered 1 through 8 do not appear in any other record type on the card.

[3] Space 9 is preempted by the printed figure "1," indicating this section is Record Type 1, essentially the "Identification" data necessary for the document as a minimum. Note the organization of the card has Record Type 5—Personalities and Record Type 7—Related Documents immediately adjacent for ease in entering these important pieces of data in the early loading phase.

[4] Space 10 is titled Tran Code and affords an opportunity to enter a code figure or number that indicates the data is added, deleted, or a change from what already is loaded in the data base. Original entries usually are left blank.

[5] Each case file is identified by a special code that is the trigger for loading that library of data. This is often unnecessary.

Appendix C: Personality Card

EXHIBIT 62

```
                                                              CASE _____

                           PERSONALITY INDEX CARD

       Last Name                          FI   First/Middle Name              MI
  1.   ⊞ ⊞                                  ⧄   ⊞                                ⧄
       Position                    Affilliation              Incl. Dates
  2.   ⊞                           ⊞                          _____
       Business Address                                      Phone Number
  3.   _____             _____
       Previous Positions          Affilliation              Incl. Dates
  4.   _____         _____      _____
       Home Address                                          Phone Number
  5.   _____             _____
  6.   Commentary:
```

Document Number	Con-text	Document Number	Con-text	Document Number	Con-text	Document Number	Con-text
⊞	☐	⊞	☐	⊞	☐	⊞	☐
⊞	☐	⊞	☐	⊞	☐	⊞	☐
⊞	☐	⊞	☐	⊞	☐	⊞	☐
⊞	☐	⊞	☐	⊞	☐	⊞	☐
⊞	☐	⊞	☐	⊞	☐	⊞	☐
⊞	☐	⊞	☐	⊞	☐	⊞	☐
⊞	☐	⊞	☐	⊞	☐	⊞	☐
⊞	☐	⊞	☐	⊞	☐	⊞	☐
⊞	☐	⊞	☐	⊞	☐	⊞	☐
⊞	☐	⊞	☐	⊞	☐	⊞	☐
⊞	☐	⊞	☐	⊞	☐	⊞	☐
⊞	☐	⊞	☐	⊞	☐	⊞	☐
⊞	☐	⊞	☐	⊞	☐	⊞	☐
⊞	☐	⊞	☐	⊞	☐	⊞	☐

[1] The name entry has blocks for the first ten characters to maintain consistency with the attorney's Document Discovery Card. It has spaces for FI—First Initial then an entry First/Middle Name, which will allow the construction of the name in the preferred use of the personality: first initial and middle name or first name and middle initial. In the event the list of personalities becomes so large that computerization is desirable, the blocks provided suggest the size of the entries to computerize.

[2] Position, Affiliation, and Inclusive Dates are insufficient in some cases to reflect the full identities needed. Either Commentary (see 6 below) or the back of the sheet may be used for greater detail.

[3] Business Address is important in the event service of papers is necessary.

EXHIBIT 63 Personality Card

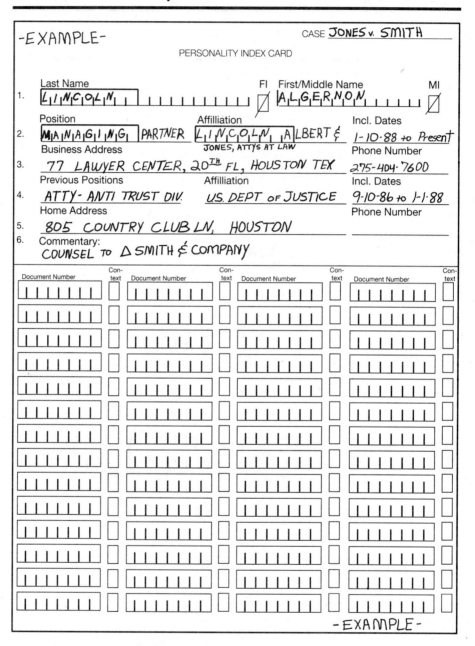

[4] Previous Positions should be recorded as they become known.

[5] Home Address and Phone Numbers are needed to allow contact or legal service.

[6] Commentary is space provided for overflow from the above entries; for short descriptions of the character of the work or material identified with this potential witness; notes the legal assistants feel might be helpful to the attorneys; or the note the attorneys wish to memorialize related to the personality.

The sets of blocks below Commentary are to allow cross-referencing the documents involving this personality in the case with the final purpose of listing every document connected with this personality whether as author, addressee, copy recipient, or mentioned in the body and so on. The lone space to the right of eight space blocks is to allow entry of the Relationship of the document to the party. These entries should be consistent with those of the ADDC (see Appendix B).

Appendix D: Production Documents

EXHIBIT 64

Case _____	Case _____
LEGAL RESEARCH TEAM FILES	LEGAL RESEARCH TEAM FILES
BEGIN	END
BOUND	BOUND
DOCUMENT	DOCUMENT

These sheets should be 8½-by-11 inches and may be color-coded for easy distinction in the file.

EXHIBIT 65

Case _____ LEGAL RESEARCH TEAM FILES BEGIN STAPLED DOCUMENT	Case _____ LEGAL RESEARCH TEAM FILES END STAPLED DOCUMENT

These sheets should be 8½-by-11 inches and may be color-coded for easy distinction in the file.

EXHIBIT 66

Case _____ LEGAL RESEARCH TEAM FILES BEGIN THREE-RING BINDER	Case _____ LEGAL RESEARCH TEAM FILES END THREE-RING BINDER

These sheets should be 8½-by-11 inches and may be color-coded for easy distinction in the file.

EXHIBIT 67

CASE _____

LEGAL RESEARCH TEAM
FILE

REDUCED-SCALE DOCUMENT

Number _____
Description _____
_____
_____
_____

EXHIBIT 68

Case _____

LEGAL RESEARCH TEAM
FILES

DOCUMENT TOO LARGE
TO COPY

Number _____
Description _____
_____
_____
_____
_____

Where filed _____
_____
_____

EXHIBIT 69

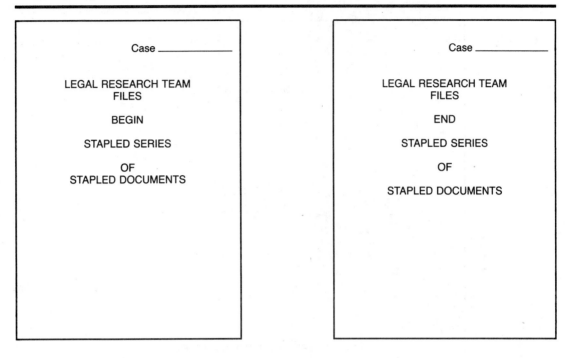

These sheets should be 8½-by-11 inches and may be color-coded for easy distinction in the file.

EXHIBIT 70

Case_____

LEGAL RESEARCH TEAM
FILES

DOCUMENT
NOT COPIED
OR MICROFILMED

SEE LARGE DOCUMENT FILE

THIS DOCUMENT IS _____ PAGES LONG AND CONSISTS OF:

_____   _____
(DATE)   (SIGNATURE)

EXHIBIT 71

Case _____

LEGAL RESEARCH TEAM FILES

PRIVILEGED DOCUMENT(S)

Page _____ to Page _____

Attachments:

Page _____ to Page _____

This sheet is substituted in the original and each copy file for the document it represents. It is used for all types of privileges and is supported by the Privilege Document Summary Sheet (see Exhibit 73, Appendix D). This sheet may be color-coded for ease of identification.

EXHIBIT 72

EXAMPLE

CASE <u>Jones v. Smith</u>

LEGAL RESEARCH TEAM FILES

PRIVILEGED DOCUMENT(S)

Page <u>0000342</u> to Page <u>0000351</u>

Attachments:

Page<u>0000352</u> to Page <u>0000356</u>

This sheet is substituted in the original and each copy file for the document it represents. It is used for all types of privileges and is supported by the Privilege Document Summary Sheet (see Exhibit 73, Appendix D). This sheet may be color-coded for ease of identification.

EXHIBIT 73

LEGAL RESEARCH TEAM FILES		
PRIVILEGED DOCUMENT SUMMARY		Case _____
Document Number		Date
Document Type		
Subject Matter		
Author(s)		
Participating Author (if any)		
Addressee(s)		
Copy Received by or Disclosed to		
Privilege Asserted		
Basis for Privilege Asserted		
Attorney-Client Privilege Claim Only	File Location Contents Confidential? Yes ___ No ___ Not Applicable ___ Response Confidential? Yes ___ No ___ Not Applicable ___ Response to a confidential communication from an employee to an attorney? Yes ___ No ___ Not Applicable ___ Does this document respond to a communication on the privileged document list? Yes ___ No ___ Not Applicable ___	
Work Product Exclusion Claim Only	Name of Lawsuit or Proceeding _____ _____ Identifying Court and Number _____ Commencement Date _____ Termination Date _____	

The Detailed Privilege Summary Sheet is used by attorneys in confirming privilege. It may be used by legal assistants with instruction.

EXHIBIT 74

LEGAL RESEARCH TEAM FILES	*EXAMPLE*	
PRIVILEGED DOCUMENT SUMMARY	Case _JONES v. SMITH_	
Document Number	*0000342*	Date *6-30-91*
Document Type	*Handwritten Memorandum*	
Subject Matter	*Atty's advice on Contract 4671-71*	
Author(s)	*A. Lincoln, Atty at Law*	
Participating Author (if any)	*G. L. Sanders, Engineer, Smith & Co*	
Addressee(s)	*J. L. Smith, President, Smith & Co*	
Copy Received by or Disclosed to	*G. R. Thompson, RCA, Denver Regional Counsel*	
Privilege Asserted	*Attorney - Client*	
Basis for Privilege Asserted	*Communication between attorney and client and participating indispensable parties*	
Attorney-Client Privilege Claim Only	File Location *Personal file. J.L. Smith*	
	Contents Confidential? Yes _✓_ No ___ Not Applicable ___	
	Response Confidential? Yes ___ No ___ Not Applicable ___	
	Response to a confidential communication from an employee to an attorney? Yes ___ No ___ Not Applicable ___	
	Does this document respond to a communication on the privileged document list? Yes ___ No ___ Not Applicable ___	
Work Product Exclusion Claim Only	Name of Lawsuit or Proceeding _____	
	Identifying Court and Number _____ Commencement Date _____ Termination Date _____	

EXAMPLE

The Detailed Privilege Summary Sheet is used by attorneys in confirming privilege. It may be used by legal assistants with instruction.

EXHIBIT 75

LEGAL RESEARCH TEAM PRIVILEGED DOCUMENT LISTING		Case _____
Document Number		Date
Type		
Subject Matter		
Author		
Addressee		
Privilege Asserted		
Basis		

EXHIBIT 76

EXAMPLE	LEGAL RESEARCH TEAM PRIVILEGED DOCUMENT LISTING	Case _JONES v. SMITH_
Document Number	0000342	Date 6-30-91
Type	Handwritten memo	
Subject Matter	Atty advice on Contract 4671-71	
Author	A. Lincoln, Atty at Law - Counsel to Smith & Co	
Addressee	J. L. Smith President, Smith & Co	
Privilege Asserted	Attorney-Client	
Basis	Advice to client on obligations and rights connected with contract EXAMPLE	

Simple privilege summary sheet from which a descriptive index can be generated if required by the court.

EXHIBIT 77

```
┌─────────────────────────┐   ┌─────────────────────────┐
│        Case _____     │   │        Case _____     │
│                          │   │                          │
│   LEGAL RESEARCH TEAM    │   │   LEGAL RESEARCH TEAM    │
│          FILES           │   │          FILES           │
│                          │   │                          │
│         BEGIN            │   │          END             │
│                          │   │                          │
│          FILE            │   │          FILE            │
│                          │   │                          │
│         FOLDER           │   │         FOLDER           │
│                          │   │                          │
│                          │   │                          │
│ DESCRIPTION: _____   │   │                          │
│ _____    │   │                          │
│ _____    │   │                          │
│ Dewey Decimal Number: __ │   │                          │
└─────────────────────────┘   └─────────────────────────┘
```

These sheets should be 8½-by-11 inches and may be color-coded for easy distinction in the file.

EXHIBIT 78

Case _____

LEGAL RESEARCH TEAM FILES

UNRESPONSIVE DOCUMENT(S)

Page Number _____ to _____

This sheet is inserted in the place of documents assembled in error. The documents themselves are removed to a special numeric file of irrelevant and unresponsive documents for possible future examination by the court.

EXHIBIT 79

Case _____

LEGAL RESEARCH TEAM FILES

THIS DOCUMENT WAS PULLED FOR ATTORNEY REVIEW

ATTORNEY _____

Pages _____   to _____

Delivered _____   by _____

This sheet is most effective if color-coded to emphasize that a document is missing from the file.

EXHIBIT 80

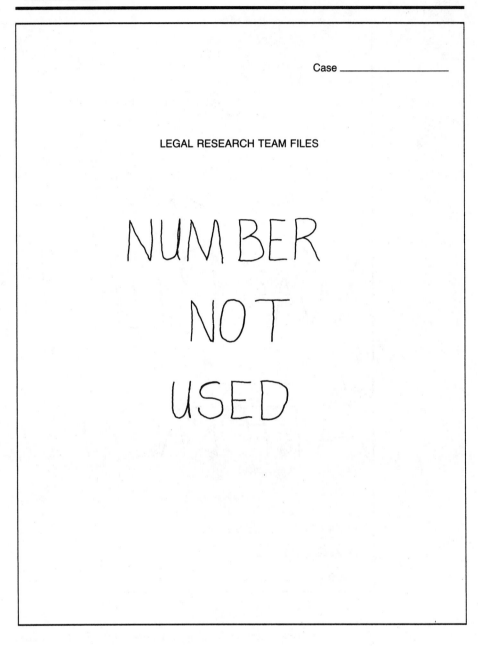

This sheet should be placed in the numeric file. The number should appear on the Numeric Sequence Justification Roster and Commentary (see Exhibit 58, Appendix A).

EXHIBIT 81

Case _____

LEGAL RESEARCH TEAM FILES

DOCUMENT(S)

NOT

PRODUCED

Was not produced BECAUSE:

It consists of: (description)

IF NEEDED, WILL OBTAIN THE ORIGINAL AND MAKE IT AVAILABLE FOR INSPECTION IN OUR OFFICE.

Date _____   Signature _____

Glossary: Legal Terminology

[Copyrighted source material: The entire section on Latin words and phrases and all other definitions followed by an asterisk have been taken from Black's Law Dictionary. *(revised fifth edition, West Publishing Company).]*

Introduction

This chapter is *not* a dictionary of all legal terms but rather a selection of frequently used terms. These words have been sorted into categories, though words found under "Business and Corporate Terms" are also used by professionals who specialize in real estate. This glossary is arranged to give legal assistants immediate and easily scanned word lists with barebones definitions that serve as memory aids or refreshers.

The definitions provided are accurate but do not constitute every possible definition or contextual meaning. They are the basic meanings generally accepted. With words commonly used in pleading causes of action, however, there is insufficient detail to provide the legal assistant with a means of outlining the elements of proof for the cause of action. For instance, *assault* in the general legal terms and phrases is defined as "an unlawful offer or attempt with force to do corporeal hurt to another." The elements for a civil action require a showing that there was no permission by the plaintiff. The legal assistant must consult the codes, annotated cases, texts, and so forth in outlining the elements of cases and their defenses.

Those seeking in-depth meanings must consult more authoritarian and detailed definitions than this book can accommodate. Black's Law Dictionary and the multivolume sets of Legal Words and Phrases are recommended.

Latin Words and Phrases

A fortiori With stronger reason; much more.

A posteriori From the effect to the cause; from what comes after.

A priori From the cause to the effect; from what goes before.

A vinculo matrimonii From the bond of matrimony.

Ab actis An officer having charge of *acta,* public records, registers, journals, or minutes; an officer who entered on record the *acta* or proceedings of a court; a clerk of court; a notary or actuary.

Ab initio From the very beginning.

Ad damnum clause A clause in pleadings praying for claimed money loss or damages or other relief.

Ad hoc For this; for this special purpose; one time only.

Ad infinitum Without limit; to an infinite extent; indefinitely.

Ad litem For the suit; for the purposes of the suit; pending the suit. A guardian *ad litem* is a guardian appointed to prosecute or defend a suit on behalf of a party incapacitated by infancy or otherwise.

Ad respondendum For answering; to make answer.

Ad satisfaciendum To satisfy.

Ad valorem According to the value. A tax imposed on the value of a property.

Adieu Without delay. A common term in the year books, implying final dismissal from court.

Aggregatio mentium The meeting of minds. The moment when a contract is complete.

Alias dictus Otherwise called. A fictitious name assumed by a person is colloquially termed an *alias*.

Alibi In criminal law, elsewhere; in another place.

Aliquot A proportional part; fractional.

Alius Other. Something else; another thing.

Alter ego Second self; the same entity under a different name or title.

Amicus curiae A friend of the court. A person who has a strong interest in but who has no right to appear in a suit but is allowed to introduce argument, authority, or evidence to protect his or her interest.

Animus Mind; intention; disposition; design; will.

Anno domini In the year of the Lord. Commonly abbreviated A.D. The computation of time, according to the Christian era, dates from the birth of Christ.

Ante Formerly; heretofore; synonymous with *supra*.

Arguendo In arguing; in the course of the argument.

Assumpsit He undertook; he promised.

Bona fide In or with good faith; honestly, openly, and sincerely; without deceit or fraud.

Causa A cause, reason, occasion, motive, or inducement.

Causa mortis In contemplation of approaching death.

Caveat Let him beware; warning.

Caveat actor Let the doer or actor beware.

Caveat emptor Let the buyer beware.

Certiorari To be informed of, to be made certain in regard to. The name of a writ of review or inquiry. The writ of a superior court directing an inferior court to send up a pending pleading, as the U.S. Supreme Court honoring a petition for writ of *certiorari*.

Civiliter Civilly. In a person's civil character or position or by civil (not criminal) process or procedure.

Civiliter mortuus Civilly dead; dead in the view of the law.

Consortium Conjugal fellowship of husband and wife and the right of each to the company, cooperation, affection, and aid of the other in every conjugal relation.

Contra Against, confronting, opposite to; on the other hand; on the contrary.

Contra bonos mores Against good morals.

Contra pacem Against the peace.

Coram Before; in the presence of. Applied to persons only.

Corpus Body; an aggregate or mass; physical substance, as distinguished from intellectual conception; main part as opposed to appendages.

Corpus delicti The body of crime. The body (material substance) upon which a crime has been committed; for example, the corpse of a murdered man, the remains of a house burned down. Fact or evidence that proves the crime.

Corpus juris A body of law. A term used to signify a book comprehending several collections of law.

Corpus juris civilis The body of the civil law.

Cum testamento annexo With the will annexed. A term applied to administration granted where a testator makes an incomplete will, without naming any executors, where he or she names incapable persons, or where the executors named refuse to act.

Curia A court.

Damnum Damage; loss.

Damnum absque injuria Loss, hurt, or harm without injury in the legal sense.

Datum A first principle; a thing given; a date.

De bonis non An abbreviation of *de bonis non administratis*. Of the goods not administered. When an administrator is appointed to succeed another who has left the estate partially unsettled, he or she is said to be granted "administration *de bonis*"; that is, of the goods not already administered.

De facto In fact, in deed, actually; legitimate or correct in fact.

De jure Of right; legitimate; lawful; by right and just title.

De minimus Short for *de minimus non curat lex*. The law does not care for or take notice of very small or trifling matters.

De novo Anew; afresh; a second time.

Dicta Opinions of a judge that do not embody the resolution or determination of the court. The plural of *dictum*.

Dictum A statement, remark, or observation.

Donatio A gift. A transfer of the title to property to one who receives it without paying for it.

Duces tecum Bring with you. The name of certain species of writs of which the *subpoena duces tecum* is the most usual, requiring a party who is summoned to appear in court to bring with him or her some document, piece of evidence, or other thing to be used to inspected by the court.

Durante During.

Durante minore aetate During minority.

Durante viduitate During widowhood.

E converso Conversely, on the other hand; on the contrary.

Ergo Therefore; hence; because.

Erratum Error.

Et al. An abbreviation for *et alii*. And others.

Et alius And another

Et cetera And others; and other things; and others of a like character; and others of the like kind.

Et seq Abbreviation of *et sequentes*. And the following; sometimes shown as *et. seq.*

Et ux An abbreviation of *et uxor*. And wife.

Ex contractu From and out of a contract.

Ex delicto From a delict, tort, fault, crime, or malfeasance.

Ex necessitate legis From or by necessity of law.

Ex officio From office; by virtue of the office.

Ex parte On one side only; by or for one party; done for, in behalf of, or on the application of, one party only. Hearing with only one party present or represented.

Ex post facto After the act; by an act or fact occurring after some previous act or fact, and relating thereto; by subsequent matter. The opposite of *ab initio*.

Ex rel From the relation of; a form of pleading by the state on a matter arising from another case. Used in citations to indicate that a case is brought on behalf of another person or entity.

Exempli gratia (e.g.) For example.

Facto In fact; by an act; by the act or fact.

Felonice Feloniously.

Feme covert A married woman.

Feme sole A single woman, including a woman who has been married but whose marriage has been dissolved by death or divorce.

Fiat Let it be done. An authority issuing from some competent source for the doing of some legal act. A command.

Filius A son; a child.

Filius familias In the civil law, the son of a family; an unemancipated son.

Filius nullius An illegitimate child; son of nobody.

Filius populi A son of the people

Flagrante delicto In the very act of committing the crime.

Forum A court of justice or judicial tribunal; a place of jurisdiction; a place where remedy is pursued.

Guardian ad litem Appointed by the court to prosecute or defend the interests of another person (usually a minor or an incompetent) in litigation.

Habeas corpus You have the body. The name given to a variety of writs having for their object to bring a party before a court or judge.

Ibid. Abbreviation of *ibidem*. In the same place; in the same book; on the same page.

Ignorantia Ignorance; want of knowledge.

Ignorantia legis neminem excusat Ignorance of the law excuses no one.

Illicit Not permitted or allowed.

Illicitum collegium An illegal corporation.

Illud That.

Impotentia excusat legem The impossibility of doing what is required by the law excuses from the performance.

In bonis Among the foods or property; in actual possession.

In camera In chambers; in private.

In esse In being; actually existing.

In extremis In extremity; in the last extremity; in the last illness.

In forma pauperis In the character or manner of a pauper. A poor person may proceed without incurring costs or fees of court.

In fraudem legis In fraud of the law with the intent or view of evading the law.

In futuro In future; at a future time.

In hoc In this; in respect to this.

In loco parentis In the place of a parent; instead of a parent.

In omnibus In all things; on all points.

In pari delicto In equal fault or guilt.

In personam Against the person. Type of jurisdiction or power that a court may acquire over a defendant's person in contrast to jurisdiction over his or her property.

In praesenti At the present time.

In re In the affair; in the matter of; concerning; in reference to; regarding.

In rem Proceedings or actions instituted against the thing, as opposed to actions against persons.

In specie Specific; specifically. In kind; in the same or like form.

In toto In the whole; wholly; completely.

Indebitatus assumpsit Being indebted, be promised, or undertook.

Infra Below, under, beneath, underneath.

Innuendo Meaning. In a pleading in libel action, a statement by plaintiff of construction that he puts upon words that are alleged to be libelous.

Inter Among; between.

Inter vivos Between the living; from one living person to another.

Interim In the meantime; meanwhile; between.

Intra In; near; within.

Ipse He himself; the same; the very person.

Ipse dixit He himself said it; a bare assertion resting on the authority of an individual.

Ipso facto By the fact itself; by the mere fact; by the mere effect of an act or a fact.

Ita est So it is; so it stands.

Jura Rights, laws.

Jura personarum Rights of persons; rights that concern and are annexd to persons.

Jura rerum Rights of things; rights that a person may acquire over external objects or things, unconnected with his or her person.

Jure divino By divine right.

Jure uxoris In right of the wife.

Juris publici Of common right; of common or public use.

Jus (pl. *jura*) Right; justice; law; the whole body of law.

Jus accrescendi The right of survivorship.

Jus ad rem A right to a thing.

Jus civile Civil law. The system of law peculiar to one state or people.

Lis pendens A pending suit. Jurisdiction, power, or control that courts acquire over property in suit pending action and until final judgment.

Locus A place; the place where a thing is done.

Locus delicti The place of the offense; the place where an offense was committed.

Mala Bad; evil; wrongful.

Mala fide Bad faith. The opposite of *bona fide*.

Mala in se Wrongs in themselves; acts morally wrong; offenses against conscience.

Mala praxis Malpractice; unskillful management or treatment.

Malo animo With an evil mind; with a bad purpose or wrongful intention; with malice.

Malum Wrong; evil; wicked; reprehensible.

Malum in se A wrong in itself; an act or case involving illegality from the very nature of the transaction, upon principles of natural, moral, and public law.

Mandamus We command. A writ issued from a court of superior jurisdiction and directed to an inferior court, a private or municipal corporation, or an executive, administrative, or judicial officer commanding performance of a particular act therein stated.

Mens Mind; intention; meaning; understanding; will.

Mens rea A guilty mind; a guilty or wrongful purpose; criminal intent.

Modus Manner; means; way.

Nil Nothing.

Nisi Unless.

Nisi pruis Trial courts where issues of fact are tried before a jury and one presiding judge.

Nolle prosequi A formal entry on the record by the prosecuting officer in criminal action declaring that the prosecutor decides not to pursue the case.

Nolo contendere I will not contest it; a plea in a criminal case that has a similar legal effect as a plea of guilty.

Non compos mentis Not of sound mind; insane.

Non obstante Notwithstanding.

Non obstante veredicto Notwithstanding the verdict.

Nudum pactum A voluntary promise, without any consideration other than mere goodwill or natural affection.

Nul No; none.

Nul tort In pleading, a plea of the general issue to a real action, by which the defendant denies that he or she committed any wrong.

Nunc pro tunc Now for then. A phrase applied to acts allowed to be done after the time when they should be done, with a retroactive effect.

Omnibus For all; containing two or more independent matters.

Pactum An agreement without consideration that might produce a civil obligation.

Pari delicto In equal fault; in a similar offense or crime; equal in guilt or in legal fault.

Particeps criminis A participant in crime; an accomplice.

Pendente lite Pending the suit; during the actual progress of a suit; during litigation.

Per annum By the year; annually; yearly.

Per capita By the heads or polls. According to the number of individuals; share and share alike.

Per curiam By the court. A phrase used to distinguish an opinion of the whole court from an opinion written by any one judge.

Per se By himself or itself; in itself; taken alone; inherently; in isolation; unconnected to other matters.

Per stirpes By roots or stocks; by representation. This term, derived from the civil law, is much used in the law of descents and distribution and denotes a method of dividing an intestate estate.

Post mortem After death; pertaining to matters occurring after death.

Persequi To follow after; to pursue or claim in form of law.

Praecipe An original writ, drawn up in the alternative, commanding the defendant to do the thing required or show the reason why he or she had not done it.

Prima facie At first sight; on the first appearance; on the face of it; so far as can be judged from the first disclosure; presumably; a fact presumed to be true unless disproved by some evidence to the contrary.

Prima facie case Such as will prevail until contradicted and overcome by other evidence.

Prima facie evidence Evidence good and sufficient on its face; such evidence as, in the judgment of the law, is sufficient to establish a given fact or group or chain of facts, constituting the party's claim or defense and that, if not rebutted or contradicted, will remain sufficient.

Pro For; in respect of; on account of; in behalf of.

Pro bono For the good; used to describe work or services done or performed free of charge.

Pro bono publico For the public good.

Pro confesso For confessed; as confessed.

Pro forma As a matter of form or for the sake of form.

Pro rata Proportionately; according to a certain rate, percentage, or proportion.

Pro se For himself; in his own behalf; in person.

Pro tanto For so much; for as much as may be; for as far as it goes.

Pro tempore For the time being; temporarily; provisionally.

Quantum meruit As much as he deserves; the extent of liability on a contract implied by law.

Quantum valebant As much as they were worth.

Quare Wherefore; for what reason; on what account.

Quasi As if, almost as it were; analogous to.

Quid pro quo What for what; something for something. Used in law for the giving of one valuable thing for another.

Quoad hoc As to this; with respect to this; so far as this in particular is concerned.

Quo animo With what intention or motive.

Quo warranto An extraordinary proceeding, prerogative in nature, addressed to preventing a continued exercise of authority unlawfully asserted.

Ratio decidenti The ground or reason of decision. The point in a case that determines the judgment.

Remittitur Power of a trial court to diminish the award of damages by a jury.

Res A thing; an object, subject matter, or status is considered as the defendant in an action or as the object against which, directly, proceedings are taken; subject matter of a trust or will.

Res gestae Things done; the whole of the transaction under investigation and every part of it.

Res ipsa loquitur The thing speaks for itself. The foundation of a legal pleading in common law in negligence, which, if accepted by the court, allows the burden of proof to be imposed on the defendant instead of the plaintiff.

Res judicata A matter adjudicated; a thing judicially acted upon or decided; a thing or matter settled by judgment.

Respondeat superior Let the master answer. Maxim meaning that a master is liable in certain cases for the wrongful acts of his or her servant and a principal for those of his agent.

Scienter Knowingly. Frequently used to signify the defendant's guilty knowledge.

***Scilicet* (SS. or ss.)** To wit; that is to say. A word used in pleadings and other instruments as introductory to a more particular statement of matters previously mentioned in general terms.

Scintilla A spark; a remaining particle; a trifle; the least particle.

Se defenendo In defending oneself; in self-defense.

Semper Always.

Semper paratus Always ready. The name of a plea by which the defendant alleges that he or she has always been ready to perform what is demanded of him or her.

Seriatim Severally; separately; individually; one by one.

Sigillum A seal; originally and properly a seal impressed upon wax.

Simplex Simple, single; pure; unqualified.

Simplex obligato A single obligation; a bond without a condition.

Sine Without.

Sine die Without day; without assigning a day for a future meeting or hearing.

Sine qua non Without which not; that without which the thing cannot be; an indispensable requisite or condition.

Situs Situation; location.

Stare decisis To abide by or adhere to decided cases. A decision that establishes precedent in law.

Status quo The existing state of things at any given date.

Sub Under; upon.

Sub nomine Under the name of; in the name of; under the title of.

Sub silentio Under silence; without any notice being taken.

Sui generis Of its own kind or class; peculiar.

Sui juris Of his own right; possessing full social and civil rights; not under any legal disability, the power of another, or guardianship.

Supersedeas The name of a writ containing a command to stay the proceedings at law.

Supra Above; before.

Terminus Boundary; a limit, either of space or time.

Tort A private or civil wrong or injury. A wrong independent of contract.

Ultra Beyond; outside of; in excess of.

Ultra vires Acts beyond the scope of the powers of a corporation, as defined by its charter or the laws of the state of incorporation.

Versus Against. In the title of a cause, the name of the plaintiff is put first, followed by the word *versus,* then the defendant's name. The word is commonly abbreviated *vs.* or *v.*

Vi et armis With force and arms.

Via Way; road. In civil law, a right of way.

Vice In the place or stead; substitution for.*

Vice versa Conversely; in inverted order; in reverse manner.

Voir dire To speak the truth. Denotes the preliminary examination that the court may make of one presented as a witness or juror, where his or her competency, interest, or other quality is objected to.

General Legal Terms and Phrases

Abrogation The destruction or annulment of a former law by an act of the legislative power, by constitutional authority, or by usage.*

Acceptance Agreeing to an offer, thereby creating a contract.

Accommodation An arrangement or engagement made as a favor to another not upon a consideration received.

Acknowledgement An admittance, affirmation, declaration, testimony, avowal, confession, or owning as genuine.

Adhesion contract Standardized contract form in which one party, normally the weaker, has little or no bargaining power or choice as to its terms.

Administrative law A body of law in the form of rules and regulations promulgated by an administrative body created by state legislature or Congress to carry out a specific statute.

Affiant One who swears to or affirms the statement in an affidavit.

Affidavit A voluntary statement in writing sworn or affirmed to before an official, usually a notary public, who has the authority to administer an oath or affirmation.

Agent A person authorized by another to act for him, one entrusted to another's business.*

Allegation The assertion claim, declaration, or statement of a party to an action, made in a pleading, setting out what he or she expects to prove.*

Amnesty A sovereign act of oblivion for past acts; often conditioned on acceptance within a trial period. Amnesty is the abolition and forgetfulness of the offense; a pardon is forgiveness.

Anticipatory breach Before the legally required performance of a contract duty, an announcement by one party to a contract to another party to the contract that he or she will not or cannot perform his or her contract duty.

Antitrust laws Federal and state laws designed to protect trade and commerce and to prevent restraint of trade, price-fixing, price discrimination, monopoly, and unfair practices in interstate commerce; for example, Sherman Act, Clayton Act, Federal Trade Commission Act.

Appraisal A valuation or an estimation of value of property by disinterested persons of suitable qualification.*

Assault A willing unlawful threat or attempt to do corporeal hurt to another by force so that the intended victim has reason to fear or expect immediate harm.

Assets All the items of value owned by an individual, association, estate, business, or corporation.

Assignment A transfer or making over to another of the whole of any property, real or personal in possession or action, or of any estate or right therein.*

Attestation The act of witnessing the signing or execution of a document by signature.

Attorney-in-fact One who is appointed by another to act for him or her in specific actions described in a power of attorney or letter of attorney.

Bailment A delivery of goods or personal property by one person to another for some particular purpose, upon a contract, express or implied, that the property will be returned to the person delivering it after the accomplishment of the purpose for which it was delivered.

Bankruptcy A state of insolvency under the Federal Bankruptcy Law in which the property of a debtor is taken over by a receiver or trustee in bankruptcy for the benefit of the creditors. A voluntary bankruptcy is brought about by the filing of a petition in bankruptcy by the debtor. An involuntary bankruptcy is brought about by the filing of a petition by the creditors against an insolvent debtor.

Battery An unlawful application of force to another's person, or other wrongful physical violence or constraint, inflicted on a human being without his or her consent.

Breach of contract Failure, without legal excuse, to perform any promise forms the whole or part of a contract.*

Capacity Legal qualification (such as legal age), competency, power, or fitness.

Censure An official reprimand or condemnation.

CLA Abbreviation for Certified Legal Assistant; a term earned through and awarded by the National Association of Legal Assistants to legal assistants who successfully complete an extensive written test of their general skills and specific knowledge of four areas of substantive law practice and procedure.

Civil law Laws adopted by local, state, and federal governments and known as codes or statutes and that concern civil or private rights and remedies, as contrasted with criminal laws.

Codes A systematic collection, compendium, or revision of laws, rules, or regulations enacted by legislation; statutes.

Code Civil The code embodying the civil law of France, framed by a commission of jurists, passed by the tribunate and legislature, and promulgated in 1804 as the *Code Civil des Francais*. When Napoleon became emperor, the code was changed to *Code Napoleon* for many years. The law of the state of Louisiana is based historically on the Napoleonic Code.

Common law All statutory and case law background of England and the American colonies; laws of legal rules that are developed as a result of decisions by judges based upon accepted customs and traditions and that do not rest upon any express and positive declaration of the will of the legislative body.

Community property Property owned in common by husband and wife, each having an undivided one-half interest by reason of their marital status.*

Conciliation The adjustment and settlement of a dispute in a friendly, unantagonistic manner. Used in courts before trial with a view toward avoiding trial and in labor disputes before arbitration.*

Consideration The price, motive, cause, impelling influence, or matter of inducement of a contract, which must be lawful in itself.

Contract An agreement between competent parties upon a legal consideration to do or to abstain from doing some lawful act.

Copyright A right of literary property as recognized and sanctioned by positive law.*

Creditor A person to whom a debt is owing by another person, who is the debtor.*

Criminal law That law that for purposes of preventing harm to society declares what conduct is criminal and prescribes the punishment to be imposed for such conduct.

Debtor One who owes an obligation.

Decree The judgment of a court of equity or chancery, answering for most purposes to the judgment of a court of law; a sentence or order of the court, pronounced on hearing and understanding all the points in issue and determining the rights of all the parties to the suit, according to equity and good conscience.*

Discharge To release; liberate; annul; unburden; disencumber; dismiss.

Duress Unlawful constraint exercised upon a person whereby he or she is forced to do some act that he or she otherwise would not have done.

Equity Justice administered according to fairness, as contrasted with the strictly formulated rules of common law.*

Evidentiary Having the quality of evidence; constituting evidence; evidencing.*

Exemptions Freedom from a general duty or service; immunity from a general burden, tax, or charge.* In bankruptcy proceedings, amounts of property allowed to be kept by the debtor.

Felony A crime of a graver or more serious nature than those designated as misdemeanors. Any offense punishable by death or imprisonment for a term exceeding one year.

Fraud Any kind of artifice employed by one person to deceive another.*

Guardian A person lawfully invested with the power and charged with the duty of taking care of the person and managing the property and rights of another person who, for defect of age, understanding, or self-control, is considered incapable of administering his or her own affairs.*

Hypothetical question A combination of assumed or proved facts and circumstances, stated in such form as to constitute a coherent and specific situation or statement of facts, upon which the opinion of an expert is asked, by way of evidence on a trial.*

Indorsement The act of a payee, drawee, accommodation indorser, or holder of a bill, note, check, or other negotiable instrument, in writing his or her name upon the back of the same, with or without further or qualifying words, whereby the property in the same is assigned and transferred to another.*

Interstate commerce Traffic, intercourse, commercial trading, or the transportation of persons or property between or among the several states from or between points in one state and points in another state; commerce between two states or between places lying in different states.*

Judgment The official and authentic decision of a court of justice upon the respective rights and claims of the parties to an action or suit therein litigated and submitted to its determination.*

Legal assistant A distinguishable group of persons who assist attorneys in delivering legal services. Within this occupational category, some individuals are known as paralegals. Through formal education, training, and experience, legal assistants have knowledge and expertise regarding the legal system and substantive and procedural law that qualify them to do work of a legal nature under the supervision of an attorney.

Legal ethics Usages and customs among the members of the legal profession involving their moral and professional duties toward one another, toward clients, and toward the courts.*

Lien A charge, security, or encumbrance upon property.*

Liquidation Payment, satisfaction, or collection; realization on assets and discharge of liabilities.*

Litigation Contest in a court of law for the purpose of enforcing a right or seeking a remedy.*

Misdemeanor Offenses lower than felonies and generally punishable by fine or imprisonment other than in the penitentiary.* Defined by local, state, and federal code and statute.

Mitigation of damages Duty of parties to minimize damages after an injury has been inflicted or a breach has occurred.

Napoleonic Code See Code Civil.

Notary Public An official authorized by law to administer oaths and to attest to and certify by his or her hand and official seal the identity of persons executing documents.

Novation Substitution of a new contract, debt, or obligation for an existing one between the same or different parties.*

Oath An affirmation of truth of a statement that renders one willfully asserting untrue statements punishable for perjury.*

Offer A promise; a commitment to do or refrain from doing some specific thing in the future.

Offeree The person to whom an offer is made.

Offeror The party who makes the offer.

Parol A word; speech, hence, oral or verbal.*

Parole A conditional release of a prisoner, generally under the supervision of a parole officer, who has served part of the term for which he or she was sentenced to prison.

Patent A grant made by the government to an inventor, conveying and securing to him or her the exclusive right to make, use, and sell his or her invention for a term of years.*

Pecuniary Monetary; relating to money; financial; consisting of money or that which can be valued in money.*

Power of attorney An instrument authorizing another to act as one's agent or attorney. Power may be made general or specific.

Privileged communication Those statements made by certain persons within a protected relationship, such as husband-wife, attorney-client, priest-penitent, and the like.*

Probation A sentence releasing the defendant into the community under the supervision of a probation officer.*

Promissory estoppel Legal theory that prevents one party to a contract from denying that consideration was given in that contract.

Rescission An action of an equitable nature in which a party seeks to be relieved of an obligation under a contract on the grounds of mutual mistake, fraud, impossibility, and so forth.*

Restitution The measure of damages according to the defendant's gains rather than the plaintiff's losses.

Revocation Taking back some power, authority, or thing granted; to make void a contract.

Specific performance The carrying out or performance of a contract according to its exact terms. Matters of specific performance are enforced by a court of equity.

Statute An act of the legislature declaring, commanding, or prohibiting something; a particular law enacted and established by the will of the legislative branch of government.*

Substantive law That part of the law that creates, defines, and regulates rights and duties. Substantive law is opposed to adjective or procedural law, which provides for the method of administering and protecting the rights, duties, and obligations created by substantive law. All states of a general nature are substantive law; those regulating administrative and court proceedings are adjective law.

Tort A private or civil wrong or injury. Three elements of every tort action are: (1) existence of legal duty from defendant to plaintiff, (2) breach of duty, and (3) damage as a proximate result.*

Trademark A distinctive mark, motto, device,or emblem that a manufacturer stamps, prints, or otherwise affixes to the goods it produces, so they may be identified in the market and their origin vouched for.*

Undue Influence Illegal threats or pressure that take away the other party's free will.

Uniform laws A considerable number of laws have been approved by the National Conference of Commissioners on Uniform State Laws, and many of them have been adopted in one or more jurisdictions in the United States and its possessions.* Some of the more important uniform laws are the Uniform Negotiable Instruments Act, the Uniform Partnership Act, the Uniform Stock Transfer Act, and the Uniform Warehouse Receipt Act.

Void; voidable That which is void is of no legal force or effect; that which is voidable may be avoided or declared void.

Business and Corporate Terms

Antitrust acts Federal and state protecting commerce and trade from unlawful restraints, price discriminations, price fixing, and monopolies.

Articles of incorporation Basic instrument filed with the appropriate governmental agency on the incorporation or formation of a business and organized under general corporation laws.*

Assumed business name The name under which an individual, partnership or corporation conducts business.

Blue Sky law A popular name for statutes providing for the regulation and supervision of investment companies and securities, offerings, and sales.

Bond A written obligation; a certificate or evidence of a debt.

Bylaws Regulations, ordinances, rules, or laws adopted by a corporation or association for the regulation of its own actions and the rights and duties of its members among themselves

Calendar year The period from January 1 to December 31, inclusive.*

Capital The principal invested in a business.

Capitalization The total amount of various securities issued by a corporation.

Clayton Act An act to supplement the Sherman Antitrust Act against unlawful monopolies and restraints.

Cooperative An organization for the primary purpose of providing economic services for its members for their benefit or gain rather than that of the organization.

Copyright A right granted by statute to the author or originator of certain literary or artistic productions, whereby he or she is invested, for a limited period, with the sole and exclusive privilege of multiplying copies of the same and publishing and selling them. A patent relates to the invention of an article; for example, a typewriter.

Corporation An artificial person or legal entity created by or under the authority of the laws of a state or nation composed, in some rare instances, of a single person and his or her successors, being the incumbents of a particular office, but ordinarily consisting of an association of numerous individuals who subsist as a body politic under a special denomination, which is regarded in law as having a personality and existence distinct from that of its several members and which is, by the same authority, vested with the capacity of continuous succession, irrespective of changes in its membership, either in perpetuity or for a limited term of years, and of acting as a unit or single individual in matters relating to the common purpose of the association, within the scope of the powers and authorities conferred upon such bodies by law.*

Domestic A corporation created by or organized under the laws of the state in which it does business;

Foreign A corporation created by or under the laws of another state, government, or country.*

CUSIP Committee on Uniform Securities Identification Procedures.

Debenture A promissory note or bond issued by a corporation as evidence of an obligation to pay money.

Depreciation An allowance for the exhaustion or wear and tear of tangible property and certain intangible assets that have a limited useful life.

Director An individual appointed or elected to manage and direct the affairs of a corporation.

Dissolution The termination of a corporation as a body politic. Dissolution may occur voluntarily or involuntarily.

Dividend The share alloted to each of several persons entitled to share a division of profits or property. Dividends may denote a fund set apart by a corporation out of its profits to be apportioned among the shareholders or the proportional amount falling to each.*

EIR Environmental impact report.

Excise tax A tax imposed by legislature on the performance of an act, the engaging of an occupation, or the enjoying of a privilege.

FELA, Federal Employers Liability Act Protects employees engaged in interstate and foreign commerce. Payments are made for death or disability sustained in the performance of the duties of employment.

Fiscal year The year between one annual time of settlement or balancing of accounts and another. A period of twelve consecutive months (not necessarily concurrent with the calendar year) with references to which appropriations are made and expenditures authorized and at the end of which accounts are made up and books balanced.

Franchise A special privilege conferred by government or individual or corporation and that does not belong to citizens or country generally of common right.* A privilege granted or sold so as to use a trade name or to sell products or services of a company. Usually conferred for a consideration.

Goodwill The favor that the management wins from the public. The fixed and favorable consideration of customers arising from established and well-conducted business.

Incorporators Individuals who join together for the purpose of forming a corporation.

Insolvency Inability to pay debts as they become due in the usual course of business.

Interstate commerce Traffic, intercourse, commercial trading, or the transportation of persons or property between or among the several states or from or between points in one state and points in another state; commerce between two states or between places lying in different states.*

Interstate Commerce Act The act of Congress of February 4, 1887, designed to regulate commerce between the states and particularly the transportation of persons and property by carriers between interstate points; prescribing that charges for such transportation shall be reasonable and just; prohibiting unjust discrimination, rebates, draw-backs, preferences, pooling of freights, and so on; requiring schedules of rates to be published; establishing a commission to carry out the measures enacted; and prescribing the powers and duties of such commission and the procedure before it.*

Interstate Commerce Commission Federal regulatory agency.

Inventory A detailed list of articles of property; an itemized list or schedule of property with appraised or actual values.

Keogh Plans An enactment by Congress that allows self-employed persons to establish and participate in tax-favored retirement plans similar to qualified pension and profit sharing plans.

Liquidation Payment, satisfaction, or collection; realization on assets and discharge of liabilities.

Majority The number greater than half of any total.

Merger The fusion or absorption of one thing or right into another.* In regard to corporations, the union of two or more corporations by the transfer of property of all to one of them, which continues in existence, the others being swallowed up or merged therein.*

Monopoly A privilege or peculiar advantage vested in one or more persons or companies, consisting in the exclusive right (or power) to carry on a particular business or trade, manufacture a particular article, or control the sale of the whole supply of a particular commodity.*

National Labor Relations Act (Taft-Hartley Act of 1947) A federal law regulating the relationship between employers and employees or their union representatives.

Nonprofit corporation A corporation or organization of which no part of its income is distributable to its members, directors, or officers.

Officer A person holding office of trust, command, or authority in a corporation with the power and duty of exercising certain functions. An officer of a corporation carries out the directives of the board of directors.

Organizational meeting A meeting of the original board of directors named in the articles of incorporation at which the adoption of bylaws, election of officers, and transaction of any other necessary business usually takes place.

OSHA, Office of Safety and Health Administration A federal agency.

Partner A member of a partnership or a firm; one who has united with others to form a partnership in business.

Partnership (general) An association of two or more persons by voluntary contract, to carry on, as co-owners, a business for profit.

Partnership (limited) A partnership formed by two or more persons that includes, along with one or more general partners, one or more limited partners, who, as such, are not bound by the obligations of the partnership.

Patent A grant made by the government to an inventor, conveying and securing to him or her the exclusive right to make, use, and sell his or her invention for a term of years.*

Pension plan A plan that requires the employer to make a certain rate of contribution into a retirement fund each year per employee.

Profit sharing plan A plan that provides the employer make contributions into a retirement fund based solely on the profits of the corporation.

Proprietorship (sole) Business completely and directly owned by a single person.

Proxy A person who is substituted by another to represent him or her and act for him or her, particularly at some meeting.* An agent representing and acting for a principal.*

Quorum The number necessary to be present in order to transact business.

Recapitalization An arrangement whereby stock, bonds, or other securities of a corporation are adjusted as to amount, income, or priority.*

Redemption A repurchase; a buying back.*

Registered agent of a corporation An individual resident (or corporation authorized to do business in the state), located at the listed registered office, upon which service or notice can be made on the particular corporation.

Reorganization The act or process of organizing again or anew. As to corporations, the carrying out, by proper agreements and legal proceedings, of a business plan for winding up the affairs of or foreclosing a mortgage or mortgages upon the property of insolvent corporations.

Resolution A formal expression of the opinion or will of an official body of a public assembly, adopted by vote.*

Royalty A payment reserved by the grantor of a patent, lease of a mine, or similar right and payable proportionately to the use mode of the right by the grantee.*

Securities Evidences of obligations to pay money or of rights to participate in earnings and distribution of corporate, trust, and other property.

Securities and Exchange Acts to provide for the regulation of securities, exchanges, and over-the-counter markets operating in interstate and foreign commerce and through the mails and to prevent unfair practices covering same. The Securities Exchange Commission (SEC) is the federal agency that administers these acts.

Shares A part or indefinite portion of a thing owned by a number of persons in common that contemplates something owned in common by two or more persons and has reference to that part of the undivided interest that belongs to some one of them. A definite portion of the capital of a company.*

Shareholder See Stockholder.

Sherman Act or Sherman Antitrust Act An act to protect trade and commerce against unlawful restraints or monopolies.

Stock (corporate) Stock is distinguished from bonds and ordinarily from debentures in that it gives right of ownership in a part of the assets of a corporation and the right to interest in any surplus after payment of debts.* Stock is the capital of a corporation, usually divided into equal shares.

Stockholder A person who owns shares of stock in a corporation.*

Taxable year Annual accounting period of a taxpayer.*

Trademark A distinctive mark, motto, device, or emblem that a manufacturer stamps, prints or otherwise affixes to the goods it produces, so that they may be identified in the market and their origin be vouched for.*

Truth in Lending Act A federal act that ensures that every person needing consumer credit is provided full disclosure of finance charges, including disclosure in the advertisement of credit transactions; amended in 1970 to regulate issuance, holder's liability, and the fraudulent use of credit cards.

Usury An illegal contract for a loan or forebearance of money, goods, or things in action, by which illegal interest is reserved, agreed to be reserved, or taken.*

Worker's compensation The name commonly used to designate the method and means created by statutes for giving greater protection and security to workers and their dependents against injury and death occurring in the course of employment.

Litigation Terms

Abatement A reduction, decrease, or diminution; the suspension or cessation, in whole or in part, of a continuing charge, such as rent.

Abstract of record A complete history in short, abbreviated form of the case as found in the record, complete enough to show that the questions presented for review have been properly reserved.

Accident report (auto) A report filed with the designated authorities by the operators of motor vehicles involved in an accident that sets forth the names of the parties and the circumstances surrounding the accident.

Affidavit A statement in writing sworn or affirmed to before an official, usually a notary public, who has the authority to administer an oath or affirmation.

Affirmative defense A new matter constituting a defense to the complaint, assuming it to be true.

Alienation of affections The robbing of husband or wife of the conjugal affection, society, fellowship, and comfort that inheres in the normal marriage relation. The deprivation of one spouse of the right to the aid, comfort, assistance, and the deprivation of consortium or society of the other spouse in family relationships.*

Allegation The assertion, claim, declaration, or statement of a party to an action, made in a pleading, setting out what he or she expects to prove.*

Allocution In criminal proceeding, the process during which the court allows the defendant to say a few words before sentencing.

Answer A pleading setting forth matters or facts as defense(s).

Appeal The complaint to a superior court of an injustice done or error committed by an inferior one whose judgment or decision the court above is called upon to correct or reverse. The removal of a cause from a court of inferior to one of superior jurisdiction, for the purpose of obtaining a review and retrial.*

Appellant A party who appeals the suit to a higher court.

Appellee The party against whom the appeal is taken.

Arbitrary Nonrational; not done or acting according to reason or judgment. Without fair, solid, and substantial cause; that is, without cause based upon the law.*

Arbitration The referring of a dispute to an impartial third party chosen by the parties to the dispute to adjudicate the dispute.

ATLA American Trial Lawyers Association.

Bail To procure the release of a person from legal custody, by undertaking that he or she shall appear at the time and place designated and submit him- or herself to the jurisdiction and judgment of the court.

Bifurcation Separation of issues, at trial.

Burden of proof The necessity or duty of affirmatively proving a fact or facts in dispute on an issue raised between the parties in a cause.

Cause of action The grounds on which a lawsuit may be brought.

Certified shorthand reporter A shorthand reporter tested and approved as to speed and accuracy by the court and empowered to administer oaths and record sworn testimony.

Circumstantial evidence Evidence of facts or circumstances from which the existence or nonexistence of a fact in issue may be inferred. The proof of various facts or circumstances that usually attend the main fact in dispute and therefore tend to prove its existence or to sustain, by their consistency, the hypotheses claimed.*

Civil action Action brought to enforce, redress, or protect private rights.

Class action An action brought on behalf of other persons similarly situated.* This refers to persons in the same situation; for example, all persons being given false information about a particular product by the manufacturer.

Codes A collection of laws; a system of law promulgated by legislative authority.

Competent Duly qualified; answering all requirements; having sufficient ability or authority. Legally fit.*

Complaint The first or initiatory pleading on the part of the plaintiff in a civil action. Its purpose is to give defendant information of all material facts on which plaintiff relies to support his or her demand.*

Conciliation The formality of bringing the parties of a case before a judge who attempts to reconcile the parties. Common in domestic relations matters.

Condemnation The process by which property of a private owner is taken for public use through the power of eminent domain.

Contempt (of court) Any act that is calculated to embarrass, hinder, or obstruct court in administration of justice or that is calculated to lessen its authority or its dignity.

Contingent fee An arrangement between attorney and client whereby the attorney agrees to represent the client with compensation to be a percentage of the recovered amount.

Conviction In a general sense, the result of a criminal trial that ends in a judgment or sentence that the accused is guilty as charged.*

Cost Expenses awarded by a court to the prevailing party.

Court reporter See Certified shorthand reporter.

Counterclaim A claim presented by a defendant in opposition to or deduction from the claim of the plaintiff.* The defendant's claim against the plaintiff set forth in the defendant's answer to the complaint.

Crime A positive or negative act in violation of penal law; an offense against the state or the United States.*

Cross-claim The claim by a party to a lawsuit against a co-party that arises out of the transaction that is the subject of the lawsuit or of a counterclaim to the original action.

Cross-examination The examination of a witness upon a trial or hearing or upon taking a deposition by the party opposed to the one who produced him or her, upon his or her evidence given in chief, to test its truth, to further develop it, or for other purposes.*

Damages A pecuniary compensation or indemnity, which may be recovered in the courts by any person who has suffered loss, detriment, or injury, whether to his or her person, property, or rights, through the unlawful act or omission or negligence of another.* The most common damages requested are: (1) general, which are to compensate the injured party for the injury sustained; (2) punitive or exemplary, which award the injured party, over and above what are general, where the wrong done him or her was aggravated by circumstances of violence, malice, fraud, and so forth; and (3) special, such as wage loss and medical expenses.

Declaratory judgment One that simply declares the rights of the parties or expresses the opinion of the court on a question of law, without ordering anything to be done.

Decree A sentence or order of the court, pronounced on hearing and understanding all the points in issue and determining the rights of all the parties to the suit, according to equity and good conscience.*

Defamation Holding up of a person to ridicule, scorn, or contempt in a respectable and considerable part of the community; may be criminal as well as civil; includes both libel and slander.

Default judgment A judgment for the the plaintiff where the defendant has failed to appear or file an answer in a timely manner.

Deposition A written record of oral testimony, in the form of questions and answers made before a public officer for use in a lawsuit.

Directed verdict Procedure whereby a judge directs that a jury reach a certain determination in cases where the evidence is such that a reasonable person could not disagree.

Discovery The ascertainment of that which was previously unknown; the disclosure or coming to light of what was previously hidden.

Dismiss without prejudice Dismissal of a case allowing a party to refile the same cause of action.

Domicile That place where a person has his or her true, fixed, and permanent home and principal establishment and to which whenever he or she is absent, he or she has the intention of returning.* Domicile is not synonymous with residence, the difference being one of intention. A person may have more than one residence, but not more than one domicile.

Due process The course that the application of law must take to result in fairness. It is prescribed by the Fifth and Fourteenth Amendments to the United States Constitution.

Enlargement Applies to the extension of time in legal proceedings.

Estoppel A bar or impediment at law that prevents one from alleging or denying a fact.

Evidence Whatever may properly be submitted to a court or jury to elucidate an issue or prove a case. Includes testimony of witnesses, documents, and admissions of parties.

Exhibit A paper or document produced and exhibited to a court during a trial or hearing, to a commissioner taking depositions, or to auditors, arbitrators, or others as a voucher or in proof of facts or as otherwise connected with the subject-matter and that, on being accepted, is marked for identification and annexed to the deposition, report, or other principal document, filed of record, or otherwise made a part of the case.*

Felony A crime of a graver or more atrocious nature than those designated as misdemeanors.* Generally, an offense punishable by death or imprisonment in the penitentiary.

Filiation Judicial determination of paternity. The relation of the child to the father.

Filiation proceeding A special statutory proceeding, criminal in form but in the nature of a civil action, to enforce a civil obligation or duty specifically for the purpose of establishing parentage and the putative father's duty to support his illegitimate child.*

Fraud A false representation of a matter of fact, whether by words or by conduct, by false or misleading allegations, or by concealment of that which should have been disclosed, which deceives and is intended to deceive another so that he or she shall act upon it to his or her legal injury.*

Garnishment A statutory proceeding whereby a person's property, money, or credits in the possession or under the control of or owing by another are applied to payment of the former's debt to a third person by proper statutory process against the debtor and garnishee.*

Guardian A person lawfully invested with the power and charged with the duty, of taking care of the person and managing the property and rights of another person who, for defect of age, understanding, or self-control, is considered incapable of administering his or her own affairs.*

Guardian ad litem A guardian appointed by the court to represent an individual during the pendency of a lawsuit.

Hearsay Evidence not proceeding from the personal knowledge of the witness but from the mere repetition of what he or she has heard others say.* Second-hand evidence, as distinguished from original evidence.

Hypothetical question A combination of assumed or proved facts and circumstances stated in such form as to constitute a coherent and specific situation or set of facts upon which the opinion of an expert is asked, by way of evidence on a trial.*

Impeachment The adducing of proof that a witness is unworthy of belief.*

Impleader A procedure by which a new party is brought into an action on the ground that the new party is or may be liable to the party who brings him or her in for all or part of the subject matter of the claim.

Indictment An accusation in writing found and presented by a grand jury, legally invoked and sworn, to the court in which it is impaneled, charging that a person therein named has done some act or been guilty of some omission that by law is a public offense, punishable on indictment.*

Inference A truth or proposition drawn from another that is supposed or admitted to be true. A process of reasoning by which a fact or proposition sought to be established is deduced as a logical consequence from other facts or a state of facts already proved or admitted.*

Information An accusation exhibited against a person for some criminal offense, without an indictment. A written accusation made by a public prosecutor, without intervention of a grand jury.*

Injunction A prohibitive writ issued by a court of equity forbidding the defendant to do some act or to permit his or her servants or agents to do some act that he is threatening or attempting to commit.

Intent Generally the same as *mens rea*. The state of mind of an individual at the time of the alleged offense.

Interpleader A procedure by which persons having claims against another person may be joined as parties to a suit and required to set up claims, if their claims are such that the person initiating such procedure is or may be exposed to multiple liability.

Interrogatories A set or series of written questions used in the judicial examination of a party or a witness.

Intervention The procedure by which a third person, not originally a party to the suit but claiming an interest in the subject matter, comes into the case in order to protect his or her right or interpose his or her claim.*

Joinder Uniting with another person or party in some legal step or procedure.

Judgment The official and authentic decision of a court of justice upon the respective rights and claims of the parties to an action or suit therein litigated and submitted to its determination.*

Jurisdiction The authority or power of a court to decide or deal with the subject matter of an issue.

Jury A certain number of citizens selected according to law and sworn to inquire of certain matters of fact and declare the truth upon evidence to be presented before them.

   Grand Jury—Considers whether the evidence presented by the state against a person accused of a crime warrants his or her indictment.

   Petit jury—The ordinary jury for the trial of a civil or criminal action. So called to distinguish it from the grand jury.

Jury panel The assembly of citizens called to court where a group will be selected for a given jury. More than one jury can be filled from one panel.

Laches An omission to assert a right for an unreasonable and unexplained length of time under circumstances prejudicial to the adverse party.

Leading question One that instructs a witness how to answer or puts into his or her mouth words to be echoed back. Questions are leading that suggest to the witness the answer desired.

Libel Almost any written language, picture, or sign that upon its face has a natural tendency to injure a person's reputation, either generally or with respect to his or occupation, and is published to a third party and is not privileged or permitted and is not true.

Litigation Contest in court of law for the purposes of enforcing a right.*

Malice The intentional doing of a wrongful act without just cause or excuse with an intent to inflict an injury or under circumstances that the law will imply an evil attempt.*

Malpractice Any professional misconduct, unreasonable lack of skill or fidelity in professional or fiduciary duties, evil practice, or illegal or immoral conduct.*

Misdemeanor Offenses lower than felonies and generally punishable by fine or imprisonment otherwise than in the penitentiary.* Defined by local, state, and federal code and statute.

Mistrial An erroneous, invalid, or nugatory trial; a trial of an action that cannot stand in law because of want of jurisdiction, a wrong drawing of jurors, or disregard of some other fundamental requisite before or during trial.*

Mitigation Alleviation, reduction, abatement, or diminution of a penalty or punishment imposed by law.*

Motion An application for a rule or order made to a court or a judge for the purpose of obtaining some act to be done in favor of the applicant or moving party.

Motive Cause or reason that moves the will and induces action. An inducement or that which leads or tempts the mind to indulge in a criminal act.*

Negligence The omission to do something that a reasonable person, guided by those ordinary considerations that ordinarily regulate human affairs, would do or the doing of something that a reasonable and prudent person would not do.*

Oath An affirmation of truth of a statement, which renders one willfully asserting untrue statements punishable for perjury.*

Opinion The statement by a judge or court of the decision reached in regard to a cause tried or argued before them, expounding the law as applied to the case and detailing the reasons upon which the judgment is based.*

Order Direction of a court or judge made or entered in writing and not included in a judgment. An application for an order is a motion.*

Paralegal See Legal assistant.

Parol evidence Oral or verbal evidence; that which is given by word of mouth; the ordinary kind of evidence, given by witnesses in court.*

Parole A conditional release; the condition being that, if the prisoner observes the conditions provided in the parole order, he or she will receive an absolute discharge from the balance of sentence, but if he or she does not, he or she will be returned to serve the unexpired term.

Paternity The state or condition of a father; the relationship of a father.*

Paternity proceeding See Filiation proceeding.

Peremptory challenge The right to challenge a juror without assigning a reason for the challenge.*

Perjury The willful assertion as to a matter of fact, opinion, belief, or knowledge made by a witness in a judicial proceeding as part of his or her evidence, either upon oath or in any form evidence given in open court, in an affidavit, or otherwise, such assertion being material to the issue or point of inquiry and known to such witness to be false.*

Personal injury A hurt or wrong to the physical body or reputation of a person or both.

Personal property (personalty) Rights or interests a person has in things movable; for example, an automobile or furniture.

Plea A pleading; more particularly, the first pleading on the part of the defendant.*

Pleadings The formal allegations by the parties of their respective claims and defenses.*

Preponderance of evidence Greater weight of evidence or evidence that is more credible and convincing to the mind. That which best accords with reason and probability.

Pretrial conference or hearing A meeting of the judge and counsel for the parties preliminary to the trial of a lawsuit.

Presumption An assumption that the law expressly directs to be made from particular facts.

Probable cause A reasonable ground for belief in the existence of facts warranting the proceedings complained of.

Probation Allowing a person convicted of some lesser offense to avoid imprisonment under a suspension of sentence, during good behavior, and generally under the supervision of a probation officer.*

Recidivist A habitual criminal.

Recission of contract Annulling or abrogation or unmaking of a contract and the placing of the parties to it in *status quo*.

Record A written account of some acts, court proceedings, transaction, or instrument drawn up, under authority of law, by a proper officer and designed to remain as a memorial or permanent evidence of the matters to which it relates.*

Relevancy The tendency of the evidence to establish a proposition that the evidence is offered to prove.

Replevin Redelivery to the owner of the pledge or thing taken in distress. A local action to be brought where property is taken or where property is detained, unless statute regulates the matter.

Rules of court Rules established by a court for the regulating of conduct of business of the court; for example, rules of civil procedure, criminal procedure, and appellate procedure.

Sequester To separate or isolate; for example, to sequester a jury by requiring it to stay apart from society until a trial is concluded and a verdict returned.

Settlement An agreement by which parties having disputed matters between them reach or ascertain what is coming from one to the other.*

Slander The speaking of base and defamatory words tending to prejudice another in his or her reputation, office, trade, business, or means of livelihood.*

Statutes See Codes.

Statute of limitations A statute prescribing limitations to the right of action on certain described causes of action or criminal prosecutions; that is, declaring that no suit shall be maintained on such causes of action nor any criminal charge made, unless brought within a specified period after the right accrued.*

Stipulation The name given to any agreement made by the attorneys engaged on opposite sides of a cause (especially if in writing) regulating any matter incidental to the proceedings or trial, which falls within their jurisdiction*; for example, agreements to extend the time for pleading or to take depositions.

Subpoena A command to appear at a certain time and place to give testimony upon a certain matter.

Subpoena _duces tecum_ In addition to being a subpoena to appear, it requires a person to produce books, papers, documents, and other materials.

Subrogation The substitution of one person in the place of another with reference to a lawful claim, demand, or right, so that the one who is substituted succeeds to the rights of the other in relation to the debt or claim and its rights, remedies, or securities.*

Summons A writ or process directed to the sheriff or other proper officer, requiring him or her to notify the person named that an action has been commenced against that person and that he or she is required to appear, on the day named, and answer the complaint in such action.*

Transcript of record The printed record as made up in each case for appeal to a superior court.

Venue The neighborhood, place, or county in which a particular lawsuit should be tried.

Verification A sworn statement confirming that the allegations in the pleadings are authentic, correct, or true.

Witness fees Fees for mileage and appearance in court or at a deposition that are paid to a witness and often prescribed by law.

Workers' compensation A procedure created by statutes that provides for fixed awards to employees or their dependents in case of employment-related accidents and diseases, dispensing with the proof negligence and legal actions.*

Real Estate Terms

Abatement The suspension or cessation of a continuing charge; for example, rent.

Abstract of title A condensed history or summary of public records relating to the title to a particular parcel of land.

Access A right vested in the owner of land to enter and leave a tract of land from a road or other highway without obstruction; the right to enter and leave over lands of another.

Acceleration clause (in a mortgage) Specifies conditions under which the lender may advance the time when the entire debt that is secured by the mortgage becomes due.

Accretion A gradual and imperceptible accumulation of land by natural causes, as out of the sea or a river.

Acre A tract of land containing 43,560 square feet of land; that is, 208.71 feet square.

Adverse possession Physical possession of land inconsistent with the right of the owner. In most states, a party in adverse possession, after satisfying fully the requirements of the relevant statutes, thereby acquires the title to the land. Usually requires: actual possession, adverse, under claim of right, notorious, open, exclusive, hostile, continuous and uninterrupted.

Air rights The right to use all or a portion of the space above a designated tract of land.

ALTA American Land Title Association, a national association of title insurance companies and title abstract organizations. This term is used most frequently as part of the indentification of standard policy forms adopted by that association.

Amortize To reduce debt by means of regular periodic payments, including amounts applicable both to principal and interest.

Appurtenances Things deemed to be incidental to the land when they are by right used with the land for its benefit.

Assessed valuation The valuation placed upon land for purposes of taxation; however, valuation does not necessarily represent the market value of the property.

Assessment A special tax levied upon property for the purpose of paying for improvements (sewer lines, sidewalks, street paving, and so on) benefiting the land.

Assessor A public official who evaluates property for the purpose of taxation.

Assignment A transfer or making over to another of the whole of any property, real or personal.* Used often in transfering interests of a mortgagee or of a lessee.

Assignee One to whom an assignment or transfer of interest is made; for example, the assignee of a mortgage or contract.

Assignor One who makes an assignment; for example, the assignor of a mortgage or contract.

Assumption of mortgage An obligation undertaken by the purchaser of land to be personally liable for payment of an existing note secured by a mortgage. As between the lender and the original borrower, the original borrower remains liable on the mortgage note.

Attachment Legal seizure of property to force payment of a debt.

Attorney in fact One who holds a power of attorney from another allowing him or her to act in the other's place and stead and to execute legal documents such as deeds and mortgages.

Base title or basic title Title to an area or tract out of which parts are subsequently conveyed or from which a subdivision or development is made. Thus, the title to farm acreage that has been subdivided would be the base title to the entire subdivision.

Beneficiary (of a trust) A person designated to receive some benefit from the trust estate.

Binder or commitment An enforceable agreement that, upon satisfaction of the requirements stated in the binder, the insurer will issue the specified title insurance policy subject only to the requirements being met prior to closing and exceptions stated in the binder. A binder sets forth status of title as of a particular date.

Bond (1) An insurance agreement under which one party becomes surety to pay, within stated limits, financial loss caused to another by specified acts or defaults of a third party. (2) An interest bearing security evidencing a long-term debt, issued by a government or corporation and sometimes secured by a lien on property.

Building (restriction) line or setback A line fixed at a certain distance from the front and/or sides of a lot or at a certain distance from a road or street that marks the boundary of the area within which no part of any building may project. This line may be established by a filed plat of subdivision, by restrictive covenants in deeds or leases, by building codes, or by zoning ordinances.

Bureau of Land Management A branch of the U.S. Department of the Interior charged with the surveying and management of natural resource lands and their resources.

Chain and links Units of length in the measurement of land. A chain is a land measurement being 66 feet in length; a link is a land measurement being 1/100th of a chain or 66/100th of a foot. *Caveat:* Modern surveyors use a steel tape 100 feet long in manual measurement, and it commonly is called a chain.

Chain of title A term applied to the past series of transactions and documents affecting the title to a particular parcel of land.

Clear title One which is not encumbered or burdened with defects.

Closing (1) A process by which all the parties to a real estate transaction conclude the details of a sale or mortgage. The process includes the signing and transfer of documents and the distribution of funds. (2) A condition in the description of real property by courses and distances at the boundary lines where the lines meet to include all the tract of land.

Closing costs Miscellaneous expenses involved in closing a real estate transaction, over and above the price of the land; for example, pro rate of taxes, insurance, or recording fees.

Cloud on title An outstanding claim or encumbrance that adversely affects the marketability of title.

Collateral Marketable real or personal property that a borrower pledges as security for a loan. In mortgage transactions, specific land is the collateral.

Commitment See Binder.

Community property A category of property existing in some states in which all property (except property specifically acquired by husband or wife as separate property) acquired by a husband and wife or either during marriage is owned in common by the husband and wife.

Condemnation The process by which property of a private owner is taken for a public use, without his or her consent but upon the award and payment of just compensation, being in the nature of a forced sale and condemner stands toward owner as buyer toward seller.

Condition precedent A specified event that must occur before all or part of a contract or document takes effect.

Conditions and restrictions A common term used to designate the uses to which land may not be put and providing penalties for failure to comply. Commonly used by land subdividers on newly subdivided areas.

Condominium A system of individual fee ownership of units in a multi-unit project, combined with joint ownership of common areas of the structure and land.

Construction loan A loan made to finance the actual construction or improvement on land; disbursements may be made in increments as the construction progresses.

Contract of sale An agreement to sell and purchase under which title is withheld from the purchaser until such time as the required payments to the seller have been completed.

Conventional loan A contract between a lender and a borrower without government loan guaranty or regulation.

Convey An act of deeding or transferring title to another.

Conveyance A document that transfers an interest in real property from one person to another; for example, a deed.

Cooperative A residential multi-unit building owned by a corporation and in which tenancy in a unit is obtained by purchase of the pertinent number of shares of the stock of the corporation and where the owner of such shares is entitled to occupy a specific unit in the building.

Cotenancy Ownership of the same interest in a particular parcel of land by more than one person.

Covenant An agreement between the parties in a deed whereby one party promises either (1) the performance or nonperformance of certain acts with respect to the land or (2) that a given state of thing with respect to the land is so; for example, a covenant that the land will be used only for residential purposes.

Cul de sac A blind alley; a street open at one end only.* Usually laid out by modern engineers to provide a circular turn-around for vehicles.

Curtesy A husband's life estate in the property of his deceased wife. By statute in most states, it is a life estate in one-third of the land she owned during their marriage. Curtesy has been abolished by statute in some states.

Deed A written document by which the ownership of land is transferred from one person to another.

Deed of trust A conveyance of a land title by a maker of a note (the debtor) to a third party, a trustee, as collateral security for the payment of the note with the condition that the trustee shall reconvey the title to the debtor upon payment of the note and with power in the trustee to sell the land and pay the note in the event of a default on the part of the debtor. Also called a trust deed.

Default Failure to perform a contractual obligation in a timely manner.

Deficiency judgment A judgment against a person liable for the debt secured by a mortgage in an amount by which the funds derived from a foreclosure or trustee's sale are less than the amount due on the debt.

Delivery The final and absolute transfer of a deed from seller to buyer in such a manner that it cannot be recalled by the seller.

Demised premises Property or a portion thereof that is leased to a tenant.

Devise A gift of land by will or to give land by will.

Devisee The person to whom property is given by a will.

Dower A wife's life estate in the property of her deceased husband. The reverse of curtesy.

Draw Disbursement of a portion of the mortgage loan. Usually applies to construction loans when partial advances are made as improvements to the property progress.

Earnest money Advance payment of part of the purchase price to bind a contract for property.

Easement A right of use over the property of another.

Egress The right to leave a tract of land. Many times used interchangeable with access. (See Access.)

Eminent domain The right of a government to appropriate private property for a public use by making reasonable payment to the owner of such property.

Encroachment An improvement, such as a house, driveway, wall, or fence, that illegally intrudes upon another's property.

Encumbrance Any right or interest in land held by persons other than the fee owner which right or interest lessens the value of the fee title; for example, judgment liens, easements, mortgages, and restrictions.

Endorsement Form issued by the insurer at the request of the insured that changes terms or items in an issued policy or commitment.

Equity (1) The interest or value that an owner has in real estate over and above the debts against. (2) A type of court of record.

Erosion Wearing away of real property by the action of water, wind, or other elements.

Escheat A reversion of property to the state in those cases where an individual dies without heirs and without a will.

Escrow Money, securities, documents, or other property deposited with a third disinterested party who completes the transaction in accordance with the instructions of the parties.

Estate (1) The degree, quantity, nature, and extent of interest that a person has in real and personal property. (2) The property comprising the assets of a decedent.

Exceptions (1) Those matters affecting title to the particular parcel of realty which matters are excluded from coverage of the particular title insurance policy. (2) In legal descriptions, that portion of lands to be deleted or excluded.

Exclusion Those general matters affecting title to real property excluded from coverage of a title insurance policy.

FNMA, Federal National Mortgage Association (Fannie Mae) A federally sponsored private corporation that provides a secondary market for housing mortgages.

Fee simple An estate in which the owner is entitled to the entire property, with unconditional power of disposition during his or her life, descending to his or her heirs upon death, intestate.

FHA, Federal Housing Administration An agency of the federal government, that insures private loans for new and existing housing and for home repairs under government-approved programs.

FHLMC, Federal Home Loan Mortgage Corporation (Freddie Mac) An affiliate of the Federal Home Loan Bank, which creates a secondary market in conventional residential loans and in FHA and VA loans by purchasing mortgages from members of the Federal Reserve System and the Federal Home Loan Bank System.

Financing statement Under the Uniform Commercial Code, used to create a public record that there is a security interest or claim to secure a dept on personal property; filed with the secretary of state or the county recorder.

Fixtures Any item of personal property so attached to real property that it becomes a part of the real property.

Foreclosure Legal process by which a mortgagor of real property is deprived of his or her interest in that property due to failure to comply with terms and conditions of the mortgage.

General warranty deed See Warranty deed.

GI or VA loan A loan for purchase of land in which the Veteran's Administration guarantees the lender payment of a home mortgage granted a qualified veteran.

GNMA, Government National Mortgage Association (Ginnie Mae) A government corporation that provides a secondary market for housing mortgages and special assistance to mortgagee financing housing under special FHA mortgage insurance programs.

Grantee A person who acquires an interest in land by deed, grant, or other written instrument.

Grantor A person who, by a written instrument, transfers to another an interest in land.

Guaranty policy A title insurance policy that insures only against defects of title appearing in the public records. Other policies insure against defects whether or not they appear in public records.

Habendum The "to have and to hold" section of a deed.

Heir The person who, at the death of the owner of land, is entitled to the land if the owner died intestate.

Heirs and assigns Terminology used in deeds and wills to provide that the recipient receives a "fee simple estate" in lands rather than a lesser interest.

Homestead, declaration of A recorded document whose primary importance to the homeowner is protection against the forced sale of property in satisfaction of certain debts.

Improvements Additions to raw lands tending to increase value, such as buildings, streets, and sewers.

Inchoate interest An interest in real estate that is not a present interest but may ripen into a vested estate, if not barred, extinguished, or divested.*

Indemnity agreement An agreement by the maker of the document to repay the addressee of the agreement up to the limit stated for any loss due to the contingency stated on the agreement.

Ingress The right to enter a tract of land. Many times used interchangeably with access. (See Access.)

Insurable title A land title that a title insurance company is willing to insure.

Joint protection policy A title insurance policy in a form suitable to insure the owner and/or lender.

Joint tenancy Where two or more persons hold real estate jointly for life, the survivors to take the interest of the one who dies.

Judgment A court's final determination of the rights of the parties in an action.

Judgment lien A statutory lien created by recording an abstract or certified copy of a money judgment.

Junior mortgage A mortgage, the lien of which is subordinate to that of another mortgage; for example, a second mortgage.

Lease A grant of the use of land for a term of years in consideration of the payment of a monthly or annual rental.

Leasehold An estate in realty held under a lease; an estate for a fixed term of years.*

Lessee One who takes lands upon a lease.

Lessor One who grants lands under a lease.

Lien A claim or charge on property of another for payment of some debt, obligation, or duty; for example, mortgage liens, judgment liens, and mechanics' liens.

Lien waiver or waiver of liens A document signed by the general contractor, each subcontractor, and each materialman of a construction project whereby the signators waive their right to mechanics' liens on the land involved in that particular project.

Life estate A grant or reservation of the right of use, occupancy, and ownership for the life of an individual.

Links See Chains and links.

Lis pendens A legal notice that there is litigation pending relating to the land, the outcome of which could affect the title to specified real property.

Loan policy, mortgage policy, or mortgagee's policy A title insurance policy in which the insurer insures the mortgagee against loss it may suffer because the title is not vested as stated in the policy and insures the validity and priority of the mortgage lien over any other lien not excepted to in the policy.

Lot A measured parcel of land having fixed boundaries.

Marketable title Such title as is free from reasonable doubt in law and fact.

Mechanic's lien and materialmen's lien The lien that by statute, a laborer or materialman may have against the land by reason of furnishing labor or material for the improvement of the property. The priority of such lien varies among the states; in some states mechanic's and materialmen's liens take priority over prerecorded mortgages.

Metes and bounds A description of a parcel of land by boundary lines in length and direction from point to point, circumscribing the parcel.

Mineral right An interest in minerals in land. A right to take minerals or a right to receive a royalty.*

Mortgage An instrument granting an interest in real property as security for payment of a note or performance of some other obligation.

Mortgage policy See Loan policy.

Mortgagor The person who borrows the money from the mortgagee and signs the mortgage as security.

Notary public An official authorized by law to administer oaths; to attest by his or her hand and official seal; and to identity persons executing documents.

Note A written promise to pay a certain amount of money at a certain time or in a certain number of installments. It usually provides for payment of interest, and its payment is at times secured by a mortgage.

Open-end mortgage A mortgage or deed of trust providing for future advances on the given mortgage and increases the amount of the existing mortgage.

Option The right, acquired for a consideration, to buy, sell, or lease property at a fixed price within a specified time.

Ownership The right to possess and use property to the exclusion of others.

Owner's policy A title insurance policy insuring the owner against loss due to any defect of title not excepted to or excluded from the policy.

Personal property Any property that is not real property.

Plat (of survey) A map of land made by a surveyor showing boundary lines, buildings, and other improvements on the land.

Points Charge imposed by a lender in consideration for making a loan secured by real property. A point equals one percent of the loan.

Power of attorney An instrument in writing by which one person, the principal, authorizes another, the attorney-in-fact, to act in his or her stead regarding the specific actions described in the instrument.

Prepayment penalty Penalty to the mortgagor for payment of the mortgage debt before it becomes due.

Prescription The doctrine by which a particular easement is acquired by long, continuous, and exclusive use and possession of property. (See Adverse possession.)

Public records Records that under the recording laws impart constructive notice of matters relating to land.

Quiet title The removal of a cloud on title by proper action in a court.

Quitclaim A deed that transfers whatever interest the maker may have in a particular parcel of land, containing no warranties as to title.

Reconveyance A document evidencing the extinguishment of the lien of the deed of trust. May be full or partial.

Redemption The right of the owner in some states to reclaim title to his or her property if he or she pays the debt to the mortgagee within a stipulated time after foreclosure.

Regress To return, go back, or reenter.

Release A deed from a mortgagee or trustee of a deed of trust that releases specific property from the lien of the mortgage or deed of trust.

Remainder An interest or estate in land in a person other than the grantor in which the right of possession and enjoyment of the land is postponed until the termination of some other interest or estate in that land.

Reserve Account The portion of funds included in a mortgage payment which are set aside for some specific purpose; e.g., insurance, taxes, etc.

Restriction or restrictive covenant Limitation imposed on a deed or lease respecting the use to which the property may be put; for example, building setback lines and limitations to residential uses.

Reversion Provision in conveyance by which, upon the happening of an event or contingency, title to the land will return to the grantor or his or her successor in interest in the land.

Riparian Pertaining to the banks of a watercourse. The owner of land adjacent to a watercourse is called a riparian owner, and the rights of the riparian owner related to that watercourse are called riparian rights.

Sale and leaseback A financial device that an owner of land may employ to raise money and still have the use of the land by selling the land to his or financier and immediately leasing it back for the period he or she wishes to use it.

Section or section of land A parcel of land comprising one square mile, or 640 acres.

Settlement See Closing (1).

Special warranty deed A deed containing a covenant whereby the seller agrees to protect the buyer against being dispossessed because of any diverse claims to the land by the seller or anyone claiming through him or her.

Standard coverage policy A form of title insurance that contains certain standard printed exceptions not included in the ALTA policies. This form of policy is used primarily in some of the western states.

Straw party Nominee; one who acts as an agent for another for the purpose of taking title to real property.

Subdivision A tract of land surveyed and divided into lots for purposes of sale.

Subordinate Placed in a lower order, class, or rank; occupying a lower position in a regular descending series;* the act of a creditor acknowledging in writing that the lien of debt due him or her from a debtor shall be inferior to the lien of the debt due another creditor from the same debtor.

Sub surface right Ownership of a right beneath the physical surface of the property.

Survey The process by which a parcel of land is measured and its contents ascertained; also a statement of the result of such survey, with the courses and distances and the quantity of the land.*

Take out loan A permanent mortgage loan that a lender agrees to make to a borrower upon completion of improvements on the borrower's land. The proceeds of the loan are used principally to pay off the construction loan.

Tax deed The deed given to a purchaser at a public sale of land for nonpayment of taxes. It conveys to the purchaser only such title as the defaulting taxpayer had and does not convey good title to that extent unless statutory procedures for the sale were strictly followed.

Tenancy by the entirety Created by a conveyance to husband and wife, whereupon each becomes seized and possessed of the entire estate and, after the death of one, the survivor takes the whole.

Tenant One who has right of possession of land by any kind of title. The word *tenant* used alone in modern times is used almost exclusively in the limited meaning of a tenant of a leasehold estate.

Tenancy in common An estate or interest in land held by two or more persons each having equal rights of possession and enjoyment but without any right of survivorship between the owners.

Title Evidence of a person's right or the extent of his or her interest in property.

Title defect Any legal right held by others to claim property or to make demands upon the owner.

Title insurance Insurance against loss or damage resulting from defects or failure of title to a particular parcel of real property; insures against past loss.

Title search An examination of public records, laws, and court decisions to determine the current ownership of and encumbrances on a parcel of land.

Torrens system A system of registering titles to lands that presumes an adjudication of title each time a deed or claim is filed.

VA loan See GI loan.

Vendee Purchaser of real or personal property.

Vendor The seller of real or personal property.

Vest To become owned by.

Waiver of liens See Lien waiver.

Warranty An agreement and assurance, binding upon the grantor of real property for the grantor and his or her heirs to the effect that he or she is the owner and will defend the title given.

Warranty deed Deed by which the seller implicitly or specifically agrees to protect the buyer against certain matters of title, usually including one or more of the following: lawful ownership of the property; rights of conveyance and quiet possession; freedom from all encumbrances; and warranty and defense of premises against all lawful claims.

Probate Terms

Abate To throw down, to beat down, destroy, quash.* To reduce a devise due to the insufficiency of property in the estate to pay all claims, expenses, and devises in full.

Ademption The act by which a testator in his or her lifetime pays his or her legatees a general legacy that, by will, he or she had proposed to give them at his or her death.

Administration of an estate The process of assembling a decedent's assets, paying debts, claims, and taxes and making distribution according to the will or the laws of succession.

Administrator An individual appointed by a court to settle the financial and legal affairs of a person who has died without a will. If the individual appointed is a woman, she is called an administratrix. In some states, this person is known under the general term of "personal representative."

Administrator *de bonis non* (Administrator d.b.n.) When the office of administrator becomes vacant for any reason, the court will appoint another person to complete the estate's administration. The new administrator is called the *administrator de bonis non,* which is an abbreviation of *de bonis non administratis,* meaning "of the goods not administered."

Administrator cum testamento annexo (CTA) An administrator of a decedent's estate appointed after the executor named in the will refused to act.* Since this person must distribute the estate under the terms of the will, rather than under the intestacy laws, he or she is called the *administrator cum testamento annexo,* meaning "with will annexed," to distinguish him or her from an administrator of an intestate estate.

Administratrix See Administrator.

Advancement That portion of an heir's inheritance given to him or her by the decedent during the decedent's lifetime.

Ancillary administration The administration of assets in the local state when the principal administration is in another state.

Annuitant A person who receives an annuity.

Annuity A yearly payment of money for life or years. A fixed sum, granted or bequeathed, payable periodically but not necessarily annually*.

Assets Property of all kinds, real and personal, owned by the decedent.

Attestation The act of witnessing the execution of a will or other document by signature.

Attesting witness A person witnessing to the genuineness of a will or other document.

Beneficiary One for whose benefit a trust is created; called a *cestui que trust* in Latin. A person having the enjoyment of property over which a trustee, executor, or other has the legal possession. The person to whom a policy of insurance is payable.*

Bequeath The act of making a bequest.

Bequest A gift by will of personal property; a legacy.* Distinguished from a devise that is a transfer of real property by will.

Codicil A supplement or an addition to a will; it may explain, modify, add to, subtract from, qualify, alter, restrain, or revoke provisions of a will.*

Death taxes Estate taxes and inheritance taxes.

Decedent A deceased person, especially one who has lately died.*

Devise A testamentary disposition of land or realty; a gift of real property by the last will and testament of the donor.* Distinguished from a bequest, which is a transfer of personal property by will.

Devisee The person to whom lands or other real property are devised or given by will.*

Distributee An heir; a person entitled to share in the distribution of an estate.

Domicile That place where a person has his or her true, fixed, and permanent home and principal establishment and to which whenever he or she is absent, he or she has the intention of returning.* Domicile is not synonymous with residence, the difference being one of intention. A person may have more than one residence but not more than one domicile.

Donee One to whom a gift is made or a bequest given or to whom a power of appointment is given.

Donor The party conferring a power. One who makes a gift.*

Duress Coercion that overcomes a person's free will.

Election Generally, the act of an heir choosing to take a statutory share of an estate in lieu of the share provided in a will.

Escheat A reversion of property to the state in those cases where an individual dies without heirs and without a will.

Estate (1) The property comprising the assets of a decedent. (2) The degree, quantity, nature, and extent of interest which a person has in land.

Estate plan An arrangement for the management and disposition of a person's property during his or her lifetime and at his or her death. Can be accomplished by a will, one or more trusts, gifts made during life, or a combination of these.

Estate tax An excise tax upon privilege of transferring or transmitting property by reason of death and is not a tax on property itself.*

Executor A person appointed by a testator to carry out the directions and requests in his or her will and to dispose of the property according to his or her testamentary provisions after his or her decease.* In some states, this person is known under the general term of "personal representative."

Expenses of administration All filing fees, costs of publication, compensation of personal representative and of his or her attorneys, and all other costs necessary to carry out the administration of a decedent's estate.

Fiduciary Any person who handles property or transacts business for the benefit of another person in a relationship of special trust.

Gift A voluntary transfer of personal property without consideration. Essential requisites of a gift are capacity of donor, intention of donor to make gift, completed delivery to or for donee, and acceptance of gift by donee.*

Gift *inter vivos* A gift between living parties and not in contemplation of death by the giver.

Gift tax The tax on a gift from one to another. A graduated tax levied by the federal government and some states on gifts made during life.

Grantor The person by whom a grant is made.*

Gross estate The total value, for federal estate tax purposes, of all a person's property before deducting debts, administrations expenses, marital deduction, charitable deductions, and so on.

Guardian A person lawfully invested with the power and charged with the duty of taking care of the person and managing the property and rights of another person, who for some peculiarity of status, or defect of age, understanding, or self-control, is considered incapable of administering his or her own affairs.*

Heir One who inherits property, whether real or personal.*

Income The return in money from one's business, labor, or capital invested; gains, profits, or private revenue.*

Income tax A tax levied by the federal and some state and local governments on a person's income, wages, and profits.

Incompetent A person legally declared to be incapable of managing his or her affairs.

Inheritance An estate or property that a person has by descent, as heir to another or that he or she may transmit to another, as his or her heir.*

Inheritance tax A tax on the transfer of passing of estates or property by legacy, devise, or intestate succession.*

Intangible property Such property as has no intrinsic and marketable value; that is, stocks, bonds, goodwill, trademarks, and so forth.

Inter vivos trust Between the living; from one living person to another.* A trust created during the grantor's lifetime.

Interested Persons Heirs, devises, children, spouses, creditors, and any others having a property right or claim against the estate of a decedent that may be affected by the proceeding, including fiduciaries representing interested persons.

Intestate One who dies without leaving a valid will, or the circumstance of dying without leaving a valid will effectively disposing of an estate. Partial intestacy occurs when the will does not dispose of all the estate.

Intestate succession Succeeding to or receiving property from a decedent as an heir, by virtue of statute rather than by will.

Irrevocable trust A trust that cannot be revoked or terminated by the grantor.

Issue Descendants. All persons who have descended from a common ancestor.*

Legacy A disposition of personal property by will. *Legacy* and *bequest* are equivalent terms.*

Legatee The person to whom a legacy is given. However, the term may be used to denote those who take under a will without any distinction between realty and personalty.

Letters of administration A certificate issued by the court identifying the administrator of the estate of a person who died intestate.

Letters testamentary A certificate issued by the court identifying the executor of a decedent's estate, as named in the will.

Life insurance trust A trust created by agreement by a person during his or her lifetime whereby the trustee receives proceeds of insurance on the life

of the creator of the trust, to be held and used as stated in the trust agreement.

Marital deduction A deduction for federal estate tax purposes measured generally by the value of property passing to the decedent's surviving spouse; under federal tax laws, the deduction is unlimited.

Minor An infant or person who is under the age of legal competence.* This age varies from 18 to 21, depending upon the state, and may even vary within a state, depending on the purpose.

Net estate The real and personal property of a decedent, except property used for the support of his or her surviving spouse and children and for the payment of expenses of administration, funeral expenses, claims, and taxes.

Net intestate estate Any part of the net estate of a decedent not effectively disposed of by his or her will.

Partial distribution A distribution of a part of the decedent's estate before administration of the estate is complete.

Per stirpes By roots or stocks; by representation. This term derived from the civil law and denotes a method of dividing an intestate estate where a class or group of distributees take the share that their deceased ancestor would have been entitled to, taking thus by their right of representing such ancestor and not as so many individuals.*

Personal representative A term used in some states to take the place of executor, administrator, administrator with will annexed, or administrator *de bonis non.*

Posthumous child One born after the father's death.

Pretermitted child A child of the testator born or adopted after the execution of the will who is neither provided for in the will nor in any way mentioned in the will and who survives the testator.

Probate The act or process of proving a will. A judicial act or determination of a court having competent jurisdiction establishing the validity of a will.*

Remainder An interest or estate in land in a person other than the grantor in which the right of possession and enjoyment of the land is postponed until the termination of some other interest or estate in that land.

Remainderman The person who is entitled to an estate after the previous estate has terminated.

Residuary estate (1) That which remains after debts and expenses and devises have been satisfied; or (2) all that has been legally disposed of by will by the residuary clause.

Reversion Provision in conveyance by which, upon the happening of an event or contingency, title to the land will return to the grantor or his or her successor in interest in the land. *Reversion* differs from *remainder* in that remainder does not come back to the grantor but goes to someone else.

Revoke To cancel or make ineffective a will or codicil.

Settlor One who creates a trust; also, one who furnishes the consideration for the creation of a trust, though in form, a trust is created by another.*

Special administrator A temporary representative appointed in an emergency situation to avoid loss, injury, or deterioration of decedent's property or to provide for disposition of decedent's remains.

Specific devise A devise of a specific thing or specified part of the estate of a testator that is so described as to be capable of identification; a gift of a part of the estate identified and differentiated from all other parts.

Surety A person or corporation executing the bond of a personal representative, thereby agreeing to make good any loss suffered by one interested in a decedent's estate by reason of the failure of the personal representative to carry out his or her duty.

Tangible property Property that has physical characteristics. It includes movable items such as jewelry, animals, furniture, and cash.

Testamentary disposition The act of disposing of property by will.

Testamentary trust A trust created by a will.

Testate Leaving a valid will at death.

Testator One who makes or has made a testament or will; one who dies leaving a will.*

Testatrix A woman who makes a will; a female testator.*

Trust A right of property, real or personal, held by one party for the benefit of another.

Trustee The person appointed, or required by law, to execute a trust; one in whom an estate, interest, or power is vested, under an express or implied agreement to administer or exercise it for the benefit or to the use of another.*

Trustor One who creates a trust. Also called settlor.*

Undue influence Improper influence to control the disposition of another's property.

Will A document that directs the disposition of the testator's property, executed in accordance with statutory requirements. The term includes codicils and a document that merely appoints a personal representative or merely revokes or revives a will.

Will contest A proceeding in probate court questioning the validity of a will or codicil.

Appendix

Appellate Brief of the National Association of Legal Assistants Submitted to the Court

Statement

The National Association of Legal Assistants, Inc. submits this brief *amicus curiae,* pursuant to Rule 36 of the Rules of the Supreme Court of the United States, in support of respondents.[1] This brief is submitted upon the written consent of petitioners and respondents.[2]

Interest of the Amicus Curiae

> Legal assistants[3] are a distinguishable group of persons who assist attorneys in the delivery of legal services. Through formal education, training and experience, legal assistants have knowledge and expertise regarding the legal system and substantive and procedural law which qualify them to do work of a legal nature under the supervision of an attorney.

National Association of Legal Assistants, Inc., Model Standards and Guidelines of Utilization of Legal Assistants (1984).

The National Association of Legal Assistants, Inc. (NALA) was incorporated in 1975 as a nonprofit organization, in recognition of and response to the burgeoning use of legal assistants in the delivery of legal services throughout the United States. Representing some 8,000 legal assistants through individual membership or affiliated associations, NALA seeks to promote professional development and continuing education for legal assistants, and to provide a strong national voice to represent this growing and significant profession.[4]

Consistent with these goals, NALA, in 1975, adopted a Code of Ethics and Professional Responsibility for legal assistants to serve as a guideline for the proper conduct by legal assistants in the performance of their duties (reprinted in full in the Appendix to this brief). In 1976, NALA administered the first national legal assistant certification examination, testing skills basic to the profession as well as substantive knowledge of law and procedure. Currently, the voluntary two-day examination program is administered three times yearly. As of July, 1988, 2,327 participants have earned the title CLA (Certified Legal Assistant).

In 1984, NALA adopted its Model Standards and Guidelines for Utilization of Legal Assistants to serve as a guide for legal assistants and supervising attorneys,

---

[1] The National Association of Legal Assistants, Inc., submitted this brief, in substantially the same form, as *amicus curiae* in support of petitioner, in the case *Blanchard v. Bergeron,* 831 F.2d 563 (5th Cir. 1987), *cert. granted,* 108 S.Ct. 2869 (June 27, 1988) (No. 87-1485), currently pending before the Court.

[2] The original of petitioners' written consent by Bruce Farmer, Esquire, counsel for petitioners, and the original of respondents' written consent by Jay Topkis, Esquire, counsel for respondents, are being filed with the Clerk of the Court under separate cover.

[3] The term "legal assistant" is preferred, as it represents those persons doing work of a legal nature under the direct supervision of an attorney, as opposed to a broader category of persons termed "paralegal," who perform work of a similar nature but not necessarily under the supervision of an attorney.

[4] Projections by the United States Department of Labor indicate an increase in the number of legal assistants from an estimated 53,000 in 1984 to 104,000 in 1995. United States Department of Labor, Bureau of Labor Statistics, *Occupational Outlook Quarterly* (Spring 1986).

by describing the role of a legal assistant in the delivery of legal services. Finally, NALA works hand in hand with local, state and national bar associations to set standards for legal assistants, and provides continuing education for legal assistants through seminars, workshops, publications and video tapes.

The legal assistant is a recognized and desirable addition to the modern law office. The delegation of work, which would otherwise be performed by an attorney, to a skilled legal assistant reduces the cost of legal services to the client and increases attorney efficiency and productivity. The benefits of this cost-reducing, cost-effective delivery of legal services to the public through the attorney-supervised use of legal assistants will be promoted and encouraged if the work of legal assistants is recognized and compensated at the market rate as part of court-awarded attorney's fees.

Were the Court to reverse the ruling below by holding that the time spent by legal assistants in the successful prosecution of a civil rights case should not be compensated at the market rate, under 42 U.S.C. § 1988, the detrimental effect upon those seeking legal representation to redress civil rights violations, as well as in other types of cases in which Congress has provided for the recovery of attorney's fees, would be substantial. Such a result would either discourage attorneys from representing victims of civil rights violations, because they could not receive full compensation for their effort, or force attorneys to perform all tasks of a legal nature, thereby decreasing the utilization of legal assistants and increasing the cost of litigation.

Summary of Argument

The widespread use of legal assistants by attorneys to perform work of a legal nature which would otherwise have to be performed by an attorney at a much higher rate has significantly reduced the cost of legal services to the public and enhanced the quality of legal representation by promoting efficient utilization of attorney time. Compensation for the attorney-supervised work of legal assistants at an hourly rate less than that charged by attorneys, but high enough to cover the cost of overhead associated with the work of a legal assistant, is customarily included in attorney's fees charged private fee-paying clients.

A reasonable attorney's fee awarded pursuant to the Civil Rights Attorney's Fee Awards Act of 1976, 42 U.S.C. § 1988, should include market rate compensation for productive work of a legal nature performed by a skilled legal assistant, under the supervision of an attorney, in order to effectuate the purpose of section 1988. Section 1988 was adopted by Congress to make available legal representation to victims of civil rights violations by fully compensating counsel for prevailing parties at a rate competitive with that charged in the private marketplace. An attorney's fee award which includes market rate compensation for the work of legal assistants is competitive with fees charged to traditional fee-paying clients, makes civil rights representation financially feasible for competent attorneys, promotes the cost-effective practice of utilizing legal assistants in the delivery of legal services, and is in accord with the goal of making available efficient and reasonably priced legal services, not only to victims of civil rights violations but also to the public at large.

Argument: The Work of Legal Assistants is Compensable at the Market Rate as Part of a Reasonable Attorney's Fee Award Pursuant to 42 U.S.C. § 1988.

   (a)   Compensating prevailing parties for the work performed by legal assistants on an hourly basis at the market rate comports with accepted practice in the private marketplace and is thus consistent with the purpose of 42 U.S.C. § 1988.

The Civil Rights Attorney's Fee Awards Act of 1976, 42 U.S.C. § 1988, provides that in federal civil rights actions, "the court, in its discretion, may allow the prevailing party, other than the United States, a reasonable attorney's fee as part of the costs." On several occasions, the Court has visited the legislative history of section 1988, finding that the purpose of the Fees Act was to provide a remedy necessary to obtain compliance with civil rights laws, and to promote respect for civil rights through effective citizen enforcement thereof. *Pennsylvania v. Delaware Valley Citizen's Counsel for Clean Air,* 478 U.S. 546, 561, 106 S.Ct. 3088, 3096 (1986) *("Pennsylvania I"); Evans v. Jeff D.,* 475 U.S. 717, 731, 106 S.Ct. 1531, 1539 (1986). Unless the attorney's fee reimbursement pursuant to section 1988 is " *'full and complete',* the statutory rights [created by civil rights legislation] would be meaningless because they would remain largely unenforced." *Pennsylvania v. Delaware Valley Citizens' Counsel for Clean Air,* 483 U.S. 711, 737, 107 S.Ct. 3078, 3093 (1987) (Blackmun, J., dissenting) (emphasis added), *("Pennsylvania II").*

Because most victims of civil rights violations are unable to afford legal representation, Congress found that the market itself would not provide adequate and effective access to the judicial process for vindication of rights violated. *Pennsylvania II,* 483 U.S. at 736–37, 107 S.Ct. at 3092 (Blackmun, J., dissenting); *City of Riverside v. Rivera,* 477 U.S. 561, 576, 106 S.Ct. 2686, 2695 (1986). Thus, to ensure that experienced competent attorneys would be willing to represent persons with legitimate civil rights grievances, Congress determined that it would be necessary to compensate lawyers for all time reasonably expended on a case, at a rate mirroring the prevailing market rate in the relevant community. *Pennsylvania II,* 483 U.S. at 742–44, 107 S.Ct. at 3095–96; *City of Riverside,* 477 U.S. at 578, 106 S.Ct. at 2696; *Evans,* 475 U.S. at 731, 106 S.Ct. at 1539; *Blum v. Stenson,* 465 U.S. 886, 895 (1984). Reasonable section 1988 attorney's fees must be competitive with the private market for lawyers' services, *Pennsylvania II,* 483 U.S. at 736, 107 S.Ct. at 3092, 3093, 3095 (Blackmun J., dissenting), and "similar to what 'is traditional with attorneys compensated by a fee-paying client.' " *Id.* at 3093 (citation omitted). *See also City of Riverside,* 477 U.S. at 575, 106 S.Ct. at 2695.

Attorneys in the private marketplace traditionally charge fee-paying clients for supervised work of a legal nature performed by legal assistants at a lesser hourly rate than that charged by attorneys. Separate billing for the services of such nonlegal personnel as legal assistants and law students in an "increasingly widespread custom." *Ramos v. Lamm,* 713 F.2d 546, 558 (10th Cir. 1983).

> In the not so distant past the court would have frowned upon the practice of billing paraprofessional time separate from attorney time just as it might if a firm separately recorded and billed the hours spent by a secretary on a specific client . . . , but the standing of paraprofessionals has improved significantly as special training has enabled them to undertake a wide variety of more sophisticated tasks previously assigned exclusively to higher priced lawyers. The advent and widespread use of the paraprofessional has meant that the cost of effective legal counsel has been reduced and its availability enhanced without impairing the quality or delivery of legal services.

In re Chicken Antitrust Litigation, 560 F.Supp. 963, 977–78 (N.D.Ga. 1980) (citation omitted). *See also Parise v. Riccelli Haulers, Inc.,* 672 F.Supp. 72 (N.D.N.Y. 1987). That attorney's fees include compensation for time spent by legal assistants reflects "the realities of the marketplace and of modern, progressive law office management." *United Nuclear Corp. v. Cannon,* 564 F.Supp. 581, 589 (D.R.I. 1983).

This court implicitly recognized and encouraged the traditional marketplace use of non-lawyer personnel in the delivery of legal services by approving an award of attorney's fees, pursuant to section 1988, which included compensation for time spent by a law clerk. *City of Riverside,* 477 U.S. at 566, 106 S.Ct. at 2690. Every federal circuit has likewise acknowledged the validity of delegating work of a legal nature to non-lawyer personnel under the supervision of an attorney by compensating for the work of legal assistants or law clerks pursuant to section 1988,[5] or to an analogous fee-shifting statute or rule.[6]

(b)   Compensating for the work of legal assistant time on an hourly basis at the market rate promotes the cost-effective delivery of legal services and enhances the quality of legal services.

Compensating for the work of legal assistant time as attorney's fees under Section 1988 "encourages cost-effective delivery of legal services and, by reducing the spiraling cost of civil rights litigation, furthers the policies underlying civil

---

[5] First Circuit: *Jacobs v. Mancuso,* 825 F.2d 559, 563 (1st Cir. 1987); *Furtado v. Bishop,* 635 F.2d 915, 920 (1st Cir. 1980); Third Circuit: *Daggett v. Kimmelman,* 811 F.2d 793, 799 (3d Cir. 1987) (fee reductions would be approved for work which should have been performed by paralegals); Fourth Circuit: *Vaughns v. Board of Educ. of Prince George's County,* 770 F.2d 1244, 1245–46 (4th Cir. 1985); Fifth Circuit: *Heath v. Brown,* 807 F.2d 1229, 1232 (5th Cir. 1987); Sixth Circuit: *Stewart v. Rhodes,* 656 F.2d 1216, 1217 (6th Cir. 1981), *cert. denied,* 455 U.S. 991 (1982); *Northcross v. Board of Educ. of Memphis City Schools,* 611 F.2d 624, 639 (6th Cir. 1979), *cert. denied,* 447 U.S. 911 (1980); Seventh Circuit: *Ustrak v. Fairman,* 851 F.2d 983 (7th Cir. 1988); *Cameo Convalescent Center, Inc. v. Senn,* 738 F.2d 836, 846 (7th Cir. 1984), *cert. denied,* 469 U.S. 1106 (1985); Eighth Circuit: *Jenkins v. Missouri,* 838 F.2d 260, 266 (8th Cir.), *cert. granted in part,* 109 S.Ct. 218 (Oct. 11, 1988) (No. 88-64), and *cert. denied,* 109 S.Ct. 218 (1988); Ninth Circuit: *Keith v. Volpe,* 833 F.2d 850, 859 (9th Cir. 1987); *Toussaint v. McCarthy,* 826 F.2d 901, 904 (9th Cir. 1987); Tenth Circuit: *Lucero v. City of Trinidad,* 815 F.2d 1384, 1385 (10th Cir. 1987); *Ramos v. Lamm,* 713 F.2d 546, 558 (10th Cir. 1983); Eleventh Circuit: *Walters v. City of Atlanta,* 803 F.2d 1135, 1151 (11th Cir. 1986).

[6] Second Circuit: *In re "Agent Orange" Prod. Liab. Litig.,* 818 F.2d 226, 238 (2d Cir.), *cert. denied,* 108 S.Ct. 289 (1987) (class action); *City of Detroit v. Grinnell Corp.,* 495 F.2d 448, 473 (2d Cir. 1974) (anti-trust class action); Third Circuit: *Brinker v. Guiffrida,* 798 F.2d 661, 668 (3d Cir. 1986) (recovery for law clerk under Equal Access to Justice Act); *Citizen's Council of Del. County v. Brinegar,* 741 F.2d 584, 596 (3d Cir. 1984) (Equal Access to Justice Act); Fourth Circuit: *Yohay v. City of Alexandria Employees Credit Union,* 827 F.2d 967, 974 (4th Cir. 1987) (law clerk under Fair Credit Reporting Act, 15 U.S.C. § 1681); *Lily v. Harris-Teeter Supermarket,* 720 F.2d 326, 339–40 n.28 (4th Cir. 1983), *cert. denied,* 466 U.S. 951 (1984) (employment discrimination); Fifth Circuit: *Concorde Limousines, Inc. v. Moloney Coachbuilders, Inc.,* 835 F.2d 541, 546 (5th Cir. 1987); *Alter Fin. Corp. v. Citizens & Southern Int'l Bank of New Orleans,* 817 F.2d 349, 350 (5th Cir. 1987) (sanctions, 28 U.S.C. § 1927); *Richardson v. Byrd,* 709 F.2d 1016, 1023 (5th Cir.), *cert. denied,* 464 U.S. 1009 (1983) (Title VII sex discrimination class action); Sixth Circuit: *Chandler v. Secretary of Dept. of Health & Human Services,* 792 F.2d 70, 73 (6th Cir. 1986) (Social Security Act, 42 U.S.C. § 406); Seventh Circuit: *In re Burlington Northern, Inc. Employment Practices Litig.,* 810 F.2d 601, 609 (7th Cir. 1986), *cert. denied,* 108 S.Ct. 82 (1987) (employment discrimination action, 42 U.S.C. § 2000e); *Spray-Rite Serv. Corp. v. Monsanto Co.,* 684 F.2d 1226, 1249–50 (7th Cir. 1982), *aff'd,* 465 U.S. 752 (1984) (anti-trust, 15 U.S.C. § 1 *et seq.*); Eighth Circuit: *Hawkins v. Anheuser-Busch, Inc.,* 697 F.2d 810, 817 (8th Cir. 1983) (employment discrimination, 42 U.S.C. § 2000e); Ninth Circuit: *Thornberry v. Delta Air Lines, Inc.,* 676 F.2d 1240, 1244 (9th Cir. 1982) (employment discrimination, 42 U.S.C. § 2000e); *Todd Shipyards Corp. v. Director, Office of Workers' Compensation,* 545 F.2d 1176, 1182 (9th Cir. 1976) (Longshoremen's and Harbor Workers' Compensation Act, 33 U.S.C. § 928); *Pacific Coast Agricultural Export Ass'n v. Sunkist Growers, Inc.,* 526 F.2d 1196, 1210 n.19 (9th Cir. 1975), *cert. denied,* 425 U.S. 959 (1976) (anti-trust, 15 U.S.C. § 1 *et seq.*); Tenth Circuit: *Kopunec v. Nelson,* 801 F.2d 1226, 1229 (10th Cir. 1986) (Equal Access to Justice Act); Eleventh Circuit: *Allen v. United States Steel Corp.,* 665 F.2d 689, 697 (5th Cir. Unit B 1982) (employment discrimination, 42 U.S.C. § 2000e); D.C. Circuit: *Wilkett v. Interstate Commerce Comm'n,* 844 F.2d 867, 877 (D.C.Cir. 1988) (law clerk; Equal Access to Justice Act); *Save Our Cumberland Mountains, Inc. v. Hodel,* 826 F.2d 43, 54 n.7 (D.C.Cir. 1987) *(en banc)* (Surface Mining Control and Reclamation Act of 1977, 30 U.S.C. § 1201).

rights statutes." *Cameo Convalescent Center, Inc. v. Senn,* 738 F.2d 836, 846 (7th Cir. 1984), *cert. denied,* 469 U.S. 1106 (1985). Skilled legal assistants are capable of performing some work of a legal nature which would otherwise have to be done by an attorney. To the extent that such work is done by supervised legal assistants at substantially less cost per hour than would have been the case had the work been done by attorneys, the overall cost of legal services to the public is reduced. A rule prohibiting recovery for legal assistant time at the market rate would discourage the cost-effective delivery of legal services.[7]

In addition to reducing the cost of litigation, the use of legal assistants enhances the quality of legal representation. Legal assistants enable the attorney to spend his or her more costly time for greater productivity in more important areas where judgment and decision-making are required. The availability of legal assistants also promotes more thorough trial preparation by permitting a more efficient and economical utilization of staff time. *Chapman v. Pacific Tel. & Tel. Co.,* 456 F.Supp. 77, 83 (N.D.Cal. 1978). *See also Todd Shipyards Corp. v. Director, Office of Workers' Compensation Programs,* 545 F.2d 1176, 1182 (9th Cir. 1976); *Beamon v. City of Ridgeland, Miss.,* 666 F.Supp. 937, 946 (S.D.Miss. 1987).

Law firms in the private marketplace routinely include an hourly rate charge for legal assistants as part of the attorney's fee charged fee-paying clients. Indeed, seventy-seven percent of 1,800 legal assistants responding to a recent survey indicated that their law firm received compensation for their work from clients on an hourly billing rate basis. National Association of Legal Assistants, Inc., 1988 National Utilization and Compensation Survey Report (1989). "Law firms, like other businesses that sell time, must set their hourly rates at an amount greater than that needed to pay their attorneys' or paralegals' salaries; they must figure into those rates all their costs of doing business." *In re Burlington Northern Inc. Employment Practices Litig.,* 810 F.2d 601, 609 (7th Cir. 1986), *cert. denied,* 108 S.Ct. 82 (1987). The hourly rate of legal assistants must reflect not only base salary, but also fringe benefits and a proportionate share of firm overhead.[8] Additionally, the routine practice of law firms seeking reimbursement for the work of legal assistants at a rate sufficient to cover both the "actual cost" and overhead costs associated with that legally related work is a fairer billing procedure.

> Unlike the work of secretaries and other supporting personnel, . . . the work of paralegals and law clerks is ordinarily charged directly to particular litigation and is therefore a clearly identifiable cost. Were it to be treated as an overhead expense, payable out of the general receipts of the attorney, the across-the-board cost of services to the attorney's clients generally would be burdened by paralegal costs incurred in connection with particular matters of no interest or benefit to other clients.

Chapman, 456 F.Supp. at 82.

Consistent with the private billing procedure, a majority of federal trial and appellate courts approve compensation for legal assistant work hours, as well as

---

[7] *See, e.g., Jacobs,* 825 F.2d at 563 Spray-Rite Serv. Corp., 684 F.2d at 1250; *Todd Shipyards Corp.,* 545 F.2d at 1182; *Shorter v. Valley Bank & Trust Co.,* 678 F.Supp. 714, 724 (N.D.Ill. 1988); *Royal Crown Cola Co. v. Coca-Cola Co.,* 678 F.Supp. 875, 880 (M.D.Ga. 1987); *Chapman v. Pacific Tel. & Tel. Co.,* 456 F.Supp. 77, 83 (N.D.Cal. 1978).

[8] *See Schwartz v. Novo Industri A/S,* 119 F.R.D. 359, 365 (S.D.N.Y. 1988) (citation omitted). *See also Williams v. Bowen,* 684 F.Supp. 1305, 1308 (E.D.Pa. 1988); *Garmong v. Montgomery County,* 668 F.Supp. 1000, 1011 (S.D.Tex. 1987); *Brewer v. Southern Union Co.,* 607 F.Supp. 1511, 1528 (D.Colo. 1984).

the legally related work of other non-attorneys such as law clerks, based upon a reasonable hourly rate set lower than the hourly rate of attorneys but higher than the "actual cost" and sufficient to defray the cost of overhead. *See Jacobs v. Mancuso,* 825 F.2d 559, 563 n.6 (1st Cir. 1987) (legal assistant expenses are most frequently reimbursed based on an hourly fee).[9] This Court, in *City of Riverside, supra,* approved an attorney's fee award which included compensation for time spent by a student law clerk, at the rate of twenty-five dollars an hour, clearly more than the actual wages paid to the individual, and obviously high enough to cover the overhead costs associated with the non-lawyer employee. *See* 477 U.S. at 566, 106 S.Ct. at 2690 & n.2.[10]

(c)   The inclusion of compensation for legal assistants in an attorney's fee award does not offend ethical and legal tenets prohibiting the unauthorized practice of law.

Any objection to including compensation for the supervised legally-related work of legal assistants in a reasonable attorney's fee award because legal assistants are not attorneys is but a "technical" one. The work performed by legal assistants is work of the type necessary to the prosecution of the litigation which would otherwise be performed by attorneys. Indeed, this Court has recognized the validity of non-lawyer personnel performing services of a legal nature. In *Procunier v. Martinez,* 416 U.S. 396 (1974), the Court affirmed the striking of a prison administrative rule banning attorney-client interviews conducted by law students or legal paraprofessionals as constituting an unjustified restriction on the right of access to the courts. The Court agreed with the trial court's finding that prohibiting the use of law students or other paraprofessionals from conducting attorney-client interviews with prisoners would inhibit adequate professional representation of indigent inmates, or alternately, increase the cost of legal representation for prisoners. *Id.* at 419–20. Likewise, in *Johnson v. Avery,* 393 U.S. 483 (1969), the Court struck down a prison regulation prohibiting any inmate from advising or assisting another in the preparation of legal documents. The Court noted that "the type of activity involved here—preparation of petitions for post-conviction relief—though historically and traditionally one which may benefit from the services of a trained

---

[9] *See also, e.g., Ustrak,* 851 F.2d 983; *Wilkett,* 844 F.2d at 877; *Save Our Cumberland Mountains, Inc.,* 826 F.2d at 54 n.7; *Tousaint,* 826 F.2d at 904; *Jacobs,* 825 F.2d at 563 & n.6; *In re "Agent Orange" Prod. Liab. Litig.,* 818 F.2d at 230, 238; *Lucero,* 815 F.2d at 1386; *In re Burlington Northern, Inc. Employment Practices Litig.,* 810 F.2d at 609; *Heath,* 807 F.2d at 1232; *Kopunec,* 801 F.2d at 1229; *Citizen's Council of Del. County,* 741 F.2d at 596; *Richardson,* 709 F.2d at 1023; *Louisville Black Police Officers Org., Inc. v. City of Louisville,* 700 F.2d 268, 273 (6th Cir. 1983); *Strama v. Peterson,* 689 F.2d 661, 663 (7th Cir. 1982); *Stewart v. Rhodes,* 656 F.2d at 1216–17; *Todd Shipyards Corp.,* 545 F.2d at 1182.

[10] To highlight the need for this Court's guidance, several courts have allowed the recovery of compensation for the work of legal assistants or law clerks based on an hourly-rate while at the same time calling it compensation for "expenses," rather than attorney's fees. *See In re "Agent Orange" Product Liab. Litig.,* 818 F.2d at 238; *Yaris v. Special School Dist. of St. Louis County,* 661 F.Supp. 996, 1002, 1003 n.9 (E.D.Mo. 1987); *PPG Industries, Inc. v. Celanese Polymer Specialties Co.,* 658 F.Supp. 555, 560, 565 (W.D.Ky. 1987), *rev'd on other grounds,* 840 F.2d 1565 (Fed.Cir. 1988). Some courts have held that law firms may only recover their paralegal "out of pocket" expenses, *see Thornberry,* 676 F.2d at 1244 (citing *Northcross,* 611 F.2d at 639), while others have permitted reimbursement for salary actually paid to a legal assistant, with no additional compensation for fringe benefits or overhead. *See, e.g., City of Detroit,* 495 F.2d at 473; *Illinois Migrant Council v. Pilliod,* 672 F.Supp. 1072, 1084 (N.D.Ill. 1987); *Campaign for a Progressive Bronx v. Black,* 631 F.Supp. 975, 983 (S.D.N.Y. 1986). Still others refuse to provide separate compensation for the work of legal assistants, taking the position that legal assistants represent overhead, such as clerical and office expenses, all covered by the attorney's hourly rate. *See Abrams v. Baylor College of Medicine,* 805 F.2d 528, 535 (5th Cir. 1986); *Roe v. City of Chicago,* 586 F.Supp. 513, 516 & n.6 (N.D.Ill. 1984).

and dedicated lawyer, is a function often, perhaps generally, performed by a layman." *Id.* at 490 n.11. *See also City of Riverside,* 477 U.S. at 566, 106 S.Ct. at 2690 (affirming attorney's fee award which included compensation for work performed by a law clerk).

Compensation for lawyer-supervised legally-related work performed by legal assistants conforms with the ethical canons and disciplinary codes governing lawyers and legal assistants. Lawyers are obligated to keep fees in check and take steps to provide efficient, cost-effective legal services. *See* ABA Model Code of Professional Responsibility EC 2-18 and DR 2-106(A)(B) (1976); ABA Model Rules of Professional Conduct, Rule 1.5(a) (1984). The delegation of tasks to lay persons is proper "if the lawyer maintains a direct relationship with his client, supervises the delegated work, and has complete professional responsibility for the work product. This delegation enables a lawyer to render legal services more economically and efficiently." Model Code EC 3–6. *See also* Model Rules, Rule 5.3.[11] Because the lawyer, or law firm, is the recipient of an attorney's fee for legal services and not the salaried legal assistant, the inclusion of compensation for the supervised work of a legal assistant as part of a reasonable attorney's fee does not offend ethical rules prohibiting attorneys from sharing legal fees with laymen. *See* Model Code EC 3-8 and DR 3-102.

Legal assistants recognize the ethical ramifications of their performance of legally-related work, and emphasize, in self-policing ethics codes and guidelines, that legal assistants shall not undertake tasks which are required to be performed by an attorney, such as setting fees, giving legal advice, or appearing in any way to a court, the client, or the public to be practicing law.[12] Additionally, the rules stress that all work of a legal nature performed by a legal assistant must be delegated and supervised by an attorney, who retains ultimate responsibility to the client and assumes full professional responsibility for the work product. National Association of Legal Assistants, Inc., Code of Ethics and Professional Responsibility (1975, as amended through 1988); National Association of Legal Assistants Model Standards and Guidelines for Utilization of Legal Assistants (1984) (both reprinted in full in the Appendix to this brief). It is the close supervision by an attorney which keeps the legally-related work of a legal assistant from treading upon the prohibited and unacceptable unauthorized practice of law, and makes the work of a legal assistant no more than an extension of the work of an attorney at a less costly rate.[13]

---

[11] The American Bar Association emphasizes that the work of a legal assistant "involves the performance, under the ultimate direction and supervision of an attorney, of specifically-delegated substantive legal work, which work, for the most part, requires a sufficient knowledge of legal concepts that, absent such assistance, the attorney would perform the task." ABA Standing Committee on Legal Assistants, Position Paper on the Question of Licensure or Certification (1986).

[12] Though the American Bar Association has shied away from defining what constitutes the practice of law, ABA Code of Professional Responsibility, it notes that "[f]unctionally, the practice of law relates to the rendition of services for others that call for the professional judgment of a lawyer." ABA Model Code of Professional Responsibility ED 3-5 (1976). Courts faced with the question have attempted to craft a definition. For example, the Florida Supreme Court has stated that the giving of advice and the performance of services which affect important rights of a person under the law, and require legal skill and knowledge of the law greater than that possessed by the average citizen, constitutes the practice of law. *The Florida Bar v. Brumbaugh,* 355 So.2d 1186, 1191 (Fla. 1978).

[13] Courts awarding attorney's fees for the supervised work of legal assistants have delineated examples of legal services which would otherwise be performed by an attorney, and thus which are compensable if performed by a legal assistant. They include: investigation of the facts relating to the action, *In re Gas Meters Antitrust Litig.,* 500 F.Supp. 956, 969 (E.D.Pa.1980); assisting with discovery, including such tasks as statistical and financial analysis, inspection and production of documents, review of answers to interrogatories, and the compilation of statistical and financial data, *Bagel Inn, Inc. v. All Star Dairies,*

(d)   Courts scrutinize attorney's fee applications to assure the hourly rates of legal assistants and the time spent and nature of the work performed by legal assistants are all reasonable.

Courts compensating for the work performed by a legal assistant in connection with the award of a reasonable attorney's fee scrutinize the reported hours, the suggested rate, and the nature of the work performed in the same manner they scrutinize lawyer time and rates. *See Pennsylvania I,* 478 U.S. at 565, 106 S.Ct. at 3098; *Hensley v. Eckerhart,* 461 U.S. 424, 434 (1983); *Ramos,* 713 F.2d at 559. Trial courts determine what portion of the work is of a clerical nature and is thus absorbed as part of the office overhead reflected in the attorney's billing rate and what portion of the work performed by the legal assistant constitutes legal services traditionally done by an attorney and which would otherwise be performed by an attorney at a costlier rate. *Ramos,* 713 F.2d at 558; *Richardson v. Byrd,* 709 F.2d 1016, 1023 (5th Cir.), *cert. denied,* 464 U.S. 1009 (1983). "Such expenses are separately recoverable only as part of a prevailing party's award for attorney's fees and expenses, and even then only to the extent that the paralegal performs work traditionally done by an attorney. Otherwise, paralegal expenses are separately unrecoverable overhead expenses." *Allen v. United States Steel Corp.,* 665 F.2d 689, 697 (5th Cir. Unit B 1982).

Indeed, when considering a reasonable attorney's fee award, courts have chastised attorneys for doing work which more properly could have been delegated to a legal assistant under the attorney's supervision, and have penalized the attorney by lowering the hourly rate charged.

It is appropriate to distinguish between legal work, in the strict sense, and investigation, clerical work, compilation of facts and statistics and other work which can often be accomplished by non-lawyers but which a lawyer may do because he has no other help available. Such non-legal work may command a lesser rate. Its dollar value is not enhanced just because a lawyer does it.

Johnson v. Georgia Highway Express, Inc., 488 F.2d 714, 717 (5th Cir.1974). Wasteful utilization of expensive legal talent for work that may be delegated to non-lawyers is not condoned. "Routine tasks, if performed by senior partners in large firms, should not be billed at their usual rates. A Michelangelo should not charge Sistine Chapel rates for painting a farmer's barn." *Ursic v. Bethlehem Mines,* 719 F.2d 670, 677 (3d. Cir.1983). Accordingly, courts regularly reduce an attorney's hourly rate

---

539 F.Supp. 107, 111 (D.N.J.1982); *In re Gas Meters Antitrust Litig.,* 500 F.Supp. at 967; *see also, e.g., Richardson,* 709 F.2d at 1023; *Spray-Rite Service Corp.,* 684 F.2d at 1250; doing legal research, *Morgan v. Nevada Board of State Prison Comm'rs,* 615 F.Supp. 882, 885 (D.Nev.1985); locating and interviewing witnesses, *Richardson,* 709 F.2d at 1023; *Garmong,* 668 F.Supp. at 1011; organizing and communicating with class members, *Richardson, supra; Edmonds v. United States,* 658 F.Supp. 1126, 1136 (D.S.C.1987); *In re Gas Meters Antitrust Litig.,* 500 F.Supp. at 970; assisting with preparation for depositions and trial, and organizing exhibits, *Easter House v. State of Illinois, Dept. of Children and Family Services,* 663 F.Supp. 456, 460 (N.D.Ill. 1987); *In re Gas Meters Antitrust Litig.,* 500 F.Supp. at 972; assisting with preparation of settlement and settlement administration, *In re Chicken Antitrust Litig.,* 560 F.Supp. 963, 978 (N.D.Ga.1980); *In re Gas Meters Antitrust Litig.,* 500 F.Supp. at 967, 972; compiling statistical and financial data, *Bagel Inn, Inc.,* 539 F.Supp. at 111; drafting pleadings, *Parise v. Riccilli Haulers, Inc.,* 672 F.Supp. 72, 75 (N.D.N.Y.1987); *In re Gas Meters Antitrust Litig.,* 500 F.Supp. at 969; and checking legal citations, *Beamon v. City of Ridgeland, Miss.,* 66 F.Supp. 937, 943 (S.D.Miss.1987).

to that traditionally charged for a legal assistant, to reflect the nature of the legal work performed.[14]

    (e)   Permitting recovery for work of legal assistants promotes the availability of legal representation to victims of civil rights violations.

If the lawyer attempts to absorb the cost of the legal assistant into his or her regular hourly rate as an overhead expense, as is done for clerical work and office supplies, or to absorb the overhead costs associated with the work of a legal assistant, then all persons employing that attorney, including victims of civil rights violations, would suffer a higher hourly rate, regardless of whether their case necessitated the assistance of a legal assistant. More likely, the work currently performed by legal assistants would be done by attorney associates and billed at the higher attorney associate rate, clearly decreasing the utilization of legal assistants and increasing the cost of litigation. The attorney performing legal tasks which could be delegated to a legal assistant, however, faces the risk that his or her fee will be reduced by a court as being unreasonably high for the quality of work performed. The only remaining alternative would be for the attorney to perform the work at a reduced rate, below and not competitive with the market rate. Such a result would make the representation of victims of civil rights violations cost prohibitive and unattractive, and discourage competent, experienced attorneys from undertaking such representation because they could not receive full compensation for their efforts.

The widespread practice of assigning less technical yet legal work to legal assistants to be performed under the supervision of an attorney promotes economy and efficiency in the administration of justice. Permitting reasonable compensation for such services at the market rate as part of a reasonable attorney's fee encourages this desirable practice, and makes legal representation more readily available to victims of civil rights violations, in accord with Congress' intent when adopting the Civil Rights Attorney's Fee Awards Act of 1976, 43 U.S.C. § 1988.

Conclusion

For the reasons set forth above, the National Association of Legal Assistants, Inc., as *amicus curiae,* respectfully urges the Court to affirm the decision of the Court of Appeals for the Eighth Circuit and permit recovery for the work of legal assistants at the market rate as part of a reasonable attorney's fee award made pursuant to 42 U.S.C. § 1988.

Respectfully submitted,

JOHN A. DEVAULT, III
Counsel of Record

---

[14] *See, e.g., Pennsylvania v. Delaware Valley Citizen's Council for Clean Air,* 478 U.S. 546, 553, 567, 106 S.Ct. 3088, 3092 (1986) ("*Pennsylvania I*") (approving a lodestar which set different hourly rates for legal work requiring varying degrees of legal ability); *Dagget v. Kimmelman,* 811 F.2d at 799 (attorney hours devoted to tasks which should have been performed by associates or paralegals would warrant an hourly fee reduction); *Northcross,* 611 F.2d at 637, (necessary services performed by attorneys which could have reasonably been performed by less expensive personnel may be compensated at a lower rate than attorney's normal billing rate); *Drez v. E. R. Squibb & Sons, Inc.,* 674 F.Supp. 1432 (D.Kan.1987) (dropping attorney billing rate to law clerk rate where three attorneys sat through trial); *Beamon,* 666 F.Supp. at 941-42 (attorney fees for purely clerical work which is easily delegable granted at reduced hourly rate); *Skelton v. General Motors Corp.,* 661 F.Supp.1368, 1385 (N.D.Ill.1987) (court reduces time of attorney spent on administrative tasks); *Metro Data Systems, Inc. v. Durango Systems, Inc.,* 597 F.Supp.244, 246 (D.Ariz.1984) (gathering information and drafting answers to interrogatories not recoverable by attorney as work which could have been performed by paralegal).

JANE A. LESTER
Counsel
BEDELL, DITTMAR, DEVAULT
& PILLANS, P.A.
The Bedell Building
101 East Adams Street
Jacksonville, FL 32202
(904) 353-0211

For *Amicus Curiae*
National Association of Legal Assistants, Inc.

National Association of Legal Assistants, Inc. Code of Ethics and Professional Responsibility

It is the responsibility of every legal assistant to adhere strictly to the accepted standards of legal ethics and to live by general principles of proper conduct. The performance of the duties of the legal assistant shall be governed by specific canons as defined herein in order that justice will be served and the goals of the profession attained. The canons of ethics set forth hereafter are adopted by the National Association of Legal Assistants, Inc., as a general guide and the enumeration of these rules does not mean there are not others of equal importance although not specifically mentioned.

Canon 1. A legal assistant shall not perform any of the duties that lawyers only may perform nor do things that lawyers themselves may not do.

Canon 2. A legal assistant may perform any task delegated and supervised by a lawyer so long as the lawyer is responsible to the client, maintains a direct relationship with the client, and assumes full professional responsibility for the work product.

Canon 3. A legal assistant shall not engage in the practice of law by accepting cases, setting fees, giving legal advice or appearing in court (unless otherwise authorized by court or agency rules).

Canon 4. A legal assistant shall not act in matters involving professional legal judgment as the services of a lawyer are essential in the public interest whenever the exercise of such judgment is required.

Canon 5. A legal assistant must act prudently in determining the extent to which a client may be assisted without the presence of a lawyer.

Canon 6. A legal assistant shall not engage in the unauthorized practice of law.

Canon 7. A legal assistant must protect the confidence of a client, and it shall be unethical for a legal assistant to violate any statute now in effect or hereafter to be enacted controlling privileged communications.

Canon 8. It is the obligation of the legal assistant to avoid conduct which would cause the lawyer to be unethical or even appear to be unethical and loyalty to the employer is incumbent upon the legal assistant.

Canon 9. A legal assistant shall work continually to maintain integrity and a high degree of competency throughout the legal profession.

Canon 10. A legal assistant shall strive for perfection through education in order to better assist the legal profession in fulfilling its duty of making legal services available to clients and the public.

Canon 11. A legal assistant shall do all things incidental, necessary or expedient for the attainment of the ethics and responsibilities imposed by statute or rule of court.

Canon 12. A legal assistant is governed by the American Bar Association Model Code of Professional Responsibility, and the American Bar Association Model Rules of Professional Conduct.

National Association of Legal Assistants, Inc. Model Standards and Guidelines for Utilization of Legal Assistants

Preamble
Proper utilization of the services of legal assistants affects the efficient delivery of legal services. Legal assistants and the legal profession should be assured that some measures exist for identifying legal assistants and their role in assisting attorneys in the delivery of legal services. Therefore, the National Association of Legal Assistants, Inc., hereby adopts these Model Standards and Guidelines as an educational document for the benefit of legal assistants and the legal profession.

Definition
Legal assistants* are a distinguishable group of persons who assist attorneys in the delivery of legal services. Through formal education, training, and experience, legal assistants have knowledge and expertise regarding the legal system and substantive and procedural law which qualify them to do work of a legal nature under the supervision of an attorney.

Standards
A legal assistant should meet certain minimum qualifications. The following standards may be used to determine an individual's qualifications as a legal assistant:

1. Successful completion of the Certified Legal Assistant ("CLA") examination of the National Association of Legal Assistants, Inc. (see attached Exhibit A);
2. Graduation from an ABA approved program of study for legal assistants;
3. Graduation from a course of study for legal assistants which is institutionally accredited but not ABA approved, and which requires not less than the equivalent of 60 semester hours of classroom study;
4. Graduation from a course of study for legal assistants, other than those set forth in (2) and (3) above, plus not less than six months of in-house training as a legal assistant;
5. A baccalaureate degree in any field, plus not less than six months in-house training as a legal assistant;
6. A minimum of three years of law-related experience under the supervision of an attorney, including at least six months of in-house training as a legal assistant; or
7. Two years of in-house training as a legal assistant.

---

* Within this occupational category, some individuals are known as paralegals.

For purposes of these standards, "in-house training as a legal assistant" means attorney education of the employee concerning legal assistant duties and these guidelines. In addition to review and analysis of assignments, the legal assistant should receive a reasonable amount of instruction directly related to the duties and obligations of the legal assistant.

Guidelines

These guidelines relating to standards of performance and professional responsibility are intended to aid legal assistants and attorneys. The responsibility rests with an attorney who employs legal assistants to educate them with respect to the duties they are assigned and to supervise the manner in which such duties are accomplished.

Legal assistants should:

1. Disclose their status as legal assistants at the outset of any professional relationships with a client, other attorneys, a court or administrative agency or personnel thereof, or members of the general public;
2. Preserve the confidences and secrets of all clients; and
3. Understand the attorney's Code of Professional Responsibility and these guidelines in order to avoid any action which would involve the attorney in a violation of that Code, or give the appearance of professional impropriety.

Legal assistants should not:

1. Establish attorney-client relationships; set legal fees; give legal opinions or advice; or represent a client before a court; nor
2. Engage in, encourage, or contribute to any act which could constitute the unauthorized practice of law.

Legal assistants may perform services for an attorney in the representation of a client, provided:

1. The services performed by the legal assistant do not require the exercise of independent professional legal judgment;
2. The attorney maintains a direct relationship with the client and maintains control of all client matters;
3. The attorney supervises the legal assistant;
4. The attorney remains professionally responsible for all work on behalf of the client, including any actions taken or not taken by the legal assistant in connection therewith; and
5. The services performed supplement, merge with and become the attorney's work product.

In the supervision of a legal assistant, consideration should be given to:

1. Designating work assignments that correspond to the legal assistant's abilities, knowledge, training and experience;
2. Educating and training the legal assistant with respect to professional responsibility, local rules and practices, and firm policies;
3. Monitoring the work and professional conduct of the legal assistant to ensure that the work is substantively correct and timely performed;
4. Providing continuing education for the legal assistant in substantive matters through courses, institutes, workshops, seminars and in-house training; and

5. Encouraging and supporting membership and active participation in professional organizations.

Except as otherwise provided by statute, court rule or decision, administrative rule or regulation, or the attorney's Code of Professional Responsibility, and within the preceding parameters and proscriptions, a legal assistant may perform any function delegated by an attorney, including, but not limited to the following:

1. Conduct client interviews and maintain general contact with the client after the establishment of the attorney-client relationship, so long as the client is aware of the status and function of the legal assistant, and the client contact is under the supervision of the attorney.
2. Locate and interview witnesses, so long as the witnesses are aware of the status and function of the legal assistant.
3. Conduct investigations and statistical and documentary research for review by the attorney.
4. Conduct legal research for review by the attorney.
5. Draft legal documents for review by the attorney.
6. Draft correspondence and pleadings for review by and signature of the attorney.
7. Summarize depositions, interrogatories, and testimony for review by the attorney.
8. Attend executions of wills, real estate closings, depositions, court or administrative hearings and trials with the attorney.
9. Author and sign letters provided the legal assistant's status is clearly indicated and the correspondence does not contain independent legal opinions or legal advice.

Comment

The United States Supreme Court has recognized the variety of tasks being performed by legal assistants and has noted that use of legal assistants encourages cost effective delivery of legal services, *Missouri v. Jenkins,* 491 U.S. 274, 109 S.Ct. 2463, 2471, no. 10 (1989). In *Jenkins,* the court further held that legal assistant time should be included in compensation for attorney fee awards at the prevailing market rate if it is shown to be prevailing practice in the relevant community to bill legal assistant time.

Except for the specific proscription contained in Section 6, the reported cases such as *Attorney Grievance Commission of Maryland v. Goldberg, supra,* do not limit the duties which may be performed by a legal assistant under the supervision of the attorney.

The Guidelines were developed from generally accepted practices. Each supervision attorney must be aware of the specific rules, decisions and statutes applicable to legal assistants within his jurisdiction.

Exhibit A

To become eligible to sit for the NALA certifying examination ("CLA"), candidates must meet one of the following requirements:

1. Graduation from a legal assistant program that is:
   a) Approved by the American Bar Association, or
   b) An associate degree program, or
   c) A post-baccalaureate certificate program in legal studies, or
   d) A bachelor's degree program in legal assistant studies, or
   e) A legal assistant program which consists of a minimum of 60 semester (or equivalent quarter)* hours of which at least 15 semester hours (or equivalent quarter hours)** are substantive legal courses.

   *900 clock hours of a legal assistant program will be considered equivalent to 60 semester hours.

   90 quarter hours of a legal assistant program will be considered equivalent to 60 semester hours.

   **225 clock hours of substantive legal courses will be considered equivalent to 15 semester hours.

   22½ quarter hours of legal courses will be considered equivalent to 15 semester hours.

2. A bachelor's degree in any field plus one (1) year's experience as a legal assistant.*

   *Successful completion of at least 15 semester hours (or 22½ quarter hours or 225 clock hours) of substantive legal courses will be considered equivalent to one year experience as a legal assistant.

3. A high school diploma or equivalent plus seven (7) years' experience as a legal assistant under the supervision of a member of the Bar plus evidence of a minimum of twenty (20) hours of continuing legal education credit to have been completed within a two-year period prior to the examination date.

The Court's Opinion: *Missouri v. Jenkins,*
109 S.Ct. 2463 (1989)

MISSOURI, et al., Petitioners

v.

**Kalima JENKINS, by her friend,
Kamau AGYEI, et al.**

No. 88–64.

Argued Feb. 21, 1989.

Decided June 19, 1989.

Prevailing plaintiffs in school desegregation case sought recovery of attorney fees. The United States District Court for the Western District of Missouri, Russell G. Clark, J., awarded attorney fees, and appeal was taken. The Court of Appeals for the Eighth Circuit, 838 F.2d 260, affirmed. On grant of certiorari, the Supreme Court, Justice Brennan, held that: (1) Eleventh Amendment did not prohibit enhancement of fee award under Civil Rights Attorney's Fees Awards Act against state to compensate for delay in payment, and (2) separate compensation award under Civil Rights Attorney's Fees Awards Act for paralegals, law clerks, and recent law school graduates at prevailing rates was fully in accord with Act.

Affirmed.

Justice O'Connor concurred in part and dissented in part and filed opinion in which Justice Scalia joined and Chief Justice Rehnquist joined in part.

Justice Rehnquist filed dissenting opinion.

Justice Marshall did not participate.

1. Federal Courts ☞265

Award of attorney fees ancillary to prospective relief in civil rights action is not subject to strictures of Eleventh Amendment. U.S.C.A. Const.Amend. 11; 42 U.S.C.A. § 1988.

2. Federal Courts ☞265

Not only is award of attorney fees in civil rights action beyond reach of Eleventh Amendment, so also is question of how

reasonable attorney fee is to be calculated. U.S.C.A. Const.Amend. 11; 42 U.S.C.A. § 1988.

3. Federal Courts ☞265

Eleventh Amendment does not prohibit enhancement of fee award under Civil Rights Attorney's Fees Awards Act against state to compensate for delay in payment. 42 U.S.C.A. § 1988; U.S.C.A. Const.Amend. 11.

4. Civil Rights ☞13.17(20)

Attorney fees under Civil Rights Attorney's Fees Awards Act are to be based on market rates for services rendered. 42 U.S.C.A. § 1988.

5. Civil Rights ☞13.17(19)

Appropriate adjustment for delay in payment—whether by application of current rather than historic hourly rates or otherwise—is within contemplation of Civil Rights Attorney's Fees Awards Act. 42 U.S.C.A. § 1988.

6. Civil Rights ☞13.17(19)
Federal Courts ☞265

Eleventh Amendment has no application to award of attorney fees, ancillary to grant of prospective relief, against state; thus, it follows that same is true for calculation of amount of fee, and adjustment for delay in payment is appropriate factor in determination of what is reasonable attorney fee under Civil Rights Attorney's Fees Awards Act. 42 U.S.C.A. § 1988; U.S.C.A. Const.Amend. 11.

7. Civil Rights ☞13.17(18)

Phrase "reasonable attorney's fee" in civil rights attorney fees statute does not refer only to work performed personally by members of bar; rather, term refers to reasonable fee for work product of attorney, and thus, to work of paralegals as well as that of attorneys. 42 U.S.C.A. § 1988.

See publication Words and Phrases for other judicial constructions and definitions.

8. Civil Rights ☞13.17(20)

Reasonable attorney fee under Civil Rights Attorney's Fees Awards Act is one calculated on basis of rates and practices prevailing in relevant market, and one that grants successful civil rights plaintiff fully compensatory fee, comparable to what is traditional with attorneys compensated by fee-paying client. 42 U.S.C.A. § 1988.

9. Civil Rights ☞13.17(20)

Separate compensation award under Civil Rights Attorney's Fees Awards Act for paralegals, law clerks, and recent law school graduates at prevailing rates was fully in accord with Act, where prevailing practice in area was to bill paralegal work at market rates. 42 U.S.C.A. § 1988.

Syllabus *

In this major school desegregation litigation in Kansas City, Missouri, in which various desegregation remedies were granted against the State of Missouri and other defendants, the plaintiff class was represented by a Kansas City lawyer (Benson) and by the NAACP Legal Defense and Educational Fund, Inc. (LDF). Benson and the LDF requested attorney's fees under the Civil Rights Attorney's Fees Awards Act of 1976 (42 U.S.C. § 1988), which provides with respect to such litigation that the court, in its discretion, may allow the prevailing party, other than the United States, "a reasonable attorney's fee as part of the costs." In calculating the hourly rates for Benson's, his associates', and the LDF attorneys' fees, the District Court took account of delay in payment by using current market rates rather than those applicable at the time the services were rendered. Both Benson and the LDF employed numerous paralegals, law clerks, and recent law graduates, and the court awarded fees for their work based on market rates, again using current rather than historic rates in order to compensate for the delay in payment.

---

* The syllabus constitutes no part of the opinion of the Court but has been prepared by the Reporter of Decisions for the convenience of the

Held:

1. The Eleventh Amendment does not prohibit enhancement of a fee award under § 1988 against a State to compensate for delay in payment. That Amendment has no application to an award of attorney's fees, ancillary to a grant of prospective relief, against a State, *Hutto v. Finney*, 437 U.S. 678, 98 S.Ct. 2565, 57 L.Ed.2d 522, and it follows that the same is true for the calculation of the *amount* of the fee. An adjustment for delay in payment is an appropriate factor in determining what constitutes a reasonable attorney's fee under § 1988. Pp. 2466–2469.

2. The District Court correctly compensated the work of paralegals, law clerks, and recent law graduates at the market rates for their services, rather than at their cost to the attorneys. Clearly, "a reasonable attorney's fee" as used in § 1988 cannot have been meant to compensate only work performed personally by members of the Bar. Rather, that term must refer to a reasonable fee for an attorney's work product, and thus must take into account the work not only of attorneys, but also the work of paralegals and the like. A reasonable attorney's fee under § 1988 is one calculated on the basis of rates and practices prevailing in the relevant market and one that grants the successful civil rights plaintiff a "fully compensatory fee," comparable to what "is traditional with attorneys compensated by a fee-paying client." In this case, where the practice in the relevant market is to bill the work of paralegals separately, the District Court's decision to award separate compensation for paralegals, law clerks, and recent law graduates at prevailing market rates was fully in accord with § 1988. Pp. 2469–2472.

838 F.2d 260 (CA8 1988), affirmed.

BRENNAN, J., delivered the opinion of the Court, in which WHITE, BLACK-

reader. See *United States v. Detroit Lumber Co.*, 200 U.S. 321, 337, 26 S.Ct. 282, 237, 50 L.Ed. 499.

MISSOURI v. JENKINS BY AGYEI 2465
Cite as 109 S.Ct. 2463 (1989)

MUN, STEVENS, and KENNEDY, JJ., joined, and in Parts I and III of which O'CONNOR and SCALIA, JJ., joined. O'CONNOR, J., filed an opinion concurring in part and dissenting in part, in which SCALIA, J., joined and REHNQUIST, C.J., joined in part. REHNQUIST, C.J., filed a dissenting opinion. MARSHALL, J., took no part in the consideration or decision of the case.

——————

Bruce Farmer, Jefferson City, Mo., for petitioners.

Jay Topkis, New York City, Russell E. Lovell, II, Des Moines, Iowa, for respondents.

Justice BRENNAN delivered the opinion of the Court.

This is the attorney's-fee aftermath of major school desegregation litigation in Kansas City, Missouri. We granted certiorari, 488 U.S. ——, 109 S.Ct. 218, 102 L.Ed. 2d 209 (1988), to resolve two questions relating to fees litigation under 42 U.S.C. § 1988. First, does the Eleventh Amendment prohibit enhancement of a fee award against a State to compensate for delay in payment? Second, should the fee award compensate the work of paralegals and law clerks by applying the market rate for their work?

I

This litigation began in 1977 as a suit by the Kansas City Missouri School District (KCMSD), the School Board, and the children of two School Board members, against the State of Missouri and other defendants. The plaintiffs alleged that the State, surrounding school districts, and various federal agencies had caused and perpetuated a system of racial segregation in the schools of the Kansas City metropolitan area. They sought various desegregation reme-

dies. KCMSD was subsequently realigned as a nominal defendant, and a class of present and future KCMSD students was certified as plaintiffs. After lengthy proceedings, including a trial that lasted 7½ months during 1983 and 1984, the District Court found the State of Missouri and KCMSD liable, while dismissing the suburban school districts and the federal defendants. It ordered various intradistrict remedies, to be paid for by the State and KCMSD, including $260 million in capital improvements and a magnet-school plan costing over $200 million. See *Jenkins v. Missouri*, 807 F.2d 657 (CA8 1986) (en banc), cert. denied, 484 U.S. 816 (1987); *Jenkins v. Missouri*, 855 F.2d 1295 (CA8 1988), cert. granted, 490 U.S. ——, 109 S.Ct. 1930, —— L.Ed.2d —— (1989).

The plaintiff class has been represented, since 1979, by Kansas City lawyer Arthur Benson and, since 1982, by the NAACP Legal Defense and Educational Fund, Inc. (LDF). Benson and the LDF requested attorney's fees under the Civil Rights Attorney's Fees Awards Act of 1976, 42 U.S. C. § 1988.[1] Benson and his associates had devoted 10,875 attorney hours to the litigation, as well as 8,108 hours of paralegal and law clerk time. For the LDF the corresponding figures were 10,854 hours for attorneys and 15,517 hours for paralegals and law clerks. Their fee applications deleted from these totals 3,628 attorney hours and 7,046 paralegal hours allocable to unsuccessful claims against the suburban school districts. With additions for post-judgment monitoring and for preparation of the fee application, the District Court awarded Benson a total of approximately $1.7 million and the LDF $2.3 million. App. to Pet. for Cert. A22–A43.

In calculating the hourly rate for Benson's fees the court noted that the market rate in Kansas City for attorneys of Ben-

---

1. Section 1988 provides in relevant part: "In any action or proceeding to enforce a provision of sections 1981, 1982, 1983, 1985, and 1986 of this title, title IX of Public Law 92–318 [20 U.S.C. 1681 et seq.], or title VI of the Civil

Rights Act of 1964 [42 U.S.C. 2000d et seq.], the court, in its discretion, may allow the prevailing party, other than the United States, a reasonable attorney's fee as part of the costs."

son's qualifications was in the range of $125 to $175 per hour, and found that "Mr. Benson's rate would fall at the higher end of this range based upon his expertise in the area of civil rights." *Id.*, at A26. It calculated his fees on the basis of an even higher hourly rate of $200, however, because of three additional factors: the preclusion of other employment, the undesirability of the case, and the delay in payment for Benson's services. *Id.*, at A26–A27. The court also took account of the delay in payment in setting the rates for several of Benson's associates by using current market rates rather than those applicable at the time the services were rendered. *Id.*, at A28–A30. For the same reason, it calculated the fees for the LDF attorneys at current market rates. *Id.*, at A33.

Both Benson and the LDF employed numerous paralegals, law clerks (generally law students working part-time), and recent law graduates in this litigation. The court awarded fees for their work based on Kansas City market rates for those categories. As in the case of the attorneys, it used current rather than historic market rates in order to compensate for the delay in payment. It therefore awarded fees based on hourly rates of $35 for law clerks, $40 for paralegals, and $50 for recent law graduates. *Id.*, at A29–A31, A34. The Court of Appeals affirmed in all respects. 838 F.2d 260 (CA8 1988).

II

Our grant of certiorari extends to two issues raised by the State of Missouri. Missouri first contends that a State cannot, consistent with the principle of sovereign immunity this Court has found embodied in the Eleventh Amendment, be compelled to pay an attorney's fee enhanced to compensate for delay in payment. This question requires us to examine the intersection of two of our precedents, *Hutto v. Finney*,

437 U.S. 678, 98 S.Ct. 2565, 57 L.Ed.2d 522 (1978), and *Library of Congress v. Shaw*, 478 U.S. 310, 106 S.Ct. 2957, 92 L.Ed.2d 250 (1986).[2]

In *Hutto v. Finney* the lower courts had awarded attorney's fees against the State of Arkansas, in part pursuant to § 1988, in connection with litigation over the conditions of confinement in that State's prisons. The State contended that any such award was subject to the Eleventh Amendment's constraints on actions for damages payable from a State's treasury. We relied, in rejecting that contention, on the distinction drawn in our earlier cases between "retroactive monetary relief" and "prospective injunctive relief." See *Edelman v. Jordan*, 415 U.S. 651, 94 S.Ct. 1347, 39 L.Ed.2d 662 (1974); *Ex parte Young*, 209 U.S. 123, 28 S.Ct. 441, 52 L.Ed. 714 (1908). Attorney's fees, we held, belonged to the latter category, because they constituted reimbursement of "expenses incurred in litigation seeking only prospective relief," rather than "retroactive liability for prelitigation conduct." *Hutto*, 437 U.S., at 695, 98 S.Ct., at 2576; see also *id.*, at 690, 98 S.Ct., at 2573. We explained: "Unlike ordinary 'retroactive' relief such as damages or restitution, an award of costs does not compensate the plaintiff for the injury that first brought him into court. Instead, the award reimburses him for a portion of the expenses he incurred in seeking prospective relief." *Id.*, at 695, n. 24, 98 S.Ct., at 2576, n. 24. Section 1988, we noted, fit easily into the longstanding practice of awarding "costs" against States, for the statute imposed the award of attorney's fees "as part of the costs." *Id.*, at 695–696, 98 S.Ct., at 2576, citing *Fairmont Creamery Co. v. Minnesota*, 275 U.S. 70, 48 S.Ct. 97, 72 L.Ed. 168 (1927).

[1, 2] After *Hutto*, therefore, it must be accepted as settled that an award of attorney's fees ancillary to prospective relief is

2. The holding of the Court of Appeals on this point, 838 F.2d, at 265–266, is in conflict with the resolution of the same question in *Rogers v. Okin*, 821 F.2d 22, 26–28 (CA1 1987), cert. de-

nied *sub nom. Commissioner, Massachusetts Dept. of Mental Health v. Rogers*, 484 U.S. 1010, 108 S.Ct. 709, 98 L.Ed.2d 660 (1988).

MISSOURI v. JENKINS BY AGYEI

not subject to the strictures of the Eleventh Amendment. And if the principle of making such an award is beyond the reach of the Eleventh Amendment, the same must also be true for the question of how a "reasonable attorney's fee" is to be calculated. See *Hutto, supra,* 437 U.S., at 696–697, 98 S.Ct., at 2576–2577.

Missouri contends, however, that the principle enunciated in *Hutto* has been undermined by subsequent decisions of this Court that require Congress to "express its intention to abrogate the Eleventh Amendment in unmistakable language in the statute itself." *Atascadero State Hospital v. Scanlon,* 473 U.S. 234, 243, 105 S.Ct. 3142, 3148, 87 L.Ed.2d 171 (1985); *Welch v. Texas Dept. of Highways and Public Transportation,* 483 U.S. 468, 107 S.Ct. 2941, 97 L.Ed.2d 389 (1987). See also *Dellmuth v. Muth,* 491 U.S. ——, —— S.Ct. ——, —— L.Ed.2d —— (1989); *Pennsylvania v. Union Gas Co.,* 491 U.S. ——, —— S.Ct. ——, —— L.Ed.2d —— (1989). The flaw in this argument lies in its misreading of the holding of *Hutto.* It is true that in *Hutto* we noted that Congress could, in the exercise of its enforcement power under § 5 of the Fourteenth Amendment, set aside the States' immunity from retroactive damages, 437 U.S., at 693, 98 S.Ct., at 2574–75, citing *Fitzpatrick v. Bitzer,* 427 U.S. 445, 96 S.Ct. 2666, 49 L.Ed.2d 614 (1976), and that Congress intended to do so in enacting § 1988. 437 U.S., at 693–694, 98 S.Ct., at 2574–2575. But we also made clear that the application of § 1988 to the States did not depend on congressional abrogation of the States' immunity. We did so in rejecting precisely the "clear statement" argument that Missouri now suggests has undermined *Hutto.* Arkansas had argued that § 1988 did not plainly abrogate the States' immunity; citing *Employees v. Missouri Dept. of Public Health and Welfare,* 411 U.S. 279, 93 S.Ct. 1614, 36 L.Ed.2d 251 (1973), and *Edelman v. Jordan, supra,* the State contended that "retroactive liability" could not be imposed on the States "in the absence of an extraordinarily explicit statutory mandate." *Hutto,* 437 U.S., at 695, 98 S.Ct., at 2576. We responded as follows: "[T]hese cases [*Employees* and *Edelman*] concern retroactive liability for prelitigation conduct rather than expenses incurred in litigation seeking only prospective relief. The Act imposes attorney's fees 'as part of the costs.' Costs have traditionally been awarded without regard for the States' Eleventh Amendment immunity." *Ibid.*

The holding of *Hutto,* therefore, was not just that Congress had spoken sufficiently clearly to overcome Eleventh Amendment immunity in enacting § 1988, but rather that the Eleventh Amendment did not apply to an award of attorney's fees ancillary to a grant of prospective relief. See *Maine v. Thiboutot,* 448 U.S. 1, 9, n. 7, 100 S.Ct. 2502, 2507, n. 7, 65 L.Ed.2d 555 (1980). That holding is unaffected by our subsequent jurisprudence concerning the degree of clarity with which Congress must speak in order to override Eleventh Amendment immunity, and we reaffirm it today.

[3] Missouri's other line of argument is based on our decision in *Library of Congress v. Shaw, supra. Shaw* involved an application of the longstanding "no-interest rule," under which interest cannot be awarded against the United States unless it has expressly waived its sovereign immunity. We held that while Congress, in making the Federal Government a potential defendant under Title VII of the Civil Rights Act of 1964, had waived the United States' immunity from suit and from costs including reasonable attorney's fees, it had not waived the Federal Government's traditional immunity from any award of interest. We thus held impermissible a 30 percent increase in the "lodestar" fee to compensate for delay in payment. Because we refused to find in the language of § 1988 a waiver of the United States' immunity from interest, Missouri argues, we should likewise conclude that § 1988 is not sufficiently explicit to constitute an abrogation of the States' immunity under the Eleventh Amendment in regard to any award of interest.

The answer to this contention is already clear from what we have said about *Hutto v. Finney*. Since, as we held in *Hutto*, the Eleventh Amendment does not bar an award of attorney's fees ancillary to a grant of prospective relief, our holding in *Shaw* has no application, even by analogy.[3] There is no need in this case to determine whether Congress has spoken sufficiently clearly to meet a "clear statement" requirement, and it is therefore irrelevant whether the Eleventh Amendment standard should be, as Missouri contends, as stringent as the one we applied for purposes of the no-interest rule in *Shaw*. Rather, the issue here—whether the "reasonable attorney's fee" provided for in § 1988 should be calculated in such a manner as to include an enhancement, where appropriate, for delay in payment—is a straightforward matter of statutory interpretation. For this question, it is of no relevance whether the party against which fees are awarded is a State. The question is what Congress intended—not whether it manifested "the clear affirmative intent ... to waive the sovereign's immunity." *Shaw*, 478 U.S., at 321, 106 S.Ct. at 2965.[4]

This question is not a difficult one. We have previously explained, albeit in dicta, why an enhancement for delay in payment

is, where appropriate, part of a "reasonable attorney's fee." In *Pennsylvania v. Delaware Valley Citizens' Council*, 483 U.S. 711, 107 S.Ct. 3078, 97 L.Ed.2d 585 (1987), we rejected an argument that a prevailing party was entitled to a fee augmentation to compensate for the risk of nonpayment. But we took care to distinguish that risk from the factor of delay:

"First is the matter of delay. When plaintiffs' entitlement to attorney's fees depends on success, their lawyers are not paid until a favorable decision finally eventuates, which may be years later.... Meanwhile, their expenses of doing business continue and must be met. In setting fees for prevailing counsel, the courts have regularly recognized the delay factor, either by basing the award on current rates or by adjusting the fee based on historical rates to reflect its present value. See, *e.g.*, *Sierra Club v. EPA*, 248 U.S.App.D.C. 107, 120–121, 769 F.2d 796, 809–810 (1985); *Louisville Black Police Officers Organization, Inc. v. Louisville*, 700 F.2d 268, 276, 281 (CA6 1983). Although delay and the risk of nonpayment are often mentioned in the same breath, adjusting for the former is a distinct issue.... We do not suggest ... that adjustments

---

3. Our opinion in *Shaw* does, to be sure, contain some language that, if read in isolation, might suggest a different result in this case. Most significantly, we equated compensation for delay with prejudgment interest, and observed that "[p]rejudgment interest ... is considered as damages, not a component of 'costs.' ... Indeed, the term 'costs' has never been understood to include any interest component." *Library of Congress v. Shaw*, 478 U.S. 310, 321, 106 S.Ct. 2957, 2965, 92 L.Ed.2d 250 (1986). These observations, however, cannot be divorced from the context of the special "no-interest rule" that was at issue in *Shaw*. That rule, which is applicable to the immunity of the United States and is therefore not at issue here, provides an "added gloss of strictness," *id.*, at 318, 106 S.Ct., at 2963, only where the United States' liability for interest is at issue. Our inclusion of compensation for delay within the definition of prejudgment interest in *Shaw* must be understood in light of this broad proscription of interest awards against the United States. *Shaw* thus does not represent a general-purpose definition of com-

pensation for delay that governs here. Outside the context of the "no-interest rule" of federal immunity, we see no reason why compensation for delay cannot be included within § 1988 attorney's fee awards, which *Hutto* held to be "costs" not subject to Eleventh Amendment strictures.

We cannot share JUSTICE O'CONNOR's view that the two cases she cites, *post*, at 2474, demonstrate the existence of an equivalent rule relating to State immunity that embodies the same ultra-strict rule of construction for interest awards that has grown up around the federal no-interest rule. Compare *Shaw, supra*, at 314–317, 106 S.Ct., at 2961–2963 (discussing historical development of the federal no-interest rule).

4. In *Shaw*, which dealt with the sovereign immunity of the Federal Government, there was of course no prospective-retrospective distinction as there is when, as in *Hutto* and the present case, it is the Eleventh Amendment immunity of a State that is at issue.

MISSOURI v. JENKINS BY AGYEI

2469

Cite as 109 S.Ct. 2463 (1989)

for delay are inconsistent with the typical fee-shifting statute." *Id.*, at 716, 107 S.Ct., at 3082.

[4, 5] The same conclusion is appropriate under § 1988.[5] Our cases have repeatedly stressed that attorney's fees awarded under this statute are to be based on market rates for the services rendered. See, *e.g., Blanchard v. Bergeron*, 489 U.S. ——, 109 S.Ct. 939, 103 L.Ed.2d 67 (1989); *Riverside v. Rivera*, 477 U.S. 561, 106 S.Ct. 2686, 91 L.Ed.2d 466 (1986); *Blum v. Stenson*, 465 U.S. 886, 104 S.Ct. 1541, 79 L.Ed.2d 891 (1984). Clearly, compensation received several years after the services were rendered—as it frequently is in complex civil rights litigation—is not equivalent to the same dollar amount received reasonably promptly as the legal services are performed, as would normally be the case with private billings.[6] We agree, therefore, that an appropriate adjustment for delay in payment—whether by the application of current rather than historic hourly rates or otherwise—is within the contemplation of the statute.

[6] To summarize: We reaffirm our holding in *Hutto v. Finney* that the Eleventh Amendment has no application to an award of attorney's fees, ancillary to a grant of prospective relief, against a State. It follows that the same is true for the calculation of the *amount* of the fee. An adjustment for delay in payment is, we hold, an appropriate factor in the determination of what constitutes a reasonable attorney's fee under § 1988. An award against a State of a fee that includes such an enhancement for delay is not, therefore, barred by the Eleventh Amendment.

III

Missouri's second contention is that the District Court erred in compensating the work of law clerks and paralegals (hereinafter collectively "paralegals") at the market rates for their services, rather than at their cost to the attorney. While Missouri agrees that compensation for the cost of these personnel should be included in the fee award, it suggests that an hourly rate of $15—which it argued below corresponded to their salaries, benefits, and overhead—would be appropriate, rather than the market rates of $35 to $50. According to Missouri, § 1988 does not authorize billing paralegals' hours at market rates, and doing so produces a "windfall" for the attorney.[7]

---

5. *Delaware Valley* was decided under § 304(d) of the Clean Air Act, 42 U.S.C. § 7604(d). We looked for guidance, however, to § 1988 and our cases construing it. *Pennsylvania v. Delaware Valley Citizens' Council*, 483 U.S. 711, 713, n. 1, 107 S.Ct. 3078, 3080, n. 1, 97 L.Ed.2d 585 (1987).

6. This delay, coupled with the fact that, as we recognized in *Delaware Valley*, the attorney's *expenses* are not deferred pending completion of the litigation, can cause considerable hardship. The present case provides an illustration. During a period of nearly three years, the demands of this case precluded attorney Benson from accepting other employment. In order to pay his staff and meet other operating expenses, he was obliged to borrow $633,000. As of January 1987, he had paid over $113,000 in interest on this debt, and was continuing to borrow to meet interest payments. Record 2336–2339; Tr. 130–131. The LDF, for its part, incurred deficits of $700,000 in 1983 and over $1 million in 1984, largely because of this case. Tr. 46. If no compensation were provided for the delay in

payment, the prospect of such hardship could well deter otherwise willing attorneys from accepting complex civil rights cases that might offer great benefit to society at large; this result would work to defeat Congress' purpose in enacting § 1988 of "encourag[ing] the enforcement of federal law through lawsuits filed by private persons." *Delaware Valley, supra,* at 737, 107 S.Ct., at 3093 (BLACKMUN, J., dissenting).

We note also that we have recognized the availability of interim fee awards under § 1988 when a litigant becomes a prevailing party on one issue in the course of the litigation. *Texas State Teachers Assn. v. Garland Independent School Dist.*, 489 U.S. ——, ——, 109 S.Ct. 1486, ——, 103 L.Ed.2d 866 (1989). In economic terms, such an interim award does not differ from an enhancement for delay in payment.

7. The Courts of Appeals have taken a variety of positions on this issue. Most permit separate billing of paralegal time. See, *e.g., Save Our Cumberland Mountains, Inc. v. Hodel*, 263 U.S. App.D.C. 409, 420, n. 7, 826 F.2d 43, 54, n. 7

[7] We begin with the statutory language, which provides simply for "a reasonable attorney's fee as part of the costs." 42 U.S.C. § 1988. Clearly, a "reasonable attorney's fee" cannot have been meant to compensate only work performed personally by members of the bar. Rather, the term must refer to a reasonable fee for the work product of an attorney. Thus, the fee must take into account the work not only of attorneys, but also of secretaries, messengers, librarians, janitors, and others whose labor contributes to the work product for which an attorney bills her client; and it must also take account of other expenses and profit. The parties have suggested no reason why the work of paralegals should not be similarly compensated, nor can we think of any. We thus take as our starting point the self-evident proposition that the "reasonable attorney's fee" provided for by statute should compensate the work of paralegals, as well as that of attorneys. The more difficult question is how the work of paralegals is to be valuated in calculating the overall attorney's fee.

[8] The statute specifies a "reasonable" fee for the attorney's work product. In determining how other elements of the attorney's fee are to be calculated, we have consistently looked to the marketplace as our guide to what is "reasonable." In *Blum v. Stenson*, 465 U.S. 886, 104 S.Ct. 1541, 79 L.Ed.2d 891 (1984), for example, we rejected an argument that attorney's fees for nonprofit legal service organizations should be based on cost. We said: "The statute and legislative history establish that 'reasonable fees' under § 1988 are

to be calculated according to the prevailing market rates in the relevant community...." *Id.*, at 895, 104 S.Ct., at 1547. See also, *e.g., Delaware Valley*, 483 U.S., at 732, 107 S.Ct., at 3090 (O'CONNOR, J., concurring) (controlling question concerning contingency enhancements is "how the market in a community compensates for contingency"); *Rivera*, 477 U.S., at 591, 106 S.Ct. at 2703 (REHNQUIST, J., dissenting) (reasonableness of fee must be determined "in light of both the traditional billing practices in the profession, and the fundamental principle that the award of a 'reasonable' attorney's fee under § 1988 means a fee that would have been deemed reasonable if billed to affluent plaintiffs by their own attorneys"). A reasonable attorney's fee under § 1988 is one calculated on the basis of rates and practices prevailing in the relevant market, *i.e.*, "in line with those [rates] prevailing in the community for similar services by lawyers of reasonably comparable skill, experience, and reputation," *Blum, supra*, 465 U.S., at 896, n. 11, 104 S.Ct., at 1547, n. 11, and one that grants the successful civil rights plaintiff a "fully compensatory fee," *Hensley v. Eckerhart*, 461 U.S. 424, 435, 103 S.Ct. 1933, 1940, 76 L.Ed.2d 40 (1983), comparable to what "is traditional with attorneys compensated by a fee-paying client." S.Rep. No. 94–1011, p. 6 (1976), U.S.Code Cong. & Admin.News 1976, pp. 5908, 5913.

If an attorney's fee awarded under § 1988 is to yield the same level of compensation that would be available from the market, the "increasingly widespread cus-

(1987), vacated in part on other grounds, 273 U.S.App.D.C. 78, 857 F.2d 1516 (1988) (en banc); *Jacobs v. Mancuso*, 825 F.2d 559, 563, and n. 6 (CA1 1987) (collecting cases); *Spanish Action Committee of Chicago v. Chicago*, 811 F.2d 1129, 1138 (CA7 1987); *Ramos v. Lamm*, 713 F.2d 546, 558–559 (CA10 1983); *Richardson v. Byrd*, 709 F.2d 1016, 1023 (CA5), cert. denied *sub nom. Dallas County Commissioners Court v. Richardson*, 464 U.S. 1009, 104 S.Ct. 527, 78 L.Ed.2d 710 (1983). See also *Riverside v. Rivera*, 477 U.S. 561, 566, n. 2, 106 S.Ct. 2686, 2690, n. 2, 91 L.Ed.2d 466 (1986) (noting lower-court approval of hourly rate for law clerks). Some

courts, on the other hand, have considered paralegal work "out-of-pocket expense," recoverable only at cost to the attorney. See, *e.g., Northcross v. Board of Education of Memphis City Schools*, 611 F.2d 624, 639 (CA6 1979), cert. denied, 447 U.S. 911, 100 S.Ct. 3000, 64 L.Ed.2d 862 (1980); *Thornberry v. Delta Air Lines, Inc.*, 676 F.2d 1240, 1244 (CA9 1982), vacated, 461 U.S. 952, 103 S.Ct. 2421, 77 L.Ed.2d 1311 (1983). At least one Court of Appeals has refused to permit any recovery of paralegal expense apart from the attorney's hourly fee. *Abrams v. Baylor College of Medicine*, 805 F.2d 528, 535 (CA5 1986).

MISSOURI v. JENKINS BY AGYEI   2471
Cite as 109 S.Ct. 2463 (1989)

tom of separately billing for the services of paralegals and law students who serve as clerks," *Ramos v. Lamm,* 713 F.2d 546, 558 (CA10 1983), must be taken into account. All else being equal, the hourly fee charged by an attorney whose rates include paralegal work in her hourly fee, or who bills separately for the work of paralegals at cost, will be higher than the hourly fee charged by an attorney competing in the same market who bills separately for the work of paralegals at "market rates." In other words, the prevailing "market rate" for attorney time is not independent of the manner in which paralegal time is accounted for.[8] Thus, if the prevailing practice in a given community were to bill paralegal time separately at market rates, fees awarded the attorney at market rates for attorney time would not be fully compensatory if the court refused to compensate hours billed by paralegals or did so only at "cost." Similarly, the fee awarded would be too high if the court accepted separate billing for paralegal hours in a market where that was not the custom.

We reject the argument that compensation for paralegals at rates above "cost" would yield a "windfall" for the prevailing attorney. Neither petitioners nor anyone else, to our knowledge, have ever suggested that the hourly rate applied to the work of an associate attorney in a law firm creates a windfall for the firm's partners or is otherwise improper under § 1988, merely because it exceeds the cost of the attorney's services. If the fees are consistent with market rates and practices, the "wind-

fall" argument has no more force with regard to paralegals than it does for associates. And it would hardly accord with Congress' intent to provide a "fully compensatory fee" if the prevailing plaintiff's attorney in a civil rights lawsuit were not permitted to bill separately for paralegals, while the defense attorney in the same litigation was able to take advantage of the prevailing practice and obtain market rates for such work. Yet that is precisely the result sought in this case by the State of Missouri, which appears to have paid its own outside counsel for the work of paralegals at the hourly rate of $35. Record 2696, 2699.[9]

[9] Nothing in § 1988 requires that the work of paralegals invariably be billed separately. If it is the practice in the relevant market not to do so, or to bill the work of paralegals only at cost, that is all that § 1988 requires. Where, however, the prevailing practice is to bill paralegal work at market rates, treating civil rights lawyers' fee requests in the same way is not only permitted by § 1988, but also makes economic sense. By encouraging the use of lower-cost paralegals rather than attorneys wherever possible, permitting market-rate billing of paralegal hours "encourages cost-effective delivery of legal services and, by reducing the spiraling cost of civil rights litigation, furthers the policies underlying civil rights statutes." *Cameo Convalescent Center, Inc. v. Senn,* 738 F.2d 836, 846 (CA7 1984), cert. denied, 469 U.S. 1106, 105 S.Ct. 780, 83 L.Ed.2d 775 (1985).[10]

---

8. The attorney who bills separately for paralegal time is merely distributing her costs and profit margin among the hourly fees of other members of her staff, rather than concentrating them in the fee she sets for her own time.

9. A variant of Missouri's "windfall" argument is the following: "If paralegal expense is reimbursed at a rate many times the actual cost, will attorneys next try to bill separately—and at a profit—for such items as secretarial time, paper clips, electricity, and other expenses?" Reply Brief for Petitioners 15–16. The answer to this question is, of course, that attorneys seeking fees under § 1988 would have no basis for re-

questing separate compensation of such expenses unless this were the prevailing practice in the local community. The safeguard against the billing at a profit of secretarial services and paper clips is the discipline of the market.

10. It has frequently been recognized in the lower courts that paralegals are capable of carrying out many tasks, under the supervision of an attorney, that might otherwise be performed by a lawyer and billed at a higher rate. Such work might include, for example, factual investigation, including locating and interviewing witnesses; assistance with depositions, interrogatories, and document production; compilation of

Such separate billing appears to be the practice in most communities today.[11] In the present case, Missouri concedes that "the local market typically bills separately for paralegal services," Tr. of Oral Arg. 14, and the District Court found that the requested hourly rates of $35 for law clerks, $40 for paralegals, and $50 for recent law graduates were the prevailing rates for such services in the Kansas City area. App. to Pet. for Cert. A29, A31, A34. Under these circumstances, the court's decision to award separate compensation at these rates was fully in accord with § 1988.

IV

The courts below correctly granted a fee enhancement to compensate for delay in payment and approved compensation of paralegals and law clerks at market rates. The judgment of the Court of Appeals is therefore

Affirmed.

Justice MARSHALL took no part in the consideration or decision of this case.

Justice O'CONNOR, with whom Justice SCALIA joins, and with whom the Chief Justice joins in part, concurring in part and dissenting in part.

. I agree with the Court that 42 U.S.C. § 1988 allows compensation for the work of paralegals and law clerks at market

rates, and therefore join Parts I and III of its opinion. I do not join Part II, however, for in my view the Eleventh Amendment does not permit enhancement of attorney's fees assessed against a State as compensation for delay in payment.

The Eleventh Amendment does not, of course, provide a State with across-the-board immunity from all monetary relief. Relief that "serves directly to bring an end to a violation of federal law is not barred by the Eleventh Amendment even though accompanied by a substantial ancillary effect" on a State's treasury. *Papasan v. Allain,* 478 U.S. 265, 278, 106 S.Ct. 2932, 2940–41, 92 L.Ed.2d 209 (1986). Thus, in *Milliken v. Bradley,* 433 U.S. 267, 289–290, 97 S.Ct. 2749, 2761–2762, 53 L.Ed.2d 745 (1977), the Court unanimously upheld a decision ordering a State to pay over $5 million to eliminate the effects of *de jure* segregation in certain school systems. On the other hand, "[r]elief that in essence serves to compensate a party injured in the past," such as relief "expressly denominated as damages," or "relief [that] is tantamount to an award of damages for a past violation of federal law, even though styled as something else," is prohibited by the Eleventh Amendment. *Papasan,* 478 U.S., at 278, 106 S.Ct., at 2940–41. The crucial question in this case is whether that portion of respondents' attorney's fees based on current hourly rates is properly characterized as retroactive monetary relief.

statistical and financial data; checking legal citations; and drafting correspondence. Much such work lies in a gray area of tasks that might appropriately be performed either by an attorney or a paralegal. To the extent that fee applicants under § 1988 are not permitted to bill for the work of paralegals at market rates, it would not be surprising to see a greater amount of such work performed by attorneys themselves, thus increasing the overall cost of litigation.

Of course, purely clerical or secretarial tasks should not be billed at a paralegal rate, regardless of who performs them. What the court in *Johnson v. Georgia Highway Express, Inc.,* 488 F.2d 714, 717 (CA5 1974), said in regard to the work of attorneys is applicable by analogy to paralegals: "It is appropriate to distinguish be-

tween legal work, in the strict sense, and investigation, clerical work, compilation of facts and statistics and other work which can often be accomplished by non-lawyers but which a lawyer may do because he has no other help available. Such non-legal work may command a lesser rate. Its dollar value is not enhanced just because a lawyer does it."

11. *Amicus* National Association of Legal Assistants reports that 77 percent of 1,800 legal assistants responding to a survey of the association's membership stated that their law firms charged clients for paralegal work on an hourly billing basis. Brief for National Association of Legal Assistants as *Amicus Curiae* 11.

In *Library of Congress v. Shaw*, 478 U.S. 310, 106 S.Ct. 2957, 92 L.Ed.2d 250 (1986), the Court addressed whether the attorney's fees provision of Title VII, 42 U.S.C. § 2000e–5(k), permits an award of attorney's fees against the United States to be enhanced in order to compensate for delay in payment. In relevant part, § 2000e–5(k) provides:

> "In any action or proceeding under this subchapter the court, in its discretion, may allow the prevailing party, other than the [EEOC] or the United States, a reasonable attorney's fees as part of the costs, and the [EEOC] and the United States shall be liable for costs the same as a private person."

The Court began its analysis in *Shaw* by holding that "interest is an element of damages separate from damages on the substantive claim." 478 U.S., at 314, 106 S.Ct., at 2961 (citing C. McCormick, Law of Damages § 50, p. 205 (1935)). Given the "no-interest" rule of federal sovereign immunity, under which the United States is not liable for interest absent an express statutory waiver to the contrary, the Court was unwilling to conclude that, by equating the United States' liability to that of private persons in § 2000e–5(k), Congress had waived the United States' immunity from interest. 478 U.S., at 314–319, 106 S.Ct., at 2961–2964. The fact that § 2000e–5(k) used the word "reasonable" to modify "attorney's fees" did not alter this result, for the Court explained that it had "consistently ... refused to impute an intent to waive immunity from interest into the ambiguous use of a particular word or phrase in a statute." *Id.*, at 320, 106 S.Ct., at 2964. The description of attorney's fees as costs in § 2000e–5(k) also did not mandate a contrary conclusion because "[p]rejudgment interest ... is considered as damages, not a component of 'costs,'" and the "term 'costs' has *never* been understood to include any interest component." *Id.*, at 321, 106 S.Ct. at 2965 (emphasis added) (citing 10 C. Wright, A. Miller, & M. Kane, Federal Practice and Procedure §§ 2664, 2666,

2670 (2d ed. 1983); 2 A. Sedgwick & G. Van Nest, Sedgwick on Damages 157–158 (7th ed. 1880)). Finally, the Court rejected the argument that the enhancement was proper because the "no-interest" rule did not prohibit compensation for delay in payment: "Interest and a delay factor share an identical function. They are designed to compensate for the belated receipt of money." 478 U.S., at 322, 106 S.Ct., at 2965.

As the Court notes, *ante*, at 2468, n. 3, the "no-interest" rule of federal sovereign immunity at issue in *Shaw* provided an "added gloss of strictness," 478 U.S., at 318, 106 S.Ct., at 2963, and may have explained the *result* reached by the Court in that case, *i.e.*, that § 2000e–5(k) did not waive the United States' immunity against awards of interest. But there is not so much as a hint anywhere in *Shaw* that the Court's discussions and definitions of interest and compensation for delay were dictated by, or limited to, the federal "no-interest" rule. As the quotations above illustrate, the Court's opinion in *Shaw* is filled with broad, unqualified language. The dissenters in *Shaw* did not disagree with the Court's sweeping characterization of interest and compensation for delay as damages. Rather, they argued only that § 2000e–5(k) had waived the immunity of the United States with respect to awards of interest. See *id.*, at 323–327, 106 S.Ct., at 2966–2968 (BRENNAN, J., dissenting). I therefore emphatically disagree with the Court's statement that "*Shaw* ... does not represent a general-purpose definition of compensation for delay that governs here." *Ante*, at 2468, n. 3.

Two general propositions that are relevant here emerge from *Shaw*. First, interest is considered damages, and not costs. Second, compensation for delay, which serves the same function as interest, is also the equivalent of damages. These two propositions make clear that enhancement for delay constitutes retroactive monetary relief barred by the Eleventh Amendment. Given my reading of *Shaw*, I do not think the Court's reliance on the cost rationale of

§ 1988 set forth in *Hutto v. Finney*, 437 U.S. 678, 98 S.Ct. 2565, 57 L.Ed.2d 522 (1978), is persuasive. Because *Shaw* teaches that compensation for delay constitutes damages and cannot be considered costs, see 478 U.S., at 321–322, 106 S.Ct., at 2965–2966, *Hutto* is not controlling. See *Hutto*, 437 U.S., 697, n. 27, 98 S.Ct., at 2577, n. 27 ("we do not suggest that our analysis would be the same if Congress were to expand the concept of costs beyond the traditional category of litigation expenses"). Furthermore, *Hutto* does not mean that inclusion of attorney's fees as costs in a statute forecloses a challenge to the enhancement of fees as compensation for delay in payment. If it did, then *Shaw* would have been resolved differently, for § 2000e–5(k) lists attorney's fees as costs.

Even if I accepted the narrow interpretation of *Shaw* proffered by the Court, I would disagree with the result reached by the Court in Part II of its opinion. On its own terms, the Court's analysis fails. The Court suggests that the definitions of interest and compensation for delay set forth in *Shaw* would be triggered only by a rule of sovereign immunity barring awards of interest against the States: "Outside the context of the 'no-interest rule' of federal immunity, we see no reason why compensation for delay cannot be included within § 1988 attorney's fee awards[.]" *Ante*, at 2468, n. 3. But the Court does not inquire whether such a rule exists. In fact, there is a federal rule barring awards of interest against States. See *Virginia v. West Virginia*, 238 U.S. 202, 234, 35 S.Ct. 795, 808, 59 L.Ed. 1272 (1915) ("Nor can it be deemed in derogation of the sovereignty of the State that she should be charged with interest *if* her agreement properly construed so provides.") (emphasis added); *United States v. North Carolina*, 136 U.S. 211, 221, 10 S.Ct. 920, 924, 34 L.Ed. 336 (1890) ("general principle" is that "an obligation of the State to pay interest, whether as interest or as damages, on any debt overdue, cannot arise *except* by the consent and contract of the State, manifested by

statute, or in a form authorized by statute") (emphasis added). The Court has recently held that the rule of immunity set forth in *Virginia* and *North Carolina* is inapplicable in situations where the State does not retain any immunity, see *West Virginia v. United States*, 479 U.S. 305, 310–312, 107 S.Ct. 702, 706–707, 93 L.Ed.2d 639 (1987) (State can be held liable for interest to the United States, against whom it has no sovereign immunity), but the rule has not otherwise been limited, and there is no reason why it should not be relevant in the Eleventh Amendment context presented in this case.

As *Virginia* and *North Carolina* indicate, a State can waive its immunity against awards of interest. See also *Clark v. Barnard*, 108 U.S. 436, 447, 2 S.Ct. 878, 882–83, 27 L.Ed. 780 (1883). The Missouri courts have interpreted Mo.Rev.Stat. § 408.020 (1979 and Supp.1989), providing for prejudgment interest on money that becomes due and payable, and § 408.040, providing for prejudgment interest on court judgments and orders, as making the State liable for interest. See *Denton Construction Co. v. Missouri State Highway Comm'n*, 454 S.W.2d 44, 59–60 (Mo.1970) (§ 408.020); *Steppelman v. State Highway Comm'n of Missouri*, 650 S.W.2d 343, 345 (Mo.App.1983) (§ 408.040). There can be no argument, however, that these Missouri statutes and cases allow interest to be awarded against the State here. A "State's waiver of sovereign immunity in its own courts is not a waiver of the Eleventh Amendment immunity in the federal courts." *Pennhurst State School and Hospital v. Halderman*, 465 U.S. 89, 99, n. 9, 104 S.Ct. 900, 907, n. 9, 79 L.Ed.2d 67 (1984).

The fact that a State has immunity from awards of interest is not the end of the matter. In a case such as this one involving school desegregation, interest or compensation for delay (in the guise of current hourly rates) can theoretically be awarded against a State despite the Eleventh Amendment's bar against retroactive mon-

MISSOURI v. JENKINS BY AGYEI   2475
Cite as 109 S.Ct. 2463 (1989)

etary liability. The Court has held that Congress can set aside the States' Eleventh Amendment immunity in order to enforce the provisions of the Fourteenth Amendment. See *City of Rome v. United States,* 446 U.S. 156, 179, 100 S.Ct. 1548, 1562–63, 64 L.Ed.2d 119 (1980); *Fitzpatrick v. Bitzer,* 427 U.S. 445, 456, 96 S.Ct. 2666, 2671, 49 L.Ed.2d 614 (1976). Congress must, however, be unequivocal in expressing its intent to abrogate that immunity. See generally *Atascadero State Hospital v. Scanlon,* 473 U.S. 234, 243, 105 S.Ct. 3142, 3148, 87 L.Ed.2d 171 (1985) ("Congress must express its intention to abrogate the Eleventh Amendment in unmistakable language in the statute itself.").

In *Hutto* the Court was able to avoid deciding whether § 1988 met the "clear statement" rule only because attorney's fees (without any enhancement) are not considered retroactive in nature. See 437 U.S., at 695–697, 98 S.Ct., at 2575–2577. The Court cannot do the same here, where the attorney's fees were enhanced to compensate for delay in payment. Cf. *Osterneck v. Ernst & Whinney,* — U.S. —, —, 109 S.Ct. 987, 991, 103 L.Ed.2d 146 (1989) ("unlike attorney's fees, which at common law were regarded as an element of costs, ... prejudgment interest traditionally has been considered part of the compensation due [the] plaintiff").

In relevant part, § 1988 provides:

"In any action or proceeding to enforce a provision of sections 1981, 1982, 1983, 1985, and 1986 of this title, title IX of Public Law 92–318, or title VI of the Civil Rights Act of 1964, the court, in its discretion, may allow the prevailing party, other than the United States, a reasonable attorney's fees as part of the costs."

In my view, § 1988 does not meet the "clear statement" rule set forth in *Atascadero.* It does not mention damages, interest, compensation for delay, or current hourly rates. As one federal court has correctly noted, "Congress has not yet made any statement suggesting that a § 1988 attorney's fee award should include

prejudgment interest." *Rogers v. Okin,* 821 F.2d 22, 27 (CA1 1987). A comparison of the statute at issue in *Shaw* also indicates that § 1988, as currently written, is insufficient to allow attorney's fees assessed against a State to be enhanced to compensate for delay in payment. The language of § 1988 is undoubtedly less expansive than that of § 2000e–5(k), for § 1988 does not equate the liability of States with that of private persons. Since § 2000e–5(k) does not allow enhancement of an award of attorney's fees to compensate for delay, it is logical to conclude that § 1988, a more narrowly worded statute, likewise does not allow interest (through the use of current hourly rates) to be tacked on to an award of attorney's fees against a State.

Compensation for delay in payment was *one* of the reasons the District Court used current hourly rates in calculating respondents' attorney's fees. See App. to Pet. for Cert. A26–A27; 838 F.2d 260, 263, 265 (CA8 1988). I would reverse the award of attorney's fees to respondents and remand so that the fees can be calculated without taking compensation for delay into account.

Chief Justice REHNQUIST, dissenting.

I agree with Justice O'CONNOR that the Eleventh Amendment does not permit an award of attorney's fees against a State which includes compensation for delay in payment. Unlike Justice O'CONNOR, however, I do not agree with the Court's approval of the award of law clerk and paralegal fees made here.

Section 1988 gives the district courts discretion to allow the prevailing party in an action under § 1983 "a reasonable attorney's fee as part of the costs." 42 U.S.C. § 1988. The Court reads this language as authorizing recovery of "a 'reasonable' fee for the attorney's work product," *ante,* at 2470, which, the Court concludes, may include separate compensation for the services of law clerks and paralegals. But the statute itself simply uses the very familiar term "a reasonable attorney's fee," which to those untutored in the Court's linguistic juggling means a fee charged for services rendered by an individual who has been licensed to practice law. Because law clerks and paralegals have not been licensed to practice law in Missouri, it is difficult to see how charges for their services may be separately billed as part of "attorney's fees." And since a prudent attorney customarily includes compensation for the cost of law clerk and paralegal services, like any other sort of office overhead—from secretarial staff, janitors, and librarians, to telephone service, stationery, and paper clips—in his own hourly billing rate, allowing the prevailing party to recover separate compensation for law clerk and paralegal services may result in "double recovery."

The Court finds justification for its ruling in the fact that the prevailing practice among attorneys in Kansas City is to bill clients separately for the services of law clerks and paralegals. But I do not think Congress intended the meaning of the statutory term "attorney's fee" to expand and contract with each and every vagary of local billing practice. Under the Court's logic, prevailing parties could recover at market rates for the cost of secretaries, private investigators, and other types of lay personnel who assist the attorney in preparing his case, so long as they could show that the prevailing practice in the local market was to bill separately for these services. Such a result would be a sufficiently drastic departure from the traditional concept of "attorney's fees" that I believe new statutory authorization should be required for it. That permitting separate billing of law clerk and paralegal hours at market rates might " 'reduc[e] the spiraling cost of civil rights litigation' " by encouraging attorneys to delegate to these individuals tasks which they would otherwise perform themselves at higher cost, *ante,* at 2471, and n. 10, may be a persuasive reason for Congress to enact such additional legislation. It is not, however, a persuasive reason for us to rewrite the legislation which Congress has in fact enacted. See *Badaracco v. Commissioner,* 464 U.S. 386, 398, 104 S.Ct. 756, 764, 78

L.Ed.2d 549 (1984) ("[c]ourts are not authorized to rewrite a statute because they might deem its effects susceptible of improvement").

I also disagree with the State's suggestion that law clerk and paralegal expenses incurred by a prevailing party, if not recoverable at market rates as "attorney's fees" under § 1988, are nonetheless recoverable at actual cost under that statute. The language of § 1988 expands the traditional definition of "costs" to include "a reasonable attorney's fee," but it cannot fairly be read to authorize the recovery of all other out-of-pocket expenses actually incurred by the prevailing party in the course of litigation. Absent specific statutory authorization for the recovery of such expenses, the prevailing party remains subject to the limitations on cost recovery imposed by Federal Rule of Civil Procedure 54(d) and 28 U.S.C. § 1920, which govern the taxation of costs in federal litigation where a cost-shifting statute is not applicable. Section 1920 gives the district court discretion to tax certain types of costs against the losing party in any federal litigation. The statute specifically enumerates six categories of expenses which may be taxed as costs: fees of the court clerk and marshal; fees of the court reporter; printing fees and witness fees; copying fees; certain docket fees; and fees of court-appointed experts and interpreters. We have held that this list is exclusive. *Crawford Fitting Co. v. J.T. Gibbons, Inc.,* 482 U.S. 437, 107 S.Ct. 2494, 96 L.Ed.2d 385 (1987). Since none of these categories can possibly be construed to include the fees of law clerks and paralegals, I would also hold that reimbursement for these expenses may not be separately awarded at actual cost.

I would therefore reverse the award of reimbursement for law clerk and paralegal expenses.

Index